The British General Election of 2015

Praise for previous editions

'The Bible of General Elections.' – David Dimbleby, BBC

'It's popular academic writing at its best, combining a clear narrative (using anecdotes and quotes garnered from more than 300 background interviews) with lots of solid, meaty number-crunching.' – *The Guardian*

'Dennis Kavanagh and Philip Cowley have penned a political thriller ... The book is distinguished by the quality of its sources: the ministers, aides and strategists who open up to these academics in a way they might not to journalists.' – *The Observer*

'Indispensable.' – Matthew d'Ancona, *The Telegraph*

'Mandelson and Blair's books will get all the attention, but if you want real insight into the last election, Kavanagh and Cowley look like they're on the money.' – *London Evening Standard*

'The quality of the analysis is as sharp as ever.' – *Fabian Review*

'... a riveting read ... this is easily the best political book of the year.' – PoliticalBetting.com

'... a formidable achievement ... The studies have become by now almost part of our democratic fabric.' – *The Listener*

'The best series anywhere on national elections.' – *Annals of American Academy of Political and Social Science*

Other books in this series

THE BRITISH GENERAL ELECTION OF 1945
R. B. McCallum and Alison Readman

THE BRITISH GENERAL ELECTION OF 1950
H. G. Nicholas

THE BRITISH GENERAL ELECTION OF 1951
David Butler

THE BRITISH GENERAL ELECTION OF 1955
David Butler

THE BRITISH GENERAL ELECTION OF 1959
David Butler and Richard Rose

THE BRITISH GENERAL ELECTION OF 1964
David Butler and Anthony King

THE BRITISH GENERAL ELECTION OF 1966
David Butler and Anthony King

THE BRITISH GENERAL ELECTION OF 1970
David Butler and Michael Pinto-Duschinsky

THE BRITISH GENERAL ELECTION OF FEBRUARY 1974
David Butler and Dennis Kavanagh

THE BRITISH GENERAL ELECTION OF OCTOBER 1974
David Butler and Dennis Kavanagh

THE BRITISH GENERAL ELECTION OF 1979
David Butler and Dennis Kavanagh

THE BRITISH GENERAL ELECTION OF 1983
David Butler and Dennis Kavanagh

THE BRITISH GENERAL ELECTION OF 1987
David Butler and Dennis Kavanagh

THE BRITISH GENERAL ELECTION OF 1992
David Butler and Dennis Kavanagh

THE BRITISH GENERAL ELECTION OF 1997
David Butler and Dennis Kavanagh

THE BRITISH GENERAL ELECTION OF 2001
David Butler and Dennis Kavanagh

THE BRITISH GENERAL ELECTION OF 2005
Dennis Kavanagh and David Butler

THE BRITISH GENERAL ELECTION OF 2010
Dennis Kavanagh and Philip Cowley

The British General Election of 2015

Philip Cowley
Professor of Parliamentary Government, Queen Mary University of London, UK

Dennis Kavanagh
Emeritus Professor of Politics, University of Liverpool, UK

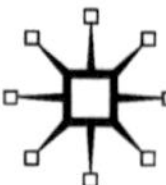

First published 2016 by
PALGRAVE MACMILLAN

Palgrave Macmillan in the UK is an imprint of Macmillan Publishers Limited, registered in England, company number 785998, of Houndmills, Basingstoke, Hampshire RG21 6XS.

Palgrave Macmillan in the US is a division of St Martin's Press LLC, 175 Fifth Avenue, New York, NY 10010.

Palgrave Macmillan is the global academic imprint of the above companies and has companies and representatives throughout the world.

Palgrave® and Macmillan® are registered trademarks in the United States, the United Kingdom, Europe and other countries.

ISBN 978–1–137–36610–8 hardback
ISBN 978–1–137–36613–9 paperback

This book is printed on paper suitable for recycling and made from fully managed and sustained forest sources. Logging, pulping and manufacturing processes are expected to conform to the environmental regulations of the country of origin.

A catalogue record for this book is available from the British Library.

A catalog record for this book is available from the Library of Congress.

To Robert John Cowley,
whose early arrival almost derailed publication

Contents

List of Tables

List of Figures

List of Illustrations

Photographs

Party Advertisements

Cartoons

List of Plates

Bound between pages 254 and 255

1 Nick Clegg and David Cameron at their first joint press conference in Downing Street, 12 May 2010. © AFP/Getty
2 Ed and David Miliband, after the former was elected Labour leader, September 2010. © Allstar Picture Library/Alamy
3 Nigel Farage, celebrating UKIP's victory in the 2014 European elections. © Prixpics/Alamy
4 Caroline Lucas and Natalie Bennett at the Green Party manifesto launch. © Jack Taylor/Alamy
5 Leanne Wood, Plaid Cymru leader since 2012. © Plaid Cymru
6 Nicola Sturgeon and Alex Salmond in Glasgow during the independence referendum campaign. © David Gordon/Alamy
7 Harriet Harman at Labour's manifesto launch in Manchester. © WENN Ltd/Alamy
8 Douglas Alexander on the old *Coronation Street* set for Labour's manifesto launch. © Gary Gibbon
9 Michael Gove, and Conservative activists, outside Labour's manifesto launch. © Gary Gibbon
10 Nick Clegg at the Lib Dem manifesto launch. © Guy Corbishley/Alamy
11 David Laws briefing the press at the back of the Lib Dem manifesto launch, near the bins. © Gary Gibbon
12 Lynton Crosby. © Alamy/Alamy
13 Lord (Andrew) Feldman. © Conservative Party
14 Stephen Gilbert. © Conservative Party
15 Ryan Coetzee. © Liberal Democrats
16 Jim Murphy, Ed Miliband and Ed Balls in Edinburgh, 10 April 2015. © Jeff J Mitchell/Getty
17 Ed Miliband rehearsing his opening statement for the first leaders' debate. © Tom Hamilton
18 Modern campaigning: Nigel Farage campaigning in the Rochester and Strood by-election. © PjrNews/Alamy
19 Modern campaigning: Boris Johnson campaigning in Uxbridge and South Ruislip. © Europa Productions

Preface

This volume is the nineteenth in a series of books which originated in 1945 in Nuffield College, Oxford. The originator of the series – Ronald McCallum – had always been infuriated by what he saw as the constant misinterpretation of the 1918 election, and he wanted to place on record the events of the 1945 contest before similar partisan myths took root. Thus began what is now the longest-running national election series in the world. This is the second volume in the series where neither of the authors is based at Nuffield, but the aim remains the same: to create an accurate and, as far as possible, impartial account and explanation of the general election.

For this volume, we conducted over 300 interviews with key players from all the main parties, and unattributed quotes in the volume are taken from those interviews. People gave generously and willingly of their time, and were very open with us, and we are extremely grateful to them. We deliberately do not list them here, as many spoke to us on conditions of strict confidentiality, but we hope they will recognise the picture we paint – even if not all of them will agree with our conclusions. Some also agreed to look at draft chapters, helping to suggest improvements and challenging our judgements, and again we are very grateful, as we are to the many friends and colleagues who also read early drafts of the book. All responsibility for any remaining errors rests with us alone.

For a long time, the authors of this series operated within a two-party and then a three-party system, from which (usually) a single-party winner emerged. By 2010, the fragmentation of the party system seemed to have inaugurated a new norm of hung parliaments and coalitions. That was certainly the widespread expectation in 2015, given the level pegging of the main parties in the polls and the rise of UKIP, the SNP and the Greens. The different party battles in different parts of the UK also made for greater complexity. Life is harder for politicians trying to navigate this system. It may be harder for voters, too, although they may welcome the greater choice. It is certainly harder for those who write about politics.

Nor is this any longer the only book on the election. We have, in various places, been able to draw on a series of excellent books already published, including Andrew Geddes and Jon Tonge's edited collection *Britain Votes 2015*, Owen Bennett's account of the UKIP campaign, *Following Farage*, Joe Pike's volume on the contest in Scotland, *Project Fear*, and Iain Watson's examination of Labour's failure, *Five Million Conversations*. Tim Ross's *Why The Tories Won* was, alas, published too close to our submission date for us to engage with properly, although it is clear that whilst we agree on some aspects of the campaign, we reach a different conclusion on others. We also await another book-length study of the UKIP campaign by Matthew Goodwin and Caitlin Milazzo, which is expected to be published just before this volume. This too all makes life more challenging for those writing about politics, but since no single book can tell the whole story of the campaign it is good news for those who like to read about it.

Like most of its predecessors, our story ends with the announcement of the result. Time will tell whether the 2015 election will prove to be a turning point in modern British politics, but there are plenty of talking points, including the comprehensive failure of the polls to anticipate the Conservative majority, the transformation of Scotland and the Scottish party system, and the scale of Labour's defeat. The fallout from the defeat and Ed Miliband's resignation will reverberate for the rest of the Parliament, and beyond.

One reviewer of the last book in this series deprecated the occasional use of industrial language in the various quotations from politicians. But much like voters, politicians do occasionally say rude words, and all we do here is to reproduce faithfully what they said to us. We estimate that out of around 185,000 words, some 0.005% of what you are about to read might not be suitable for minors.

We have a debt to all our contributors whose names appear in the table of contents and who met demanding deadlines and repeated editorial requests. In addition to writing Appendix 1, John Curtice, Stephen D. Fisher and Robert Ford also supplied the data from which Appendix 2 has been compiled. This book follows the broad structure of previous volumes in the series. But each election is different. For the first time since the volume on the 1979 election, we have included a chapter specifically on Scotland, which had, even after devolution, mostly been a fairly predictable and uneventful part of the Westminster battle. Not this time. Attentive readers will also note the absence of a column on the Communist vote in the Table on page 432. An ever-present feature in all volumes since the first in 1945, it is no more.

We are indebted to all those who supplied, or allowed us to reproduce, material. Labour, the Conservatives, the Liberal Democrats, the SNP, the Greens, Plaid Cyrmu, UKIP and the National Union of Students all generously allowed us to reproduce campaign posters or images. Martin Rowson, Steve Bell, Howard McWilliam, Morten Morland and *The Telegraph* (for Adams, Matt and Bob) granted us permission to print their excellent cartoons. The majority of photos in the plates come courtesy of either Getty or Alamy, although other pictures, some thanks to the now-ubiquitous camera phone, come from Plaid Cymru, Gary Gibbon, the Conservative Party, the Liberal Democrats, Europa Productions, North News and Pictures, Alexandra Coyle, Tom Hamilton and Jonathan Dean. Other photos come from the National Union of Students, Reuters and Niall Paterson. The photo of Labour's results board in Chapter 8 comes from someone who would prefer to remain anonymous. Mirrorpix supplied the content for Figure 8.1, and Populus, YouGov and Ipsos MORI all provided polling data. The Polling Observatory team kindly supplied the graph for Figure 1.1 and Lizz Loxam from the BBC provided help with election data. We are grateful to all of them.

The social media data used in Chapter 5 draws on a project on Scottish independence funded by the UK Economic and Social Research Council (ESRC) in conjunction with the Applied Quantitative Methods Network (AQMeN) as part of the 'Future of the UK and Scotland' research programme. The research in chapter 12 was supported by a grant from the British Academy/Leverhulme Trust (grant reference SG142216). We also acknowledge help from the British Academy small grants scheme (SG141982). Matthew Bailey, Abigail Taylor, Gemma Rosenblatt, Eilidh Macfarlane and Melissa Lee provided research assistance.

The team at Palgrave have been supportive and encouraging, and have allowed us to tell what we think is a fascinating story.

Philip Cowley
Dennis Kavanagh
October 2015

1
I'm Afraid There is No Money: Five Years of Coalition

In the early hours of 8 May 2015, during his victory speech at Conservative Campaign Headquarters, David Cameron described the general election as one where 'pundits got it wrong, the pollsters got it wrong, the commentators got it wrong'.

It was a fair complaint. A couple of months before, a collection of academic experts had met at the London School of Economics to forecast the result of the election. No matter what model they used or how they set about crunching the numbers, they all reached the same conclusion: no single party would win enough seats to command a majority in the House of Commons. A survey of over 500 academics, journalists and pollsters in early March came up with the same finding.[1] You could add bookmakers to David Cameron's list of the mistaken as well: just before the polls closed on 7 May, Paddy Power, for example, was offering odds of 1/25 for a hung parliament.

But you could add one other group too, a group who almost universally got the election wrong: the political parties. After the election was over, and with Cameron back in Number 10, there was an attempt by some of the participants in the election to rewrite history and to claim that they had known all along how it was going to play out. As we will show, whilst the parties' private information was different from much of the public polling – Labour's private polling had long been more pessimistic than the public polls and Conservative strategists had been more optimistic – these were differences of scale, not outcome. As the polls closed, even the most optimistic Conservative strategists were predicting a hung parliament, whilst Labour strategists all believed they had a real chance of entering government.

The apparent inevitability of a hung parliament – and one in which the Scottish National Party (SNP) would play a major role – had dominated discussion of the election. It became impossible to avoid conversations about the various post-election scenarios, with dozens of seminars and articles on the subject: what conditions the parties would have for a deal; what were their red lines; who would deal with whom. It even looked likely that a two-party deal would not be enough to produce a majority. Whereas in 2010 the Conservative and Liberal Democrat Coalition had produced a clear majority in the House of Commons, which, despite many difficulties, had lasted for five years, in 2015 it seemed as if the post-election negotiations might require a deal encompassing three or even four parties to secure a majority in the Commons.

Yet against almost all expectations, David Cameron pulled off one of the most unexpected election victories. The opinion polls – on which almost all of the pre-election analysis had been based – turned out to be fundamentally wrong, triggering a post-election crisis amongst pollsters to match that amongst opposition politicians. The election of 2015, then, was the surprise election – Cameron called it 'the sweetest victory of all'. Speaking to celebrating Conservative staff the day after polling, his long-time friend and party vice-chair, Lord Feldman, described it more bluntly: as a big 'fuck you' to all those who said it could not be done.

It was true that it was achieved on only a very slight increase in the Conservative vote – up by 0.8 percentage points – and to levels that many previous Conservative leaders would have scoffed at.[2] But much like Dr Johnson and his dancing dog, what is impressive is that it happened at all. Since 1945, there have only been three occasions in the UK when a party in government has increased both its vote and seat shares in consecutive elections; they had all involved either very short periods between election (as in 1964–6 and February–October 1974) or mid-term changes of Prime Minister (1951–5). None was comparable to what had happened in 2015. David Cameron was a rarity: an incumbent Prime Minister who had been in power for a full term and who had still managed to increase support in both his party's votes and seats. There is no comparable modern example, at least dating back to the Great Reform Act of 1832.

For all these reasons, the Conservative victory of 2015 is noteworthy. But it is also noteworthy for the many sub-plots. The collapse of the Liberal Democrats, the Conservatives' coalition partners for five years, who fell from 57 seats down to just eight, undoing at least a generation's work building the third force in British politics; the rise, but ultimately still the failure, of the United Kingdom Independence

Party (UKIP), who piled up almost four million votes, the best result for an 'other' party in modern British politics, but who achieved a paltry single seat as a reward; and, perhaps most spectacularly of all, the rise of the SNP, taking 56 of the 59 seats in Scotland, an increase of 50 seats on their 2010 performance, utterly destroying the Scottish Labour Party in the process, in what the former First Minister of Scotland described as an electoral tsunami – and which constitutes probably the most significant change in the British party system since the formation of the Labour Party.

The paradox of the last of these is that on election night itself, it was not all that surprising, but just a year before it would have seemed unimaginable. Whilst the polls may have been wrong about the overall outcome of the election, they were broadly right in Scotland and had been predicting a SNP landslide since shortly after the independence referendum of late 2014. Until then, Labour had assumed that its hegemony at Westminster elections would continue, whilst the SNP similarly had had no great expectations for the general election. In late 2014, one Scottish Labour MP was joking with his colleagues about how much his majority was going to rise at the next election. He is an MP no longer.

Then there was the performance of the pollsters; polls that had been more numerous than in any previous contest proved to be as flawed as they had been in 1992, the Waterloo of the polls; there were the developments in campaign techniques, and especially the rise of hyper-targeted campaigning; and the changes in the composition of the Commons. The massive expansion of the SNP Westminster group is the largest sudden growth of any party since the arrival of Sinn Fein MPs in 1918, whilst the 2015 Parliament returned more women and ethnic minority MPs than in any previous parliament, and more gay and lesbian MPs than in any parliament in the world. There is the role of the press, with a combined readership that is lower than in any post-war election, but which still packs a punch, and the broadcasters, struggling to adapt to multi-party politics.

It is too early to tell if 2015 marks a fundamental realignment in British electoral politics – too many supposed realigning elections in the past have turned out to be more transient than they seemed at the time – but it clearly has the potential to be so. For the first time since the rise of the Labour Party, Britain's third party was no longer the Liberals or its successor party. In votes, UKIP was now third; in seats, it was the SNP. And for the first time since 1832, a different party topped the polls in each part of the UK: in England, it was the Conservatives;

in Scotland, the SNP; in Wales, Labour; and in Northern Ireland, the Democratic Unionist Party (DUP). The potential consequences for the British state are also clear. The Conservative victory paved the way for an in/out referendum on Britain's membership of the European Union to be held within two years of the election. Regardless of the result of that, the likelihood of a second Scottish independence referendum occurring also increased. Campaigning in Leeds during the election, David Cameron mistakenly described the election as 'career-defining', quickly correcting himself to 'country-defining' – but both were right.

As in most general elections, most of the significant events of the election took place outside of the formal six-week campaign. Some did not even take place during the five years of the Parliament. This chapter sets out the background to the surprise election.

The Coalition formed on 12 May 2010 was Britain's first peacetime coalition since 1931.[3] That coalition had initially been formed as a short-term one to deal with an economic crisis. But the Coalition in 2010 was designed to be longer-lasting, recognised in the plans for a fixed-term five-year parliament. 'The next general election', said William Hague in one of the Coalition's first announcements, 'will be held on the first Thursday of May, 2015.' There were plenty of observers – as well as a few of its participants – who wondered if the Coalition could really last that long. Such doubts persisted throughout the first half of the Parliament, with prophecies of early elections coming thick and fast, but Hague's initial prediction turned out to be correct.[4]

During the five days of coalition negotiations, William Hague had privately described the Conservative Party as an absolute monarchy, 'qualified by regicide'. David Laws remarked that the Liberal Democrats were an 'absolute democracy, moderated by very little'.[5] To agree their participation in the Coalition, the Lib Dems undertook a formal process of internal party democracy, with the Conservatives looking on somewhat bemused.[6] Cumbersome as it was, the Lib Dem process had important consequences. It meant that for good or ill, the decision to go into coalition with the Conservatives was a decision of the party, not of the leadership. It was thereafter very difficult for any Lib Dem to say that they had been bounced into anything. For the Conservatives, however, the coalition process was essentially top-down, driven by David Cameron and his team, and involving other elements in the party sporadically and only when necessary. A senior member of the Conservative 1922 Committee described it as 'a sort of British Leyland car park ballot, except we didn't even have a show of hands'. There were also complaints within the Conservative parliamentary party about what they saw as the leadership's 'deceit', having been told that they needed to offer the Lib Dems a referendum of voting reform to head off Labour's competing offer, only for Labour's competing offer to turn out not to exist.[7] From the beginning, this meant that there were a significant group of Conservative MPs who were unhappy with the Coalition and felt that they had not been consulted over its creation.[8] The Coalition had produced a paper majority in the Commons of almost 80, the sort of majority that had it been achieved by one party would have been described as a landslide. It served as a useful buffer against backbench unhappiness on both sides of the Coalition (and at times probably encouraged some MPs to rebel, safe in the knowledge they could do so without consequence), but it was not sufficiently large to protect the government entirely.

The distribution of Cabinet posts was quickly announced, with the top jobs going to George Osborne (Chancellor), Theresa May (Home Secretary) and William Hague (Foreign Secretary). The first two were to remain in post for the full five years of the government, while Hague remained until 2014. The Lib Dems took five Cabinet positions, including Clegg as Deputy Prime Minister, Vince Cable at Business and David Laws as Chief Secretary to the Treasury. Ten Lib Dems were given departmental junior minister posts and a further seven gained other government offices. The decision was taken to have Lib Dem ministers in almost every department rather than have the party 'own' particular ministries (as tends to be the case in some European coalition governments), with the aim of the party being able to influence every area of government policy. Later, several senior Lib Dems would look back on this as a mistake.

Within two years, two of the five Lib Dem members of the Cabinet had resigned amid scandals over their private lives. Laws lasted just 17 days as Chief Secretary, resigning following the disclosure of his improper parliamentary expenses claims. He was replaced by Danny Alexander. Charged with conspiring to pervert the course of justice over a driving offence, another Lib Dem minister, Chris Huhne, resigned his Cabinet post in February 2012. He vigorously protested his innocence, which he continued to do right up to the point a year later at which he pleaded guilty and announced he would resign his seat.[9] He was jailed for eight months, as was his former wife who had taken penalty points for speeding on his behalf.

The two parties were represented on all Cabinet committees. An institutional innovation was the 'Quad' – in essence, an inner cabinet – consisting of two Conservatives (Cameron and Osborne) and two Lib

Dems (Clegg and Alexander). It acted as a clearing house for potentially difficult issues and for important ones, like the Budget. It involved hard bargaining, but once the four had agreed a line, the Cabinet was presented with a virtual *fait accompli*. At one point, annoyed by accusations that they were simply the Conservatives' patsies, the Lib Dems floated the idea of allowing a fly-on-the-wall documentary team to film the Quad in action; the Conservatives, unsurprisingly, were not keen.

That the Coalition lasted for the full five years owed much to the good personal relations between the two party leaders; as is often the case with coalitions, decision making worked better at the top than below. But there was also an electoral incentive to hold together. Both political parties calculated that the longer the Parliament went on and as the economy improved, the better their chances of electoral success would be. This was one of the reasons why the length of the fixed term was set for five years rather than four, and nothing in the polls, right up until polling day itself, indicated that going earlier than that would be beneficial. There was never a point when the polls indicated that it might have been in either party's interests to collapse the Coalition early.[10]

The legacy of the 2008 financial crash shaped the formation of the Coalition and dominated its life. Given the size of the deficit (10% of the economy in 2010) and the continuing Greek financial crisis, it was inevitable that the economy would dominate the Coalition's thinking. The Queen's Speech in 2010 stated that the government's first priority was 'to reduce the deficit and restore economic growth'. Both were achieved, but not in the way that was planned.

George Osborne was inevitably cast as an austerity Chancellor.[11] He had hoped he would make sufficient progress in reducing the deficit to allow room for tax cuts before a 2015 general election. He brought in an emergency Budget in June 2010 and announced the first in what would be a series of cuts to spending programmes, including a halt to infrastructure projects and restrictions on entitlement to welfare benefits. The most notable of these were a VAT increase from 17.5% to 20%, child benefits frozen for three years, a two-year public sector pay freeze and Capital Gains Tax increase from 18% to 28% for the highest earners. *The Guardian* headlined it 'The Axeman Cometh'. This was Plan A.

But progress in cutting the deficit fell behind schedule, in part because of the stagnant Eurozone economy, modest income tax receipts from low-paid workers and the economic impact of cuts in government spending which tipped Britain onto the edge of recession. Osborne's standing was hit in 2012 by what became known as the 'omnishambles' budget, after a phrase in the satirical comedy *The Thick of It*. Osborne announced a cut in the 50p top tax rate by 5p. The government's claim was that the money raised by the additional 5p on the marginal rate was essentially negligible and simply encouraged tax avoidance, but privately many Conservatives saw it as a political mistake, giving an easy attack line to Labour that the government was in favour of tax cuts for millionaires whilst cutting services for ordinary people. The budget was also marked by a series of low-level cock-ups and retreats. The most obvious was the extension of VAT onto cooked food that was 'designed to cool down'. What Labour quickly labelled 'the pasty tax', and which they seized on as another example of the government being unconcerned with ordinary people, resulted in a bizarre series of exchanges in which Cabinet Ministers were asked to prove their proletarian credentials by identifying when they had last bought a pasty (and with the existence of said pasty shops then becoming a matter of debate) and members of the Shadow Cabinet staging a photo opportunity in a branch of Greggs. The story might have been even worse if it had become known that the Treasury's pre-budget analysis had identified rotisserie chicken as potentially problematic, yet no one had thought about the pasty. The tax was hastily reversed, but the same budget also generated a granny tax, a charity tax, a churches tax and a caravan tax (the last also delayed after protests). None of these was especially important individually, but collectively they smacked of political failure. At a Conservative political cabinet in the summer of 2012, Osborne told Conservative colleagues that 'the tunnel has become longer and the light further away'. His standing was low. 'We no longer hung on his every word', said a Cabinet minister. When Osborne appeared on the platform of the London Paralympic Games in August 2012, he was met with a chorus of boos. Commenting on rumours that Osborne would be moved, a senior adviser to Miliband said in July 2012 that 'we hope he stays as Chancellor until the end'.

Yet gradually the Chancellor, without announcing it, shifted to Plan B, a form of disguised Keynesianism to stimulate the economy. He relaxed the pace of deficit reduction and announced a series of infrastructure projects in the 2012 autumn spending statement. Such measures as his Funding for Lending in 2012 for firms and Help to Buy in 2013 to boost the housing market, a cut in corporation tax and his decision to scrap the planned rises in fuel duties all aimed to stimulate economic growth. Economic recovery was also assisted by low interest rates and continuing quantitative easing by the Bank of England. Prompted by the Lib Dems, he incrementally raised the personal income tax allowance from £6,500 to £10,600 by the end of the Parliament, freeing many low-paid workers from paying income tax. The 2014 Budget gave pensioners freedom to access part of their pensions before retirement and announced limits on spending on welfare, excluding pension benefits. That Budget, he boldly declared, was for 'the workers, the doers and the savers'.

Economists could present a damning assessment of Osborne's five-year record at the Treasury. He missed his target to eliminate the deficit, only halving it over the Parliament. That had been the aim of the last Labour Chancellor, Alistair Darling, which Osborne had derided at the time. Eliminating the rest of the deficit was postponed until the next Parliament. There was no progress in rebalancing the economy via more exports and manufacturing, the performances on the balance of payments and productivity were poor, and living standards declined over the lifetime of the Parliament. For all the cuts in benefits, the total welfare bill rose during the Parliament largely because of the protection given to pensioner entitlements. For the first three years, official forecasts for growth were revised downwards. Average income per head declined, except for the over-65s, who saw their real incomes rise. Labour attempted to make political capital from what they called the cost of living crisis.

On the other side, the increase in numbers in work (over two million in five years) was remarkable; the increase was bigger than in the rest of the EU combined. By 2014, Britain was the fastest-growing economy among the major Western states. Unemployment fell from 8% in 2010 to 5.5% in the first quarter of 2015 (see Table 1.1) The chief economist of the International Monetary Fund (IMF), who in 2013 had criticised Osborne's policy for cutting too much too fast, ate humble pie a year later and praised the record of the British economy. Inflation was low (below 2% in 2014), helped by falling oil prices. By 2015, the Office for Budget Responsibility (OBR) reported that household incomes had returned to pre-crisis levels.

Politically, the government could be reassured by both public and private polling on the need to tackle the deficit. Private Conservative polling in late 2011 reported that a large majority of voters accepted that what it was doing was clearing up 'Labour's mess'. When asked who was to blame for the cuts, voters blamed the banks, the last Labour government and the Eurozone countries ahead of the Coalition. When appointed Chief Secretary to the Treasury, David Laws found a note left by the outgoing Labour minister, Liam Byrne. It read: 'I'm afraid there is no money.' Byrne had meant it as a light-hearted friendly private note and was mortified both when Laws revealed its existence and even more so when the Conservatives made repeated use of it during the 2015 campaign.[12] Even when Labour was comfortably ahead in voting intentions, the Coalition, or at least the Conservative half of it, basked in a commanding lead in the opinion polls over Labour on questions of economic trust and competence. When asked, at the end of the Parliament, why Labour's attacks on Conservatives had failed, a member of the Shadow Treasury team summed it up simply: 'We were in charge when it went wrong. And the Tories were making progress. So we could tell people that George Osborne had failed to hit his own targets, but they'd say, "so what, it's your fault, and they are making it better".'

Nick Clegg and *that* pledge in 2010

Credit: NUS

The decision of the two parties to agree a 'Programme for Government' meant that their election manifestos were superseded. The Lib Dems made many gains in the policy negotiations. One analysis suggested that 75 per cent of Lib Dem manifesto commitments had been included in the Coalition agreement, compared to only 60 per cent of those of the Conservatives.[13] But they had made politically damaging concessions on tuition fees and spending cuts, two issues that would come to define the Parliament. Quantitatively, they were the clear winners; qualitatively, the outcome was not so clear.[14] The priority accorded to cutting the deficit meant that Departments, except for those at the protected Health, Education and Overseas Development departments, faced big reductions across Whitehall. Local government was particularly badly hit.[15]

Table 1.1 Economic indicators, 2010–15

	(1) *Real Household disposable income per head (£)*	(2) *Average earnings (seasonally adjusted average weekly earnings)*	(3) *Retail Sales Index*	(4) *CPI, annual rates*	(5) *Unemployment*	(6) *Working days lost to labour disputes*	(7) *GDP (GDP growth, chained volume measure, seasonally adjusted)*
		2000=100	*2011=100*	*%*	*%*	*(thousands)*	*%, quarter on quarter*
2010 1	4,480	141.5	99.9	3.3	8.0	284	0.4
2	4,453	141.4	101.2	3.5	7.9	22	0.8
3	4,494	142.4	101.9	3.1	7.8	15	0.5
4	4,432	143.4	100.7	3.4	7.9	44	0.1
2011 1	4,375	145.5	100.7	4.1	7.8	60	0.7
2	4,354	145.2	100.0	4.4	7.9	296	0.3
3	4,329	145.7	99.4	4.7	8.3	17	0.8
4	4,299	146.2	99.9	4.6	8.4	1015	0.2
2012 1	4,358	146.5	100.9	3.5	8.2	55	0.2
2	4,455	147.7	101.5	2.8	8.0	153	–0.2
3	4,454	148.3	101.9	2.4	7.9	25	1.0
4	4,424	148.1	101.2	2.7	7.8	16	–0.1
2013 1	4,332	147.3	100.8	2.8	7.8	95	0.7
2	4,393	151.1	102.5	2.7	7.8	121	0.6
3	4,395	149.5	103.5	2.7	7.6	21	0.9
4	4,336	149.7	104.5	2.1	7.2	207	0.6
2014 1	4,258	150	106.4	1.7	6.8	149	0.6
2	4,333	150.9	107.4	1.7	6.3	63	0.9
3	4,320	151	108.9	1.5	6.0	416	0.6
4	4,381	152.9	111.3	0.9	5.7	158	0.8
2015 1	4,388	152.9	111.7	0.1	5.5	69	0.4

Sources: (1)–(9) ONS; (10) Yahoo Finance; (11)–(13) Bank of England; (14)–(15) Ipsos MORI

(8)	(9)	(10)	(11)	(12)	(13)	(14)	(15)		
Balance of Payments (current account balance)	*House Price Index*	*FTSE 100 share index (3-month average)*	*US$ to £*	*Sterling exchange rate index*	*Interest (base) rates*	*Ipsos MORI Economic Optimism Index*	*Ipsos MORI polls (voting intention)*		
% of GDP	*Q1 2002 = 100*			*Jan 2005 = 100*			*C*	*L*	*LD*
–2.4	172.8	5,408	1.56	79.62	0.5	11.0			
–2.0	175.5	5,220	1.49	79.89	0.5	6.7	39.0	31.0	19.0
–3.3	178.4	5,344	1.55	81.76	0.5	–9.0	38.5	37.5	14.5
–3.4	174.5	5,701	1.58	80.30	0.5	–17.7	37.7	38.0	13.0
–1.1	172.9	5,922	1.60	80.82	0.5	–31.3	34.3	42.3	12.0
–0.1	172.3	6,002	1.63	79.45	0.5	–15.7	37.3	40.3	10.0
–2.8	175.6	5,446	1.61	79.22	0.5	–30.3	33.7	38.7	13.0
–2.6	173.7	5,541	1.57	80.30	0.5	–44.0	36.3	39.3	11.7
–2.4	173.7	5,774	1.57	81.16	0.5	–23.7	36.3	35.3	11.7
–3.4	175.7	5,543	1.58	83.13	0.5	–24.3	33.0	40.3	10.3
–3.1	178.9	5,696	1.58	84.04	0.5	–22.7	31.0	42.3	12.0
–4.2	177.7	5,849	1.61	83.61	0.5	–15.7	33.3	44.3	9.0
–4.2	177.5	6,350	1.55	80.31	0.5	–24.7	29.0	41.7	8.7
–3.2	180.8	6,410	1.53	80.50	0.5	–6.7	30.3	35.7	10.0
–4.6	185.3	6,499	1.55	81.22	0.5	16.0	31.0	39.0	10.0
–6.0	187.4	6,710	1.62	83.55	0.5	16.0	33.3	36.7	8.7
–4.5	191.6	6,640	1.65	85.57	0.5	22.7	31.0	34.0	12.7
–4.2	199.2	6,789	1.68	86.91	0.5	29.7	31.0	35.0	8.7
–5.4	207.1	6,724	1.67	88.01	0.5	27.0	33.0	33.7	7.3
–6.3	206.1	6,612	1.58	87.29	0.5	12.0	31.3	30.3	8.7
–5.2	207.8	6,832	1.51	89.43	0.5	14.7	33.3	34.7	7.3

The Lib Dems wanted to demonstrate that hung parliaments and coalitions did not inevitably lead to weak government and instability. They wanted, in the words of one of Clegg's advisors, 'to detoxify the idea of coalition'. This required them 'owning' the entire Coalition – good policies and bad – and required internal discipline in the meantime; 'coalition cracks', said the aide, was the easiest story for a journalist to write. The first test of that position was tuition fees. The Lib Dem manifesto had pledged to phase out tuition fees and Lib Dem MPs, including Clegg and Cable, had signed the National Union of Students' 'Vote for Students' pledge 'to vote against any increase in fees in the next Parliament and to pressure the government to introduce a fairer alternative'. The Coalition agreement allowed the Lib Dems to abstain on any vote on the issue if they were unhappy with the recommendations of the Browne Review into university funding. The party ended up splitting three ways – a debacle discussed in more detail in Chapter 4.

The Conservative manifesto in 2010 had promised that there would be no more 'top-down reorganisation' of the health service. But they were not the words of the new Health Secretary of State, Andrew Lansley, but those of Oliver Letwin, who had written the manifesto. Lansley proceeded to introduce far-reaching reforms which alienated many in the profession. He carried an increasingly unconvinced Cabinet with his reforms.[16] He was eventually replaced by the more conciliatory Jeremy Hunt, whose brief was essentially to close the issue down. Health had been a key issue for Cameron from the time of his election as leader in 2005. The NHS had long been an electoral minus for the party and identifying the Conservatives with it had been important in helping to demonstrate the party's compassion. In government, it turned out to be a losing issue for the Coalition parties, even though it was one of the few departments where spending was protected. When in 2011 a frustrated Cameron received a private polling report on the voters' dissatisfaction with the government's record on health and suggestions for tackling it, he scribbled on the top page: 'Well, let's do something about it!!'

Europe was a similar headache throughout. As a young Special Adviser to Cabinet ministers in John Major's government, David Cameron had a ringside seat as the party had self-destructed over Europe. He knew voters were more concerned about issues such as schools and the NHS, and in his first party conference speech as party leader in 2006, he had said that the Conservatives should 'stop banging on about it'. He favoured British membership, but – like many British Prime Ministers in recent years – the more dealings he had with the EU, the more sceptical about it he became. Increasingly, he came to the view that the EU needed reform to meet global competition and respond to Britain's needs. Number 10 staff liked to repeat Chancellor Merkel's (disputed) dictum: '7, 25, 50'. The EU had 7% of the world's population, produced 25% of its output, but accounted for 50% of the world's welfare bill. The EU was falling behind more dynamic Asian countries. Cameron wanted to curb the increasing scope of the interventions of EU institutions and reclaim more autonomy for national bodies.

Conservative MPs, reinforced by activists and Conservative-inclined newspapers, had become more Eurosceptic and a substantial number favoured withdrawal. Therefore, any scepticism the Prime Minister had was compounded by his backbenchers, who spent the five years of the Parliament pushing and prodding the leadership into a more Eurosceptic position. It did not help that the Prime Minister and the Chancellor had little to show for their efforts to assert British authority in Brussels. They failed to block a financial transactions tax which would bear heavily on the UK because of its large financial sector. They failed to stop the election of Jean-Claude Juncker as President of the EU Commission (Britain was in a minority of two against 26 other countries), despite Cameron's condemnation of Juncker. As we show in Chapter 2, Conservative MPs kept up unremitting pressure on the government to move in a more Eurosceptic direction, pressure to which Cameron frequently had little choice but to bend. The party began the Parliament ruling out a referendum on the EU, but by January 2013, the Prime Minister had given in and in a speech at Bloomberg agreed that one would be held by 2017 after a renegotiation of terms. In his 2006 conference speech, he had said the Conservatives had been banging on about Europe, 'while parents worried about childcare, getting the kids to school, balancing work and family life'; he gave the 2013 speech at 8 am, precisely when parents were getting their kids to school.

Some of Cameron's MPs wanted the referendum to be held much earlier than 2017; even more doubted that the renegotiations would amount to much and as long as Cameron did not spell out his negotiating position, they remained suspicious. However, he had to deal with these increasingly Eurosceptic MPs whilst balancing the views of his party with those of the more pro-European Lib Dems, and demands by his Eurosceptic MPs for more overlooked the reality of coalition. Also hovering over Cameron's relations with the EU was UKIP, which called for Britain to leave the EU and which from 2013 onwards began to surge in the polls. Cameron was confident that the Conservatives had the

European policies to nullify UKIP's appeal, particularly the promise of an in/out referendum which Labour and the Liberal Democrats opposed. But what mattered more for UKIP voters was halting immigration, most of which came from EU countries. Immigration was frequently among the top choices when voters were asked about the most important issues or problems facing the country. Academic studies pointed to the benefits that the British economy gained from immigration. But the complaints that low-skilled immigrants were depressing the wages of low-paid British workers and placing strains on the services in the towns where immigrants concentrated gained more publicity. There was not much Britain could do about this given the EU's commitment to freedom of movement across its Member States, and other EU leaders made clear that freedom of movement was not negotiable. Cameron's pre-2010 pledge to reduce immigration to 'the tens of thousands' with 'no ifs no buts' lay in ruins as net migration figures increased remorselessly. During 2014, net immigration rose above 300,000.

The Coalition, driven by the Conservative half, tightened the rules on the entry of overseas students and placed a cap on the entry even of skilled non-EU migrants. These policies irritated Vince Cable at the Department for Business, Innovation and Skills, as well as universities (which were relying on overseas graduate students) and businesses (which were dependent on skilled workers from other countries). Some business leaders were already complaining about the uncertainty being caused by an in/out EU referendum. But no party could compete with the stark simplicity of UKIP's policy of withdrawal from the EU, which was the only way to stop unrestricted entry from Member States.

In January 2011, Andy Coulson, David Cameron's Director of Communications, resigned amid continuing allegations of phone hacking by journalists under his editorship at the *News of the World*. The phone hacking story had forced his resignation from the paper in early 2007, after which he had gone to work for the Conservatives. But renewed claims about phone hacking had appeared in late 2010, and by January he resigned from his post in Number 10, saying that 'continued coverage of events connected to my old job at the *News of the World* has made it difficult for me to give the 110% needed in this role', adding that 'when the spokesman needs a spokesman, it's time to move on'. The phone hacking scandal had major impacts on the press, on the police and on politics. In July, it was revealed that the paper had hacked into the voicemails of murdered schoolgirl Milly Dowler. The new Labour leader, Ed Miliband, who had been elected in late 2010, seized the initiative by demanding an independent inquiry into the role of the press as well as the resignation of Rebekah Brooks, the former chief executive of News International, which owned the *News of the World*. Within a few days Coulson had been arrested, as had Brooks. After 168 years of publication, the *News of the World* closed down in July 2011.

To answer the growing concern over newspaper ethics and the relationship between the press and politicians, Cameron announced that Lord Justice Leveson would head an inquiry into press regulation and the relations between the press and politicians. Amongst other things, the inquiry confirmed the very close relationship between Cameron and Brooks; they apparently exchanged texts once a week. In May 2012, Brooks was charged with perverting the course of justice and Coulson was charged with perjury. Leveson published his report in November 2012, recommending independent regulation of the press backed by statute.[17] The episode was one of a series of attacks Miliband would make throughout the Parliament on vested interests and boosted his self-confidence. But at the height of the scandal, the weekly Populus question asking over 2,000 voters what topic they would raise with David Cameron if he came to their door found only 38 people (1.9%) raising the issue of hacking.

The expenses scandal which had marred the previous Parliament rumbled on. In 2011, two years after the scandal first surfaced, a number of (sitting and former) parliamentarians were sentenced to jail for their fraudulent expense claims. They included David Chaytor, Eric Illsley, Jim Devine, Denis MacShane and Elliot Morley (all Labour MPs), The Tory peers Lord Taylor of Warwick and Lord Hanningfield were also jailed.

In 2013, Maria Miller, the Culture Secretary, was accused of providing a home for her parents at the taxpayers' expense. She repaid some of the expenses and made such a perfunctory (30 seconds) apology to the Commons on 3 April that criticism only increased. She resigned six days later. More generally, the decision of MPs to delegate decisions about their pay and conditions to a new Independent Parliamentary Standards Authority (IPSA) did nothing to reduce public opprobrium on the issue. Each release of information about MPs' expenses continued to attract headlines focusing on the apparently trivial or extravagant – and when, in 2013, the IPSA recommended an 11% pay rise for MPs, it did not matter that the recommendation was coming from an independent body or that the overall deal was cost-neutral.

Of even more public concern were the riots that began in August 2011, following the shooting by police of Mark Duggan. A protest in Tottenham on 6 August turned violent; this violence spread to other parts of London in the following days and to other English cities. The riots caused five deaths and 16 serious injuries across England. By 15 August, 3,100 people had been arrested and 100 charged. Cameron cut short a family holiday in Tuscany and recalled Parliament to allow MPs to 'stand together in condemnation of these crimes and also to stand together in determination to rebuild these communities'.

There were more opinion polls between 2010 and 2015 than in any other parliament in British political history. These came from a variety of different firms and were conducted under a variety of different methods, but they told a fairly consistent story. Using data from the Polling Observatory team, Figure 1.1 shows the pooled estimates of every poll from the beginning of the Parliament until 1 April 2015, at the beginning of the official short campaign.[18]

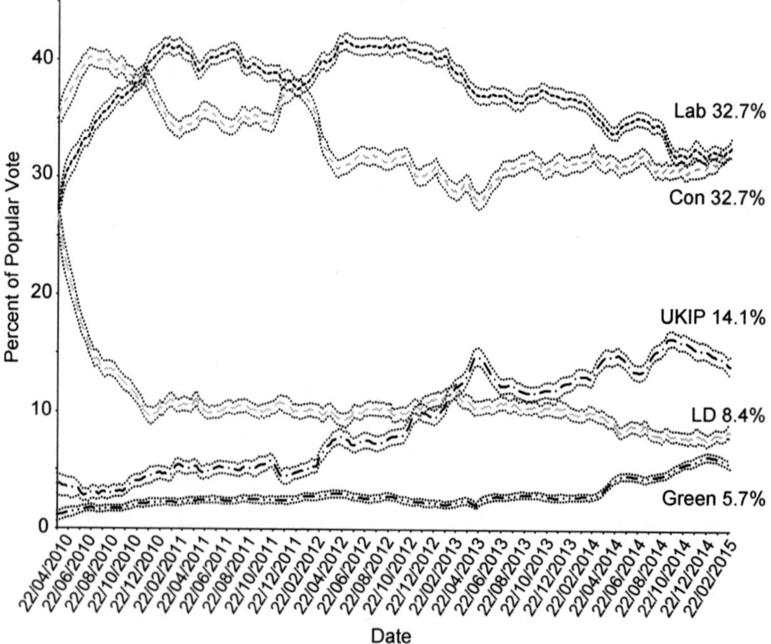

Figure 1.1 Estimated party vote intention, May 2010–April 2015

Source: Polling Observatory

Within months of the Coalition forming, Lib Dem support virtually halved, then dropped yet further by the end of the year after the tuition fees vote, before trending very gently downwards for the rest of the Parliament. At first, the leakage was largely to Labour, and there was an immediate rise in Labour support, with Labour moving ahead of the Conservatives in the polls by the end of 2010. The gap between the two main parties briefly narrowed, only to widen again after the omnishambles Budget of 2012. Labour regularly polled over 40% in public polls after the 2012 Budget, leading the Conservatives by double figures. Labour's support then declined from late 2013 and the two parties were closely matched in the last 12 months of the Parliament, at around 33%. The Polling Observatory team's April 2015 estimates had the two parties exactly tied at 32.7% just as the short campaign began. Figure 1.1 also shows the clear and dramatic rise in support for UKIP, from below 5% at the start of the Parliament, rising to a peak of around 16% in late 2014, before dipping very slightly thereafter. UKIP moved ahead of the Lib Dems from early 2013. There was also a noticeable rise in support for the Greens in the last 12 months of the Parliament, as well as – not shown here, but discussed in Chapter 5 – support for the SNP in Scotland.

We discuss the issue of opinion polling, and especially questions about its accuracy, in more detail in Chapter 9. But here it suffices to note that these same broad trends were seen in the various elections that took place during the Parliament. The Lib Dem collapse, for example, was clear right from the start of the Parliament. In the local elections in May 2011, the Lib Dems lost (net) almost 750 councillors, more than 40% of the seats they were defending; things got no better in 2012, 2013 or 2014. Across the Parliament as a whole, they lost 2,000 councillors and lost control of 16 councils. In the Scottish elections of 2011, in the face of an exceptional performance by the SNP (see below and also Chapter 5), the Lib Dem performance was catastrophic, falling from 17 to 5 MSPs. The party lost every mainland constituency and their vote more than halved to just 7.9%.[19] The European elections in 2014 saw the Lib Dems reduced to just one MEP. Of the 19 by-elections held in seats in Great Britain (see Table A2.7), 14 saw double-digit percentage drops in the Lib Dem vote share. They lost their deposits – that is, polled below 5% – in 11 of these. Apart from the Eastleigh by-election in 2013, caused by Chris Huhne's resignation and which they held (despite a 14.5% decrease in their vote share), the party only retained one deposit from 2013 onwards. They finished fourth in nine by-elections, fifth in one and even – at the Rotherham by-election in late 2012 – eighth. In Rochester and Strood, they failed even to poll 1%.

UKIP's rise was equally clear. They made impressive gains in the 2013 and 2014 local elections.[20] Over the course of the Parliament, the party made a net gain of 477 councillors. They began to be a serious performer in parliamentary by-elections, finishing first or second in more than half of the Westminster by-elections they contested, winning two in 2014 with defections from the Conservatives, and only narrowly missing out on taking Heywood and Middleton from Labour in October 2014. From the mid-point of the Parliament, every by-election saw their vote share increase noticeably, almost always by 10 or more percentage points and often by more than 20. They also topped the poll in the European Parliament elections in May 2014 with 27.5% of the vote, the first time a party other than Labour or the Conservatives had done so in any nationwide electoral contest for over 100 years.

The electoral pain inflicted on the governing parties was asymmetric, with it being inflicted disproportionately on the Lib Dems rather than the Conservatives. In the 2011 local elections, the Conservatives even made a small net gain in terms of seats. They lost councillors in each further round of elections, but never catastrophically. They lost the Corby by-election in 2012, but managed to hold Newark in 2014. They polled poorly in the European elections, coming third, but only narrowly behind Labour, and they managed to hold the London Mayoralty (albeit with a candidate in Boris Johnson who has the ability to rise above party). And whilst Labour made gains in almost all elections it participated in, they were never quite of the scale to convince people – both inside and outside the party – that they were on course for a clear victory at the general election. They gained seats in every round of council elections, making a net gain of over 2,000 councillors throughout the Parliament, as well as gains in the European elections. They had few chances to shine in by-elections (which mostly occurred in seats that were not going to change hands), took Corby from the Conservatives, but lost Bradford West to George Galloway's Respect Party. It was an upward trajectory, but it was not clear whether it was steep enough.

The exception to Labour's upward trajectory was the elections to the Scottish Parliament in 2011, where the party lost seats – as did the Conservatives and the Lib Dems – as the SNP stormed to a majority that the electoral system was supposed to make impossible, as discussed in more detail in Chapter 5. By putting the SNP in a position where they could initiate a referendum on independence for Scotland, it was probably the most significant electoral moment of the Parliament. Indeed, all the electoral shocks of the Parliament were delivered by supposedly minor parties – UKIP, the SNP and Respect – but never by Labour.

If the Coalition agreement had been implemented in full, the Parliament had the potential to be a constitutionally radical one.[21] Elected on five-year fixed terms, the House of Commons returned in 2015 would have been a smaller body with more equally-sized constituencies. It could have been elected by the Alternative Vote and would have had control over its own timetable. Members of the public would have had the power to initiate recall against MPs accused of wrongdoing and to initiate proceedings in the Commons, including bringing forward bills. There would have been widespread all-postal primaries to select candidates for election. There would be elected Police and Crime Commissioners. And there would have been the first steps towards a wholly or at least mainly elected House of Lords. Had this all taken place, the election in 2015 would have been qualitatively different from that of 2010. But most of the reforms died, from neglect or abuse. Where they survived, they were often a pale imitation of what had first been promised.[22]

One of the changes that did take place was the Fixed-Term Parliaments Act 2011. Despite its name, it provides for semi-fixed-term Parliaments.[23] General elections are to be held every five years on the first Thursday in May, and the Act removes the Prime Minister's ability to use the Royal Prerogative to call an election at the time of his or her choosing. Early elections could only take place if more than two-thirds of the House of Commons voted to call an election or if the Commons passed a vote of no confidence in the government and a new government was not formed within 14 days. Fixed-term parliaments had long been a Lib Dem policy, but there was also a political imperative: the party wanted a safeguard to prevent the Conservatives dumping them at a moment's notice. The original intention had been for the length of the parliament to be four years, but during the coalition negotiations, George Osborne suggested five. Both the principle and the specifics – especially the length of the term – were controversial, but the government got its way.

Less significant were the elections for 41 Police and Crime Commissioners in England and Wales which took place in November 2012, with the public responding in an underwhelming way, seeing turnouts of between 10 and 20%.[24] Overall turnout was 15%, the lowest ever in a nationwide election.

The Parliamentary Voting System and Constituencies Act 2011 was deliberately two measures in one. One provided for a referendum on whether to replace first-past-the-post electoral system with the Alternative Vote (AV) for Westminster elections. The other provided for a reduction in the number of Westminster constituencies to 600, with constituencies being of a more equal size. AV had been a sticking point in the coalition negotiations, but was a key Lib Dem demand. It was not that they wanted AV per se – prior to 2010, Clegg had called it 'a miserable little compromise'– but it was, in the words used by a member of the party's Federal Executive at their first meeting after the election, 'as good as it's going to get'.[25] AV might not be a proportional electoral system and it would not generate an especially large increase in Lib Dem seats, but the party still estimated it would increase its number of MPs by about 20, making future hung parliaments more likely and thus giving them more chances to push for further reforms in the future. As we noted in 2010: 'The Liberal Democrats accepted a referendum on AV on the basis that it was the best they could get; that something was better than nothing; and that it could be a stepping stone to future reform.'[26]

The AV referendum was held in May 2011. It was a disaster for the Lib Dems.[27] The Yes campaign was worthy and naïve; the no campaign was cynical, partisan and victorious. The latter turned the issue into one of cost, claiming the system would cost £250 million.[28] One poster featured a picture of a newborn baby with the slogan: 'She needs a new cardiac facility NOT an alternative voting system'; another featured a soldier: 'He needs bulletproof vests NOT an alternative voting system.' The *New Statesman* complained that the ads were 'beyond parody', but they worked. When No to AV ran focus groups in October 2010 – when Yes was ahead in the polls – not one person had talked about cost; when they re-ran the groups in March 2011, every group mentioned the £250 million figure.[29] Nick Clegg deliberately kept a relatively low profile in the campaign; he acknowledged that voters wanted the opportunity to punish him ('people want to poke me in the eye and signal their displeasure'), but the No campaign targeted him, wanting to make the campaign about Clegg and his broken promises over tuition fees. Cameron initially took a relaxed approach to the vote, until his backbenchers voiced their concern, at which point he put the party machine behind the 'No' campaign, and campaigned vigorously. No triumphed by more than two to one. The Coalition agreement had been explicit in allowing the Coalition parties to take a different stance on the issue from each other, but the vehemence with which the Conservatives had attacked Clegg personally damaged relations between the parties.

'Psephology'

Martin Rowson, *The Guardian*, 26 May 2014

Even worse was to come over House of Lords reform, another proposal close to the Lib Dems' hearts. In July 2012, the government won the second reading vote on the House of Lords Reform Bill, although 91 Conservative MPs defied a three-line whip to vote against. The second reading was achieved thanks to Labour support, but this did not extend to the bill's programme motion. In the face of certain defeat, the government withdrew the motion and realising that it would be impossible to proceed without control of the timetable – fearing opponents of the bill would filibuster – the Coalition officially shelved plans to reform the House of Lords.

The Lib Dems were furious, both because of the loss of the Bill and also because they believed (despite plenty of allegations of strong-arm tactics from the Conservative whips) that the Conservatives had not tried sufficiently hard to get the legislation through.[30] As one of Clegg's advisors said: 'They [the Lib Dems] accept that, as the junior partner in a coalition, you will get stiffed, but when you do, you've got to hit back.' To retaliate, the Lib Dems withdrew their support for the new electoral boundaries created as part of the Parliamentary Voting System and Constituencies Act.[31] The Lib Dems claimed that Lords reform and the new boundaries were part of a package of reforms; if one fell, then so did the other. When the issue came before the Commons, Lib Dem MPs – including ministers – joined with Labour to vote against the Conservatives, postponing the boundary changes until 2018.[32] One of the ironies of the row was that the Lib Dems had been in favour of a reduction in the size of the Commons – the 2010 Lib Dem manifesto had promised an even greater reduction, down to 500 MPs – but the party had begun to realise how disruptive it could be for incumbent MPs to have their constituency boundaries altered. Anyway, even if some Lib Dems had still wanted the measure, it was clear the Conservatives wanted it even more, which made it an obvious target.

The Conservatives had also entered the 2010 election promising a reduction in the size of the Commons. This was justified on the basis that it would reduce the cost of politics (fewer politicians never being an unpopular message), but the real goal was to equalise the size of constituencies, with the reduction in the size of the Commons being the trigger for an immediate boundary review. Conservative strategists were well aware of the pro-Labour bias in the electoral system. After 2010, to gain a 20-seat majority, Labour needed to be four percentage points ahead of the Conservatives; to gain the same majority, the Conservatives needed to be 11% ahead of Labour.[33] The Conservatives had calculated that moving to more equal-sized constituencies would be worth around 20 seats to them at the next election. This would not be enough to negate the pro-Labour bias in the electoral system, but it would at least ameliorate it.[34] Conservative MPs and strategists were furious with the Lib Dems for blocking the boundary changes. The episode led to a more transactional relationship between the two parties and a proposed Coalition 2.0 document for the second half of the Parliament was abandoned. This was now a peculiarly British form of coalition, in which governing parties voted down government legislation which had formed part of their Coalition agreement and yet remained governing parties.

The government pushed ahead with plans for individual electoral registration (IER), a change from a system where one member of the household ('the head of the household') would register all those within the household who were eligible to one where everybody was expected to register individually. This had originally been introduced by the Labour government in 2009, although the Coalition announced its intention to 'speed up' the introduction of IER in the Electoral Registration and Administration Act 2013. The Act provided for a phased introduction of IER, with only those not found on the Department for Work and

Pensions database having to register afresh.[35] This initial matching exercise was undertaken to reduce the risk of people dropping off the registers, although even then the absolute number of entries on the registers in England and Wales published in December 2014 had gone down.[36] Labour began to talk about the 'missing million' voters. The reality was less dramatic than this: there was particular concern about the number of students registered (several registers in areas of high student population saw numbers decline), but since many students can be registered at both home and term-time addresses, the concerns about disenfranchisement of students may have been somewhat overplayed. Talk of people missing from the register, alongside the traditional campaigns to register that take place ahead of a general election, started to have an impact on registration, resulting in a big increase in the run-up to the deadline, enhanced by the ability to now do so online. On every day in March 2015, there were between 18,000 and 80,000 applications to vote, rising to a peak on the last day for registration, 20 April, which saw almost half-a-million applications on that one day.[37]

Equally controversial was the Lobbying, Non-Party Campaigning and Trade Union Administration Act 2014. A proposal to regulate lobbying had formed part of the Coalition agreement and had been anticipated for a number of years. Less expected were the restrictions on non-party campaigners (known as 'third parties') that formed Part 2 of the Bill. Their inclusion, explained the government, was to prevent unregulated spending by vested interests having undue influence in elections, although critics claimed that it was a way of preventing charities and non-governmental organisations (NGOs) campaigning properly. The Bill aimed to significantly reduce the amount of money that third parties could spend in elections and broadened the definition of campaign expenditure to include activities such as canvassing and rallies as well as electoral material.[38] The Bill ran into much controversy in the Lords and had to be watered down to ensure its passage, but it still presented charities and other lobbying organisations with a harsher climate in which to try to influence elections.

Cameron preferred to keep ministers in post for a good innings if possible. He regarded the frequent turnover of ministers as the bane of British politics. Liam Fox had resigned as Defence Secretary in 2011 following revelations that he had taken a friend with him on several official trips. Cameron's first major Cabinet reshuffle in September 2012 saw Jeremy Hunt move from Culture to Health and Chris Grayling replaced Kenneth Clarke as Justice Secretary. Justine Greening was controversially moved from Transport to International Development. Patrick McLoughlin moved to Transport and was replaced as Chief Whip by Andrew Mitchell. The reshuffle (with the exit of the pro-European Clarke to a position as Minister of State without Portfolio) was widely regarded as repositioning the party towards the Eurosceptic and right of centre in advance of the 2015 election, and away from the Lib Dems.

Mitchell did not stay long in post, brought down within weeks by the so-called 'plebgate' affair. On 19 September, he had a row with the Downing Street police officers who refused him permission to take his bike through the main gates. Two days later, *The Sun* reported that Mitchell had sworn at officers and called them 'plebs', a term that fed into charges that the Conservatives were wealthy snobs. Amid further claims and counterclaims about what he had actually said, Mitchell came under mounting pressure and, on 19 October, he resigned due to the 'damaging publicity' that prevented him from doing his job. He was replaced by Sir George Young, who had just been dismissed as Leader of the House of Commons.

The initial story gradually unravelled as the police version of events was challenged, amid claims that an officer had given false evidence. Over the following months, eight people were arrested and bailed as part of the investigation, five of whom were police officers. Four officers ultimately lost their jobs over the affair for gross misconduct. It proved a Pyrrhic victory for Mitchell, who was not reinstated and who lost an expensive libel case against *The Sun* in November 2014.

In July 2014, Philip Hammond replaced William Hague as Foreign Secretary, who became Leader of the Commons (and simultaneously announcing that he would be standing down from the Commons at the election), and Michael Gove moved from Education to be Chief Whip. Gove had won plaudits from supporters with the extension of free schools and academies and a more rigorous testing regime in schools, but he had attracted brickbats from the teaching profession and irritated other ministers with his habit of intervening on their patches.

Cameron was comfortable on the international stage and, despite his scepticism about the grander schemes of European integration, forged good relations with President Nicolas Sarkozy of France and Chancellor Angela Merkel of Germany. He and Sarkozy set the pace in getting the Security Council to authorise a no-fly zone over Libya and to use military force to protect Libyan civilians against Colonel Gaddafi. However, he suffered a rebuff over plans to intervene in Syria.

Having recalled Parliament on 29 August 2013 to debate the situation in Syria, Cameron was confident of receiving Miliband's support. This was not forthcoming and the government whips discovered significant discontent among Tory MPs about the prospect of military action. The government retreated, promising that no military action would take place without a further vote, but even this was not enough to satisfy some Conservative opponents of military action (or the Labour front bench), who voted against it, resulting in defeat of the government motion by 285 votes to 272. The USA had been poised for action, but, following the Commons vote, did not proceed.[39]

The UK government condemned as illegal the Russian annexation of the Ukraine territory of Crimea in March 2014. It joined other EU states in imposing sanctions and supported the suspension of Russia from the G8. In September 2014, Parliament was again recalled, this time to vote on British air strikes against Islamic State forces in Iraq. The government motion this time was approved by 524 votes to 43. British troops handed over Camp Bastion to Afghan security forces on 26 October, bringing an end to British combat operations in Afghanistan. Defenders of the armed forces – including many Conservative MPs – complained about the limits on the defence budget and how it was close to falling below the 2% of GDP target set by NATO.

In October 2012, in the 'Edinburgh Agreement', David Cameron and Scottish First Minister Alex Salmond agreed that a referendum on Scottish independence would be held by September 2014. The unionist parties, Conservative, the Lib Dems and Labour, joined in a Better Together ('No') campaign to preserve the Union. Leading positions were taken by Labour, much the strongest party of the three in Scotland. Although Cameron took a back seat in the campaign, he visited Scotland at least six times to give speeches and discussed it regularly with his aides. He did not want to go down in history as the Prime Minister who 'lost Scotland' and, had he done so, his party critics would almost certainly have called for a leadership contest – although those close to him believe he would have resigned before they could do so.[40] The lead-up to, and consequence of, the referendum is discussed in Chapter 5. Along with the departure of Coulson, Cameron regarded it as the most stressful episode of his premiership. Despite the victory for the No side, the political fallout of Scotland then dominated the remaining months of the Parliament; the SNP continued the momentum of the campaign into the general election, transforming the political landscape. Although the Union survived in September 2014, British electoral geography was completely transformed.

Prior to the referendum in 2014, it was commonplace for Scots to argue that those south of border – journalists, politicians and academics – did not understand what was happening in Scotland. There was doubtless some truth in this. But the events after September 2014 demonstrated that it was not just those south of the border who were ignorant; many of those north of the border – journalists, politicians and academics – did not have much of a clue either. After the rise of the SNP became clear, there was no shortage of post-hoc explanations; everyone could retrospectively explain what had happened; it was obvious. But it was not so obvious that anyone had managed to predict it.

The 2010 Parliament defied many expectations by lasting its full term, although increasingly the two Coalition parties had been differentiating themselves for the forthcoming general election. Many Lib Dems complained that they were not receiving due credit from the Conservatives or the public for the sacrifices they had made; one Cameron aide said that the public saw the coalition as 'a Tory government with Lib Dem window-dressing'. According to opinion polls, most voters wanted a return to single-party government, but according to those same polls, there was next to no chance of that happening. The general election would decide whether the 2010 experience would be the start of a new norm of multi-party governments or whether it had been a one-off and single-party government would be restored.

Chronology of events from May 2010 to December 2014

2010

11 May	Con–LD coalition formed.
12 May	Coalition Cabinet (includes five LD): N. Clegg, Deputy Prime Minister, G. Osborne, Chancellor, W. Hague, Foreign Secretary and T. May, Home Secretary.
17 May	Osborne announces new Office for Budget Responsibility.
20 May	Tory MPs oppose Cameron's plans to alter the 1922 Committee.
25 May	Queen's Speech includes plans for free schools and abolition of identity cards.
29 May	Chief Secretary to the Treasury, D. Laws resigns after allegations he broke rules on parliamentary expenses. Danny Alexander replaces him.

1 Jun	Cameron makes apology for Bloody Sunday killings.
22 Jun	Emergency Budget includes rise in VAT from 17.5% to 20%.
6 Jul	Government caps redundancy payments for 0.5 million civil servants.
8 Jul	M. Gove, Education Secretary, apologises for publishing incorrect list of school building projects.
30 Jul	Work and Pensions Secretary, I. Duncan Smith, announces simplification of benefits system.
9 Aug	Government U-turn over scrapping free school milk.
25 Sept	E. Miliband elected Labour leader.
29 Nov	EU rescue package agreed for Ireland.
9 Dec	Student protests in London over tuition fees.
20 Dec	Government U-turn over cuts in school sports funding.
26 Dec	Government partial U-turn over free books for children scheme.

2011

7 Jan	Former Lab MP, D. Chaytor, jailed for fraudulently claiming parliamentary expenses.
20 Jan	A. Johnson steps down as Shadow Chancellor for personal reasons; replaced by E. Balls. Y. Cooper becomes Shadow Home Secretary; Douglas Alexander Shadow Foreign Secretary.
21 Jan	A. Coulson, No 10's Director of Communications, resigns.
10 Feb	Barnsley Central Lab MP, E. Illsley, jailed for expenses fraud.
11 Feb	H. Mubarak, President of Egypt, resigns after 18 days of mass protests.
17 Feb	Government ditches planned sale of forests.
18 Feb	Government drops cut of housing benefit for long-term unemployed.
21 Mar	House of Commons votes to endorse no-fly zone over Libya.
23 Mar	Budget: measures introduced include: personal tax allowance to rise by £630; inflation rise in fuel duty delayed until 2012; annual 1p above inflation 'fuel escalator' rise scrapped until 2015; £2bn extra taxes on North Sea oil firms; 2% above inflation rise in excise duties for wine, spirits and beer; tobacco duty rates up by 2% above inflation.
6 Apr	Government pause National Health Service Bill.
1 May	O. bin Laden killed by American Special Forces.
5 May	AV referendum sees 67.9% oppose changing voting system. Local elections; LD lose 748 councillors; Lab gain 839; Con

gain 86. In Scottish parliamentary elections SNP win 69 seats and form first majority government at Holyrood. In Wales Lab gain 4 seats, giving them half the seats in the Assembly. In Northern Ireland DUP gain 2 seats and Sinn Fein one.

18 May	Justice Secretary, K. Clarke, appears to suggest that some rapes are more serious than others.
19 May	D. Strauss-Kahn resigns as Managing Director of IMF following arrest on rape charges.
19 May	Government U-turn over coastguard cuts.
14 Jun	Government agrees major concessions to NHS Bill.
21 Jun	Government drops plans to allow prisoners 50% off their sentences if they plead guilty.
23 Jun	Miliband abolishes elections for Labour Shadow Cabinet.
4 Jul	Revelation that *News of the World* hacked voicemails of murdered schoolgirl M. Dowler.
9 Jul	Arrest of Coulson over phone hacking.
10 Jul	*News of the World* closes.
17 Jul	Former News International Chief Executive R. Brooks arrested over phone hacking. Sir P. Stephenson, Metropolitan Police Commissioner, also resigns over his involvement.
18 Jul	Assistant Police Commissioner, J. Yates, resigns over phone hacking.
19 Jul	R. and J. Murdoch and Brooks give evidence to the Culture, Media and Sport Select Committee over the phone hacking scandal.
22 Jul	A. Behring Breivik bombs government buildings in Oslo, killing eight, before going on a mass shooting spree, killing 69 people.
6–10 Aug	Major riots and looting across UK.
6 Oct	Bank of England announces £75bn of fresh quantitative easing.
7 Oct	Miliband reshuffles Shadow Cabinet.
12 Oct	UK unemployment up 114,000 to 2.57 million, a 17-year high.
14 Oct	Defence Secretary, L. Fox, forced to resign following controversy over his relationship with lobbyist and unofficial adviser; replaced by P. Hammond.
18 Oct	Inflation rises to 5.6%, highest since June 1991.
20 Oct	M. Gaddafi is killed.
24 Oct	Eighty-one Con MPs rebel over an EU referendum.
27 Oct	EU bailout deal for Greece provisionally agreed.

1 Nov	World stock markets plummet at news of Greek referendum on EU bailout plan.
9 Nov	G. Papandreou resigns as Greek Prime Minister, as referendum plans abandoned due to EU pressure.
9 Dec	Cameron vetoes EU-wide treaty change designed to solve Eurozone crisis.

2012

11 Jan	Government unveils plans for in/out referendum on Scottish independence.
31 Jan	F. Goodwin, former Chairman of RBS, stripped of his knighthood.
3 Feb	Energy Secretary, C. Huhne, resigns after being charged with perverting the course of justice. E. Davey replaces him.
9 Feb	Bank of England announces another £50 billion of quantitative easing.
15 Feb	UK unemployment 2.67 million, a 16-year high.
21 Mar	Budget: cut in top rate of income tax from 50p to 45p; new 7% stamp duty for houses worth more than £2 million and 15% duty for properties bought by a company; personal allowance for lower-income taxpayers increased by £1,100. U-turn on child benefit, gradually removing it for those earning between £50,000 and £60,000 a year. VAT on freshly cooked pasties, static caravans and changes to listed buildings. Cap on tax relief for charitable donations.
30 Mar	G. Galloway wins Bradford West by-election for Respect Party with swing of 36.59%.
25 Apr	UK growth falls 0.2% in the first quarter of 2012, putting country back into recession.
15 May	Brooks arrested for perverting the course of justice.
25 May	Houla massacre in Syria.
28 May	Government U-turn on pasty tax and VAT on static caravans.
30 May	Coulson arrested for perjury.
31 May	Government U-turn on cap on tax relief for charitable donations.
2–5 Jun	Diamond Jubilee celebrations for Queen Elizabeth II.
26 Jun	Government halts 3p fuel increase.
27 Jun	Government publishes Lords reform proposals.
2 Jul	Cameron announces parliamentary inquiry into banking.
3 Jul	B. Diamond, Chief Executive of Barclays Bank, resigns over LIBOR rate fixing.

5 Jul	Bank of England announces another £50 billion of quantitative easing.
10 Jul	Government wins House of Lords Reform Bill second reading vote, but 91 Con MPs rebel. Fearing defeat, programme motion is withdrawn.
16 Jul	Coalition is re-launched by Cameron and Clegg.
18 Jul	Coalition announces £50 billion of infrastructure projects.
24 Jul	Eight people including Coulson and Brooks charged with phone hacking. Last day of Leveson Inquiry.
27 Jul	London Olympic Games begin.
6 Aug	Coalition abandon plans for reform of House of Lords; Clegg withdraws support for boundary changes in retaliation.
3 Sep	N. Bennett elected leader of Greens.
4 Sep	Cabinet reshuffle: J. Hunt promoted to Health Secretary. C. Grayling replaces K. Clarke as Justice Secretary. New Chief Whip is A. Mitchell.
12 Sep	Cameron apologises to victims of Hillsborough disaster.
15 Oct	Cameron and Salmond sign a deal on Scottish independence referendum.
19 Oct	Mitchell resigns as Chief Whip after allegations he called Downing Street policeman a 'pleb'. Replaced by Sir G. Young.
31 Oct	Coalition suffers first Commons defeat on cuts to EU budget.
6 Nov	US President B. Obama re-elected.
15 Nov	15% turnout for Police and Crime Commissioner elections. Lab win Corby from Con, hold Manchester Central, and Cardiff North and Penarth.
29 Nov	Lord Justice Leveson recommends statutory control of press. Lab hold three by-elections in Middlesbrough, Croydon North and Rotherham. UKIP perform strongly.

2013

23 Jan	Cameron says there will be an EU in/out referendum in 2017.
29 Jan	LD and Lab unite to delay Coalition proposals to redraw parliamentary constituencies and to cut number of MPs.
4 Feb	Huhne quits as MP, pleading guilty to driving offences.
21 Feb	LD launch internal party review into allegations of sexual misconduct by Party's former Chief Executive, Lord Rennard.
22 Feb	UK's credit rating downgraded from AAA to AA1.
1 Mar	LD hold Eastleigh.

20 Mar	Budget: planned increase in personal allowance brought forward a year; corporation tax down to 20%; increase in fuel duty cancelled; additional £15 billion for infrastructure projects; cancellation of the duty escalator on beer.
22 May	Clegg abandons illegal immigrant amnesty proposal.
27 Mar	D. Miliband to resign as MP.
1 Apr	Government instigates new benefits cap and under-occupancy penalty that becomes known as 'the bedroom tax'.
8 Apr	Death of former Con Prime Minister, M. Thatcher.
12 Apr	Cameron and A. Merkel meet in Germany to discuss EU reform.
15 Apr	Boston Marathon bombings.
17 Apr	Thatcher's funeral.
24 Apr	May admits Abu Qatada will not be deported for months. Government exploring temporary withdrawal from European Convention on Human Rights.
25 Apr	LD refuse to support proposals to monitor internet and social media use.
2 May	Local elections: Labour 29%, Conservatives 25% (lowest share since 1982), UKIP 23% and LD 14% (lowest ever). Direct Mayoral elections in Doncaster and North Tyneside. Lab win South Shields by-election; UKIP second; LD seventh.
14 May	Con publish draft parliamentary bill setting terms for an in/out EU referendum by 2017.
16 May	On a free vote, 114 Cons MPs vote for motion regretting absence of EU referendum bill in Queen's Speech.
22 May	Soldier, L. Rigby, is murdered in the street in Woolwich.
25 May	J. Prescott calls on Miliband to promise an in/out EU referendum.
27 May	US officials say UK would probably be excluded from trade agreement if it leaves EU.
31 May	Con MP P. Mercer resigns from party in 'cash for questions' scandal.
2 June	Two British Lab peers suspended by party following allegations of offering to undertake parliamentary work for payment. Ulster Unionist peer Lord Laird, accused of same offenses, resigns party whip.
17–18 Jun	UK hosts G8 summit.
1 Jul	M. Carney becomes Governor of the Bank of England.
3 Jul	Egyptian President Mohamed Morsi deposed in military coup.

6 Jul	Prescott resigns from Privy Council in protest over delays to changes in press regulations.
9 Jul	Miliband says he will end the automatic 'affiliation' fee paid by union members to Lab. Option of imposing whole-life tariff for worst murders in England and Wales ruled illegal by European Court of Human Rights.
11 Jul	Party leaders criticise IPSA recommendations to increase MPs' salaries to £74,000 from 2015.
16 Jul	Hunt announces 11 hospitals will be placed in special measures because of major failings.
17 Jul	Same-sex marriages legalised in England and Wales.
22 Jul	Prince George born to Duke and Duchess of Cambridge.
21 Aug	Chemical attacks in Damascus sees President Obama threaten military strikes. Cameron pledges British support subject to parliamentary approval.
27 Aug	Badger cull begins in Somerset and Gloucestershire despite controversy.
29 Aug	House of Commons recalled four days early to debate backing military intervention in Syria. Government is defeated by 285 votes to 272.
4 Sep	US Senate Foreign Relations Committee backs military action against Syria.
10 Sep	Charged with sexual offences, N. Evans MP resigns as Deputy Speaker.
20 Sep	G. Bloom MEP makes outburst about 'sluts' at UKIP conference and is later expelled from the party.
24 Sep	Miliband vows to freeze energy prices at Lab Party Conference.
26 Sep	UN Security Council agrees resolution requiring Syria to hand over its chemical weapons.
27 Sep	Cameron rejects invitation for head-to-head TV debate on Scottish independence with Salmond.
28 Sep	*Daily Mail* declare E. Miliband's father as 'The Man Who Hated Britain'.
7 Oct	Launch of the National Crime Agency.
11 Oct	Government publishes Royal Charter aimed at underpinning self-regulation of the press following an agreement between the three main political parties.
17 Oct	Osborne announces that UK will allow Chinese companies to invest in British nuclear industry.

22 Oct Sir J. Major, former PM, calls for government to levy a windfall tax on Britain's energy companies.

23 Oct Owners of Grangemouth oil refinery announce its closure due to industrial action. Decision is later reversed. Cameron announces review of green energy taxes.

28 Oct *News of the World* phone hacking trial begins.

30 Oct Privy Council grants Royal Charter on press regulations.

6 Nov BAE Systems announces it is cutting 1,775 jobs, resulting in the end of shipbuilding in Portsmouth.

18 Nov Cameron welcomes decision by search engine companies Google and Microsoft to block online images of child abuse.

20 Nov General Synod of the Church of England votes in favour of legislation to allow the ordination of women bishops by 2014.

24 Nov Iran agrees to limit its nuclear development programme.

26 Nov Salmond unveils the SNP's independence blueprint.

5 Dec N. Mandela, South Africa's ex-President, dies.

16 Dec May announces draft legislation for tougher prison sentences for people convicted of human trafficking.

20 Dec EU credit rating downgraded from AAA to AA+.

22 Dec Cable attacks Con over migrant 'panic', likening rhetoric to E. Powell's 'Rivers of Blood' speech; also calls for an end to public spending cuts.

23 Dec Former MP D. MacShane jailed for expense fraud.

24 Dec Enigma codebreaker A. Turning receives Royal Pardon for conviction of homosexual activity in 1952.

26 Dec UN refugee agency condemns proposed immigration laws.

28 Dec Cameron, Clegg and Miliband call for unhindered humanitarian access as figures show 9 million are suffering in Syrian conflict.

29 Dec UKIP leader N. Farage calls on government to let Syrian refugees into the UK.

2014

8 Jan Inquest jury decides that death of M. Duggan by police, which sparked 2011 riots, was lawful.

19 Jan UKIP suspend Oxfordshire councillor who blamed bad weather on legalisation of gay marriage.

29 Jan Governor of Bank of England says that Scotland would need to give up some powers in return for a currency union with UK in the event of independence.

31 Jan	European Union (Referendum) Bill rejected by House of Lords.
6 Feb	PC K. Walls, who claimed to have witnessed the 'plebgate' incident, sentenced to 12 months' imprisonment. Royal Marines sent to Somerset Levels to help with flood protection. Government also provides extra £30 million to help relief efforts.
7–23 Feb	Sochi Winter Olympics. Britain's best performance at a Winter Games since 1924.
8 Feb	Immigration Minister, M. Harper, resigns after disclosure that his cleaner did not have permission to work in UK.
11 Feb	1,600 troops deployed to help flood relief effort.
6 Mar	May announces public inquiry into undercover policing.
16 Mar	Referendum on the status of Crimea.
19 Mar	Budget. Measures include: rise in 40p income tax threshold; inheritance tax waived for members of emergency services who give their lives in service; VAT waived on fuel for air ambulances and inshore rescue boats; 10p tax rate for savers abolished; and new £1 coin to be introduced in 2017.
21 Mar	Russia formally annexes Crimea.
24 Mar	Russia temporarily suspended from G8.
27 Mar	UN General Assembly passes resolution recognising Crimea within Ukraine's international borders and rejecting referendum result.
9 Apr	Culture Secretary, M. Miller, resigns over expenses row; S. Javid is replacement.
24 Apr	Danny Alexander announces Cornish people will be granted minority status under Council of Europe.
29 Apr	Former Cons MP P. Mercer resigns his Newark seat.
22 May	European parliamentary elections (results announced 26 May): UKIP top share of vote.
5 June	Obama says US's interest in Scottish independence referendum is to ensure it retains a 'strong, robust, united and effective partner'. Newark by-election; Con hold seat but with large rise in UKIP vote.
12 Jun	2014 FIFA World Cup begins.
24 Jun	Coulson found guilty of conspiring to hack phones.
25 Jun	Jury in the phone hacking trial dismissed after failing to reach verdict on outstanding charges against Coulson. Trial's judge rebukes Prime Minister for commenting on Coulson's conviction while trial still ongoing.

7 Jul	May announces major review and inquiry into allegations of historical child abuse across all areas of UK society.
10 Jul	Cameron announces emergency powers giving police the ability to access phone and Internet records will be rushed through Parliament after existing legislation overturned by European Court of Justice.
14 Jul	Church of England votes to allow women to be ordained as bishops. Hague steps down as Foreign Secretary as D. Cameron reshuffles Cabinet.
15 Jul	Hammond appointed Foreign Secretary; M. Gove becomes Chief Whip; N. Morgan appointed Education Secretary.
21 Jul	N. Griffin ousted as BNP leader.
23 Jul	2014 Commonwealth Games opens.
5 Aug	First televised debate between Salmond and A. Darling on Scottish independence.
6 Aug	Mayor of London, B. Johnson, announces intention to seek re-election to Parliament.
25 Aug	Second televised debate between Salmond and Darling.
26 Aug	Publication of Independent Inquiry into Child Sexual Exploitation in Rotherham concludes that at least 1,400 children in the area subjected to sexual abuse between 1997 and 2013. UKIP leader Farage chosen to fight South Thanet at election.
28 Aug	Con MP D. Carswell defects to UKIP and will contest by-election as UKIP candidate.
29 Aug	UK's terror alert raised from 'substantial' to 'severe'.
5 Sep	MPs back the Affordable Homes Bill, designed to relax controversial housing benefit cuts.
6 Sep	YouGov poll on Scottish independence gives Yes campaign a majority for the first time, 51% to 49%.
7 Sep	Osborne pledges 'plan of action' for further devolution to Scotland if Scots vote No in referendum.
8 Sep	Duchess of Cambridge expecting second child. G. Brown sets out timetable for transferring more powers to Scotland after No vote.
9 Sep	Scottish leaders of three main UK parties back greater devolved powers for Scottish Parliament.
12 Sep	Johnson selected as Con candidate for Uxbridge and South Ruislip.
13 Sep	Cameron condemns killing of British hostage D. Haines after release of video showing aid worker's beheading.

18 Sep	Scottish independence referendum. 'No' wins by 55.3% to 44.7%. Turnout of 84.5% a record high for any election in UK since universal suffrage in 1918.
19 Sep	Cameron announces plans for further devolution of powers to Scotland (as well as to other countries of UK) and establishes Smith Commission to convene talks. Salmond announces resignation as First Minister of Scotland and leader of SNP.
24 Sep	N. Sturgeon launches campaign to lead SNP and therefore Scottish First Minister.
26 Sep	Parliament recalled to debate and agree bombing of Isis in Iraq. Government wins majority of 481.
27 Sep	Con MP M. Reckless defects to UKIP, triggering by-election.
1 Oct	SNP membership trebles from 25,000 to 75,000 in 13 days following independence referendum.
3 Oct	Cameron says Britain will do all it can 'to hunt down [and bring] to justice' the killers of British hostage A. Henning after video posted online showing his beheading.
9 Oct	Clacton and Heywood and Middleton by-elections. Carswell wins Clacton, becoming UKIP's first elected MP; Lab hold Middleton, but with significant rise in UKIP vote.
15 Oct	Sturgeon becomes leader of SNP unopposed.
24 Oct	J. Lamont resigns as leader of the Scottish Lab.
3 Nov	LD Home Office Minister, N. Baker, resigns, claiming working in the department is like 'walking through mud'.
7 Nov	Osborne criticised as he reveals the UK will pay its EU budget surcharge in two interest-free sums next year totalling £850 million instead of a larger lump sum of £1.7 billion by 1 December.
17 Nov	Church of England adopts legislation paving the way for appointment of women bishops.
19 Nov	Sturgeon becomes First Minister of Scotland.
20 Nov	Rochester and Strood by-election. Reckless wins for UKIP. Launch announced of *The National*, Scotland's first daily newspaper to take pro-independence stance.
25 Nov	Report into Rigby murder by Parliament's Intelligence and Security Committee suggests MI5 could have prevented the killing had they been allowed access to online forum in which the murder had been discussed five months previously.

27 Nov	Smith Commission publishes report recommending Scottish Parliament be given the power to set income tax rates and bands. Mitchell loses libel action against *The Sun*.
1 Dec	Brown announces he is to stand down as MP at next election.
3 Dec	Autumn Statement: Osborne replaces flat rate of stamp duty for graduated scheme.
7 Dec	Salmond confirms intention to contest Gordon constituency at election.
13 Dec	J. Murphy elected Scottish Lab leader.
16 Dec	Hague sets out Con plans for 'English votes for English laws'.

Notes

1. 'A Distribution of General Election Forecasts', blogs.lse.ac.uk, 27 March 2015; and 'Politics Experts Predict Conservatives and Labour Will Be "Virtually Inseparable" in Terms of Both Seats and Votes', www.psa.ac.uk, 2 March 2015.
2. The Conservatives polled 36.9% of the UK vote in 2015. This was lower than the party had polled in all but eight general elections since 1832.
3. Of the many accounts of the negotiations leading to the Coalition, see Dennis Kavanagh and Philip Cowley, *The British General Election of 2010*. Palgrave Macmillan, 2010, Chapter 10, as well as Rob Wilson, *5 Days to Power: The Journey to Coalition Britain*. Biteback, 2010; David Laws, *22 Days in May: The Birth of the Lib Dem–Conservative Coalition*. Biteback, 2010; and Andrew Adonis, *5 Days in May*. Biteback, 2013.
4. See, for example, Patrick Dunleavy, 'Fixed Term Parliaments are a Mirage – it's All Downhill from Now to a June 2014 General Election', blogs.lse.ac.uk, 20 February 2012.
5. Laws, *22 Days in May*, p. 102. It is regularly misquoted as 'an absolute monarchy, moderated by regicide'.
6. It is often forgotten that David Cameron had become Prime Minister before the Liberal Democrats had formally agreed to join the Coalition.
7. Kavanagh and Cowley, *The British General Election of 2010*, pp. 213–15.
8. Some, mainly on the right, opposed any deal with the Lib Dems and would have preferred Cameron to form a minority government, with the aim of calling a second election later in 2010. With Labour and the Lib Dems short of money and the former locked in a divisive leadership election, they claim the Conservatives would have swept the board. But anyone who makes such an argument does not understand what was – and was not – realistically on offer in 2010. Given that Labour were the incumbent party and were offering the Lib Dems a coalition arrangement (albeit one that only secured a majority with the support of other parties), had the Conservatives attempted to govern alone as a minority, the Lib Dems and Labour would almost certainly have formed an alternative governing coalition. Rather than be in a minority government, the Conservatives would have remained in opposition.

9. Indeed, he was so persistent in his private claims that he was innocent and the case was about to collapse that those around Nick Clegg had begun working out ways in which they would be able to bring him back into government when he was acquitted.
10. In retrospect, it may indeed have been better for the Lib Dems to have exited earlier, but there was never a point at which their position in the polls made that clear.
11. On Osborne, see Janan Ganesh, *George Osborne: The Austerity Chancellor*. Biteback, 2012.
12. See Liam Byrne, '"I'm Afraid There is No Money." The Letter I Will Regret for Ever', *The Guardian*, 9 May 2015. As he said: 'I knew my successor's job was tough. I guess I wanted to offer them a friendly word on their first day in one of government's hardest jobs by honouring an old tradition that stretched back to Churchill in the 1930s and the Tory chancellor Reginald Maudling, who bounced down the steps of the Treasury in 1964 to tell Jim Callaghan: "Sorry to leave it in such a mess, old cock".' But in the same article Byrne notes that the phrase was one he had used, repeatedly, when negotiating spending cuts with fellow Labour ministers in the run-up to 2010. It was not *just* a joke.
13. 'Inside Story: How Coalition Government Works' (Constitution Unit, June 2011).
14. For a good discussion of this, see Thomas Quinn *et al.*, 'The UK Coalition Agreement of 2010: Who Won?', *Journal of Elections, Public Opinion and Parties*, 21(2) (2011): 295–312.
15. See Anthony Seldon and Mike Finn (eds), *The Coalition Effect 2010–2105*. Cambridge University Press, 2015; Matthew D'Ancona, *In it Together*. Penguin, 2014; and Matt Beech and Simon Lee (eds), *The Conservative–Liberal Democrat Coalition*. Palgrave Macmillan, 2015.
16. Nicholas Timmins, *Never Again? The Story of the Health and Social Care Act 2012*. Institute for Government and King's Fund, 2012.
17. Technically, this was just part 1 of the Inquiry. Part 2 could not start until the various police investigations and criminal proceedings had finished, although it was not clear it ever would.
18. That is, Robert Ford (University of Manchester), Will Jennings (University of Southampton), Mark Pickup (Simon Fraser University) and Christopher Wleizen (University of Texas at Austin). Rather than reporting individual poll figures, the team pool each month's polls, controlling for different company's different methodologies (what are called 'house effects'). The methodology is explained at: pollingobservatory.wordpress.com/methodology.
19. Scottish leader Tavish Scott resigned the day after the elections. That the Welsh result was considered relatively good within the party, despite Lib Dem support falling by almost a third, was an indicator of just how bad things were elsewhere.
20. And in the local elections held on the same day as the general election, they took control of their first council, Thanet.
21. For an excellent overview of the Coalition's constitutional reform programme, see Martin Loughlin and Cal Viney, 'The Coalition and the Constitution' in Seldon and Finn (eds), *The Coalition Effect*.

22. Here we discuss the major constitutional or electoral reforms. But the same applies to many of the others, such as all-postal primaries (abandoned very early on), recall (introduced in a very limited form), MPs' control of parliamentary business (only half-implemented) and public initiation of bills (not implemented). See Philip Cowley, 'Parliament' in Seldon and Finn (eds), *The Coalition Effect*.
23. Andrew Blick, 'Constitutional Implications of the Fixed-Term Parliaments Act 2011', *Parliamentary Affairs*, 2015 (online).
24. J. Garland and C. Terry, *How Not to Run an Election: The Police & Crime Commissioner Elections*. Electoral Reform Society, 2012.
25. In the same interview, Clegg called it a 'baby step in the right direction', although this phrase was quoted much less often.
26. Kavanagh and Cowley, *The British General Election of 2010*, p. 226. In the event, even this calculation was wrong. By 2015, the evidence appears to be that AV would not have helped the Lib Dems (see below, p. 424).
27. See Paul Whiteley, Harold D. Clarke, David Sanders and Marianne C. Stewart, 'Britain Says NO: Voting in the AV Ballot Referendum', *Parliamentary Affairs*, 65(2) (2012): 301–22.
28. The figure was, at best, debatable and, at worst, highly dubious, given that the single largest component of additional cost was for automated voting machines, for which there were no plans. But it was effective.
29. Dylan Sharpe, 'AV: How No Won', nottspolitics.org, 9 May 2011.
30. One unnoticed consequence of the Fixed-Term Parliaments Act is that it removed the Prime Minister's ability to make votes, like this one, into votes of confidence. See Philip Norton, 'The Fixed-Term Parliaments Act and Votes of Confidence', *Parliamentary Affairs*, 2015 (online).
31. David Rossiter, Ron Johnston and Charles Pattie, 'Representing People and Representing Places: Community, Continuity and the Current Redistribution of Parliamentary Constituencies in the UK', *Parliamentary Affairs*, 66(4) (2013): 856–86.
32. The Bill itself had already passed, but the key vote was to approve the Order implementing the recommendations of the Boundary Commissions. The Lib Dems first defeated the measure in the Lords and then joined Labour to stop the Commons reversing the vote.
33. Kavanagh and Cowley, *The British General Election of 2010*, p. 338. These figures were to change, first, as the Lib Dem vote collapsed, and then, second, as Labour collapsed in Scotland, but these were the estimates at the beginning of the Parliament.
34. Those involved in drawing up the policy understood that the unequal size of constituencies was not the only, or even the main, reason for the pro-Labour bias in the electoral system – but the gains were still worth making. As one of those involved noted, the more Conservatives thought that smaller boundaries were largely responsible for the pro-Labour electoral bias – that is, the less they really understood the policy – the more they were in favour of it, which made it easy to persuade them of its value.
35. The preference of the Minister in charge, Mark Harper, had been to include an 'opt-out' to allow people to choose not to register – which would potentially have meant millions falling off or not joining the registers. The opt-out provisions did not make the final Electoral Registration and Administration

Act. Had they done so, the state of the registers may have entered a period of decline and even greater politicisation.

36. *Analysis of the December 2014 Electoral Registers in England and Wales*. Electoral Commission, 2015.
37. Like so much in this debate, this figure is also potentially misleading. It means that there were half-a-million *applications* to vote. Since the system did not allow anyone to check whether or not they were already on the register, many will have done so on a just-in-case basis (why not?); the actual number who registered as a result was significantly smaller. In total, between 1 January and the final day for registration, there were just short of 5 million applications to register in England and Wales, yet the numbers registered grew by just 1.35 million, indicating a lot of people were applying who were already registered or not eligible to vote.
38. The total amount that non-party campaigners can spend during the regulated period was set at: £319,800 in England; £55,400 in Scotland; £44,000 in Wales; and £30,800 in Northern Ireland.
39. See Juliet Kaarbo and Daniel Kenealy, 'No, Prime Minister: Explaining the House of Commons' Vote on Intervention in Syria', *European Security*, 2015 (online).
40. Anthony Seldon and Peter Snowdon, *Cameron at 10*. William Collins, 2015, p. 422.

2
How Hard Can it Be? The Conservatives

For much of the Parliament, there was disagreement among Conservatives about how to interpret the 2010 election. David Cameron's critics never forgave him for failing to win the election outright, especially against such an unpopular Prime Minister as Gordon Brown. Partly, this was a criticism of the party's tactics – most obviously the decision to take part in the television debates which gave Nick Clegg so much visibility and credibility – but it was also a criticism of the fundamental messages on which the party had fought the 2010 election. Critics dismissed the manifesto's idea of a Big Society, both intellectually and as a doorstep message, and criticised the lack of emphasis on Europe, immigration and tax cuts. The election post-mortem conducted by the Conservative-Home website regarded it as a missed opportunity, one made worse by Cameron then forming a coalition with the Liberal Democrats.[1]

The party's so-called modernisers – of which David Cameron was initially one – argued that this missed the point spectacularly.[2] A core vote strategy, directed at the party's strong supporters and emphasising tax cuts, hostility to the EU and restrictions on immigration, had been tried in both 2001 and 2005, and had failed badly.[3] The core was not large enough and catering to it would alienate other voters needed to win an election. Repeating such a campaign strategy would do little to help the party recover in Scotland (where it had just one seat) or the north of England, or overcome its weaknesses among ethnic minorities or public-sector workers (both groups which were less likely to vote Conservative). Party researchers found that the biggest single predictor of the party doing badly in a seat on polling day in 2010 was a large non-white electorate.[4]

When he was elected Conservative leader in 2005, Cameron and his close colleagues had been determined to change how the party was perceived. They had been struck by surveys which showed that levels of approval for policies fell as soon as these policies were linked with the party. To use the terms in vogue at the time, the Conservative brand was 'toxic' and needed to be 'decontaminated'. The real failure in 2010, they argued, was that the modernisation was at best an incomplete project by the time of the election. Lord Ashcroft's 2010 report *Minority Verdict* concluded that the party failed to get a working majority largely because it was still not seen to be on the side of ordinary people, was not trusted on public services and its motives were suspect.[5] In one telling image, voters identified the Conservatives with a picture of a posh family standing outside a large house.

Cameron and his close colleagues were determined to change that image. The Tory modernisation strategy was the attempt to do for the Conservatives what Tony Blair had done for Labour – to make it electable – hence the drive before 2010, via the A-list of candidates, to change the composition of the party's MPs by recruiting more women and ethnic minority candidates. It complemented efforts to work in cooperation with the professionals in health and education; encouragement of volunteering; and the adoption of policies to address social issues, protect the environment and show more tolerance of alternative lifestyles (such as same-sex marriage).

But in office, the David Cameron of the Big Society, environmental protection, 'wellbeing', hugging-a-hoodie and the A-list of candidates was a pale version of what had been promised. There was a continuing tension between addressing core voter concerns and the modernisers' agenda. In trying to balance both sets of interests, Cameron often left both sides disappointed. Some on the anti-EU and right wing of the party complained that he had no deep beliefs and he seemed just to like being Prime Minister. One colleague, on arriving to work at Number 10, was told 'if you're looking for his irreducible core, you'll not find it'.

Despite the coalition with the Lib Dems, immigration and Europe rose up high on the list of Cameron's concerns and pulled him to the right. His early ambition may have been to stop the party obsessing about the EU, but the issue dominated his time in office. As Prime Minister, he rarely spoke on climate change, once casually dismissing it as 'green crap', and many of his MPs were sceptics about the claims made by the green lobby. He abandoned the A-list of candidates. His firm response to the summer riots in 2011, including stiffer sentences for looters and curbing their welfare benefits, prompted charges that he was reverting to a more traditional form of Conservatism. Despite all the efforts the Conservatives had made in opposition to show their commitment to the NHS and despite its budget being protected, Andrew Lansley's mammoth and controversial Health and Social Care Act damaged the party's reputation on the issue. The Chancellor's cut in the 50p top tax rate in the 2012 Budget gave a gift of a soundbite to Labour that the party was indeed only interested in looking after the interests of the rich. Cameron could – and did – point to the raising for the personal tax allowance, which took many of the low paid out of tax altogether, but as this was a Lib Dem policy, it was both an audacious and disingenuous defence against claims that the Conservatives favoured the wealthy.[6] But essentially much of the modernisers' programme had fallen victim to austerity. There was no flowering of Big Society projects. After just a few months, references to the Big Society or 'we are all in it together' produced giggles among some Number 10 staff.

Yet one of the curiosities of the Cameron government was that whilst those on the left saw it as a brutal ideological exercise in cutting social programmes and creating a smaller state, those on the right – including many within Cameron's party – saw it as a vacuous holding operation by someone who had few beliefs and who was afraid of pursuing genuinely Conservative policies.[7] A paradox of the 2015 election is that had Cameron failed to secure re-election, those on the right would have seen it as a vindication of their view that modernisation was an electoral dead end, whereas modernisers had long been despairing of the Prime Minister and his agenda.

Cameron took with him into Number 10 most of the senior staff who had served with him in opposition before 2010. They included Ed Llewellyn, his chief of staff, Kate Fall, deputy chief of staff, Andy Coulson, press secretary, Ameet Gill, at first Cameron's speech-writer and then given charge of strategic communications, and Steve Hilton, head of strategy. A significant appointment, as party co-chairman, was Lord (Andrew) Feldman of Elstree, a friend of Cameron's from their student days at Oxford who had raised the money for his leadership campaign in 2005.

Compared to the confusion that had sometimes reigned in Number 10 under Gordon Brown, David Cameron's operation was relatively calm and orderly. Officials were impressed with how Cameron's political team persisted with the daily 8.30 am and 4.00 pm meetings that his team had used in opposition. These lasted half an hour and combined a review of the day with a look ahead to events for later that day or tomorrow. Officials, including Jeremy Heywood, the Number 10 Permanent Secretary, attended, but were supposed to withdraw when the discussion turned to party matters. In making decisions, Cameron liked to hear a range of views and was slow to narrow the discussion if it would mean closing down options. But he did not respond well to questions which posed either/or options. Before the 2012 Budget, George Osborne asked him whether it should be a package for growth or for tackling the deficit. Cameron thought for a moment and then replied 'Both'.

Two of Cameron's original appointments, both with the highest salaries and highest profiles, did not stay to the end. Steve Hilton was the arch-moderniser, radical and close to Cameron. But by the time he left Number 10 in May 2012, Hilton had become impatient with the obstacles he felt were in the way of his reforming plans. These included the civil service ('the bureaucracy'), the EU, health and safety legislation, the legal system, the Lib Dems and his leader's timidity. In Number 10 he had become more radical and wanted to use the economic constraints as a pretext for bold measures and shrinking the state. In particular, he wanted more devolution of power to parents, neighbourhoods and patients. He told bemused officials that he wanted the Coalition to become 'missionary and transformative'.[8] The originator of the Big Society still believed in it, even if very few others did. His critics would argue that one of the biggest obstacles to Steve Hilton's progress within Number 10 was Steve Hilton. 'He can be astonishingly childish and emotional', said one Number 10 staffer in 2011. As one Lib Dem Special Advisor wrote: 'He did not so much collide with reality, as arrive late to meetings with it, shout at it, question what makes it tick and then storm off, appalled at reality's obstinacy.'[9] His departure, regretted by Cameron but few others within Number 10, was widely seen as marking the end of the Big Society agenda.

The departure of Andy Coulson after serving just eight months in post was a more damaging episode. He had been appointed as the party's communications director in 2007 after assuring Cameron that he knew nothing of the phone hacking undertaken by the *News of The World* when he was editor. Cameron came to rely on him heavily. Despite warnings to Cameron that damaging revelations would come out, Coulson was appointed as communications director in Number 10. His previous experience as a tabloid newspaper editor, his more modest social background (very different from the upper-middle-class one of most of the Number 10 personnel) and his common touch ('Andy knows what the punters think', said a Cameron aide) gave him great credibility. When he resigned in January 2011 to face charges over illegal phone hacking, his appointment reflected badly on the judgment of both Cameron and Osborne.

Most press or communications directors in Number 10 had, like Coulson, come from a newspaper background. His successor, Craig Oliver, from the BBC, regarded the broadcast media as more important and strengthened Number 10's resources in digital and social media. 'He didn't care about the lobby', said one Number 10 staffer, 'and the feeling was reciprocated.'[10] Collectively, these were the people, along with Osborne, Cameron was most comfortable with – and to whom he usually turned when making big political decisions.[11]

In 2011 Cameron appointed Andrew Cooper, the Director of the polling firm Populus, to act as his director of strategy. Cameron called him an 'uber-moderniser' and told him one of his tasks was 'helping to make a modern compassionate Conservative Party'. When he appointed Lynton Crosby later in the Parliament, he said that his job was to win the election. There was a constant tension between the two goals.

From 2010 to 2012, Feldman's co-chairman at Conservative Campaign Headquarters (CCHQ) was Baroness (Sayeeda) Warsi, a forthright and energetic media spokesperson for the party, and the first Muslim woman to serve in the Cabinet. Her main task was to visit local associations and keep the activists in good heart, although being in the Lords limited her contact with the party's MPs. Feldman ran the organisation and was an immensely successful fundraiser, paying off the party's debt and raising a substantial war chest for the election. He shed staff in party headquarters and, like Labour, employed more in the regions and constituencies. In 2012 Warsi was replaced by the MP Grant Shapps, who proved to be a ready and skilful communicator, if with what turned out to be baggage from his business dealings before Westminster. He also kept in closer touch with MPs than his predecessor. But the appointment of Crosby clipped his wings when it came to the general election. The days of Tory party chairmen like Cecil Parkinson, Norman Tebbit and Chris Patten deciding election strategies and running campaigns had gone.

An increasingly influential figure in recent Conservative election campaigns has been the campaigns director Stephen Gilbert; he had been in charge of field operations since 1993 and had served four different party leaders. He was also Cameron's political secretary, in part because of the relationship he had built up with MPs during elections. He divided his time between Number 10 and CCHQ, but from 2014 concentrated more on the latter role. His main task was to choose the 2015 election battleground, the seats which the party would be defending and those it would be trying to win.

Just before David Cameron entered Downing Street, one of his best friends remarked to him how strange it was that one of his old friends might become Prime Minister. 'Mr Cameron looked at him bemused and said: "How hard can it be?".'[12] Most colleagues, officials and staff working for a party leader want to know what makes him or her 'tick', what their priorities are and how they like to take decisions. In Cameron's case, the question often posed was: what kind of Conservative is he?

Asked by the *Sunday Times* just after the death of Lady Thatcher whether he was a Thatcherite, Cameron first attempted to side-step the question; when pressed, he admitted to being a big supporter of Thatcher, if not a Thatcherite, arguing that such labels were misleading and that contemporary challenges were different from those in the 1980s.[13]

Two years earlier, in 2011, he had answered an interviewer's question if he was a compassionate Conservative by describing himself as 'common sense'. Cooper remonstrated with him over this disavowal of the compassionate label, arguing that it would be seen as a retreat from modernisation and a move towards William Hague's 2001 agenda ('the commonsense revolution'). Was he then simply a pragmatist? Note the ease with which – to the ire of many of his party – he seemed to take to coalition government rather than a dictating and driving zeal, and not for nothing did Cameron make it known that his political hero was not Thatcher, but Harold Macmillan.

But the danger in this approach and the uncertainty over whether Cameron held to a particular creed was the risk of being seen as merely an entitled and happy adventurer. At best this might fit with his political hero, but at worst he was simply a toff with a sense of entitlement and a sense that politics might be a jolly good wheeze. The latter tied in with perceptions of him as lazy ('chillaxing', holidaying and fond of watching DVD box sets) and last-minute (the phrase 'the essay crisis Prime Minister' began as early into his premiership as 2010).

But there were beliefs, if worn lightly. The perceptive Matthew D'Ancona described the essence of Cameron's Conservatism: 'It was not just personal responsibility that he called for but – more ambitiously – "social responsibility"' that would, for instance, inspire parents to set up free schools, and charities and volunteers to become involved in socially useful activities.[14]

As the head of a coalition, Cameron immediately found himself denied a large part of the Prime Minister's armoury – patronage, and in particular government jobs. Over a quarter of government posts went to Lib Dems. Many senior Conservative MPs who had laboured through the long years of opposition as opposition frontbenchers and the ambitious (and often able) intakes of 2005 and 2010 were inevitably disappointed. Cameron tried to compensate with appointments to various advisory bodies, such as the Conservative Policy Board, but he left many of his backbench MPs frustrated and in some cases bitter.

It did not help that the Prime Minister gained few marks for good party management. Colleagues wondered if his neglect was because he had spent such a short period on the backbenches – from the beginning, he and Osborne had operated at elite levels in the party, and he became party leader after just five years in the Commons – or whether his aloof manner was a result of his social background, or indeed whether it was both. Whatever the reason, a good number of backbenchers thought he took them for granted and they resented it. His tough line on MPs' expenses, following the expenses scandal in the 2005 Parliament, and his opposition to an increase in their pay did not impress many of them, who would comment on his private wealth. It was, they would say, easy for him. He and his friends, the Cameroons, were an almost exclusively upper-middle-class social set, whose friendships dated from being students at Oxford and desk officers at the Conservative Research Department (CRD).[15] It was something of a chumocracy ('a coup of chums' was a phrase bandied about in the early days of his leadership) rather than a group who shared a political philosophy. Yet whilst the leadership may have been a social elite, the party in Parliament was changing, becoming less privately and Oxbridge-educated. David Davis, who had lost to Cameron in the leadership election in 2005, called in 2012 for a change in the ethos and type of people around the leader: 'please, please, no more old Etonian advisers'. The maverick Conservative MP Nadine Dories touched a nerve when she dismissed Cameron and Osborne as 'two posh boys who did not know the price of a pint of milk'.

Cameron got off to a bad start with a cack-handed attempt to bring the 1922 Committee of Conservative backbenchers to heel.[16] His proposal that ministers should have full voting rights was an attempt to influence the forthcoming election of a new chairman. The intervention smacked of arrogance, met with strong protest and was eventually abandoned. He had opposed the election of the new chairman, Graham Brady, who had resigned from Cameron's frontbench in 2007 over a disagreement on grammar schools. Brady proved more independent of the party leader than some of his more recent predecessors. 'Not helpful to us' was the verdict of a Cameron aide about Brady. Number 10 tried to work around the 1922 Committee by calling meetings of all Tory MPs through the auspices of the Chief Whip rather than the 1922. This was, not surprisingly, deeply resented.

The Prime Minister was good at doing the formal parts of consulting with his parliamentary party – he would regularly tour the Members' Dining Room, invite MPs over to Number 10 and so on – but he was less good at genuinely engaging with their concerns.[17] As one senior member of the 1922 Committee put it: 'In quantitative terms, considerable. In qualitative terms, not so good ... Colleagues don't think he really wants to know what they think. There's lots of contact, not much listening.'

In their defence, the leadership faced significant structural problems – most notably the competing pressures of many long-serving MPs with such a large intake in 2010, especially given the constraints created by the Coalition. Creating space for the promotions inevitably involved sacking people. As one of Cameron's Chief Whips observed, 'in almost no other occupation do you sack people and then still need them to help you'. But the leadership was not good at dealing with these competing demands. There was a widespread feeling that questions of merit did not play much of a part in decisions about advancement or defenestration. This was partly a result of a pledge Cameron had given in 2009 that by the end of his first term, a third of his ministers would be women. When he made it, people pointed out how difficult this would be to achieve, given the usual lag between initial election as an MP and ministerial office, and so it proved.[18] He had also not anticipated that his scope for appointments would be limited by a coalition. Throughout the 2010 Parliament, he was routinely criticised by (some) male MPs for disproportionately promoting women MPs and was routinely criticised by (some) commentators for not having enough women on his frontbench and in Cabinet. He received little thanks or praise for his efforts to deal with the latter, whilst the former perception just stored up more resentment on the backbenches. But gender was not the only source of complaint; there was also the issue of disproportionate promotion of allies and friends of the Chancellor, whatever their gender. The Chancellor's hand was detected in a number of government appointments; the fortunate ones were known by the excluded as 'friends of George'. As one senior backbencher said: 'It's just so capricious. Even if you escape unscathed, you see how unfair it is.'

For a Prime Minister who elsewhere aimed for stability in his ministers, the Prime Minister got through four Chief Whips during the Parliament; each time a new Chief Whip took office, there was discussion of how he (it was always a he) would shake up the Whips' Office and solve the party management problems the party was facing and, each time, it made little difference. The result was a record level of backbench dissent, with Conservative MPs defying their whips in 35% of divisions, a figure without precedent in the post-war era.[19] An analysis of the composition of the parliamentary party in this period estimated that just 14% of MPs could be classed – along with David Cameron – as 'modernisers'. Even when combined with another group, so-called 'radicals', many of whom were not hostile to the Cameron project initially, the total still only reached a third of the parliamentary party.[20] On core economic matters, there was now relatively little dispute, but on both Europe and questions of social liberalism, the divisions were significant.

The single biggest source of dispute on the Conservative backbenches throughout the Parliament came over the issue of Europe. Other issues would come and go, flaring up and then subsiding, but the EU was a constant. What Euroscepticism the Prime Minister had was encouraged – they might say strengthened – by his backbenchers.

In 2011, the Conservative MP David Nuttall introduced a debate calling for an in/out referendum on the EU 'in the next session'; 81 Conservative MPs defied a three-line whip to support him.[21] With Labour support, the motion was defeated, but it was a foretaste of the problems that Europe was to give Cameron throughout the rest of the Parliament. It was already what one Conservative whip called an 'existential threat' to the Prime Minister; there was, he said, 'a discernible ideological faction, which you could see reforming'.

In October 2012, the government suffered its first Commons defeat as a result of these divisions.[22] Some 53 Conservative MPs voted against their whip on an amendment moved by Mark Reckless calling for a reduction in the EU budget. Although smaller than the 2011 rebellion, this time Labour joined forces with the rebels to defeat the government. The rebels were further emboldened by the government's reaction. As one member of the 1922 Committee put it, 'they resisted [the amendment] on the grounds that it was impossible to achieve, then achieved it, and then took the credit for it'.

Similarly, having ruled out an in/out referendum repeatedly, in January 2013, the Prime Minister gave in and moved to a position of offering a referendum after he had tried to negotiate better terms. He

'Come to Crosby Country'

Steve Bell, *The Guardian*, 18 July 2013

would be a Eurosceptic wanting to remain in a reformed EU. He rejected the goal of moving towards an ever closer union, but said that if the renegotiation went well: 'I will campaign for it with all my heart and soul. Because I believe something very deeply: that Britain's national interest is best served in a flexible, adaptable and open European Union.' Plenty of his backbenchers did not trust him to deliver on this pledge and moved a hostile amendment to the Queen's Speech in May. Faced with the possibility of a very large rebellion, the Conservative leadership backed down and promised support for an immediate private members' bill on the subject.[23] Despite this, the rebels still pushed ahead with their amendment – their persistence a measure of their lack of trust – and, faced with what would have been an enormous rebellion, the Conservatives allowed a partial free vote on the issue: ministers would abstain, while backbenchers could do what they liked. More than 110 Conservative MPs went on to vote for an amendment 'regretting' the absence of a referendum bill from the Queen's Speech.

This new policy bought temporary unity in the party, but the Prime Minister's refusal to state his demands in future negotiations fuelled suspicion among the already suspicious. Reformers for a time placed some store on a 'balance of competencies' review by the Foreign

Office, which studied the relative powers of the UK and the EU across a range of policy areas and hoped to extend the discretion of the UK. It led nowhere. The Prime Minister was aware that some of his Cabinet colleagues – Philip Hammond, Michael Gove, Iain Duncan Smith and Oliver Letwin – were already disposed to vote for an exit. If Cameron led the party to victory in 2015, the next stage in the troubled history of the Conservative Party and Europe would centre on the renegotiation and the referendum. But the pragmatic Cameron calculated that that hurdle lay in the future and could wait on events.

Polling evidence was salutary; the EU invariably ranked near the bottom of voters' concerns when compared with the economy, the NHS or immigration. But the pressure helped to make Cameron look a weak Prime Minister. It was difficult to disagree: the government's position on Europe was driven by the parliamentary party, and the more they got, the more they wanted.

Cameron was personally a strong supporter of same-sex (or 'equal') marriage, but the proposal ran against the grain of his party. He was encouraged by polling (showing that young people overwhelmingly supported it) and his advisors argued that the fuss would have died away by 2015 (which it did), but it soon became clear that the Prime Minister had misjudged the mood of Conservative MPs. On a free vote, Conservative MPs voted against the Second Reading of the Bill in February 2013 by 136 to 126, with the Prime Minister finding himself in a minority of his party.[24] The measure passed thanks to the votes of the other parties. In itself, this division was remarkable, but perhaps the most striking feature of the vote was the anger and bitterness the issue generated amongst the parliamentary party. Free votes normally take the poison out of arguments like this; in this case they did not. Partly this sprang from a feeling that the legislation was unnecessary (it was not in the manifesto and it divided the party, so why do it?) and partly amongst some Conservative MPs a feeling that the issue was, as one senior member of the 1922 Committee put it, being raised specifically 'to generate division, and to demonise bits of the party. It was to denigrate the dinosaurs who took a different view'. Many Conservative MPs reported receiving considerable pressure from their activists over the issue, and some reported being leant on to support the Prime Minister's position (not all free votes are all entirely free, and this one was no different). There was a heavy postbag to Number 10 which was overwhelmingly hostile. There were claims that many members, often elderly and socially conservative, were deserting the party in protest

('The further from London, the worse it was', as one whip put it). The socially conservative wing of the party was well-organised and articulate, but their claims about the number of defections were exaggerated. Party membership had been declining for years and Andrew Feldman would claim that the losses were no greater than would normally occur due to the deaths of members. Membership continued its steady decline and was down to 140,000 (a decline of 10% since 2010) by the end of 2014.

The Prime Minister was later variously quoted as saying that had he known the difficulties the issue would cause, he would not have taken it on, a claim he disputes – although he did accept that he underestimated the extent of the unhappiness the issue would cause amongst his party.[25]

Conservative MPs were also involved in helping to defeat the Coalition's plans for House of Lords reform (see p. 21) and preventing the government from taking military action in Syria (see p. 25). By 2011, a YouGov poll found that 64% saw the Conservatives as divided; by 2013, that figure had risen to over 70%. And in October 2014, a ComRes poll for ITV News found that the one phrase most associated with the Conservatives – out of a list of eight – was divided. The in-fighting had been noticed by the public.

Exacerbating the divisions over both the EU and same-sex marriage was the rise of UKIP and concerns about the effect it was having on Conservative support. UKIP offered a clear alternate home to Conservatives alienated by the party's modernisers – or just plain alienated.[26] As an internal note to the Prime Minister argued in late 2012, whilst UKIP voters did have particular policy concerns, 'policies in general are, in fact, of secondary importance in the mix of things that attract people to UKIP. It is much more about general outlook'. One of the factors contributing to the intra-party hostility around the same-sex marriage vote was that it took place, as one of the whips office put it, as 'people were just revising their views about UKIP, and realising that they were here to stay'. Pressure on the Prime Minister to strengthen his position on Europe was often justified with the argument that it would help head off the UKIP challenge – although those putting forward such a case were often committed better-off-outers in any case.

The Conservative Party had initial hopes of victory at the Eastleigh by-election in February 2013, but was forced into third place behind the Lib Dems and UKIP. Conservative concern then increased over the course of 2013 as UKIP made inroads in local and by-elections, and in 2014 finished top in the Euro elections. A poll in January 2014 reported that over a third of Conservative voters from 2010 had left the party, with half of them fleeing to UKIP.[27] The right of the party felt vindicated at the apparent ease with which UKIP picked up voters from traditional Conservatives. Here, they argued, was proof that only a stronger line on immigration and exit from Europe would bring victory in 2015. Many Conservative MPs (some of them 'the usual suspects', as Number 10 called them) agreed in principle with Nigel Farage's demand that Britain should leave the EU. Some had more partisan electoral fears, concerned about the loss of scores of seats because of UKIP's rise. Michael Fabricant, a party vice-chairman (albeit one of nine), called for a pact. The MP for Somerset North East, Jacob Rees-Mogg (who liked to talk of UKIP as part of 'the Conservative family') pressed for an accommodation, extending to an electoral pact between the parties. Cameron himself accepted that he had been too complacent about the rise of UKIP; he came to regret his insult in 2006 to its supporters as 'loonies, nutters, fruit-cakes and closet racists'.

Cameron (and other mainstream party leaders) struggled to come up with an effective answer to the UKIP question. In a Conservative political cabinet, Ken Clarke argued that ministers should avoid talking up UKIP issues ('you can't outkip UKIP'), to which Cameron replied that they could not promote their own agenda until they had removed what he called 'this roadblock'. Populus always added a question to its weekly polls, asking voters what topic they would raise with David Cameron if he knocked on their door. Every week for two and a half years, with almost no exceptions, the top issue was immigration.[28] Conservative internal polling was quite clear on the fact that insofar as UKIP voters had policy concerns, it was immigration and not Europe that was of primary importance. As was noted in Chapter 1, the Coalition, notably the Conservative part of it, gradually stiffened policies on immigration and the EU, although EU membership, with its policy of free movement, imposed constraints on what could be done. Theresa May, the Home Secretary, tightened rules for the entry of non-EU immigrants.

This renewed emphasis on immigration was not without costs. The party had been trying to boost support within ethnic minorities and had paid several private fact-finding visits to the Canadian Conservatives who had built support among such groups. Many minority voters agreed with the Conservative position on issues such as crime or welfare, but did not vote Conservative because of the party's historical image and rhetoric. Similarly, some business leaders, already complaining about the uncertainty being caused by a possible in/out referendum, now expressed concerns about the immigration policy cutting off the supply of much-needed skilled workers. But all this paled in comparison with the pressure to do something to head off the rise of UKIP. Tory campaigners were consoled by research which found that among UKIP voters in the Euro elections, only 48% said they were sure to vote UKIP in a general election, and yet Conservative policies and warnings did not initially seem to make much of a dent in support for UKIP in the opinion polls.

In August 2014, Douglas Carswell, the MP for Clacton, announced that he was leaving the Conservatives to join UKIP. Carswell had been one of the most critical of Conservative MPs over a host of issues, including Europe, but he had recently become more on board.[29] In March 2014, he had written on Twitter: 'Only the Conservatives will guarantee and deliver an In/Out referendum. It will only happen if Cameron is Prime Minister.' His decision to defect came like a bolt out of the blue. With it came his resignation from the Commons, Carswell taking the rare decision to fight his seat under his new party colours. Very quickly, CCHQ realised they would lose the by-election. Carswell was popular locally, and his constituency was demographically the most UKIP-friendly in the country. Their bigger worry was how many other Conservative MPs might follow him.

One of the government whips remembers hearing the news of Carswell's defection. His first thought was: 'Where's Reckless?' The calculation in the Whips' Office, as soon as they knew Carswell had defected, was that the odds of Mark Reckless, the MP for Rochester and Strood, joining him was 50/50, which he promptly did in September, announcing his defection at the UKIP Conference in Doncaster. Rochester and Strood was initially considered a more winnable seat for the Conservatives, and Reckless was less popular amongst his former Conservative colleagues ('We never had any problem getting people to go to Rochester', said one Conservative campaigner), but Reckless hung on, albeit with a majority down to under 3,000, which the Conservatives judged would help dissuade other potential defectors. There were a score or so of other Conservative MPs who the party's whips were concerned might jump ship; with each, they individually put the odds of a defection at no more than 15% and often less – although there were enough potential defectors to make the possibility of at least one of them going significant. The whips moved to make potential defectors box themselves in by giving statements of support, and after Reckless' by-election, the Chief Whip's calculation – which proved to be correct – was that there would be no further defections.

UKIP was a problem for both the Conservatives and Labour. But there were two differences between the parties. The first was that the Conservatives woke up earlier to the potential threat that UKIP might pose to them – not least because their calculation was that most of UKIP's initial rise in the polls had come at their expense – and therefore had longer to work out how to deal with it. Although Number 10 aides were frequently criticised for being complacent about UKIP, they were privately well aware of the potential problem from 2012 onwards and undertook significant work to try to understand the nature of the UKIP vote. In 2013, they were predicting privately that UKIP would win at least one by-election during the Parliament and would top the polls in the European elections; neither event came as a surprise to them. However, after the Newark by-election in 2014 – which the Conservatives held – party strategists had been surprised at how poorly organised UKIP were and 'how aimless many of their so-called activists seemed'. They also felt, by mid-2014, that those voters who they had lost to UKIP had already gone, whereas Labour's problems in this respect were only beginning.

Second, party strategists always felt that they would, eventually, be able to win back many, but not all, of the voters that they had lost.[30] They concluded early on that UKIP's vote was 'soft', and squeezable, especially on the issue of leadership and the choice between Ed Miliband and David Cameron, which would become more of an issue for ex-Conservatives as the election approached; 'Go to bed with Farage, wake up with Miliband', the Prime Minister joked in 2014. And insofar as policies mattered, they believed they had a better policy offer than Labour to win back UKIP defectors. However, they were also aware that overt efforts to win over UKIP voters could easily alienate others. In 2012 an internal note for the Prime Minister noted: 'There is nothing we could realistically say to persuade UKIP considerers that David Cameron's Conservative Party shares (or even sympathises with) their general sense of cultural threat and anger about the pace of change in modern society.' Or rather, there was, but only at the cost of driving away other voters 'upon whom our prospects of electoral victory depend'.

The party targeted UKIP defectors remorselessly, under the radar, using social media, direct mail, phone calls and canvassing to inform potential UKIP voters about Conservative plans for curbing immigration and the in/out referendum. Stephen Gilbert's view was always that a sufficient number would eventually come to the Conservatives, 'although reluctantly and late in the day', almost holding their noses on 7 May once they were faced with a choice of Miliband or Cameron.

With an election to win and the economy expected to be decisive, George Osborne could be pleased with the opinion polls showing that he and his government were well ahead of Ed Balls and Labour on economic competence and economic trust. Some of the advantage stemmed from his success in portraying the last Labour government as incompetent and profligate, and the turnaround in the party's poll ratings for economic competence was remarkable. For nearly two decades after the humiliating exit from the ERM in 1992, the Conservatives had trailed Labour in public perceptions of the economy. In the 2010 election, they had been just narrowly in the lead, but in the five years that followed, they were always ahead, often by a large margin. Nevertheless, the Chancellor was aware that colleagues and the public were tiring of the programme of austerity. In a Conservative focus group in Bolton, a voter commented: 'We have to take the medicine but it may end up killing us.' Osborne confided to a colleague that he knew he had three years to turn the economy around. If he had not, he would have failed.

A highly political Chancellor, Osborne made a point of contacting MPs defending marginal seats and asking what he could do to help. Such constituencies often seemed to be the recipients of a new bypass or A&E department. In 2014, he announced his northern powerhouse project, involving more investment for infrastructure and improving transport links, and devolution of spending to local politicians, all to encourage economic revival in the northern cities. The project had a political edge; the local political leaders he had won over and to whom power was to be devolved were largely Labour. Osborne was also hoping to boost Conservative support in the north where it had been in decline for decades.

Of Osborne and Cameron, the former was very much the strategist and no important decisions were taken without his input.[31] As well as the Quad (see p. 5), Osborne also attended the daily 8.30 am and 4.00 pm meetings in Number 10 and, in Cameron's absence, chaired them. Apart from the few months following his 2012 omnishambles Budget, his influence across a range of policies was immense. One aide who attended the daily meetings said that when a proposal was aired: 'We, including Cameron, wait for George to speak.' He was such a regular presence in Number 10 that some aides wondered how much of the Treasury work was being left to his chief of staff, Rupert Harrison. If there had been a post of political director in Number 10, Osborne would have held it.

In December 2014, however, Osborne over-reached himself with his plan to wipe out the deficit by 2017. The IFS calculated that achieving this would reduce spending as a proportion of GDP to 35%. Labour seized on this figure to warn of the 'savage' cuts in spending that would follow the election, as Britain went back to spending levels seen in the 1930s. Osborne's Treasury team – and the party's election campaign strategists – quickly realised their mistake. 'Thank God we had the Budget to come and time to row back', said a Treasury advisor.

While Cameron's ratings as party leader and as Prime Minister were never brilliant, they ran far ahead of those for Ed Miliband (except for a time in 2012) and Nick Clegg, and increased over the course of the Parliament. The party regularly polled on its brand, issues and perceptions of the Prime Minister. Cameron outscored Miliband among voters when it came to being decisive, prepared to take unpopular decisions and good in a crisis. Some of this advantage may have derived from being Prime Minister, with Miliband just another party leader, but it was an undeniable asset. An internal polling presentation delivered to Conservative MPs in 2013 labelled Miliband 'an unprecedented liability'.

However, Cameron's private polls did not overlook his downsides and occasionally were nearly as deflating for him as Miliband's so often were for the Labour leader. In May 2012 (a bad time after the Budget), they reported that many voters saw him as being 'out of touch with people like me', less than a third agreed that 'he really understands how tough things are for families' and 61% thought his policies 'benefit the rich at the expense of people like me'. Being out of touch was consistently the biggest negative voter perception of Cameron throughout. All Prime Ministers come to be seen as out of touch over time, but Cameron's ratings started worse (presumably because of he was the son of privilege) and deteriorated quicker. Just two years into his premiership, internal Conservative polling found that his ratings for being out of touch were as bad as Tony Blair's had been after a decade as Prime Minister.

A Conservative strategy memo in 2012 warned that 'the perceptions of you are especially worrying'. It added on the theme of Cameron being on the side of the rich: 'But to be thought **only** on the side of the rich is toxic and to favour the rich <u>at the expense of</u> ordinary voters is highly likely to be fatal' (emphasis in original). Whereas Labour's private polling on leadership for Miliband was confined to a handful of people, polling for Cameron was distributed more widely, at least until Lynton Crosby's arrival. Some in Number 10 regarded negative perceptions as a challenge, while others just shrugged their shoulders and said they were 'in the price'. Cameron himself was not fazed by negative findings; after some poor polling findings on the NHS in 2011, he scribbled on one memo: 'Give me the right language in speeches & physically attack me with the right words before an interview. I will do what I am told...' He remained extremely good at sticking to top lines in interviews if briefed properly.

Some linked the negative aspects of the party's image with its alleged 'women problem'. Every few months, there would be a poll in which the Conservatives were behind Labour among women voters, which would prompt concern amongst some MPs and some of those in Number 10. And periodically there would be some event that would trigger discussion of the Conservatives' 'women problem' – such as the Prime Minister's dismissive remark to the Labour MP Angela Eagle to 'calm down, dear' or the occasion on which the Conservative frontbench was all male. This issue was taken seriously – the party carried out multiple pieces of analysis on the nature of the gender gap and a briefing paper was prepared by the policy unit and CCHQ, listing policies that were seen to have helped, or were judged to appeal to, women. But the analysis within Number 10 never saw it as a major problem. The real picture was more nuanced; although women were more critical than men of the government's record, there was much less of a gender gap in voting intentions.[32] True, the Conservatives did poorly among some women – those who were young (under 55), rented, worked in the public sector and/or were dependent on benefits, groups particularly affected by the spending cuts – but the analysis Number 10 conducted showed the overall gap was never more than two percentage points. The predominant view in Downing Street was that the 'women problem' existed mostly in the minds of the media and opposition politicians. As one of Cameron's aides put it, 'the Conservatives – and Cameron personally – had a "women problem" only in the sense that a number of female journalists and commentators didn't like him or the framing and language for some policies and their journalistic intuition led them to think that many other women saw things the same way'. That constructed women problem remained for the entire Parliament and became a media frame through which the failure to have more women MPs and ministers as well as 'cuts' were reported. However, the problem was taken seriously enough that there were multiple exercises in aggregating data in order to check the scale of any gender effects, and in 2012, one of Cameron's aides wrote him and Osborne a strategy memo entitled 'Why We Lost in 2015'. Written as a 'what if', it identified four areas with the potential to be responsible for a defeat: lack of support among non-white voters, weakness in urban Britain, loss on values – and women voters.

More generally, the party's private polling showed strong support for the government's welfare reforms. In September 2012, by 51% to 43% voters approved of taxing the disability living allowance and freezing working age and child benefits for three years. Other reforms, above all the introduction of a cap on welfare so that no one could receive more in benefits than the average working family earned, were even more popular with voters, with support in the 70–80% range. 'We felt at the time', said one of Cameron's aides, 'that it was a massive error by Labour to have opposed the benefit cap, revealing that they didn't understand what a critical issue welfare reform was for most voters.' Voters also supported the need for cuts in public spending, although many doubted that they were being done fairly. Andrew Cooper's verdict on the polling in May 2012 was that the best way for the Conservatives to show they were on the side of 'hardworking people who want to get on' was to persist with welfare reform.

The party invested heavily in survey research into key target voter groups. A political cabinet in October 2012 was presented with research identifying eight distinct voter segments.[33] The four that the party intended to focus on were: Steady Tories (11% of the electorate); Disaffected Tories (14% of the electorate); Anxious Aspirationals (18% of the electorate); and the In-play Centre (11% of the electorate).

Collectively, these groups amounted to more than half of the electorate. Further analysis was conducted into the demographics, locations, values and concerns of voters in the segments and the messages that might appeal to them. Asked about the most important issues for 'me and my family', the Disaffected Tories were overwhelmingly concerned about immigration, wanted an in/out EU referendum and were moving to UKIP. Anxious Aspirationals and the In-play Centre, on the other hand, were more concerned about the cost of living and the NHS, and only small numbers mentioned immigration and an EU referendum.

There were sharp differences between the groups on values. Disaffected Tories were mainly older and by a large margin disapproved of equal marriage, but the other groups were socially liberal and relaxed about equal marriage. At the political cabinet meeting, Cameron referred to the challenge of winning back the Disaffected Tories without alienating the other three segments. It was less obvious how that might be done.

In April 2013, Jo Johnson, younger brother of Boris, was made head of the Number 10 policy unit. He was the first MP to hold the post since the unit was created in 1974. For the government's previous two years, it had been a Coalition policy unit, staffed by civil servants and reported to both Cameron and Clegg. With two years to go to the general election, it was given a more party political remit, worked just for Cameron and consisted of 20 special advisors and 12 civil servants. Its main task was to prepare the manifesto for 2015 and it was led by a manifesto steering committee consisting of Oliver Letwin, Ed Llewellyn and Kate Fall. There were five policy commissions, chaired by Cabinet Ministers William Hague, George Osborne and Iain Duncan Smith (co-chairing), Theresa May, Eric Pickles and Michael Gove. They reported the results of their work to Cameron in October and then to MPs at an away-day in the same month. Over Christmas, Johnson completed a first draft of the manifesto, organised into three sections: the (inevitable) long-term economic plan, strong society and Britain in the world. Being in coalition with the Lib Dems imposed a brake on more right-wing measures, covering plans for a British Bill of Rights and changes on welfare, immigration and the EU.

Meanwhile, the party pruned its candidates' list by over 200 and was more active in head-hunting suitable candidates, usually looking for a commitment to working in the constituency. The party may have abandoned the A-list of candidates, but by stealth there were efforts to recruit more female and minority candidates (see p. 344).The party also expected an incumbency bonus to accrue to the Conservative MPs newly elected in 2010. In that election, it had been worth an extra 2.6% in votes to the Conservative MPs first elected in 2005 compared to longer-serving MPs. However, Lord Ashcroft, regarded in Number 10 as a gleeful bearer of gloom, cast doubt on the bonus. He found no consistent pattern in his various constituency polls (see p. 242) and warned that 'the advantage to candidates is earned, not bestowed'.[34] Stephen Gilbert's view was that it had been earned, and on Gilbert's watch there was probably more central oversight of candidates in key seats, choice of messages, and monitoring and targeting of voters than ever before.

As the Conservatives failed to open a poll lead over Labour in 2013, some in the party pressed for the appointment to Number 10 or CCHQ of Lynton Crosby, the Australian campaign strategist. Known as the 'Wizard of Oz' because of his role in guiding John Howard in four successive Australian elections, he had also managed Boris Johnson's successful mayoral campaigns in 2008 and 2012 in largely Labour-voting London. He had a reputation in Australia as a right-winger because of his hard line on immigration, and some right-wing Conservative MPs thought he might be more sympathetic to their policies. Modernisers within the party certainly feared such an agenda. Andrew Cooper cautioned Cameron: 'You don't get Lynton without Lyntonism.' Crosby had managed the Conservative general election campaign in 2005, during which he had learnt of David Cameron's unease at the party's emphasis on immigration in the election. He had then been privately very dismissive of social liberals such as Cameron, whom he regarded as out of touch with voters living on an average wage in very difficult circumstances.

It was an exaggeration to say that the departure of Cooper (whose return to Populus had been long planned) and arrival of Crosby spelt the end of the modernising agenda – Tory modernisation had been ailing for a while and Crosby did not live up to the caricature often painted. He disapproved of the language of 'shirkers' for some welfare claimants and wanted no accommodation with UKIP, which some on the party's right were floating. But Cameron and Osborne were less interested in his views (they decided the policies); more important for them was their expectation that he would provide a clear direction and discipline to the campaign. The 2010 campaign had suffered from confused lines of authority between Osborne, Andrew Coulson and Steve Hilton. The last two had left and Osborne had allegedly later admitted 'I hated every minute of it'.

Crosby's reputation rested on his success in identifying the issues and language which would appeal to key voters and enforcing message discipline. Once in post, full time from January 2014, he set up a top table for general election purposes in the Matthew Parker Street headquarters to which the party had moved in February 2014. He hated what he termed 'process stories' where the media reported real or fabricated accounts of tensions in his team. Insiders noted that in CCHQ no seat had been allocated for Steve Hilton despite rumours that he would return for the campaign. Crosby was widely reported as telling Conservative MPs that he wanted to get rid of what he called the 'barnacles', issues which had been dividing the party, like gay marriage and Europe. Some of these barnacles were distractions, while others were things that the government was doing that core voters or activists did not like. His fixation was that the

'The Higher Politics'

Martin Rowson, *The Guardian*, 19 November 2012

party had to stop antagonising its base; it needed instead to consolidate the base and then look at where the extra percentage points of votes could come from. He thought the existing strategy did not place enough emphasis on the government's record of 'competence', particularly in bringing the economy back from the brink.

Crosby had long been influenced by the work on voters' values conducted by Dick Wirthlin, the pollster for President Reagan in the 1980s. Wirthlin believed that sharing a voter's values was the most important shaper of the voters' choice of a party or politician. The party's existing message – designed to last until the general election – had been crafted by Cooper and Oliver and was the centrepiece of Cameron's 2012 conference speech. Cameron responded positively to the suggestion that they integrate the government's economic plan with the welfare and education reform agenda. Their message tried to spell out 'a strategic narrative beyond deficit reduction', warning that the world had changed and so must Britain. There was a global challenge as emerging economies 'push ahead with energy and drive' and the country needed to 'step up to meet the big long-term challenges'. The party's private polling showed that 67% agreed with the Conservative message that Britain was on course to become an 'aspiration nation', in which people who worked hard would be rewarded. Labour, by contrast, did not get that the world had changed and the Cooper message ('our narrative on Labour') was that its answer to debt was to incur more debt – 60% agreed with this proposition about Labour's stance. But guided by the survey into voters' values, Crosby dumped talk of the global race. 'Talk of meeting global competition alienated the UKIP voters we needed. They are already losing from globalisation and are looking for security', according to a Cameron aide. Crosby won support for his suggestion that the party needed a plan for the future which offered security for hard-pressed people at all stages of their lives and policies to demonstrate that the sacrifices being made would be worthwhile.

Crosby relied on intensive survey research by his business partner Mark Textor to locate and then target such voters. Textor, who regarded most British polling as 'hopeless', came up with the message of Conservative competence versus Labour chaos. His work on values concluded that ultimately the most important thing for British voters was 'security and peace of mind'. This had the added benefit that the politicians found it clear and simple enough to adopt. Crosby and Textor were expensive recruits, but Andrew Feldman, the party co-chairman, managed to raise the funds. In late 2014, Conservative focus groups found that the argument that the election could produce 'competence or chaos' was a very effective one – and that this message especially worked with Lib Dem waverers if they could be persuaded that their vote was important. This became the front-page message in a leaflet printed in December 2014, ready to be distributed in all Conservative target seats in early January – and which formed the main thrust of Conservative messaging thereafter.[35]

Textor began an ambitious polling programme in 80 marginal seats with samples of up to 1,000 voters each. It dwarfed what Labour was doing (see p. 247). Crosby was at best lukewarm about the recruitment of an advertising agency, but Cameron and Osborne wanted and hired M&C Saatchi, a link with the famous Thatcher election victories.

Osborne worked closely with Crosby. He readily accepted Crosby's suggested phrase of 'the long-term economic plan' to describe the government's economic project and, under pressure, periodic reminders that cutting the deficit and improving the economy were not ends in themselves, but were for a purpose. This was a point that had strongly come out of private polling and focus groups from the earliest days of the Coalition.

To Crosby's question 'what's in it for the ordinary voter?', Osborne could claim he was creating the conditions for an improvement in living standards and public services. A ComRes poll in October 2013 reinforced the point of Crosby's question and showed that voters were aware of the different nuances of the economy. They accepted that the Conservatives were ahead of Labour when it came to economic growth, but Labour led on bringing down the cost of living, creating jobs and making families better off. Crosby urged ministers to use the term 'long-term economic plan' at every possible opportunity.

Crosby's themes for the party's campaign were, unsurprisingly, leadership, or the choice of Cameron or Miliband for Prime Minister, and the economy. Confident that Miliband was 'unelectable', he warned Cameron against taking part in any head-to-head TV leadership debates. Cameron did not need persuading. Bruised by his experience in the debates in 2010, he had already decided that incumbents were always at a disadvantage in these encounters; the trick would be to find a plausible reason for refusing to take part. On three key issues – welfare, the economy and immigration – the Conservatives led Labour, but talking about anything other than the economy and leadership was, for Crosby, time wasted.

However, standing in the way of all of this was still the issue of immigration. Crosby initially felt they needed to remove the problem immigration caused them before they would be listened to on other issues. Trying to deal with this resulted in a significant dialling-up of rhetoric from Cameron and others on the issue. None of it seemed to work, and Crosby reluctantly concluded – before the Prime Minister did – that it was impossible to move perceptions on the issue. The final attempt at this came with a big (and much trailed and postponed) speech by the Prime Minister on immigration in November 2014. It was therefore only really only in the final six months that they properly narrowed their messaging to focus on the economy and leadership. From then on, the strategy was that, unless they could be linked with the economy, to avoid Europe and immigration – 'take them off the table', he said. Message discipline was important to Crosby. He was aware of how off-message MPs and ministers could be, and his ruthless single-mindedness won praise from his rivals. One Lib Dem strategist noted: 'You've got to admire Crosby's ability to get them in line, saying and doing the same things, even when they didn't entirely believe them ... They had a clarity of message from 2013 that we lacked.'

Crosby did not attend Cameron's daily Number 10 meetings at 8.30 am and 4.00 pm and had no pass to Downing Street or to Portcullis House. Given that he was not one for large meetings, this did not matter; he had insisted on one-to-one discussions with Cameron and

Osborne as a condition of taking the job. These three and Number 10 staff Craig Oliver, Catherine Fall and Ed Llewellyn formed a so-called 'Chequers Group', which met monthly at Number 10 and quarterly at Chequers to review strategy; Crosby chaired the meetings. He was credited (or blamed) for the decision in July 2014 to move Michael Gove from Education to Chief Whip on the basis of hostile opinion polling and feedback from worried Conservative MPs. Crosby's alleged role in Gove's dismissal from Education provoked criticism which was not confined to the radical minister's admirers. It seemed to be a case of the pollster exercising too much influence and reflected badly on Cameron's loyalty to a colleague.

Another overseas recruit to the campaign team was Jim Messina, an expert in voter identification and mobilisation. He had worked on the Obama 2012 presidential campaign and Conservatives regarded it as a political coup to have captured a major figure from the US Democrats, given that traditionally the Conservatives had had closer relations with their sister Republican Party. He came with the explicit approval of President Obama.[36] His expertise was in identifying and messaging target voters. For the Obama 2012 campaign, he had concentrated on key voters in just 11 states. He had made heavy use of Facebook and other social media to collect information on voters so that Obama could send them personalised messages. The challenge was to do the same for Cameron in 2015. He was another very expensive hire. The prime mover in the recruitment of Messina was Feldman and in 2013 he accompanied his co-chairman Shapps, Crosby, Gilbert and a donor on a visit to Messina at his Washington DC headquarters and the deal was done. Messina's line all the way through was that all that mattered was the economy. When he spoke at an away day for the party's MPs in October 2014, he told them that every second spent talking about anything other than the economy was a second lost.

Conservatives left the 2014 party conference in good heart, buoyed in part by Ed Miliband's poor performance the previous week in Manchester. Cameron and Osborne held out the prospect of tax cuts and a British Bill of Rights under a future Conservative government. The party led decisively on what the pollsters regarded as campaign fundamentals: the economy and leadership.[37] Campaign managers made a reasonably upbeat presentation on the battleground seats to MPs at an away day in November. No seat figures were mentioned, but at this point among senior staff in CCHQ there was an expectation that the party would win between 310 and 320 seats. But because the advantages on the fundamentals were not reflected in a lead in voting intentions in the public polls, outsiders expected a closer contest. The public polls suggested a reason for this. In October 2014, a ComRes/ITV News poll reported that 72% agreed that 'despite the economic recovery I don't feel better off'. To those who wondered if this might be a voteless recovery, like John Major suffered in 1997, the optimists answered that Miliband's Labour was not New Labour and David Cameron, unlike Major, was not running against Tony Blair.

Notes

1. 'ConservativeHome General Election Review', www.conservativehome.blogs.com, 2010.
2. For a moderniser's analysis of interpretations of the election, see Janan Ganesh, 'A Party in Agony Over a Misunderstood Election', *Financial Times*, 21 May 2013.
3. See, for example, Lord (Michael) Ashcroft, *Smell the Coffee: A Wake-Up Call for the Conservative Party*, 2005.
4. Dennis Kavanagh and Philip Cowley, *The British General Election of 2010*. Palgrave Macmillan, 2010, pp. 335–7.
5. Lord (Michael) Ashcroft, *Minority Verdict: The Conservative Party, the Voters and the 2010 Election*, 2010.
6. Moreover, the policy's actual impact was more complicated than the rhetoric. As the Institute for Fiscal Studies (IFS) noted, whilst increasing the personal allowance benefited lower-paid individual-income taxpayers, the policy was not progressive in terms of families, 'as relatively few of the poorest families contain a taxpayer and two-earner couples gain twice as much in cash terms as one-earner families', and thus 'the highest average cash gain occurs in the second-richest tenth of the income distribution'. See 'A £10,000 Personal Allowance: Who Would Benefit, and Would it Boost the Economy?', www.ifs.org.uk, 9 March 2012.
7. For a highly partisan and critical view, see P. Toynbee and D. Walker, *Cameron's Coup: How the Tories Took Britain to the Brink*. Guardian Faber, 2015. For the alternate view, see Tim Montgomerie, 'Cameron Must Find Some TLC for the Right', *The Times*, 4 March 2013.
8. Hilton later developed some of his ideas in a book, *More Human: Designing a World Where People Come First*. W.H. Allen, 2015.
9. Giles Wilkes, 'Steve Hilton: The Tory Guru Out of Step with Political Realities', *Financial Times*, 22 May 2015.
10. To compensate for Oliver's weakness with the press, in August 2013, Number 10 hired *The Sun*'s deputy political editor, Graeme Wilson.
11. On Cameron, see Francis Elliott and James Hanning, *Cameron: Practically a Conservative*. Fourth Estate, 2012; and Peter Snowden, *Back from the Brink*. HarperPress, 2010.
12. This story, now in wide circulation, came from Tim Shipman, 'A Nod and a Wink Here, Finger-Jabbing There, This Rebellion is a Mess of the Prime Minister's Making', *Daily Mail*, 11 July 2012.

13. 'I Have Problems with the Thatcher Legacy', *Sunday Times*, 28 April 2013. For an early attempt to trace Cameron's debt to Thatcher, see Stephen Evans, '"Mother's Boy": David Cameron and Margaret Thatcher', *British Journal of Politics and International Relations*, 32(3) (2010): 325–43.
14. Matthew D'Ancona, *In it Together*. Viking, 2013, p. 151.
15. As well as Cameron, CRD alumni included Osborne, Hilton, Fall, Llewellyn, Cooper and Oliver Dowden, later Cameron's deputy chief of staff.
16. Philip Norton, *The Voice of the Backbenches*. Conservative History Group, 2013.
17. Those inside Number 10 were always frustrated by the claim that they did not engage with the parliamentary party, itemising all of the things that they did. As one said, 'an inordinate amount of time and effort was devoted to trying to improve relations with MPs: dinners at Chequers, drinks in the Downing Street flat, small groups coming in to discuss policy issues. None of it helped – if anything it seemed to make them resent DC even more'.
18. Philip Cowley 'The Parliamentary Party', *Political Quarterly*, 80(2) (2009): 214–21.
19. Philip Cowley, Mark Stuart and Tiffany Trenner-Lyle, 'The Parliamentary Party' in G. Peele *et al.* (eds), *Modernizing Conservatism*. Manchester University Press, 2016.
20. *Ibid.*
21. Philip Cowley and Mark Stuart, 'The Cambusters: The Conservative European Referendum Rebellion of October 2011', *Political Quarterly*, 83(2) (2012), 402–6.
22. There was one earlier Commons defeat, but this was the result of an ambush by Labour MPs, not Conservative rebellions.
23. They could not offer support for a government bill because the Lib Dems blocked it.
24. The Conservative MPs who voted for same-sex marriage were disproportionately female, younger and from the new 2010 intake; the problem for the modernisers was that two of these groups of disproportionate support were relatively small, whilst amongst the numerically large 2010 intake, support might have been stronger than amongst the older lags, but it was hardly overwhelming. At every one of the last three elections, there have been claims about how the new intake of Conservative MPs would be more socially liberal and would shift the balance of power in the party. The reality has always been more mixed.
25. See, for example, the Andrew Pierce article in the *Daily Mail* ('I Never Expected Gay Marriage to Cause Such an Uproar, Admits Cameron in Private Meeting at Party Conference', 8 October 2013), but also its later correction (see 'Daily Mail Apologises for Wrongly Stating that David Cameron "Regretted" Equal Marriage', *Pink News*, 8 October 2013). But also note the claim in D'Ancona, *In it Together*, p. 350: 'If I'd known what it was going to be like, I wouldn't have done it.'
26. Lord Ashcroft, *'They're Thinking What We're Thinking'. Understanding the UKIP Temptation*, 2012.
27. Lord Ashcroft, 'Project Blueprint Phase 4', lordashcroftpolls.com, 2014.
28. The exception was the NHS during the height of the row over the Lansley reforms in the spring of 2012.

29. Mark Wallace, 'Carswell Abandons Rebellion – Because a Conservative Victory in 2015 is the Only Way Britain Can Leave the EU', www.conservativehome.com, 30 January 2014.
30. Many, but not all. There was a realisation, early on, as one of Cameron's team noted, that 'we couldn't alter the reality that now UKIP existed as a more credible option, there were some previously Tory voters for whom UKIP was simply a better representation of their views than a mainstream Conservative Party ... could, would, or should be'.
31. On this relationship, see A. Seldon and P. Snowdon, *Cameron at 10*. William Collins, 2015; and Janan Ganesh, *George Osborne: The Austerity Chancellor*. Biteback, 2012.
32. See Roger Mortimore, Gideon Skinner and Tomasz Mludzinski, '"Cameron's Problem with Women": The Reporting and the Reality of Gender-Based Trends in Attitudes to the Conservatives, 2010–2011', *Parliamentary Affairs* (2015): 97–115; 'Ladies in Red', *The Economist*, 19 April 2014; and Lord Ashcroft, "The Conservatives don't attract too few women. They attract too few of anyone", www.conservativehome.com (4 March, 2014).
33. The others were: Urban Welfare (18%); Inner-City Dwellers (4%); Core Labour (16%) and Metropolitan Elite (8%). These were all considered less fertile territory for the Conservatives.
34. Lord Ashcroft, 'A Lesson from the Blue-Yellow Marginals. Incumbency is Not Enough', www.conservativehome.com, 27 September 2014.
35. It is sometimes said that the Conservative focus groups found the SNP coming through as an important issue around this time; the groups were, though, slightly more nuanced. What they showed was that arguing that the election could produce an unstable outcome was powerful – with the SNP a part of that instability. Hence the messaging in the January leaflet: 'Ed Miliband would need to be propped up by one of the minor parties – the Lib Dems, the SNP, Greens or UKIP... Amidst all this uncertainty, only the Conservatives can claim to have a chance of forming a stable, majority government.' Moreover, it was crucial to emphasise that the choice made by voters was important in affecting the national outcome: 'Your vote at the 2015 General Election really could be the most important vote you cast in your lifetime.'
36. On election night in May 2015, Andrew Feldman would tell celebrating party staff that Obama had told Messina to work for the Conservatives to stop the 'socialist' Miliband getting to Number 10.
37. Peter Kellner, 'The fundamentals favour Cameron, so the general election is his to lose', www.yougov.co.uk, 14 April 2014.

3
Brand Failure: Labour

Ed Miliband was elected Labour leader on 25 September 2010.[1] He defeated his older and politically more senior brother, David, on the fourth and final round of voting by a wafer-thin margin, 50.65% to 49.35%. David Miliband had led in all three earlier rounds of voting, and even in the final round led amongst both Labour MPs/MEPs and party members, but Ed Miliband's lead amongst trades union and affiliated bodies was just sufficient for victory. Inherent in a voting system like the one used by Labour is the idea that the various components of the electoral college might differ in their preferences (if not, there is no point in having them), but the nature of Miliband's victory thereafter allowed critics, both within and without the party, to say that he owed his victory to the unions.[2]

For many involved, however, this was a convenient allocation of responsibility – not least for David Miliband, who had thought very seriously about what he would do after winning the leadership, but not seriously enough about how to win it. As Churchill said of Rosebery, he would not stoop; he did not conquer: a handful of MPs less alienated by his slightly aloof style, a slightly more conciliatory tone at the hustings, and the crown would have been his. But David Miliband found his defeat hard to take. He wrote, shortly after the result, to Hillary Clinton: 'Losing is tough. When you win the party members and MPs doubly so. (When it's your brother...).'[3] At a personal level, relations between the two were never the same afterwards and the idea that Ed had somehow betrayed his brother – 'stabbed him in the back' – would surface throughout the Parliament and again during in the election in May 2015.[4] Surveys of party members and trade unionists showed that David Miliband was by large margins regarded as the most likely to be the best leader of the party, lead it to election victory and be the best Prime

Minister. The argument that the party had picked 'the wrong brother' would also be made repeatedly and was picked up in both Labour and Conservative private focus groups; the Conservatives considered, but eventually rejected, an advertising campaign on that theme. But the reality was that for all that the five years between 2010 and 2015 would reveal Ed Miliband's weaknesses as a party leader and would-be Prime Minister, it was not as if David Miliband was an unflawed candidate either. Under David Miliband, the five years from 2010 would certainly have been different for Labour; it is less clear whether they would have been more positive overall.

Neil Kinnock, the former party leader, was ecstatic at the result and was reported as saying that 'we have got our party back'.[5] But this overlooked the votes of local members and elected MPs and MEPs. Kinnock would have been encouraged by the new leader's promise to be a candidate of change and his declaration that 'the era of New Labour is over'. In private Miliband had been more explicit, saying to friends that he wanted to bury New Labour.

Ed Miliband's plan to appoint his brother as Shadow Chancellor was foiled when David announced he would not stand for election to the Shadow Cabinet. This was one of a number of occasions on which he declined offers to serve in a frontline position, and he would resign from the Commons in 2013. Ed Balls was the obvious appointment, but was, significantly, overlooked, partly because he was too associated with the economic legacy of the Gordon Brown government and partly because of a lack of trust between him and Ed Miliband.[6] Alan Johnson was instead the surprise appointment. He was a popular and an experienced minister, but had previously shown little interest or expertise in his new brief. Other key appointments were Yvette Cooper as Shadow Foreign Secretary, Balls as Shadow Home Secretary and Andy Burnham at education. Within eight months, all three had changed posts. Miliband's office drew attention to the sacking of the experienced chief whip Nick Brown and his replacement by Rosie Winterton, which they presented as a symbolic rejection of a style of politics that Miliband wanted to leave behind.

In his speech accepting the leadership, Miliband used the word 'generation' 41 times, and declared that 'a new generation has taken charge of Labour'. Within a year, he had persuaded the party to abandon the system of MPs electing members of the shadow team and leave selection to the leader. The change enabled him to promote several of the 2010 intake of MPs rapidly, including Chuka Umunna as Shadow

Business Secretary and Rachel Reeves as Shadow Chief Secretary, both reaching the Shadow Cabinet within 18 months of their election to the Commons. His close friend and political ally Stewart Wood was awarded a peerage in 2011 and had right of attendance at the Shadow Cabinet. The big beasts of the Blair/Brown years – David Blunkett, Jack Straw, Alistair Darling and Alan Milburn, as well as Brown and Blair themselves – had either left the Commons or no longer wanted a frontbench role.

It took time for the 40-year old leader to assert his authority, not least because he had not been the first choice of most Labour MPs or his Shadow Cabinet. He regarded Shadow Cabinet discussions as a forum in which to clarify his thinking, but few regarded it as a decisive body. It was never clear how many shadow ministers shared his political project or accepted that it was an election-winning one.

Miliband was forced into an early reshuffle of his shadow team when Alan Johnson resigned for personal reasons in January 2011. The role of Shadow Chancellor was again offered first to David Miliband, who turned it down, after which there was little choice but to give Balls the post, although there was unease among some of Miliband's team. One of Miliband's aides had, semi-jokingly, told him to think carefully about the decision because it might be the last one he ever made.[7] The two men were not always as one and there was little warmth in their relationship, although in contrast to the Brown/Blair years, they managed to keep their disagreements private and there were relatively good relations between their staffs.[8] Yvette Cooper moved to home affairs and Douglas Alexander replaced her at foreign affairs. Miliband grumbled to an aide after the reshuffle, 'not one of them said "thank you"'. All three remained in post for the rest of the Parliament. Like the leader, all had started as Brownites and all had benefited from Brown's patronage. Labour, as Janan Ganesh noted in the *Financial Times*, was now 'led by people who spent a decade believing that Tony Blair was a problem and Gordon Brown was the answer'.[9]

In policy terms, Miliband said that he would start with a 'blank page'. But it soon became clear that the public did not. During the five months of the leadership contest, and with the candidates reluctant to defend the record of the last Labour government, the Conservatives and the Liberal Democrats had been free to create and reinforce a narrative about the state of the economy. 'Clearing up the mess we inherited' figured prominently in ministers' speeches, not least when defending spending cuts. Five years later, Labour politicians were still complaining about how voters' negative views of the last Labour government coloured their perceptions of the party. One member of the Treasury team noted that these attacks had especial impact because of the role that the Lib Dems played in the Coalition:

> They formed a national government, working in the national interest, pursuing a national purpose, to put right Labour's reckless spending. It was all nonsense, but the public totally bought it. The image was untrue, but powerful ... At every stage, Clegg used the economic situation to justify his decision. It's integral to why they were in coalition.

From the start, Miliband's private polls reinforced what the public polls were saying. Many voters blamed the last Labour government for mismanaging the economy and over-spending, allowing too much immigration and being too 'soft' on welfare claimants. By the end of the Parliament, the party's policies had moved significantly on all three points. But the movement was grudging, gradual and invariably in the direction of the Coalition government. It was so delayed and ineffectively communicated (albeit not helped by a predominantly right-wing press) that Labour got little credit. The image from 2010, particularly on the economy, stuck.

Even before Miliband was elected party leader, focus groups with potential Labour voters were so negative about the party that Miliband's pollster James Morris wrote: 'A Labour leader who argues that we should keep spending to secure growth is flying in the face of common sense and would need a *volte face* by the entire media to have a chance of success.' A year later, in late 2011, an internal Labour strategy document noted: 'Labour has not repaired its image at all.' It warned that on the economy: 'The Tories have a focused message and vernacular language.' George Osborne's 'analogy with paying off your own credit card bill is very powerful. It provides very strong support for the Tory position' and Labour's polling found cuts were strongly preferred over tax rises as an answer. In October of the same year, the new Shadow Cabinet was played a recording of the views expressed in a focus group about the last Labour government. It was highly critical, with voters looking for an apology for the perceived over-spending.

Labour tested multiple ways of dealing with the Conservatives' 'vernacular language' in focus groups. The conclusion, according to one of those involved, was simple: 'Nothing worked.' One attempt was to try to combat the image of the mortgage by arguing that no one pays off their 25-year mortgage in two years and still expects to have food on the table. 'But it was all self-defeating. Because all it does is remind people about the mortgage.'

Balls and Miliband decided at the outset that they would not apologise for the structural deficit and the level of debt the Labour government left in 2010. Their reasoning was both intellectual and political. Intellectually, they believed that the recession had been caused by the global economic crisis, not Labour's spending, and they defended the last Labour government's increased spending on health and education. But, politically, they argued that this would simply hand the Tories a weapon to bash them with until 7 May 2015. 'The Tories would have loved it', said one of the Shadow Cabinet. 'It would have stood up the untruth. Spending had no relation to any of it. It would have just stood up the Clegg/Cameron narrative.' There was also relatively little pressure in the Shadow Cabinet for any such apology. As one of Miliband's advisors put it: 'Most of the shadows accepted Ed Balls' argument that the coalition was cutting too far and too fast and that seemed correct at the time. So we did not [apologise].' Balls would later admit that regulation of the banks had been too lax and that Brown had been wrong to say that he had ended the cycle of boom and bust. But this was as far as the two Eds would go and it was not the prelude to any sort of apology that some within the party had thought would be necessary.

At first, Balls' charge that the government, by cutting spending too far and too fast, was killing off economic growth appeared to have some purchase. George Osborne was missing his deficit reduction targets, the economy flatlined and living standards were falling. Balls called for a slower pace of deficit reduction and offered a plan for growth, including a cut in VAT, more apprenticeships and house building, and financing infrastructure projects. As Balls appeared to be vindicated, it became more difficult politically for those around Miliband to warn that the party needed to adopt a tougher stance on spending.

There remains a debate about whether the refusal early on to apologise was decisive. Some of those close to Miliband, as well as prominent figures less close, urged him and Balls to do so. The refusal may have fed into the fear of some voters that the party had not learnt its lessons and that a Labour government would again resort to borrowing and too much spending. One of Miliband's aides said: 'Without that apology from the start all our policies on the economy rested on a weak economic foundation.' Another quoted the late Philip Gould's dictum: 'Concede and move on.' But those around Balls rejected this argument:

'You couldn't concede and move on', one said, 'because no one would move on. All you'd have done was concede.'

The other alternative was to defend the record of New Labour, but Miliband – keen to distance himself from the Blair and Brown governments – was never able to do this properly. One of Miliband's aides summed it up: 'We did not confront, concede or convince. We simply hoped to move on.'

It also took time for Miliband to recruit his political team. The most senior member was Stewart Wood, who had worked closely with him in Number 10 under Gordon Brown. Before 2010, Miliband and Wood had already decided that after Brown, they wanted to adopt policies which would break with New Labour. Wood was soon appointed Shadow Minister without Portfolio and had a deliberately ill-defined role. Also key in the early period was Lucy Powell, who had managed the leadership campaign and was made acting chief of staff. It was well known that she would be seeking to become an MP, which she did at a by-election in 2012. The journalist Tom Baldwin became director of communications strategy, whilst Bob Roberts, former political editor of *Daily Mirror*, became head of press.

After some comings and goings, the key members apart from the above were: Greg Beales, at first adviser on policy but who from 2012 took over from Baldwin on strategy; Marc Stears, an academic and speechwriter; Torsten Bell, a former Treasury official and adviser to Alistair Darling, who became director of policy and rebuttal; and Anna Yearley, who was political secretary and Miliband's link with MPs and the unions. Tim Livesey, former adviser to the Archbishop of Canterbury, succeeded Powell as chief of staff in late 2011.

In an effort to achieve closer integration of the leader's team with the party headquarters, Miliband turned to the businessman Charles Allen for ideas. The result was the creation of a new board to oversee the party organisation. Allen chaired it and three of the seven directors came from Miliband's team (Bell, Beales and Roberts) and a further two of Miliband's team joined the board. Many party officials regarded it as a blatant takeover.

From the beginning, there were repeated complaints about the way the leader's office functioned. These are not unusual in politics, although they were made strongly and repeatedly in the case of Miliband's team. There were complaints that staff were unwilling to share information with shadow ministers and that too many were like-minded former Oxford Philosophy, Politics and Economics (PPE) alumni, North

London-based and lacking experience of life outside the Westminster bubble. 'The rest of us were in the cheap seats', complained one member of the National Executive Committee (NEC). 'If you weren't part of that scene, you were a tier below.' Some northern MPs in particular spoke of a 'metropolitan clique' and party officials muttered the leader's appointments taking up so many positions on the new board. But perhaps most damaging of all, there were complaints that the set-up was ineffectual. 'Decisions just didn't get made', complained one of the Brewer's Green campaign team. 'And when they were made, they didn't happen. I just couldn't get anything done.' Or, as a Shadow Cabinet minister said of the core team around Miliband: 'Four of them in a room and nothing coming out.' Several saw this as reflecting Miliband's personality, and especially his tendency to appoint multiple people to similar jobs: 'Look at Baldwin and Roberts. Look at Douglas Alexander and Dugher. He does not like one-on-one confrontation. He does not like saying no directly to a person. It is better if he deals with a couple of people.' A key member of the campaign team described the operation as characterised by three features: centralisation, chronic indecision and resulting paralysis. 'Indecision is Ed's weapon', he said.

Helped by the immediate post-election collapse in the Lib Dem vote, Labour soon took a lead in the opinion polls, which they then held almost continuously for the next four years. Labour's private polling was, however, never quite as positive as the national polls. It was conducted by Stan Greenberg's company Greenberg, Quinlan Rosler, although most of the work liaising with Labour was done by James Morris, the firm's London partner. There were repeated complaints about the secrecy of the private polling, which often was presented to Miliband with just Beales, Morris and sometimes Greenberg present.

These private polls – of which there were 22 between 2010 and the start of the election campaign in March 2015 – never showed the party's vote share above 38%; by contrast, more than half of the public polls during the Parliament had Labour over 39%. Labour's lead over the Conservatives in 2012–13 in its private polling was consistently lower than in the average of the public polls, sometimes by six or seven percentage points, although from June 2013 onwards there was not much difference in the gap compared with the average of the published polls. Labour's polling in marginal seats, however, also found that the pro-Labour swing was lower than that in its national polls and in the average of the public polls.[10]

Despite the government not hitting its economic targets and despite the sluggish growth in the economy for much of the period, Labour still lagged behind the Conservatives on economic trust. Conservative private polling showed that voters preferred Balls' slower pace of cuts by 2:1 over the Osborne plan. But when the pollster added that this would entail more borrowing, debt and higher interest rates, voters preferred the Conservative plan by 55% to 45%.Voters thought cuts were necessary even if many complained that they were being carried out unfairly. Soon after Osborne's 'omnishambles' Budget in 2012, a YouGov survey found that voters trusted Labour to make the economy fairer, but the Conservatives to make it grow faster.[11] Yet, crucially, when voters were forced to choose between the two, their preference for the latter trumped the former decisively.

In May 2013, two years ahead of the general election, and with Labour 11% ahead of the Conservatives in public polling, the pollster Peter Kellner noted that in modern times no opposition had returned to office after one term without leading at the mid-term by 20% (Labour's best was in the low teens). Given Labour's deficit on leadership and economic competence, both of which suppressed its support or made it conditional, and the likelihood of the Coalition government benefiting from an economic recovery, he concluded that his surveys were 'profoundly troubling for Labour'.[12] Kellner's regular articles for *Progress* magazine giving multiple warnings about Labour's fundamental vulnerabilities irritated Ed Miliband's political office, although his findings were not dissimilar from their own focus groups and private polls. In September 2013, one of Labour's private polls listed the positive attributes voters associated with the Labour and Conservative Parties. Labour were ahead for being 'on the side of ordinary people', but were behind on all the others, including competence, being careful with taxpayers' money and having the right approach to the economy. 'Do you have to be so negative?', Miliband said to Stan Greenberg at one point.

Although everyone in Miliband's team accepted that the party needed to attract former Conservative voters and make inroads in the south, they also had other voters in mind. If, some of his team argued, the party retained the bulk of its 2010 vote (which was taken for granted), regained some of the 1997 Labour voters who had drifted away (always said to be five million), appealed to non-voters, students (alienated by the hike in tuition fees) and kept hold of disaffected Lib Dems, the party could forge a winning coalition. Here was the basis of Labour's alleged '35% strategy'. This figure was never a target, let alone a strategy, but there was an expectation that it would be enough for Labour to win, particularly given the pro-Labour bias in the electoral system and the likelihood that the Conservatives would not get more than 32–33% of the vote. After all, no governing party had increased its share of the vote after one full term since 1955. Although the 35% figure was rarely mentioned among party strategists, it seemed implicit in the policy positions taken. 'Many of us assumed it', said one.

At the time, there were complaints that this figure was not ambitious enough – although the longer the Parliament went on, the less ambitious it seemed. The bigger problem was that whilst polling 35% might have been enough to reach Number 10, the composition of that 35% was crucial. There was ample public research pointing out the problems with pulling together a coalition of the disgruntled. Many of the supposed lost five million voters were in fact now dead, and research into the views of those still alive showed that they were less likely to be in a trade union, social housing, work in the public sector or regard themselves as left of centre.[13] And contrary to the idea that most non-voters were inclined to be left of centre, the available evidence suggested the opposite on issues like law and order, immigration and welfare.[14]

All of this was confirmed by Labour's own research. A polling presentation in 2011, based on detailed analysis of a combination of public and private data, made it clear that a strategy based on appealing to the core vote and non-voters was 'a dead end'. It recommended making an appeal across the board and emphasised the need to do better in the south (outside London). But such voters disapproved of the party's record on welfare and the economy. 'There were many questionable assumptions in Ed's thinking. The coalition of voters was chosen to fit the politics. It had more to do with ideology than polling evidence', said one party official.

Miliband believed that the global financial crisis in 2008 marked a turning point in political economy, necessitating a new approach to the economy. The crisis had shown the downside of the neo-liberal model of free markets and deregulation. Contrary to claims that a growing economy ensured a trickle-down of benefits, the reality was that the living standards of ordinary people stagnated as those at the top, particularly in banking and financial services, gained the most. There was a disconnection between economic growth and living standards, and ample evidence of greater inequality in the UK and the USA. In both countries, the already wealthy rather than wage-earners had for several years grabbed most of the benefits of growth. Miliband and Wood believed that these developments made a modern social democratic message more relevant than ever. They calculated that the electorate was ready for a new political economy, one that would work for ordinary people.[15] If New Labour had been 'relaxed' about inequality, Miliband cared passionately about it and wanted to use the resources of the state to combat it.

That, at least, was the indictment. But Miliband was better at diagnosing the problems than coming up with solutions. It took a long time to develop policies to remake the economy and tackle the cost of living crisis he had identified. In his 2011 conference speech, he called for a more socially and economically responsible capitalism, and drew a distinction between predator firms (which were bad, for example, paying their workers such low wages that they relied on tax credits) and producers (which were good, training for workers and investing).[16] Miliband's private focus groups, conducted *before* the conference, had found the terms 'predator' and 'producer' confusing, and even his colleagues struggled to place well-known firms in one or other category.

At the party conference the following year, Miliband spoke of 'One Nation Labour', bringing a cultural and patriotic dimension to his generally economistic politics. It contrasted his concern for the welfare of all sections of society with the Coalition's policies, which, Labour claimed, were dividing north from south, the public from the private sector and the rich from the poor. Shadow ministers were urged to plug the 'One Nation Labour' theme in all policy announcements and interviews. Developed largely by Marc Stears (despite doubts by other aides), the theme was a daring steal from modernising Conservatives who had long been associated with it. Miliband was never entirely happy with it, wanted something more cutting, and Beales presented polling which showed voters were equally unsure about what it meant. Within a year, it too had been largely dropped. Some of Miliband's team regretted that they seemed too keen to find new themes for his major public speeches, but did not allow sufficient time to allow an argument to gel with the public. Other concepts such as the 'squeezed middle' or 'pre-distribution' or the 'British promise' would be launched, have some resonance, only to be forgotten shortly afterwards.

When George Osborne in his 2012 Budget reduced the top rate of income tax from 50% to 45%, Labour promised to reverse this 'tax cut for millionaires' and party spokesmen regularly used this powerful soundbite. In his 2013 conference speech, Miliband announced a two-year energy price freeze while a Labour government began the process to 'fix' the market (the idea had been enthusiastically endorsed in focus groups). Other proposals included a cap on landlords' ability

'I have remembered to mention the deficit' (Christian Adams, *Daily Telegraph*, 12 December 2014)

to increase rents, a mansion tax on properties worth over £2 million and breaking up big banks. Wood, an admirer of the US President 'Teddy' Roosevelt's attacks on oligopolistic rail and oil barons in the early twentieth century, encouraged the leader to take on today's vested interests: the banks and rail and energy companies. Miliband, who had been successful with his attack in 2011 on News International over the phone hacking scandal, liked this approach, which he also took in August 2013 when he led the party in opposition to the government's proposed armed intervention in Syria alongside the USA.[17]

Collectively, many of these policies and the rhetoric provided the opportunity, however unfairly, for opponents and internal critics to say that Labour was 'anti-business'. As one Shadow Cabinet member said:

> If you sat down with him [Miliband], he'd agree about the importance of business, in a rational discussion. But the desire to get cut through, and be the insurgent, to be attacking vested interests, had such a big impact, that the cumulative impact of all of that was to make him appear anti-business. Plus, any time he sat down with business

> people, they all left thinking he didn't get them. He didn't have any empathy with them, and he was bored by them.

Charles Dunstone, the founder of Carphone Warehouse and a Labour sympathiser, organised a series of dinners for Miliband to meet business leaders. The first, a month before the election, went so badly because of Miliband's disengagement that the rest were cancelled.[18] There was a widely circulated story about the occasion Miliband asked the chairman of a FTSE 100 company: 'Why exactly do you need to pay your shareholders dividends?' The story was probably apocryphal – the company involved changes depending on who is telling the story – but plenty of those who know him felt it was plausible.[19]

In order to deal with the blank policy page, Miliband first appointed Liam Byrne, the Shadow Cabinet Office Minister, to coordinate a policy review and he took this remit with him when he moved to become Shadow Work and Pensions Minister. Byrne had 23 groups, each headed by the relevant shadow minister, which were supposed to feed in ideas for a 2015 manifesto rather than for day-to-day policy. He organised a 'listening exercise' to inform the groups about the public mood. The latter largely reinforced the gloomy message for the party of the opinion polls, particularly on immigration and welfare. On his own departmental watch, his recommendations for restoring a measure of the contributory principle and more conditionality were opposed by many on the left, including Len McCluskey, leader of the Unite union, who dismissed them as 'failed Blairite policies' and called for Byrne's dismissal.

Another source of ideas was so-called Blue Labour, whose main spokesman was the recently ennobled academic Maurice Glasman. The group invoked Labour's traditions of localism, mutualism and pluralism, and the need for a politics of identity. As well as joining the now-widespread call for more devolution, it also called for a greater sensitivity to the sections of the English working class who felt left behind by globalisation, the decline of manufacturing and cultural change. Glasman complained, controversially, about the effects of mass immigration on communities and, less controversially, advocated a living wage. He was tapping into a mood that UKIP soon exploited.

The Dagenham MP Jon Cruddas took over from Byrne as policy coordinator in 2012 and corralled the number of policy groups to three, covering politics, society and the economy. Given spending constraints, his proposals were less about making spending proposals than redistributing power. He recommended more devolution to local and regional bodies, the creation of regional banks, greater control of public services by users, integration of health and social care, and an ambitious and expensive package of universal childcare for pre-school children.

Because Miliband's office was thought to be unsympathetic to the drift of Cruddas' work, various centre-left think tanks wrote to *The Guardian* complaining that Miliband's policy team was cherry picking and watering down proposals; Cruddas was overheard complaining of 'the dead hand of the centre', which was too bureaucratic and frightened of bold ideas.

As head of policy, Torsten Bell was a key figure in Miliband's office. Other teams reporting to the leader's office included Lord Adonis on transport and economic growth and Sir Michael Lyons on housing. Many of the key policies that Labour would unveil at the election – including the 10p tax rate, the cut in tuition fees, the energy price freeze and an increase in the minimum wage – were initiated by Bell's policy team. At the National Policy Forum, the party described its policy package as 'big reform not big spending', accepting the Coalition's spending plans for 2015–16.

Many of these individual policies were popular – as both Labour's polling and public polling confirmed – but they were not connected into a persuasive or even coherent narrative. 'Ideas are important, of course they are', said one member of the NEC. 'But for Ed, they're everything. But they're not. You need more than good ideas.' And they had no impact on Labour's weaknesses on perceived competence or trust on the economy compared with the Conservatives. Labour's focus groups would simultaneously find support for individual Labour policies – cutting tuition fees, imposing a 50% tax rate, an energy price freeze – and more fundamental doubts about the party: too likely to borrow and add to the deficit, and too soft on undeserving welfare claimants. A close observer of the groups said: 'Ed and his people listened attentively but there was no great appetite for doing anything about it.' Bagehot in *The Economist* wrote of 'an increasingly unpopular party with lots of popular policies'.[20]

In January 2013, Ed Balls risked his standing with the left and the unions when warning that a Labour government would not be able to reverse all the government's cuts – although the party had opposed many of them – and would restrict pay in the public sector. In June 2013, in a major speech at Reuters, he accepted Osborne's plans for spending in 2015–16 and for attaching more conditionality to some welfare benefits. At the end of 2013, he introduced a zero-based spending review to stop colleagues making promises involving more spending. In his 2014 conference speech, he was booed when he mentioned the party's proposal to restrict child benefit. If the message of a fiscally responsible Labour Party was not cutting through to the public – and it was not – Balls and his team could and did fairly claim that much of the responsibility must lie with the rest of the leadership for not making the case more frequently and strongly.

Party managers gradually restored financial stability, helped in part by party membership increasing to 200,000 by the end of 2014. Following the 2005 general election, the party's debts (including loans) had amounted to £24.5 million. Prudent housekeeping by the general secretary Ray Collins and, from 2011, his successor, Iain McNicol, resulted in the debts being steadily reduced and on course to be paid off by 2016. Drawing on the annual £6 million Short money paid to the opposition, the party expanded the policy and digital teams in its London headquarters and boosted the number of regional directors and organisers in key seats.

For a time, the party drew on the volunteer work of the American Arnie Graf, who had helped train the young Barack Obama as a community organiser, to train teams in the key seats. Graf influenced Miliband in the early years of his leadership, and some of the Labour team found his work helpful ('inspirational'), but he returned to the USA in 2013 amid queries over his visa status shortly after Douglas Alexander and Spencer Livermore took charge of Labour's campaign. As one NEC member put it: 'They hated that airy-fairy kind of nonsense.'

In February 2012, Eric Joyce, the Labour MP for Falkirk, was involved in a drunken altercation in the Strangers' Bar of the House of Commons, during which he punched several people and headbutted a Conservative MP. Charged with multiple criminal offences, Joyce was suspended from the Labour Party and announced his decision to stand down at the next election. The brawl set in train a series of events that were to have profound and unintended consequences for the party after Ed Miliband's resignation as leader in May 2015.

The role of the Unite union in influencing candidate selections had already raised eyebrows, but things came to a head in the selection for Joyce's replacement, amid reports that Unite was involved in signing up scores of members, some without their knowledge, to determine the selection in Falkirk.

The reports and the negative media coverage of the unions 'running' the party led Miliband to take action in 2013. He invited Lord (Ray) Collins to head a working party to examine the links between the party and the unions. The Collins Report into Labour Party Reform was revealed in February 2014. It backed Miliband's preferred reforms by proposing that in future, union members should opt in individually to the party rather than being affiliated collectively by the union if they had not opted out of paying into the union's political fund. At the same time, the electoral college would be dissolved. Miliband could fairly claim that this represented 'real' One Member One Vote (OMOV) and that membership would be an individual's deliberate choice. In private, some complained about the ending of the electoral college, which gave the parliamentary party a third of the vote in leadership elections. And some worried that the creation of the registered form of membership (for a nominal £3 annual fee), while opening up the party, also gave scope for entryism by groups which would damage the party. What was widely regarded as a bold stroke at the time was envisaged by very few as providing an opportunity for a leader to be elected over the opposition of the great majority of Labour MPs, as was to happen in September 2015.[21]

But there were two more immediate consequences of the row over Falkirk. One was the resignation of the party's election campaigns director, Tom Watson, who was close to the Unite leader, amid accusations that he had been involved in the alleged misdeeds. The second was financial. For all the financial progress made, the party still relied on the affiliated trade unions for its running costs, and the reforms led to a reduction in the funds coming to it. Unite, Unison and the GMB cut their affiliation fees to the party immediately, and the resulting loss of £2.7 million in funding for the year 2013–14 created significant problems for the campaign effort, especially on the ground, where the party did not have sufficient resources. In March 2014 at a special conference, 86% of delegates approved the Collins package and it was backed by the general secretaries of the big unions. Miliband had emerged from an embarrassing situation with some credit – but less money. One of those involved in Labour's campaigning described the party's ground war operation at this point as 'absolutely broke'. Union money was switched back on in late 2014 with some discretionary donations, but those involved claim this was far too late for a properly targeted ground operation in marginal seats.

Ed Miliband lacked electoral appeal. In early 2012 a Conservative polling note for the Prime Minister described Miliband's ratings with YouGov – just 18% thought he was 'doing well', 71% 'doing badly' – as 'the worst... for any party leader ever'. This verdict depended on the data analysed; in the early 1980s, for example, MORI had found worse satisfaction scores for Michael Foot than for Miliband after 2010 – but to poll slightly better than Michael Foot is not a sign of great electoral appeal. Where David Cameron polled ahead of his party, Miliband trailed his. His supporters would point out that Ted Heath in 1970 and Margaret Thatcher in 1979 were opposition leaders who were less popular than the Prime Minister of the day, but went on to win the subsequent general election. Now, however, the greater frequency and publicity of focus groups and opinion polls heightened awareness of the leadership factor; perceptions of Miliband's weakness and alleged fratricide were set early on. From the start, focus groups among voters Labour needed to win over said that he was not prime ministerial. He was failing to inspire a large minority of Labour voters – at times under half agreed he was doing a good job – and he trailed Cameron among UKIP and Lib Dem supporters as a possible Prime Minister. Perhaps most wounding was a private poll in September 2013 which asked voters to give 'the best three reasons for not voting Labour'. The top reason mentioned was 'Ed Miliband', followed by immigration and welfare. Such information was deleted from presentations beyond the smallest group of Miliband's advisors.

Comment about the 'Ed problem' was not confined to unsympathetic commentators.[22] If he was inconsistent in the Commons, he was confident and relaxed when handling question-and-answer sessions with groups around the country and (at least until 2014) with addresses, always notes-free, to party conferences.

Some of the problems were of Miliband's own creation. In May 2014, taking part in a local election campaign event, he went to a café in New Covent Garden Market to promote a policy on small business. A bacon sandwich was presented to him. All of his aides told him not to be photographed eating it. He ignored their advice. The photo became widely circulated, demonstrating apparent gaucheness and an inability even to do basic things such as eat.[23] As Owen Jones wrote in *The Guardian*, it presented him as 'a sad pathetic geeky loser who cannot even eat a bacon sandwich with any dignity'. Jones went on: 'You can easily select photographs to make any politician look undignified, or generally reinforce whatever narrative you have selected.'[24] True, it was all unfair, but in this case self-inflicted. Miliband followed the incident with a speech arguing that a Prime Minister needed other qualities than being good at photo ops and soundbites. It was the sort of thing you say if you are not good at photo ops and soundbites.

However, for all the grumbling about the leader being an electoral handicap, there were few obvious alternatives. By the end of 2013, most shadow ministers accepted that Miliband would lead the party in the general election, although following his unfortunate conference speech in September 2014, there were fitful attempts among backbenchers to organise a challenge. But once Alan Johnson again ruled out any interest in returning to the frontline, Miliband was secure until the election. Peter Kellner's review of the polling evidence in November 2014 concluded that the party's problems went beyond the leader: 'My guess is that getting rid of Ed Miliband would make little difference (and) the biggest weaknesses belong to the party as a whole.'[25] This, however, was not a view shared within the Conservative camp. Based on extensive polling, their view was that, at any point, replacing Ed Miliband with someone more credible as a potential Prime Minister would have made a significant difference.[26]

In 2011, Miliband had invited Douglas Alexander and Spencer Livermore to work with Beales on a paper suggesting themes for a War Book for the election. Alexander had managed the bruising 2010 campaign; Livermore had worked on the 2005 campaign and as a strategy adviser to Gordon Brown in Number 10 until 2007. They had both written the party's War Books for previous elections and their involvement paved the way for their eventual appointment to run the campaign. They presented the paper to Miliband just before Christmas 2012. It suggested likely Conservative lines of attack, including Labour as a 'Back to Brown' risk with the economy. The authors recommended that Miliband counter the attacks by making a clean break with the Blair/Brown years, deploying the 'One Nation' theme as an alternative vision in order to frame the election around the question 'whose side will you be on?'.

Once Tom Watson resigned as the party's election campaigns coordinator in July 2013, it was largely inevitable that Alexander and Livermore would be installed to direct the general election campaign. They formed an uneasy team with Michael Dugher, who was in charge of attack and rebuttal. The grandees associated with Labour's previous campaigns – Peter Mandelson, Philip Gould and Alastair Campbell – were for different reasons no longer involved, although the latter continued to provide advice, not all of it welcome.

In 2013, Tim Livesey confided privately that he thought Labour needed to be 15 points ahead as they came into the general election. If they were ten points ahead, they might be OK, but equally might be in trouble. 'And if we're five points ahead, we'll be putting a brave face on it.' Yet during 2014, Labour's lead in the public polls narrowed to low single figures and Miliband's already poor ratings fell further. In May, two polls actually reported a lead for the Conservatives. Although YouGov regularly found that over half of the electorate thought the government was doing badly, only around a third supported Labour. A lack of clarity about the party's message and what it stood for remained. Morris's polling in September 2013 had revealed that when voters were asked what the parties stood for, 14% said they did not know and another 16% said 'nothing' for the Conservatives; the figures for Labour were 41% and 23% respectively, with a further 9% mentioning just 'opposing the Conservatives'. Some of the lack of clarity may have been a consequence of not being in government or of having too many messages. Miliband's party critics complained that he was too often looking to say something new or different and did not develop and repeat themes enough. As noted earlier, the more inclusive 'One Nation' theme, which had been so prominent following the 2012 annual conference, had virtually disappeared by the 2013 conference. Some of the differences reflected different outlooks among aides and advisers. Stears, Cruddas and Baldwin favoured One Nation Labour; Beales, influenced by the polls, wanted a sharper message on immigration and 'offers' for voters; and Wood a more ideological line. This all led to a failure to stick to a coherent message. A note from Greenberg and Morris to Miliband following the 2013 party conference pointedly complained 'we are already slipping into multiple messages and losing the main values that motivate you and Labour'. According to one Shadow Cabinet member: 'The view in Ed's office was: "once you've said it once, it's been said". But that's no good. You have to say it again, and again, and again.'[27]

The rise of UKIP initially pleased some in the party, who felt that it would largely take votes away from the Conservatives ('If it was bad for the Tories', said one Labour MP, 'it must be good for us'). But as more became known about the nature of the UKIP vote and as more and more Labour MPs found UKIP support growing in their constituencies, with UKIP making inroads among Labour's elderly, white working-class supporters in England, concern grew. UKIP's message was appealing to many traditional Labour voters and Nigel Farage could sound like Len McCluskey when attacking Labour leaders as members of a Westminster elite, ignorant of the concerns of ordinary people.

There was a feeling on the backbenches, however, that the leadership never really grasped the nature of the problem, at least partly because of who the leadership were. 'They never understood UKIP at all', said one member of Labour's NEC. 'If you're Scottish or from London, you just don't get that demographic ... They totally under-estimated the threat.'

Miliband resisted pressure in the Shadow Cabinet to support an EU referendum, notably from Ed Balls, Andy Burnham and Jim Murphy, and eventually ruled it out. Douglas Alexander was adamantly opposed. Miliband's view was that any referendum was risky and would in any case dominate the first two years of a Labour government. However, he did waver, at one point authorising Beales to write a paper preparing the ground for it. When he was told that Miliband was going to come out against an EU referendum, the veteran Labour MP John Spellar, who had long been warning of the UKIP threat, accused Alexander of not understanding UKIP because he sat for a seat in Scotland; in turn, Alexander accused Spellar of being racist.

There had been some fencing between Miliband and Yvette Cooper over the line to take on immigration, another core UKIP concern, with the aides of the two blaming the other for not coming up with proposals. Cooper's view was that a major policy announcement, to be effectively communicated, had to be made by the leader. Yet Miliband probably made more speeches on immigration than any other topic apart from the economy. Both Miliband and Cooper recognised the voters' concerns – immigration in 2014 had overtaken the economy as the top issue – and the pressures it was imposing on some communities. Miliband admitted that the last Labour government had been wrong to allow in so many East European immigrants – it was one of the areas where he felt they could sensibly concede past errors – and he and Cooper incrementally toughened the party's position, while trying to operate within the party's traditions of integration, contribution and fair wages, and within the reality of EU membership and the free movement of people. They said that Labour would act to prevent employers recruiting and exploiting cheap immigrant labour, would strengthen the border force, and would stop immigrants from claiming benefits for two years after arriving and from transferring welfare benefits to family members living overseas. Labour had moved far on immigration, but if the package did not prevent Labour voters turning to UKIP, it was probably both because it was not enough (and, whilst the UK was a member of the EU, could never be enough), and because it was communicated *sotto voce*; the son of immigrants, Miliband never seemed comfortable talking about the subject.

By the May 2014 local and European elections, the realisation of the UKIP threat was widespread, and there were several Shadow Cabinet discussions on how to handle it. A party strategy note warned that if UKIP exceeded 16% in the national polls, it would start to hurt Labour more than the Conservatives. Unease was strengthened following the near-loss of Heywood and Middleton to UKIP in a by-election in October 2014, after which an internal 'task force' was established to oversee the party's attacks on UKIP. It was noticeable that it involved MPs from the north of England. In December 2014, the *Daily Telegraph* published a leaked version of a lengthy party document advising local activists how to deal with voters who were receptive to the UKIP message. The document was a ground war response, accompanied by detailed constituency-specific material, identifying the parts of each constituency whose demographic profile most looked like those of voters that had or were considering switching from Labour to UKIP.

Miliband believed that he also had an intellectual response to UKIP in his critique of global capitalism. 'But', as one Labour MP said, 'you also needed an organisational response and an emotional one, and you needed the right people to carry the message ... We looked like the establishment, telling people they were so lucky to have us.' Even in 2014, a senior member of Miliband's team was heard saying that he was more worried about the electoral effect of the Greens than UKIP.

In 2013, following the May local elections, Miliband and his team held a review session at his North London home. Whilst he often had such weekend sessions with his closest aides, this one was challenging as some called for a change in direction and a stronger stance on deficit reduction. Miliband rejected the advice as tantamount to asking for a return to New Labour and a betrayal of why he had stood for the leadership. When appointing Alexander and Livermore as his new campaign managers later that year, both of whose politics had become more New Labour over time, he overrode any doubts they had and made clear that the main themes had been set and were not for revising.

'We still hoped for a reappraisal by Ed', recalled one of them. 'But it did not happen.' There was another inquest-cum-review at Miliband's house following disappointing analysis of the local and European elections in May 2014, which showed that the party was not on course for a general election victory. Again there were calls for change, particularly on economic policy, and again Miliband refused. If Labour won or lost the election, it would be on his terms. As he said more than once to aides, 'You guys have got to trust me' and 'I must be true to myself'. If Blair had claimed that Britain was a Tory country, Miliband was gambling that it was now a progressive one.

The party's campaign staff were still of the impression that Labour was on course for victory. Stan Greenberg, apparently convinced that the Conservatives could not go higher than 32–33% of the vote – they needed all of their 2010 vote, would lose support to UKIP and were hindered by the electoral system – said in December 2013 that the above factors made it structurally impossible for Labour to lose, and was still of that view in the autumn of 2014, prior to the Scottish referendum.[28]

In April 2014, Miliband and Alexander recruited another American, David Axelrod, who had worked on the successful Obama presidential campaigns in 2008 and 2012. The fee for his involvement was never disclosed, although it was said to be around £300,000. Even within the core Labour team, there were doubts about Axelrod's utility and the value-for-money that his appointment represented. He was variously described as 'a comfort blanket for Douglas Alexander' and 'a very expensive process story'. One senior member of the Labour campaign claimed simply: 'No idea what he did.' Some of the criticism was based on a misunderstanding of Axelrod's role. He was often compared to the Conservatives' Lynton Crosby – but Crosby was the campaign manager, whereas Axelrod was an advisor, albeit a significant one, whose role was necessarily more sporadic. He rarely visited the UK, but had regular conference calls with the core Miliband team. He commented on drafts of speeches and helped with debate preparations. His main contribution was in forcing Labour to compose a narrative or overall story; without that, he said, the narrow retail offers were equivalent to 'Vote Labour and get a microwave'. 'Make a big argument', he urged Miliband, 'and it will elevate you.' He helped the party create the message 'Britain only succeeds when working families succeed'. He was more active and influential than he was usually given credit for, although that would not be difficult.

In June 2014, with the Scottish referendum campaign beginning to build towards its conclusion, Gordon Brown rang Michael Dugher to discuss the unfolding situation. He was not positive. 'We'll lose seats over this', he warned. It was, Dugher later recalled, the first time anyone, anywhere, inside the party had mentioned to him the possibility that the referendum campaign was going to have electoral consequences for Labour. 'Losing seats in Scotland isn't part of our key seat strategy', he told Brown.

As explained in Chapter 1, Labour had joined other pro-Union parties in the cross-party campaign, Better Together, urging Scots to vote 'No' in the referendum. Joining with other parties in this way left Labour in Scotland vulnerable to the SNP charge that they were working with the (hated) Conservatives, that they were part of 'them', part of the 'Westminster' system, working against Scotland's interests.[29] As James

Mitchell noted, the Labour Party had been successfully 'othering' the Conservatives in Scotland for years.[30] Now they found the same tactic being used against them, with equally brutal results. The cross-party nature of the campaign denied Labour a distinctive voice for the best part of two years. And the campaign had also exposed the decay of the party's political machine north of the border. It was not just the decline in membership – down, on some estimates, to 13,000 – but it was also a deep organisational rot.

Some Labour politicians had been aware of this, but – having grown complacent – had turned a blind eye. Others were unaware until they became involved in the referendum. But almost every Labour figure south of the border who got involved in the referendum campaign was appalled by what they found. 'We had the wrong people, not enough people, no ground operation and some incredibly lazy politicians', said one of the Brewer's Green team. 'We have seats with, literally, zero contact data, where doors haven't been knocked on for 20 years.' Or as another put it: 'We were always being told: the worst thing that you could do would be for London to get involved. We're having to now, though.' Shortly after the referendum, one member of the party hierarchy was told, in pleading terms by a Scottish Labour MP, that they needed to realise what was happening and that the national party had to send extra resources. The reply came back: 'But you're the Labour Party in Scotland. What have you been doing?'

In the final days of the referendum campaign, the party diverted over half of its professional staff, and considerable money, to help the 'No' campaign. The Shadow Cabinet held a meeting in Scotland and over 100 MPs went by train a week before polling day to campaign. This was all a huge distraction from a general election that was now less than a year away.

Despite winning the referendum, the consequences of the campaign were catastrophic for Labour in Scotland. The SNP became the voice of opposition to the Coalition government and to austerity in Scotland. Within a month, some public polls put the SNP at over 50% (see p. 137). Labour's private polling confirmed this, putting the SNP ahead of it by 49% to 25% in November 2014. If this level of support were to be sustained until 7 May, it would be enough to cost Labour virtually all its seats in Scotland and remove – at a stroke – the chance of a Labour majority government. It could still manage to become the largest party in a hung parliament, but the party was now fighting on multiple fronts – against the Conservatives, UKIP and the SNP – a very different terrain from that which Miliband thought he would be facing when he became leader in 2010.

In the speech he had prepared in the event of winning the leadership in 2010, David Miliband planned to warn Labour against being deficit deniers. He would have described the deficit as 'the biggest argument in politics, and the biggest danger for us'. An internal polling memo to Ed Miliband in early 2011 had similarly warned that the deficit had to be taken seriously: 'Because we start with low credibility on the deficit, our determination to reduce the deficit should be over-emphasised. It should be in every script, and is even more important where we are opposing a cut.' The warning was not acted on.

Ed Miliband's notes-free speech to the party conference in Manchester in September 2014 was notable for the omission of a key passage dealing with precisely that subject. Amongst other things, he forgot to say:

> In the four years since we lost the last election, we have learnt hard, important lessons. They start with government having to live within its means. If people feel cynical now – and they do – think how much worse it would be if we made false promises. There won't be money to spend after the next election. Britain will be spending £75 billion on the interest on our debt alone. That's more than the entire budget for our schools.

The speech was a major setback for those hoping to strengthen the party's economic message and for showing Miliband as a prospective Prime Minister. His team regarded the conference as the last major platform on which he could establish his leadership credentials.[31] Miliband was distraught when, leaving the stage, he realised the omission (and muttered to an aide that he would deal with the deficit in interviews). The omission was highlighted when the party's digital team posted an unedited version of the original speech online. Without that, the criticism might not have been so vehement, although even before it became clear that the omission had been accidental, the Conservatives had already leapt on the lack of any mention of the deficit.

Apologists said Miliband had spent much of the first weeks in September in Scotland not fully engaged with the speech and that events in Syria had forced a reordering of the speech, and it is easy to see this as a simple slip-up, the downside of the obsession for politicians giving notes-free speeches to try to appear authentic. One of his team just blamed the leader's 'vanity': 'He wanted it to be notes-free but had not mastered the text.' But plenty of those around Miliband – and not just those hostile to him – saw the omission as something more significant, almost Freudian. Even his conference speech the previous year had referred to the deficit in just one sentence.

And for all the talk of 'tough choices' on spending, the party opposed virtually every government cut and offered very few of its own. Miliband chose to address The People's Assembly Against Austerity and later joined a Trades Union Congress (TUC) march against the cuts. He did not enjoy complete freedom of manoeuvre. The leadership faced difficulties in persuading Labour MPs on the need for some austerity. In an effort in March 2013 to show that Labour could make a 'tough choice' on welfare, the party imposed a three-line whip to abstain on a government bill to sanction benefit claimants who did not seek work, but 44 Labour MPs – congratulated by Len McCluskey – defied the whips to vote against it.[32] A full quarter of Labour voters even thought the government ran a budget surplus.[33] But the leadership was not completely comfortable with the agreed policy. An adviser later reflected: 'At the end of the day the two Eds simply did not want to be the guys making the big cuts. It would be bad for the poor. They were social democrats and this was not the centre-left politics they had signed up to.'

Less noticed, but equally annoying to some of those around Miliband, was the fact that the forgotten section of the 2014 speech also included material on immigration: 'Immigration benefits our country but those who come here have a responsibility to learn English and earn their way. And employers have a responsibility not to exploit migrant workers and undercut wages.' These were, and had been since 2010, Labour's two biggest strategic weaknesses, and both slipped the party leader's mind. The speech was also noticeable for what was completely absent, even in the prepared draft. An irate Balls, and others, had been pressuring Miliband to include some business-friendly rhetoric, but had made no progress.

The tension between Alexander and Dugher was resolved in November 2014 when the latter was moved to shadow transport and was replaced by Lucy Powell, formerly Miliband's chief of staff. As vice-chair of the campaign team, her brief was to manage the campaign grid. Her arrival was not universally welcomed, but she took some weight off a heavily burdened Alexander and was credited with making sure that decisions were taken and implemented. 'People will pour a tonne of shit on Lucy', said one of Miliband's team, 'because there was lots of bitterness and jealousy when she got involved. But she was a breath of fresh air.

Very no nonsense, and she could chair meetings well, which most politicians can't.' More than anybody, Alexander continued to provide the strategic thinking for the general election. But he was also Shadow Foreign Secretary, had been heavily involved in the Better Together campaign in Scotland and now had to worry about the SNP threat to his own seat in Paisley.

Osborne's autumn spending statement in December 2014, in which he aimed to produce a spending surplus by 2019–20 and reduce government spending to 35% of GDP, provided Labour with an opportunity. Labour warned of the damage to public services, including, inevitably, the NHS, that would follow the 'savage' level of cuts that Osborne would have to make if he reached his 35% target. Balls refused to match the scale of Osborne's deficit target, but said Labour would balance the books on current spending by 2020, two years after Osborne. This was combined with 'fairness' measures such as action on tax evasion and zero-hours contracts, a levy on bank bonuses, a reversal of the 2012 cut in the 50p top rate of income tax, and a mansion tax on properties valued at more than £2 million.

Labour launched the first of their election pledges later that month, which was to cut the deficit-year-on-year. They launched the second – on immigration – a few days later. It was a deliberate decision to lead with these two issues, both troublesome for the party, before Christmas in order to attempt to deal with what were still seen as fundamental problems with the Labour brand, leaving the three more positive pledges to follow in the new year. All of the pledges came in two parts – a short statement, together with more detailed policy claims – and all were tested in focus groups.

Miliband could claim some credit for the party not lapsing into the faction-fighting that often accompanied the defeat of previous Labour governments. In part this was due to the decline of left-right factionalism, in part to a reaction against the past Brownite–Blairite infighting, and in part to Miliband's emollient style. On his watch, there were no major party conference bust-ups over policy and Labour's relative unity contrasted with Conservative divisions over issues like same-sex marriage and Europe. He helped to place rising inequality on the agenda and the need to reset markets in finance and energy. He recognised the problems facing social democratic parties which wanted to pursue goals of social justice when there was little money to spend.

But unity was also achieved at a cost of avoiding some hard choices. The party had few plans for public service reform (a New Labour theme

Labour's five pledges

which had been taken on by the Coalition government) and, for reasons of party management, was often left opposing or half-heartedly accepting the government's measures. But efficiency-enhancing reforms in the major spending programmes in education and health were essential when spending would be restrained for years to come. Also lacking were plans for wealth creation, apart from a proposed infrastructure commission and expanded apprenticeship scheme.

Never properly resolved was the leadership's public assessment of the last Labour government, of which Balls and Miliband had been members. The subject was rarely mentioned, perhaps as part of the decision not to apologise for the economic record. Alastair Campbell urged Miliband in vain to mount a defence and in the end irritated the team with the persistence of his advocacy. Miliband was never going to defend the record; he wanted to distance himself from New Labour.

Following the 2014 party conference, Labour MPs' doubts about their leader intensified. In the public polls, there had been no crossover, but in Labour's private polling, there was a clear post-conference slump, with the Conservatives narrowly ahead by the end of 2014. Miliband's private polling in the battleground seats at the time showed that on a forced choice question about preferring a Conservative government led by David Cameron or a Labour government led by Ed Miliband, the former now led by 45% to 37%.

Yet despite this and the electoral catastrophe that seemed likely to hit Labour in Scotland, the chances of Labour entering government in May 2015 still seemed good. A small team led by Lord (Charlie) Falconer and Tim Livesey was working on preparations for a Labour government. It consulted with senior civil servants and had prepared a draft 400-page document setting out how every significant policy in each department would be moved forward in the first 100 days. Some of those involved wondered if the party had prepared its supporters, let alone the country, for the scale of cuts any government would have to make if it formed a government after the general election. But even sceptical colleagues had come round to accept the probability that Ed Miliband would, without Labour necessarily winning the most seats, be the next Prime Minister and in a position to decide on their political futures. Many were still of that view when the polls closed on 7 May 2015.

Notes

1. On Miliband, see M. Hassan and J. McIntyre, *Ed: The Milibands and the Making of a Labour Leader*. Biteback, 2011. For an excellent account of the Labour Party under Ed Miliband, see Tim Bale, *Five Year Mission*. Oxford University Press, 2015.
2. This claim went beyond the mere numbers of ballots cast: many of the unions canvassed heavily for Ed Miliband and some distributed ballots with their recommendations in the same packages as the voting slips. See Richard Jobson and Mark Wickham-Jones, 'Reinventing the Block Vote? Trade Unions and the 2010 Labour Party Leadership Election', *British Politics*, 6 (September 2011): 317–44.
3. 'David Miliband Tells Hillary Clinton: My Heartache at Losing Labour Leadership Contest', *Daily Telegraph*, 1 September 2015.
4. Bale, *Five Year Mission*, p. 11.
5. This has joined a list of political misquotes. Kinnock (approvingly) quoted someone sat behind him in the hall, who said to him: 'Neil, we've got our party back.' Kinnock later claimed that he replied: 'No, we never lost it!' (*New Statesman*, 9 October 2013), although at the time in 2010, he was more gung-ho about the claim.
6. Labour's focus groups found that members of the public, if aware of Balls at all, tended to think of him as the former Education Secretary (or, more formally, as the Secretary of State for Children, Schools and Families, which he was between 2007 and 2010), but the media associated him with Gordon Brown and with economic policy.

7. Patrick Wintour, 'The Undoing of Ed Miliband – and How Labour Lost the Election', *The Guardian*, 3 June 2015.
8. For example, Balls did not think that the proposed HS2 railway link was good value for money, whereas Miliband and many Labour leaders in northern cities were in favour of it. He also favoured the expansion of Heathrow, which Miliband opposed.
9. Janan Ganesh, 'Tories Ignore Signs in Rush for the Exit', *Financial Times*, 1 April 2013.
10. Labour's marginal polling was carried out in 68 Conservative-held and 10 Lib Dem-held seats.
11. *Sunday Times*, 25 March 2012.
12. Peter Kellner, 'Majority Rules', *Progress*, May 2013, pp. 14–21.
13. Peter Kellner, 'A Class Apart?', *Progress*, November 2012, pp. 12–13.
14. Peter Kellner, 'Stuck in the Middle', *Progress*, November 2013, pp. 16–17.
15. A reader of this chapter in draft recalled a passage about a previous Labour leader, Michael Foot, in Peter Jenkins' *Mrs Thatcher's Revolution and the End of the Socialist Era* (Cape, 1987): 'through the self-indulgence of pure principle, patrician sentimentality and an old man's vanity the working people of Britain, for the first time since 1945, lacked a proper champion' (p. 121). He added 'substitute "young" for "old" and we have it'.
16. He linked this with welfare reform to discourage shirkers, but at the last moment dropped suggestions for promoting greater equality of opportunity (for example, ensuring wider access to top universities).
17. For sympathetic assessments, see Rafael Behr, 'Ed Miliband's Leadership Style Could Put Him in No 10', *The Guardian*, 23 July 2014; and Steve Richards, 'Ed Miliband is at His Best When He Defies Convention', *The Independent*, 30 December 2013.
18. Peter Mandelson, who chaired the event, told the diners: 'it's even worse than you think – he's not saying what he says because he does not understand you – it's because he really means it'.
19. *The Times* journalist Philip Collins recalls first meeting Miliband. After a discussion of political theory – on which Collins had written a doctorate – Miliband discovered that Collins worked in the City; 'he said "but ... how ... what". He then proceeded to question me with fascination and revulsion, as if I had just said I was a rat catcher'.
20. 'Running out of Road', *The Economist*, 24 May 2014.
21. For one of the few prescient articles at the time, see James Forsyth, 'Labour's Internal Reforms Will Have Consequences', blogs.new.spectator.co.uk, 6 February 2014.
22. See, for example, Rafael Behr, 'Labour Has Given Up Expecting to Be Impressed by Miliband', *The Guardian*, 15 October 2014; Rachel Sylvester, 'Labour Has No Clue How to Solve its Ed Problem', *The Times*, 11 November 2014; and the formerly supportive Jenni Russell, 'Aloof Miliband Alienating His Own Supporters', *The Times*, 27 March 2014.
23. Perhaps the saddest part of the whole story is that he did not even eat all of the sandwich.
24. 'The Most Important Political Issue of the Moment? Ed Miliband's Kitchens', *The Guardian*, 13 March 2015.
25. 'Should Miliband Go?', yougov.co.uk, 10 November 2014.

26. The single most important – and, on the Conservatives' post-election analysis, critical – voter type in battleground seats was the group who leaned strongly to Labour, but thought Miliband so unfit for office that they were considering voting Tory. Conservative post-election analysis revealed that across its key seats, more than 80% of people in this group did indeed vote Conservative in the end.
27. After the election, an internal Labour analysis of debates in the Commons found that Conservative speakers were much more on message than Labour MPs, using the phrase 'our long term economic plan' in debates at least twice as often as Labour MPs talked about the 'cost of living crisis'.
28. When reminded later of his claim, he would reply simply: 'Did you expect the SNP to surge?' One individual who can claim that he did – one of very few – was the former Labour Home Secretary, Charles Clarke. In March 2014, he privately predicted a post-referendum SNP advance to a member of the Better Together leadership, and by the summer of 2014, it was what one of its members called 'a mainstream view within the Better Together campaign'. Yet even Clarke, prescient as he was, was not anticipating anything on the scale that eventually transpired.
29. There is a whole book to be written on the semiotics of the term 'Westminster' in Scottish politics (especially 'the broken Westminster system'). It is variously a way of talking about Britain without having to use the word itself, a way of linking expenses and corruption, a code for distance and remoteness, and, for some, a way of being rude about the English without having to be overt.
30. See James Mitchell, 'Sea Change in Scotland' in Andrew Geddes and Jon Tonge (eds), *Britain Votes 2015*. Oxford University Press, 2015. See also A. Convery, '2011 Scottish Conservative Party Leadership Election: Dilemmas for Statewide Parties in Regional Contexts', *Parliamentary Affairs*, 67(2) (2014), 306–27.
31. A YouGov poll on the eve of conference found that only 20% of voters thought 'he has made clear what he stands for'.
32. An Ipsos MORI poll of parliamentary candidates in 2015 found not a single Labour one who selected 'the deficit/spending' as one of the most important issues facing Britain. True, the sample size was small and many did select 'the economy', but it was still indicative of the pressures facing Miliband.
33. Labour voters were, by some way, the most ill-informed about the state of the nation's finances. In 2013, YouGov found that over 60% of Conservative and Lib Dem voters (and over 50% of UKIP voters) knew that the government spent more each year than it raised; the figure for Labour voters was just 42%, with 26% thinking that the government raised more each year than it spent.

4
Zugzwang: The Liberal Democrats and Others

The share of the popular vote garnered by the two major parties in a post-war British general election first fell below 80% in 1970. It then dropped below 70% in 2005 and reached a record low of 65% in 2010.[1] Throughout the 2010 Parliament, with the rise of UKIP, the Greens and the SNP, there was talk about how the party system was continuing to fragment, although there was no evidence that the two-party share was in further decline. What was happening, and dramatically so, was that the composition of the 'others' – as they used to be referred to rather dismissively – was changing. These parties matter in their own right, as the democratic choices of millions of voters, but in a close election there was also much discussion of how they would affect the outcome of the election, either by taking votes from other parties or as a result of their involvement in post-election deals. The rise of the SNP is considered separately in Chapter 5. Below we discuss the significant other parties, both those on the rise as well as those for whom 2010–15 turned out to be electoral hard times.

The Liberal Democrats

Everyone connected with the Liberal Democrats accepted that there would be an electoral cost to entering into a coalition with the Conservatives. Chris Huhne remarked privately that he expected the party's opinion poll ratings to fall into single figures. This was typically seen as a short-term cost. In the medium to long term, though, most of those around the party leadership believed support would pick back up again once the party was seen to have taken tough decisions in

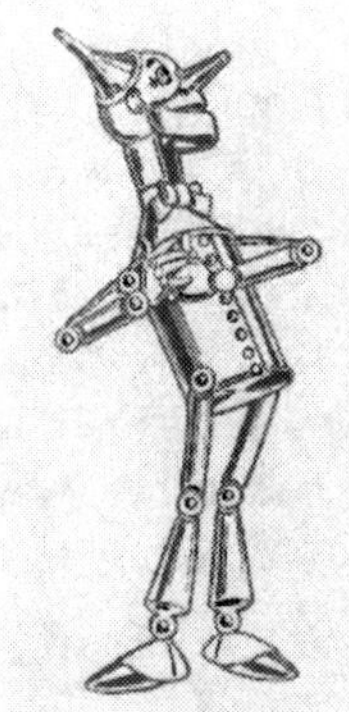

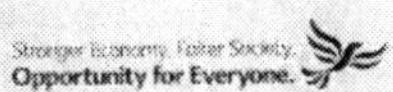

government and had received the credit for what it had delivered. It might never reach the levels of popularity seen during the 2010 election – when the party had been in first place in some opinion polls – but it would rise sufficiently to prevent the Lib Dems suffering too much at the 2015 election. The party also had well-entrenched MPs whose local popularity would help protect them from any downturn in the polls.[2] In the long term, going into government would change the way the Lib Dems were seen: from being a party of protest and opposition, it would become a party of government and would be taken seriously thereafter. By making a success of the Coalition, the party would also change the way in which the public viewed hung parliaments; instead of the fear that they would lead to unstable government, the Lib Dems could show how well coalitions could work. Plus, of course, the referendum on the Alternative Vote (AV) – promised as part of the Coalition Agreement – would deliver a change to the electoral system that would ensure there would always be a larger number of Lib Dem MPs thereafter. The party planned for the 2010 Parliament to be transformational – which indeed it was, if not quite in the way intended.

Almost every aspect of this strategy failed. There was no upturn in support; after its initial slump, Lib Dem support trended moderately downwards for the entire Parliament. The public did not take to coalition government, nor did they learn to respect the party for the tough decisions it took in government. Individual policy decisions which the Lib Dems went along with – most obviously the rise in university tuition fees – damaged their standing with the public, whilst they appeared to get next to no credit for the policies which they blocked or the influence which they exerted within government.[3] As detailed in Chapter 1, the AV referendum failed spectacularly. The party would end the Parliament praying that incumbency would be enough to protect their MPs, only to find that these prayers were not answered.

It was easy to criticise the choice the party made in 2010, but it was often not realised how constrained the Lib Dems were. There is a term used in chess, *zugzwang*, for when a player has to move, but where any move will make them worse off. In 2010, the Lib Dems were in *zugzwang*. There were no good moves. It would have been possible, just, to have put together a deal with Labour instead, but that was not without significant problems of its own, and almost certainly not sustainable for a full term. Just as going with the Conservatives cost the party its left-of-centre support, so going with Labour would have cost it right-of-centre support, whilst staying out of office altogether was felt to be an abdication of responsibility as well as equally damaging. The party could perhaps have tackled the coalition negotiations differently, demanding different ministerial posts or digging its heels in on certain policies, but all of these options would have come with their own costs.[4] The same applied to some of the policies enacted during the Parliament. The Lib Dems would frequently act to block or reform policies proposed by the Conservatives, but this was part of ongoing negotiations, in which the Conservatives would demand things in return. As one of Clegg's team said, in frustration, at one point about critics from within the party: 'They think you can just say no all the time.' But, still, even in *zugzwang*, the skill consists in finding the least damaging move that can be made. The longer the Parliament went on and as no upturn in the polls took place, the less obvious it became that the party had chosen correctly in 2010. But however much it failed – and five years on, it was difficult to argue that it had been a success – this was the strategy which explained what the Lib Dems did for their time in government.

The shift from opposition to government came as a shock to many within the Lib Dems. The party struggled to adapt to the change in public attitudes: Lib Dems were used to being ignored, or ridiculed, but many found outright hostility difficult. The first year was exceptionally hard. 'I wouldn't wish it on my worst enemy', said one Lib Dem Cabinet member. Nick Clegg himself had a fairly thick skin, but still found the personal abuse difficult to take. He was spat at (as was his child minder) and had faeces pushed through his letterbox.[5] In late 2010, the Deputy Prime Minister spotted some graffiti in his Sheffield constituency, which read: 'Kill Clegg.' His Special Advisor argued that it was at least better than 'Who's Clegg?' Clegg was not convinced. The party lost Short Money – the state funding given to opposition parties – and many of the staff from its Cowley Street headquarters moved into government as special advisors to ministers, leaving a hollowed-out party organisation behind. One Special Advisor recalls being asked by Conservative colleagues if he could get the Lib Dem policy team to research something, to which he replied that the Lib Dem policy team was him 'and Google'.

The reality of government, with its hard edges and difficult choices, was also a shock. 'We didn't have a clue what government was like', admitted one of Clegg's team. 'Every day brings bad news', said another in late 2010, 'with some messy compromise.' The party's staff was used to working with a small close-knit team of people; the shift to having to work with what one of Clegg's advisors called 'the machine' was 'indescribable'. The media was another headache. Previously, the problem had been attracting attention.[6] Going into government solved that problem, only to create another: deflecting negative press attention. 'We'd had a taste of it during the election, with all that Nick Clegg is a Nazi stuff', said one of Clegg's media team. 'But it's now like that every day ... You think you'll go into government and make a difference. But I spent all yesterday [in 2011] denying that he'd dyed his hair.' He estimated that there were just two journalists in the entire lobby who he trusted 'not to fuck us'. It was 'immensely frustrating'. After the 2015 election, *The Guardian* carried an editorial in which it bemoaned the departure of the Lib Dems from government and praised their contribution to the Coalition.[7] You have to search hard for many similar editorials published during the Coalition.

In turn, Whitehall had to get used to the Lib Dems being part of the government and to what was – in modern terms – a new way of working. A constant complaint of the Lib Dems was that they suffered from being the second, smaller party in a system that was not used to coalition, and received diminished visibility as a result. As one of Clegg's team put it: 'If people don't see what you've delivered in government, you've got no chance.' Clegg later argued that his decision to sit next to David Cameron during Prime Minister's Questions was the worst he took in office: 'Sitting mute next to David Cameron at Prime Minister's Questions every week was a sort of terrible encapsulation of what our critics said about us, that we were somehow just sort of passengers in the Government when in fact we were active architects rather than observers of the Government.'[8] Olly Grender, who worked as Deputy Chair of the party's election campaign, put it more bluntly: 'The only time most people saw Nick was every week, sat next to David Cameron at PMQs, sitting there silently, whilst Cameron talked bollocks.' Those around Clegg felt that the party made a mistake initially in agreeing to Whitehall's under-resourcing the Deputy Prime Minister's Office, preventing him from better fighting the Lib Dem corner. It was a deliberate decision of Gus O'Donnell and Jeremy Heywood to stop another Blair and Brown split, and was accepted by the Lib Dems as part of a desire to be one government rather than establishing separate centres of power, but they soon came to see this as naïve.

As noted in Chapter 1, a key part of the party's strategy was to 'own' the entire coalition, good and bad. Richard Reeves, who was Clegg's Director of Strategy between June 2010 and 2012, produced a graph, which he would scribble for anyone who wanted to see it, in which there was a trade-off over time between stability and independence. At the start of the Parliament, the party had to demonstrate that coalition worked and could produce stable government, even at the cost of the Lib Dems' own identity; as time went on, the party could increasingly demonstrate independence, even if it meant the government looked less stable. At times, during the early phase, the Lib Dems even gave the impression that the Coalition's policies were better than their own. In his 2010 conference speech, Clegg went so far as to say that the Coalition was 'more than the sum of our parts'.[9] One of the criticisms often made of the Clegg approach was that this cooperative attitude did not allow for enough differentiation between the parties of government. But the reality is that Clegg and those around him were aiming to differentiate the parties for much of the Parliament after the first year.[10] One week after the local election results of 2011 – which had been disastrous for the party – Clegg gave a speech at the National Liberal Club outlining the new approach. It was to be more 'muscular': 'Does this mean the end of the Coalition? No. Does it mean the Coalition is going to change? Yes.' 'It's not as if we didn't see the perils of being strapped to the Conservatives', said one of the Lib Dem leadership. But as time went on, it became clear that being muscular was not making much of a difference. There was also a limit as to how far this approach could be taken. Some blithely called for a more 'transactional' approach to the Coalition, with the Lib Dems making clearer which bits of policy they disagreed with. Yet the nature of the Coalition would still have required them to vote for such policy once it had been agreed; the idea that ranks of Lib Dem MPs voting for legislation they had publicly disowned was likely to rebuild support for the party seems unlikely.

There would, every now and again, be stories about how the rows between the two governing parties were stage-managed so that the Lib

Dems could be seen to be standing up to the Conservatives. There was something in this ('We understand each other's needs', as one of Clegg's team put it), but these stories often exaggerated the choreography involved. 'I read all these articles explaining why X has said something', said one of Clegg's press team, 'and I think if only if was that organised.' In particular, anything involving Vince Cable was much more likely to be the result of Cable choosing to go off-piste than part of any media strategy. There was no love for Cable amongst the Lib Dem's Downing Street team, a view that was reciprocated.

The party did not emerge well from any encounters with the voters. In the first set of local elections after the formation of the Coalition, the Lib Dems lost 40 per cent of the council seats they were defending; in terms of local authority strength, this took the party back to its 1993 level, and the overall projected national vote was just 15 per cent, worse than any result since the last local elections the Liberal Party had contested before the formation of the SDP (13 per cent in 1980). Losses were particularly heavy in the northern cities which the party had taken from Labour over the preceding ten years. In northern England, which was more dependent on the public sector than the south, the Coalition's programme of cuts was deeply unpopular, and in any case there were few Conservative councillors left to bear the brunt of the Labour assault.[11] It was not as if this was a one-off either. With one exception, the Lib Dems performed disastrously in every set of elections they contested after 2010.[12]

The exception was the Eastleigh by-election – held by the Lib Dems in 2013 after Chris Huhne's resignation – which appeared to give the party some hope. Internally, however, the leadership were aware of just how poor their performance had been. Eastleigh was the Lib Dems' fifth-best seat in terms of voter contact, and the in-house tracking poll that the party ran during the campaign showed the Conservatives and UKIP gaining on them throughout. Eastleigh, often presented as demonstrating the party's resilience, in fact demonstrated its weakness. We 'flattered to deceive', said one senior Lib Dem. Clegg realised just how bad things were: 'This could kill us', he said shortly afterwards to a colleague.

Of all the policy decisions taken during the five years of the Coalition, tuition fees is probably the most emblematic of the Lib Dem time in government. On one level, it is a fairly straightforward story of a party promising something in opposition, performing a U-turn in government and then being punished for it by voters. But the full story of tuition fees is more complicated than this.

The Lib Dems had gone into the 2010 election pledging to remove tuition fees altogether. This was not a decision on which they were united. Clegg and Cable had long fought to remove this policy, believing it unsustainable ('a policy made for perpetual opposition' is how one senior Lib Dem described it), but despite an extensive fight, the pair eventually lost in the Party's Federal Policy Committee.[13] Although the policy was thought to have played well in some university seats, it was not one of the Lib Dems' main policy pledges at the election. However, matters were compounded during the campaign by Lib Dem MPs, including Clegg, signing the pledge promoted by the National Union of Students (NUS) not to raise fees – and being photographed doing so. Lib Dem MPs were often criticised for their tactical naïvety in giving this hostage to fortune, but they were advised to do so by the party's campaigns team and, given that the policy on which they were fighting the election was to abolish fees, it would have been difficult to refuse to commit to being against any rise.[14]

In recognition of the difficulties that the issue might cause, the Coalition Agreement explicitly allowed for the Lib Dems to abstain if they was not happy with the decision of the Browne report into student finance – one of just a handful of policies for which abstention was agreed. The problem was that when Browne reported, recommending removing the upper limit for undergraduate fees, the parliamentary party found itself split. In a break with Browne, which had recommended no upper limit, the government's proposal was for a maximum fee of £9,000 per year, but some Lib Dem MPs refused to abstain and insisted on voting against the measure regardless. The parliamentary arithmetic was fairly simple. Had the party abstained *en masse*, the measure passed. But if only some abstained and enough voted against, there was a real chance that the vote might be lost. Whilst this would have pleased opponents of the policy, the Lib Dem leadership

felt that a defeat of a high-profile government policy so early in the Parliament would be too destabilising to the Coalition.

Matters were not helped by the Department responsible for the policy (Business, Innovation and Skills) being headed by Vince Cable – and by Cable's insistence that he would not abstain, but would vote for the policy. Cable was convinced that the system he was introducing was better than the one it was replacing.[15] 'He was adamant', said one of those involved, 'as Secretary of State that he could not abstain on a policy that was his.' It is not true – as sometimes claimed – that the party did not realise the potential fall-out from the issue. Indeed, Clegg attempted but failed to get the issue delayed by at least a year.[16] However, as well as Cable, many of those around Clegg were becoming even less convinced by their original policy position and more convinced by the new policy – what one of Clegg's advisors called ending 'the middle class gravy train, the single biggest transfer from the poor to the rich, that this was the single most progressive element of the Comprehensive Spending Review'. The party's previous stance made it impossible to argue this case with any conviction (as it would have promoted the counter-argument 'well, if it was so terrible, why did you support it before?'). In the teeth of strong opposition from backbenchers and during a protracted meeting of the parliamentary party, Cable and Clegg announced that they were prepared to abstain to preserve party unity – as the Coalition Agreement permitted – as long as the rest of the parliamentary party followed suit. But those who were opposed would not be dissuaded from voting against and, fearing defeat in the Commons, the Lib Dem ministers decided to vote for the rise in the cap. The result was a three-way split: 28 Lib Dem MPs, mostly ministers, voting for; 21, including party president Tim Farron and former leaders Charles Kennedy and Menzies Campbell, voting against; and eight, including deputy leader Simon Hughes, abstaining or absent.

This policy is often said to be responsible for the collapse in support experienced by the Lib Dems. But the party's most serious drop in the polls occurred before the Browne report was published in October, and certainly before the key vote in December 2010. Indeed, immediately prior to the vote, one poll already put the Lib Dems on just 8%. It was going into coalition with the Conservatives that destroyed the Lib Dems' poll rating, not any particular policy. Thereafter, the policy U-turn became associated with the party, and it may perhaps be that tuition fees prevented the Lib Dems winning new support, but it was not what led voters to leave it initially. There were those within the leadership who in any case believed that tuition fees were merely the excuse people gave for disliking the party, and if it had not been that issue, it would have been something else instead. But others, including Clegg, thought that there was something specific about the issue of student fees – something visceral, about education, about the idea of young people being burdened with debt – that made the issue particularly difficult. It did not help that the party had always traditionally polled well with university graduates and students, or had some areas of strength in university seats, or indeed had made a party election broadcast in 2010 criticising parties that did not keep their promises.

In September 2012, Clegg apologised for the debacle – in a much-ridiculed party political broadcast – yet the apology was not for the policy, but for making the initial pledge:

> It was a pledge made with the best of intentions – but we should not have made a promise we were not absolutely sure we could deliver. I shouldn't have committed to a policy that was so expensive when there was no money around. Not least when the most likely way we would end up in government was in coalition with Labour or the Conservatives who were both committed to put fees up.[17]

Indeed, as the Parliament went on and the doomsayers' predictions of a collapse in student numbers failed to materialise, it was striking how Lib Dems became more positive about the policy *qua* policy, if increasingly depressed by the politics of it. One felt that this was exactly the problem: 'We thought about it in policy terms. People responded with their hearts.'

The party departed its Cowley Street HQ in 2011 and moved into a more modern, open-plan office in Great George Street, just off Parliament Square. A new Chief Executive, Tim Gordon, was appointed the same year. In 2012 Clegg appointed Ryan Coetzee, a South African with a background in the country's Democratic Alliance, as his Director of Strategy, replacing Richard Reeves. Coetzee later moved to the Lib Dem HQ in 2014 as General Election Director of Strategy. 'Ryan is keen on stripping the message back to basics', said one of Clegg's team. 'He's not interested in strategy in a Richard-Reeves-here's-an-interesting-pamphlet-from-a-think-tank-way, he's into polls and focus groups. It's all about votes.' Coetzee conducted a significant polling exercise – or at least a significant one for a cash-strapped party – involving around 12,000 respondents to try to uncover what he termed the party's 'market', those people who were instinctively attracted to what the

'Doomed but chipper'

Steve Bell, *The Guardian*, 7 January 2014

party had to offer, now that it could no longer rely simply on being a party for those who did not like the other parties.[18] It identified around a fifth of the public who might support a liberal party which prioritised economic credibility and social justice. This work informed the party's 'Stronger society, fairer economy' strapline which it was to use on its 2015 manifesto. But the research also showed that the party's brand was 'weak and fuzzy'. Even in their own market, amongst their own would-be supporters, the Lib Dems did not own many issues. There was not a single policy area even amongst their own potential supporters in which the Lib Dems had the support of at least 40%, and they were frequently beaten by other parties. As one Lib Dem strategist noted: 'When ordinary people look at us, it's like a short-sighted person watching TV. They can see light, and movement, but not really what's going on.' Even amongst their own 'market', respondents preferred the Conservatives on the economy, Labour on the NHS, or UKIP on immigration.

Coetzee also attempted to instil some message discipline on Clegg and his colleagues. His mantra was 'On message, in volume, over time', trying to use the multiple platforms the party had to promote simple messages about what it had achieved in government. The party had to focus on a handful of achievements and talk about them relentlessly. Clegg himself was not inherently good at message discipline. He was, according to one of those close to him, 'too intellectually curious' ('It's fine to be an intellectually curious politician ... but you have to do that in your spare time'). He still had a worrying tendency to try to engage with the question asked in interviews rather than stick to his top line and, when tired, could become self-righteous and tetchy. He also often wanted to use humour in speeches and interviews, much to the dismay of his advisors. 'We have to stop him', said one of his press team. 'A Nick Clegg joke goes: my dog has no nose and smells terrible.'

In January 2013, Clegg began a weekly radio phone-in show on LBC Radio ('Call Clegg'). It was a first for a frontline government politician, and a gamble, but one which the party felt it could afford to take, given its poll ratings.[19] Occasionally Clegg would face hostility from callers, but he mostly handled it well, enjoyed the format, and the party felt it was a good way to try to articulate its key messages. Its success spawned a media strategy that was to run until the election in which the party attempted to make Clegg look as accessible, and 'normal', as possible.[20] The same approach informed the (less successful) decision to debate the subject of Europe with Nigel Farage in early 2014 ahead of the European Parliament elections. In two debates, the first on LBC, the second televised on BBC ('The European Union: In or Out'), the Deputy Prime Minister took on UKIP's leader and, according to the post-debate polls, was comprehensively bested both times. 'Nick was making arguments. Nigel was emoting', said one of the Lib Dem team who had helped prepare Clegg.

The party's former leader, Lord (Paddy) Ashdown was appointed to chair the party's general election campaign in late 2012. Those who worked with him praised his work rate, energy, and ability to encourage and motivate. By the middle of the Parliament, the party realised it was essentially fighting a series of rearguard actions in seats it already held.

One of the greatest what-ifs about the party during this period was what if it changed its leader? Clegg came close to resigning after the disaster of the European Parliament elections in 2014, with the party reduced to just one MEP. Throughout the Parliament, there were also assorted plots to force him out, of which the most significant came to a head in late May 2014 when a series of constituency polls were published claiming to show the party would do better under Vince

Cable's leadership. Lord (Matthew) Oakeshott was soon outed as the individual who had organised and funded the polls. Oakeshott had long been a critic of Clegg's leadership, as well as acting as an unofficial spokesperson for Vince Cable. Cable claimed to know nothing about the polls carried out in any other seats (although he did admit to knowing about polling undertaken in his own Twickenham constituency). It later became clear he had known all along, and the plan had been for the polls to trigger pressure on Clegg to leave; John Pugh, the Lib Dem MP for Southport, had been collecting signatures from fellow MPs, designed to force Clegg out, and two days after the elections, Pugh and Adrian Sanders, the MP for Torbay, had publicly called for Clegg to step aside, only for other MPs to get cold feet. The plot came to nothing when Cable's bluff was called whilst he was on a trip to China and he was forced to repudiate the polling.[21] Oakeshott subsequently resigned from the party, saying that it was 'heading for disaster if it keeps Nick Clegg'. There were plenty of other Lib Dems who feared he was right, but who doubted that changing the leader would make much of a difference.

UKIP

During the 2010 election campaign, the UKIP leader, Lord Pearson, admitted that he had not read his party's manifesto, while on polling day, the former party leader, Nigel Farage, almost got himself killed in a plane crash. The next five years were to see UKIP play a much more significant role.

Pearson stood down in August 2010, admitting that he was 'not much good at party politics' and that the party 'deserved a better politician to lead it'. Farage was comfortably elected leader for a second time. Despite the party's name, Farage had always been keen for UKIP not to be seen as a one-issue party, and to try to link the issue of EU membership with policies which were more salient with the public, most obviously immigration.[22] And for all that UKIP's performance in 2010 had seemed a disappointment – especially after the 2009 European elections, where the party had come second, pushing Labour into third place – it polled 3.1%, a record share of the vote for a minor party.[23] By entering into coalition with the Conservatives, the Lib Dems had negated their status as the obvious destination for voters unhappy with the establishment and 'the same old parties', and the British National Party – which had also achieved a record performance in 2010, but which competed for some of the same voters as UKIP – fell in on itself shortly after the election and soon ceased to function as a substantive political force (see below, p. 120).[24] The conditions for a UKIP advance were propitious. As noted in Chapter 1, by 2013, UKIP had moved ahead of the Lib Dems in the polls and performed well above most commentators' expectations in the 2013 local elections, before achieving first place in the European Parliament elections in 2014.

Once it became clear that UKIP's support was rising, one of the first major polling exercises into the party was undertaken by Lord Ashcroft; it noted that whilst UKIP voters and sympathisers might have particular policy concerns, 'these are often part of a greater dissatisfaction with the way they see things going in Britain':

> Schools, they say, can't hold nativity plays or harvest festivals anymore; you can't fly a flag of St George anymore; you can't call Christmas Christmas anymore; you won't be promoted in the police force unless you're from a minority; you can't wear an England shirt on the bus; you won't get social housing unless you're an immigrant; you can't speak up about these things because you'll be called a racist; you can't even smack your children.[25]

In the second of the EU debates with Nick Clegg in 2014, the UKIP leader urged voters to 'take back our own country' and to 'join the people's army' in order to 'topple the establishment who've led us to this mess'. Farage's anti-establishment rhetoric (party insiders would also refer to themselves as an 'insurgency') was one of the many paradoxes of UKIP. He would rail against the political class, yet he had been an MEP since 1999. He was in favour of curbing immigration and prioritising jobs for British workers, but had a German wife who worked as his assistant. He would present himself as speaking up for the common man or woman, yet he had been educated at Dulwich College, before a career in the City.[26] Perhaps the biggest irony, however, was the change that UKIP wrought to the British party system. Most European countries have just such a radical right, anti-immigration party. 'One of the greatest ironies of the rise of UKIP', wrote Matthew Goodwin, 'is that the success of a party founded to take Britain out of Europe has ended up making the British party system look much more European.'[27]

As the journalist Matthew D'Ancona noted in an article in the *Evening Standard* in 2012: 'Consult the polls of its members and spend a little time reading its literature and you quickly grasp that what it [UKIP] objects to is modernity: the pluralist, globalised, fast-changing world in which we live.'[28] This helps explain why the other parties struggled to attack it, or why UKIP's multiple problems over its policy platform

or over its personnel rarely harmed it in the polls. When, in January 2014, Farage got into difficulties answering question about UKIP policy on an LBC phone-in programme, he simply disowned the entire 2010 manifesto: 'I didn't read it', he said (despite having signed its foreword). 'It was drivel. It was 486 pages of drivel ... It was a nonsense. We have put that behind us and moved on to a professional footing.' New policy was going to be formulated, he claimed, and he could not be held to account for previous policy. No other mainstream party would have got away with such a manoeuvre. UKIP policy was still frequently open to challenge and, when challenged, often immediately changed. In September 2014, the party's economy spokesman Patrick O'Flynn put forward a luxury goods tax, a 25 per cent rate of VAT that would have hit items like designer handbags, shoes and sports cars, and which soon became known as the 'wag tax'; Farage vetoed the policy just days later. Between the party's pre-election conference in 2014 and the beginning of the election campaign six months later, it ran into problems on economic policy, its approach to the NHS, sex education, immigration and even the question of animal slaughter. The website Conservative-Home ran a series of blogposts entitled 'Pinning Down Farage'. Yet such inconsistencies – which would have caused headaches for more established parties – were not a particular problem for UKIP. The fact that it was not a slick and disciplined operation, and therefore not like the established Westminster parties, was what made it attractive to some voters, and would-be UKIP voters were not looking for policy coherence. One study which looked at the motivations of voters found that UKIP voters were, of all the parties, the most likely to see their vote as sending a message rather than requiring a coherent policy programme.[29]

The same applied to many of the more curious utterances of UKIP's members or candidates. There was the local councillor who saw floods as divine retribution for legislation on gay marriage, or the MEP who objected to sending foreign money to 'Bongo Bongo Land' and was forced to resign the whip after calling female party members 'sluts', or the councillor who disliked black people ('something about their faces'), or the prospective candidate who called gay people 'disgusting old poofters'. In an interview with *The Times* at the beginning of 2014, Farage said that he would no longer tolerate 'Walter Mittys seeking a role in politics' and admitted that UKIP had had a 'struggle with talent in the early days'. Yet the party appeared to retain its fair share of Walter Mittys and was plagued by a number of candidates with foibles ripe for headlines right up and into the general election campaign (see below, pp. 154, 193). But part of the very attraction of UKIP was that it would say the things that people claimed needed to be said, but which they thought mainstream politicians were too scared to utter.[30] As a Conservative briefing note for the Prime Minister noted: 'UKIP considerers see themselves as the last defenders of old-fashioned common sense values.'

This was particularly true of UKIP's leader. One piece of polling, noted by the journalist Stephen Bush, identified what he called the Mr Bean/ Sean Bean effect. Asked which actor should play Nigel Farage in a film, the top choice of those who did not support UKIP was Rowan Atkinson, who played the hapless Mr Bean. The top response from supporters of UKIP was the much more heroic Sean Bean.[31] UKIPers saw both the world, and their party, differently from everyone else.

For all that UKIP's appeal was not primarily about policy, there was one policy area which the party deliberately set out to prioritise: immigration. The issue had obvious appeals for UKIP. Unlike the issue of Europe, it was not niche, but was one of the main issues – and sometimes *the* main issue – prioritised by the public; it was one where both major parties had records they found difficult to defend; and it was one which could easily, and logically, be linked to the issue of party's raison d'etre. Membership of a European Union in which free movement was an underpinning principle meant that control over borders would only be regained in the event that Britain voted to leave. This allowed the party to present itself not as racist or against immigration per se, but against uncontrolled or unlimited immigration. By the time of the 2015 election, the party successfully 'owned' the policy. People overwhelming thought UKIP took immigration seriously and would try to reduce immigration, and – less overwhelmingly, but still significantly more than any other party – that they would be successful in doing so.[32]

'Old Allure'

Adams, Daily Telegraph, 6 April 2015 (© Adams/*The Telegraph*)

As we have shown (see p. 64), having lost their previous ownership of the subject, the Conservatives eventually gave up trying to engage on the topic and attempted instead just not to talk about it.

One of the biggest debates about UKIP was over their source of voters – and the damage they might inflict on the other parties. It was a right-of-centre party and because many of its leading figures – including both Pearson and Farage – were former Conservatives, and of a similar social background to many Conservatives, the initial view was that it predominantly drew support from the Conservatives. A rising UKIP vote would therefore be a threat predominantly to Conservative MPs at the general election. But examination of the party's electoral support produced a more nuanced finding: UKIP supporters were in fact predominantly blue-collar, poorly educated, old, white and male. They were socially not similar to mainstream Conservative voters. UKIP was attracting a group that Ford and Goodwin, who wrote the first major study of the party, called the 'left behind', those who were not benefiting from globalisation and the economic and social transformation of Britain:

> UKIP are not a second home for disgruntled Tories in the shires; they are a first home for angry and disaffected working-class Britons of all political backgrounds, who have lost faith in a political system that ceased to represent them long ago.[33]

The party did initially seem to draw its support disproportionately from the Conservatives rather than Labour, although much depended on the part of the country being discussed, and examining the past votes of UKIP supporters *before* 2010 often revealed an even more complicated picture.[34] A large part of UKIP's electoral strategy was to appeal explicitly to Labour voters (or former Labour voters) as well as Conservatives. Farage would frequently castigate the Labour Party for having forgotten its roots, suggesting that the Labour's elite had 'taken a conscious decision to stop speaking for working-class people. It is that they are so out of touch that they just do not know how to speak for working-class people anymore'.[35] It was no coincidence that this anti-Labour rhetoric was ramped up after the Conservative leadership acquiesced over the issue of an in/out EU referendum. Having achieved success with one party that might form the government, it became important for UKIP to try to achieve the same result with the other one – and, as we have shown on p. 87, they almost succeeded. But equally, in the medium term, the party had come to realise that it had a significant electoral opportunity in Labour-held seats in the Midlands, northern England and Wales. UKIP's so-called 2020 Strategy was to establish a beachhead of victories (literally so, given the types of seats they were realistically hoping to win) in 2015, but also to come second in sufficient seats, especially Labour seats, to use as a launchpad for an election in 2020. The attraction of Labour seats was partly their socio-economic composition, but also that these were often seats in which the Lib Dems had been the second-place party, only for their support to have fallen away, creating a vacuum for UKIP to fill.

Douglas Carswell's decision to resign his seat and fight a by-election immediately after joining UKIP was not universally welcomed within the party. Whilst Carswell might win easily – as he did – it set a precedent which some other would-be defectors were less keen to follow. The precedent having been established, Reckless' relatively narrow victory in Rochester and Strood was then not encouraging to those who might want to swap parties. At least a dozen Conservative MPs were mentioned as possible defectors to UKIP (see also p. 54) and UKIP constantly played up the possibility of others following Carswell and Reckless, but none did. Rumours persisted, encouraged by research suggesting that a number of Tory MPs might fare better at the forthcoming election under UKIP colours.[36]

Carswell's Euroscepticism made him a natural convert to UKIP, but it was about the only thing that did. There were many other Conservative MPs who would have felt much more naturally at home within the party. There were multiple policy areas as well as differences in temperament and outlook where UKIP's new MP and its leader looked at odds with one another, most obviously immigration.[37] Moreover, there was a faction (crudely if usefully) described as 'Red UKIP' within the party – focused on securing votes among traditional working-class voters in the north of England – which was also at odds with many of the policies Carswell would advocate. Had a less iconoclastic Conservative been the first to be lured across the floor, it might have been better, but beggars cannot be choosers.

Looking forward to 2014 and that year's European elections, UKIP's head of policy, Tim Aker, told the BBC that the party 'would completely change British politics'. Press reports during the autumn of 2014 had UKIP winning anywhere between 25 and 128 Westminster seats. Following victory in Rochester and Strood in November 2014, one of UKIP's major donors, Paul Sykes, urged the party to take on 'that Oxbridge lot' and called for a much more ambitious set of targets at the general election: 'We have the tiger by the tail here, we can start widening the list, we had 30 odd in mind, then 40, this blows the whole thing open, I don't have a number in mind, but 65, 70, or more now. What is a marginal for us now?'

Party insiders were noticeably more cautious, talking about a dozen targets, and even that figure was reduced as time went on. However, a successful 2020 strategy still required a decent result in 2015.

The Green Party

The Green Party of England and Wales that fought the 2015 election was, as James Dennison notes, 'in a completely different position from that of 2010' and was almost unrecognisable from that of ten or so years before. It had a single leader, and was a more professional 'and, much to the lament of some of its supporters, more orthodox political party'.[38]

The party had emerged from the 2010 election with its first MP when its leader, Caroline Lucas, won Brighton Pavilion. A year later, the Greens won control of Brighton and Hove City Council. Lucas, who was a confident and articulate media and Commons performer, used her position in Parliament to give the Greens much greater visibility than they had previously enjoyed.[39] In 2012, she stood down as leader to concentrate on her role at Westminster. In her place, the party elected the Australian-born former journalist Natalie Bennett. It is the only case thus far of any major party in Britain where one female leader has handed on the baton to another female leader. Despite formally renouncing the leadership, Lucas remained a significant force within the party. Her base in Brighton was described by one of the party's staff as 'a party within a party', and her position in the Commons gave her both increased visibility and greater resources. It did not help matters that she was, in many ways, a more impressive politician than her successor. Bennett was a much less assured media performer than Lucas – as would become painfully clear during the election campaign – and struggled to generate the same sort of coverage.[40] To be fair to Lucas, her decision to resign the leadership had been entirely strategic – predicated upon giving the Greens both a leader and an MP as a way of maximising the party's profile – but the talk of tensions between the two were not invented by the media.

The party had always been on the political left, but Bennett took it even further left, aiming to make it an explicitly anti-austerity party, quite clearly to the left of Labour.[41] In England, at least, it would be the only party standing on such a platform. The Greens were happily knocking around on 2–3 percentage points in the polls, with no

obvious indication that they were going to do anything else. In the local elections of 2013, they made a net gain of five seats; the following year, they made a gain of 18 – and then broadcasters announced that whilst Nigel Farage and UKIP would be part of the proposed leaders' debates, the Greens would be excluded. Protests against this decision provided the catalyst for an increase in Green support in the opinion polls – at least trebling, occasionally hitting double figures and pushing the Lib Dems down into fifth in some polls – as well as a surge in members. Collectively, this became known as the 'Green Surge'. The Prime Minister even supported the call to have the Greens included in the debates, hoping that their participation would hurt Labour. By January 2015, the party had more members than either UKIP or the Lib Dems, and although its poll ratings dropped somewhat as the election approached, membership continued to rise, reaching 60,000 in England and Wales by April.

All of this was extremely welcome for the party, but was not without problems. By 2015, the majority of Green Party members had been members of the party for less than a year. Not all of the older members were particularly welcoming ('It's like someone is interfering in their little social club', as one Green staffer put it). Whilst the rise in membership brought with it an increase in funds, which enabled the party to field the largest number of candidates in its history in 2015, those within the party felt this all had occurred too near to the election to be really useful. 'The surge happened just a bit too late for us', said one senior Green. For example, the party had long seen the potential of social media – which allowed it to by-pass the mainstream media – but it lacked the funds to appoint a full-time digital staff member until March 2015, just months before the election.

This all gave the Greens a stronger base going into the 2015 election than in any previous Westminster election. Publicly, they were targeting 12 seats, where they claimed they were aiming for first or second place. 'That was for public consumption', said one of their election team. 'No one really believed that.' In reality, they were targeting just three and were hoping to build support elsewhere.

Plaid Cymru

Plaid Cymru enjoyed nothing like the rise in popularity that the SNP were to experience. In 2011, while the SNP were storming to majority control in the Scottish Parliament (see Chapter 5), Plaid slipped from second into third place in the National Assembly, being overtaken by the Welsh Conservative Party. It was their worst result in a devolved election, whether measured in terms of Assembly Members elected or the share of the vote in either the constituency or regional ballot parts of the electoral system. It brought to an end their time in government in Wales – the so-called One Wales government, in coalition with Labour – after just four years.[42] 'This was', wrote one analysis of the results, 'a hugely disappointing election for the nationalist party, especially when juxtaposed against some remarkable successes for its sister party, the SNP, in Scotland.'[43]

The same month Ieuan Wyn Jones announced that he would stand down as leader, and in 2012 Leanne Wood, one of the party's Assembly Members since 2003, was elected as the new leader with 55% of the party vote. She was not expected to win – she did not herself expect victory when she stood – and had not been one of Plaid's ministers during the coalition. She was the first non-native Welsh speaker to lead the party, as well as the first woman. She was on the left of the party and a republican (one of her claims to fame is being the first person to be ordered out of the chamber of the Assembly, having referred to the Queen as 'Mrs Windsor'). The party's inquiry into the 2011 elections resulted in the reform of the party's constitution, more powers for the membership and a streamlining of the leadership structure. Plaid support fell again, by over three percentage points, in the 2014 European elections, although against expectations, they hung on, just, to their seat in the European Parliament.

One consequence of Plaid's spell in office, however, was a referendum, held in March 2011, to substantially strengthen the Assembly's law-making powers. On a low turnout of just over a third, the yes vote won.[44] It was a significant policy gain for the party. Within the party,

Wood would be judged on how she performed in 2016 in Wales rather than in 2015 at Westminster.

Respect

Respect was responsible for perhaps the biggest by-election shock of the Parliament. Caused by the resignation of the sitting Labour MP, Marsha Singh, due to ill health, the Bradford West by-election saw George Galloway pull off a stunning victory – a majority of 10,140 over his Labour opponent on a swing of 36.6%.[45] The result took Labour completely by surprise; until the ballot boxes were opened, they had believed they would hold the seat. Echoing events in the Middle East, Galloway hailed the victory as the 'Bradford Spring' and used his moment in the spotlight to castigate the mainstream political parties: 'If a backside could have three cheeks then they are the three cheeks of the same backside. They support the same things, the same wars, the same neoliberal policies to make the poor poorer for the crimes of the rich people. And they are not believable.'

Galloway's hyperbole soon got the better of him. In August 2012, during one of his regular podcasts, he chose to comment on the allegations of rape brought against WikiLeaks founder Julian Assange. His remarks, including the claim that 'not everybody needs to be asked prior to each insertion', were described by Respect's leader, Salma Yaqoob, as 'deeply disappointing and wrong'. Within weeks, she had resigned her post as leader and left Respect, blaming a breakdown in 'relations of trust and collaborative working'. Her replacement as party leader, Arshad Ali, lasted just over a month in the job before resigning after it was revealed that he had a spent conviction for electoral fraud.

Having stood 30 candidates at the 2005 general election and 11 in 2010, the number of Respect candidates more than halved again in 2015, with the party contesting just four seats: Galloway in Bradford West; Halifax; and two seats in Birmingham (Hall Green and Yardley).

The British National Party

Amidst all the talk of the rise of insurgent parties, it was useful to remember that parties – like stocks and shares – can go down as well as up, as the collapse of the British National Party (BNP) demonstrated. In 2010, the BNP had fielded a record 338 candidates, garnering over half a million votes. Five years later, they were to field just eight candidates who won 1,667 votes *between them*.

If the total figures looked impressive for the BNP in 2010, they could not hide a night of disappointments. The party's leader, Nick Griffin, failed to capitalise on a well-publicised bid to become the MP for Barking and Dagenham – he ended up in third place. In the BNP's other target seat, Stoke Central, the party's deputy leader Simon Darby could only manage fourth place. The same night saw the BNP lose its only councillor in Leeds; in Stoke, where it had said it was poised to take control of the council, it was pushed back to just five councillors, and right under Griffin's nose in Barking, the party lost all 12 of its councillors.

Amid already simmering tensions within the party's upper echelons (only a month before the party's publicity director, Mark Collett, had been arrested on suspicion of threatening to kill the party leader), these results triggered recriminations and infighting. Late 2010 saw the formation of a breakaway British Freedom Party (which only lasted two years) and a leadership election in July which Griffin narrowly won, defeating his fellow MEP Andrew Brons by 1,157 votes to 1,148. By October 2012, Brons had left the BNP, leaving Griffin as the party's one and only MEP. The following years saw the BNP's vote fall back heavily in the local elections of 2012 and 2013.[46] None of this dampened the discontent within the party.

Griffin was declared bankrupt at the beginning of 2014 and in May he lost his seat as an MEP at the European elections. The party's electoral representation was now down to just two local councillors. In July 2014 Griffin was replaced as leader by Andrew Walker, a former teacher.[47] Griffin was given the post of Honorary President, but by October he had been expelled for allegedly 'trying to cause disunity by deliberately fabricating a state of crisis'. Griffin accused the party of playing 'plastic gangster games'.

By 2015, it was reported that the BNP had an estimated membership of just around 500, little more than the number of candidates it had put up for election in 2010 – and Griffin, their most successful leader, was urging supporters to vote for UKIP. The BNP appeared to be a spent force in British politics.

Northern Ireland

Throughout the five years between the 2010 and the 2015 elections, the power-sharing coalition in Northern Ireland continued its fragile existence, never far away from revealing the tensions at its heart. Yet for all the underlying friction, there were continuing reminders of how far the province's politics had come. The period saw the Deputy First

Minister, Martin McGuinness, formerly a member of the IRA, shake the hand of the Queen, and he was among the first to pay tribute when one of the giants of Northern Irish politics, Dr Ian Paisley, died in 2014. 'I have lost a friend', McGuinness said. Having once allegedly plotted Paisley's assassination, this was a testimony to reconciliation and democratic politics.

Reconciliation only went so far, however. Northern Irish politics continued to be deeply communal; within each communal bloc, the Democratic Unionist Party (DUP) and Sinn Fein continued their dominance. In the Northern Ireland Assembly elections in May 2011, the DUP gained two seats and Sinn Fein one extra.[48] On a reduced turnout, the Ulster Unionist Party (UUP) even fell behind the Social Democratic and Labour Party (SDLP) in terms of first preference votes (albeit with 16 seats against the SDLP's 14); both the SDLP and the UUP were down two seats.[49] The following year, UKIP gained its first Member of the Legislative Assembly (MLA) when former UUP MLA David McNarry joined the party; in 2013 he was elected as UKIP's leader in Northern Ireland.

There were considerable personnel changes. Both Gerry Adams and McGuinness stood down from a Westminster Parliament in which they had never taken their seats, with Sinn Fein holding both by-elections comfortably. Reg Empey stood down as leader of the UUP in 2010; Tom Elliott was chosen as his successor on a promise to reconnect with the party's grassroots. However, Elliott's election was seen as a move to the right for the UUP and swiftly prompted three of the party's 2010 general election candidates to resign and join the Alliance Party. Elliot resigned in 2012 and, less than a year after becoming an MLA, the former TV presenter Mike Nesbitt became the latest leader of the party. The SDLP leader Margaret Ritchie had come under pressure following poor results at both the 2010 general election and the Assembly elections in 2011, and stepped down in 2011, being succeeded by Alasdair McDonnell.

Having fought the 2010 general election with an agreed list of candidates under the banner of Ulster Conservatives and Unionists New Force (UCUNF), the Conservative Party in Northern Ireland chose to part company with the UUP, and in June 2012 launched themselves as 'a fresh, pro-Union, centre-right party, which is proudly and distinctively Northern Irish'.

The new SDLP leader, Alasdair McDonnell, explicitly ruled out any form of electoral pact with Sinn Fein, describing such deals as being based on 'sectarian, selfish interests'. McGuinness described McDonnell's decision as mistaken and a lost opportunity for nationalism. On the other side of the sectarian divide, there were no such qualms. In

March 2015 the DUP and the UUP announced that they had agreed an electoral pact in which the DUP would step aside in Fermanagh and South Tyrone, and Newry and Armagh, with the UUP doing the same in East and North Belfast. McGuinness immediately renewed his appeal to the SDLP to do a similar deal with Sinn Fein, an appeal which was again rejected. Criticised at the time, the pact would pay off for both unionist parties at the election.[50]

As the general election approached, many of the parties began to set out their stalls for possible wooing by the mainland parties in the event of the widely believed likelihood of a hung parliament. It would be a rare occasion when Northern Ireland would impinge upon the mainstream campaigning. Despite the DUP and Sinn Fein threatening legal action over their exclusion from the ever-growing list of participants in the proposed TV debates, the next the majority of voters would hear about the parties in Northern Ireland would be if either Mr Cameron or Mr Miliband came a-courting on 8 May.[51]

Notes

1. That is, as a percentage of the total UK vote. The trend is similar as a percentage of GB votes, although the absolute levels are (slightly) higher.
2. Craig Johnson, 'The Importance of Local Parties and Incumbency to the Electoral Prospects of the Liberal Democrats', *Politics*, 34 (2014): 201–12.
3. There was a contrast throughout the Parliament between the way the party was perceived by many right-of-centre Conservative MPs – who saw it as continually blocking 'true' Conservative policies – and the way the public perceived the party as irrelevant.
4. For example, it is perfectly plausible that the Lib Dems could have persuaded the Conservatives to put any reforms to university finance on hold. But had they insisted on that during the coalition negotiations, what would the Conservatives have wanted in return?
5. See Jasper Gerard, *The Clegg Coup*. Gibson Square, 2011, p. 192.
6. As one of Clegg's aides said to him shortly after going into government: 'Opposition is wasted on the young.'
7. 'The Guardian View on the Liberal Democrats: Missing Them Already', *The Guardian*, 15 May 2015.
8. *Newsnight*, 13 October 2015.
9. The foreword to the full Coalition programme talked of 'a programme for government which is more radical and comprehensive than our individual manifestos'. See Philip Cowley and Martin Ryder, 'Into Government: Coalition (2010–2011)' in Robert Ingham and Duncan Brack, *Peace, Reform and Liberalism*. Biteback, 2011, p. 366.
10. See the comments in 'Richard Reeves: Parting Shots from Clegg's Right-Hand Man', *The Independent*, 6 July 2012. Indeed, even in late 2010, several Lib Dem ministers were already freelancing, regardless of what the leadership thought.

11. Cowley and Ryder, 'Into Government', p. 368.
12. By the end of the Parliament, the party had effectively stopped trying. By-election candidates were given a miserly £5,000 for election expenses and were effectively left to their own devices.
13. Dennis Kavanagh and Philip Cowley, *The British General Election of 2010*. Palgrave Macmillan, 2010, pp. 108–10.
14. Similarly, even if Clegg had been victorious in the party's Federal Policy Committee and had removed the abolition of fees from the manifesto, it would still not have been the party's position to *raise* fees. So even if he had fought harder to remove the policy from the manifesto – and it was hardly as if he did not try – it would not necessarily have avoided the problem caused by the NUS campaign.
15. There were multiple elements to the package that were appealing to Lib Dem MPs – the removal of up-front fees, the raising of the threshold below which no money had to be repaid and the extension of the scheme to part-time students – and so privately some would argue that they had not really broken the NUS pledge (which talked of supporting a fairer alternative). Wisely, this argument was rarely heard publicly.
16. Cable and David Willetts, the Conservative Universities Minister, argued that they needed to move quickly to allow universities to print their prospectuses and that vice-chancellors would be very unhappy if they delayed. In retrospect, one of those close to Clegg thinks that a few angry vice-chancellors may have helped enormously: 'It would have been good if there had been a good crisis. The problem would have them helped make the case for the solution.'
17. The last sentence is not entirely true, since both Labour and the Conservatives were pledged to await the Browne review recommendations (although it was hardly a shock when Browne recommended removing the cap on fees).
18. This involved two online surveys, each of around 6,000 respondents, the first to identify their potential market and the second to examine how they responded to specific policies. The large number of respondents overall was to ensure that the number of potential Lib Dem supporters in each poll was sufficient for analysis.
19. The idea had come from Ryan Coetzee and Lena Pietsch.
20. This included appearances on Channel 4's *The Last Leg*, as well as bids to appear on *Soccer AM*, *Jonathan Ross* and *The One Show* – although the party turned down (and then regretted doing so) an offer for Clegg to appear on the *Graham Norton Show*.
21. Patrick Wintour and Nicholas Watt, 'The Clegg Catastrophe', *The Guardian*, 24 June 2015.
22. Kavanagh and Cowley, *The British General Election of 2010*, p. 116.
23. Kavanagh and Cowley, *The British General Election of 2010*, p. 404.
24. UKIP supporters can get very touchy about the overlap between their support and that of the BNP. The evidence for some overlap is, however, pretty comprehensive. See Robert Ford and Matthew Goodwin, *Revolt on the Right*. Routledge, 2014, Chapter 4.
25. Lord Ashcroft, *'They're Thinking What We're Thinking'. Understanding the UKIP Temptation*. 2012, p. 5.
26. This paradox is perhaps the easiest to explain. Yes, Farage went to a public (that is, private) school, and yes he went to work in the City and not down

a mine or in a factory. But he did not go to university and working in the City is still a job, and one that is in the private sector. His pre-political career was therefore completely different from the standard university-public sector-special advisor route of many mainstream politicians.

27. Matthew Goodwin, 'Not Who You Think: UKIP Voters' in P. Cowley and R. Ford (eds), *Sex, Lies and the Ballot Box*. Biteback, 2014, p. 235.
28. 'The PM Should Avoid UKIP – It's a State of Mind, Not a Party', *Evening Standard*, 28 November 2012.
29. Respondents were asked to choose between two statements ('When I vote in the general election, the party I choose must have coherent policies which they could implement in government' or 'When I vote in the general election, the party I choose will be about sending a message about the sort of society I want to live in'). For UKIP voters, the figures were 30% policy, 63% message. Green voters took a similarly symbolically focused approach to voting. See Philip Cowley, 'What's More Important to Voters? Coherent Policy or the Chance to "Send a Message"'. blogs.new.spectator.co.uk, 5 February 2015.
30. Indeed, this was a defence Farage himself used when one of the above-mentioned cases blew up. The candidate was a 'a council house boy from the East End of London, left school early and talks and speaks in a way that a lot of people from that background do ... I think we are very snobbish in London about condemning people for the colloquial language they use, particularly if it's not meant with really unpleasant intent'.
31. 'Who Would Play Nigel Farage in a Film?', *Daily Telegraph*, 22 December 2014. Also see the comments in Lord (Michael) Ashcroft and Kevin Culwick's *Pay Me Forty Quid And I'll Tell You* (London, Biteback, 2015, p. 39) in which Farage is seen by voters as either Ray Winstone or Sid James.
32. James Dennison and Matthew Goodwin, 'Immigration, Issue Ownership and the Rise of UKIP' in Andrew Geddes and Jon Tonge (eds), *Britain Votes 2015*. Oxford University Press, 2015, p. 181. However, they also thought UKIP talked about the issue too much, and that their approach was intolerant. See Sunder Katwala and Steve Ballinger, *The Politics of Immigration*, British Future, 2015.
33. Ford and Goodwin, *Revolt on the Right*, p. 270, although to be really accurate, the final sentence needs a 'they feel' inserted before 'ceased'.
34. Go back beyond 2010 and it becomes clear that many of those backing UKIP in 2014 were former Labour voters who had defected from Labour before UKIP support took off. By 2010, therefore, they may have been Conservatives or BNP or non-voters subsequently tempted by UKIP, but they were previously Labour supporters. See Geoffrey Evans and Jon Mellon, 'Working Class Votes and Conservative Losses: Solving the UKIP Puzzle', *Parliamentary Affairs*, 2015 (online).
35. 'Nigel Farage: The Main Parties Don't Listen to the Working Classes', *Evening Standard*, 10 March 2015.
36. See 'Research Fuels Speculation of More Tory Defections', *Financial Times*, 12 October 2014, which identified four seats where it was claimed Conservative MPs would do better to defect to UKIP. In the election in 2015, the Conservatives held each one, with UKIP coming third.

37. This was most evident after Farage's controversial but calculated remarks during the election campaign about the cost to the NHS of immigrants with HIV. It was an area where the two had already differed previously, with Carswell saying that Farage's views could not be taken 'seriously'. Carswell had spent his childhood in Uganda, where his father was one of the doctors who first diagnosed HIV and campaigned for greater attention to be paid to the disease; his differences with Farage over this were deeply held.
38. James Dennison, 'The Other Insurgency? The Greens and the Election' in Geddes and Tonge (eds), *Britain Votes 2015*, p. 189.
39. Her account is in Caroline Lucas, *Honourable Friends*. Portobello, 2015. It is not a book riddled with self-doubt.
40. For all her flaws, which would become obvious during the election campaign, those who work with Bennett will stress her skills. She is good at much of the behind-the-scenes work needed in a political party, building up local parties, inspiring activists and engaging with students. 'She'd be a brilliant Chief Executive', said one of the Green team in what was a deliberately double-edged comment.
41. Neil Carter, 'The Greens in the UK General Election of 7 May 2015', *Environmental Politics*, 24(6) (2015): 1055–60.
42. Roger Scully, 'More Scottish than Welsh? Understanding the 2011 Devolved Elections in Scotland and Wales', *Regional & Federal Studies*, 23(5) (2013): 591–612.
43. Laura McAllister and Michael Cole, 'The 2011 Welsh General Election: An Analysis of the Latest Staging Post in the Maturing of Welsh Politics', *Parliamentary Affairs*, 67(1) (2014): 172–90.
44. Richard Wyn Jones and Roger Scully, *Wales Says Yes: Devolution and the 2011 Welsh Referendum*. University of Wales Press, 2012.
45. Lewis Baston, *The Bradford Earthquake*, Democratic Audit, 2013.
46. Matthew Goodwin, 'Forever a False Dawn? Explaining the Electoral Collapse of the British National Party (BNP)', *Parliamentary Affairs*, 67(4) (2014): 887–906.
47. Walker had taken Michael Gove, the Education Secretary, to court in an attempt to overturn his ban from teaching, claiming that his BNP membership had been prejudicial in the decision to ban him.
48. Neil Matthews, 'The Northern Ireland Assembly Election 2011', *Irish Political Studies*, 27(2) (2012): 341–58.
49. By comparison, the Alliance Party managed to gain one seat and saw its share of the vote rise significantly; success that paid out in the form of an extra departmental position in the coalition executive. Among the other parties, the Progressive Unionist Party lost its single seat in the Assembly, whilst the leader of Traditional Unionist Voice, Jim Allister, became his party's first MLA.
50. Jonathan Tonge and Jocelyn Evans, 'Another Communal Headcount: The Election in Northern Ireland' in Geddes and Tonge (eds), *Britain Votes 2015*, pp. 118–19; also see below, p. 219.
51. In the event, of course, they did not, and the province's politics 'slid back to its default positions of obscurity and parochial communalism' (Tonge and Evans, 'Another Communal Headcount', p. 117).

5
The Long and the Short of the SNP Breakthrough

Richard Rose and Mark Shephard

The 2015 election campaign saw the Scottish National Party (SNP) abruptly transformed from a largely irrelevant minority party to one with a major impact on British politics. For two generations after Scottish Nationalists began contesting elections in 1929, their efforts had demonstrated the commitment of Scots to the two British governing parties. Together, the Conservative and Labour Parties took up to 97% of the Scottish vote, while the Nationalists averaged only 1%, and did not win a single seat at a general election until 1970. The SNP first gained significance when the share of the two British governing parties fell to 75% at the 1974 British general elections. While in England the Liberals benefited, in Scotland it was the SNP that gained most. In the February 1974 British general election its vote almost doubled and it won seven MPs, enough to hold the balance of power in an almost evenly divided House of Commons. In October 1974 the SNP won 11 seats and its share of the Scottish vote reached 30%, only six percentage points less than the Labour vote. The Labour government introduced a bill for the devolution of a minimum of powers to a Scottish assembly, but many Labour MPs were hostile and the proposed assembly was rejected because of insufficient turnout at a 1979 Scottish referendum.

In reaction to the repeated election of a Conservative government under Margaret Thatcher, the Labour Party became pragmatically committed to devolution. It assumed that Labour's dominance in Scottish MPs would be paralleled by Labour permanently dominating a devolved Scottish Parliament and crushing the challenge of the

SNP. Opinion polls showed that devolution was popular with the Scottish electorate. When offered a choice between three alternatives – the status quo option of a unitary Parliament making all decisions at Westminster; the devolution of some powers to a Scottish Parliament; or an independent Scotland – the median voter consistently endorsed the principle of devolution rather than the status quo or independence. George Robertson, a senior Scottish member of the Labour government, declared: 'Devolution will kill nationalism stone dead.' Conservatives tended to be opposed, fearing devolution would become movement along a slippery slope leading to independence. The SNP did not endorse Labour proposals because they fell far short of its goal of independence. However, the leadership did accept the challenge of contesting seats in the Scottish Parliament in the hopes of turning the election of a Scottish Parliament with devolved powers into a vehicle that could lead to independence.

The introduction of a two-election system

The victory of the New Labour Party of Tony Blair at the 1997 British general election was followed by prompt legislation setting up a devolved Scottish Parliament in Scotland. In the first three elections of the British Parliament following devolution, the SNP was irrelevant for the British government because it only contested Scottish seats and won only a handful of Scottish constituencies. The Labour Party did not gain additional support for delivering devolution; instead, its Scottish vote fell as it did elsewhere in Britain. The Conservatives did not lose any votes because of their initial opposition to devolution; they took 17% of the vote in 1997 and the same in 2010. The SNP vote remained stable too. It won 20% in 2001 and the same share at the 2010 election. When the Conservatives fell 20 seats short of an absolute majority in 2010, the SNP had little impact on the political arithmetic of government formation because it had just six MPs.

In the 2010 British general election the first-past-the-post (FPTP) system gave Labour more than two-thirds of Scotland's MPs with just over two-fifths of the Scottish vote. Labour appeared in a strong position to continue benefiting from a Scottish bonus of seats, holding most of its seats by margins so large that by any conventional analysis they would be regarded as very safe. The median SNP challenger was 28 percentage points behind a Labour MP and in more than half its seats the Labour MP had won more than 50% of the vote in 2010. By contrast, the Nationalists' six Westminster MPs held their seats with an average lead of only 10%.

For the first four years of the 2010 Parliament, Labour's Westminster position was hardly affected by the SNP controlling Scotland's government. Labour continued to be the preferred choice in 17 of 18 Scottish polls asking Scots how they would vote in a British general election. In September 2013 Labour had a lead of nine percentage points over the SNP. While this was a 3% reduction in Labour's lead compared to its 2010 showing, it was no threat to Labour's hegemony. On a uniform swing, this poll implied that the SNP would not gain a single seat from Labour and only two seats from the Liberal Democrats.

While the SNP was irrelevant at Westminster, devolution institutionalised a separate system of elections in Scotland to elect a devolved Parliament at Holyrood. A complex Mixed Member Proportional System of election was intended to prevent any party winning an absolute majority of Members of the Scottish Parliament (MSPs). Voters were given two ballots. The first ballot was to vote for individual candidates in single-member constituencies won by coming first-past-the-post (FPTP). The other ballot was to cast a vote for a party that listed candidates for more than two-fifths of seats chosen by a compensating system of proportional representation. Westminster politicians assumed that the Scotland Act 1998's limitations on the powers of the Scottish Parliament would keep it subordinate and that there would be no spillover from a second-order Scottish election to a first-order election deciding which party governed Britain.

The SNP welcomed the opportunity to compete under an electoral system that guaranteed it a minimum of dozens of seats at Holyrood, with the resources and Scottish media attention that went with it. To enhance its appeal, it evolved from an introverted movement about independence into an organisation seeking votes from a broad cross-section of Scottish society with the valence claim that it could govern Scotland better than its opponents. At a time when British political parties were steadily losing membership, that of the SNP more than doubled.[1]

From the first election of the Scottish Parliament in 1999 onwards, votes and seats differed substantially between Scottish and Westminster elections. The decline in Labour's British vote under Tony Blair had a parallel in elections to the Holyrood Parliament.[2] Nonetheless, in the first two elections the Labour Party and the Liberal Democrats together won enough MSPs to form coalition governments. The SNP did well enough to become the official opposition in the Holyrood Parliament.

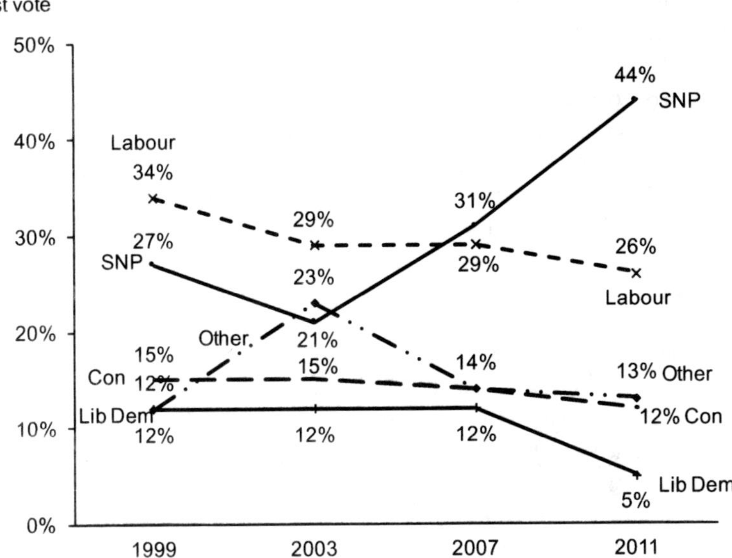

Figure 5.1 Party competition in Holyrood elections, 1999–2011

Source: C. Rallings and M. Thrasher, *British Electoral Facts*, 1832–2012. Biteback, 2012, pp. 214–16.

In 2007 the SNP finished first in both the list and single-member ballots, winning 47 seats, one more than Labour. Since the Labour and Liberal Democrat coalition was also short of a majority, the SNP was able to form a single-party minority government headed by Alex Salmond. To carry its annual budget, the SNP Finance Minister John Swinney was adept at making deals with other parties, including the Conservatives. Since much legislation is not controversial along party lines, the SNP could appear as a party that could govern in keeping with a consensus of Scottish opinion. Because it had less than two-fifths of the 129 seats at Holyrood, the SNP did not have a political mandate to call an independence referendum.

The 2011 Holyrood election dramatically demonstrated that when the same parties compete in different electoral systems, the outcome can be categorically different. Twelve months after a British general election in which Labour returned more than two-thirds of Scotland's MPs with 42% of the vote, the SNP staged a breakthrough. It won 44% of the list vote and three-quarters of the FPTP single-member seats in the Scottish Parliament. Doing so enabled it to take advantage of the tendency of proportional representation systems to give a bonus in terms of seats to the party that wins the most votes. The result was that the SNP gained an absolute majority in the Scottish Parliament. Although Holyrood constituency boundaries are not identical with Westminster constituencies, the SNP victory was a caution that Labour's Westminster MPs would become vulnerable if Scottish voters ever decided to align their Westminster vote with how they voted for Members of the Scottish Parliament.

The referendum: a different question and outcome

The SNP's election manifesto pledged it to call a referendum on independence and its absolute majority at Holyrood gave it the power to do so. However, the Westminster Act that devolved powers to the Scottish Parliament did not authorise it to call an independence referendum. The SNP government recognised that it needed the British government to accept the principle of the right of Scots to leave the UK in order for a Scottish vote to take effect. With less than one-fifth of the Scottish vote, a British Conservative government was in a weak political position to veto a referendum, but was in a strong position to bargain about the conditions under which a referendum was held. Since opinion polls showed those in favour of the status quo were a limited minority, the SNP wanted to offer voters two choices: independence or more devolution of powers to Edinburgh. The latter was seen as a second-best alternative, but as something that would keep up the impetus towards Scottish self-government. The British government wanted a simple choice between voting for independence or rejecting it, a phrasing that invited those in favour of the status quo and more devolution to join together in rejecting independence. Following inter-governmental meetings to iron out differences, the Edinburgh Agreement of 15 October 2012 confirmed the British government's acceptance of a referendum that could lead to the break-up of the UK with the condition that the ballot offered a straight Yes/No choice: should Scotland be an independent country?

The officially recognised organisation campaigning for independence, Yes Scotland, was launched in May 2012. It was formally independent of the SNP, recruited some supporters from the Green Party and had the backing of Scottish celebrities such as Sean Connery as well as people who had not previously been identified with any political party. There were also recruits from Labour; Dennis Canavan, a former Labour MP, chaired its advisory committee. Nicola Sturgeon, deputy leader of the SNP, was also a member. The Yes campaign received a grant of £342,797 from the SNP to fund its launch. Most of its workers were SNP voters. In effect, there were three institutional groups campaigning for independence: the ad hoc referendum organisation, the established SNP party organisation and the Scottish government led by Alex Salmond.

The Yes campaign regarded the 45% vote it took at the 2011 Holyrood election as giving it the potential core of support. However, a referendum is not decided by a plurality of voters, but by an absolute majority, and the SNP's support was short of that figure. The campaign made the case that the performance of the SNP in charge of a devolved Scottish government since 2007 showed that Scots could govern an independent Scotland. It argued that Scotland could do an even better job if independence removed the complications of devolution, in which major powers remained at Westminster and each general election raised the risk that the party governing Britain had little support in Scotland.

The SNP had the advantage of being the dominant political presence in Scottish politics thanks to its control of the Edinburgh government since 2007. In Alex Salmond as First Minister, it had a leader whose presence was much more familiar to Scots than Ed Miliband. It had built a membership that had been growing substantially, while that of Labour had been contracting or even ossifying. Although the issue of independence divided Scots, the SNP's approach to the electorate sought to be inclusive, claiming to be the party to represent everyone who lives in Scotland, whatever their religion, race or ethnicity. In this way it attracted support from residents from Europe and Third World countries. A small-scale study of referendum voting found that Polish and Pakistani immigrants were more likely to favour independence and prefer a Scottish to a British identity.[3] By contrast, the Labour Party had traditionally adopted an Us versus Them approach to the Scottish electorate. This was successful as long as it could convert a plurality of votes into a big majority of seats at Westminster.

Devolution gave the Scottish press and broadcasting services much more Scottish news than before on topics that directly affected virtually all their readers. It added a Scottish government focus that could compete for attention with news of the British government at Westminster. The Scottish media were glad to play up the Scottish dimension at a time of increased competition for audiences with British papers whose primary audience was English. The BBC was under particular pressure from the SNP government to give more attention to Scottish news and not treat it as just a regional follow-up of news coming from London.

British papers took advantage of developments in technology to set up printing facilities in Scotland and recruit Scottish staff who were given substantial autonomy in competing with papers only aimed at a Scottish audience. While remaining Unionist in outlook, *The Times*, the *Sunday Times* and the *Daily Telegraph* sought to run a Scottish story on their front page in every issue. Whether a paper was reporting or attacking the activities of the Scottish government, it was raising awareness – and after 2007 this meant awareness of the SNP. The Yes campaign also made use of social media such as Twitter and Facebook to encourage its supporters to mobilise friends and neighbours on behalf of a Yes vote. Passive online support measures such as liking Facebook messages saw the Yes side's lead over the No campaign rising from 10,000 in December 2013 to more than 100,000 by the time of the referendum. Concurrently, Yes Scotland followers on Twitter increased from 25,000 in December 2013 to 107,000 by the referendum. This contrasted markedly with Better Together, whose followers rose from 15,000 to 41,000 in the same period.

The news that English media audiences received about Scotland was often different from as well as less than what Scottish audiences received. At the time of the 2007 Holyrood election, the headline in the Scottish edition of *The Sun* – 'Vote SNP today and you put Scotland's head in the noose'– would match London views. But by the 2015 British general election, *The Sun* offered Scottish and English readers conflicting advice. Its page one splash headline told Scottish readers 'Why it's time to vote SNP'. However, it advised its English readers to vote Tory.

The No campaign organisation, Better Together, was a coalition bringing together the Labour, Conservative and Liberal Democrat parties. Given Labour's position as the largest party in Scotland, its members took the lead role in steering the No campaign. Alistair Darling, a Labour MP representing an Edinburgh constituency since 1987, was the Director. Its senior full-time staff had worked with Labour politicians previously. Westminster party leaders were kept at a distance so that the organisation could avoid an SNP attack that the group spoke for Westminster rather than Scottish interests. Most of its funds came from a small number of businessmen, including Ian Taylor, who had formerly given £550,000 to the Conservatives. The author J.K. Rowling gave the No campaign £1,000,000.

While the three sets of partisans shared a common goal in the rejection of independence, they were more accustomed to campaigning against each other. In May 2013 the Scottish Labour Party leader Johann Lamont, Gordon Brown and Anas Sarwar, a Glasgow MP, launched

United with Labour on the grounds that the Labour movement had a different view of Scotland's future than did the Tories and the Liberal Democrats. Notwithstanding its positive name, Better Together's campaign emphasised a simple negative message: independence was risky. The Scottish *Sunday Mail* complained on 17 February 2013: 'If, as their campaign complains, we will be better together, they need to start telling us why.'

From the perspective of Labour campaigners, the demand for independence was irrelevant to what they deemed the real economic interests of voters. The No campaign stressed the economic benefits conferred by the existing system, including the disproportionate transfer of British tax revenue to the Scottish government that was inherent in the Barnett formula. Even more, it emphasised the economic risks of being cut off from the use of the pound sterling and the uncertainties that independence could create for Scotland's economic relations with England and with the European Union. The Conservative government underscored these arguments by publicising the fiscal benefits that Scotland would lose if it could not draw on British tax revenues and the threat of higher taxes with independence.

The conventional British view that it was the economy that motivated voters ignored the lesson of Northern Ireland, where nationalism and religion have sustained political conflict with bombs and bullets as well as ballots. Although the UK was constructed as a multi-national state,[4] British politicians avoided the use of this term because it encouraged demands for a federal state. The terms 'Union' and 'United Kingdom' were evoked as symbols of what the No campaign represented, but they were a pale shadow of the appeal of Crown and Empire when Unionism was at its height. Moreover, the numerous Scots of Irish origin saw Unionism as the rejection of national self-determination in Ireland. References to Britain were ambiguous, for it could be a secondary identity for a majority of Scots or a term that referred to a population that was five-sixths English. In addition, the flow of immigrants from other continents has made London-based politicians describe the UK as a multi-cultural society in which British people formed one culture. In his distinctive Scots accent, the then Labour Foreign Secretary Robin Cook celebrated chicken tikka masala as a 'true British national dish'.[5]

By contrast, the No campaign was confident of victory. Collectively, the parties backing the No campaign had polled 80% of the vote at the 2010 British general election. It recognised that the No vote had to 'win well' in order to settle the issue for a generation on the grounds that a slim margin of victory, as a slim majority would fuel a nationalist clamour for another referendum in which a one-vote margin in favour of independence could mean the break-up of Britain. Darling did not set a numerical target, but colleagues briefed that pushing the Yes vote below 40% should keep independence off the political agenda for decades.

Opinion polls consistently showed that Scots who preferred the status quo or more devolution formed a majority and those endorsing independence were always a limited minority. An average of polls conducted in 2013 found 61% against independence with 39% in favour and in December 63% rejected independence (Figure 5.2). These responses offered assurance to No campaigners that the Union would not be broken up. However, opinion polls always showed a very strong rejection of the status quo. When Scots were asked how they would vote if there were three choices in the referendum, three-quarters rejected the status quo. The largest group, 41%, said they would vote for more devolution and one-third would endorse independence.[6]

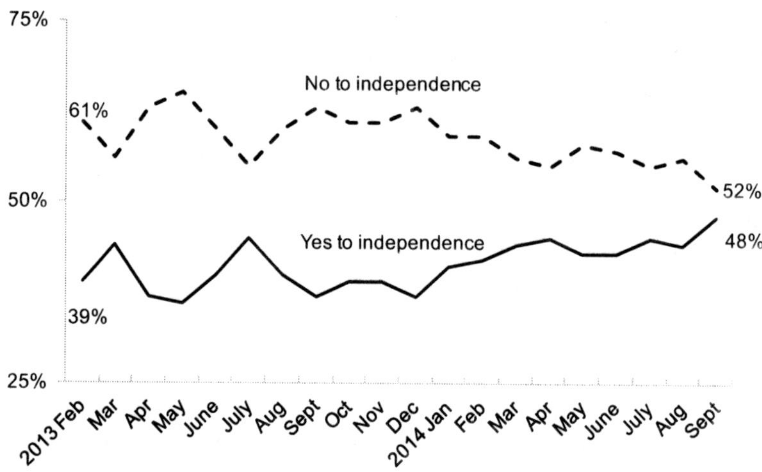

Figure 5.2 Independence support in polls rises as vote nears

Source: unitedkingdompollingreport.co.uk; don't knows excluded.

The logic of a referendum ballot pushed off the fence the plurality of Scots for whom more devolution was their first choice. The Better Together campaign hoped that they would be overwhelmingly against independence. However, this was not the case. By early September 2014, poll results indicated that up to a quarter of those who had been in favour of more devolution had decided to vote yes for independence (Table 5.1). The size of the group wanting more devolution did not shrink, however, because two-fifths of those who had previously favoured the status quo came to prefer more devolution. Thus, a substantial majority of those who rejected independence also rejected the status quo. Barely one in seven Scots endorsed the terms that the Westminster Parliament had set for the powers of the Scottish Parliament.

Table 5.1 From opinion poll to referendum ballot

Q. How would you vote in the referendum if there were three options?

	March	*Sept*	*Referendum*
Independence Yes	35%	45%	45%
More devolution	40%	39%	–
Combined No	–	–	55%
Keep as is	25%	15%	–

Source: YouGov surveys for *The Times* (26 March 2014) and the *Sunday Times* (7 September 2014). Don't knows and would not vote omitted.

Twelve days before the referendum, a YouGov poll dropped a bombshell: it showed 51% of its respondents were planning to vote yes for independence. This pointed and public reminder that the outcome of a referendum isn't over until the last ballot is counted caused panic among British party leaders. David Cameron and Ed Miliband missed Prime Minister's Question Time on 10 September 2014 to fly to Scotland. Instead of defending the Union as it was, they switched to promising a greater devolution of powers to Scotland than either the government of David Cameron or Gordon Brown had been prepared to tolerate. On 16 September 2014 the party leaders promised in a front-page story in Scotland's largest and most Labour-leaning paper, *The Daily Record*, to give 'extensive new powers for the Scottish Parliament' if independence was rejected.

In the referendum on 18 September, 55% voted No and 45% Yes to independence. Among the few who had voted Conservative in the 2011 Holyrood election, 91% voted No. Among SNP voters, 81% voted Yes. By contrast, 30% of those who had voted Labour or Liberal Democrat in 2011 endorsed independence, more than offsetting the number of SNP voters who favoured it as the devolved Scottish government but did not want to leave the UK. Reflecting the very high level of engagement achieved through political mobilisation, the referendum turnout was 84%, higher than at any UK general election since suffrage became virtually universal in 1918.

The 45% of the vote cast for the SNP cause was bigger than either the Labour or Conservative parties had secured in Scotland in ten of the 11 previous Westminster elections. The four council areas that registered a majority for independence included three Labour strongholds in the west of Scotland and Dundee. In Glasgow, where all the MPs were Labour, there was a 53% Yes vote. If all who voted Yes in the referendum supported the SNP candidates in the forthcoming British general election, in a FPTP general election ballot the SNP stood to make massive gains from Labour.

While the No campaign was immediately successful in defeating the SNP's first bid for independence, it failed to meet the test of winning a big enough majority to put paid to the challenge that the SNP presented to the government of the UK. Within a fortnight of its defeat, the Yes campaign's advisory board issued a statement promising to maintain the momentum of placing Scotland's future in Scotland's hands. It identified its immediate task as ensuring that Westminster parties delivered on the promises they had made to give substantial additional powers to the Scottish Parliament. The political calendar offered two opportunities for maintaining its momentum: the British general election in May 2015 and a Scottish Parliament election in May 2016.

FPTP puts the SNP first

In his speech the day after the referendum vote, David Cameron promised to deliver more devolution to Scotland, a promise consistent with the vow that the British party leaders had made in their last-minute visit to Scotland before the vote. Since the pledge was very general, the government established a Commission under Lord Smith of Kelvin to make recommendations about what should be devolved. It reported on 27 November 2014. The Conservative government followed this up with draft legislative proposals. Cameron sought to address concerns in the party's English electoral base about England being disadvantaged by devolution. He declared: 'We have heard the voice of Scotland – and now the millions of voices of England must also be heard. The question of English votes for English laws, the so-called West Lothian question, requires a decisive answer.'

The SNP tactic was to take advantage of its momentum in order to win enough Westminster seats to hold the balance of power if there was another hung parliament. In doing so, it had the advantage of having its membership rise from 25,000 by the time of the independence ballot to more than 100,000 before the general election. By contrast, the demoralised Scottish Labour Party Labour claimed about 13,000 members. Alex Salmond's resignation as First Minister immediately after the referendum defeat resulted in the SNP having a fresh face as leader, Nicola Sturgeon. Behind Sturgeon's attractive personality and presentational skills was a very firm commitment to secure much more devolution than any British party would grant. Salmond did not leave politics, but instead turned his attention to Westminster.

For the forthcoming British election, the SNP sought to make the big issue which party could best represent Scotland's interests at Westminster.[7] The readiness of British leaders to offer more devolution as a consequence of the referendum campaign was cited as proof that the SNP could increase the powers of the Scottish Parliament. In the FPTP contest for Westminster seats the SNP did not need to win an absolute majority to be successful. Given the division of Unionist support between Labour, the Conservatives, the Liberal Democrats and UKIP, a 45% vote would be sufficient to return dozens of SNP MPs to Westminster.

A month after the referendum, an Ipsos MORI poll showed that the Nationalist momentum was being maintained. The poll punctured any hopes British politicians had that defeat in the referendum would deflate the SNP appeal. It reported that 52% of Scots supported the SNP and that Labour was down to 23%. If such a swing occurred uniformly across Scotland at the general election, it would leave Labour with just one Scottish MP and the Liberal Democrats wiped out. Averaging October polls made the Ipsos MORI result appear an outlier. Nonetheless, it showed the SNP with 43% of the vote compared to 27% for the leading Unionist party, Labour (Figure 5.3). On a uniform swing, this would be enough to deliver three-quarters of Labour-held constituencies to the SNP plus substantial gains from the Liberal Democrats. By Christmas the pattern was clear: the SNP was consistently maintaining sufficient support to win the most Scottish seats at the general election. A significant bloc of Scots who had voted Labour in 2010 and for independence in 2011 now preferred the SNP to speak for them at Westminster. This contrasted with England, where those who defected from Labour while its vote was falling by almost one-third between 1997 and 2010 switched to the Liberal Democrats, the Greens or UKIP.

The loss of dozens of Scottish seats threatened Labour's hopes of winning control of the British government, since seats lost in Scotland

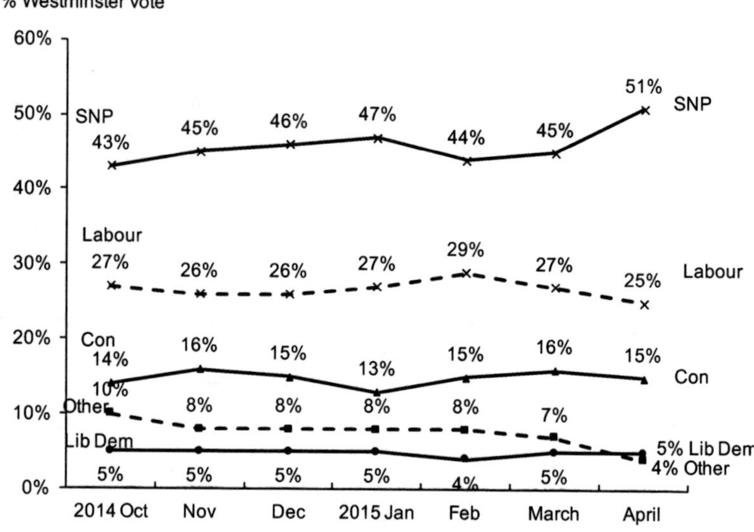

Figure 5.3 The SNP breaks through in Westminster polls

Source: monthly poll averages from whatscotlandthinks.org/questions.

required it to compensate by winning more seats in England. The Labour Party leadership in London interpreted this loss as due to the shortcomings of its Scottish politicians. Its lack of confidence was made evident in the press and its handling of relations with the Scottish branch of the party organisation. Johann Lamont, the leader of the Labour Party in opposition in the Holyrood Parliament, responded by resigning in late October. She publicly attacked the London leadership of the party for failing to devolve more power to the Scottish branch of the party and denounced Labour MPs as dinosaurs for failing to recognise the change in the Scottish political climate. Two of her predecessors as Labour first minister in the Scottish government backed her complaints.[8]

The turnover of Labour leadership following Gordon Brown's loss of office in 2010 meant that the most prominent figures in the British party no longer included many Scots, as had been the case when Tony Blair formed his Cabinet in 1997. The leadership backed Jim Murphy, a Westminster MP, to become the leader of the Scottish party and he was duly endorsed by its Scottish branch. Murphy announced that he would campaign to regain defecting Labour voters by reminding them that only by voting Labour could they prevent the return of another Tory government. This appeal was consistent with the lack of support that the Conservatives had in Scotland and with the view that a Westminster election is about who governs Britain. It was also consistent with the Conservatives' hope that Labour's loss of seats in Scotland would leave the Conservatives with the most seats in the next House of Commons. Labour campaigners also hoped that stressing left/right economic issues common from one end of Britain to the next would regain votes from the SNP, whose supporters were a mixture of voters inclined to the right and the left.

By January 2014, successive Scottish polls had confirmed that the SNP was poised to achieve a breakthrough at Westminster. Poll results indicated that the SNP would dominate Scottish representation at Westminster, winning a minimum of 45 seats of Scotland's 59 seats.[9] Given a virtual wipeout of the Liberal Democrats in Scotland and a big loss of its English seats, this would make the SNP the third largest party at Westminster. Since British polls made another hung parliament appear likely, it would give the SNP the power to decide whether there was a Conservative or a Labour government. In spite of losing the independence referendum a few months earlier, the SNP now appeared to be at the heart of British politics.

Notes

1. James Mitchell, L. Bennie and R. Johns, *The Scottish National Party*. Oxford University Press, 2012. See especially Chapter 3.
2. See Gerry Hassan and Eric Shaw, *The Strange Death of Labour Scotland*. Edinburgh University Press, 2012.
3. Neil McGarvey and Gareth Mulvey, 'Identities and Politics in the 2014 Scottish Independence Referendum' in R. Medda-Windischer and P. Popilier (eds), *Emerging Trends in Independence and Migration*. Brill Academic, in press.
4. See Richard Rose, *Understanding the United Kingdom*. Longman, 1981.
5. In a speech to the Social Market Foundation, London, 19 April 2001.
6. whatscotlandthinks.org.
7. See the discussion of the displacement of conflict in E.E. Schattschneider, *The Semi-Sovereign People*. Holt, Rinehart and Winston, 1960.
8. On the problems that Labour has had in understanding how the SNP's ideology competes with its own, see Gerry Hassan, 'The Auld Enemies: Scottish Nationalism and Scottish Labour' in G. Hassan (ed.), *The Modern SNP*. Edinburgh University Press, 2014, pp. 141ff.
9. Richard Rose, *The 2015 UK Election Outcome*. Tosca Fund, January 2015, pp. 7–10.

6
Roads and Car Crashes: The Election Approaches

From the beginning of January 2015 to the dissolution of Parliament on 30 March, the parties' campaigns moved up a gear. They used the period to try to set the agenda, to announce or re-announce policies, launch posters, hold rallies and press conferences. It was a period in which they could test policies and prepare the grid for the short campaign covering each day, each week and each month. However, unlike in most previous elections, this period was also dominated by a constant discussion about post-election outcomes, as the parties came to grips with the reality of the new political landscape.

The 2015 election campaign saw a noticeable decline in the use of the campaign poster. Many poster 'launches' were merely media events to generate publicity, with the poster being unveiled on a moveable board (and then used online), but never hitting a paid poster site. Lynton Crosby was particularly sceptical about the value of posters as a campaign tool, and so even the Conservatives, who continued to use posters, spent around one-sixth of what they had spent in 2010 on them. But the year began with one of the few genuine poster launches of the election, the Conservatives unveiling 'Let's stay on the road to a stronger economy' on 5 January. The implied contrast – none too subtle – was with Labour's road to ruin and the choice between competence and chaos. The poster suffered from an unfortunate pre-history. Initially M&C Saatchi had presented a poster design which was met with silence by Cameron and his team. Its proposed tag line – 'WELL DONE YOU' – was dismissed for its *de haut en bas* tone. George Osborne described it as 'patronising and insensitive'. The substitute 'road' poster was

Steve Bell, 'Organise', *The Guardian*, 6 January 2015

then produced in-house, only for embarrassment to ensue when it was revealed that the road in the picture was in fact in Germany. Osborne had on three occasions asked for assurances that the road was in Britain and had been misinformed. It was much mocked, especially online, where spoofs soon circulated.

On 12 January, David Cameron announced the party's six so-called guiding principles for the election, covering the deficit, jobs, education, housing, taxes and retirement. Critics noted the omission of the NHS and immigration from the six themes, even though they were two of the three most important issues for voters. The party's response was that these were subsumed into the economy; without a strong economy, the NHS could not be resourced properly, and limiting their access to welfare benefits would remove any 'pull' factor to immigrants. To the backdrop of the slogan 'Britain Living Within its Means', Cameron's warning that a Labour government would involve more borrowing, more debt interest and less to spend on schools and hospitals was a variant on the increasingly well-worn mantra of competence versus chaos. But it was an example of how the party was weak on individual issue areas, one a traditional weakness, but also one which was a new-found vulnerability. As *The Spectator* noted: 'The Tories want to talk about things where they think a debate will benefit them, no matter what the discussion.'[1] Talking about immigration in isolation only helped UKIP and talking about the NHS would play into Labour's hands.

At the beginning of January, Ed Miliband, Ed Balls, Harriet Harman, Douglas Alexander and their teams moved to the party headquarters in Brewer's Green. For the first time since 1997, party HQ and not 10 Downing Street would be the base from which Labour would fight the campaign.

Labour turned to the NHS to open their campaign on 5 January. It was helped by media accounts of pressures from patients on A&E departments, operations being cancelled and letters to the press by doctors' leaders attacking the Coalition's health record. A large-scale polling exercise on the issue of health by Lord Ashcroft reported that 51% of the electorate thought that the NHS had got worse under the Coalition and just 15% thought it had got better. At a cost of around £1 million, Labour sent leaflets to every home in 80 target seats appealing to voters to save the NHS from David Cameron.[2] The strategy spoke to Labour's perceived strengths. One reason why there was quite so much Labour material about the NHS published online was that party staff found it easier to get such material agreed. 'It was', said one of Labour's digital team, 'much easier to get content signed off about the NHS than any other issue. Things about the economy, until literally the final weeks, were much harder.'

But Labour soon became bogged down in a row over whether Miliband had told a private meeting of BBC executives in November 2014 that their campaign would involve 'weaponising' the NHS. On 11 January, Miliband faced an awkward interview on the *Andrew Marr Show*, declining on seven separate occasions to admit that he had used the phrase. At Prime Minister's Questions on 28 January, David Cameron said the phrase was 'disgraceful' and 'appalling'. Tactically, the controversy allowed the Conservatives to accuse Miliband of using the NHS as a political football (which, of course, he was) and thus close down discussion of the issue itself (which is, of course, what the Conservatives wanted).[3] Miliband repeatedly refused to confirm he had used the word (he had) and Labour continued to weaponise the NHS throughout the campaign. Indeed, at times, it looked as if it was close to being their only weapon (see Figure 6.1). Alan Milburn, a reforming health secretary under Blair, complained that the party was campaigning in its 'comfort zone' and regretted the absence of an NHS reform programme. Labour had been unhappy about what they had seen as SNP 'fear-mongering' over the NHS during the independence referendum, because, as Rafael Behr of *The Guardian* wrote, 'only Labour [is] allowed to fear-monger over NHS'.[4]

During the last session of the Parliament, the Liberal Democrats increasingly tried to differentiate themselves from their coalition partners. Nick Clegg demanded more spending on mental health, a policy which George Osborne was privately prepared to concede. Clegg also objected to Conservative plans to curb civil liberties by allowing intelligence agencies to break into encrypted communications of suspected terrorists. Liberal Democrat ministers let it be known that they were prepared to accept the recommendations of the teacher's pay review, to which the Conservatives were objecting. Much of this related to positioning in relation to future coalition negotiations with the Conservatives or Labour. Clegg began the year claiming that the Lib Dems would 'provide heart to the Conservatives and spine to Labour' if it found itself in coalition after May, borrowing less than Labour and cutting less than the Conservatives. The heart and spine comparison would be used for the rest of the campaign, although it soon transformed into heart and head.

Speaking in Oxford West and Abingdon – a Conservative-held seat that the party was officially targeting – on 12 February, Clegg launched the front page of the party's 2015 manifesto. Since the manifesto had not yet been formally agreed, this provoked some mutterings within the party about due process, but it had the impact of both drawing attention to the party and allowing the Lib Dems to begin to set out their negotiating positon ahead of the hung parliament which everyone assumed was coming. Clegg said he would insist on £8 billion more for the NHS in the next Parliament, raising the tax-free personal allowance

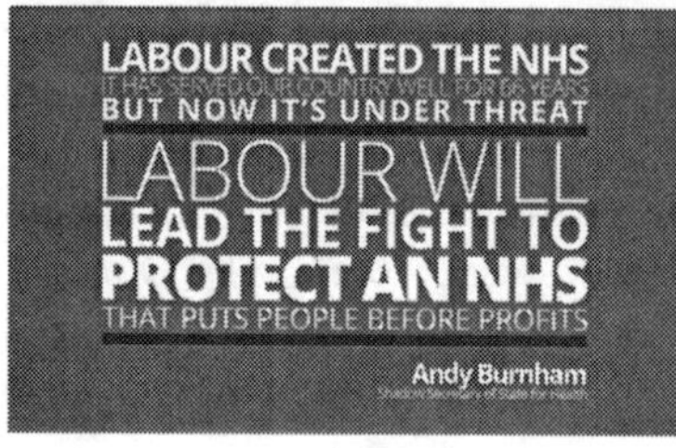

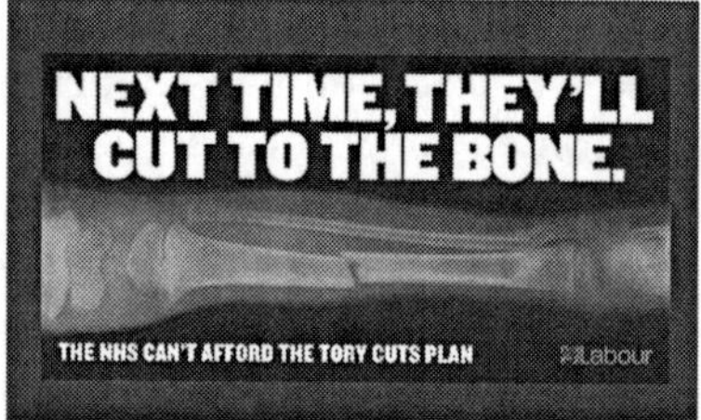

Figure 6.1 Scaremongering (part 1)

to £12,500 and a guarantee for the school budget in real terms. The Conservatives had offered to protect pupil expenditure, but without any allowance for inflation, which the Institute for Fiscal Studies (IFS) calculated would amount to a 7% cut over the course of the next Parliament. At this stage, the Lib Dems refused to call these positions negotiating 'red lines', although during the short campaign they would come to admit that this was exactly what they were.

It was not just the Lib Dems who attempted to stake out their ground prior to any post-election negotiations either. The Democratic Unionist Party (DUP), another potential king-maker in a hung parliament, started to set out their terms. In February, Nigel Dodds, the party's deputy leader, said the DUP could 'do business' with Labour in a hung parliament.[5] By March, they were even more explicit, identifying an extra £1 billion funding for Northern Ireland as the price for supporting either the Conservatives or Labour in a minority government. 'It was basically a shopping list', said one of those tasked with dealing with the DUP. 'It even had the prices marked up.' Or, as one of Labour's putative post-election negotiating team noted: 'There were a lot of roads that needed redoing around Belfast.'

On Labour's grid for February was the theme of young people. Speaking to a largely student audience at Leeds College of Music on 27 February, Miliband repeated a pledge he had made in 2011 to reduce annual university tuition fees to £6,000, which would take effect in September 2016, with the money coming from cutting the tax relief on pension contributions of the wealthiest. This policy caused considerable unease within the party. Many wondered why one of the few groups on which a Labour government would shower largesse was wealthier graduates and whether this was a sensible use of almost £3 billion a year.[6] As *The Observer* noted: 'If Labour's priority is improving social mobility, there are many ways it could have invested this valuable extra cash more wisely.'[7] Miliband dug his heels in. He had two justifications. The first – articulated publicly – was that having promised to reduce fees in 2011, he would not now break his word ('I made you a promise on tuition fees. I will keep my promise'); to u-turn on the same issue that had caused Nick Clegg such difficulties was considered foolhardy, especially with the student vote. The second reason was that far from being about dealing with issues of student poverty or access, the policy was in fact a carrot deliberately designed to appeal to wealthier middle-class families. As one of Miliband's aides said: 'The research showed that a top anxiety for middle class parents was the amount of debt their children might take on. I know all the problems with the policy, but that's what it was trying to address.' Not surprisingly, this aspect of the policy was not articulated publicly.

The same month saw the launch of Labour's 'Woman to Woman' campaign. The campaign was based on the claim that women were increasingly unlikely to vote and the belief that the best way to get them engaged was to have Harriet Harman and other female politicians drive around the country in a pink bus. The first claim was demonstrably untrue (there was no reliable evidence that women were any less likely to vote than men), whilst the second was, at best, dubious.[8] As well as an argument over the colour of the bus – was it pink, magenta or cerise? – and in part prompted by it, there followed a debate about whether this was a patronising way of reaching women voters. It was possible – just – to defend it as a way of reaching out, although many commentators saw the exercise as at best confused and at worse condescending.[9] One of the few certainties was that had the Conservatives attempted such an exercise, Harriet Harman and most of those being driven around in the bus would have slaughtered them for being so patronising, but it was yet another an example of issue ownership. As one of Labour's core team, initially sceptical of the idea, said: 'You can't be attacked for being anti-women if you've got Harriet involved. She's the high priestess of parliamentary feminism.'

On 14 March, Miliband announced what appeared to be the last of Labour's promised five election pledges – on the cost of living – at a party pre-election rally in Birmingham, along with the party's pledge card. The five pledges collectively covered a strong economic foundation, control over immigration, rising living standards for working families, the NHS and a country where the next generation could do better than the last. On 20 March, the party also revealed another NHS poster, albeit a virtual one. Designed by Trevor Beattie, 'Next Time They'll Cut to the Bone' even featured a broken leg in case the message was too subtle.

The SNP's preparations for the election had, of necessity, been put on hold until after the referendum. Insofar as they had thought about the election, they had assumed it would be what one of Nicola Sturgeon's team had called 'a fairly standard Westminster election'. They would have focused on a handful of seats – the six they held, plus a handful where they hoped they might perhaps make gains, but with little hope of doing so. Indeed, there were plenty within the party who had worried that in the face of a No vote, the party would fall in on itself, descending into infighting and paralysis, much as happened after 1979. The immediate post-referendum boost in members and support came as a pleasant surprise, although it took the party until November just to get on top of processing the quantity of membership applications. The SNP also had to resolve a series of questions about whether to stand as part of a broad Yes-Alliance group in the election (no), to waive the length of membership requirement for candidates to enable those who had been brought into politics by the referendum to stand for the SNP (yes) or to allow them to take part in selections (also yes). All of this took up most of what was left of 2014.

In December 2014, the SNP conducted some focus groups in order to try to understand the nature of their apparent rise in the polls. They were taken aback by just how positive the groups were. Indeed, the results were so positive that a cautious Sturgeon, worried that support might be transient or that the groups might just have been unusually pro-SNP, asked for them to be re-done. The new focus groups in January 2015 were just as supportive.

Along with the Conservatives, the SNP were one of the few parties to continue to use posters, at least in the urban parts of Scotland (with local newspaper ads using the same imagery in more rural areas), and in early January 2015 the party launched a poster showing a series of tartan benches in the House of Commons: 'The more seats we have here, the more powers for Scotland.' The aim of the campaign was to hit the New Year with a running start. 'We had to stay relevant', said one of the SNP team, 'which is always our problem.' The SNP leadership were pleased with the imagery, but focus groups helped them realise the message was not quite right. It was not powers, plural, that were important to people, but *power*. The debate had already moved on from the referendum. This election was going to be about fighting for resources – who would get the most for Scotland? – rather than about the constitution. A later version of the poster, launched during the short campaign, therefore talked of: 'More SNP Seats. More Power for Scotland.'

On 22 January, an Ipsos MORI poll showed the SNP poll some 28 points ahead of Labour, suggesting the party could win all but four of the seats in Scotland. The Scottish media, as well as that south of the border, were initially sceptical about the polls showing the SNP on course to make such massive gains. 'And not all of us were totally believing', one

of Sturgeon's team said. But as the weeks went on, and more and more polls came out, all with broadly similar figures – and especially once a series of Scottish constituency polls confirmed the national picture (see p. 242) – it became clear that the early polls were not freaks or outliers. By the end of February, and with canvass returns confirming the polls, there was a realisation within the SNP that there had been a genuine shift in attitudes in Scotland. Rather than a standard Westminster election, this was going to be extraordinary.[10] 'Suddenly, we were the market leader. Whatever you do, don't mess up', said one of their team.

Many in the Labour Party had reached a similar conclusion about what was going to happen in Scotland. One of Jim Murphy's first acts as Scottish Labour leader had been to announce that his party would have autonomy from Labour south of the border. This autonomy did not stop him demanding more resources from party HQ in London or declaring that some of the proceeds of a mansion tax (paid mainly by wealthy homeowners in London and the south-east) would be used to employ more nurses in Scotland. There was a constant tension between what Murphy thought was electorally realistic in Scotland and the view of the team at Brewer's Green in London. Early in the New Year, some of the London party staff had visited Scotland; they 'looked at the data, sniffed the air, and took some pretty hard-headed decisions'. Yet Murphy was still insisting to disbelieving senior party officials in London that Labour could hold on to 34 Scottish seats. The party began organising mailshots to voters in Scottish constituencies, but with little or no contact data in many seats – and relatively few activists – it was of necessity fairly unfocused and untargeted work. 'We're chucking resource at it', said one of Labour's campaign team, 'but there's not much infrastructure there.' They were not unlimited resources, either. Although Murphy's requests for additional funding were not fully met, the party transferred resources from defensive English marginals to Scotland, angering English MPs and candidates. 'We are now fighting 20 key seats in Scotland and have not prepared for it', said a senior organiser.[11]

The rise of the SNP had removed, almost at a stroke, any hope Labour might have had that they could win a majority in the Commons. The decision of the SNP then to rule out any post-election deal with the Conservatives also removed, at a stroke, the most obvious anti-SNP argument that Labour could have deployed: that only by voting Labour could Scots guarantee not getting a Conservative government. In Scotland, Labour tried to counter this by arguing that the party that won most seats at Westminster would form the government, but this too put it at odds with those in the party south of the border, who were desperate to establish that what mattered was whether a party could enjoy the support of the Commons, not whether it came first in seats or not.

Questioned on the *Andrew Marr Show* in January, Miliband four times refused to rule out forming the coalition with the SNP. Many around the Labour leader would later accept that they were too slow to see the problem the issue was causing and too slow to rule out such deals. From the start, Douglas Alexander believed that the party needed to rule out coalitions and should try to close the subject down entirely. Others, most notably Lord (Charlie) Falconer, charged with Labour's post-election planning, did not.[12] 'The significance of this issue in the public mind grew as the campaign progressed', said a senior member of Miliband's team. 'We had an understandable reluctance initially to rule out deals, because we were never sure when we might need it. And we would have been stronger [in government] had we been able to do some deals. So we tried to keep our options open, until it became clear that it was hurting us.' Moreover, Falconer, in particular, was aware that ruling out a coalition would probably not close the subject down, but would simply move it on to other, even trickier, areas. It was also yet another example of where the interests of the party were diverging north and south of the border. In Scotland, Murphy and his colleagues wanted to delay ruling out any post-election deals with the SNP. They knew how this would come across to their electorate; it would not be seen as rejecting the SNP, but as a rejection of Scotland. Labour focus groups with swing voters produced a reaction to the idea that was 'violently negative, as if it would be a slight against Scotland'.[13] Miliband had intended to rule out a coalition on 7 March at an event in Scotland, but Murphy persuaded him to delay, and it took until 16 March before Labour ruled out a formal coalition, at an event in England ('there will be no SNP ministers in any government I lead', Miliband said). But since the SNP had in any case already ruled out a coalition with Labour, this changed little and – as Falconer had feared – merely raised other questions. If not a coalition, what about a confidence and supply arrangement in which the SNP formally agreed to support a Labour minority government without being in government themselves? What about other deals on a vote-by-vote basis? The SNP, helpfully, made it clear that they would be open to such arrangements. Nicola Sturgeon argued that the SNP would ensure that Labour was 'honest'. Alex Salmond was filmed joking that he would write a Labour government's budget. It was a joke – albeit not a very good one – but the SNP leader and ex-leader were, in Labour's view, playing the Conservative game.

The Conservative attacks were relentless (see Figure 6.2). In late January, the party released an image of Miliband and Salmond together: 'Your worst nightmare ... just got worse.' After Miliband visited Northern Ireland a few days later, Gerry Adams, the President of Sinn Fein, was added to the picture: 'Your worst nightmare ... just got even worse.' (It was a sign of how fevered possible post-election speculation was getting that the idea of the abstentionist Sinn Fein taking their seats at Westminster was even being discussed.) A Scottish equivalent followed ('Vote Eck, Get Ed'), as did online attack clips: Gerry Adams and Ed Miliband set to Grieg's 'In the Hall of the Mountain King' ('The SNP and Sinn Fein propping up Ed Miliband? Chaos for Britain') or Alex Salmond making Ed Miliband dance ('Put Mr Miliband into power. And then call the tune'). On 9 March, the Conservatives released a poster, featuring Alex Salmond looking down at a tiny Ed Miliband in his pocket, which they deployed in and around marginal constituencies in England and Wales.

The parties' digital campaigns also stepped up a gear. 2015 saw a clear qualitative change in the use of digital campaign tools from any previous British election. 'Everyone claimed that 2010 was the first digital election in British political history', wrote Craig Elder and Tom Edmonds, who ran the digital team for the Conservatives. 'Well we worked on it, and trust us – it really wasn't. None of the parties had a clue how to use digital effectively. But 2015 was different.'[14] Or, as one of Labour's digital team noted: 'This was the first digital campaign with firepower. We could cut through.' The debate over whether digital campaigning works is now essentially over: all the parties do it and they all think it is effective. Indeed, in different ways, they can all show that it works.[15]

One of Elder and Edmonds' maxims was: 'Be where your audience is – and ignore the places they aren't.' For almost all the parties, that meant Facebook, with almost all other platforms coming a poor second. Twitter, for example, was considered an elite platform – one used by journalists and commentators, but not swing voters. 'I'm not bothered about it at all', said one digital staffer. 'It's where the journalists are, it's not where people are. We'd do a bit, just to keep the hacks happy, but it's not important.' But Facebook, in the words of one of the SNP team, 'was the real deal'.[16] In their best month, Labour reached almost 16 million people from their Facebook page, with just over 11 million video views on it alone. The Conservatives claimed to be reaching

Figure 6.2 Scaremongering (part 2)

17 million people a week in total during the campaign. These figures are deceptively impressive – a video is counted as being watched on Facebook if someone watches the first three seconds – and many of these interactions will be little more than a video or graphic appearing on someone's Facebook page, but even allowing for this, the potential reach is now clearly considerable.

The parties also made extensive use of pre-roll adverts – the adverts that appear on YouTube before the video can be watched – and especially their extensive email lists, which were essential for fundraising and activist mobilisation. Indeed, plenty of digital staffers still consider email the most important digital tool available, particularly because of its ability to raise funds, although Facebook is now closing in fast. Labour's digital team raised over £3 million, which they claimed was a British record in online donations – 'and that buys a lot of mailshots or balloons'.

The Conservative SNP–Labour attack ads – and Labour's multiple NHS ads – are themselves good examples of how political campaigning has changed significantly in recent years as a result of the rise of digital. It has meant that much more varied creative imagery was generated and shared online in a way in which the formal campaign poster never used to be, and many of the more memorable graphics of the 2015 campaign only ever appeared online. The Web now also allows parties to make broadcast adverts much more like US campaign ads. These are much shorter than traditional party election broadcasts – the Conservative 'In the Hall of the Mountain King' clip ran for just 16 seconds – and often much more negative. They are posted on YouTube or on the party's own website, but the main mechanism for delivery to voters is through social media such as Twitter or Facebook, increasingly subverting the British ban on television advertising. The parties also put considerable efforts into targeting online material to swing voters in marginal constituencies (in a way that they cannot with party election broadcasts). The digital campaign is as much part of the ground war as it is the air war.

These adverts are usually produced quickly and inexpensively in-house, and allow parties to react very swiftly to events, and to innovate and adapt their message. The parties all use what is known as A/B Testing – or split testing – sending out two different versions of an email or posting different versions of a graphic to small samples of their audience in order to see which one gets greater interest and then tweaking the message accordingly. Some were sceptical about the difference that this could make.[17] 'It's crazy to get too distracted by this', said one of the parties' digital team. 'A one percent difference in [email] open rates for the Obama campaign was a massive difference.

A one percent difference in open rates for the Liberal Democrats is less important. You can get too complicated with this stuff.' But the differences could still be significant: a one-word change in a Labour fundraising email (changing 'the future' to 'our future') was estimated to increase revenue by £15,000 over a year. And in general, one of the key attributes of the digital campaign, as one of Labour's team put it, 'is that you can fail quickly'. Parties can discover something is not working and then move on.

When the Internet was first developing as a political tool, there was a debate about whether it would work to level the playing field between the parties. In retrospect, that debate looks naïve. Labour would make much of how their online campaign was organic and did not rely on paid adverts or similar. As one of their briefing notes said:

> The Tories are spending more than £100k a month on Facebook advertising, backed by donations from hedge funds and city donors, so they can afford to make sure their message is shown to people on social media. We don't have the budget to be able to do the same (in November last year, we spent 7% of what they did on online advertising) so instead we focus on making shareable campaigns that surprise and delight and rely on supporters to get the message out online by sharing.

Labour had particular success with two platforms: a personalised NHS timeline, which had more than a million users, and 'How many voters share your name?', which had more than 750,000 users. Both were very successful in harvesting emails and contact data. But where they could afford it, they were using paid online adverts – as did almost every other party – and privately they would admit to being envious of the amount of money that the Conservatives were able to spend on their digital campaign. As one of Labour's digital team noted: 'If we had five million in the bank, I'd be doing the same as the Tories.'

The rise of the SNP had one other significant impact on the election: it almost certainly reduced the profile of UKIP and Nigel Farage. They were no longer the new insurgent face of politics. In January 2015, *BuzzFeed* published an article entitled '25 Things That Will Definitely Happen in the General Election Campaign'. Number 6 was 'A UKIP candidate will say something ridiculous and be forced to resign'. Numbers 13, 17 and 25 all said the same thing. The *BuzzFeed* examples were deliberately far-fetched ('UKIP Candidate Says Gays Cause Ebola', 'UKIP Candidate Claims Bulgarian Immigrants are All Witches'), but they were only slightly more ridiculous than the real-life examples that did take place. In January, the party suspended its parliamentary candidate for Charnwood after he said that benefits claimants should not be allowed to drive ('These people really could catch the bus'). In March alone, the candidate for Carmarthen East and Dinefwr was suspended over financial irregularities, the candidate for Scunthorpe was briefly suspended after a complaint of harassment was made against him (although this was lifted a few days later), the candidate for Folkestone and Hythe (also an MEP) was suspended amid allegations of fraudulent expenses claims, and the following day the party suspended its candidate in Sunderland over allegations of workplace harassment, and the candidate for Westmorland and Lonsdale candidate resigned claiming 'open racism and sanctimonious bullying within the party'.

UKIP would, fairly, complain that there were plenty of other examples in other parties of candidates saying daft or offensive things. On 22 March, in perhaps the most bizarre example, the Conservative candidate in Dudley North, Afzal Amin, was suspended over allegations he had sought to collude with the English Defence League (EDL); he had discussed with the EDL a plan to march against a proposed mosque; the march would then be called off, enabling him to take the credit, and he pledged to act as the group's 'unshakeable ally' in Parliament if elected. He was swiftly dropped. Earlier that month, the Lib Dem candidate for Brent Central was forced to stand down after allegations that he was advising donors how to circumvent party funding laws. But still, this problem was worse for UKIP, and their candidate vetting was clearly a problem. It provided easy pickings for a press that was no longer as supportive.[18]

Despite these setbacks, UKIP started the year with high expectations. At a campaign launch on Canvey Island on 12 February, Farage announced ambitious spending plans for the NHS and defence, to be financed by cuts in overseas aid, the abandonment of HS2 and withdrawal from the EU. On 12 March, the party's immigration plans were set out. They included setting up a new immigration watchdog, a ban on unskilled immigrants for five years and the introduction of an Australian points-style points system for skilled applicants. But the main impact would be made by withdrawal from the EU and its commitment to freedom of movement.

Always eager for media opportunities, Farage did not want to be left out of the post-election speculation about coalitions. He declared that UKIP would not be part of any coalition (which, given both the likely number of seats they would win and the other parties' declared refusals to have anything to do with UKIP, was no great sacrifice). He added that a condition for supporting a minority government would be an in/out EU referendum to be held before the end of 2015, knowing full well that this would not happen, given that it precluded David Cameron's policy of having negotiations before a referendum. Nick Clegg stated the obvious when he said that he would not entertain a coalition which included UKIP.

UKIP's problems were not confined to their local candidates. The party did not avoid confusion over some of its policies, notably the different views expressed by spokesmen over anti-discrimination legislation and the role of private insurance in the NHS. The manifesto, due to be launched at Margate on 7 March, was not ready in time. When cynics wondered if the delay was to allow less time for scrutiny of the party's proposals, Farage countered by saying that it would enable the exciting policies to have more impact. Meanwhile, Suzanne Evans, the party's vice-chairman was given the task of trying to complete the manifesto.

For all their problems, however, UKIP still appeared on course for an electoral breakthrough. Matthew Goodwin, one of the academic experts on UKIP, told the *Daily Telegraph* that four seats for the party were already 'in the bag' and that it should win 'at least two more'. These included 'a far more convincing win for Farage [in Thanet South] than people currently acknowledge'.[19]

The Greens formally launched their election campaign on 24 February. The day did not go to plan. That morning, Natalie Bennett was interviewed by Nick Ferarri on LBC Radio and had what was widely described as a car crash interview. 'To be fair to Ms Bennett', wrote the *Daily Telegraph*'s sketch writer, 'Ferrari did ask her a lot of tough questions, such as what her policies were and how she would fund them.' The worst part came during a discussion of social housing:

> Ferarri: The cost of 500,000 homes, let's start with that. How much is that going to be?
> Bennett: Right, well, that's, um. You've got a total cost... Um. That we're... That will be spelt out in our manifesto.
> Ferrari: So you don't know?
> Bennett: No. Well. Er...

Some things are worse in print than in real life; this however was worse than it reads, and got worse as the interview went on.[20] Publicly, Bennett blamed a cold and what she described as 'brain fade'. Privately, her staff got blamed. 'There was a complaint that we didn't brief her', said one of her team. 'We did. It just didn't stay in.' There then followed the campaign launch event, a joint event with Caroline Lucas, who had heard the interview and was unimpressed. When journalists tried to question Bennett about her radio appearance, the chair of the meeting refused to let Bennett answer. It did little to rebuild her confidence.

Nor was this Bennett's first disastrous interview. She had also come unstuck in a *Daily Politics* interview with Andrew Neil in January, when she had been unable to explain details of party policy, repeatedly having to advise people to visit the Green Party website if they were interested in how the policies might work. Even when she was able to explain policy, she had problems justifying it. Neil asked her about the Green's policy for it not to be a crime to be a member of a terrorist organisation. Bennett at first attempted to deflect the question by suggesting it was a hangover from past party policy towards the African National Congress and then defended it on the principle of free speech. The policy was subsequently dropped within a fortnight. The Greens were discovering that surges have a downside. They bring with them an increase in scrutiny – and they were not well enough prepared for it.

Throughout this period private discussion – and public posturing – about the possibility of televised leadership debates continued, before being resolved on 21 March, just prior to the campaign formally beginning. The negotiations and their outcome are discussed further in Chapter 11. Labour were desperate for the debates to take place: they saw them as a chance to build up Ed Miliband's role and character, and to cut through some of the misunderstandings about him ('to see the real Ed Miliband'). Privately, though, they were not optimistic about them taking place: at the first meeting with the broadcasters, one of Labour's team declared that there was not 'a cat in hell's chance of this happening'. He added: 'If I was one of Cameron's advisors, I'd not let him do it, and nor will they.' This was a view the Conservatives shared. In late 2014, one of Cameron's team admitted that they were especially keen to avoid debating with Farage: 'We don't want UKIP but if we have to have Farage then we will insist that all minor parties take part.' He added that 'this will kill it as a spectacle'. This view was endorsed by Jim Messina, and Cameron's team also expected Sturgeon to do more damage to Miliband than Farage could inflict on Cameron.

Behind the scenes, the parties began their preparations for whatever debates might occur. Labour began first, in late 2014, and when it was still hoping for a more conventional series of head-to-head contests.

Believing that these were worth investing significant time and effort in, they undertook multiple full rehearsals, which were filmed, as well as sessions spent discussing phrasing and attack lines. Everyone involved felt the work had improved Miliband's performance significantly, whatever happened in the debates themselves. 'I wish we'd done that four years before', said one of those in his debate team. 'It made a huge difference to his ability to get his message across. It gave him a confidence that he could deal with anything that was going to come up. The slog – and it is a slog – of going through what works, what doesn't, how best to frame your message, really helped.' Preparing for the debates was one of the areas where even the more sceptical Labour insiders felt David Axelrod earned his money. 'If you want help with debate preps you have got to get an American', said one of Labour's team. 'They are just so familiar with the problems.'[21]

The Conservatives began later, once it became clear that they were not going to be able to dodge at least one debate. The US consultant Bill Knapp was used, as in 2010, to help develop lines, and they also performed multiple full rehearsals with seven podiums. Lib Dem rehearsals focused much more on the strategy than the messaging. Slightly scarred by his experience debating with Farage in 2014, Clegg felt it was important to spend less time on policy detail and more on delivery. 'Debates are emotional, not factual', said one of those involved, who felt that they had got this aspect wrong in the debates with Farage. The party carried out one full dress rehearsal, in the Ministry of Sound, with special advisors and party staff playing the other candidates.[22] Plaid Cymru carried out a full rehearsal, as well as having sessions in which they discussed lines to take.

The Greens were annoyed by the eventual decision to involve the SNP and Plaid in the debates as it diluted their impact. As one of the Greens team said: 'We were no longer the only woman on the panel presenting an anti-austerity message. What we say, and what they say, isn't really all that different.' The internal party dynamics were also difficult. Partly because of Bennett's lacklustre media performances, Caroline Lucas was said to be 'chomping at the bit' to take part in one of the debates, and the party put forward a bid to the broadcasters to have Lucas and Bennett participate in one debate each. The official line was that the two 'felt it was right that they share the responsibility, as leader of the party and its MP'. 'It would have killed our leader', said one of the Greens' staff, who was not disappointed when the broadcasters turned the bid down. The party had originally intended to do just one full rehearsal, but ended up doing a second in order to try to rebuild

Bennett's confidence, only partially successfully. The Greens filmed both of their rehearsals, but as one of those involved said: 'We didn't look at the videos. Natalie didn't like the way she came across on video, and we didn't want to do anything more to damage her confidence, which by that stage was already a problem.'[23]

Both the SNP and UKIP held sessions to discuss tactics and phrasing, but with no formal rehearsals. Farage is the sort of person who does not pre-plan speeches, let alone rehearse debates. Similarly, 'That's not Nicola's style' said one of the SNP team about the idea of formal rehearsals, although Sturgeon was building on extensive experience in debates in the referendum, where she had routinely bested rival politicians. She was by far the most experienced of any of the seven candidates in the format.

The Lib Dems had to be persuaded by George Osborne to agree to a Budget on 18 March. It was fiscally neutral. Aware of the misgivings that his December spending statement had caused among Conservative MPs, Osborne slowed the pace of future spending cuts. He introduced Help to Buy ISAs for first-time house buyers and abolished the tax on savings for all but the rich. Measures that pleased the Lib Dems included raising the personal tax allowance and the bank levy, and providing extra funding for mental health services in England. Osborne also held out the prospect of abolishing inheritance tax on properties worth up to £1 million. The Lib Dems had by now tired of the Budget being seen as an 'Osborne moment' in which he took all the credit and, the following day, in a symbolic final act of differentiation, Danny Alexander presented a Lib Dem alternative budget – complete with yellow despatch box – to a virtually empty Commons chamber. It was not the party's finest moment.

By the end of March, the parties had advanced drafts of their manifestos and some idea of their red lines or not-so-red lines in the event of coalition negotiations. In February, at Cameron's request, Jo Johnson rewrote his pre-Christmas draft of the manifesto (see p. 60). The changes were in language and structure. There had been three sections to the manifesto – the long-term economic plan, a strong society and Britain in the world. It was then decided to make the economic plan more relevant to people and highlight the theme of security and opportunity at all stages in life. Some of the ideas were discussed at the regular Conservative political cabinet meeting on Tuesdays. Johnson visited Cabinet ministers to discuss the relevant section of the manifesto with them, but deliberately so late in the day that it was difficult to change much. And given that Cameron and Osborne had agreed the text beforehand, Johnson was in a strong position. Osborne was aware that some of the policies might have to be traded away, including his fiscal plans, if the party entered a coalition.

The Labour manifesto was largely the work of the leader's office and relied heavily on Torsten Bell and his team of policy researchers. From January, it was discussed at regular Wednesday morning meetings. John Cruddas and Jonathan Rutherford wrote a lengthy first draft that was, according to readers, 'heavy on big ideas and philosophy but short on practical policies'. It was then taken over by Bell. The document incorporated many of the policies accepted at the National Policy Forum in the summer. It was left to Angela Eagle, chair of the Policy Forum, to agree with shadow ministers the sections relating to their responsibilities. The title was to be 'Britain can be better', together with a line on the front cover: 'Britain only succeeds when working people succeed.' Miliband had used the phrase in a speech in November 2014 and again in March 2015. It was a suggestion of David Axelrod's and had tested well in focus groups.

Both Labour and the Conservatives had already formed teams to negotiate with other parties, particularly the Lib Dems, in the event of a hung parliament. The prospect of such a coalition caused some resentment among staff in Number 10. 'They [the Lib Dems] will lose a lot of votes and seats but they are the only people here who can be sure of returning after 7 May', said a member of Cameron's staff. On 24 March, Lord Falconer and Tim Livesey handed the Cabinet Secretary their plans for reorganising Whitehall departments and their policy proposals if Labour won the election.

On the Monday of the last week of the Parliament, the BBC aired an interview with the Prime Minister in which he was asked how long he wanted to remain in Number 10. He made it clear that he would stay for a full second term, 'but I think after that it will be time for a new leadership'. 'Terms are like shredded wheat', he said: 'two are wonderful but three might just be too many'.[24] The interviewer, fellow old Etonian James Landale, had not been tipped-the-wink to ask the question, and the story caused consternation among Cameron's aides and surprised his media team. The aim of the interview had been for the Prime Minister to rule out standing down after any proposed EU referendum, not to announce that he would do so by the end of the Parliament.

'If the election has just begun...'

Matt, *Daily Telegraph*, 31 March 2015 (© Matt/*The Telegraph*)

'Sometimes', Landale said, 'you ask a politician a question and they answer. It's a rare occasion.'[25]

On Wednesday, the Conservatives regained the initiative at the final Prime Minister's Questions (PMQs) of the Parliament with another straight answer. Labour had launched a poster warning about Conservative plans on VAT the day before and Ed Miliband asked whether the Prime Minister would 'rule out a rise in VAT'. The Prime Minister's direct response – 'The answer is yes' – was not what Labour had expected.[26] 'The look on Mr Miliband's face', wrote Michael Deacon, in the *Daily Telegraph*: 'It was as if an eagle had swooped out of the sky and swiped the sandwich from his hands.'[27] The focus shifted immediately onto Labour's plans for National Insurance; within hours, Labour had been forced to rule out any rise in National Insurance and basic tax rates. The IFS (which had by now acquired an almost oracle-like status) noted that in the space of 12 hours, the main parties had ruled out increases on the taxes that raise 60% of revenues and had thus boxed themselves in in the event of an economic downturn.[28] 'This is', wrote the BBC's Nick Robinson, in his *Election Notebook*, 'no way to make tax policy.'[29]

The Conservatives claimed they had lured Labour into this trap, when the Chancellor had refused to rule out an increase in VAT in evidence to the Treasury Select Committee. But this sort of tricksy political manoeuvring could easily backfire, and Tory delight at their tactical genius lasted just 24 hours, with the final day of the Parliament then seeing a too-clever-by-half attempt by the Conservatives to stitch up the Speaker, John Bercow, backfiring. With no warning and no discussion with the Opposition (or the Speaker), the Conservatives put down a motion to change the method by which the Speaker was re-elected; the move was so transparent that it galvanised support for the Speaker.[30] Labour MPs – down after the debacle of PMQs the day before – rushed back to Westminster and, along with a handful of Conservatives, voted down the plans. When the Labour field team complained about MPs losing a day's campaigning, the response from the Labour whips was straight-forward: if the election resulted in Labour being a minority government, they would need the Speaker's goodwill, as they would if they ended up in opposition. 'What a strange end to a Parliament that has been crawling along for a good long while', wrote Isabel Hardman, 'it is ending in uproar.'[31] Parliament was prorogued later the same day.

That evening saw the first of the TV programmes designed to replace the head-to-head debates that had so dominated the 2010 election – and which the Conservatives had been so keen not to repeat. The replacement programmes of 2015 had nothing like the same impact on the campaign as the debates had had in 2010. It was not just that they had smaller audiences, but that in 2010 they had been the key structural moments of the campaign, around which everything else had been organised. In 2015, by contrast, the mixture of formats and lack of head-to-head challenges meant that whilst the various programmes remained important moments – and ones for which the parties prepared carefully – they were not to be defining moments.

This did not stop the broadcasters pretending otherwise. The first programme, *Cameron and Miliband Live: The Battle for Number 10,* was hosted jointly by Channel 4 and Sky, and was given the sort of hyperbolic build-up that would have accompanied a Foreman–Ali rematch. The programme was a hybrid: half interview by Jeremy Paxman, half Q&A with members of the public (see p. 285). Cameron was widely felt to have under-performed, being discomforted on questions on food banks and zero-hours contracts (the Conservatives had taken a deliberate decision not to rise to Paxman's provocations, which they regretted afterwards); Miliband, by contrast, was felt to have performed relatively well and above expectations. However, as one member of the Shadow Cabinet put it: 'Expectations were so low that he could knock over the podium, while the belt snapped on his trousers and people would still say "he was better than I thought".' In all of these events, there is a tendency for partisans and commentators to get very excited about individual moments – supposed gaffes, zingers, game-changers – despite the lack of any evidence that the watching public think that way. The immediate *Guardian*/ICM poll had Cameron ahead, but Miliband's team took heart from the fact that he had performed better amongst undecided voters and that he had emerged unscathed. Ironically, given how much Labour had prepared and practised for the various broadcasts, the one most memorable line of Miliband's performance – 'Am I tough enough? Hell yes, I am tough enough' – was ad-libbed. 'It's fair to say', said one of his advisers, 'that if anyone had suggested he was about [to] say "Hell yes" in the interview, I would have run across the room to stop him.'[32] By contrast, Cameron's team accepted privately that he had under-performed and stepped up preparations for the next debate.

Even with the election now just weeks away, election fever was not sweeping the nation. The polling company Populus asked a regular open-ended question asking people to name the top news story that they had noticed that week. In the last week before the election formally began, the top story was a plane crash in the Alps, mentioned by 63% of people. Just 1% mentioned David Cameron ruling out a third term in office and 1% mentioned the TV election debates; this was the same percentage as mentioned Zayn Malik leaving the boy band One Direction.

Table 6.1 YouGov monthly average vote shares, January–March 2015

	Con	*Lab*	*Lib Dem*	*UKIP*	*Greens*	*Others*	*Con lead over Lab*
Jan	32	33	7	15	7	5	–1
Feb	33	34	7	14	7	5	–1
March	34	34	7	14	6	5	0

Nothing the parties did appeared to make much of a difference. The polls took it in turns to provide sporadic encouragement for the main parties. ICM on 17 February reported a swing in the battleground seats to the Conservatives of 1.5% and a 6% Conservative lead. A week earlier, the *Sunday Times* YouGov poll had reported a 4% lead for Labour. But once the mass of polling was averaged out, there was essentially a remarkable stability in the polls over the three months prior to the campaign beginning (see Table 6.1). The polls were unanimous in showing that unless something major changed during the short campaign, it was very unlikely that any party would end up with an overall majority, that Labour and the SNP would have more votes and seats than they had gained in 2010, and that the Conservatives and the Lib Dems would have fewer of both. Thanks to its collapse in Scotland, Labour may have had next to no chance of winning a majority, but with the SNP refusing to support the Conservatives under any circumstances, it appeared to *The Spectator*'s Fraser Nelson at the end of March that: 'Red Ed is home and dry.'[33]

Right at the end of the Parliament, in a near-deserted Portcullis House, we interviewed one of Labour's campaign team. If you could change one thing about your campaign, we asked, what would it be? 'Money', he replied immediately.

He paused: 'And no point hiding it, the leader ratings are poor.' Another pause: 'And they lead on economic competence.'

'Yet you're still in with a real chance of winning', we said.

'I know', he said, '*amazing*, isn't it?'

Chronology of events from 1 January 2015 to 29 March 2015

1 Jan D. Cameron unveils Con campaign poster, 'Let's stay on the road to a stronger economy'.

4 Jan Cameron tells *Daily Mail* he 'won't rule out' leaving EU if negotiations aren't successful.

5 Jan E. Miliband launches Lab election campaign. G. Osborne warns of £1,200 hidden tax and debt 'bomb shell' under Lab. J. Murphy announces extra 1,000 nurses in Scotland funded by Lab UK-wide mansion tax.

6 Jan Parties clash over A&E 'crisis'.

7 Jan Gunmen kill 12 at satirical magazine *Charlie Hebdo* in Paris.

8 Jan Police officer shot dead in Paris.

9 Jan Osborne says tackling terrorism is 'the national priority'. *Charlie Hebdo* gunmen killed outside Paris, while four killed with gunman at siege in Paris shop.

11 Jan Cameron joins world leaders for solidarity march in Paris. Asked four times on *Andrew Marr Show* whether he'd consider deal with SNP, Miliband refuses to answer.

12 Jan Cameron outlines the six key election themes: deficit, jobs, taxes, education, housing and retirement.

13 Jan IFS warns Lab spending plans risk adding £170 billion to national debt.

14 Jan Miliband, N. Clegg and N. Farage write to Cameron saying that they will go ahead with TV debates without him.

15 Jan IMF hails UK economic recovery.

18 Jan Clegg rules out being part of coalition including UKIP. Farage launches campaign to become MP for Thanet South.

19 Jan Lord Mandelson attacks Labour's mansion tax as 'crude' and 'short-termist'.

20 Jan P. Hammond says Britain 'wide open to abuse' by 'freeloading' EU migrants.

22 Jan Ipsos MORI poll gives SNP 28-point lead over Lab, suggesting party could win all but four seats in Scotland. P. Robinson says DUP could work with either Labour or Conservatives in a hung parliament.

23 Jan	Former Conservative Home Secretary L. Brittan dies. Broadcasters say they will 'empty chair' party leaders who do not take part in television debates. Con launch poster: 'Your worst nightmare ... just got worse.'
25 Jan	Greek election victory for Syriza, which had pledged to renegotiate country's bailout terms.
26 Jan	Mandelson advises Lab to prepare thoroughly for coalition talks. Syriza and Independent Greeks form new coalition government.
27 Jan	Cameron and Miliband mark 100 days until election by focusing on key messages – cuts in benefits for working-age people and greater resources for the NHS respectively. A. Milburn and Lord Hutton criticise nature of Lab campaign.
29 Jan	Lord Kinnock criticises critics of Labour's campaign.
30 Jan	G. Shapps rules out deal with UKIP after the election. Unite union pledges £1.5 million to Lab in run-up to election.
1 Feb	Acting chief executive of Boots says that Lab victory would be 'a catastrophe' for UK.
3 Feb	W. Hague outlines plans to stop Scottish MPs from voting on English issues. Attempting to calm growing rows between Lab and business, E. Balls struggles to recall name of prominent Lab business backer on *Newsnight*. Greens ditch policy of decriminalising membership of terrorist organisations.
4 Feb	Survation poll for Unite union shows Clegg 10% behind Lab in his seat.
5 Feb	LDs outline financial policies.
6 Feb	Kings Fund publishes report criticising Coalition's NHS reforms.
9 Feb	No. 10, Treasury and Bank of England hold emergency talks over possible repercussions to Greece leaving the Eurozone.
10 Feb	Cameron tells British Chambers of Commerce that as economy recovers they must give employees a pay rise. Miliband criticised for not attending the same conference.
11 Feb	Lab launches 'Woman to Woman' tour. Miliband accuses Prime Minister of being 'dodgy' at PMQs regarding HSBC tax avoidance scandal. N. Dodds says DUP could 'do business' with Lab in a hung parliament. Greece and Eurozone in stalemate as negotiations fail to produce framework for further talks over relieving Greece's debt crisis.
12 Feb	Farage launches UKIP's election campaign. Clegg launches front page of LD manifesto, identifying key policies for coalition negotiations.

14 Feb Gunman kills one and wounds three in attack on café in Copenhagen.

15 Feb Perpetrator of attack in Copenhagen kills security guard and wounds two. Attacker then killed in shootout with police.

16 Feb Talks between Greece and Eurozone creditors break down. ICM poll for *Guardian* puts the Con up 6 points on previous month, 4 points ahead of Lab.

17 Feb H. Yeo, former chair of Labour's National Executive Committee, resigns from party to support UKIP.

18 Feb ECB agrees €3.3 billion more in emergency funds for Greek banks. Kinnock defends Labour's mansion tax, describing it as costing 'little more than a slap up lunch'.

20 Feb Eurogroup brokers agree an agreement between Greece and Eurozone for four-month loan extension.

22 Feb A. Rosindell queries whether a pregnant Lab shadow minister could have her baby and give possible Cabinet job 'her full attention'.

23 Feb Two former Foreign Secretaries – Sir M. Rifkind and J. Straw – are suspended from their respective party's whips after being filmed apparently offering access for cash.

24 Feb M. Rifkind announces that he will step down as an MP at the election and resign Chair of the Intelligence and Security Committee. Greens launch campaign following disastrous interview by their leader, N. Bennett, on LBC Radio. UKIP's LGBT chair quits, concerned party leadership had 'failed to set a gay friendly tone'.

26 Feb Net flow of immigration into UK in 2014 announced as 298,000.

27 Feb Coalition announces 'St David's Day Agreement', handing more powers to Welsh Government. Plaid denounces it as 'third-rate devolution'.

28 Feb Farage at UKIP Spring Conference denies rumours about his health.

4 Mar Farage sets out UKIP's immigration policy. Following longest decline in living standards this century, average household incomes are back to the levels before banking crisis. Cameron rules out head-to-head debate with Miliband.

5 Mar Ex Lab Prime Minister T. Blair donates £1,000 to 106 Labour Party candidates. Several make point of rejecting it.

6 Mar Former Con Prime Minister J. Major says that Miliband must 'summon up the courage' to rule out a deal with the SNP.

7 Mar	Lord Baker suggests the need to consider a Tory–Labour coalition to stop SNP creating a constitutional crisis in a hung parliament. N. Sturgeon rules out coalition with Con, but says SNP would support minority Lab government to make it 'effective'.
8 Mar	Lab to legislate for leaders' debates at every election. Cobra beer founder, Lord Bilimoria, says deal between Lab and SNP 'terrifying' and 'disaster' for UK economy.
9 Mar	Con launch poster depicting Miliband in the pocket of Salmond.
11 Mar	Mandelson predicts Lab will not win majority.
12 Mar	Former LD chief fundraiser and candidate for Brent Central resigns after being taped advising supporter how to avoid funding laws. Dodds says DUP's coalition demands include referendum on Europe, but excludes partnership with the SNP. Farage forced to clarify remarks implying he wanted to abolish anti-discrimination legislation. Businesswoman and star of *The Apprentice,* K. Brady, says Miliband 'does not understand business'.
13 Mar	Miliband exposed as having two kitchens at his £2 million town house.
14 Mar	Miliband announces five key election pledges. Farage says UKIP would support a minority Con government in return for EU referendum before Christmas.
15 Mar	*Sunday Times* reports one-third of Shadow Cabinet have complaints about Miliband's 'miserable' campaign. Lord Heseltine compares Farage to E. Powell. Farage will quit as UKIP leader if he fails to become an MP. Clegg tells Spring Conference that LD 'will do so much better than anyone thinks'. Danny Alexander calls for tactical voting in Scotland to stop SNP.
16 Mar	Sturgeon argues SNP will be a benefit to Britain acting as 'constructive' partner at Westminster. Miliband rules out coalition with SNP. Ofcom grants UKIP two PEBs, Greens one.
17 Mar	Cameron backs BBC's plan for one-off debate between leaders of seven main parties. DUP and UUP agree electoral pact to stand one unionist candidate in four Northern Ireland seats.
18 Mar	Budget. Savings of £30 billion forecast during next Parliament. Key announcements include: crackdown on tax avoidance; 20% reduction in Corporation Tax; increase in minimum wage; rise in bank levy; introduction of 'Help to Buy' ISA for first-time buyers; abolition of employers' National Insurance

for under-21s; rises in tax-free personal allowance and rate at which 40p rate paid; first £1,000 of interest on savings made tax free; cut in tax relief on pensions from £1.25 million to £1 million; freeze on duty for petrol and wine, cuts for beer, cider and whisky.

19 Mar UKIP MEP and Folkestone and Hythe candidate, J. Atkinson, suspended from the party amid allegations of plot to make fraudulent expenses claims. Danny Alexander announces LD 'alternative' budget in Commons.

20 Mar LD Lord Strasburger resigns after fundraising scandal. UKIP suspends candidate in Sunderland due to allegations of workplace harassment, and Westmorland and Lonsdale candidate resigns claiming 'open racism and sanctimonious bullying within the party'.

21 Mar Broadcasters and parties agree format of TV debates. UKIP faces claims it has failed to kick out three senior figures with links to National Front.

22 Mar Con candidate in Dudley North, A. Amin, suspended over allegations he sought to collude with EDL. Salmond says SNP landslide will allow him to dictate Lab budgets.

23 Mar Cameron tells the BBC that he will not serve a third term as Prime Minister. UKIP expel Atkinson. Amin quits as Con candidate. DUP outline extra £1 billion funding for Northern Ireland as price for supporting Lab or Con minority government.

24 Mar E. Balls vows no VAT rises under Lab. Before Treasury Committee, Osborne refuses five times to say he will not raise VAT. Cameron heckled at Age UK's rally. Inflation falls to 0%.

25 Mar Con attack Salmond's 'deeply sinister' plans to oust Con government. Mandelson concerned by Miliband's campaign strategy. Cameron rules out VAT rises at PMQs.

26 Mar Attempt by the government to oust Speaker backfires. Cameron and Miliband interviewed by Jeremy Paxman.

27 Mar Miliband launches Lab campaign proposing cap on profits that private companies can make from NHS.

28 Mar Con promise extra £8 billion funding for NHS.

29 Mar *Sunday Times* reports post-interview 'bounce' for Miliband, with poll putting Lab 4 points ahead. Lab donor, Dr A. Allam, says Cameron has best economic policies. Lab election vice-chair, L. Powell, admits the party would borrow more money if it won the election. E. Balls denies this next day.

Notes

1. Isabel Hardman, 'Tories Drop Weak Policy Areas for "Six Election Priorities" Launch', blogs.new.spectator.co.uk, 12 January 2015.
2. One of many examples where Labour's lack of funding hurt their campaign: these were mass leaflet drops rather than targeted direct mail, where the message could be segmented for individual audiences. Some in Brewer's Green also queried whether it was wise to mention Cameron by name.
3. See Nick Robinson, *Election Notebook*. Bantam, 2015, p. 257.
4. On Twitter: @rafaelbehr (8 September 2014).
5. Labour's calculation was that the DUP would, almost inevitably, end up preferring a deal with the Conservatives, whatever the offer, but that it was still worth trying.
6. When Labour originally announced their plan to introduce a cap of £6,000 in 2011, the policy had been attacked for precisely that reason, but Labour's position then had been that it was an interim measure, before moving to a graduate tax, a defence that had gone by 2015.
7. *The Observer*, 1 March 2015.
8. Rosie Campbell, 'Following the Pink Battle Bus: Where are the Women Voters in 2015?', www.britishelectionstudy.com, 16 February 2015. Even when this had been pointed out (repeatedly) to Labour, they carried on repeating the claim.
9. For a slightly anguished attempt, see Sarah Childs, 'Pink Stinks But Labour's Bus is a Welcome Sight on the Road', www.theconversation.com, 12 February 2015.
10. Quite how extraordinary, however, still only dawned on people as the months went on. The bookmakers Paddy Power had an over/under seat market for SNP seats. In mid-January, the cut-off was at 31.5 seats; by mid-February, this had increased to 38.5 and, by mid-March, to 43.5, where it stayed for April. Only in May did it tip over the 50 mark.
11. See also the excellent *Project Fear* by Joe Pike (Biteback, 2015).
12. Iain Watson, *Five Million Conversations* (Luath Press, 2015) is very good on the strategic problems that Labour faced over this, p. 49.
13. Pike, *Project Fear*, p. 214.
14. Craig Elder and Tom Edmonds, '2015 Really was the First Digital General Election: Here are 7 Lessons You Should Know', *Daily Telegraph*, 23 July 2015.
15. One of the advantages of digital campaigning is that the data on things like click-through rates, or the length of time a video is watched or how often it is shared, can be constantly monitored in a way that more traditional campaigning cannot be.
16. It was not just that Facebook has higher audience penetration, especially amongst the groups that the parties wanted to target; it was also that it was easier, and cheaper, for the parties to target its use geographically.
17. One thing about A/B Testing that most of the parties agreed on was as follows: 'It's completely random. You can't predict what will work and what won't' (which is why it is important to test). But they did learn tricks, over the campaign, to encourage people to share content. One was to say something had been just announced, even when the substantive part of the policy had long been public. 'People will share it, because it makes them seem in the know. It's "look, I know, I know politicians, I know stuff, I'm important".'

18. After the election, Suzanne Evans was to write on Facebook: 'Much better candidate vetting needed. Can't weed out every idiot but I think we could do better' (20 May 2015).
19. 'UKIP Already Has Four Seats "in the Bag", Says Leading Expert Matthew Goodwin', *Daily Telegraph*, 4 March 2015.
20. Once he had finally got some estimates from her, Ferrari exclaimed: 'Five hundred thousand homes? £2.7 billion? What are they made of? Plywood?'
21. Axelrod was in fact just one of four American advisors Labour used; there was also Labour's pollster Stan Greenberg, Mike Sheehan, who had been involved in coaching for every US presidential debate since 1988, and Mike Donilon, who had advised Joe Biden on debate preparation.
22. For the Conservatives, Rupert Harrison played Ed Miliband, Jeremy Hunt played Clegg (as he had done in 2010), Oliver Dowden was Farage, Andrew Dunlop was Sturgeon, Meg Powell-Chandler was Bennett, and Laura Trott was Wood. It perhaps says something for how peripherally the Conservatives viewed Plaid that the last was described to us by our source as 'the Plaid lady'. The Labour team varied, although Alastair Campbell often played Cameron and Kezia Dugdale, Labour's Deputy Scottish Leader, was a very convincing Nicola Sturgeon.
23. There was a particular problem getting Bennett to deliver answers of the right length. She is not a fan of scripted text; she disdains what she calls 'The Tony Blair thing' and would keep going off on tangents, over-running. 'You want to say to her', said one of those involved, "I'm sorry but you are a politician, this is what you have to do".'
24. He added: 'I'm not saying all prime ministers necessarily go mad or even go mad at the same rate.'
25. See James Landale, 'Has David Cameron Opened Pandora's Box?', www.bbc.co.uk, 23 March 2015. The filming had been done on the preceding Saturday, but Craig Oliver had not been present and the Conservatives did not make their own audio recording of the interview. The party initially tried to argue that the Prime Minister was – as planned – simply ruling out standing down after the referendum, but the transcript of the interview made that line untenable.
26. Labour had a VAT attack film ready for use after the last PMQs of the Parliament; it just required a clip of the Prime Minister prevaricating to be dropped into it. His answer ruling out any increase meant that ad was never seen.
27. Michael Deacon, 'PMQs Sketch: David Cameron Drops Ed Miliband into a VAT of Gunge', *Daily Telegraph*, 25 March 2015.
28. 'Tories and Labour Have Boxed Themselves in on Taxation, Claims IFS', *The Guardian*, 25 March 2015.
29. Robinson, *Election Notebook*, p. 317.
30. The merits of the case – why should the Speaker, now elected by secret ballot, not be re-elected the same way – became secondary to the way in which the Conservatives had tried to bounce the vote onto the Commons.
31. Isabel Hardman, 'Parliament Finishes in Uproar over Speaker Vote', blogs.spectator.co.uk, 26 March 2015.
32. Patrick Wintour, 'The Undoing of Ed Miliband', *The Guardian*, 3 June 2015.
33. 'YouGov/*Sunday Times* Poll Puts Labour 4 Points Ahead. Be Afraid', blogs.new.spectator.co.uk, 28 March 2015.

7
Dead Cats and Bogy Men: The National Campaign

Launching Labour's election campaign at Olympic Park on 27 March, Ed Miliband declared: 'Like so many races here during the Olympics, it will go to the wire. Neck and neck.'[1] This was not just the sort of thing that has to be said by any politician running for office; it was what the parties, behind the scenes, all genuinely thought. Throughout the campaign, the polls consistently appeared to indicate that no one party would win a majority in the House of Commons. There would be an occasional flutter of interest caused by a poll indicating a small shift in the parties' standing (although such a shift was almost never larger than the margin of error inherent in polling), only for everyone to calm down again when the next poll showed that everything had returned to normal. Later, after the results were declared, Miliband and most of those around him came to believe that Labour were probably behind throughout the whole of the short campaign. But at the time, he and his campaign team believed the race was neck-and-neck – as did those in the other parties. Even though the Conservative campaign team had higher predictions for the number of seats they might gain than those predicted by the public polling (see p. 250), not a single Conservative strategist's predictions during the campaign were for an outright majority. By the end of the campaign, every strategist in every party was expecting a hung parliament.

'If the polls had reflected reality', said one of Miliband's closest advisers, 'it would have been a totally different campaign. The agenda would have been about a second Tory term.'[2] Or as one of Nick Clegg's advisers put it: 'Had we realised what the result would have been, there would have been a different message: "The Tories are going to win, and they're going to eat your baby".' There was therefore a significant disjuncture between the campaign as fought – what people thought they were doing at the time – and what it now appears, with the benefit of hindsight, was happening. As one senior broadsheet journalist admitted after the election: 'I feel we reported something that was fundamentally untrue. I've never been so angry as a journalist. Our entire coverage was flawed.' But campaigns are not fought or reported with the benefit of hindsight, and the almost universally held view that the election would result in a hung parliament, in which either of the main parties could emerge as the winner, dominated the campaign and determined the way it was fought.

After the election, a myth developed that the role of the SNP and its possible future influence on the government only became significant as a result of Nicola Sturgeon's excellent performances in the party leaders' debates (discussed below). But the future role of the SNP was an ever-present issue throughout the campaign. When Labour launched their campaign at Olympic Park, Conservative activists turned up outside the event wearing Alex Salmond masks. Similar Conservative disruption of Labour events continued throughout the campaign and aggravated the already poor relations between the party and *The Sun* newspaper, which Labour believed was involved in passing information about their events to the Conservatives. That weekend, when the SNP held their largest ever campaign conference in Glasgow, interviews with Sturgeon focused on the role that SNP MPs could play in any hung parliament and the 'progressive alliances' that could be built with other parties. 'We'd be open to some arrangement [with Labour]', she said, such as a confidence and supply deal, 'but if there wasn't an arrangement like that that was possible, then we would use our influence on an issue by issue basis.' The Conservative response was 'it is the SNP's sworn intention to hold Ed Miliband hostage in Downing Street and dictate terms on how Britain is governed ... We cannot let this happen to our country'. It was a message they were to repeat relentlessly throughout the campaign.

The Conservative focus on Ed Miliband as an individual was also ever-present. At the party's Spring Forum that weekend, Cameron had said: 'I know what this role needs – and frankly, I don't think Ed Miliband has it. Some might say "don't make this personal" ... but when it comes to who's Prime Minister, the personal is national.' Parliament was dissolved on Monday 30 March; after visiting the Queen, David Cameron's speech outside Number 10 mentioned Miliband by name

'They're off'

McWilliam, *The Week*, 4 April 2015

three times. Britain faced a 'stark choice', he said. 'The next Prime Minister walking through that door will be me or Ed Miliband.' As the campaign went on, the Conservatives were to merge both messages into one, to talk about an 'SNP–Ed Miliband government', or the extent to which the SNP would dominate Miliband: 'we saw how Nicola Sturgeon and the SNP would walk all over Ed Miliband'; 'he's in the pocket of Alex Salmond and Nicola Sturgeon has him on a leash'; 'Nicola Sturgeon knows she will be pulling Ed Miliband's strings if he gets into Downing Street'.[3] More than 60% of the press releases put out by the Conservatives during the short campaign mentioned the SNP or Nicola Sturgeon. These attacks intensified as the campaign went on, but they were ever-present.

Nick Clegg had a separate audience with the Queen on the same day (30 March), before which he told reporters: 'It is my view that the era of single-party government is now over in British politics' (in getting this wrong, he was at least in good company), emphasising a message that was to run throughout the Lib Dem campaign: 'About the very last thing the country now needs is a lurch to the left or the right and yet that is exactly what the Conservative and Labour parties are now threatening.'

In policy terms, the election began, as the year had begun, with the NHS. Labour's NHS policy, launched at the Olympic Park event, introduced a profit cap on NHS contracts worth more than £500,000. Labour always struggled publicly to explain why this cap was arbitrarily set at 5% or, indeed, why it applied to some organisations working in the NHS but not to others, and behind the scenes there was doubt about the wisdom of leading on the issue of NHS 'privatisation'. Those involved admitted it was difficult to write a serious press release bemoaning an increase of private finance in the NHS from 4% to 6% as somehow marking the end of civilisation, and whilst Labour's own polling found health to be an important issue, the public's concerns focused on waiting times and quality of care rather than the involvement of private finance. One staffer who queried the wisdom of the approach was told that the policy would at least appeal to Labour's base. The Conservatives too began with health policy, stressing plans for seven-day NHS service and additional investment, agreeing to fully fund the five-year plan drawn up by Sir Simon Stevens, the head of NHS England. Labour felt they could not match these pledges without breaking their spending limits, which led to the election beginning with a sense of political cross-dressing, Labour being out-spent on the NHS, but appearing to be economically more cautious. Both parties were trying to close down issues they knew were potentially difficult for them.

Throughout the campaign, the Conservatives often struggled to explain where money was coming from to fund their policies – or indeed where the £12 billion of welfare cuts they had promised would materialise. George Osborne made it clear that the Conservatives would only publish details of planned welfare cuts after the election. This issue would dog them throughout the campaign, but it was a conscious strategic choice on their part. As one of those in the Treasury team said, 'we didn't want lots of detail on cuts and the correct calculation was that our track record and economic competence ratings would see us through'. Labour could only look on in admiration and frustration. 'We would never have got away with that', one of Labour's team noted. 'And that was because we never got the fundamentals right ... We were never off the hook of economic credibility.'

The only TV debate in which David Cameron and Ed Miliband would appear on stage together took place on 2 April. Filmed at MediaCity UK in Salford, *The ITV Leaders' Debate* featured seven party leaders, including two, Nicola Sturgeon and Leanne Wood, who were not even standing as candidates in the election. Despite being two hours long, the number of participants meant there was time for just four questions and discussion, along with an opening and closing statement.[4]

Although the parties had no advance knowledge of the questions to be asked, they did not find it difficult to predict the sort of topics that would come up, with questions focusing on the deficit, the NHS, immigration and (the only one which slightly surprised the panellists) the future for young people in Britain. In addition to rehearsing specific answers ('Sixty seconds allows you to tell a little story, with a start, a middle and an end, and each of those has to have a point', as one of those involved put it), the parties' preparations also involved strategic choices about how to approach the debates. With seven and then five participants, they all knew that the dynamics of these debates were going to be much messier than in the three-way debates in 2010, and the parties had to work out what message they wanted to get across – and who they wanted to talk to.[5] For the three largest parties, the plan was mostly to focus their fire almost entirely on each other. As one of the Labour team who had helped Miliband prepare for the debates put it: 'We didn't want to be in any fucking 5– and 7-way debates in the first place, so we had to make them into something else.' Labour's plan was therefore to attempt to draw the contrast with David Cameron, summed up as: 'There's a big fundamental choice in this election. These other people are lovely, but it's me or him. Who do you want?'[6] The Lib Dems, similarly, wanted to turn the debate into an ersatz three-way: Cameron versus Miliband versus Clegg. 'We didn't want to engage directly with the others', said one of those working with Clegg. 'We didn't want to spend the time fighting with them.'[7] During the only formal seven-person rehearsal they held, the Lib Dems stood Clegg between Wood and Bennett deliberately in order to work out how best to avoid getting sucked into debate with the minor parties. The Conservatives' goal was to try to remain aloof, to bracket all the opposition parties together, and to present Cameron as Prime Ministerial and a cut above.

This would all give the smaller parties freedom to land blows without much risk of retaliation. As *The Economist* noted of Ed Miliband's general lack of engagement with Nicola Sturgeon: 'Jim Murphy, the leader of Scottish Labour, must have been tearing his hair out.'[8] In turn, their targets were primarily to be the larger parties and not each other. Three – the SNP, Plaid Cymru and the Greens – had a de facto non-aggression pact, as what one of them called 'an anti-austerity alliance';[9] rather, their main targets were to be Cameron (in anger) and Miliband (more in sorrow). Clegg was to be largely ignored. With Natalie Bennett's confidence at rock-bottom following her various disastrous media appearances prior to the campaign, the Green strategy was summed up by one of those involved in the debate preparation simply as 'survival'.[10] 'This was', they said, 'the biggest exposure we'd ever had, so if it went wrong – and it really could have done – it could have been disastrous.'

Given that the debates would be relatively gender-balanced, the male participants were also aware of the risk of appearing to be condescending towards one of the female participants.[11] 'It's so easy with a dismissive hand gesture to appear patronising', as one of those involved put it. 'You can't pile in on the women, or you'll look like a bully' said another.

'So they will get free shots, and the men will have to be careful about how they phrase any response ... Piling in on Natalie Bennett will be like torturing a kitten.'

The approach taken by Plaid Cymru and the SNP differed. Sturgeon's strategy was to try to speak to voters in both Scotland and beyond, and to appear constructive and collaborative, with a focus on both the general election and the post-election negotiations, to try to appeal to Scottish voters but also to make the SNP look acceptable to voters south of the border.[12] Wood's focus was much more on the Welsh audience, to frame herself as 'the voice of Wales', focusing not so much on the general election, but to try to raise her profile prior to the Welsh elections in 2016. Her team felt this worked, but that she slightly overdid it, and in the second debate (see below), she attempted a broader appeal. Natalie Bennett did at least avoid a catastrophe.[13]

With the exception of the Greens, who wanted to try to present themselves as 'anti-UKIP', almost everyone had decided that they would largely try to ignore Nigel Farage.[14] In turn, Farage had decided to raise his profile and energise his core vote by presenting himself as distinct from all the others, not afraid to say things others would not. His most remembered intervention was on the issue of immigrants with HIV being treated by the NHS, a tactic described by his own campaign team as 'shock and awful' – although both the tactic and its appellation caused disagreement within the UKIP camp.[15] He had tried to position himself as distinct from the others throughout the debate, from his opening statement, through to challenging the idea that there was austerity ('we've got to get real'), talking about money being sent 'over Hadrian's Wall' and finishing with his closing statement ('I warned

Vote Conservative X

you at the beginning, they are all the same'). A ComRes poll halfway through the debate found that Farage topped the poll of those seen as doing best in the debate, but also the poll of those doing worst, a finding that was entirely consistent with his strategy of motivating his core vote and ignoring the rest of the public.[16]

For each of the TV debates, there was a 'spin room' filled with journalists and party spinners.[17] As one journalist described it: 'Journalists watch politicians being interviewed by other journalists or members of the public on a big television, and then other politicians tell journalists what they have just seen and why what they have just seen shows that the politician from their party is so much better than the politician from the other party.'[18] 'Utter waste of time', said one party press advisor, 'but you sort of have to do it.' 'We get very little out of going', said another journalist: 'It's only worth it to build up relationships: you're being nice to them, so that one day they'll be nice to you.' The real spinning was in any case not done in the spin room, but back at the various party HQs, where there was a much bigger team of people, fact-checking, tweeting and emailing out material both during and after the debate. As one Lib Dem put it: 'The spin operation in the spin room begins five minutes after the debate ends. The one here begins five minutes after the debate starts.' Or as one Labour staffer put it, the spin room is 'a sort of wet dream for spin doctors who want to pretend they're in the US in the 1990s and they're James Carville'. He added that 'the polls can immediately change everything anyway'.

Except that this time who 'won' the debate depended on which polling company was used. Of the seven participants, four were judged to have 'won' the debate by at least one pollster.[19] (There was also various analyses of social media, of varying methodological sophistication, but all of pretty limited value.) Given how responses to such questions tend to be driven by the partisanship of the respondent, it was not surprising that both Cameron and Miliband did relatively well, and both the Labour and Conservative teams were happy: Miliband because he had outperformed expectations and Cameron because he had emerged unscathed. Nicola Sturgeon polled between 15% and 28% (the latter the highest polled by any of the participants in any of the surveys), despite drawing on a much smaller group of partisans than any of the British leaders. In part, perhaps, this was because, for the majority of the audience – or those outside of Scotland at least – she was a fresh face. A YouGov focus group earlier in the week had found that not a single person knew who she was.[20] But being a fresh face was on its own not sufficient, as both Wood and Bennett demonstrated. And whilst

Sturgeon may have been relatively unknown to most of the audience, those participating were well aware of how good a debater she was and did not under-estimate her. 'Presentationally', said one of her rivals' teams, 'she was brilliant ... She had gravitas, and came across exactly as an equal to Miliband.'

During the 1951 election, Nye Bevan had claimed that 'the Tories, every election, must have a bogy man. If you haven't got a programme, a bogy man will do'. In 2015 the Conservatives started with a bogy man, who – after the seven-person debate – transformed into a bogy woman. To coincide with the debates, the Conservatives released a revised version of their Miliband-in-pocket poster, this time with Sturgeon in place of Salmond, and from then on Conservative activists picketing Labour events turned up in Sturgeon masks.

Throughout the campaign, as they had done in the run-up, the SNP made it clear that there were no circumstances under which they would do any post-election deal with the Conservatives. Former Labour voters in Scotland could, the party argued, vote SNP without any risk that by doing so they would prop up a Conservative government. However, the weekend after the leaders' debate, the *Daily Telegraph* led with a story claiming that the Scottish First Minister was on record as wanting a Conservative victory at the election. Headlined 'Sturgeon's Secret Backing for Cameron', the paper drew on a government memorandum, written on 6 March, which was a record of a telephone call with the French Consul-General, relaying a conversation the French Ambassador had had with the First Minister. It included the claim that 'she confessed that she'd rather see David Cameron remain as PM (and didn't see Ed Miliband as PM material)'.

The idea that the SNP might be better off politically with a Conservative government at Westminster, against which they could then rail furiously, thus building support for independence, had long been claimed by Labour. But no SNP politician could be seen to say so. The story had the potential to be dynamite. However, even the civil servant writing the memo had appeared surprised by the claim ('I have to admit that I'm not sure the FM's tongue would be quite so loose on that kind of thing in a meeting like that, so [it] might well be a case of something being lost in translation').[21]

The First Minister immediately denied saying it. The French Ambassador concurred. The story, which was first published online late on 3 April, had all but collapsed by the time the newspaper was formally published on 4 April. It was a good example of how social media has sped up the political body clock. 'It would have taken longer to turn the story round before', said one of the SNP team. 'Now you can tweet your rebuttal, and it's almost instantaneous ... It was out of date by the time the paper was physically published.' A leak enquiry was then established, which, almost uniquely for a leak enquiry, found the source of the leak. 'It gives leaking a bad name', as one former Special Advisor put it.[22]

One of Labour's largest policy announcements of the campaign came on 8 April: to abolish (in reality severely restrict) the non-domicile tax rule ('non-doms'), which allowed around 110,000 people to avoid paying UK tax on some of their income by claiming not to be based in the UK.[23] Labour had been pondering the idea for two years and had considered launching it earlier, concerned that the Conservatives would announce a similar policy in their final budget and thus steal their thunder. The shine was slightly taken off Labour's announcement when a video surfaced of Ed Balls, from an interview given in January, in which he said that abolishing non-dom status would reduce the tax take in the UK, but Labour still felt that the policy would guarantee them positive coverage for a few days.[24]

The Conservative response was to throw a dead cat on the table. Boris Johnson, for whom Lynton Crosby had worked on his campaign for the London Mayoralty, summed it up: 'Let us suppose you are losing an argument. The facts are overwhelmingly against you, and the more people focus on the reality the worse it is for you and your case. Your best bet in these circumstances is to perform a manoeuvre that a great campaigner [Crosby] describes as "throwing a dead cat on the table, mate"':

> There is one thing that is absolutely certain about throwing a dead cat on the dining room table – and I don't mean that people will be outraged, alarmed, disgusted. That is true, but irrelevant. The key point, says my Australian friend, is that everyone will shout, 'Jeez, mate, there's a dead cat on the table!' In other words, they will be talking about the dead cat – the thing you want them to talk about – and they will not be talking about the issue that has been causing you so much grief.[25]

This particular dead cat was deployed by the Defence Secretary, Michael Fallon, who launched a personal attack on Ed Miliband the next day, claiming that he would surrender Trident to reach a deal with the SNP: 'Miliband stabbed his own brother in the back to become Labour leader. Now he is willing to stab the United Kingdom in the back to become prime minister.' The over-the-top and personal nature of the attack was authorised by the Conservative campaign team – the phrase 'stab in the back' was not of Fallon's creation – although there was concern about it, and several senior Conservatives worried that it made them look too negative. But there was grudging admiration within the Labour camp for the Conservative response. 'I thought non-doms would run for three days', said one of Miliband's closest aides, 'with them defending wealthy foreigners not paying tax. I thought it was really clever of them. It wasn't true, but it was clever.'[26]

The majority of party manifestos launched in the week beginning 13 April, starting with Labour (on Monday), then the Conservatives and the Greens (Tuesday), and the Lib Dems and UKIP (Wednesday).[27] The Conservatives had originally planned to launch on the Monday as well, but decided to pull back a day in order to give the media more time to examine (by which they meant criticise) Labour's manifesto.

Launched at the old Granada studios in Manchester, Labour's manifesto, *Britain Can Be Better*, opened with a 'Budget Responsibility Lock', including the line: 'The first line of Labour's first budget will be: "This Budget cuts the deficit every year".' An early April polling presentation stressing Labour's continued economic weakness had been leapt on by Spencer Livermore. 'Spencer had long been worried about this, and seized his opportunity', said one of Labour's team. Miliband agreed to the page's inclusion, but it was not included in the version presented to the meeting which signed off the manifesto, which provoked complaints within the party. It had been held back for fear it would leak, Labour wanting to make a splash with the announcement.[28]

The Conservatives launched the next day in Swindon. At the heart of the imaginatively entitled *The Conservative Party Manifesto 2015* was the claim that the party was the 'real party of working people', with the Prime Minister stressing tax-free income for those on the minimum wage and 30 hours of free childcare. The long-term economic plan was at the forefront, but the manifesto promised to provide security 'for every stage of your life'. The manifesto also included the extension of right-to-buy policy to the 1.3 million families in housing association properties. Cameron's speech was more upbeat than many of his stump speeches, absent the routine the attacks on Ed Miliband and the SNP, instead talking of wanting to create 'a country where a good life is there for everyone willing to work for it'. Having launched the front

'Match the clothes to the leader'

Adams, *Daily Telegraph*, 14 April 2015 (© Adams/*The Telegraph*)

cover of their manifesto in February, along with the key policy pledges, the formal launch of the Lib Dems' *Manifesto 2015* took place at a nightclub in Battersea, arranged at short notice when the Conservatives changed the date of their launch, which necessitated the party moving from the Tuesday to the Wednesday. The launch event suffered from power and microphone failures, and saw Clegg pledge to 'add heart to a Conservative government and add a brain to a Labour one'. Or as Danny Alexander put it: 'Whose hand do you want around the throat of the next government?'

UKIP's manifesto, *Believe in Britain,* was noticeably more professional than in previous elections. Ironically, given that the party made so much of being different, it felt, and read, much more like a normal party manifesto. To buttress its search for credibility, UKIP made much of the fact that its economic commitments had been independently audited by the Centre for Economics and Business Research, and the manifesto ran to a sizeable 28,000 words.[29] However, the UKIP launch at a hotel in Purfleet, in the key UKIP target of Thurrock, descended into farce when a *Daily Telegraph* journalist queried why the only non-white face in the entire document was on the page about overseas aid. Farage did not answer; instead, ethnic minority members of UKIP in the audience stood up to visibly demonstrate their presence in the party, whilst the room began to heckle the journalist. If the goal of the manifesto was to demonstrate that the party was serious, this rather undermined it.[30] It also demonstrated a continuing lack of sensitivity to such issues. The Green manifesto (*For the Common Good*) was only available to download, with no hard copies being printed.[31] It was launched at an event in Dalston, hosted jointly by Bennett and Caroline Lucas, designed to damp down continuing rumours of a split between the two. None of the manifestos flowed with beautiful prose, each being the creation of many authors, although Labour's was perhaps the ugliest; normal people do not write sentences like: 'We will support this model of knowledge clusters.'

In addition, most of the parties put out multiple alternate manifestos, targeting specific demographics. The Greens alone had supplementary manifestos for: young people, animals (that is, animal welfare, not actually targeted at animals – although one pledge was 'Giving animals a voice in policy-making'), Lesbian, Gay, Bisexual, Trans, Intersex and Queer (LGBTIQ) voters, and Black and Minority Ethnic (BAME) voters. They also had an additional manifesto for Wales (with versions in both English and Welsh); Braille and audio versions of the main manifesto; and a mini manifesto of just 16 pages. Moreover, the Scottish Greens put out their own manifesto (*An Economy for the People, a Society for All*, albeit just 20 pages long), as did Scottish Young Greens and the Green Party in Northern Ireland (*For the Common Good*) – 10 manifestos in total, in a variety of formats.

Labour was the only party to create a specific women's manifesto, launched by Harriet Harman from the Woman to Woman campaign bus. The Lib Dems released a funny online retort video dismissing the need for such an approach ('we may have ovaries, but we also have brains ... our manifesto is for men and women'), but then the Lib Dems had specific manifestos for younger people, older people, families, the environment, the disabled, mental health and BAME voters, which rather undercut any claims of universality. Most of these additional manifestos never existed in hard copy, but were available for download.

The party HQs were packed with the extra staff taken on for the campaign. The main floor for each had a focal point where the senior figures in the party would make key decisions. In Conservative Campaign Headquarters (CCHQ), there was a 'pod' – known as the 'power pod' to those not in it – occupied by Crosby, Stephen Gilbert and Andrew Feldman, along with Tom Edmonds (head of digital) and Alex Dawson (the head of the Conservative Research Department). Election campaigns are not for those who need a lot of sleep: the team's meetings would start at 5 am each day, with Cameron and Osborne taking part in a phone conference call around 7.30 am, before going off for campaign visits. In Brewer's Green, on Labour's so-called top desk were Spencer Livermore, Tim Livesey, Lucy Powell and Greg Beales. Facing them were Douglas Alexander, Marianna McFadden, Harman and Balls, with the last two absent most of the time campaigning. There would be an early morning conference call with Ed Miliband around 7.30 or 7.45 am. The time varied, but the call always happened.[32] The Lib Dem campaign team was known as the wheelhouse. The wheelhouse executive consisted of ten people, chaired by Paddy Ashdown. They would have three formal meetings per day: a morning one, a noon one (focusing on individual seats) and an evening one, deliberately timed after the BBC/ITN bulletins, with the media coverage being the first agenda item. Clegg would participate in two key conference calls each day: a morning one, with a large number of participants, and a much more restricted evening call.

Party election broadcasts (PEBs), which ran throughout the short campaign, were mostly short and unimaginative. The majority ran to a maximum of three minutes and were a fairly predictable mixture of voiceover and footage – often of, or by, the party leaders. All three UKIP broadcasts, for example, featured a mixture of Nigel Farage to camera together with clips of him on the campaign trail, sometimes using the same footage in different broadcasts. Labour made use of celebrities – Martin Freeman, Jo Brand and Steve Coogan – talking to camera, along with closing voiceovers by David Tennant. One of the few PEBs to run for longer was 'Ed Miliband. A Portrait', an attempt to do for Miliband what had been done for Neil Kinnock in 1987 or Tony Blair in 1997. Directed by Paul Greengrass and running for five minutes, it featured clips of Miliband discussing his life and what motivated him. It included an odd gloss. At one point, remembering his father, Ralph, he said he was 'a removal man by day', which is not how one of Britain's most prominent Marxist authors is usually remembered.[33]

The most imaginative were probably Plaid Cymru (in which individuals 'outed' themselves as Plaid voters – 'Mum, Dad, there's something I need to tell you') and the Greens (whose one PEB featured a mock boyband containing the male party leaders, which was either hilarious or cringeworthy depending on your sense of humour). PEBs are now usually released online the day before their formal broadcast in order to generate news stories, and then have an ongoing life online after they have been broadcast on TV. On the whole, the parties design different, shorter, material specifically for online transmission (see p. 152), although the Green 'boyband' PEB was an exception, being deliberately designed to be a viral success.[34] Almost by universal consensus, the Lib Dem PEBs, all on the theme of 'Look Left, Look Right, then Cross', were poor, although the production values were at least better than the one broadcast from the Trade Unionist and Socialist Coalition, which ran for five minutes, but which felt much longer.

The parties still think the PEBs matter – 'How many other organisations would die for four minutes of TV?' said one senior staffer – and they row over the number each party should receive (the Greens feeling particularly aggrieved at being allocated just one). But they matter less than they once did. The Conservatives ran two of their broadcasts twice; the SNP ran the same broadcast – a car journey through Scotland, narrated by the actor Martin Compston ('this is our place, our country') – four times. The messages in the PEBs also remain a good insight into core party strategies (see Box 7.1).

One campaign tradition now all but abandoned was the morning press conference. In a cost-saving plan, the Conservatives, Labour and the Lib Dems had provisionally agreed to hire a shared venue to use for press conferences, only for the idea to be scrapped when they realised that they would hardly use it.[35] UKIP continued to hold occasional press conferences at One Great George Street in Westminster, with (usually) Suzanne Evans and Patrick O'Flynn fronting for the party, but they were fairly brief and poorly attended events. The norm now was to have campaign events at which the press and broadcasters might attend; questions were usually limited and the presence of the party activists made it harder to quiz the politicians in detail. 'Please don't boo the journalists' became a regular plea from politicians to their activists, although activists rarely followed the advice.

Access on campaign buses was also limited. Although the major parties all had a campaign bus – or buses – Labour and the Conservatives limited the number of press and broadcasters who could go on them, and there was no guarantee that the party leader would accompany the journalists.[36] The Conservatives were the most restrictive, but Labour also rarely allowed journalists much time with Ed Miliband. The buses were for the most part just a way of moving journalists around – and of charging media organisations money for the privilege. The Lib Dems were deliberately more open, allowing (almost) anyone onto their bus in an attempt to make Clegg seem the most accessible of the leaders

Box 7.1: Party election broadcast themes

The Conservatives emphasised support for young families, support for those 'who get up early, who put in the hours ... Not something for nothing, but where people who work hard get rewarded', and, in their final broadcast, one of those broadcast twice, the risks of allowing Ed Miliband to be 'propped up by the SNP'. The imagery was never subtle. One Conservative PEB had someone throwing their curtains open, playing on the Conservative theme of supporting those who go off to work whilst others' curtains stay closed. The final broadcast opened with an image of a bell jar clock; the message of the broadcast was not just that Labour would turn back the clock, but – cue sledgehammer descending onto the bell jar – that Labour would *destroy* the clock.

Labour stressed the NHS, which was the sole focus of two of its PEBs ('Little by little, the NHS is being pulled apart ... If they get back in, the NHS as we know it, wouldn't survive five years') and which featured in others as well. In addition to the various celebrities, the party also used Harry Smith, born in 1923, to talk about his life, the death of his sister in the workhouse infirmary and the arrival of the NHS ('a miracle'). No one watching Labour's PEBs could have doubted that Labour thought the NHS was a Good Thing. Quite how many people needed persuading of that, however, was more debatable.

The Lib Dems focused on their role as a constraint on the other parties ('a government of self-interest and grievance or a coalition of tolerance and decency') and UKIP played up their anti-establishment values ('the rich are getting richer, the poor are getting poorer', 'I'm an ordinary bloke, doing an extraordinary job'), as well as their focus on immigration ('the debate on immigration has been closed down') and patriotism (with images of Farage looking wistfully at the white cliffs of Dover).

The SNP broadcast emphasised the extent to which Labour no longer stood for ordinary people ('I remember when Labour used to stand up to the Tories, but that's just not happening anymore') and the extent to which they could push for more power for Scotland ('The question for us here in Scotland isn't which Westminster party will become the next UK government. The question is who's really going to stand up for Scotland?'). In response, Scottish Labour used the Freeman broadcast that had also been broadcast south of the border, but others PEBs put out by Labour north of the border featured Jim Murphy more prominently, as well as using a noticeably different language ('working-class families punished', 'working people can come together') and imagery, including black-and-white footage from the early years of the Labour Party, featuring James Keir Hardie.

(and 'to challenge the image of us as beaten, and downtrodden'), although the Lib Dem campaign events themselves were just as artificial and formulaic.

Knowing that much of the print media were out to get him, Labour played particularly safe with its campaign events, putting Ed Miliband behind a lectern, surrounded by activists, for almost all photo calls.

Miliband had been resistant, wanting to do more free-form, notes-free events, but as one of his team put it: 'We're dealing with an incredibly hostile media, and you can do loads of these things really well, and then you do one badly, and that's the one they focus on. People are out to get him. Let's not take any chances. We're not throwing it away because he looks like a wally walking down the street.' At one point, the Labour leader even gave a lectern-based talk in a back garden. 'It's pretty fucking absurd to put a podium in someone's back garden', said one of their press team, 'but then it's no more absurd than most photo ops. And the embarrassing pictures of Twitter showing what it really looks like are hugely outnumbered by the six million or so people who will see it on the news.'

The same applied to Conservative press events, which were ruthlessly stage-managed. Occasionally, the mask would slip – as when a wide shot of a Conservative campaign rally was published, showing just how tightly corralled the activists had been to give the impression of a mass rally – but again most people only see the staged shot, and there was praise from their rivals for the quality of the Conservative tour operation, and especially the behind-the-scenes work of Cameron's aide Liz Sugg (described by one of her rivals as the 'master of the brand'). 'It makes us groan, but it totally works', said a member of another party's press team. 'The pictures [she produces] are brilliant and culturally relevant.'

In general, though, as one experienced journalist put it, 'the trajectory of access to anyone who might be prime minister continued downwards in this election', and the media complained constantly. 'Back in the 1960s', wrote Marina Hyde in *The Guardian*, 'Daniel Boorstin defined a pseudo-event as one that would not happen if the cameras were not there. It's almost as if he could foresee the day when journalists would travel to Somerset to watch George Osborne smile at a vacuum cleaner.'[37] Part of this frustration was a lack of being able to get close enough to probe on details of policy – although the media's desire for 'genuine' interactions between the public and politicians is often just code for wanting scenes in which politicians get embarrassed, preferably involving members of the public shouting at them in a vaguely incoherent manner.

Such moments were rare. The Prime Minister had been heckled at an Age UK event just before the start of the campaign; a heckler was ejected from the seven-way leaders' debate; a ukelele-playing busker in Alnwick told David Cameron 'to fuck off back to Eton'; in Twickenham, a man complained that the Conservative focus on the SNP was racism; and a questioner at a Conservative event in Hendon asked whether voter

7 April 2015. Conservative rally, Wadebridge, Cornwall. Close up

REUTERS/Toby Melville

7 April 2015. Conservative rally, Wadebridge, Cornwall. Wide shot

Niall Paterson/Sky

apathy was caused by the fact that the Prime Minister, the London Mayor and the Chancellor 'were all in the same class at school?'.[38] The very scarcity of such events rendered them newsworthy when they occurred. There was no 2015 equivalent of Gillian Duffy (2010) or Sharon Storrer (2001).

The parties concentrated their leaders' visits mostly on marginal seats (although some Lib Dem incumbents explicitly rejected a visit from Nick Clegg), balancing individual visits with a need to hit different broadcast and press regions in a way that maximised coverage in local and regional media.[39] In the case of the SNP, planning such visits presented a problem, since all of Scotland was now a potential destination. Privately, the SNP began to realise their vote share could approach 50%, and although they refused to discuss their number of target seats, this meant that every seat was in play. 'You'd look at her diary and try to work out where she could be sent', said one of those involved in planning Nicola Sturgeon's campaign visits, 'and you could pretty much send her almost anywhere.' The party transported Sturgeon around in a purple helicopter to try to cover as many constituencies as possible – although even with a helicopter, a visit to Orkney and Shetland was considered too remote.[40] Praise was regularly heaped upon Sturgeon's more accessible campaign, in which she would mingle with crowds of enthusiastic voters in public in a way that few other senior politicians do. Yet this often confused cause and effect. Nicola Sturgeon was not getting this sort of reaction because she was campaigning in that way; she was able to campaign in that way because of the reaction she would get. Had David Cameron attempted a meet-the-people event in Glasgow, the results would have been less impressive.

The 'Challengers' debate – containing representatives of the main five non-government parties – took place on 16 April. Of all the planned TV events, this was the one that had caused most consternation in Labour's camp: the fear was that Ed Miliband would end up representing the establishment, attacked from both left and right by parties who could promise to shower gold on the electorate. Several months before, Labour had attempted a six-way debate rehearsal in case David Cameron had boycotted the seven-way debate. It was not a success, with Miliband getting sucked into arguments with those playing Wood and Sturgeon. Watching on, David Axelrod's advice was: 'You have to assume David Cameron is on the stage, even if he isn't', which was the approach they then adopted for the Challengers' debate. Privately, all of Miliband's team conceded that Cameron had been politically savvy to avoid as

'The Seven Dwarfs'

Adams, *Daily Telegraph*, 2 April 2015 (© Adams/*The Telegraph*)

many debates as possible, but Labour attempted to make use of the Prime Minister's absence. Farage, again, tried to raise his profile, complaining about the composition of the audience. Unlike his controversial comments in the seven-way debate, this was an unplanned, off-the-cuff comment borne out of frustration with the audience's reaction to him.[41] Despite their fears, Miliband did well and (according to Survation) narrowly won the debate, polling 35%. Sturgeon and Farage came next 31% and 27%, respectively. Throughout the campaign, Miliband's team were relatively pleased with his performance in the various TV debates, and they felt that they had succeeded in raising his profile and challenging perceptions about him. But afterwards, several of them wondered if they would have been better, once they realised a head-to-head with the Prime Minister was not going to happen, to have avoided the debates altogether given the extra profile they allowed the SNP. Bennett and Wood again picked up the wooden spoon; offered prime-time opportunities, they again failed to make any significant impact.

The SNP manifesto, *Stronger for Scotland*, was launched on 21 April, later than the other parties, and on a date deliberately chosen to coincide with the arrival of postal votes on voters' doormats.[42] That weekend the party had launched a new poster campaign ('My vow is to make Scotland stronger at Westminster') and a leaflet with the same imagery had been sent out to would-be postal voters. The strapline was a deliberate play on Better Together's use of Vow in the referendum ('we were tweaking their tail', one of Sturgeon's team admitted), although the back of the leaflet focused on more bread-and-butter matters, such as the NHS, education and protecting bus passes. The manifesto launch event at Edinburgh International Climbing Centre had a touch of the revivalist meeting about it. Sturgeon's mere use of the word 'independence' triggered a standing ovation – even though the First Minister was keen to stress that that was not what the election was about. Sturgeon promised voters in Scotland that the SNP would make their voice heard at Westminster 'more loudly than it has ever been'. Asked what she thought of Boris Johnson's claim that putting the SNP in power in Westminster was akin to putting Herod in charge of a baby farm, she said that it was 'entirely offensive' and as in the leaders' debates, she attempted to speak to an audience south of the border in order to counter this image: 'Although you can't vote SNP your views do matter to me and you have a right to know what to expect of my party if the votes of the Scottish people give us influence in a hung parliament ... If the SNP emerges from this election in a position of influence we will exercise that influence responsibly and constructively, and we will always seek to exercise it in the interests of people not just in Scotland but across the whole of the UK.'[43] The party noted explicitly that this was 'a manifesto for delivery UK-wide'.

For a party so widely seen as to the left of Labour, what was remarkable about the SNP manifesto was how similar its policies were to those of Labour. It proposed the reintroduction of the 50p top tax rate, a tax on bankers' bonuses, a mansion tax, a bank levy, targeting tax avoidance, abolishing 'non-dom' status, removing the married couples' tax allowance and a review of the pension tax relief available to the wealthiest. As George Eaton noted in the *New Statesman*, 'every one of these measures is already supported by Labour. Indeed, it was arguing for them long before the SNP'.[44] The obvious exception was the renewal of Trident, but in general, as the Institute for Fiscal Studies (IFS) noted, the party's 'stated plans do not necessarily match their anti-austerity rhetoric'. The IFS argued that the reality was that 'all four parties' plans imply further austerity over the next parliament', although there were substantial differences in terms of scale between the Conservatives on the one hand and Labour and the SNP on the other. The problem, the IFS noted dryly, was that: 'None has managed to be completely specific about how much they want to reduce borrowing or exactly how they would do it ... the electorate is at best armed with only an incomplete picture of what it can expect from any of these four parties.'[45] However, as one outgoing Labour MP noted, in dealing with the SNP, Labour were not fighting a set of policies, but an alternative narrative.[46]

Within the Labour camp, how best to deal with that narrative continued to be a constant tension. One view, strongly advocated by Douglas Alexander, was that the party needed to challenge the issue, to 'talk it up in order to close it down'. But the alternate view was that 'every day spent on Scotland and the SNP was a bad day. We should say the minimum'. This clash was most keenly felt over a speech that Miliband gave on foreign affairs at Chatham House on 24 April. Publicly, it generated a synthetic row over a line which Conservative spin doctors said blamed the Prime Minister for the deaths of refugees drowning in the Mediterranean as they tried to reach Europe.[47] That had never been Labour's intention. As one of Labour's team put it: 'If we had wanted to smear the Prime Minister, believe me, we wouldn't have buried it on page three of a press release about a foreign policy speech.'[48] Behind the scenes, though, there had been a much bigger row within the Labour camp about the speech. Miliband had wanted to use it to apologise for the Iraq War, but many in his team felt it was a wasted opportunity. Alexander and others instead wanted him to use it to tackle the SNP issue head-on, making the speech about Britain's place in the world and criticising Cameron for fanning nationalism. It would, wrote Iain Watson, 'have accused the Prime Minister of putting party interests ahead of the national interest – caving in to Eurosceptic demands for a referendum, and fuelling Scottish nationalism with his plan for English Votes for English Laws'. But Spencer Livermore and others felt that this would just give the SNP yet more publicity. 'The result was a no-score draw, a much weaker speech.'[49] The concern by now was less the party's fate in Scotland itself, where the London party (if not Scottish Labour) had accepted it had lost most of its seats, but much more how the issue was playing out in England and (to a lesser extent) Wales. MPs and canvassers of all parties began to report the issue of the SNP coming through on the doorstep south of the border.

A formal coalition had been ruled out before the campaign began (on 16 March; see p. 149), but a confidence and supply arrangement with the SNP was not categorically ruled out until 26 April. Even then, the issue did not go away, since the SNP had always made it clear that they were prepared to do vote-by-vote deals to get legislation through.

Labour's polling found that the Conservative attacks were working – and Labour's denials were not. As one of those conducting focus groups for the party said: 'No one believed it! No one believed that a party wouldn't cut deals to get into government. Why should they? I didn't believe it.' And despite Labour's attempts to close down the issue of deals with the SNP, the perception that the SNP would be likely to play a role in government after the election *increased* during the campaign.[50] Labour spent the campaign playing down the chance of the SNP being involved in government, while the Tories spent the campaign playing it up – and the Tories won. In the last few days of the campaign, Miliband's pollster warned that in the battle of the 'squeezes', Labour's appeal to vote for it to save the NHS was not as strong as Conservative warnings about the dangers of Labour being dependent on the SNP.

One of the most googled phrases during the seven-way leaders' debate had been 'Can I vote for the SNP?' and because Sturgeon had done so well in the debates, a belief grew up in some quarters that people throughout the UK had been transformed into disenfranchised SNP supporters. At her party's manifesto launch, Sturgeon had claimed that: 'My inbox is heaving with people from other parts of the UK asking if they can vote SNP.' Maybe it was, and there were certainly *some* people who liked the SNP. But the feeling was far from universal. For the first time, the British Election Study began to ask respondents outside of Scotland for their views on the SNP (previously, the question was understandably felt to be rather superfluous). In England, the mean score for the likeability of the SNP was exactly the same as the mean score for the Conservatives in Scotland – in other words, low. Whilst some liked the SNP, most people in England were noticeably more negative.[51] When YouGov asked voters for their views on particular post-election scenarios in late March, nearly three-fifths said they would be 'dismayed' by a Labour/SNP deal (a worse score than any of the other options about which they were asked); a later poll by the same company, in late April, similarly found any deals involving the SNP scoring worse than any others.[52] A similar poll by ComRes found that whilst 32% of people in Britain wanted to see Farage and UKIP in government, the figure for the SNP was just 19%; majorities did not want either Sturgeon (54%) or the SNP (59%) to play a role in the next government.[53] If Scottish politics had long been a process of the parties 'othering' the Conservatives, then the 2015 election saw the Conservatives get their revenge.

Although the issue had been ever-present throughout the campaign and had been causing problems even before it, from the seven-way

debate onwards, it caused what one of Miliband's team called 'anguish' within Labour's camp. 'It was a process story about the SNP that was damaging us. It just had cut through like nothing else.' The problem was not just the direct damage that this was causing to the party – it was also that it prevented Labour from being able to get other stories running that were more to their advantage. As one of Labour's press team observed: 'We couldn't get a story up there, just didn't happen. It was immensely frustrating.' Because of their lack of cheerleaders in the press, Labour were particularly dependent on the BBC for coverage – and thus were even more annoyed when it too began to focus on this story. As another of the Brewer's Green team said: 'All we had was the *Mirror*, and to a lesser extent the *Guardian* and the *Indie*, but no one reads those. We are really reliant on the broadcasters giving us a fair wind. And it's not that the SNP isn't a story – it is – but it was relentless.' Tom Baldwin complained repeatedly about the way the BBC were handling the issue and, on 22 April, Lucy Powell wrote to the BBC's Director of News, James Harding, to complain about coverage that she said had become 'disproportionately focused on the SNP and Tory claims that Labour would enter into a deal which would damage the rest of the UK ... We strongly object not only to the scale of your coverage but also the apparent abandonment of any basic news values, with so much reporting now becoming extremely repetitive'.[54]

In a desperate attempt to gain media attention, the party added a sixth policy pledge, on housing, on 27 April. As with the earlier five pledges, it had a short, snappy (if vague), promise ('Homes to buy and action on rents'), then a longer, more detailed, version ('Biggest house building programme for a generation with priority for first-time buyers and their stamp duty cut to zero. Secure three-year rents capped by inflation'). It was another policy that was popular in its own right, even if it did little to deal with voters' fundamental concerns about the party.

UKIP had launched their campaign with a pledge card on 30 March, focusing on five policies: leaving the EU, controlling immigration, more cash for the NHS, cutting foreign aid and no tax for those on the minimum wage. The next day, in Dover, they launched a billboard focusing on immigration (very similar to one used in 2014, but now with three escalators rather than one).

There was a constant tension between the team accompanying Farage in Kent and those in the London HQ. They did not like, trust or respect each other, and tensions were permanently simmering. Farage himself focused his campaigning mostly in the south-east of England, not least as a result of having to work hard to try to win his own seat.[55] The *Daily Telegraph* estimated that during the campaign, Cameron travelled around 7,900 miles, Clegg around 6,600, Miliband around 5,600 and Farage just 3,500. One trip to the European Parliament in Strasbourg aside, all of Farage's campaign trips were within England and almost all in the south-east. UKIP were standing candidates almost everywhere, but they were not fighting a genuinely national campaign. Also not helping was Farage's health. Having previously denied claims that there was anything wrong, on 25 April, he admitted that he was suffering from a recurrence of an old spinal injury and had been prescribed Temazepam. He said the pain meant he had not been 'firing on all cylinders' during the early weeks of the election campaign, but was now 'back on form'.

UKIP also continued to make headlines for the wrong reasons. During the short campaign alone, the UKIP candidate for North East Hampshire was suspended from the party after he told undercover reporters from the *Daily Mirror* that he would 'put a bullet between the eyes' of his Conservative rival ('His family have only been here since the 70s. You are not British enough to be in our parliament. I've got 400 years of ancestry where I live. He hasn't got that'), while the candidate for West Lancashire was suspended for comments made about South Africa and remarks made to a Jewish Labour MP ('Protect child benefits? If you had it your way you'd send the £ to Poland/Israel'). Although not suspended, the candidate for Sedgefield was forced to apologise after it was found that he had written that the journalist Yasmin Alibhai-Brown 'needs a good shag' and made other sexualised remarks.[56]

In an interview with the *Daily Telegraph* on 7 April, the Prime Minister targeted UKIP voters: 'This election is about choosing a government. It's not a moment of protest ... I would say to those voters who have concerns – message received and understood.' He added: 'Come with us, come back home to us rather than risk all of this good work being undone by Labour.' Boris Johnson made similar remarks in an interview with *The Sun*: 'My message to Kippers is this: grit your teeth, screw up your eyes, take a deep breath and do the right thing for this country. Come home Ukippers. Help us stave off the nightmare of a supine, useless, federalist Miliband/SNP government — because that's the choice we face.'[57] It was easy to critique this on the basis that not all UKIP voters were former Conservatives (and many of them did not like Cameron), but this missed the point. The plea was not aimed at all UKIP voters, just at those who were ex-Conservatives, and the party had, by now, evidence that it was beginning to work.

All election campaigns have things that go wrong, moments that give cheer to their opponents and have supporters with their heads in their hands, but which then have almost no impact on the outcome of the contest.

For the Conservatives, that moment came on 25 April when the Prime Minister was outlining his vision for ethnic minority communities. 'We are', he said, 'a shining example of a country where multiple identities work. Where you can be Welsh and Hindu and British, Northern Irish and Jewish and British, where you can wear a kilt and a turban, where you can wear a hijab covered in poppies. Where you can support Man United, the Windies and Team GB all at the same time'. He then added, in what appeared to be an ad lib: 'Of course, I'd rather you supported West Ham.' Social media exploded and he was soon having to explain why he wanted anyone to support West Ham when he had always insisted he supported Aston Villa, who play in the same colours. For his critics, this revealed how he was a phony who would say anything to get elected. The Prime Minister blamed a Natalie Bennett-style 'brain fade' ('sometimes these things happen when you are on the stump').[58]

Labour's head-in-hands moment was more carefully planned and more monumental: an 8-foot 6-inch limestone tablet inscribed with Labour's six policy pledges, unveiled in a car park in Hastings. 'Our six pledges form the basis of our plan for working people', said Miliband. 'These six pledges are now carved in stone, and they are carved in stone because they won't be abandoned after the general election.' The claim was that the stone would be placed in Number 10's garden (unlikely, given planning regulations) or in Labour HQ (more likely, although it apparently did not fit through the door), so that every day it would remind the government of its promises. What soon became known as the 'Ed Stone' was unveiled on Saturday 2 May, with the photos released to the media the next day. Reaction was not positive. The stone was variously described as a policy cenotaph, a tombstone or the heaviest suicide note in history. 'You wonder why we stopped doing *The Thick of It*', said Simon Blackwell, one of the show's writers.

The plan had originated with Torsten Bell, Miliband's head of policy (and pre-launch had been known within Labour as the Torstone), and he was soon outed as the person responsible. But whilst the idea was originally Bell's, it had been signed off collectively by the campaign team. As one of Miliband's closest aides put it: 'Politicians take the credit when it all goes right, and when it doesn't, it's a staff member's fault. You want people to come up with ideas that are a bit different, and then it's for the rest of us to veto them if they're daft. We didn't ... You can't blame Torsten.' Several members of the Shadow Cabinet had been enthusiastic supporters of the stone, but only before its launch. Lucy Powell then compounded matters by giving an interview in which she appeared to say that just because the pledges had been written in stone, it did not mean Labour would necessarily keep them. It was a simple slip of the tongue, but it did not help.[59]

There was a post-election coda to the story, as journalists set off to try to find the stone, eventually locating it in storage in a warehouse in South London. 'It's still a problem now', said one of Labour's press team a month after the election. 'Everything else has gone. But we're still getting effing questions about a stone.'[60]

On 6 April, the *Daily Telegraph* had reported that: 'Senior Tory strategists now believe that the party's path to electoral success is by taking a "couple" of Labour seats and "destroying" Nick Clegg's party in the south, south west, parts of London and even a few seats in the north.' It was a remarkably accurate forecast of what was to come, although at the time it passed most people by. Labour, in particular, had little intelligence on what was happening in Conservative–Lib Dem contests, given that in most such seats they had so little infrastructure or members. Like a battle happening over a hill, they knew something was going on – they could see the seats the Prime Minister was going to visit, for example – but they had no idea how those contests were going. Even some Cabinet ministers were confused; one recalls being sent to visit Bath and Yeovil, both Lib Dem-held seats, and wondering to himself:

'Take us to Ed Miliband'

Matt, *Daily Telegraph*, 2 May 2015
(© Matt/*The Telegraph*)

'What am I doing here?' When David Cameron visited Yeovil – even going to Paddy Ashdown's village – the party attempted insouciance. 'The poor chap is confused again', said Ashdown of Cameron. 'He's come to the wrong place entirely.' 'If they want to waste their energy and money in Yeovil then they are very welcome'.

But the reality was that the Lib Dems knew exactly what was going on. Their canvass returns were finding that the Conservative message about the consequences of a Labour–SNP deal, coupled with the claim that the Conservatives only needed 23 extra seats to win, was having an impact on the doorsteps. A meeting at party HQ a month before polling day decided that the Liberal Democrats had to do all they could to shore up what they called their 'blue-yellow switchers'.[61] This meant redoubling efforts to attack Labour in order to try to dispel the view that they would be happy to do a deal with Labour. By that stage, the party felt they had just one Labour-facing marginal seat left in play; the others were either constituencies they thought they would hold or seats that were now considered beyond hope.[62] Their focus therefore had to be on holding their Conservative-facing seats, especially in the south-west and parts of London. At the constituency level, this led to a change in who the party targeted in those seats and how they did so (discussed on p. 269), and at the national level, this led to a deliberate heightening of the noises against Labour. 'We can't rule out a coalition with Labour', said one of Clegg's team. 'It would split the party. But we had to try to make it look as if we didn't really want it.' In an interview with the *Financial Times* published on 24 April, Clegg appeared to rule out any deal with Labour if it depended on support from the SNP. 'I would', he said, 'never recommend to the Liberal Democrats that we help establish a government which is basically on a life support system, where Alex Salmond could pull the plug any time he wants.'[63]

This caused dismay in both Lib Dem and Labour ranks. Much of Labour's preparations for government had been made on the basis of a possible deal with the Lib Dems, and whilst Labour were prepared to rule out any deals with the SNP, they also knew that they would need the tacit agreement of the SNP to govern. Clegg's statement appeared to block what was one of the most likely routes to government for Labour. Similarly, many Lib Dems could not see the value in effectively ruling out one of only two serious government partners – let alone one that many of them would have preferred to work with. A day later, on 25 April, Clegg and Miliband spoke privately at events to mark the centenary of Gallipoli, with Clegg acknowledging that he had gone too far in his *Financial Times* interview. In return, he asked Miliband why he wasn't ruling out a deal with the SNP: 'It's going to kill you', he said. David Laws then similarly backed off from the *Financial Times* position slightly during various broadcasts on the Sunday. Clegg still refused to be in any government that *formally* involved the SNP (or for that matter UKIP), but such deals were not on the table and he was careful not to go so far again as to rule out any post-election deal which was at least dependent on the SNP.

More generally, as they had done in 2010, the Lib Dems attempted to set out the rules by which they would engage with the other parties in any post-election negotiations. They would talk first to the party with the biggest 'mandate' (although, as in 2010, they ducked whether that meant votes or seats) and only then to the runner-up, although both publicly and especially privately, Clegg expressed scepticism about the legitimacy of deals done with any party that had clearly 'lost'. Constitutionalists did not approve; Vernon Bogdanor described Clegg's statements as 'absurd', pointing out the lack of any historical basis to them.[64] But they were an attempt to deflect questions about Clegg's preferences, or those of the people around him, and to claim that it was the voters who would decide what happened. Moreover, historically absurd or not, it was up to the party who they dealt with, and under what conditions; as one senior Lib Dem put it: 'Thank God constitutional experts don't run politics ... Just because it happened in 1924 or whenever doesn't mean we should still work like that.' And to speak first with one party was not quite the same as saying they would speak only to that party; in 2010, the party had begun negotiations with the Conservatives first, but then initiated contact with Labour whilst discussions with the Conservatives were still underway. They assumed they would do the same this time.

The Lib Dems also began to issue, publicly, their red lines for post-election negotiations. Beginning on 27 April, the party highlighted a series of policies that they considered non-negotiable, mostly taken from the front cover of their manifesto. This had the benefit of trying to make it clear what was, or was not, up for grabs (so that no one could later claim the party had sold them out), but it had the added benefit of generating extra coverage for policies that were already in the manifesto.[65] The Lib Dem red lines noticeably did not include ruling out an EU referendum, thus facilitating a deal with the Conservatives. Appearing on the *Andrew Marr Show* the weekend before polling, Clegg was asked eight times if he would accept a referendum in 2017 as the price of a coalition. Labour also watched this with some concern, worried that it indicated that the Lib Dems were more inherently likely to go into any post-election deal with the Conservatives, especially if Clegg survived in Sheffield Hallam. But equally, they did not see anything in the Lib Dem red lines that would have blocked a Labour–Lib Dem deal.[66] Although the precise nature of a deal would have depended on how reliant Labour were on the Lib Dems to secure a Commons majority, Labour intended to offer a formal coalition, involving a significant policy offer and three Lib Dem Cabinet positions: Deputy Prime Minister, Chief Secretary to the Treasury and Secretary of State for Education. This was partly to make a serious effort to rope the Lib Dems into a 'progressive alliance', but also so that if the Lib Dems walked away, it was clear they had made a conscious choice to do so, to show that they preferred working with the Conservatives rather than that there had been no chance of working with Labour.[67] They wanted no repeat of 2010, when the Lib Dems were plausibly able to argue that Labour had not been serious about coalition.

Labour's private position on the SNP was by this stage of the campaign the same as its public one: there would be no deal with the SNP. They were going to call their bluff. Having ruled out any deal with the Conservatives, the SNP had less negotiating power than many realised when it came to government formation. 'If anything they did allowed the Tories into power, then they were completely fucked', said one of Labour's negotiators. 'We had to offer them nothing to get the Tories out.'[68]

Although we talk about polling day, the widespread use of postal voting means that there are now multiple polling days. Postal votes began to be issued around 13 April, as the parties' manifestos were published, and after nominations had closed on 9 April. Most postal votes were cast from 20 April onwards.[69] The parties make considerable efforts to sign supporters up for postal votes, knowing that they are more likely to be cast than conventional votes, and they target specific literature at registered postal voters. The Conservatives sent out their one Royal Mail

freepost mailing deliberately to coincide with postal votes arriving; the SNP timed their one paid direct mail of the campaign specifically to hit postal voters.

The parties also use the postal votes as an early indicator of the level of support they are enjoying. Postal votes are opened for verification in council offices prior to polling day, with representatives of the parties in attendance to ensure nothing untoward occurs. The votes are not counted at this point and are sorted face-down, but an activist with a sharp pair of eyes can attempt to track the level of support for the various parties and then pass on that information to party headquarters. The parties used to do this openly, but late in 2014, and much to their surprise, the Cabinet Office announced that it intended to prosecute anyone behaving in this way. As far as the parties were concerned, the Cabinet Office and the Electoral Commission were misinterpreting the law, but they became more discreet in how they went about observing votes.[70]

It was from their analysis of the postal voting that the Liberal Democrats received the first clue that things were not going as well as they might have hoped. Early Conservative postal vote intelligence had reached a similar conclusion. It suggested the party was winning a significant number of seats that would not be won given the public polling and it was the final factor in convincing the party that the whole Liberal Democrat battleground was in play. There was also a claim that it was Labour's poor performance in the postal votes that was responsible for one of the more unexpected events of the campaign – when Ed Miliband was interviewed by the actor and comedian Russell Brand. The Labour Uncut website claimed that: 'Labour insiders familiar with the latest figures have told Uncut that the picture for Labour in marginal seats, where it is fighting the Tories, is almost uniformly grim ... With just a few days to go until the election, Labour desperately needs new voters. This is why Ed Miliband suddenly changed his plans and went to Russell Brand's home to be interviewed.'[71] Yet at that stage, the information reaching Labour about postal voting was not especially worrying.[72] Rather, the visit had been organised by Lucy Powell, who had been in contact with Brand, with the latter keen to arrange an interview.

The broadcast interview, which took place in Brand's modish kitchen, lasted almost 16 minutes, with the interviewer speaking for as long as the interviewee. The two perched awkwardly on stools, with Ed Miliband occasionally lapsing into mockney as he attempted to respond to Brand's questions-cum-monologue. What became known as the Milibrand interview was released on 29 April. But on 4 May, a second tranche of the interview was released, after which Brand formally endorsed Labour, claiming to have been persuaded by Miliband's answers.[73] Three separate sources within Labour say that Brand had agreed to do so before Miliband took part in the interview.

The case for doing the interview was obvious: Brand had an appeal that no established politician could match, especially with groups not easily reached; he had almost 10 million Twitter followers, with more than a million people watching his YouTube channel. But the case against was also fairly clear. As one of Miliband's team put it: 'The papers kicked us to death over it. The people who vote, read those papers. The people who don't, maybe liked it, but they don't vote. The young people in the office, all said, it's going well, my friends all like it on Facebook, it's all sort of under the radar – but then they didn't vote. The whole thing was pointless ... No, worse than that. It was harmful.' Brand would later say that he felt personally responsible for the election result. The truth was that he was not that influential.

The last TV 'debate' took place on 30 April in Leeds Town Hall, a special edition of the BBC's *Question Time*. The leaders appeared before the studio audience one after another, each for 30 minutes, starting with David Cameron, then Ed Miliband and ending with Nick Clegg. This was the only TV event at which Miliband's team felt he under-performed. The audience were more punchy than in previous programmes to all three leaders; just as Farage had complained about the audience in the BBC Challengers' debate, behind the scenes, Miliband's team had been furiously complaining to the BBC about the audience selection process, which they claimed produced an anti-Labour bias in the audience.[74]

Miliband's trickiest moment came with a question about spending: did he accept that the last Labour government spent too much? His initial response ('No, I don't') produced an audible intake of breath in the studio, followed by heckling, and an aggressive follow-up question in which he was accused of being ludicrous and lying. Miliband had a standard, rehearsed, response to any question about spending: acknowledge that not all spending by the last Labour government could be justified; yes, things could have been different; but he was proud of the investment in schools; and it was important to realise that it was not spending on schools and Sure Start centres that caused the financial crisis. He made most of these points, but not in that order, and his gaffe was seized on by the Conservatives throughout what was left of the campaign. He then stumbled slightly as he left the stage, reinforcing the sense of a below-par performance. As soon as he left the stage, he admitted to his team that he knew he had got it wrong.

Labour were, however, more pleased with the way he had dealt with a question about the SNP. He again ruled out a 'deal' and a coalition, adding: 'If it meant we weren't going to be in government, not having a coalition, not doing a deal, then so be it.' He specifically ruled out confidence and supply deals, but attempts by both David Dimbleby as chair and the audience member who asked the question to winkle out what would happen in the event of a Labour government putting forward a Queen's Speech and being dependent on the SNP to carry it were skilfully swerved.

Cameron and Clegg's teams both felt they had performed well, despite tough questioning. As in many of his stump speeches, Cameron waved around Liam Byrne's 'There is No Money' letter. An ICM poll for *The Guardian* had Cameron 'winning' (on 44%), Miliband second (38%) and Clegg last (19%). Despite coming last, Clegg's team thought he had performed well in all of the debates. As one of his team put it: 'The disappointing thing was that, as with the first seven-way debate, a good performance didn't shift support for the party in any meaningful way', adding that 'nothing shifted the dial at all over the course of the campaign'. This was not quite true. The British Election Study, which was monitoring support across the campaign, found Clegg's rating slowly improved during the campaign, increasingly more than any other leader, but just not by enough to make much of a difference.

The Duke and Duchess of Cambridge's second baby was due to arrive days before polling day, which led to (serious) discussion as to whether it could influence the outcome of the election. It was a sign of how close the election was felt to be – and how even the slightest changes of votes might affect the outcome – that such an argument was given any time at all. There was a related, and marginally less daft, concern that the event might swamp media reporting, but the birth of Princess Charlotte on 2 May meant that even this was not a major issue. According to Populus, the event was the most noticed news story that week for just 1% of the population.

On 30 April, *The Guardian* ran a story about 'secret' Conservative plans to cut child benefit, which were being 'exposed' by Danny Alexander.[75] The reality was more prosaic – the document was an options document discussed and rejected in 2012 – but the source of the material was more significant than the content. Having worked together closely for five years, there was no shortage of similar material that could be spun damagingly by either of the coalition parties. Yet there were limits in terms of how far they could go in washing their dirty linen in public. 'There are emails and notes that we've all saved', said one Special Advisor, 'and they know, and we know, that if we cross a line, it will all come out. But that is mutually assured destruction.' The child benefit story provoked several angry phone calls from the Conservatives to the Lib Dems – including one from the Prime Minister's Chief of Staff, Ed Llewellyn, pointing this out. 'We still thought there might be a second coalition and it would be too messy if we'd used all of this stuff', said one Lib Dem aide. It was another example of where things might have been different if the likelihood of a hung parliament had not seemed so great. Even so, there would have been more leaks had the *Daily Telegraph* story on Nicola Sturgeon not gone so badly. 'If that hadn't backfired, there would have been more zingers in the last week', said a key member of the Lib Dem team.

When on 4 May, Lord Scriven, a Lib Dem peer and close confidant of Clegg, accused Cameron of 'lying' over the Tories' chances of victory, claiming he had privately admitted to the Deputy Prime Minister that they 'won't win a majority', the Prime Minister denied the story, but added: 'I could tell you all the things [Nick Clegg] has said to me in private. That would certainly surprise you.' Clegg refused to comment on Scriven's claim, but said: 'They are not going to win with a majority ... they know that. Nobody thinks they're going to win a majority, they need 323 seats and there's absolutely no way they are going to get that.' This was again something Clegg got wrong, but where he was in good company.

Crosby had long told the media that there would soon be 'crossover' in the polls, with the Conservatives pulling ahead of Labour. Plenty of journalists – and even some of those around Ed Miliband – had expected the same. But as the campaign crawled on, there was no evidence that it was happening. With every week that passed, optimism began to grow in the Labour camp – and a sense of frustration began to grow at Conservative HQ. 'The pollsters caused an immense amount of stress, forcing us to do some things that we had not planned', said one of the Chancellor's aides. This included the £8 billion promised for the NHS at the beginning of the campaign, a pledge that regulated train fares would not rise by more than inflation made on 10 April, and the idea of using fines imposed on Deutsche Bank for its involvement in rigging interest rates to fund 50,000 apprenticeships, announced in late April.

Moreover, there was frustration within the Conservative camp at how the lack of any polling crossover was manifesting itself in media coverage of the election. Just as Labour were frustrated by the focus of the media on the post-election scenarios and the role of the SNP, so the Conservatives began to get annoyed with the focus on their lack of any breakthrough. 'We were', one said, 'all getting upset by the commentariat, particularly the BBC, providing so much comment and not news. We had to break the narrative, which was being driven by the polls.' There was particular annoyance at the idea that their campaign was lacklustre and that Cameron himself did not seem particularly energised. The former Labour spin doctor Alastair Campbell had written that he was 'beginning to doubt that Mr Cameron really wants to win, and beginning to wonder whether he may be, as they say in maternity circles, too posh to push'.[76] Campbell may have been *parti pris*, but there were similar complaints from Conservative supporters.

Crosby's view was that you should largely ignore the commentariat – until there was a problem. And then you should then do something that would get noticed. A fortnight from polling day at a meeting at Chequers, the Conservative team made a conscious decision to up the tempo of the campaign – and to brief the media that that was what they were doing. In practice, this meant that the Prime Minister shouted a bit more during his speeches, went red-faced, gesticulated wildly and told people that he was 'pumped up'. Questioned by journalists about his new approach, he roared: 'If I'm getting lively about it, it's because I feel bloody lively about it!' It was easy to mock, and plenty did, but it filtered through, and Conservative focus groups said they had noticed the difference. Much to his surprise, Rupert Harrison, one of George Osborne's Special Advisors, found that his mother-in-law had noticed: 'It's good to see the Prime Minister has entered the campaign', she said.

And yet still the polls did not seem to move – and Labour confidence increased further.

As the campaign closed, the almost universal assumption was that the election had been just the *amuse-bouche*. Behind the scenes, all the parties were preparing for what would follow election night. George Osborne, encountering Nick Robinson in mid-April, told him not to hurry back to work after his cancer treatment: 'Don't worry about rushing back to cover the campaign ... The time your judgement will be needed is on election night and in the days that follow.'[77] Osborne then spent election day sending Nick Clegg texts calling for another coalition.[78] Former Cabinet Secretary Gus O'Donnell – who was clearly enjoying his role as a constitutional authority – predicted 'weeks' of negotiations.[79]

The leaders pursued a hectic schedule to the end. Cameron, as he had done in 2010, completed a virtually non-stop 36-hour tour of marginal seats. Clegg travelled from Land's End to John O'Groats and forecast that the Lib Dems would be 'the surprise story' of the election (this was something he got right, if not quite for the reasons he expected). Miliband spent 6 May campaigning in marginal seats in the Pennines. On polling day, all three adjourned to their constituency homes and with their aides waited to learn from the exit poll what their fates would be. Miliband's team provided the waiting journalists camped outside his Doncaster house with bacon sandwiches; this time no photographs were taken.

Plenty of people within the Labour Party had been apprehensive ahead of the campaign. They feared that Miliband would crack under the pressure and increased scrutiny of the campaign, the polls would begin to shift and Labour's campaign would collapse. But after the first few weeks of the campaign, when Conservative attacks appeared to have come to nothing, they felt emboldened; even after being on the back foot for the last few weeks of the campaign, the public polling had still refused to shift, and even the most pessimistic within Labour felt that they might manage to pull it off. Whilst expecting to gain fewer seats than the Conservatives, they knew that they had a greater number of would-be partners than the Conservatives in any negotiations, almost certainly enough to get Ed Miliband into Number 10.

Private doubts, however, remained. The core Miliband campaign team were aware of the party's private polling – not as positive as the public polls – and on 5 May, the former Labour leader Neil Kinnock gave an interview to the *New Statesman* in which he wondered whether the polls might be under-estimating Conservative support. He recalled the campaign in 1992, when the polls had given false hope to him and

Labour.[80] Twenty-three years later, his daughter Rachel was in charge of organising Ed Miliband's campaign events – and with less than a week to go, Miliband turned to her and said that he too worried that the election could be a re-run of 1992.

Campaign chronology

30 Mar	Dissolution of Parliament. D. Cameron warns voters they face £3,000 extra tax under Lab; IFS calls figure 'unhelpful and of little value'. E. Miliband launches Lab business manifesto.
31 Mar	N. Farage says leaving the EU could cut immigration from 300,000 to 30,000 a year, which is contradicted by UKIP's immigration spokesman, who puts the figure at 50,000. Plaid Cymru launch manifesto, *Working for Wales.*
1 Apr	103 business leaders write to the *Daily Telegraph* saying that Lab threatens UK recovery. Miliband promises zero-hours workers regular contracts. UKIP vice-chair, S. Evans, contradicts both her leader and party spokesman saying that the party has no net migration targets.
2 Apr	Seven-way TV debate.
3 Apr	*Daily Telegraph* publishes story that N. Sturgeon told French Ambassador she would 'rather see' Cameron as Prime Minister than Miliband. Sturgeon denies story and calls for inquiry.
4 Apr	Civil service inquiry into leaked Sturgeon memo announced.
5 Apr	Sturgeon offers to help Lab into government and to form an anti-austerity alliance after election.
6 Apr	J. Murphy launches Scottish Lab 10-point pledge card.
7 Apr	Former Lab PM T. Blair backs Miliband and warns of chaos of EU referendum. Cameron calls on UKIP voters to 'come home'. First Scottish leaders' debate.
8 Apr	Lab announce they will restrict 'nom-dom' tax status. Over 140 senior doctors write to *The Guardian* attacking Con NHS reforms. Second Scottish leaders' debate (including UKIP and Greens).
9 Apr	Con Defence Secretary, M. Fallon, claims Lab would 'barter away our nuclear deterrent' dealing with SNP. Three polls give Lab a lead over Con; one finding (for the first time) that Miliband has more positive personal approval ratings than Cameron.
10 Apr	*The Guardian* headline: 'The Day the Polls Turned.'
12 Apr	Farage calls on voters to back Con in seats where UKIP can't win.

13 Apr Lab launches manifesto, *Britain Can Be Better.* Con take a six-point lead with ICM. 100 small business owners write to *The Sun* fearing Lab government.

14 Apr Con launch manifesto, *The Conservative Manifesto*; Green Party launch manifesto, *For the Common Good.*

15 Apr Lib Dem launch manifesto, *Manifesto 2015.* UKIP launch manifesto, *Believe in Britain.* SDLP publish *Prosperity Not Austerity.* Cameron tells BBC's *Newsnight* he will have failed if the Con do not get overall majority.

16 Apr 'Challengers' debate involving main opposition leaders. *Daily Express* owner, R. Desmond, donates £1m to UKIP.

17 Apr Con launch 'jobs manifesto'. UUP launch manifesto, *One Chance for Change.*

18 Apr A. Salmond says Miliband been 'foolish' in ruling out coalition with SNP. Miliband sets out Lab's immigration policy.

19 Apr Con release poster depicting Miliband as puppet of Sturgeon. Cameron urges Lib Dem and UKIP voters to 'lend their vote' to Con to stop Lab–SNP government.

20 Apr SNP launch manifesto, *Stronger for Scotland.* Sinn Fein launch manifesto, *Equality Not Austerity.*

21 Apr Former Con PM J. Major says SNP will 'create merry hell' if they hold balance of power. Former Con Cabinet Minister N. Tebbit calls on Con to vote Labour in Scotland to stop SNP. DUP launch manifesto, *DUP Westminster Manifesto 2015.*

23 Apr G. Osborne says that a Lab–SNP government would leave families £358 worse off per year. IFS says voters 'left in the dark' on where cuts would fall by main parties' manifestos.

24 Apr Row over the suggestion Miliband will say that deaths of refugees crossing the Mediterranean is 'in part a direct result' of PM's intervention in Libya. Cameron says remarks 'ill judged'. Con launch 'English manifesto'.

25 Apr Cameron appears to forget which football team he supports. N. Clegg says Lib Dem would ensure 'legitimate and stable government' if no party wins outright.

27 Apr Lab add sixth election pledge. Con publish 'small business manifesto'. J. Wells resigns as Northern Ireland health minister after linking same-sex relationships to child abuse.

28 Apr Miliband confirms that he has been interviewed by the comedian R. Brand.

29 Apr Cameron announces Con will legislate to outlaw rises in income tax, VAT and NI before 2020. Lab claim Con cuts will

leave families up to £2,000 worse off. Ipsos MORI poll for STV suggests the SNP could win every seat in Scotland. Brand interview with Miliband broadcast.

30 Apr ComRes poll puts Lab and Con neck-and-neck; later Ipsos/MORI gives Con five-point lead. *Question Time Election Special* with Cameron, Miliband and Clegg.

1 May B. Johnson urges UKIP voters to 'come home' to Con. Meaning to describe the election as 'country defining', Cameron calls it 'career defining'.

2 May Duke and Duchess of Cambridge's second child born. Miliband says 'no special deals' for the SNP.

3 May Miliband unveils 8ft 6in stone plinth engraved with Lab's election pledges. Final Scottish leaders' debate.

4 May Brand releases second part of interview and urges voters to back Miliband. Murphy forced to abandon campaigning by SNP activists.

6 May UKIP candidate for North East Hampshire is suspended for threatening to shoot Con opponent. Polls show Con and Lab neck-and-neck.

Notes

1. Like quite a lot of races at the Olympics, it didn't.
2. Patrick Wintour, 'The Undoing of Ed Miliband – and How Labour Lost the Election', *The Guardian*, 3 June 2015.
3. All taken from Conservative press releases during the campaign. There are a lot more where they came from.
4. Both the positions in which the leaders stood and the order in which they spoke was decided by lots – beginning with Natalie Bennett's opening statement for the Greens and ending with David Cameron, who would give the final closing statement. The original intention had been for the programme to have no advert breaks, but during ITV's rehearsal, it had become obvious that the participants would probably need a toilet break at some point.
5. Who the parties think they are speaking to can then determine the language used. The SNP, for example had a discussion about the use of the word 'austerity'. 'There was concern that it wasn't an ideal word, but it's the word that's used', as one of those involved put it. 'People sort of know what it means, they know it means cuts ... Basically, austerity is bad.' The Greens reached a similar conclusion, but for different reasons. Not everyone may know what austerity means, but they concluded that potential Green voters did. 'We're not speaking to the entire electorate', said one of the Green debate team. 'At this stage in our development, there's about 10% of the electorate who might vote Green. If you use mainstream messaging, there's a risk you alienate that group.'

6. The answer to this became clear on 7 May.
7. With so many SNP-facing MPs, there would have to be some engagement with Nicola Sturgeon, he said, but 'we really didn't want to engage with Wood or Bennett [or Farage]'.
8. 'Nicola Mania', *The Economist*, 6 April 2015. In rehearsal, Labour had discovered that when Miliband attacked Sturgeon it tended to elevate her and diminish him; the staffer playing Cameron would ostentatiously stand back, gesture towards them and say 'See? That's the chaos you'd see every day under a Labour-SNP government'. It was especially difficult to challenge the SNP's record in government: if Miliband talked about Scotland, then he was showing the majority of the public that his government would get bogged down in issues that were not relevant to them; if he did not talk about Scotland, then the only person in the room making any sort of appeal to Scottish voters was Sturgeon – and she could spend all of her time appealing to a tiny segment of the overall electorate. 'There was,' one of Labour's debate team concluded, 'no right answer', adding: 'those who thought Ed did the wrong thing in the debates had generally not thought about how the opposite approach gamed out'.
9. Sturgeon and Wood in particular were in frequent contact by text ('I would be amazed if there wasn't some coordination', said another of those involved in the preparation work) and the former was seen popping into the room of the latter just before the debate, but even without formal collaboration, there was, as one Plaid Cymru staffer put it, 'nothing to be gained' by any of those three parties attacking one another.
10. There was a further below-par interview to come. On 7 April, Bennett went on the *Today* programme on Radio 4 and again struggled, with the interview then ending with the presenter confusing her with Caroline Lucas.
11. In the first debate, there were four male and three female participants, plus a female chair; in the second, there were two male and three female participants, plus a male chair.
12. In the various Scotland-only debates which took place during the campaign, she was much more combative, not least because she had a record in government to justify, and therefore the other parties did not treat her so gently. As one of her team said: 'It was 3 to 1 there, and we had a record to defend. The goal then is one of survival. You need to get in, and get out, without a blow.' Or, as another of her team put it, the Scottish debates were 'four people talking at the same time'.
13. Although it was hardly an impressive performance. One Lib Dem advisor, watching on, was horrified by Bennett's performance: 'You're *reading* it. It's a closing statement of 60 seconds long – and you're having to *read* it? *Really?*' But the Green closing statement had only been prepared earlier that day, in the hotel room, and it had not been properly memorised. Fearing another media disaster, she opted for the safety of a script.
14. In *Project Fear* (Biteback, 2015, pp. 224–5), Joe Pike claims that Labour had planned to engage with Farage, albeit with some difficulty. Our sources differ on this. In practice it was Wood (in the first debate) and Sturgeon (in the second) who did most to confront him, and both did so spontaneously.
15. See Owen Bennett, *Following Farage*. Biteback, 2015, pp. 257–8.
16. Farage topped the 'best' poll with 24% and the 'worst' poll with 22%.

17. This was true not just of the genuine debates, but also for some of the other programmes, even those – such as the three-way *Question Time* event – which had managed perfectly well without 'spin rooms' in previous elections.
18. Bennett, *Following Farage*, p. 252.
19. ICM, for *The Guardian*, had Miliband (25%) marginally ahead of Cameron (24%); ComRes, for ITV, had Cameron, Miliband and Farage all on 21%; YouGov, for *The Times* and *The Sun*, had Sturgeon top on 28%; Survation had Cameron and Miliband both on 25%. The question of who 'won' each debate is a largely meaningless one (for an excellent discussion, see Lewis Baston's 'The TV Debate: Colourless Green Ideas Sleep Furiously', www.lewisbaston.com, 3 April 2015), but it is a meaningless one that dominates the way the debates are reported.
20. People in Scotland occasionally express surprise at this: how could voters in England and Wales not know who the First Minister was? But given that voters have, on the whole, relatively limited knowledge about those who govern them, why should we expect people to have knowledge of someone who doesn't govern them?
21. The initial conversation was conducted in English, but this did not rule out some misunderstanding occurring.
22. Reporting after the election, it revealed that the dark arts of spin are not always sophisticated. The memo had originated out of the Scottish Office; the Special Advisor concerned had used his official phone to contact the *Daily Telegraph*, and – despite having denied knowledge of it publicly – the Liberal Democrat Secretary of State, Alistair Carmichael, had agreed with its leaking. Carmichael admitted that he had been involved and said that, had he still been in office, he would have resigned from government. He came under pressure to resign his seat, being the subject of one of the few post-election petitions. It was still on-going as this book went to press. In July 2015, the Independent Press Standards Organisation upheld a complaint about what it described as a 'significantly misleading' front-page story.
23. In reality, Labour would retain the ability for those genuinely non-domiciled in the UK to avoid paying UK tax on non-UK income and would have consulted on the details.
24. Technically, Balls' earlier statement and Labour's policy were not inconsistent, since Balls had been talking about the problems with abolition, and Labour's policy was not to abolish, but to restrict non-dom status, yet Miliband and the party frequently talked about abolishing or ending the non-dom rule, and so the distinction became (understandably) lost.
25. Boris Johnson, 'This Cap on Bankers' Bonuses is Like a Dead Cat – Pure Distraction', *Daily Telegraph*, 3 March 2013. See also Isabel Hardman, 'Is the Tory Trident Row an Example of a "Dead Cat" Strategy?', blogs.spectator.co.uk/coffeehouse, 9 April 2015.
26. Once the personal insults were removed, the claim was ridiculous. With Conservative support, it would have been very easy for even a Labour minority government to get Trident renewed, and Fallon came unstuck on this, but the dead cat distracts from such detail.
27. Labour's manifesto felt – and indeed was – the briefest, coming in at 84 A5 pages, including multiple photos, and just 20,000 words. The Conservative manifesto had a similar number of pages (81), but was A4 in size, and even

if more padded with photos, it came in noticeably longer at 31,000 words. The Lib Dem manifesto had more pages than both those of Labour and the Conservatives put together, at 188 pages (even in A5 size, this weighed in at 36,000 words and was widely seen as too long. It had an index and even supplied a page so that the really keen reader could take notes).

28. Several around Miliband had wanted to hold back even more from the Clause 5 meeting to sign off the manifesto, but the probity of the party's rules won out.
29. Nigel Farage made much of the fact that there were no special interests represented in the UKIP manifesto – although the only specific policy pledge on airports concerned Manston Airport, which happened to be in the constituency Farage was fighting.
30. The launch of UKIP's Scottish manifesto on 4 May was even more farcical. No copies of the manifesto had arrived, a problem the party blamed on the Bank Holiday post, but no online copies were available either.
31. It was the longest of all, just 81 pages, but some 43,000 words.
32. Never earlier, we were told, as Miliband was an evening person, and was not at his best early in the morning.
33. Ralph Miliband was indeed a removal man after arriving in Britain in 1940, but he was also the author of (amongst others) *Parliamentary Socialism*, *The State in Capitalist Society*, *Marxism and Politics*, *Capitalist Democracy in Britain*, *Class Power and State Power* and *Socialism for a Sceptical Age*, none of which got a look in.
34. Not all the Greens liked it, though. As one member of the campaign team said: 'I hated that PEB. We're going around saying: "We're competent. We're serious. Vote for us to govern", and then we put out something like that. Yes, it was funny, but we weren't trying for funny.'
35. The Conservatives withdrew first, to no great disappointment from the others.
36. Much less publicly, the Prime Minister was often transported by helicopter or plane, then meeting up with the campaign bus at the venue.
37. Marina Hyde, 'The Great Unvetted Public Locked Out as Party Leaders Tour Sanitised Britain', *The Guardian*, 10 April 2015.
38. *The Independent* said this was 'the kind of question we have all been waiting for one of the political leaders to be asked during this dull and stage-managed campaign'. By this, it presumably did not mean a question in which the premise was factually wrong, given that the Chancellor and the Prime Minister did not even go to the same school. 'David Cameron and Boris Johnson Told They're Elitist and Out of Touch Because They Went to Eton', *The Independent*, 5 May 2015.
39. Visits are planned with the two key aims: to hit important media regions (the region matters much more than the individual constituency that the visit takes place in) and to generate good pictures. When searching for ideas for visits, policy staff tend to suggest venues linked to a policy that is to be promoted; those with experience planning visits think about the pictures that will be generated. 'Where do you not go?', we asked one of those involved in planning visits. 'A lifeboat factory.' There is evidence that such visits work: see Alia Middleton, 'The Effectiveness of Leader Visits During

the 2010 British General Election Campaign', *British Journal of Politics and International Relations*, 2014 (online).

40. Despite the logistical problems involved and despite the fact that it was, on paper, such a safe seat, the SNP seriously considered a Sturgeon campaign visit to Orkney and Shetland, a sign of just how confident they were at targeting every seat in Scotland. But in the end the opportunity cost – of other seats not visited in the time that trip would take – was considered too great. She did, however, visit the only Conservative-held seat on four separate occasions, so keen were the SNP to achieve a Conservative wipeout.
41. Bennett, *Following Farage*, p. 298. Even if frustrated, it is difficult to imagine any of the other participants attacking the audience in this way.
42. By contrast, Plaid's manifesto, *Working for Wales* (c. 18,500 words), was launched right at the beginning of the campaign, on 31 March.
43. Boris Johnson, 'If Ed Miliband's in the Driving Seat, Nicola Sturgeon Will Be Steering Him to the Left', *Daily Telegraph*, 19 April 2015. He went on: 'If Miliband somehow manages to form a minority government, he will be peeping from Alec Salmond's sporran like a baffled baby kangaroo.'
44. George Eaton, 'Why the SNP Wouldn't Drag Labour Far to the Left', *New Statesman*, 27 April 2015.
45. Rowena Crawford *et al.*, *Post-election Austerity: Parties' Plans Compared*, IFS Briefing Note BN170, 2015.
46. David Torrance, 'The Reinvention of the SNP', *The Guardian*, 21 May 2015.
47. As Labour's briefing note said, 'the refugee crisis and tragic scenes this week in the Mediterranean are in part a direct result of the failure of post conflict planning for Libya. The tragedy is this should have been anticipated, it could have been avoided'.
48. Iain Watson, *Five Million Conversations*. Luath Press, 2015, p. 149.
49. Watson, *Five Million Conversations*, p. 149.
50. See Philip Cowley, 'Voters Wrong, But Still Revealing', revolts.co.uk, 15 June 2015.
51. Because this question only started to be asked midway through the campaign, it is, alas, not possible to discover whether this animosity was always present or whether it grew during the campaign. The overall figure is slightly misleading, and the SNP scored relatively well with Labour, Lib Dem, and especially Green and Plaid supporters, but it scored very badly with Conservative and UKIP supporters. The mean likeability score given by SNP voters for the Conservatives was 1.2; Conservatives returned the favour, scoring the SNP at 1.3.
52. Will Dahlgreen, 'What Kind of Coalition Do You Want?', yougov.co.uk, 14 March 2015, and, by the same author, 'Majority Conservative Government the "Least Bad Option" – Voters', yougov.co.uk, 24 April 2015.
53. Amongst those aged 65 and over, opposition to Sturgeon rose to 71%. 'ITV News Index – Coalition Partners', comres.co.uk, 20 April 2015.
54. Wintour, 'The Undoing of Ed Miliband'.
55. Rowena Mason, 'Boozy Farage Holds Impromptu Victory Party after Thanet Poll Boost', *The Guardian*, 24 April 2015.
56. The candidate for Charnwood, who had been suspended in January for saying that those on benefits should not be allowed to drive, had his suspension lifted in February and stood as an the official UKIP candidate.

Shortly after the election, the suspended candidate for West Lancashire joined the BNP.

57. 'Boris Tells UKIPers: Come Home to the Tories', *The Sun*, 1 May 2015.
58. Cameron had previously admitted not to being a particularly involved football fan, but given that his connection with Aston Villa was that his uncle, Sir William Dugdale, was Villa chairman, it seems implausible that he would have simply forgotten the name of the club, no matter how slight – or not – his interest in football and no matter how tired he was. His other verbal slip, this time more straightforward, came on 1 May, when he claimed the election was 'career-defining', quickly correcting himself to 'country-defining'.
59. In an interview with Radio 5, she said: 'I don't think anyone's suggesting the fact that he's carved them into stone means that he is absolutely not going to break them or anything like that.' The context of the interview made it clear enough what she was trying to say, but the phrasing was a gift to her opponents.
60. Several of Labour's press team attempted to get the stone destroyed the weekend after polling, but were unable to get authorisation.
61. This is how they were known within the party, although in practice the switching was more yellow-blue than blue-yellow.
62. As it was, this calculation proved optimistic. Several of the supposedly safe seats were to fall to Labour on election day.
63. George Parker and Kiran Stacey, 'Clegg Dismisses Any Coalition Deal with Labour Involving SNP', *Financial Times*, 24 April 2015.
64. 'Nick Clegg's Rules on Coalition-Building are "Absurd", Says Constitutional Expert', *The Guardian*, 25 April 2015.
65. The six red lines were very similar to the five key policies announced in February (see p. 143) when the party had launched its manifesto front page – when it had said explicitly that it would not be issuing red lines.
66. Only two Lib Dem policies were seen as causing difficulties: the pace of deficit reduction and the issue of tax rates/allowances for the low paid. Neither was seen by Labour as insurmountable. 'I think we should have been able to do a deal in which we taxed the less well-off less without too much difficulty', said one of those involved.
67. Unlike in 2010, when Labour had conducted almost no preparation for coalition negotiations, in 2015 the preparation was considerable. The briefing on the Lib Dems, for example, ran to around 250 pages.
68. This was probably true of getting into power. Once in government, however, the SNP would have been able to exercise considerable influence on a vote-by-vote basis. Labour's view was that they would deal with that once it happened, but that having pledged so publicly that there would be no deals, it was crucial that they delivered on this promise.
69. See Philip Cowley, 'Postal Voters – and Fibbers', www.revolts.co.uk, 23 June 2015.
70. The relevant legislation is the Representation of the People Act (1983), which makes it illegal to 'attempt to ascertain the candidate for whom any vote is given in any particular ballot paper or communicate any information with respect thereto obtained at those proceedings' (s. 66(4)(d). The dispute was over the phrase 'particular ballot paper'. Did that mean any individual

ballot paper or did it mean a specific ballot paper (such as John Smith's ballot paper or Fred Bloggs' ballot paper)? The parties' interpretation was the latter, which therefore made general monitoring of votes acceptable; the Electoral Commission's was the former, which meant it was not.

71. Atul Hatwal, 'Revealed: Ed's Night-Time Dash to Casa Brand Driven by Postal Ballot Panic', labour-uncut.co.uk. This story itself provoked complaints to the Electoral Commission and pleas to prosecute Labour.
72. Given the eventual result, this lack of concern within Labour about their postal votes might be thought to support those who argue that the election was decided by a late swing to the Conservatives. It might, however, be that the quality of information reaching the party was not as good as it might have been, given the requirement to monitor votes so much more discreetly.
73. At least he did in most of England – he had also endorsed the Greens in Brighton Pavilion, in a separate interview, and suggested that people in Scotland should vote SNP. However, he had previously advocated not voting, and the interviews took place after the deadline for registration had passed, so anyone who followed his advice religiously would have been unable to vote anyway.
74. There were supposed to be equal numbers of Labour, Conservative and Lib Dem supporters; Labour argued that this meant two-thirds of the partisans in the room would be, broadly, for the Coalition. After the debate, Labour supporters kept identifying the links that various audience members who asked difficult questions had with the Conservative Party.
75. Patrick Wintour, '"Secret" Tory Plans for £8bn in Welfare Cuts Exposed by Danny Alexander', *The Guardian*, 30 April 2015.
76. 'The Lethargy of the Cameron Campaign – Is He Too Posh to Push?', www.alastaircampbell.org.
77. Nick Robinson, *Election Notebook*. Bantam, 2015, p. 332.
78. Andrew Rawnsley, 'George Osborne is the Master of All He Surveys... Except the Economy', *The Observer*, 12 July 2015.
79. 'Lord O'Donnell: Former Cabinet Secretary on the Election and Life Away from the Levers of Power', *The Independent*, 3 May 2015.
80. Neil Kinnock, 'If Campaigns Win Elections, We are Doing Well. But I Do Recall that I Got the Prize for the Campaign and Still Didn't Win', *New Statesman*, 5 May 2015. There were occasional discussions of this in the media. See, for example, Asa Bennett, 'What if the Polls are Wrong? Shy Tories Could Deliver an Election Surprise', *Telegraph* blog, 1 May 2015.

8
Different Scripts Required: Election Night

Election night was to be a battle for legitimacy. Before being despatched to the TV and radio studios, politicians from both Labour and the Conservatives were briefed by their parties on the key constitutional precedents in the event of a hung parliament: what had happened in 2010, but also what had happened in the elections of 1924 or 1974, when no party had won a majority, as well as the wording of the *Cabinet Manual* ('A guide to laws, conventions and rules on the operation of government'), and in particular paragraph 2.12, on what happened in the event of a hung parliament. Labour's 13-page briefing document for its studio guests, replete with quotes from assorted constitutional experts, included historical examples back to 1892.

Both parties felt it was important to control the narrative of election night from the beginning. The Conservatives expected to be the larger party and intended to argue that this gave the Prime Minister the right to remain in office to try to form a government and – citing Baldwin's behaviour in 1924 – to bring a Queen's speech before Parliament even if the chance of that speech passing the Commons was slim.

Although they did not expect to be the largest party, Labour expected there to be what they termed a lock-out majority, with more than half the House of Commons being unwilling to support the Conservatives under any circumstances.[1] They intended to argue that the government had lost its majority and – citing Heath's behaviour in 1974 – that as soon as it became clear there was an anti-Conservative majority, the Prime Minister should resign and the Queen should then invite Ed Miliband to attempt to form a government.[2] Senior Labour figures had earlier in the day taken part in a significant briefing operation, contacting various journalists and assorted constitutionalists in an attempt to ensure their interpretation of the manual was the same as Labour's.[3]

In the event that such an anti-Conservative majority did exist but the Prime Minister did not resign, once Parliament resumed, Labour intended to put down a motion of no confidence as an amendment to the Queen's Speech – but they were keen to avoid any such vote taking place.[4] As one of those involved in Labour's planning put it: 'It was incredibly important for us not to be written off. Our legitimacy would have been ruined by the belief we had lost. Imagine if people thought the Tories have won, but whoops, Labour is now the government.' Whilst Labour knew that they would under these circumstances be able to force David Cameron out of Number 10 – the inevitability of the parliamentary arithmetic would eventually have told – they were concerned about the time this would take and the damage that it could do to how they were perceived by the electorate, especially in the face of what they assumed would be a predominantly hostile media. 'We'd have been seen as illegitimate', as one put it. 'We wouldn't have been able to do anything. We'd have been in office but not power.' They also did not want to be seen to be reliant on the votes of the Scottish National Party (SNP) in order to oust David Cameron. Once installed in Downing Street, there was an acknowledgement that the SNP would be a political reality that would have to be dealt with, but having ruled out any formal deals with the SNP so firmly during the election campaign, Labour wanted to avoid the SNP being involved in the government's formation. Labour had accurately predicted what the Conservative attack would have been: to argue that it would not be democratic for Labour to take power on what they would have called 'a constitutional nicety'. 'If they think they can rule without a democratic mandate', as one Conservative put it just before 10 pm, 'they've misjudged how the British voters feel.'

At the bookmaker's, you could, at this point, get odds of just 1/25 on a hung parliament and a massive 11/1 on a Conservative majority.[5]

And then, at 10 pm, the exit poll came out – and everything changed.

Broadcast simultaneously on the BBC, ITV and Sky News, it predicted that the Conservatives would win 316 seats and Labour just 239. The Liberal Democrats would be reduced to ten, down a full 47, and the SNP were predicted to win 58, an almost clean sweep of Scotland's 59 seats. (The exit poll's methodology and accuracy is discussed in more detail on p. 238.) These were figures completely out of line with the campaign polls – and with almost everyone's expectations. Although it still put the Conservatives just shy of the number required to form an outright majority, they were near enough that it was relatively easy to see how they could do a deal with either the Democratic Unionist Party (DUP) or the Liberal Democrats to stay in office. Just as in 2010, there was initial scepticism about its predictions. Paddy Ashdown offered to eat his hat on TV if the exit poll turned out to be true; Alastair Campbell said he would eat a kilt if the Scottish figures turned out to be true; senior SNP figures said that the poll should be treated with 'huge caution'.

Those who wanted the exit poll to be wrong leapt on two other polls released during the night – a poll by Lord Ashcroft of some 12,000 people who had voted, predicting a much less dramatic three-point Conservative lead, and a YouGov poll, often discussed as if it were an exit poll, but which was merely an exercise the firm had done re-contacting those it polled previously to see if there was any need to change its final numbers (which there was not). Labour and Lib Dem supporters initially clung to these two polls, as they did John Curtice's earlier public pronouncements on the difficulties of conducting the 2015 exit poll given the rise of the SNP and UKIP.[6] But just as in 2010 and 2005, the exit poll was to prove astonishingly accurate.

The BBC's first announcement, that the Conservatives would be the biggest party, did not overly concern anyone at Brewer's Green. It was entirely in line with their expectations. But as soon as the party projections were released, Labour's HQ was stunned. One of those present described the feeling as 'sheer horror'. 'I have never known a period of silence amongst so many people for quite so long', recalled Ed Balls' Special Advisor, Alex Belardinelli.[7] It was Lord Falconer who broke the silence, telling staff not to over-react – polls had been wrong before, he said, they could be wrong again, and staff should just carry on with what they were supposed to be doing. Labour politicians in broadcast studios initially persisted with their line that David Cameron might lose his majority. It would not have taken the exit poll to be very wrong for this to be true, although several of those parroting this line did it with less than total enthusiasm. One studio guest who texted Labour HQ to find out what line to take was told to be as bland as possible until it became clearer what was going on; Harriet Harman similarly spent 30 minutes kicking her heels whilst Labour tried to work out a potential line to take before letting her appear on air.

Ed Miliband was in Doncaster, watching TV with his wife and close team. They had spent the evening tense but optimistic and believed the results would be good enough to see them into government. Amid the shock at the exit poll, Miliband remarked how it confirmed some of

Labour's internal polling ('that squares with James's poll', see p. 247). He then left the room briefly to talk privately with his wife, Justine, before returning and saying: 'If this is right, I'll have to go.' He then spoke by phone to various aides, including Spencer Livermore at Brewer's Green – who was equally stunned – and before too long the team were receiving phone calls with information from election counts, all of them containing bad news. The claim – variously made – that Miliband was writing a victory speech as the exit poll came through is erroneous.[8] His team had earlier prepared two speeches, each slightly different in tone for use depending on how the results unfolded; both had been read through earlier in the day. Miliband would later say privately that the act of reading the more negative speech had at least partly prepared him for what was to come – although neither speech was downbeat enough for what was now unfolding.

The first seat to declare was Houghton and Sunderland South, maintaining Sunderland South's record of declaring first in every contest since 1992.[9] The speed at which Sunderland conducts its count – combined with the relative lack of speed elsewhere – means that it is now possibly the most over-analysed city in British politics, with the ever-present danger of drawing false conclusions from a handful of atypical seats. But the Sunderland seats in fact proved remarkably prescient.

A Labour hold as expected, Houghton and Sunderland South saw a swing of 3.9% from the Conservatives to Labour. On the face of it, this appeared better than might have been expected from the exit poll, but the exit poll had found Labour doing better in the north-east than in other parts of the country and had predicted a swing to Labour of 5% in the seat, which was larger than what occurred. Next came Sunderland Central (with a slightly larger swing to Labour) and Washington and Sunderland West (slightly smaller). Taking the three constituencies together, there should, according to the exit poll, have been a 3.5% swing to Labour; the actual swing was 4%.

UKIP came second in Houghton and Sunderland South (and second or third in all three Sunderland seats), the first of many seats in which that would be true, followed by the Conservatives, with the Greens in fourth place, pushing the Lib Dems into fifth, with just 2.1% of the vote. In 2010, the Liberal Democrats had not lost a single deposit throughout all of Great Britain; in 2015, they lost their deposits in the first three seats to declare – and then went on to do so in more than half of the seats they were fighting. The Sunderland seats were also the

Figure 8.1 The difference punctuation makes

Front pages of the *Daily Mirror*, as released after the exit poll and later, revised, as results started to come through. © Mirrorpix.

first signs that for all the talk of a very close election having engaged the electorate, turnout was only up very marginally.

Where the Sunderland seats were atypical is that all three were held by female MPs. As in 2010, by midnight on election night in 2015, the Westminster Parliament was 100% female.

The odds on a Conservative majority had now fallen to 11/2.

Next came Swindon North, held by the Conservatives. There should, according to the exit poll, have been a small swing to Labour. In fact, there was a 4.3% swing to the Conservatives. Nine minutes later came Putney, also a Conservative hold, with a tiny 0.4% swing to Labour. Neither were target seats for Labour – although Labour had won Swindon North as recently as 2005 and Putney in 2001 – but they were not exactly promising signs for the party either.

The first marginal to declare was Battersea, where Conservative activists had described Labour's 'Get Out The Vote' operation earlier that day as 'massive'. The result of all that work on the doorstep was a 1.7% swing *from* Labour to the Conservatives, with the Conservative MP Jane Ellison increasing her majority. It was the moment that those around Ed Miliband began to realise that if it had erred, the exit poll may in fact have slightly over-estimated Labour support. 'We didn't particularly expect to win [in Battersea]', said one of those sat with the Labour leader in Doncaster, 'but it was the lack of any shift.'

At 1.51 am came the result from Nuneaton in the West Midlands, an absolute key target seat for Labour. A swing of 3.0% from Labour to the Conservatives saw the Conservative majority more than double. David Cameron would later compare it to Basildon in 1992, the moment when it was clear that the Conservatives had won. For those at party HQs, however, watching intelligence pour in from the counts, the realisation that the exit poll was on the money was there long before the results were formally announced. 'People say it's Nuneaton', said one of Miliband's team. 'But we knew Nuneaton had been lost long before it was declared. Way before then we knew it was all over.'

The mood was rather different at Conservative HQ. When the BBC flashed up the exit poll with the news that the Conservatives were projected to be the largest party, there had been a muted cheer. Someone shouted 'Come on, give us the numbers!' – and when they appeared, the room exploded. It was what one of those present called 'a sort of stunned euphoria'.[10] There was a small private room, in which sat Lynton Crosby, Jim Messina, Mark Textor and Stephen Gilbert. They watched the results sitting together on a sofa, leaping to their feet as one whenever good results came through. For particularly impressive results, Crosby would stand up and play a rough approximation of a fanfare on a bugle as party staff cheered. By 2 am, the Conservative exercise in briefing about the constitutional position had been put on hold indefinitely.

The first seat to change hands was South Antrim in Northern Ireland, taken from the DUP by the Ulster Unionist Party (UUP) with a majority of 949. It was one of three seats to change hands in Northern Ireland, a high proportion by the standards of the province. In addition, Belfast East was gained by the DUP, regaining it from the Alliance Party. It was one of the four seats in which the DUP and the UUP had a pact not to stand against each other. The same was true in Fermanagh and South Tyrone, taken by the UUP from Sinn Fein (who had held it at the last election with a majority of just four) and which UUP leader Mike Nesbitt described as 'the best result unionism has had for over a decade'.[11] After their complete wipeout in 2010, the UUP were at least back in the House of Commons. And a new record was established in Belfast South, where the winning Social Democratic and Labour Party (SDLP) candidate, Alasdair McDonnell, emerged victorious from a nine-way contest with just 24.5% of the vote, a record low, ending

Russell Johnston's 23-year reign as the MP with the lowest victorious percentage at a Westminster election.

On election night in 2010 not a single Scottish constituency had changed hands.[12] No one thought that was likely this time. Just after 2 am, Kilmarnock and Loudoun was taken by the SNP on an astronomical Labour–SNP swing of 25.9%. This was enough to change a majority of over 12,000 for Labour into one of almost 14,000 for the SNP, but it was also the sort of swing that indicated that no seat was safe. Within the next two hours alone, the SNP took 35 seats, almost all from Labour, as what Alex Salmond called an 'electoral tsunami' swept through Scotland and in particular the Scottish Labour Party. Casualties included the Shadow Foreign Secretary, Douglas Alexander, in Paisley and Renfrewshire South at around 2.30 am, deposed by a 20-year old student with a Labour–SNP swing of 26.9%, and at 3.15 am the leader of the Scottish Labour Party, Jim Murphy, in Renfrewshire East, with a Labour–SNP swing of 24.2%. It mattered not whether they were seats the Labour Party had abandoned or, like Murphy and Alexander's, where they had been pouring resources into a rear-guard action. They almost all fell.

By the end of the night, the SNP had failed to take just three of the 59 seats in Scotland. Just before 4 am, the Lib Dems managed to cling on in Orkney and Shetland, but with a majority down to under 1,000 in what had been their safest seat.[13] They were now back down to the same number of Scottish seats – indeed, the same seat – they had held in the 1950s. Just before 4.30 am, Labour holding a seat in Scotland became a news story when Ian Murray became the only Labour MP in Scotland, holding Edinburgh South, helped by an SNP candidate who had made injudicious comments on Twitter.[14] Even in 1906, when Labour had first won seats in Scotland, they had at least managed to win two. And just before 5.30 am, the Conservative MP David Mundell held Dumfriesshire, Clydesdale and Tweeddale with a reduced majority of just 798. For all the praise that had been heaped on the Scottish Conservative leader Ruth Davidson and her energetic campaigning, the Conservative share of the vote was the lowest ever recorded in Scotland.[15]

The SNP had come within 4,255 votes of a clean sweep.[16] In total, 50 of the seats in Scotland changed hands, on swings of up to 39.3%, with the SNP taking 50% of the vote in Scotland, the highest proportion the party had gained in a Scottish-wide election and higher than Labour had ever managed.[17] 'The tectonic plates of Scottish politics shifted', said Nicola Sturgeon.

The SNP had begun the night playing down expectations, whilst being aware that they could potentially win anywhere in Scotland. 'We hoped and believed', said one of Sturgeon's team, 'but we didn't want to say.' Information from counts soon made it abundantly clear early on that it was going to be a landslide. By midnight, they were clear they would win at least 56 seats. 'You know every campaign has someone who's really pessimistic?', said another of Sturgeon's team. 'When that person is sending you texts saying, we're walking it, you think, alright, OK.' The SNP ended up winning more seats in 2015 than the party had won in every previous general election in its history combined.

South of the border, things were less seismic, although in terms of the outcome of the election probably more significant. Just before 3 am, Labour made their first gain of the night, taking Burnley from the Lib Dems. A few minutes earlier, the Conservatives had held on in Peterborough; just after 3 am, they held Worcester. And at 3.06 am, they held Warwickshire North, which they had taken in 2010 with a majority of just 54. That had been transformed into a Conservative majority of almost 3,000. Whereas Conservative resilience in some of their most marginal seats could be attributed to the work of first-term incumbent MPs – who, as John Curtice and his colleagues demonstrate in the Appendix, outperformed their colleagues – in Warwickshire North, the Conservative candidate had only been in place since September 2014 and he had still held the party's most marginal seat. As well as Warwickshire North, Labour also failed in seats such as Thurrock (albeit with special circumstances, discussed below), Hendon (a Conservative majority of 106 transformed into one of 3,618), Cardiff North (194, into 2,137), Sherwood (214, into 4,433), Stockton South (332, into 5,046), Broxtowe (389, into 4,287), Amber Valley (536, into 4,205), Waveney (769, into 2,408), Morecambe and Lunesdale (866, into 4,590) and Carlisle (853, into 2,274). Of the 13 seats which the Conservatives had won with a majority of 1,000 or under in 2010 and where they were facing a Labour challenge, Labour took just two. Of the Conservatives' 30 most marginal seats where they were facing a Labour challenge, Labour took just seven.

The odds on a Conservative majority had fallen briefly to evens around 2 am, after Nuneaton declared, before drifting out again, but by 3 am they were back at 5/4.

Labour's first gain from the Conservatives came just before 3 am, when they took Ealing Central and Acton. It was evidence of Labour's slightly better – although still not great – performance in London. Of the ten seats they were to take from the Conservatives during the night, four were in London. Partly because of the fact that the London seats declared earlier (helped by the absence of any local elections), but also because of Labour's poorer performance outside of London, Labour did not take a seat from the Conservatives outside of London until just after 5 am, when they won Wirral West – which had been a particularly vicious contest – after a re-count. By then, the Conservatives had even started to take seats from Labour. At about 3.15 am, they won Vale of Clwyd, the first of eight seats that the Conservatives would take from Labour; outside of London, the Conservatives took more seats from Labour than vice versa.

In 2015 Labour took more seats (12) from the Liberal Democrats than they did the Conservatives (10). Labour were to end the night on 232 seats, a lower number than in 1992 or 2010, back down almost to the level of 1987. Neil Kinnock's (attributed) remark about getting his party back seemed more accurate than he might have realised back in 2010.

Given that it was the closest and most unpredictable result in a generation, there had been a widespread expectation that turnout might be up. As the night wore on, it became clear that, however close and unpredictable the contest might have been, it had not driven voters to the polls in larger numbers than before. Across the UK as a whole, turnout rose by just one percentage point to 66%. Turnout in Northern Ireland was, as in 2010, the lowest in the UK, at 58%. The only exception was Scotland, where a turnout was up 7.2% on 2010 to 71%, a legacy of the referendum. It was, at least, the third election in a row in which turnout had risen, but only to levels still below those seen in 1997 or before.

Despite Paddy Ashdown's public hat-eating bravado, the Lib Dems had quickly realised that they were in for a terrible night. The first seat to contact Lib Dem HQ had been Eastleigh, a seat they had thought touch and go, but where with five ballot boxes having been opened, the Conservatives were comfortably ahead. Then a source contacted them from Cheltenham, a seat that the party thought should have been safe, but where the Tories were also clearly ahead. Soon feedback was pouring in from election counts, all of it negative. Ryan Coetzee would text each piece of news he received to Nick Clegg. After a few texts, all equally depressing, he asked: 'Do you really want to hear all of this?' Yes, Clegg replied. Five depressing texts later, Coetzee asked, 'Are you sure?'

The first Lib Dem seat to fall was Dunbartonshire East, where Jo Swinson was swept away in the Scottish tsunami.[18] Seven minutes later, the party lost Brecon and Radnorshire and, one minute after that, Burnley. In those eight minutes, they lost seats to Labour, to the Conservatives and to the SNP, and in all parts of Great Britain. 'Our campaign was fought on three fronts', Coetzee was to write later, 'and we lost on all of them.'[19]

At about 3.45 am, Ed Davey lost Kingston and Surbiton, the first Cabinet minister to lose his seat, but not the last. At 4.11 am, Simon Hughes lost in Bermondsey and Old Southwark, a seat he had held, with varying boundaries, since 1983. At 4.17 am, the party lost Eastleigh, held in the by-election earlier in the Parliament. When Nick Clegg had visited during the campaign, he had said that the party was 'fighting 60 Eastleighs'. As the results started to come through, it became clear he was right. Just before 5 am, the Lib Dems lost Sutton and Cheam, Eastbourne, Bath, Cheltenham and then Twickenham, where the Business Secretary, Vince Cable, was defeated. Just before 6 am, David Laws lost in Yeovil. Paddy Ashdown, by now back at Lib Dem HQ, found it difficult to comprehend the party losing the seat which Ashdown himself had held for 18 years. According to one of those present: 'He just stared at the TV, in utter shock, even when the coverage had moved on to other things, he just carried on staring.' At 6 am, former party leader Charles Kennedy lost in Ross, Skye and Lochaber, another seat held since 1983. He characterised it as 'the night of the Long Skean Dhus'. The party also lost their Chief Secretary, Danny Alexander, in Inverness, Nairn, Badenoch and Strathspey. Of the Lib Dem team that negotiated the Coalition Agreement in 2010, none was left.[20]

The seats the Lib Dems lost to Labour had mostly been expected, as were most of their losses to the SNP, but what destroyed the Lib Dems was the 27 defeats to the Conservatives, more than they lost to Labour and the SNP combined, and including many seats that they had considered pretty much safe, such as Lewes, Colchester, Thornbury and Yate, and Eastbourne (which they had thought they would win by ten percentage points). In total, they lost 49 seats and lost their deposit in 341, the same number as in every general election from 1979 to 2010 combined. In some of these seats, they did not even manage to come second. In four constituencies, the Lib Dems went from first to third place, whilst in Norwich South, they went from first to fourth.[21] The party came fewer than 25,000 votes from being wiped out completely and were left with not a single seat in what had been their south-west stronghold.[22] All eight remaining seats were held by incumbent MPs – all men – but incumbency alone had been shown not to be enough. At least a generation's work building the party had been reversed. The party was now the fourth-place party in both seats (behind the SNP) and votes (behind UKIP). They were to end the election with the same number of seats as the DUP.[23]

Just before 5 am, Nick Clegg hung on in Sheffield Hallam, despite a vigorous local campaign by Labour, but with a much reduced majority. His acceptance speech noted that it was 'painfully clear that this has been a cruel and punishing night for the Liberal Democrats'. While at the count, the news came through that Vince Cable had lost his seat; the Labour activists in the hall gave their biggest cheer of the night to a Conservative victory.

In Wales, just three seats changed hands. Labour increased their vote by just 0.6% on what had been a terrible performance in Wales in 2010, achieving the second worst result since 1918, and they ended the night with a net loss of one seat. Unlike in Scotland, where UKIP did not save a single deposit, in Wales they saved every one and pushed Plaid Cymru into fourth in terms of votes, albeit without winning a single seat. The Lib Dems survived in Wales with just one seat. The Conservatives won 11, up three on their performance in 2010. Their gains included Gower, now the seat with the smallest majority of any constituency in the UK, of just 27 votes. Wales remains a stronghold for Labour, but one in which the party is in danger of stagnating.

The results board at Labour HQ, showing the seats lost. Gower was such a surprise that a handwritten sign had to be created for it.

It was not a night for going to bed early. By 2 am on election night in 1992, around 70% of seats had declared. By 2010, both because of the concurrent local elections and the requirement to verify postal votes, that figure had fallen to just 9%. In 2015, it fell yet further to under 3%. Even by 3 am, less than 11% of seats had declared. The three hours between 3 am and 6 am accounted for more than half of the declarations.[24]

At 6.07 am, George Galloway lost in Bradford West, Labour re-taking the seat he had won at the by-election of 2012. He did not go gracefully. 'The hyena can dance on the lion's grave', he said during his speech, 'but it'll never be a lion.' He added: 'I'm not in my grave, in fact I'm off to plan my next campaign.' He later announced he was planning an election petition against the result, but it did not materialise.[25]

Just before 6 am, the bookmaker's odds on a Conservative majority slipped into odds-on, and by 7 am, the BBC was predicting a Conservative majority, albeit still marginally smaller than the one eventually achieved.

The SNP had had a small negotiating team ready to fly to London on the earliest morning flight. They were well aware that Labour would do no overt negotiating with them, but they wanted to be seen to be available and to plug into any official civil service networks that were created as part of the process of government formation in the event of a hung parliament. 'We wanted to demonstrate we would be willing to help, to work in good faith', said one of those involved. 'If he [Miliband] didn't want to talk, then who looks responsible, [and] who looks unresponsive?' But with a Conservative majority now on the cards, there really was nothing to negotiate and the team was disbanded. There were a lot of empty seats on that flight to London that morning.

For UKIP, the night was the best of times and the worst of times. They polled a total of just under 3,900,000 votes, the best performance by any 'other' party since records began, and more than the SNP and Lib Dems polled combined. By any standards, this was an astonishing achievement. But no party had ever piled up so many votes for so little return, and they failed to make anywhere near the breakthrough they had hoped for. At 4.19 am, they won Clacton, taken in the by-election of 2014 – and which was at least a nominal gain from the Conservatives – although even this was with a much reduced majority of just under 3,500. Just before 4.30 am, they failed to take the key target of Thurrock, coming third (albeit less than 1,000 votes behind the victorious Conservative). They also failed in a string of other seats, such as Castle Point (second, with 31%, but a full 17% behind), Great Grimsby (25%, but third and 15% behind the winner) or Boston and Skegness (second, with 34%, but 10% behind the winner). At 8.11 am, they lost Rochester and Strood, their other by-election victory, Mark Reckless exiting the Commons to much Conservative delight. Claire Perry, the Conservative MP for Devizes, tweeted: 'Hallelujah. Mark

Reckless out. Don't let the door hit your fat arse as you leave.' She spoke for many Conservative MPs.

'If we can win here we can win across the country', Reckless had said in his by-election victory speech in 2014. But they could not and they did not. Seats that had been described as 'in the bag' turned out to be categorically outside of it. The party stacked up 120 second places, many of which were achieved with not much more than paper candidates, but 2015 was meant to be about more than just coming second. For all their efforts, UKIP had still failed to win a seat at a general election without the advantage of a defection, and they were not even able to hold both of those.

By then the rumours that Nigel Farage was in trouble in Thanet South were widespread, and at just gone 10.37 am on 8 May, the Conservatives held the seat with a majority of 2,812. Farage had said repeatedly that he would resign as party leader if he failed to win in Kent. It was, he had written in his pre-campaign book, *The Purple Revolution*, 'inconceivable' for him to remain. He did indeed resign within an hour of the declaration, although he then remarked that he might stand for the leadership of the party again, and within a few days he had in any case withdrawn his resignation, claiming the party's National Executive Committee had refused to accept it. The party then descended into a bout of post-election infighting, from which Farage emerged bruised but victorious. There is said to be a rule within UKIP that 'Nigel always wins', but it only applies to intra-party contests; this was his seventh unsuccessful attempt to get into Westminster.

The Greens had a similar night of contrasts. At 7.36 am, Caroline Lucas held Brighton Pavilion, increasing her majority substantially, and the party won 3.8% of the UK vote, up almost three percentage points on 2010, their highest ever share of the vote (only partly as a result of standing more candidates). But in the two seats that the Greens had been seriously targeting – Bristol West and Norwich South – they failed in both, coming second in Bristol West, but third in Norwich South, where their vote fell slightly, ending up a full 12,000 votes behind first place. In Holborn and St Pancras, the party leader Natalie Bennett came third. Elsewhere, they managed another three second places and lost 442 deposits. The much-vaunted Green surge of a year before had fallen short.

For most of the night there had been rumours that the Shadow Chancellor, Ed Balls, was in trouble in his Morley and Outwood seat. Balls had done some TV and radio early in the night, after which he spent most of the early hours of the morning in a Premier Inn hotel avoiding the media. At 7.30 am, he was called into a room at the count by the returning officer, and his and the Conservative numbers were read out. The result was close enough that Labour were allowed a re-count, but far enough apart that they knew it would make little difference; about an hour later, the Conservatives took the seat, Andrea Jenkyns unseating one of the biggest figures in British politics on a 1.6% swing. There were to be private complaints within Labour that so many resources had been put into Sheffield Hallam, whilst leaving the Shadow Chancellor vulnerable. But Balls himself had been diverting resources into other, nearby, marginal seats, unaware of how precarious his position was. The national party were similarly unconcerned. There were Labour-held seats that they were worried about – some of which they lost, others of which they held – but although Morley and Outwood was monitored, there were no concerns about it or about how Balls was operating. 'He was doing everything right', said one of those at Brewer's Green. It was not much consolation.

After his declaration, Nick Clegg travelled down to London, where he resigned as party leader at 11.30 am. In his resignation speech, he described the result as 'immeasurably more crushing and unkind' than he had expected. 'Fear and grievance have won. Liberalism has lost. But it is more precious than ever and we must keep fighting for it ... This is a very dark hour for our party but we cannot and will not allow decent liberal values to be extinguished overnight.' He was later quoted as saying 'live by the sword, die by the sword – I just didn't realise there'd be so many swords'.[26] The day before polling, Clegg and his team had learnt of a plot to install Vince Cable as leader in the event that Clegg had tried to remain in charge; not only had Clegg stood down but Cable had lost his seat – and so yet another Lib Dem plot did not go quite to plan.

Speaking at his count at Doncaster Racecourse, Ed Miliband had described the result as 'a very disappointing and difficult night for the party'. It was a speech which clearly signalled his intention of resigning. He then returned to London by car with police protection, along with Justine, Bob Roberts, Greg Beales and Stewart Wood, with the rest of the team following by train. At Brewer's Green, where he spoke to party staff, there were attempts to persuade him to stay on as leader. Falconer, Alastair Campbell, Harriet Harman and Tom Baldwin all argued that he should remain as caretaker for six months while a more considered leadership election took place. They argued this would be better for his reputation (because he would not see his record trashed so badly), for the party (because demoralised, exhausted, defeated parties rarely make great decisions) and for the country (because it needed effective opposition in the crucial months after a general election). Their model was Michael Howard in 2005, who had stayed on long enough to allow David Cameron to emerge as a rival leader to David Davis. But Miliband was not convinced and he resigned as leader just after noon.[27] 'This', he said, 'is not the speech I wanted to give today because I believe that Britain needed a Labour government. I still do, but the public voted otherwise last night ... I take absolute and total responsibility for the result and our defeat at this election.' A party that had begun election night thinking it had a serious chance of going into government had within 24 hours seen its leader resign and its Shadow Foreign Secretary and Shadow Chancellor lose their seats.

David Cameron and his team had spent election day in Oxfordshire. In the afternoon, Cameron and speech-writer Clare Foges had prepared speeches for three different scenarios, ranging from the Conservatives putting together another coalition to outright defeat.[28] In the early evening, on the patio of his constituency home, he had rehearsed the last, his resignation speech, in front of the closest members of his team.[29] It had been an emotional moment and he appears to have convinced himself that he was about to lose, a mood that only passed when the exit poll was released, to much jubilation.

But, just like Ed Miliband, none of Cameron's pre-prepared speeches now fitted what was unfolding and so a new speech was written, whilst waiting for his result at Witney's Windrush Leisure Centre, amid the smell of stale sweat.[30] After his declaration, around 5.45 am, he said: 'I want my party, and I hope the government I would like to lead, to reclaim a mantle that we should never have lost, the mantle of one nation, one United Kingdom.'

Cameron then travelled to Conservative campaign HQ where he was recorded talking to party workers: 'Now I'm not an old man, but I remember casting a vote in '87, and that was a great victory; I remember working just as you've been working in '92, and that was an amazing victory; and I remember 2010, achieving that dream of getting Labour out and getting the Tories back in, and that was amazing, but I think this is the sweetest victory of all.'

He arrived at Buckingham Palace to see the Queen just a quarter of an hour after Ed Miliband had resigned.

The last seat to declare, just before 3.30 pm on the Friday, was St Ives. It completed the wipeout of the Lib Dems from their former heartland of the south-west. It was now possible to walk from Land's End to the Scottish border and not leave a Conservative constituency, although north of the border things looked rather different. By then, David Cameron was already back in Downing Street, Prime Minister of the first majority Conservative government to be elected for 23 years.

Notes

1. Labour assumed this would be the case, without requiring the votes of the Liberal Democrats and the Democratic Unionist Party (DUP).
2. The discussion would have focused primarily on just two words in paragraph 2.12 of the Cabinet Manual: what did 'clear alternative' mean? Did this mean a clear alternative Prime Minister (obviously Ed Miliband) or did that Prime Minister need to demonstrate they had a majority (less obviously Ed Miliband)? We should perhaps just be grateful that the nation avoided such a discussion.
3. This led to some speculation in the press about the Conservatives planning a 'constitutional coup' to try to hold on to office. Labour insiders admitted this was overblown language, but they felt it was a useful way to draw attention to the battle for legitimacy that was about to take place.
4. The amendment would have been similar to that deployed in 1924; it would deliberately not have contained the wording that triggered the Fixed-Term Parliaments Act (FTPA) which gave a 14-day period to form an alternative government. This was partly because it would be quicker – Labour's understanding was that the FTPA motion could only be put down *after* the debate on the Queen's Speech – but also because, in the event that the process of negotiation with the other parties dragged on, the party did not want to be up against a 14-day deadline.
5. All bookmakers' odds quoted in this chapter are from Paddy Power. Other bookmakers will have had slightly different prices, but none were very different, and the trends were almost identical.
6. See, for example, Robert Hutton, 'UK Election Exit Pollster Says His Poll May Be Vague or Wrong', *Bloomberg*, 1 May 2015: 'Prepare for disappointment', said Curtice. 'It's almost guaranteed.'
7. Part of an excellent series of recollections by various special advisors, recalling election night, recorded for BBC Radio 4's 'The World at One'. Bellardinelli's was broadcast on 5 August 2015.
8. See, for example, Andrew Pierce, 'Ed Miliband was Writing His Victory Speech – Then Came that Exit Poll', *Daily Mail*, 8 May 2015; Dan Hodges, 'Inside the Mili Bunker', *The Spectator*, 16 May 2015.

9. The BBC records the declaration time as 10.51 pm, but Sunderland Council (and the House of Commons library) record it as 10.48 pm.
10. There were what one of those present described as 'just shrieks of disbelief – many in the form of four-letter words'.
11. The pact also worked in Belfast North, where the DUP increased their majority, even in a seat which now has a slight Catholic majority. See Jonathan Tonge and Jocelyn Evans, 'Another Communal Headcount: The Election in Northern Ireland' in *Britain Votes 2015*. Oxford University Press, 2015, Chapter 8.
12. That is, excluding those where there had been by-elections during the Parliament.
13. The SNP's analysis indicates that they won in Shetland, with the Lib Dems hanging on thanks to Orkney.
14. The SNP candidate, Neil Hay, had been found to have used an anonymous Twitter account – under the name Paco McSheepie – to hurl abuse at unionists, including describing referendum 'No' voters as 'Quislings'. This became public after his selection; he apologised and his comments were condemned by the SNP leader, yet he still managed a 10.9% swing. Murray was saved by the complete collapse of the Lib Dem vote; in a seat that had been a top Liberal Democrat target in 2010, the Liberal Democrats came *fifth* in 2015, with just 3.7%, and lost their deposit.
15. Such a comparison is slightly unfair, given that anti-SNP tactical voting will have eaten into the Conservative vote in 2015 in a way it might not have done previously. But still, there was no evidence of Conservative support rising.
16. That is, the majority of those three seats combined plus three. On the basis that those switching from one party to another are worth double, it would have required just over 2,000 voters in Scotland to change their votes for the party to achieve a clean sweep.
17. More accurately, it rounded *up* to 50.0%, with the SNP's vote accounting for 49.97% of the votes cast in Scotland. There was some very slight frustration within the party at not achieving a majority of the votes cast, given the symbolic benefit that would have given, although that frustration was minor compared to the joy at the overall result. And even this still comes behind the 50.1% achieved by the Conservatives (and allies) in 1955. But as one of Sturgeon's closest advisors said: 'It gets a bit churlish when you start to be annoyed you're not winning every seat.'
18. Within an hour, her husband, Duncan Hames, had lost his seat in Chippenham. They became the first husband and wife team to be defeated at a general election since John and Gwyneth Dunwoody in 1970.
19. Ryan Coetzee, 'The Liberal Democrats Must Reunite, Rebuild or Remain in Opposition', *The Guardian*, 22 May 2015.
20. One had retired, two had lost their seats and one went to prison.
21. Brent Central, Aberdeenshire West and Kincardine, Bristol South, and Berwickshire, Roxburgh and Selkirk.
22. The eight surviving MPs' majorities combined came to 24,968. It would therefore have only required 12,500 or so people to have changed their votes and the party might have been wiped out at Westminster completely.

23. Given the scale of their wipeout, it is not surprising that the Lib Dems were not successful in the handful of seats which they had hoped they might gain. In Maidstone and the Weald, visited by Nick Clegg twice during the campaign, the incumbent MP (who the Lib Dems had said had the worst ratings of any MP they had polled) saw her majority increase to one of more than 21%. In Watford, where the popular Lib Dem mayor was standing and where they thought they had a real chance, the Lib Dems came *third*, more than 14,000 votes behind the winning Conservative. They were similarly unsuccessful in Montgomeryshire, and Oxford West and Abingdon.
24. There were 107 declarations between 3 and 4 am, 123 between 4 and 5 am, and 137 between 5 and 6 am.
25. There were three election petitions in total: one against Alistair Carmichael (for grounds explained on p. 209); one against Nadine Dorries in Mid-Bedfordshire (dismissed) and one against Jonathan Lord in Woking (which failed due to lack of security for costs).
26. See for example 'Britain is in a perilous state, warns tearful Clegg', *The Times*, 9 May 2015.
27. Patrick Wintour reports Justine as being in favour of an immediate resignation, arguing that he should not have to be repeatedly mocked by Conservative MPs at Prime Minister's Questions. See Patrick Wintour, 'The Undoing of Ed Miliband – And How Labour Lost the Election', *The Guardian*, 3 June. Also arguing against the caretaker role were Greg Beales and Bob Roberts.
28. Anthony Seldon and Peter Snowdon, *Cameron at 10: The Inside Story*. William Collins, 2015, p. 522. Seldon and Snowdon reveal that in the event of the second speech being required – if Labour put together a government propped up by the SNP – the Conservatives intended to support the Queen's Speech in the interests of national interest, but insist on a second election later in the year, as occurred in 1974. It is not at all clear how they thought they would trigger this second election.
29. This was first revealed in James Forsyth, 'Revealed: David Cameron's Rehearsed Resignation Speech', *The Spectator*, 13 June 2015.
30. Seldon and Snowdon, *Cameron at 10*, p. 529.

9
Margin of Error: The Polls

The 2015 general election was the most polled in the history of British elections.[1] The story the polls told over the final year of the Parliament was essentially one of stability, albeit with a slight Labour decline, and with virtually all polls pointing to deadlock between Labour and the Conservatives. Of over 1,000 polls conducted in the three years after the 2012 Budget, only one had placed the Conservatives above the 37.8% they achieved in May 2015. Of the 92 polls reporting during the six-week campaign, 33 reported a Conservative lead, 41 a Labour lead and 18 a dead heat. Virtually all the leads were within the margin of error inherent in polling.[2] Of the 28 polls conducted in the final week, 9 had a Conservative lead, 9 a Labour lead and 10 a tie.

The polls were frustrating for the parties, whose initiatives seemed to have so little impact on the voting numbers, as well as for commentators, who ran out of ways to say how close the election was (or, in Scotland, how dramatic). Slight shifts in the figures for a party, even when within the margin of error, did not stop the media exaggerating the movements in their desperation for a story, but cumulatively the polls conditioned commentators and campaigners for a hung parliament, and one in which there would be a massively expanded Scottish National Party (SNP) contingent. It led to an explosion of coalitionology, debating hung parliaments, possible coalitions, constitutional process and the 'legitimacy' of various outcomes, as everyone prepared for post-election deals. Yet as soon as the results started to come in, it became clear that the polls had got it badly wrong.

At least they had in England. For one of the paradoxes of 2015 was that while the polls were widely believed in England, where they turned out to be badly wrong, they were often doubted in Scotland, where they turned out to be accurate (as they were, less spectacularly, in Wales). Ever since the referendum of 2014, they had pointed to a landslide for the

SNP, and from April onwards the SNP were at least 20 percentage points ahead of Labour in every poll. But in terms of the overall outcome, 2015 joined 1970 and 1992 as elections the polling industry would rather had never happened.

It was not an inconsequential error. As Martin Kettle wrote in *The Guardian*, 'politics reflected the polls' rather than vice versa.[3] Party spokespeople felt especially aggrieved at the poll-driven media and how the polls had shaped so much of the narrative of the election. As we discuss in Chapter 7, Labour complained officially to the BBC about its extensive coverage of possible SNP demands on a minority Labour government. Had the polls been reporting a clear Conservative lead, the party's warning about the SNP 'threat' would not have carried much weight and the media attention would probably have turned to the policies that a majority Conservative government would carry out. As one Labour strategist complained after the election: 'No one believed all of our the-NHS-is-going-to-die-in-ten-minutes-and-the-end-of-the-world-is-coming stuff, because they were told there wasn't going to be a Conservative government. It de-risked a majority Conservative government, because it ruled it out. It was safe to vote Conservative, because you couldn't get a Conservative government. Except you could.' Equally, the failure of the public polls to report a Conservative breakthrough reinforced media criticisms of a 'lacklustre' Tory campaign and forced the Conservatives into policy stances they would otherwise have preferred to avoid, whilst the Liberal Democrats believed the polls undermined their vote in Conservative–Lib Dem marginals. And in Scotland, by emphasising both the rise of the SNP and the hung parliament overall, the polls helped reinforce the SNP's message that they could hold the balance of power.

On balance, the polls' inaccuracy in England and Wales helped the Conservatives more than other parties, although after the election, Lynton Crosby still castigated 'so-called experts', the commentators and pollsters 'living in the Westminster bubble', and called for the prohibition of public polls two weeks before polling day. Safely back in Chicago, David Axelrod urged the British polling industry to have a root-and-branch examination of its methods because he had 'never seen so stark a failing'. Similarly aggrieved were those who had been commissioning the polls: one newspaper political editor, noting the outcome of the election, complained that 'three party leaders have resigned but not one pollster has'.

The expansion in polling was a result of three factors. First, most of the established polling companies which had been carrying out political polling between 2005 and 2010 continued to do so. Second, a year before the election, they were joined by a newcomer, in Lord Ashcroft, the former Conservative Deputy Chairman, who had published several pieces of polling-informed research in the past, and from May 2014 started a weekly national survey as well as a series of polls in battleground constituencies, the seats which would decide the election. He also published the highlights of weekly focus groups.[4] The scale of his operation was unprecedented, involving 167 constituency polls in all, at a reputed cost of approximately £3 million. Ashcroft described himself as a 'pollster', although Crosby's view was that 'he's not a pollster, he's just a rich bloke who buys polling'.[5] And, third, the Internet polling company YouGov, which had begun polling on a daily basis during the 2010 election campaign, continued to do so, polling every weekday during the Parliament. Of these three factors, it was the last which had most impact on the quantity of polling data generated during the Parliament (out of more than 2,000 polls during the Parliament, YouGov conducted over 1,200 of them), although the second made a qualitative difference to the nature of that data. It meant that on almost every day there was at least one poll published and frequently more. The days of polls appearing once a month were over. Plus, for the first time, there was detailed data about individual constituencies, data that everyone assumed would be a more accurate guide to the election than national polling. The irony, of course, was that despite all of this data, election day arrived with no one the wiser as to who was likely to emerge victorious – and then the outcome was the only thing that the polls had said was practically certain not to happen.

The methodological catholicism of previous elections continued. Pollsters aim to interview a demographically representative sample of the electorate, but this is easier said than done. As one pollster put it: 'We don't always get it right and we certainly didn't this time, but the fact that it is difficult to get right is an inescapable part of the process.' They employ different methods to gather respondents, using online surveys, telephone polling or (rarely) face-to-face contact. Having done this, they then utilise increasingly complicated methods of filtering and weighting to translate the raw data of question answers into the eventually published figures.[6] Even though they differed in terms of how they went about dealing with them (and would have frequent arguments about how best to do so), all pollsters were well aware of the multiple problems that can be caused by differential turnout, selection bias and false reporting. Prior to 10 pm on 7 May, however, they thought they had worked out ways of dealing with them.

The pollsters had different regular outlets for their findings. ICM was commissioned by and published in *The Guardian*; YouGov in *The Times*, the *Sunday Times* and *The Sun*; Ipsos MORI in the *Evening Standard*; Opinium in *The Observer*; ComRes in the *Daily Mail* and ITN News; and Survation in the *Daily Mirror* and the *Mail on Sunday*. Some papers ran regular expert analyses of the public polls, whilst for the aficionado, there were also a growing number of blogs hosting more detailed discussions. Well-established sites such as politicalbetting.com or ukpollingreport.co.uk were joined by more recently established ones such as the *New Statesman*'s May2015.com or a variety of academic blogs, such as electionsetc.com or electionforecast.co.uk, all of which provided analysis and forecasts.[7] The combination of the quantity of polling and the depth of analysis meant that it would have easily been possible to spend all of the campaign reading about polls, if that is what one wanted to do.

In retrospect, it would not have been that useful a way of spending time, given that they were so wrong. Almost all of the more complicated forecasts which drew on the polls were also wrong. Of the 12 academic forecasting teams who presented their models at an event at the LSE on 27 March, six projected Labour to gain more seats than the Conservatives. The average estimate was for Labour to end up with 283 seats to the Conservatives' 279. Just two of the 12 models had the Conservatives above 290 seats and none had them above 300.[8] The final forecasts of most of the more regular forecasting models all had the Conservatives ahead in terms of seats, at least. Election Forecast predicted 281 to 266, Elections etc. forecast 289 to 257, and Peter Kellner, who was one of the boldest pollsters in making seat calculations, put the Conservatives on 284 seats and Labour on 263.[9] But still, none had the Conservatives above 290. Nate Silver, the celebrated American forecaster for elections and sporting events, proved as inaccurate in 2015 as he had been in 2010. His final forecast, borrowed from the Election Forecast team, was for 278 seats for the Conservatives and 267 for Labour. He provided little added value, despite the media hype – including an entire edition of *Panorama* – that had accompanied his visit.

More accurate, and challenging for the public polling, was the work of Matt Singh, a former city trader, who set up the Number Cruncher Politics blog.[10] Before 7 May, he was forecasting a Conservative lead over Labour of eight percentage points, with the Conservatives ahead of Labour by 302 to 249 in seats. Many of those involved in forecasting had built in an allowance for polling error, but Singh was one of the most vocal in raising it as an issue, and relied much less on voting intention data and instead on the respective ratings for the party leaders and economic competence, a method that had been more accurate as a prediction for every election since 1979.

Pollsters are always careful to remind people that polls are not predictions; they are snapshots of public opinion at the time they are taken.

The final polls published before polling day, however, are meant to be more than just a snapshot. Their poor collective performance in 2015 (see Table 9.1), with an error on the lead of just less than 7%, rivalled their previous disasters. In 1970 four of the final five polls had the wrong winner (Labour) in the lead and by large margins. The error between the average of the polls and the result was 7.1%. In 1992 the polls gave Labour an average lead of 0.9%, but the Conservative margin of victory was 7.6%, an error of 8.5%. In all three cases the error was a consequence of overstating Labour's support and understating that of the Conservatives.

The individual forecasts in 2015 varied, but were all wrong – and all wrong in the same direction. The final polls all put the Conservatives between 31 and 36%, with every poll under-estimating their eventual vote share. Labour were on 31–35%, with all but one poll over-estimating their eventual vote share. The average prediction of the final polls had the Labour and Conservative Parties tied. Of the 11 polling companies, just four had the Conservatives ahead, and never by more than one percentage point. Despite their varied sampling methods and sizes, weightings and whether they were conducted online or by telephone, no poll came even close to predicting the 6.8% gap between Labour and the Conservatives They were more accurate in measuring the support for the other parties, but this was small consolation.

The first indicator of how inaccurate the opinion polls had been came with the announcement of the exit poll just after polls closed on 7 May. Television companies have used seat prediction exit polls for British general elections since 1974. For the 2005 general election, the BBC and ITN joined forces to commission a joint poll conducted by Ipsos MORI and GfK NOP. In 2010 they were joined by Sky News, and the trio and the same two polling companies continued for 2015.

The 2015 exit poll interviewed approximately 22,000 people in 141 locations across a sample of 133 constituencies. Rather than being

Table 9.1 Final published polls

	TNS–BMRB	*BMG*	*YouGov*	*Opinium*	*Panelbase*	*Ashcroft*	*Survation*	*Populus*	*ComRes*	*Ipsos MORI*	*ICM*	*Result*
Con	33	34	34	35	31	33	31	33	35	36	34	38
Lab	32	34	34	34	33	33	31	33	34	35	35	31
LD	8	10	10	8	8	10	10	10	9	8	9	8
UKIP	14	12	12	12	16	11	16	14	12	11	11	13
Green	6	4	4	6	5	6	5	5	4	5	4	4
Other	6	5	6	5	7	8	7	6	6	5	7	6
Mean error	1.5	1.8	2.0	1.7	2.3	2.5	2.3	1.8	1.3	1.7	2.0	
Fieldwork end	4.5	5.5	6.5	6.5	6.5	6.5	6.5	6.5	6.5	6.5	6.5	

a conventional sample of the population, the exit poll – as its name implies – involves stopping those leaving polling stations and asking them to complete (in secret) a form revealing how they have just voted. The locations chosen are deliberately not a representative sample of constituencies, but are instead chosen because of what they help identify about different types of places. The aim is to calculate the scale of the change in the vote in different locations and then use that to estimate it across the country. The exit poll does not assume uniform swing, but rather attempts to identify the type of constituencies (both demographically and geographically) which are switching, and then uses that information to model change across the country. From that model is generated a series of predictions for individual constituencies – and from that a total number of seats.[11]

The changed political geography made the exit poll particularly challenging in 2015. The poll five years before had deliberately been conducted disproportionally in contests between the Conservatives and Labour (and sometimes the Lib Dems), and much less in the sort of seats that had since seen rises in support for either the SNP or UKIP. Additional polling locations were chosen to deal with this, but because they were new additions, the team had no data from the previous exit poll to help identify the amount of change in those areas.[12] Data gathered at polling stations is passed to the team analysing the exit poll throughout the day in batches in order to help them develop and refine their models. Unlike in 1992, when the exit poll had picked up a late swing to the Conservatives as the day went on, in 2015 it was clear to those analysing the data what was happening from the beginning. The very first batch of data analysed showed the Conservatives doing significantly better than the public polls had indicated.

The poll was a major surprise – perhaps the biggest single surprise of the entire campaign – because it predicted such a clear Conservative lead. The seat predictions were: Conservative 316 (+9), Labour 239 (–19), Lib Dem 10 (–47), SNP 58 (+52), Plaid Cymru 4 (+1), UKIP 2 (+2), Green 2 (+1), Others 19 (+1).[13] As noted in the last chapter, the poll was treated with some scepticism when it was first published, with some pointing to the problems inherent in the exercise this time. But if it erred, the poll slightly under-estimated how well the Conservatives had done.

The exit poll team thus became known as the only people to predict the election correctly.[14] But for all their skill, exit polling and 'normal' polling are two very different activities. The former has two huge inherent advantages. The first is that it entirely avoids the issue of (differential) turnout, over which normal pollsters agonise. The second is that by talking to people after they have voted, it entirely dodges the problem of people changing their minds. Conventional polls ask people how they think they will vote if they vote, but exit polls ask them how they have voted. Asking why normal polling cannot be done in the same way as exit polling is like asking why we cannot make aeroplanes out of the material that they use for the black box flight recorder.

The exit poll came as a shock not only to politicians and campaigners but also to the pollsters. Peter Kellner, appearing on the BBC's *Election Night* programme, looked greatly discomforted. The pollsters had little option but to admit that they had got it wrong, although some responses looked like an exercise in reputation retrieval. Some pointed to the margin of error, noting that (some) of their party share estimates fell (just) within. But for this to be a valid excuse, the estimates of the various companies should have scattered around the actual result rather than all being on one side of it. The argument might just about hold for an individual company, but it did not hold for the polling industry collectively.

Most notably, Survation drew attention to a phone poll it had conducted on the afternoon and evening of 6 May, which named candidates in the voter's constituency and spoke only to the named person from the dataset, and called mobile and landline telephone numbers to maximise the reach of the poll. It had a sample of 1,045 and produced a lead of 37:32 for the Conservatives over Labour, which was very close to the final result. The company's final published poll (for the *Daily Mirror*) polled over 4,000 voters between 4 and 6 May and predicted a 31:31 tie for Labour and the Conservatives. The latter was published, but the former was not. The chief executive, Damian Lyons Lowe, said he had 'chickened out' of reporting the former poll because it was out of line with other polls, an admission that reflected badly on the pollster. He said it was 'something I'm sure I'll always regret for the rest of my life'.[15] Yet unpublished but accurate polls are like unplaced but winning bets.

The British Polling Council (BPC) immediately announced it would set up a committee to conduct a post-mortem. It was in the interests of all polling companies to come up with the right answer to why they had got it wrong.[16] Questions would arise about the following issues:

- The type of polling, in particular online versus phone polling: does the former attract unrepresentative samples in terms of their relatively greater interest in politics, and shortage of over-60s, who voted heavily Conservative? Perhaps the boldest polling claim made during the campaign had come from Adam Ludlow of ComRes. On 14 April, he argued that the Conservatives 'have been leading all year' and that the long-awaited crossover had already occurred in January.[17] Both online and phone polls were used by ComRes, and he noted that the latter were producing more favourable scores for the Conservatives. But because online polls were more common, the Conservative lead in phone polls was not making much of a dent in the regular poll of polls that some newspapers conducted. Yet in the end, there seemed to be no difference between the various online and phone forecasts on 7 May, and the ComRes final poll on 7 May showed just a 1% Conservative lead. There were also some calls to revert to more face-to-face polling, even though it was the problems of generating sufficiently representative samples that had driven the initial shift away from face-to-face polling after 1992.
- Sampling: was the sampling upmarket enough, a failure that had occurred in 1992 and which pollsters thought they had corrected? Did it take account of the subsequent growth in size of the middle class? One pollster found his samples had slightly over-represented the number of welfare recipients, the disabled and people living in densely populated areas – all of which would increase Labour numbers. And even if demographically representative, are the people interviewed too politically engaged and too likely to vote?
- Questionnaire design, especially the order in which the questions are asked: Labour's pollsters, Greenberg, Quinlan Rosler, led their surveys with questions on voters' preferences on issues, leaders and parties, before asking about voting intention. James Morris claimed that this approach was more likely to put respondents in 'a ballot box mindset' and to think seriously about how they would vote. It also seemed to reduce the number of 'Don't Knows'. From October 2014, his private polling for Labour (see below) had the Conservatives in the lead, while the average of the public polls had the parties tied.[18]
- The importance of contextual questions: should polls attach more significance to contextual questions, not least in allocating the 'Don't Knows'? For example, at Populus, Andrew Cooper had long

been focusing on around 18% of voters who were either 'Don't Knows' or supporters of other parties than the Conservatives, but who preferred Cameron over Miliband as Prime Minister and the Conservatives on the economy. He persistently found 3% who were not planning to vote Conservative, but who, if they voted, might do so. To his regret, he did not use these contextual questions to 'squeeze' that group of 'Don't Knows' in his final forecast, which gave Labour a 1% lead.[19]

- Differential turnout: Ipsos MORI complained after the election that the large number of 'lazy' Labour voters, who did not turn up to vote, had confounded its predictions of Labour's vote share. It had drawn its final voting intention figure from those who claimed to be 'absolutely certain to vote', a group who made up over 80% of its respondents. Its problem was not that people exaggerated turnout – because they have always done this – but that it was more exaggerated than in the past and that the increase in exaggeration seemed to be disproportionate among those intending to vote Labour.[20] People might say they will vote Labour, but if they do not even manage to vote at all, this will not matter much.
- Response rate: it is becoming increasingly hard to get people to take part in polls. In evidence to the enquiry, ICM's Martin Boon said that in 1995 it would take around 3,000–4,000 phone calls to generate 2,000 interviews. By 2015, it took around 30,000. This inevitably leads to questions about the people who are choosing not to participate – and those who do.
- Groupthink: was there an element of groupthink among pollsters? 'Rogue' polls, a regular feature of British general elections, were largely absent in 2015 and all erred in the same direction rather than scattering either side of the mean. This seems unlikely – pollsters are in fierce competition – and their data are released, under BPC guidelines and are scrutinised.
- A late swing to the Conservatives: there was some anecdotal evidence of voters shifting to the Conservatives very late on in the campaign. The Lib Dems in particular detected some evidence of undecided voters moving to the Conservatives in the last week, as did a handful of Labour candidates.[21] But surveys in the last week found no evidence for this, and when pollsters re-contacted their respondents after the election, they found that switching was largely self-cancelling.[22]

This book is published before the conclusion of the panel's work. But it is already clear that there is not going to be a single or simple answer to the problem. Immediately after the election, the British Election Study (BES) tested some of the above suggestions. It found no evidence of 'Don't Knows' shifting to the Conservatives, or of a late swing, or of 'shy' Tories who refused to reveal their preferences. Using split sample experiments, it found no difference in Labour and Conservative support depending on question placement. It did find a slight problem with sampling – too few very old respondents in the case of the BES – which induced a small pro-Labour bias. But it argued that differential turnout was more likely to be a major part of the explanation. More of the BES panel claimed to have voted than had in reality, but it was able to test the honesty of voters by noting claims to have voted in local elections where none were held. It found that 'the fibbers lean significantly more to Labour than other respondents'.[23] This might indicate that those who leant towards Labour were more likely to tell Labour they would back them and that they would vote, but were then less likely to do so in reality. Yet even this was not of a scale that would explain the polls' failure away. Given that none of the discussed solutions seems very plausible on its own, it may be that the polling failure in 2015 was a combination of multiple factors, each contributing a small part of the error. This might be the worst outcome for pollsters, as it will make it harder to correct in the future.

It was not a coincidence that the man responsible for the explosion of constituency polling in the UK was a billionaire. Constituency polling, on any significant scale, is an expensive business.[24] Lord Ashcroft was not the only person to commission constituency-level polling in the run-up to 2015, but he was responsible for more of it than everyone else combined. Excluding private polls not released, there were constituency level polls undertaken, by Ashcroft and others, in more than 150 separate constituencies.[25] Many of these saw multiple polls; seven were conducted in Sheffield Hallam alone and eight were conducted in Thanet South. By their very nature, those chosen tended to be battleground or otherwise significant constituencies and were not a representative sample of seats. Nevertheless, they helped to establish or confirm three narratives about the election.

First, they confirmed the findings from the Scotland-wide polling that showed the SNP were on course for major gains in Scotland. Ashcroft released his first tranche of Scottish constituency polling in early February 2015. Polling in 16 Labour-held seats, some with massive majorities, including all of the Glasgow constituencies, found the SNP on target to take 15 of them. In total, of the 36 constituency polls undertaken in Scotland (all but one paid for by Ashcroft), the SNP were ahead in 34. It was one thing to see polling which had the SNP doing really well in Scotland as a whole; it was quite another to see constituency polls which put them ahead in seats such as Glasgow East.

The second narrative – which the constituency polls helped establish – was that Labour was outperforming the Conservatives on the ground. Ashcroft's polls included a question about whether respondents had been contacted by a political party or not. These data constituently showed more people reporting contact from Labour than from the Conservatives. Of the 31 constituency polls Ashcroft released in April and May 2015 in Conservative–Labour fights, Labour were ahead of the Conservatives in terms of voter contact in all of them. Even in Scotland, the Ashcroft polls tended to show Labour outperforming the SNP.[26] We discuss this further in Chapter 10, but for now suffice to say that the reality was not as positive for Labour.

And, third, the constituency polls confirmed the picture from the national polls in England and Wales, showing that the Lib Dems were in trouble (although they might hang on where they had well-entrenched incumbent candidates), UKIP had a chance in a handful of seats, and Labour and the Conservatives were pretty much neck and neck in the marginal seats. Here the constituency polling turned out to be no more accurate than the national polling. Ashcroft himself was a firm believer in the mantra that the polls were snapshots, not predictions, but compared to the eventual results, a full third of his polls put the wrong party in the lead and on average substantially under-estimated the Conservative vote and overstated Labour's. The Lib Dems complained publicly that his policy of not asking about specific candidates under-estimated the level of support for incumbent Lib Dem MPs, but if anything, Ashcroft's polling overstated the Lib Dem position.[27]

Because Ashcroft's previous general election surveys, reported in *Smell the Coffee* (2005) and *Minority Verdict* (2010), had made the case for Conservative modernisation, some Tories saw him as having an agenda. He regularly reported that voters did not see the party as being on the side of ordinary people, although that was common currency across all polls, both public and private, and (the Lib Dems aside) there were few criticisms of his polling methods per se. But his widespread polling – and the free availability of the data – caused some irritation in Conservative Campaign Headquarters (CCHQ) because it was seen as giving aid to Labour and the Lib Dems, who could not afford the same level of private polling as the Conservatives. Ashcroft's constituency polls could also be an aid to tactical campaigning and voting (at least if they were right); the results might be reported in the local press and candidates could, where it was advantageous, exploit the findings.

Chapter 1 outlined the story of the Parliament as seen through the polls: shortly after the coalition's formation, Lib Dem support collapsed and never recovered, triggering an immediate rise in Labour's vote. UKIP's vote rose throughout the Parliament, only dipping slightly at the end, with the Greens nudging up after mid-2014. There was a dip in Conservative support following the 'omnishambles' budget in 2012, after which Labour were clearly ahead, but Labour's lead slowly diminished over the last couple of years, with the two parties ending up roughly neck and neck. There was never, in the public polling at least, the crossover in votes between Labour and the Conservatives that Lynton Crosby had been predicting.

But was this what happened? Given that the final polls were so wrong, how do we know that they were right at other points during the Parliament? It depends on why we think the polls were wrong. If it was because of some sort of late swing, then we have no reason to doubt the earlier version of events. In that case, the polls were right all along, but at the very last minute, voters changed their minds. But if the problem was something more systematic, then it is plausible that the polls were wrong for much (or all) of the preceding five years.

For example, if we assume that the polls were as wrong throughout the Parliament as they were on election day and adjust the voting intention polling data accordingly, then polling crossover occurred sometime around July 2013, with the Conservative lead increasing slowly but steadily after that. Indeed, Labour probably only led – and then only narrowly – for around 18 months, between (roughly) March 2012 and July 2013. If this, or anything like it, was right, then it is easy to see how the five years of the Parliament could have been very different had the polling been more accurate. For example, had Labour slipped behind the Conservatives in the polls with almost two years to go, would Ed Miliband have survived as leader until the election? Would the Parliament have even lasted five years or would the Conservatives have attempted to collapse the coalition early to take advantage of a poll lead?[28] And how would an election in Scotland have played out if it had looked likely for more than a year that there would not be a hung parliament? We will obviously never know, but it does seem unlikely that the preceding five years would have been the same had the polls been different. If so, this is a much bigger democratic problem than the polls being wrong during the six weeks of the short campaign.

We then face a similar problem with almost all data drawn from those same polls – on things such as leadership, perceptions of the parties, of their leaders, of the economy and so on. The explosion of polling in general had led to an equal increase in this sort of data, yet if the headline figures are wrong because of problems with sampling, then perhaps so too are these other data. Here, the problem is somewhat less serious. For one thing, many of these underlying trends were always more pro-Conservative than the headline voting intention figures – which was one of the reasons why the headline polls appeared curious to many observers. As we reported in Chapter 2, the fundamentals always looked poor for Labour (see also p. 163). And some of the differences pollsters found are so large that even the sort of adjustment that might be required does not change the basic finding. The irony of the polls' failure in 2015 is that they had long presented ample data on the underlying strength of the Conservative position – notably on leadership and the economy – and the rise in the approval of the government's record. Between March 2013 and April 2015, the net score for economic optimism (optimism minus pessimism) with Ipsos MORI moved from –30% to +26%. It would have been a first in British elections for these indicators (almost all pointing the same way) not to predict the winning party. Voting intention responses pointed one way, but many of the responses to polling questions decisively signalled a different result. The dilemma was choosing which data to rely on. Greg Cook, Labour's polling analyst and a sceptic about the constant polling reports putting Labour being close to or ahead of the Conservatives, summed it up on 8 May: 'The result would not have been a surprise but for the polls.'

For all that politicians say they do not pay attention to the polls, they do. 'We were all obsessed with the polls', said one of the Conservative team; this obsession extended right up to the Prime Minister, who would regularly check his phone for polling updates. All of the parties take full advantage of the public polling, but they also conduct their own surveys and focus groups to help with strategy and tactics, identify target voters and test messages.

The most ambitious polling programme was undertaken by the Conservatives, whilst the other parties found that a lack of finance placed severe limitations on what they were able to do. Between March 2011 and October 2013, the pollster Andrew Cooper was based in Number 10

'Today is SATURDAY?'

Matt, *Daily Telegraph*, 9 May 2015
(© Matt/*The Telegraph*)

as David Cameron's Director of Political Strategy, the first such appointment in Downing Street, and his Populus firm conducted the party's polling. When Lynton Crosby was appointed as the general election director in late 2012, he insisted that the polling move to his Crosby Textor firm – and the pace of polling increased considerably. The voter segmentation work by Populus was discarded by Textor, although it did inform the messages used in the party's ground war campaign.

Textor's polls for the Conservatives in the marginal seats were held more frequently than Labour's and with larger samples. The overnight findings and focus groups summaries were reported to Cameron, George Osborne and Crosby. The polls concentrated ruthlessly on a smaller number of key seats than Labour, used a mix of telephone and online methods, and, in contrast to most other polls, mentioned the candidates' names in the constituencies. The polls were conducted in four clusters of seats and were held weekly. Textor would then use regression analysis to assess the salience and party favourability in order to choose the issues on which to campaign. High salience issues on which voters favoured the Conservatives were, predictably, the economy and leadership, while education and the NHS were 'Labour issues'.

Focus groups registered voters' potential concern about the SNP's likely influence over a minority UK government as early as autumn 2014. Crosby had decided that this concern might prove to be a useful lever for the party in a tight contest, as long as it was linked to the risk that an SNP–Labour alliance might pose to the economic recovery. Focus groups and reports from constituencies especially showed that this was cutting through in the last two weeks of the campaign.

Financial constraints meant that Labour conducted only two quantitative polls in the first 18 months of the Parliament. As explained in Chapter 3, the findings were often challenging and perhaps for that reason, but not that alone, circulation was highly restricted. During the short campaign, the Labour Party planned two polls, but added a third in late April. The second, in early April, had showed a 3.5% swing to Labour in the marginals, the minimum needed for Labour to be the largest party in seats, and it was decided to commission another poll for 30 April. This poll was discouraging. It showed Labour trailing 37:36 to the Conservatives with a swing of only 1% among those likely to vote; Morris thought this slight shift was caused by Conservative warnings about a Labour government being dependent on deals with the SNP. Even worse, when voters were asked to choose between a Miliband-led Labour government and a Cameron-led Conservative government, the latter's lead between the two polls had increased from 2% to 8%. The decision not to circulate the poll to more than a handful led to some excitable post-election comment about an alleged 'secret poll'.[29] 'It was only one poll, it was within the margin of error and anyway, what could we have done with it? We just held our breath', said one recipient of the poll. The research also reported that a quarter of the supporters of 'other' parties still thought of voting Labour or Conservative and were evenly divided between the two. However, the research note which accompanied the poll added that the Tory 'squeeze' about the potential influence of Nicola Sturgeon on Labour was more powerful than the Labour message. When Miliband heard the exit poll at 10 pm on 7 May and remarked 'That squares with what James was saying', it was this poll to which he was referring.

Labour's focus groups were mainly conducted by Morris, Greg Cook and Michelle Napchan, Douglas Alexander's special adviser, and were held mainly with former Labour voters in Conservative marginals and some with UKIP and Lib Dem waverers. Reactions to Miliband in focus groups were often disheartening; 'terrible' was the verdict of one of those involved. Those involved in surveying voters over the Parliament reflected that their challenging findings on the trio of weaknesses – welfare, immigration and the deficit – had not produced enough of a response from Miliband. Focus groups during his leadership campaign had warned that he was seen as 'too backwards looking' and 'fitted the Labour mould too closely' with his links to the unions and 'the lack of a focus on benefits cheats'.

As noted in Chapter 4, on arrival as Nick Clegg's strategist, Ryan Coetzee had commissioned two large online polls of some 6,000 voters, attempting to find the groups of the electorate to whom the Lib Dems' message might be most appealing. As the Parliament ran on and as Lib Dem poll ratings did not increase, this knowledge became less useful, and the party retreated back into a largely defensive exercise of trying to hold as many seats as possible, rendering this work largely redundant.

As part of this more defensive strategy, the Lib Dems also conducted private polling in the seats they held – and a handful they were targeting. The samples were around 400, much smaller than ideal, but were all they could afford and were believed by the Lib Dems to still be useful. 'It couldn't tell you if you'd win', said one of their team, 'but could tell you if it was worth fighting.' The Lib Dems claimed that the degree of name recognition and appreciation of the work of their MPs was encouraging. Leaving aside the smallness of the samples, prompting with questions about the name of the candidates may have overstated the strength of their position. One hard-headed Lib Dem reflected that it had a touch of 'comfort polling'. The surveys were selectively released to generate 'good news' stories about name recognition of the party's MPs and the conversions being made from Conservatives among women and the young, features not being detected in the national polls.[30] Yet it was striking that the polls that the party chose to release were not all that positive. These were good news stories without much good news, uncomfortable comfort polling. Even this polling ceased at the end of February 2015 when the money ran out. 'We took the decision that the money was better spent on leaflets', said one of Clegg's campaign team.

We noted in Chapter 4 that the SNP used focus groups to help refine their message after the referendum (and had used them extensively before). The feedback from SNP canvass returns was so positive that the party felt that they did not need to do much additional polling during the campaign. They did, however, commission two private telephone polls in the final week of the campaign, just to provide a double-check on levels of support, to calm any nerves and to help prepare for the result.

For both the Conservatives and Labour, the findings of the private polls were made available to very few people. Miliband shared the findings with Greg Beales, Stewart Wood, Marc Stears, Torsten Bell and, after their appointments, Douglas Alexander, Spencer Livermore and Lucy Powell. Crosby's polling was even more restrictive, being shared on a regular basis only with Osborne, Cameron, Lord Feldman and Jim Messina, but even then, this was mainly by Crosby's oral presentations and little data was made available. If the Conservatives had not won, some were ready to complain about Crosby 'marking his own homework'. There is continuing debate among strategists about the wisdom of confining the data that drives the strategy to a small handful. Veterans of the Clinton 'war room', like James Carville and Stan Greenberg, thought it useful to share the information widely and the private polls were circulated to a larger number of senior Labour and Conservative personnel in the past. A consequence of confining the private polls to a handful of insiders may accidentally or intentionally empower them in internal debates about strategy.

The private polls were not primarily designed to make forecasts, but to test messages and themes. All parties use focus groups for this as well, and we give examples of this throughout the book: from Labour desperately seeking solutions to the Conservatives' vernacular language on the economy to the SNP changing their message after the referendum.

However, the combination of internal polling and canvass returns allow the parties to make predictions. For the Conservatives, Messina and Crosby on the morning of 7 May predicted to Cameron that the party would win 305 seats. The director of campaigning, Stephen Gilbert, predicted 295. The aggregate figures of reports from his field directors to Gilbert suggested a figure of 328 seats, but, influenced by the consensus of the opinion polls, he feared that was too optimistic and lowered that figure by 33 – to his subsequent regret. For Labour, Patrick Heneghan's calculation on the day, based on polling and feedback from the marginal seats, was that at best Labour would get 262 seats to the Conservatives' 283 (a deficit of 21 seats) and at worst 256 against the Conservatives' 288 (a deficit of 32). The belief that the Lib Dems would hold some 20 seats was the basis for the Labour expectations that the Conservatives would not be able to combine with other likely partners to reach 323 seats, but that Labour, with more coalition options and with the SNP ruling out any arrangement with the Conservatives, would be able to enter government. In the event, the Conservative lead in seats over Labour was 98. The Lib Dems ended the campaign with at least 14 seats they thought they were going hold. The SNP ended the campaign expecting to win at least 50 seats, being only slightly concerned about the effect of turnout.[31]

After the result, Crosby and Messina dismissed the public polls and claimed that they had known that Conservatives were clearly in the lead all along. Messina complained about the methods of the British pollsters, observing that he named the candidates in the seats, used bigger samples, and employed a mix of phone and online polls.[32] He also claimed that voters have become more tactically aware and that this was crucial in helping to attract Lib Dems, fearing SNP influence on a Labour government, into the Conservative camp. For such voters, the outcome which they wished to achieve or avoid was more important than party loyalty.[33] James Morris sparked some anger amongst Labour politicians when he went public with his claims that Labour's private polling had long shown the party in a worse position than the public polls.[34]

Labour's private polling was more negative than the public polls, and the Conservatives' polling was more positive. Yet none of the polling – whether private or public – accurately predicted an outright majority. No one in the Conservative Party or the Labour Party had prepared for any party achieving an overall majority. If Labour's predictions had been right, they would have been able to lock the Conservatives out of Downing Street. The Conservatives' internal predictions were closer to the actual result, but were also tantalisingly close to the point at which they might not have been able to cling on to Number 10. Even with Crosby's prediction to Cameron of 305 seats on the morning of 7 May, there was no guarantee that the party would be able to cobble together a figure of 323 seats with other parties to form a government. Cameron, at his home on polling day, was braced for bad news. If the Conservatives were really so confident, why was there so much tension in Cameron's house and in CCHQ on election night? The mood of plenty on the Conservative top table was sombre as they heard reports of on-the-day polling by YouGov. As one of the key members of the team put it: 'Don't let anybody tell you we thought we were going to win on that day.' For Labour, if the party really knew they were going to lose, why had the preparations for government been conducted so vigorously in the last few days of the campaign? As one of those involved put it: 'We thought we were going to be the government. We wouldn't have done all of that work otherwise.' Ditto for their briefing of journalists: 'We'd have looked daft doing that if we knew we were going to lose.'

When it comes to election predictions, the private polls compete with the public ones. But the latter are more numerous, up-to-date and accessible to a wider number of party workers, even those at the centre. In 2015 the private polls were of marginal seats and were not representative of the nation. Some Labour HQ staff who understood Stan Greenberg to have been claiming that Labour could not lose (see p. 88) felt let down. But they and the very few readers of the private polls were more buoyed by the public polls indicating that, even by finishing second in the total number of seats, Labour would be in the driving seat to form a government. They discounted the more pessimistic internal polls.

When Parliament had resumed, Lord (Daniel) Finkelstein gave an account of his last visit to Downing Street before the election:

> I was taken down in the lift by Kevin, the messenger who had accompanied me to the ground floor many times over the previous five years. As we reached the bottom I said, 'Well Kevin, this could be the last time we do this'. He looked at me, shook his head slowly and said, 'Naaah'. This turned out to be more perceptive political analysis than most of what was written in the media over the following two months.[35]

Those pundits whose view on the election had been guided more by a sense of intuition (albeit historically guided intuition) had long been confident that the Conservatives would win; they included Matthew Parris and Philip Collins (*The Times*), Dan Hodges (*Daily Telegraph*) and John Rentoul (*Independent on Sunday*). They were more accurate in their predictions than those who followed the polls religiously. That is not a good outcome for polling.

In part, the blame for this lies with the polls, but it must also rest on the shoulders of those who reported them so heavily and relied on them for their analysis. Did the media have to be so beholden to the polls? They as well as the pollsters had lessons to learn.

The year 2015 was an *annus horribilis* for the public polls – and for pollsters. Those who predicted the death of the poll, however, were soon disappointed. Although newspapers immediately scaled back their reporting of voting intention polls, they continued to be conducted and, within months, polls were being conducted on the possible outcome of an EU referendum as well as the Labour leadership contest. Those running those polls, however, knew that they needed to be more accurate next time.

Notes

1. The total of 92 polls in the 2015 campaign compares with 81 in 2010, 52 in 2005 and 31 in 2001.
2. The margin of error is commonly said to be +/– 3%, although in reality it varies depending upon sample size (and strictly speaking derives from the sample being randomly drawn from a knowable universe, which is not the case for most commercial polls). Moreover, the margin of error applies to

each data point – in this case, support for each party. The lead is calculated from two data points, each with their own margin of error. As we note (p. 236), however, in 2015 the scale and direction of the polls' failure was such that technicalities of this sort became largely irrelevant.

3. 'It's Vital to Know Why Labour Lost – Yet More So to Know Why the Tories Won', *The Guardian*, 14 May 2015.
4. These were amusing and sometimes wounding. In Oscar week the pollster asked who would play each leader in a film biography. Miliband was allocated Rowan Atkinson as Mr Bean. Clegg had Tom Cruise and Cameron had Hugh Grant or Colin Firth. When asked about the leaders' favourite beverage, Farage was linked with a pint of bitter, Cameron a good red wine, Clegg a Babycham and Miliband a crème de menthe, 'the sort of drink nobody would order'. They were later published in Lord (Michael) Ashcroft and Kevin Culwick's *Pay Me Forty Quid and I'll Tell You*. Biteback, 2015.
5. 'Lynton Crosby in Pollster "Scream" Attack', www.politicshome.com, 2 June 2015.
6. Although methodologically fairly sophisticated, the reasons for such adjustments are fairly simple and easy to understand: pollsters want to ensure that their respondents are broadly representative of the public, and then – for any discussion of voting – further adjust to take into account that not every respondent will vote. YouGov surveys members of its online panel and weights according to how respondents voted at the previous election, discounting 'Don't Knows'. TNS interviews people in their homes, weighted for previous vote and likelihood to vote. ICM uses telephone interviews and weights for previous vote and likelihood of voting. Opinium uses telephone surveys and respondents are drawn from its panel. Ipsos MORI conducts telephone interviews, does not weight according to vote at the previous general election and includes only those certain to vote in its final calculation. Populus conducts its surveys online and weights for vote at the previous general election, level of party support in previous Populus surveys and likelihood to vote. The Ashcroft polls were carried out by telephone (Ashcroft refused to say which company carried them out, although insiders in the polling industry believed that most of them were conducted by Populus) and were weighted for likelihood to vote and past vote. ComRes used both phone and online methods and weighted for vote at last general election and likelihood to vote.
7. This was obviously mostly for a niche rather than a mass audience, although in its last month May2015.com alone had a not unimpressive 2.9 million page views from 1.3 million people and ukpollingreport.co.uk had 6.2 million pages views from 1.2 million people.
8. Not all of these models drew on polling data – using other data, such as local election results – but most used polling data for all or at least part of their model.
9. His calculation allowed the Conservatives an incumbency advantage of some 20 seats from their first-time MPs and a swing back to the government of the day. He also thought the Lib Dems were well entrenched and would do better than indicated by their projected vote share.
10. 'The Blogger Who Beat the British Political Pollsters', www.bloomberg.com, 31 July 2015.

11. There is a useful, pre-2015, explanation in John Curtice, 'Iain Dale, Naked' in Philip Cowley and Robert Ford (eds), *Sex, Lies and the Ballot Box*. Biteback, 2014. The team then update their model as the night progresses with the results from individual seats.
12. Instead, in these locations, they used data from the constituency as a whole, having chosen the polling locations to be as typical of the constituency as possible.
13. Although not released at the time, the underpinning vote shares predicted by the exit poll also proved very accurate: Con +1 (reality was +1); Lab +1 (+1); Lib Dem –16 (–15); SNP (in Scotland) +33 (+30); UKIP +10 (+10); PC (in Wales) +2 (+1); Green +3 (+3).
14. 'John Curtice: The Man Behind the Only Poll That was Right', www.may2015.com, 8 June 2015.
15. Damian Lyons Lowe, 'Snatching Defeat from the Jaws of Victory' www.survation.com, 8 May 2015.
16. Among a number of more immediate post-mortems, see Alberto Nardelli, 'Election Polls Made Three Key Errors', *The Guardian*, 11 May 2015; Robert Booth, 'Why Did the Election Pollsters Get it So Wrong?', *The Guardian*, 15 May 2015; David Cowling, 'Election 2015: How the Opinion Polls Got it Wrong', BBC News, 17 May 2015; Sebastian Payne, 'How the Pollsters Got it Wrong and Why Labour Lost', *The Spectator*, 12 May 2015; Peter Kellner, 'Where it All Went Wrong for the Polls', *The Times Guide to the House of Commons 2015*. Times Books, 2015
17. 'Look Past the "Polls of Polls", the Conservatives Have Been Leading All Year', www.comres.co.uk, 14 April 2015.
18. James Morris, 'Late Swing? Labour's Private Polls Showed the Tories Ahead before Christmas', *New Statesman*, 11 May 2015.
19. Informed by this research, Daniel Finkelstein wrote that the challenge for the Conservatives was to move the 'yes, yes, no' voter to a 'yes, yes, yes' one. See 'Cameron Needs to Convert the Yes, Yes, Nos', *The Times*, 1 May 2015.
20. Ipsos MORI's predictions for turnout had never been 80%, despite this figure. As it noted at the time: 'Our experience suggests that this figure tends to overstate the actual turnout. On this basis we would expect a turnout of between 72 and 74%.'
21. The Lib Dems conducted a large canvass in Kingston and Surbiton on the last weekend of the campaign involving 5,000 contacts. It found no great difference in their squeeze category or their definite/probable voters. But of the unknowns, they found a large Tory surge. This was only one seat – it was the only seat where there was sufficient data to be sure about the trend – and it may be that Kingston and Surbiton was not typical of other constituencies, but it did at least indicate some late switching.
22. Of the polling companies, YouGov, Populus, Opinium and ICM all had re-contact data showing no late swing. The only exception was Survation.
23. Jon Mellon and Chris Prosser, 'Why Did the Polls Go Wrong?' www.britishelectionstudy.com, 15 July 2015.
24. Apart from Ashcroft, the only two other significant commissioners of constituency-level polls were also wealthy individuals: Lord Oakeshott, whose polls were leaked earlier in the Parliament to try to destabilise Nick Clegg's leadership (p. 108), and Alan Bown, one of UKIP's main donors.

25. Ashcroft's polling was conducted in Great Britain only; the one constituency poll in Northern Ireland, which was undertaken by Lucid Talk for the *Belfast Telegraph*, (accurately) showed the Democratic Unionist Party (DUP) on course to take Belfast East from the Alliance Party of Northern Ireland (APNI).
26. See Philip Cowley, 'The SNP Has an Army of Activists, But is it Winning the Ground War in Scotland?', www.may2015.com, 20 April 2015. Even at the time, this seemed unlikely, as well as clearly not mattering very much, given the leads that the SNP appeared to be generating in those same constituencies.
27. For example, in September 2014, Ashcroft polls reported the Lib Dems comfortably ahead of the Conservatives in Cheadle, Eastleigh, Sutton and Cheam, and Eastbourne. All of these seats fell to the Conservatives on large swings (9.2% in Cheadle and 12% in Eastleigh).
28. The Fixed-Term Parliaments Act (FTPA) made this tactic harder to pull off, but not impossible. It is possible to imagine a scenario under which the Conservatives decide to end the coalition and call for an early election ('it is time to put these important questions to the people'); they urge Labour to vote to trigger an early election; under the FTPA, Labour can refuse and instead enter into an arrangement with the Lib Dems (and others) putting Ed Miliband into Number 10 without an election; but amid concerns that such a deal could look illegitimate and make Labour look frit of putting its case before the electorate, they decide to back the election instead. The point is that, given the polls throughout the Parliament, such questions never really arose.
29. See Sam Coates, 'Team Miliband Hid Poll Warnings of Looming Defeat from the Party Faithful', *The Times*, 9 May 2015.
30. See Patrick Wintour, 'Lib Dem Polling Brings Hope of Future Coalition Role', *The Guardian*, 20 February 2015.
31. As one of the SNP team put it: 'We knew the vote had turned out, but we were still a little cautious about turnout. Turnout had burned us in the indyref. Then good was good, but very good was bad. And so we were a bit cautious until we saw the turnout figures.'
32. The comparison was hardly fair. Messina was conducting big data analytics rather than polling and operated with vastly more data points than the pollsters.
33. 'Mercenary Voters Decided UK Election Says Pollster Who Predicted Tory Victory', *The Guardian*, 6 August 2015.
34. Morris, 'Late Swing?'. Critics within the party claimed that his public statements were a breach of contract.
35. HL Debs, 27 May 2015, col. 13.

1. Nick Clegg and David Cameron at their first joint press conference in Downing Street, 12 May 2010.

2. Ed and David Miliband, after the former was elected Labour leader, September 2010.

3. Nigel Farage, celebrating UKIP's victory in the 2014 European elections.

4. Caroline Lucas and Natalie Bennett at the Green Party manifesto launch.

5. Leanne Wood, Plaid Cymru leader since 2012.

6. Nicola Sturgeon and Alex Salmond in Glasgow during the independence referendum campaign.

7. Harriet Harman at Labour's manifesto launch in Manchester.

8. Douglas Alexander on the old *Coronation Street* set for Labour's manifesto launch.

9. Michael Gove, and Conservative activists, outside Labour's manifesto launch.

10. Nick Clegg at the Lib Dem manifesto launch.

11. David Laws briefing the press at the back of the Lib Dem manifesto launch, near the bins.

12. Lynton Crosby.

13. Lord (Andrew) Feldman.

14. Stephen Gilbert.

15. Ryan Coetzee.

16. Jim Murphy, Ed Miliband and Ed Balls in Edinburgh, 10 April 2015.

17. Ed Miliband rehearsing his opening statement for the first leaders' debate.

18. Modern campaigning: Nigel Farage campaigning in the Rochester and Strood by–election.

19. Modern campaigning: Boris Johnson campaigning in Uxbridge and South Ruislip.

20. Modern campaigning: Nick Clegg campaigning in Solihull.

21. Modern campaigning: Nicola Sturgeon at the SNP conference in Perth in November 2014.

22. The ITV Leaders' Debate.

23. George Osborne in the spin room after the Leaders' Debate.

24. Nicola Sturgeon visiting Berwickshire, Roxburgh and Selkirk on 30 April 2015.

25. Hard-working families: David Cameron and George Osborne.

26. A polling station in Herne Hill, South London.

27. Bridget Phillipson, the first MP elected to the 2015 Parliament in Houghton and Sunderland South.

28. Neil Coyle defeats Simon Hughes in Bermondsey and Old Southwark.

29. Nick Clegg and his wife Miriam at the Sheffield Hallam declaration.

30. Ed Miliband and his wife Justine arriving at Labour HQ, the day after the election.

31. The new SNP MPs at the Forth Bridge, with Nicola Sturgeon, 9 May 2015.

32. David Cameron and his wife Samantha arriving back at Conservative HQ, the day after the election.

33. Victors and vanquished at the VE Day Service, 8 May.

10
Where to Drop the Bombs: The Constituency Battle

There have been significant changes in local campaigning in recent years. The parties have had to adapt to a general long-term decline in members – the Green and SNP surges notwithstanding – as well as the opportunities offered by technology and social media.[1] For Labour and the Liberal Democrats especially, the local or ground war is important because the preponderance of press support for the Conservatives places them at a disadvantage in the mass-media or air war. In communicating with voters, parties have learnt from commercial marketing tools and have become eager students of the latest developments in US elections; in 2015 the Conservatives and Labour imported key staff who had worked on the Obama 2012 presidential campaign. They also learn from each other. The Conservatives were impressed at how Labour held on to so many marginal seats which they would have lost on a uniform swing in 2010 by exploiting their superior rates of activity and voter contact; Labour organisers had boasted that they had gained a 1992 share of seats for a 1983 share of votes. Alicia Kennedy, Labour's then campaign director, had claimed 'where we work, we win', and it was a lesson the Conservatives had taken to heart.

In 2015 the media were fascinated with the arcane techniques of the parties' use of big data and social media. Much of this activity was directed from the parties' headquarters and operated under the radar. Local candidates and organisers as well as the media often had little idea of what was happening in the key seats; the national campaign directors had a better picture, although even they could be blind-sided in seats they were not targeting.[2] Local campaigning is local only up to a point. In key or target seats, the centre is heavily involved in selecting target seats, the target voters, the kinds of messages to send to voters and the amount of help to send to local organisers. It is only in seats which are considered completely safe or hopeless that local campaigning remains genuinely local. Above all, the centre is involved in collecting data from a range of sources and providers and in collating it. Parties still need members – for fundraising, representing the party in the community and delivering leaflets, contacting and collecting information about voters, and mobilising supporters on polling day – but in target seats, they are supplemented by other forms of contact with voters. The traditional distinction between the ground war (the local contest) and the air war (the national contest) remains useful, but in addition – to continue the military metaphor – there is a considerable amount of artillery, fired over the heads of the ground troops, directed from the centre and about which local party workers (or even staff) will be largely or completely ignorant. A Conservative organiser compared the vote-targeting operation to 'telling the aircraft where to drop the bombs'. Or as one of Labour's field team claimed: 'This is a case where the man in Whitehall, or Brewer's Green, actually knows best.' Much of this is not picked up in conventional analysis of campaign activity – or, crucially, in measures of local campaign expenditure.

Despite Labour and the Conservatives drawing lessons from the 2012 Obama campaign, the differences in scale between Britain and the United States are significant. In the latter there are greater amounts of money, paid television advertising and much longer campaigns. Jim Messina, working for the Conservatives, compared Obama's 30,000 field operatives in 2012 with the 120 available for the Conservatives in 2015. Despite Labour's heavy investment in a digital team, their 15 team members were dwarfed by Obama's 300 in 2012. However, the various commercial companies which the parties use as part of their campaigning often speak very highly of their work, noting that it is at least as sophisticated as anything being done by private sector clients. As one data supplier noted, compared to their other clients, the parties 'put a lot more time into sweating the data ... It's not about return on investment. It's about winning. No one's going to thank you for saving some money if you lose'.

The key term in modern campaigning is targeting: target voters and groups of voters, target seats, and targeted messages. Campaigners increasingly concentrate their efforts on particular seats and particular voters in those seats. There is nothing new about the former; marginal seat campaigning is a long-established practice. But new technology enables parties to garner large amounts of data about individuals and to personalise their communications accordingly. Combined with extensive opinion polling, campaigners can create micromodels of potential target voters, building up a portrait of each one, including information about past vote, likelihood of voting and issue concerns.

Addressing the Conservative annual party conference at Birmingham in 2012, Stephen Gilbert announced what was known as the party's 40–40 strategy, identifying 40 attack and 40 defence seats, based on a mix of electoral margins and local activity. If the party held the latter and gained the former, it would have a clear working majority. Labour started with 86 attack seats, enough for a 40-seat majority. The Lib Dems began with the 57 seats won in 2010 and identified another dozen which were then regarded as potentially winnable. That was the initial electoral battleground for 2015, but it was soon to change. The Conservatives expanded their number of battleground seats, as did Labour (only then to narrow their focus and later have to adapt to the SNP surge). The Lib Dem battleground narrowed as the Parliament progressed as the party increasingly opted for a defensive strategy. The SNP, by contrast, began the Parliament with a largely defensive battleground – consisting of six held seats and a handful of possible targets – only to see it expand to cover all of Scotland.

Even within a constituency, segmentation is key. The parties use a mixture of voter ID (what used to be called canvassing) and commercially available data to map messages on to voters. Almost all parties use the commercial Mosaic data, which splits the population into 15 broad categories (from A, 'City Prosperity', to O, 'Rental Hub') and then within these into 67 sub-groups.[3] They will supplement this with other commercially or publicly available data. Labour, for example, ran two targeted mailshots to parents of children born in 2014 to inform them of the party's childcare policies, as well as targeted mailings on the party's energy price freeze pledge to those facing increases in their energy bills. The most complex of the Labour segmentations targeted 13 different sub-groups of voters within the scope of one mailing. Targeted campaigning has become personalised campaigning.

This can make it very difficult for any observers – and some participants – to understand what is taking place. As one Labour organiser put it: 'What's going on in the key seats and the marginals is so different from what's going in in safe seats that it's sometimes difficult for politicians to understand what we're doing.'[4] At one Conservative meeting, Craig Oliver, David Cameron's press secretary, listened to an account of the party's ambitious mailing programme and wondered aloud why, given that he lived in a target seat, he had received nothing from the Conservatives, but lots of material from Labour. The response was that he was identified as a strong Conservative with a high propensity to vote, so he was not being targeted by his own party. The Conservative ground team asked him who he thought was fighting the most effective campaign: them for not spending any money on someone who would vote for them anyway or Labour for spending loads of money on someone who would not.

To segment properly requires both good data and an accurate delivery mechanism for the message. It requires a means of getting the right message to the right target at the right time. Even where they exist in large enough numbers, local activists are not always considered reliable enough for highly segmented targeting. As one party strategist put it: 'Local parties are not always great at getting the material out when it needs to be out.' The parties thus have two options: one, used increasingly, is social media (discussed below); the other is direct mail, which is used by all the major parties to some extent – and to a huge degree by the major British parties. The Conservatives were often critical of what they called Labour's 'spraying and praying' approach to campaigning, an impression reinforced by Labour's continual boasting about their numbers of grassroots contacts.[5] But it was not that Labour's field team eschewed direct mail, just that they could not afford to do as much of it as they would have liked. Labour's relatively limited direct mail programme was driven by finance, not preference. As a cheaper alternative, Labour would often resort to what the Royal Mail calls 'door drops', deliveries which can blanket a specific postcode – roughly 5,000 voters – at a much cheaper cost (around 4p per leaflet, noticeably cheaper than individualised direct mail).[6] This at least ensured that leaflets were delivered at the right time, to match national messaging. But there is a trade-off between cost and the ability to segment accurately, and Labour lacked the resources to campaign in the way their field team would have liked, a complaint they were making privately long before the election. The result was that the Conservatives were able to target their message more precisely, and for longer, on potential swing voters.

Ideally, a party will select candidates, appoint organisers and canvass voters in key seats well in advance of the short campaign. The adage 'early money works best' holds if the party has sufficient funds. Both Labour and the Lib Dems received ad hoc sums of campaign funds late in the day and which they feel might have been better used if received earlier. All parties have long abandoned the idea of having full-time agents in key seats and instead now train local and regional staff in campaigning and mobilising voters.

The parties are also all aware of the potential benefits of incumbency as a campaign resource. There is a clear pattern over recent general elections that first-time incumbent MPs do better than would be predicted from the uniform national swing.[7] The effect is especially strong for Lib Dem MPs, but it also existed to a lesser extent for both Labour and the Conservatives.[8] Even though the MPs' 'communications allowance' had been abolished early on in the Parliament, the visibility of incumbency was still significant. One Labour campaigner estimated it as worth around £130,000 over a five-year period. 'You can't be party political', he said, 'but it's still profile raising.' There was much discussion of how this might enable the Lib Dems to survive their national poll ratings, but the party with the most to gain from incumbency was the Conservatives, as they had a large number of MPs defending seats they had first gained in 2010 and which Labour would have to retake if they were to enter government.

The parties' HQs drafted scripts for activists with advice and potential responses to questions for use in doorstep encounters with voters. The Conservatives built their national databases on voters' responses to a series of 12 questions, based on a 14-page script.[9] The aim was not to ask people how they were going to vote, but to deduce it from the key questions. The first two questions were about asking voters if they thought it was important to have a strong government so that it could deliver a strong economy. The second was whether they approved of a government being reliant upon the SNP. Using statistical modelling, Labour identified which parts of each constituency would be most rich in what it termed 'persuasion targets', those voters who were most likely to consider voting Labour. The party also experimented with data on the time of voting in order to ensure that people were more likely to be in when contacted on polling day. As noted above (p. 88), it also distributed a doorstep strategy for dealing with UKIP sympathisers, to show how Labour policies might address the voters' concerns (usually on immigration) as well as 'moving the conversation on' from immigration.

As the Conservative Party has suffered a steady decline in membership (down to 140,000 in 2014), it has relied more on volunteers and technology for local campaigning. Grant Shapps, who had replaced Sayeeda Warsi as party co-chairman in 2012, set up Team 2015, a mix of volunteers who were party supporters, as well as members, and recruited largely by email and Facebook.[10] The idea was to bring in new people as well as motivating and organising existing members. He did not mind that they were not in full agreement with all the party policies and recognised that not being a member of a political party might be a canvassing asset. The scheme, based on his own experience as the MP for Welwyn Hatfield, had nearly 100,000 volunteers on its database within two years. He negotiated a substantial sum from Andrew Feldman to fund the volunteers' weekend visits (covering travel and accommodation) to marginal seats. But for all the publicity Team 2015 attracted, particularly in the Newark by-election in 2014, privately Conservative party strategists viewed its occasional visits as no substitute for the regular work of committed local activists who knew the constituency and its problems.

In April 2014, in a sign of growing confidence and available resources, Stephen Gilbert added ten seats to the Conservatives' offensive target list, mostly Lib Dem-held seats, and in December added ten to the defensive list. Entering the election, the party therefore had a 50–50 seats strategy. It had invited candidates to apply for selection in its attacking seats in 2012 and, within 12 months, candidates were in place in target seats and all had full-time campaign managers. Conservative Campaign Headquarters (CCHQ) looked for a commitment by successful applicants that they would embed themselves in the constituency over the following two to three years. In particular, in seats with well-established Lib Dem MPs, the Conservative candidates were expected to be highly visible and raise their profile to offset the personal vote that many of the MPs had garnered over the years. The Lib Dems certainly believed that this strategy worked. As one Lib Dem strategist noted: 'They neutralised our local advantage. Did just enough. It wasn't very convincing, and our people were cynical about it. But if you go on about it for 3 to 4 years, it's enough.'

As noted on p. 60, there was no repeat of David Cameron's 'A-list' of favoured candidates, designed to recruit more female and ethnic minority candidates in winnable seats. This had caused much local resentment before 2010. But the candidates' list had been revised to make it more socially diverse. CCHQ mostly limited its role to supplying information about the demography of the constituency to local officers in the hope that they would choose a 'suitable' candidate, but in some cases Gilbert's team head-hunted for suitable candidates and usually joined with local officers to select the shortlist. In the attack seats, CCHQ discreetly monitored the candidates' media profiles and how active they were. With some prodding from the centre – 'soft pressure' was the term used – the party ended up with record numbers of women, local and ethnic minority candidates in the winnable seats and, in the new Parliament, among its MPs too (see chapter 13).

In 2012 the Conservative Party started to compile a list of different types of target voters. Each voter was placed on a scale of 1 to 10 depending on the likelihood of him or her voting Conservative, with 10 being strongly likely to vote for the party. For the 2014 European and local elections, the party reworked Andrew Cooper's categories of voters (see p. 59). The ten new categories included, *inter alia*, former Conservatives now leaning towards UKIP and soft Labour voters who preferred David Cameron as leader and/or preferred the Conservatives on the economy, Conservatives who were least likely to vote, and most Liberal Democrats. For each category, there were distinctive messages to be delivered by phone, direct mail, social media or on the doorstep.

During the campaign, all voters received leaflets with the core Conservative message of offering to secure a better future for Britain. In addition, personalised direct mail was delivered in 4,000 different versions depending on the type of voter and type of seat. These figures can sound deceptively large: with 100 target seats, within each constituency this means a less impressive 40-fold segmentation, but during the six weeks of the campaign, a typical target voter would receive at least eight personalised messages from the Conservatives.

Jim Messina's work on the motivations of voters was intensive. His approach required large amounts of data and used commercial call centres to explore consumers' political attitudes, values and demographics. This information was integrated with Mosaic data and other publicly available data about a voter's lifestyle choices, shopping habits and other information to develop a propensity model for different types of voters who might be persuaded to vote Conservative. Textor's polling in the marginal seats was used to monitor the views of voter types. The selected potential Tory switchers were then bombarded with direct mail, phone calls, social media and personal visits. Messina was working with samples of between 1,000 and 2,000 voters per key seat and an admiring colleague commented: 'Because of how they [voters] had been identified and targeted it was essentially invisible. The Liberal Democrats were blindsided and the media were unaware of what was happening.' Messina then tracked the overall probability score of each of his voter types voting Conservative. In cases where the score dropped further, targeted communications were directed at voters.

Specific mailshots were delivered to help in individual seats. One Conservative candidate reported his concern about Conservatives defections to UKIP; when an Ashcroft poll showed Labour in the lead, CCHQ arranged for the delivery a few days before polling of 4,000 personalised direct mail messages aimed at Conservative voters who were leaning towards UKIP. During the campaign, CCHQ added the highly marginal Croydon Central seat to its defensive target list and, when it looked as if the seat would be lost (Labour organisers had written it up as a gain a few days before polling), arranged for the delivery of personalised emails to doubtful and to UKIP-leaning Conservatives. The incumbent won by 167 votes.

During the short campaign, Gilbert received nightly reports from his 25 field directors (each responsible for four seats), which he then reported to Lynton Crosby the following morning. On polling day, the Conservative Party phoned tens of thousands of target voters. Whatever fears Gilbert might have had about trailing Labour in a get out the vote (GOTV) operation on 7 May, the feedback was encouraging. By lunchtime, over 50% of Conservative identifiers had already voted compared to just over 30% of other voters. By 10 pm, the party calculated that it had been supported by some 80% of two important categories of its target voters: the original Conservative-leaning but UKIP supporters and the anti-UKIP supporters who had not been minded to vote Conservative. Gilbert and Messina had worked hard on these types of voters. Messina spent election day analysing his latest data, assessing the probability of a Tory vote for each voter type in each seat and then updating his forecast. He predicted particular seats, not vote shares, and on polling day he upgraded his predictions for Conservative seats from 305 to 319 shortly before the polls closed. Some of his seat predictions were correct, but, less well publicised, a number were not. Because confidence about making predictions increases with the size of the data sets, a successful operation requires large sums of money, and here the Conservatives were better resourced than other parties.

For all its sophistication, however, things still went wrong. The Conservatives had replaced their unreliable Merlin software programme with Vote Source. But on polling day, due to the heavy demand and in part due to the lack of training of some users, it effectively crashed.[11] Had the Conservatives lost the election, the narrative would doubtless have been one of Labour's old-fashioned grassroots campaigning defeating too-clever-by-half technology.[12]

Patrick Heneghan succeeded Alicia Kennedy as Labour's director of field operations in late 2012. Virtually all the seats on the party's initial target list had been lost in 2010 to the Conservatives. The list was revised in November 2012 when the campaigns coordinator, Tom Watson, prodded by the leader's office, added a further 20 seats, mainly in the south-east, to fit in with Ed Miliband's One Nation theme. More controversially, the party for the first time went public with the list of target seats. This decision raised expectations among candidates and organisers in the target seats and resentment among those which had been passed over. Realistically, there was no way that 106 seats could be properly resourced. In June 2014, Douglas Alexander agreed, without publicity, to cut back the number to 70. If the party could win 40 of its 50 'A' category or most winnable seats, it could reach 310 seats and would almost certainly be involved in forming a government. If it reached 60, it would have small majority.

Labour invested heavily in recruiting and training field operations staff on a two-year course. Each key seat had at least one organiser, 120 in all, and 30 organising staff based in party headquarters. The marginal seats were graded according to their winnability and some of the so-called must-win seats were so well resourced that they had two or three organisers. Labour had placed organisers in most of their must-win seats in 2013 and set them ambitious contact targets. Local activity – such as contact with voters, recruitment of volunteers and raising money – was monitored from the party's London HQ, and candidates were called in for stern talkings to if they were failing to hit the required activity levels.

Following the controversy over the selection of the Labour candidate in Falkirk (see pp. 82–3), some unions, including Unite, GMB and Unison, cut back their affiliation fee contributions to the Labour Party in 2014 and diverted funds to their political funds, from which they supported sponsored candidates with substantial grants (reportedly between £40,000 and £70,000). The distribution did not always square with the party's views about the most effective allocation. For example, the Unite-backed Clive Lewis in Norwich South, an anticipated easy Labour gain, was much better resourced than Labour's candidate in neighbouring marginal Norwich North, Jessica Asato. Lewis was on the left of the party, while Asato was not – Lewis won easily, Asato lost.

Like the Conservatives, Labour used a mix of polling and canvassing data to build a voting propensity model for each voter, measuring the likelihood he or she would vote Labour. The party used its Contact Creator software to keep a record of voters' views and the contacts with them, and Nation Builder, an established platform for recruiting and mobilising volunteers. The party also built a model of the voter's propensity to turn out on polling day. When it seemed likely the contact might vote Labour, it was left to the GOTV team to mobilise the voter on 7 May.

In early January 2015, Miliband announced a much-publicised goal for party workers of holding four million 'conversations' by 7 May with target voters. The target was achieved ahead of schedule and by the end of April, the party released a regional breakdown of the figures and a total of 4,085,962 'conversations'. A target of a further million was then announced.[13] This reinforced the impression that Labour, with their larger and younger party membership, were conducting a formidable ground operation. It was certainly true that Labour felt they had more activists and supporters out on the streets. As one of their campaign team noted: 'Last time, we might organise a weekend canvass session and we'd get four or five people turn up. Now it'll be 25. Things are probably better than at any time since 1997. It's the only benefit of being in opposition.' The party's press team also played up the Ashcroft surveys which showed Labour 'winning' the ground war.[14] Ashcroft's surveys in Conservative-held marginals showed Labour almost always outscoring the Conservatives in terms of voter contact. In Milton Keynes South, for example, local activists appeared to be almost twice as active in contacting voters as the Conservatives; with a similar disparity in Finchley and Golders Green. In both seats, Labour were ahead on voting intention.[15] In Southampton, where the Labour MP John Denham was standing down, Labour were buoyed by an Ashcroft poll in March showing them 8% in the lead. The candidate had worked the seat for over two years and claimed to be contacting 3,000 voters a week.[16]

However, the field operations teams in the various party headquarters were always more sceptical of the Ashcroft claims. 'I just don't believe those figures', said a key organiser in the SNP's ground campaign. 'I know how many canvasses we'd done. There's no way we got those canvassing returns.' Or as one of Labour's field team put it: 'In some of those surveys, you'll find 30% of people saying they've had nothing from the parties. But I know we've been in touch with every single household.' Moreover, the Ashcroft question about contact was a fairly broad one, asking about any contact.[17] This set the bar low (one piece of literature from a party qualified), was binary (and therefore did not measure intensity of contact) and did not distinguish between types of contact (an intensive face-to-face chat counted the same as a pamphlet pushed through the door). In Scotland, where the Ashcroft data often showed Labour outperforming the SNP in terms of contact, this was largely a result of mass Labour mailshots rather than much doorstep activity. Even at the time, a critical reader of the figures might have noted that the half-million 'conversations' recorded in Scotland were not reversing or even denting the large swing from Labour to the SNP in the polls.[18] In mid-April, Andrew Cooper at Populus made a rigorous analysis of all the Ashcroft constituency polls then conducted and found that the superior Labour scores for campaign awareness and contact rate did not correlate in any way with an above-average swing to Labour in the seats in question.

One criticism of these 'conversations' was that they were not really conversations. They were mostly highly instrumental exercises in data gathering, establishing and recording if the voter would be supporting Labour, if they had voted Labour last time and whether they preferred a Labour government, the standard trinity of canvassing questions which Labour had used for previous elections. Arnie Graf's work on local organising had, as noted above (p. 82), come to nothing. One organiser stressed to us the need for brevity in the conversations – 'Time is at a premium' – and another dismissed the difference between long and short conversations as false. 'Getting people to answer any questions is progress. The dichotomy isn't between rich conversations and simple ones. It's between simple and none.'

The other impact of the Ashcroft polls was that where they indicated that the contest was close, candidates often used the survey as a lever to extract more resources from the centre and/or energise local activists. By showing how close the race was, they boosted activity. In a number of his constituency polls, Ashcroft showed the local Lib Dem MP doing better than the national picture and his reports of Labour leads in Conservative seats prompted the local candidate to press Brewer's Green for more resources. On polling day, Labour organisers in Finchley and Golders Green were calling for more resources because (already encouraged by an Ashcroft constituency poll) they claimed they could win the seat. In the end, Labour lost by nearly 6,000 votes.

As noted in Chapter 6, most of Labour's social media campaigning was organic – that is, most of the content someone would see on Facebook or other social media platforms would be as a result of a friend of theirs 'liking' or sharing something. This severely limited Labour's ability to target their digital campaign. It was not just that the Conservatives were able to target content directly at voters in marginal seats – whereas much of Labour's digital campaign would only be hitting marginal seats if they were lucky – it was also that the Conservatives therefore had more ability over the type of message that they were able to disseminate. As one of Labour's digital team noted:

> What they [Labour supporters] want to share are the things they most care about. If we write, 'we want to reduce the deficit', no Labour supporters – or not enough, anyway – want to share it. Basically, they don't want to share the messages that we want people to hear. So you can end up talking to your base.

Paid promotion of social media avoids this problem, allowing parties to reach the sort of people they want to reach in the right constituencies, and with the right messages. This is why all the major parties did it – including Labour – but none had the resources to do it on the same scale as the Conservatives. The upside for the Labour campaigners – indeed, those on the left more generally – was that their supporters were more likely to be posting material online, which at least generated more chance of some of it being seen by marginal voters, but this only increased the problems of the echo chamber and of it being the 'wrong' message. Even when resources began to flow into Labour's campaign after the fallout from Falkirk had subsided, the decision was taken to put most of that money into direct mail rather than digital campaigning. Because of this lack of finance, Labour only began to deploy targeted Facebook adverts in 2014. 'The Tories had had a year of putting their message out there before we even began to compete', said one of Labour's digital team. It perhaps says something about how narrow Labour's ambitions were in Scotland that their digital target seats included just seven in Scotland. This sort of campaigning is not just centrally directed, it is campaigning of which the activists based in the constituency may be completely unaware.[19]

After the election, the Conservatives made much of how they had won the digital war – and how this had translated into greater number of seats.[20] But they were doing nothing that the other parties would not have done had they had comparable resources.

However good the sales operation, it cannot make up for a flawed product. Individual Labour policies – action on zero-hours contracts, energy prices and 'the bedroom tax' – were often received well on the doorstep, but more generally, as one Labour strategist put it, the four million conversations 'were often miserable conversations for people to have'. As another stated:

> We didn't lose the election because of our ground operation. We lost the election because of a position set out in 2010 and of which we could not persuade people on the doorstep ... It was obvious when you looked at the canvass returns that we had a problem with a particular group. They were very stubborn. They wouldn't say to your face, 'I'm voting Conservative', because we're English and most people don't behave like that, but they were very stubborn in saying 'I don't know', which means 'I'm voting Conservative'. We had nothing to convince these people.

Another senior organiser put it simply: 'You only had to knock on the door to realise our problem.' A disappointed James Frith, who lost the target seat of Bury North by less than 1,000 votes, felt compromised by the national message which he regarded as too anti-business and pro-welfare for the voters he needed to persuade. 'Our offer was a complaint', he said. One senior Labour staffer who campaigned in 30 marginal seats reported a chastening encounter with one voter who mentioned that he was not receiving tax credits or housing support and did not work in the public sector. 'Where', he then asked, 'is Labour's offer to me?'

Conservative feedback was not universally positive either. Some of the feedback reported concerns about the NHS under a Conservative government (but often added that it was not affecting voting intentions) and claims that the party was out of touch with ordinary people. However, Textor's polling repeatedly showed that Ed Miliband was a drag on Labour in the Conservative–Labour marginal seats and that there was growing concern in the Conservative–Lib Dem marginal seats about the influence the SNP might have on a minority Labour government. Labour and Lib Dem organisers reported similar reactions on the doorstep. The forecast of a close race was crucial because it increased the credibility of the 'threat' of Miliband becoming Prime Minister. As one Conservative strategist put it: 'We need voters to believe that in some circumstances he can become Prime Minister.' A Labour strategist resignedly said: 'The Tories claimed to segment their messages but I'm not sure if I ever saw anything that veered off the lines of warning about the dangers of an "Ed Miliband government propped up by the SNP".'

There was confusion and dismay in Labour headquarters in the early hours of 8 May as the results, particularly the number of Conservative gains from the Lib Dems, came in. One official said: 'Our ground campaign was stronger than the Conservative one and had we won that would have been the story of the election. But the gap in messaging (and the message carrier) was too great.' Much of this disappointment was reflected in a frank internal party post-mortem for Labour's senior party officials '2015: What Happened?'. It noted tactfully: 'Anecdotally, canvassers found it difficult to navigate issues surrounding the popularity of the leader and the impact of a potential coalition with the SNP.' The view at Brewer's Green was replicated in the campaign feedback to CCHQ. Campaigners also struggled to convince voters of the manifesto's economic responsibility because 'the rhetoric used in the first half of the Parliament shaped public and media perceptions of our final policy offer'. The report, again diplomatically, noted: 'This mismatch between our policy and its perception made it difficult to overcome two key challenges' – convincing voters that Labour could be trusted with the public finances and winning over swing voters with measures that would benefit them and their families.

The Lib Dems operated under severe financial and political constraints. As noted on p. 103, entering the Coalition meant the loss not only of voters but also of activists and the Short Money granted to opposition parties. Losing a third of its local councillors during the Parliament as well as disillusioned members deprived the party of many of its active and experienced party workers. In one target seat just days before polling day, only one activist could be found canvassing. There were too few activists to move activists from hopeless seats to more competitive ones and many refused to be so directed in any case, preferring to canvass locally for local council candidates or to build support ahead of elections in 2016. As one organiser commented, 'people didn't join the Liberal Democrats to be told what to do'.

The party was effectively fighting a series of by-elections in the seats it held, with just a handful of potential, long-shot, targets.[21] It was having to fight on three fronts: in Scotland against the SNP, and in England and Wales against both Labour and the Conservatives. The Lib Dems started with a grid assessing the amount of help seats would get based on the level of local activity (rated from A to D) and their likelihood of being won (rated from 1 to 6, taking particular account of the party's polling, the various Ashcroft polls and assorted election results). As the election approached, they moved to a simpler classification: Green, Yellow, Amber and Red. As polling day neared and the opinion polls brought no comfort, Paddy Ashdown, the campaign chair, concentrated resources on a reduced number of seats where victory seemed possible. The first to be effectively let go – long before the campaign formally began – was Norwich South, but even in seats where the party concluded it was almost certain to lose, some campaign activity continued. In retrospect, several of those involved in the party's campaign wondered if they should have been even more brutal in their marshalling of resources.

In 2013, the Conservatives had carried out private polling in Lib Dem-held seats and concluded that the seats were vulnerable, but only if the election could be framed so as not to be about the local MP. They had found that Lib Dem MPs polled well if they were named as individuals, but never well if they were not. As long as they could make the election about a national choice – and as long as the Conservative local candidate was seen to be half-decent – the Conservatives would have a chance at turfing out even well-entrenched incumbent Lib Dem MPs. Another, expensive, re-polling of Lib Dem-held seats in 2014 confirmed this finding and led to the Conservatives expanding their Lib Dem battlegrounds. But for this strategy to work, the party had to demonstrate to swing voters in those seats that their vote could matter.

It worked. Throughout 2015, Lib Dem feedback to the party's Cowley Street HQ emphasised the growing impact of the Conservative warnings about the SNP – 'very palpable on the doorsteps', 'incredibly powerful' – and the claim that the Conservatives only needed an additional 23 seats to form a majority. Lib Dem warnings about a Blukip alliance (a Conservative government supported by UKIP and the DUP) paled in comparison. As one Lib Dem organiser noted, despairingly, increasingly the praise canvassers encountered on the doorstep for the local MP and even sometimes for the party nationally would be followed by: 'I can't vote for you this time. I can't do it.' The party re-orientated its national campaign to focus more on what it called the blue-yellow switchers (see above, p. 196), and this was reflected in the party's ground operation. 'We littered leaflets with quotes from Professor X saying the Conservatives can't win a majority', said one of the party's strategists. 'Professor X is now famous for being very wrong.' The party shifted its canvassing away from switchers or squeeze voters, or unknowns, and on to definites and probables. As one strategist said: 'We needed to firm up the base ... It didn't remotely work.'

The Lib Dems' aim was to get a total number of seats in the high 20s, with anything over 30 being a best-case scenario. 'Everything we were doing was to get us to 30', said one of the key campaign team. Even by the end of the campaign, the party had 14 seats it considered safe and 22 others that it thought might make it. 'We erred on the side of pessimism', said one Lib Dem staffer, 'not quite enough as it turned out.' But for all that the election result was a shock to the Lib Dems, their overall classification of seats was about right. 'We weren't that wrong, in that the seats we thought were safer held up. But we had the line in the wrong place.'

Labour had not planned on Scotland being an important part of their 2015 election battleground. Their inability to counter the post-referendum surge in support for the SNP in part revealed the consequences of their complacency in their safe seats over the years. Many local parties had collected little data on voters and this neglect undermined any attempt to launch a last-minute targeting exercise. It was not just Labour either. Some Scottish Lib Dem MPs also had next to no canvass data. One Lib Dem campaigner, sent to try to help the Scottish Lib Dems fight back, complained: 'It's like campaigning in the 1950s.' Some incumbent Labour and Lib Dem MPs did almost nothing until 2015 began. 'You try to emphasise that they can't do all of this stuff in a few months – it has to be week-in, week-out for years', said one staffer. 'But some just won't listen.' That said, it is at least a moot point as to whether even the most organised local campaigns would have been sufficient to withstand the SNP surge. Although some Labour and Lib Dem MPs had taken their constituencies for granted, not all had, and some had impressive records working the constituency. The hard-working lost their seats along with the indolent.[22]

Three weeks before polling day, with the polls pointing to an SNP landslide, Murphy was still claiming that Labour could win 20–25 seats. One London official thought the claim 'delusional' and a bid for more resources; they were reconciled to heavy losses. In March one London staffer had already estimated that Labour would be down to as few as ten Scottish seats. By the end of the campaign, they were hoping for, at most, five, with the hope that one of them at least would be someone symbolically important.

The SNP campaign was, in many ways, an old-fashioned one. With a small professional staff at party headquarters, local SNP parties were left largely to their own devices, with leaflets and similar provided by

HQ. The first post-referendum orders from local parties were for the maximum number possible to cover all 2.4 million households in Scotland. In the event that polls or canvass returns had shown the campaign operating on too broad a front, SNP HQ was prepared to step in and try to focus efforts more, and to narrow down the range of targets, but the need never arose. The party soon realised all 59 seats in Scotland were potentially in play and let activists take the lead.

Party membership had already surpassed 100,000 in March 2015 and was said to be over 110,000 by the time of the election. The SNP had become the third-largest party in the UK, but for a party fighting just 9% of seats, it was, proportionally, the largest political party in Great Britain by a long way. It averaged more than 1,500 members per constituency, members who were said to be very fired-up and energetic. It was, in other words, the sort of grassroots army that any other political party would kill for. 'We can deliver leaflets to the whole of Scotland in a couple of days', as one SNP organiser put it. It was not always possible to use people strategically – the party would decide to leaflet a village of 500 people and have 50 volunteers turn up – but these are the problems of success, the sort of problems that British parties rarely experience. There was almost no segmentation in terms of the appeal the party put out, with party staffers feeling that there was little need to complicate the message.

The SNP were enthusiastic users of Facebook as a campaigning tool – skills they had honed during the referendum campaign – but they did relatively few targeted adverts, the exception being three segmented appeals to young, the elderly and women voters, and the party did just one targeted direct mailshot to would-be postal voters.[23]

Despite the massive increase in the number of Green and UKIP candidates, the bulk of campaigning for both parties was noticeably less sophisticated than for the more established parties. Both parties still relied on hand-delivered leaflets rather than the more expensive direct mail and the centre gave modest sums of money to the key seats. There were very different levels of expertise in the Green seats. Caroline Lucas' Brighton Pavilion operation was highly professional, but beyond the top three or four targets, the Green grassroots operation was very patchy. The Greens did some unsegmented mail drops in Brighton, Bristol and Norwich, but, as noted in Chapter 4, the surge in Green members had come too late for the party. 'Many of our people are still learning how to canvass', said one Green staffer. Even in one of the main Green target seats, the canvass returns were still held on an

Access database on a local activist's hard drive. The difference with the larger parties – where canvass returns are uploaded instantly to national HQ, allowing them to track support in real time – is stark. Some of the Green local parties, particularly in London, use Mosaic to analyse their support. 'But there is a huge difference between the quality of some of our local parties', said one Green staffer. 'A handful are really advanced. Most aren't.' The continuing success in Brighton aside: 'It was pretty obvious, pretty quickly, that we were not going to win in either Bristol or Norwich.'

UKIP's target seat operation was run by Chris Bruni-Lowe, who defected from the Conservatives with Douglas Carswell, ran the resulting by-election campaign in Clacton and subsequently aimed to professionalise the party's operation. Clacton was the first time the party used a voter ID system, with a database of information of voters, and the first time it segmented its message – and it was to take this approach into its target seats in the general election.[24] 'Our aims are quite simple', Bruni-Lowe said in an interview in 2015: 'Get Nigel elected in South Thanet, win a good number of seats, and then come second in more than 100 northern constituencies.'[25] Despite professionalising their ground operation, it is striking that UKIP were to fail in all three of these objectives.[26] The party had thrived in the European elections (with low turnouts) and by-elections where it could focus its resources. But a general election in which it fought virtually every seat was a bigger challenge, and in most seats its campaign remained generic and unfocused. Its main efforts were concentrated in half-a-dozen seats, defending the two by-election victories, in Clacton and Rochester and Strood, and a handful of others, of which Nigel Farage's campaign in Thanet South was the single most important. In early April 2015, after a poll showing he was no longer the favourite to win in Thanet South, Farage asked UKIP followers for a 'personal favour' of 'one or two days' support' in Thanet, much to the annoyance of some other UKIP candidates.

Table 10.1 shows the type and extent of contact which voters said they received from the parties, drawing on data from the British Election Study (BES). As with any opinion poll from the 2015 election, it should be treated with some caution, but whilst it would be unwise to put too much weight on any one figure, there is no reason to doubt the overall trends. The BES specified six types of contact, from phones to (the rather quaintly named) SMS.[27] In total, 52% of respondents claimed to have read a campaign leaflet, letter text or email from a party and 6% to have displayed a party poster. The question asked about contact in the 'past four weeks' and therefore probably slightly under-estimates total contact made during the campaign itself – and, as noted above, the parties were sceptical about the absolute value of such figures like this, just as they were sceptical about Ashcroft's figures for contact. For example, even in marginal seats in England, held by Labour or the Conservatives, and with a majority of less than 10% – constituencies in which almost every house will have been contacted – the figure reporting some contact was still only 64%.[28] Such data are therefore probably too low in absolute terms, even if they are useful in relative terms.

Table 10.1 Types of voter contact during the campaign (%)

	Con	*Lab*	*LD*	*SNP*	*PC*	*UKIP*	*Green*
Phone	2	3	1	4	1	–	–
Leaflet/letter	34	38	23	49	25	21	11
Home visit	7	10	3	14	4	1	1
Street	2	3	1	10	2	1	1
Email	9	9	4	10	2	1	1
SMS	1	1	–	3	1	–	–
Overall	39	43	25	53	28	22	12

Source: Wave 6, BES, core weighting. The figures in each row do not sum to the overall figure because some people may have been contacted in more than one way; figures for the SNP and PC are for Scotland and Wales only respectively; – indicates >0, but <0.5.

Two features of Table 10.1 are striking. The first is the importance played by leaflets and letters, the main method of communicating with voters for all parties; indeed, for UKIP and the Greens, they are basically the only method of contact. But even for the other more established parties, leaflets and letters dwarf other means of contact.[29] As one strategist said: 'I have never understood why journalists don't focus on leaflets more. If you want to know what our message is, look at what we're putting through people's doors.' Unfortunately, like many surveys, the BES does not differentiate between the ability of a party to deliver leaflets for free to the door personally and those that a party pays someone, such as Royal Mail, to deliver. For the reasons explained above, the parties see a real difference between these types of contact – but it is understandable methodologically (will survey respondents really know or remember how a leaflet got through their door?). The data also do not reveal whether the leaflet or letter is generic or more segmented (again because there will be no way for the respondent to know).

A second feature of the table is the reach of the SNP's ground operation. The SNP figures are the highest for every type of contact. If we take the various forms of face-to-face contact together, then over the final four weeks of the campaign, 11% of voters claimed face-to-face contact with a Labour canvasser (which equates to five million people) and 8% with a Conservative canvasser, but 21% in Scotland with an SNP canvasser. Face-to-face contact with voters is still more effective than more impersonal types of campaigning, something that played to the SNP's advantage.[30]

As in 2010, Labour claimed that their best results were in seats where they had their highest contact rates. In Ilford North, a Labour gain, the local party had the most doorstep conversations of any seat.[31] According to Jon Ashworth, a Shadow Cabinet office minister, across the top ten best-performing seats in terms of voter contact, the Labour vote increased by 5.1% on average, and among the top 30, the increase was 4.8%.[32] But across the top 100 seats for contact, the average increase in vote share was 1.7%, just above the average for all seats of 1.4%

These were the contact successes. But the party's internal analysis showed only a modest if positive relationship between number of contacts and increase in Labour vote, and overall some key seats performed slightly worse than the national swing. The results led some Labour organisers to query the effectiveness of the targeting and the quality of the earlier 'conversations', five million or not. The party's post-election internal report noted the familiar theme that the difficulty was 'the policy and messaging offer for which ... there was a clear and substantial advantage for the Conservative Party'.

That the Conservatives usually outspend Labour and other parties is nothing new. Only the Conservatives had the funds to have four-page messages wrapped around local newspapers, for example. However, this advantage has become even more pronounced with the availability of digital and direct mail campaign techniques. Moreover, these are campaign techniques that will not be noticed in measures of campaign spending at constituency level. One rival campaigner estimated – with a sense of admiration and envy rather than complaint – that the Conservatives would be spending up to £100,000 on some seats that would be counted as 'national', not local spending – thus driving a proverbial coach and horses through supposed constituency spending limits.[33]

Yet, for all the interest in the ground war and the latest technology, a sense of perspective is required. Even the best ground war campaign is thought to make no more than couple of percentage points of difference to the final result. Voters' perceptions of the parties' records and leaders and their national messages still decide elections. 'Nobody ever thinks you win an election with a field operation', said one of Labour's organisers. 'It means 2–3 points at the margins. The notion that we could have been delivering a 40% strategy through running a different field operation is nonsense.' Yet in a close general election, as 2015 was expected to be, and/or in very closely contested seats, this small margin might be crucial, and the parties all put significant resources into their local campaigning activities.

And it remains the case that campaigning, in the form of organisation and activity on the ground, will not compensate for a weak message. In Labour's case in 2015, even the most outstanding ground campaign would not have compensated for the weakness on leadership and the economy. Party activists could reflect that even if they targeted the right voters and bombarded them with messages, if the voters did not believe the message, did not trust the bearer of the message or were not interested, there was not much to be done. And the local campaigns could not make up for the collapse of the party's support in Scotland and of the Lib Dems in the Conservative–Lib Dem marginals.

The verdict of a detailed study of the local campaigns was that 2015 'was the election when the Conservative Party became genuinely effective in terms of the delivery of electoral payoffs'.[34] It added that for Labour and the Lib Dems, 'the results could have been even worse had their [local] campaigns not been so well-managed'.

Notes

1. One senior campaigner put it bluntly: 'party membership is no longer a social plus'. Or as a Labour candidate, in a safe Tory seat, said: 'The only people you've got left helping you are the sort of people who shouldn't be let anywhere near the public.'
2. For example, the case of Labour and their perception of how the Lib Dems were performing in Conservative–Lib Dem seats.
3. There is a separate Mosaic categorisation for Scotland, and Plaid Cymru report the data being less useful in Wales because it does not adequately capture the extent to which Plaid support is underpinned by language and identity. 'If you ran an analysis using Mosaic', said one Plaid staffer, 'you'd be better if you ran it against Williams, Jones, Evans, Thomas...'
4. He added: 'If you were a mother in Mosaic Group G, living in a marginal seat, you will have been hammered by direct mail, from us and them.' However, other, less crucial swing voters will have experienced a much less intensive election.

5. Craig Elder and Tom Edmonds, '2015 Really was the First Digital General Election: Here are 7 Lessons You Should Know', *Daily Telegraph*, 23 July 2015.
6. Royal Mail also offer something call Day Drops, which allow the delivery to be targeted at a specific day, at slightly more cost. Labour did two of these in key seats in the last week of the campaign.
7. See Peter Kellner 'Incumbency Matters', www.progressonline.org.uk, 27 November 2014. For a counter to this, see Lord Ashcroft's, 'A Lesson from the Blue-Yellow Marginals. Incumbency is Not Enough', www.conservativehome.com, 27 September 2014.
8. T. Smith, 'Are You Sitting Comfortably? Estimating Incumbency Advantage in the UK: 1983–2010 – A Research Note', *Electoral Studies*, 32(1) (2013): 167–73.
9. Labour were very sceptical about trying to ask quite so many questions of voters. As one of Labour's field team argued: 'The Tories are telling porkies if they claim that every conversation they had on the doorstep involved 12 questions. Imagine doing that in the rain!'
10. Andrew Gimson, 'Team2015 is More Formidable, and Traditional, than it Looks', www.conservativehome.com, 30 March 2015.
11. As one Lib Dem organiser said of the party's Connect software: 'It's like a washing machine with eight cycles, but you only really use two. But then someone will use the seventh.'
12. Mark Wallace, 'The Computers that Crashed. And the Campaign that Didn't. The Story of the Tory Stealth Operation that Outwitted Labour Last Month', www.conservativehome.com, 16 June 2015.
13. 'Miliband Says Labour Members Have Had 4 Million Conversations and Aim for Another Million', labourlist.org, 29 April 2015.
14. See the coverage in M. Savage, 'Labour Pulls Ahead in the Ground War in Key Marginals', *The Times*, 14 April 2015; D. McBride, 'The Armchair General Marching Ed Miliband to Victory', *Sunday Times*, 5 April 2015; S. Brown, 'Labour's Ground Campaign is Better than the Tories and Here's Why', labourlist.org, 30 July 2015; and R. Behr, 'Brute Organisational Force Can Still Carry Labour Over the Line', *New Statesman*, 13 February 2015.
15. In the event, the Conservative lead over Labour in Milton Keynes increased from 5,220 in 2010 to 8,700, and the margin in Finchley and Golders Green was 5,600.
16. Archie Blair, 'Online and on the Street. Labour Tests Modern Methods', *The Guardian*, 2 May 2015. In the event, on a swing of 2.8%, the Conservatives gained the seat with a 2,300 majority.
17. 'I would like to ask whether any of the main political parties have contacted you over the last few weeks – whether by delivering leaflets or newspapers, sending personally addressed letters, emailing, telephoning you at home or knocking on your door. Have you heard in any of these ways from the Conservatives, Labour, the Lib Dems, or UKIP?' The question was adapted in Scotland or Wales.
18. P. Cowley, 'The SNP Has an Army of Activists, But is it Winning the Ground War in Scotland?', www.may2015.com, 20 April 2015.
19. Some local candidates did their own social media work – a handful even arranged for paid social media adverts to go out – but this sort of campaigning

is secondary to the power of targeted social media adverts funded from the centre.

20. As an example, see the account of the Conservative digital campaign in 'Sir Mick Jagger Knew the Conservatives Would Win the Election Weeks Before Polling Day, Says US Guru', *Daily Telegraph*, 17 May 2015, which details the work the Conservatives were doing on social media. There is nothing identified in the report that Labour were not also doing.
21. How long a shot only became clear after the election result.
22. Of all the Scottish Lib Dem MPs, Jo Swinson had the best contact data and almost hung on. But it was not enough.
23. Between them, these three categories – young, old and women – cover a large proportion of the electorate, and their very breadth is an indication of how unsegmented the SNP campaign was. But they were groups with whom the SNP either had normally struggled or who needed to be encouraged to vote.
24. Matthew Goodwin, 'Ukip's Days of Amateur Campaigning are Over', *Daily Telegraph*, 17 November 2014.
25. Sebastian Payne, 'What UKIP Wants: Get Farage Elected, Then Prepare for a Labour Collapse in the North', *The Spectator*, 7 March 2015.
26. As well as failing in Thanet South and everywhere else apart from Clacton, the party came second in just 35 constituencies in the north of England, along with 14 constituencies in the Midlands.
27. Wave 6 of the BES was conducted by YouGov on 8–26 May 2015 and had a sample of 30,027. The answer options for this question also included an 'other', but very few selected this, so it has been excluded from the table.
28. By contrast, in safe seats in England held by Labour or the Conservatives with a majority of 30% or more, just 44% said they had been contacted.
29. The figures in the table are the percentage of the entire population contacted; seen as a percentage of those contacted in any way, the figures for contact by leaflets or letters are never lower than 89%.
30. Justin Fisher, David Cutts, Edward Fieldhouse and Bettina Rottweiler, 'Constituency Campaigning at the 2015 General Election', unpublished paper presented at Elections, Public Opinion and Parties conference, September 2015.
31. Although in Ilford, as in several other London seats, there were also demographic changes that worked to Labour's advantage (see p. 396).
32. Jon Ashworth, 'Does Canvassing Matter?' *New Statesman*, 13 July 2015.
33. This was well discussed in Mark Pack, 'Constituency Expense Limits are Dying off in the UK, But Neither Politicians nor the Regulator Will Act', www.markpack.org.uk, 10 March 2015.
34. Fisher *et al.*, 'Constituency Campaigning at the 2015 General Election'.

11
The Battle for the Stage: Broadcasting

Charlie Beckett[1]

In this election, broadcasting tried to reflect a changing political landscape. Television in particular was challenged to adjust to the impact of the smaller parties such as the Green Party, UKIP and the SNP. Editorially, broadcasters had to cover a diverse range of issues of varying degrees of scale, importance and relevance to different audiences. All journalists, but most obviously broadcasters, found themselves limited in terms of scope by the unprecedented levels of party stage-management. There were the usual concerns about delivering impartiality and information, but perhaps the hardest task for the broadcast journalists was to fulfil their key democratic functions at election time: to engage the public and to hold politicians to account. The strategic reluctance of the main parties to conduct more open campaigns meant that the desire for dramatic broadcasting to match the significance of the stakes was frustrated. Like all journalists, broadcasters were also misled by erroneous polling to construct a false narrative around the relative success of the two main parties. Indeed, the way in which the campaign was conducted and reported by all news media was arguably a distraction from any serious attempt to have an honest, critical argument about the big issues such as the deficit, welfare, national identity and the nature of British society.

British broadcasters are required by law to be impartial and have regulatory codes covering their output during election campaign periods.[2] This is tricky at the best of times, but it was made more complex because of the rise of UKIP, the surge in support after the

2014 independence referendum for the SNP and the continued niche popularity of the Green Party. This more plural political context provided a technical problem in the negotiations for the TV election debates. There was also a more direct political context for the regulated public service broadcasters of having to deal with the politicians from the major parties who could be deciding their organisations' fate after the election. This was most keenly felt at the BBC, which faces a renewal of its Charter in 2016. All parties subjected the BBC to regular complaints, which its Director of News, James Harding, found 'astonishing' in their 'ferocity'.[3] The BBC's Political Editor, Nick Robinson, said that at one point on the campaign trail, he was told that the Prime Minister had threatened to 'close down the BBC'.[4] This might just be part of the rough and tumble of media/political relations, but it was also a background factor in the struggle for journalistic independence – and in the extensive discussions about the TV debates.

Debate negotiations

In 2010 the TV debates formed 'the spine' of the campaign.[5] The three 90-minute leaders' programmes reached an average audience of 22.5 million and shaped the rhythm of the campaign. They created a dominant dynamic in a period where a sense of momentum and direction of travel is seen as important for the 'optics' or public perception of the political struggle. So whether and how they would happen in 2015 became an important (pre–)campaign issue in its own right.

The broadcasters assumed that the default position was to repeat the structure of 2010, albeit with some adjustments. However, there were external pressures for further reform. The downside of the 2010 debates was that their novelty and timing meant they had monopolised media attention. Each dominated the media space for three days. They probably did not 'suck the life out of the campaign' as alleged by David Cameron; indeed, the strong viewing figures for each of the lengthy programmes suggested a high degree of public interest. But they unbalanced the campaign. There was a growing sense that the programmes had to change in style as well as substance to reflect the new political realities. However, discussions between the broadcasters and politicians were always going to be uncertain because no binding agreement on process or aims was made following 2010.

Although there were some preliminary discussions early in the Parliament, the most important player, the Conservatives, put off detailed talks until after the 2014 party conferences. The political context of 2010 had been favourable because it was in the interests of all party leaders to take part, including the Labour Prime Minister Gordon Brown, who was lagging behind in the polls. But by 2014, the incumbent David Cameron had more to risk than the various challengers. The Liberal Democrat leader Nick Clegg received an opinion poll boost from his TV debate appearances in 2010 and that precedent meant that in 2015 the Tories feared sharing a platform with rivals. Any kind of publicity would be good publicity for Ed Miliband, Nick Clegg and Nigel Farage. This would distract from Conservative campaign advisor Lynton Crosby's strategy of a relentless focus on the economy and the choice between Cameronian 'competence' and Milibandian 'chaos'. It was understandable tactics for the Conservatives to resist raising the profile of their competitors. However, Cameron's long track record of support for the principle of TV debates meant there was a political risk of looking weak if he ducked out. As late as April 2014, Cameron said: 'I've just always believed that these need to happen. It's good for democracy.'[6] Despite the widespread belief at the time that the Conservatives were trying to force the collapse of the debate discussions, his team insist they always assumed there would be debates, but reserved their right to delay a final decision in an effort to secure the best format from their point of view. Labour, however, were very keen to participate, almost whatever the format. They saw the debates as a way of raising Miliband's profile and countering what they saw as the misleading impression so many people had of him. But they also had a preference for as tightly focused a debate as possible, and especially one that would allow them to attack David Cameron's record. 'He doesn't like to have to defend his record', said one of those involved in Labour debate preparation. 'Every time we'd practised a head-to-head [debate], we'd found we could really get stuck into him.'

In their opening formal proposal on 13 October 2014, the broadcasters produced a more flexible format than 2010 to reflect the new context of the campaign.[7] It was designed to respond to the core political reality that either David Cameron or Ed Miliband would be Prime Minister, but it also sought to recognise the special status of the Lib Dems as the coalition government partner and the rise of UKIP, both in the opinion polls and the fact that it had a growing number of MEPs and councillors. Nigel Farage had taken part in two debates with Lib Dem leader Nick Clegg in the run-up to the 2014 European elections, which acted as a taster, if not precedent, for his inclusion.

The proposed format was also created to reflect more accurately the range of mainstream broadcast media. Channel 4 and Sky News were to share one of the programmes and all of them were to be online. A detailed schedule was published with programmes planned for 2, 16 and 30 April in a 2–3–4 structure (though the actual order would be decided by lot): Cameron and Miliband; Cameron, Miliband and Clegg; and Cameron, Miliband, Clegg and Farage. Former BBC *Newsnight* presenter Jeremy Paxman was lined up by Channel 4 to chair a 'debate' between the two main leaders, with Sky News' main presenter Kay Burley as the anchor of the programme who would steer the 'post-debate analysis'. The second debate would be produced by the BBC with David Dimbleby chairing. The third debate would be chaired by *ITV News*' Julie Etchingham. Unlike in 2010, when each of the debates focused on a different policy area, this time each debate would cover all subject areas. They would all be in front of audiences selected by the broadcasters. The audience would submit questions to be put to the politicians. The broadcasters promised to work with social media organisations like Twitter and Facebook to ensure the widest possible audience engagement. Each broadcaster would also make its debate available live to all other media outlets.

The difficulty of including UKIP but not the Green Party, which already had one MP and was at around 4% in the opinion polls, was immediately raised, and not just by the Greens. The SNP, the Northern Irish unionists and Plaid Cymru also made claims that their status was of UK-wide significance. The Conservatives accused the broadcasters of naivety in thinking that they could include a party that was widely seen as a threat to the Tory vote (UKIP), but not one that was more a threat to Labour (Greens). Equally predictably, some newspapers, still smarting from the dominance of broadcast in 2010, felt that they distracted from the 'real' campaign and fostered 'presidential'-style politics. Many pointed out the harsh political logic that the Conservatives had no self-interest in taking part. Others argued that, for all their flaws, the debates attracted public attention to the campaign and tested the mettle of the politicians.

On 8 January the broadcasting regulator Ofcom ruled that UKIP was a 'major' party for the purposes of election coverage in England and Wales, but that the Greens were not.[8] This decision was based on a detailed consultation and a thorough analysis of a series of indices such as vote share, MPs and opinion polls. But, in short, it was decided that there had to be a cut-off and that the Greens were on the wrong side of it. The nationalist parties were to continue as before to get major party treatment in their own countries. However, Ofcom could only advise the broadcasters about the minimum requirements in this respect and the overall need for fair treatment. So the broadcasters were still free to think again for themselves when the next political initiative opened up.

The debate about the debates came to a head during the 14 January Prime Minister's Questions. Labour leader Ed Miliband taunted the Prime Minister with selected quotes from Cameron supporting TV debates and their role in democracy.[9] Cameron's response was that it was impossible to have the Lib Dems and UKIP involved, but not the Greens. As the Prime Minister put it: 'Why is Labour so frightened of debating with the Greens?' This was going beyond Ofcom, but it allowed him to be in favour of debating while putting up yet another obstacle. The broadcasters side-stepped that by adapting their offer to include the Greens, but they felt that this meant the SNP should also be involved. And if one nationalist party was involved, they felt obliged to have Plaid Cymru too. Logically that might have also meant the Democratic Unionist Party (DUP), but it was argued that the Northern Ireland campaign was historically and politically separate. The new proposal was still for three programmes, on 2, 16 and 30 April, but this time they would be made up of two seven-way debates on the BBC and ITV plus a head-to-head between Cameron and Miliband jointly hosted by Channel 4 and Sky. The broadcasters never used the phrase 'empty chair' at this point, but they made it clear that they would go ahead even if one party refused to take part. This is less dramatic than it sounds. It can refer simply to the presenter pointing out that someone had been invited and had declined. No actual chairs need be involved. However, Ofcom did warn at that point about the risk to 'impartiality' and it infuriated the Conservatives, who saw the prospect of an 'empty podium' as a political act on the part of the broadcasters.[10]

In early March, Downing Street made a 'final offer' to take part in one debate with all seven leaders to be held before the official campaign began. This apparent logjam was broken in a dramatic weekend of talks, with the BBC's Head of News, James Harding, and Channel 4's Chief Creative Officer, Jay Hunt, dealing directly with Number 10. These individuals had not been directly involved in the discussions before, which might have helped them to arrive at a compromise that delivered most of what the broadcasters wanted. There would be no genuine head-to-head debate between Cameron and Miliband, but every channel and (almost) every party would get a programme and the BBC would also put on a special edition of *Question Time*.

In the week before that crucial weekend, many journalists had been briefed that the mainstream broadcasters' proposals were likely to be completely rejected and that an alternative proposal from a consortium of digital and newspaper platforms was a contender. As the mainstream proposals stalled, the digital alternative debate plan went from being a maverick, hypothetical proposition to a real option. The consortium of Google with *The Guardian* and the *Daily Telegraph* had been arguing that they should have at least one of the slots to break the conventional broadcaster monopoly and to recognise the new realities of video consumption in the UK. Their late offer of a one-off, seven-leader debate held before April would have allowed the Conservatives to say they had contributed to a debate. However, despite its digital logic, it never stood much of a chance of surviving the crossfire of media and party politics. The main broadcasters would always be the most important players as far as the politicians were concerned because of their established audiences. This is significant because unless there is a complete failure to stage a mainstream broadcaster debate next time, it looks for now as if the main TV companies will remain the dominant election broadcast organisations, not newspapers, social networks or digital platforms.

The final format (see Figure 11.1) completely reshaped the debates from 2010 in terms of the makeup of the programmes and their participants, while the more spread-out timing meant they were less likely to swamp the campaign.

---

26 March: Sky/Channel 4: sequential leaders' interviews with Cameron and Miliband by Jeremy Paxman, with the studio audience moderated by Kay Burley.

2 April: ITV: debate with the leaders of the Conservatives, Labour, the Liberal Democrats, UKIP, the Greens, the SNP and Plaid Cymru, chaired by Julie Etchingham.

16 April: BBC: debate with the 'challenger parties', Labour, UKIP, the SNP, Plaid Cymru and the Greens, chaired by David Dimbleby.

30 April: BBC *Question Time* with Cameron, Miliband and Clegg taking questions from the audience sequentially, chaired by David Dimbleby.

Figure 11.1 TV 'debates', as finally agreed

From a starting point of three debates with four participants, through to the prospect of no debates or debates with empty chairs, had emerged four special election programmes featuring seven people – including two, SNP leader Nicola Sturgeon and Plaid Cymru leader Leanne Wood, who were not even standing in the election – and only one programme where any kind of direct exchange was allowed between the Prime Minister and the man most likely to replace him.

The TV debates

The TV special 'debate' programmes did not 'suck the life out of the campaign' in the way that the 2010 debates had dominated media coverage. No longer a novelty, the total average audience figures for the 2015 debates were down from 22.5 to 15.2 million, though including the fourth BBC *Question Time* programme audience brings the figure to 21.2 million, including people who watched simulcasts of the debates on other channels. So the numbers were lower than 2010, but they still helped shape the campaign.

Table 11.1 Proportion of bulletins referring to TV debates

Campaign week	*TV debate referenced in news bulletin*
Week one	48%
Week two	9%
Week three	18%
Week four	2%
Week five	18%
Week six	5%

An analysis of 211 lead broadcasts during the six-week campaign indicated that 16% of broadcast news bulletin lead items were about the election debate strategies or featured the debates themselves.[11] Overall, the TV debates were referenced in about 19% of these bulletins, although this varied hugely from week to week, as Table 11.1 shows. This suggests that they weaved their way through the editorial narrative, but only occasionally dominated the news agenda. Sky News staged live broadcasts from debates hosted by the other channels, but overall debate-related stories were covered with relative restraint in the bulletins. This should be put in the context of what was otherwise a dull and incident-free campaign for the broadcasters. The novel arrangements and new participants might have helped freshen up the interest. Certainly, they represented and articulated the idea that this was a less predictable and more complex election. The fact that the opinion polls told us that the race was close meant that more attention was paid to every gesture and utterance – especially of the two main leaders – in case it might create momentum or drama in a static and closed-down campaign. In this sense the debate coverage unwittingly played into the false narrative of a neck-and-neck race.

The battle for Number 10

The first joint production was watched by 2.6 million on Channel 4 and 0.3 million on Sky. Both were decent figures for those channels and the overall viewing figures edged up to 3.5 million including on-demand and the BBC News Channel broadcast. It was broadcast before the official short campaign, but on the day of prorogation, and since the phoney war had begun in January, it helped signal that battle really was about to commence. Cameron had 18 minutes with Jeremy Paxman followed by 18 minutes with the studio audience asking questions refereed by Sky's Kay Burley. Miliband followed in reverse order, facing first the audience and then Paxman. The Prime Minister had chosen to go first, but appeared defensive in his interview, where he struggled with classic awkward questions on the number of food banks and whether he could live on a zero-hours contract. Burley was noticeably more interventionist when Miliband took his turn with the audience. This resulted in complaints to Ofcom of bias, but was more likely just an attempt to inject life into what was turning out to be a fairly routine piece of political TV.[12] One study of the interviews showed that Paxman was more aggressive towards Miliband, intervening more often and asking more aggressive questions. It also showed that Cameron got to speak 22% more.[13]

Before, during and after the programme (and all those to follow) there was a spin-battle as party politicians and officials at press rooms at the venues and on social media sought to talk up their candidate's performance. The verdict on Miliband was relatively positive, an impression reinforced by polls of Twitter 'sentiment' that showed the Labour leader had performed well according to the highly unrepresentative sample of those who were on Twitter and bothered to tweet about the contest. According to the Centre for the Analysis of Social Media, Cameron got 35% 'cheers' and 65% 'boos' on Twitter, while the figures for Miliband were 62% positive and 38% negative. Social media – especially when used by broadcast journalists – is now an integral part of the television coverage and reaction to it. The TV debates largely drove content on social media, but social media also acted as a distorting feedback loop for journalists and the public. Even when a *The Guardian*/ICM instant opinion poll came out 54–46 in favour of Cameron, it was still reported as encouraging for Miliband on the basis that Cameron should have been further ahead. The instant reactive judgements were encouraged by other aspects of the debate programming such as the optional live on-screen graphic 'worm' that allowed viewers to see how other people were responding to what speakers said as the debate unfolded. It was meant to be a tool for engagement with no claims of accuracy, but it too may have added to the skewing of perceptions.[14]

More detailed analysis coverage of the data regarding audience reaction showed that Miliband's gains were minor and that Cameron was still scoring well ahead on the key indicators such as trust and competence. In his analysis 24 hours after the programme, *The Guardian*'s political data journalist, Alberto Nardello, made a thoughtful dissection of the evidence before making this prescient judgement:

> Based on the past, Thursday's Q&A is unlikely to noticeably shift voting intention once opinion stabilises. There are at least three debates (or sort-of debates) to go, but for now don't hold your breath.[15]

The ITV Leaders' Debate

The ITV Leaders' Debate on 2 April presented by Julie Etchingham was the highest rating of the programmes with a total average audience of 8 million viewers. The presence of the smaller parties meant that there was little time for anyone to engage with each other, including Cameron and Miliband, although the director tried hard to generate drama with cut-aways of the leaders responding when attacked. Each was allowed to make a short opening statement before taking questions from the audience. The critical first half hour when audiences are highest and most attentive was dominated by a discussion on the deficit. It set the pattern for the evening, allowing the SNP's Nicola Sturgeon to attack both the main parties. Her direct, passionate style got a positive reaction from viewers. Nigel Farage also cut across the other speakers, often literally interrupting their responses.

'Here's your tea'

Matt, *Daily Telegraph*, 17 April 2015 (© Matt/*The Telegraph*)

The second question on sustainability of funding for the NHS demonstrated why health never really became a hot issue during the broadcast campaign. All the leaders promised more money. Only Farage took a different tack, raising the spectre of 'health tourism', but otherwise all the leaders were divided only by the different ways they promised to increase the NHS budget.

Despite the logistical challenge of so many speakers, it did at least demonstrate the existence of multi-party politics. Memorable moments included Leanne Wood telling Nigel Farage that he should be ashamed of himself, but there were no breakthroughs. This was reflected in the various instant opinion polls afterwards that gave mixed results.[16] A YouGov poll asking who had 'won' the debate had Nicola Sturgeon ahead on 28%, with Farage on 20%, Miliband on 18% and Cameron on 15%. But both a ComRes and Survation instant polls had Cameron and Miliband level as 'winners'. An ICM poll gave Miliband a slender lead. Yet whatever momentum Miliband thought he had created was diverted by the attention paid to his Scottish rival. Again, this played into the overarching false narrative of the campaign: that it was 'too close to call' and that the minor parties could have a significant role in the outcome and in a subsequent government. However, the regular opinion polling on intended voting preferences appeared to be unchanged.

The BBC Election Debate

Presented on 16 April by David Dimbleby, the BBC's 'challengers' debate without David Cameron and, more controversially, without Deputy Prime Minister Nick Clegg, only attracted an average audience of 4.7 million viewers. Each leader was allowed one-minute opening remarks and then answered questions from the audience in turn. The politicians had no advance notice of the questions, but Dimbleby had, and he asked follow-up questions and allowed some further interaction between the politicians. The choreography of the reduced cast did have some significance. Miliband was forced to engage directly with Sturgeon in a heated way that sent a strong visual signal to voters that theirs was a relationship that mattered. It established a juxtaposition that was critical in the last phase of the campaign, reinforcing the narrative of the SNP holding Labour to account.

After the debate, Emily Maitlis presented a further reaction programme from the 'spin room'. This allowed William Hague to give a detailed response on behalf of the Conservatives that sought to characterise the debate as confused and chaotic. He was quick to highlight the exchanges between Miliband and Sturgeon as evidence that the SNP would have a hold over a Labour minority government. The critical exchange was when Sturgeon called on Miliband to 'work with us to keep the Tories out of government'. Miliband insisted curtly that 'we're different', but she replied: 'If we work together we can lock Cameron out of No. 10.' The *Daily Telegraph* front-page lead the next day featured that offer to back Labour if they agreed to take an anti-austerity stance: 'Sturgeon Offer to Miliband: I'll Make You PM.'

An instant Survation poll 90 minutes after the programme put Miliband ahead on 35% and Sturgeon second on 31%.[17] At one point Farage criticised the studio audience itself for what he saw as BBC-engineered left-wing bias, but the audience at home seemed to like him enough to give him a 27% score in the Survation poll. As the programme ended, the three female leaders embraced, leaving Miliband looking on forlornly. Some felt it symbolised a new female order, but in fact only one woman really broke through into public consciousness. Just 5% thought Natalie Bennett had 'won', while just 2% thought the same of Plaid Cymru's Leanne Wood.

The BBC *Question Time* Special

The BBC had always hoped to have editions of *Question Time* during the campaign, but it had not been part of the official debate discussions between the politicians and broadcasters group. Until the final stage of discussions, the BBC saw it as an alternative, not an addition to the other debates. All the broadcasters were surprised that the Conservatives agreed to this confrontation with the public, but Cameron's team insist they were always happy to see their man engage directly with voters. Each leader faced 30 minutes of questioning from the Yorkshire audience who had asked to take part. It was a rare moment in the campaign where the politicians were forced to engage directly, at length and in public with voters. An average audience of 4.7 million people watched the leaders weathering the storm in contrasting styles, but Miliband's worst moment came with a question about the deficit, where he did not give the prepared answer and instantly regretted it (see pp. 200–1). But as Table 11.2 shows, the key thing about the subject matter was that public spending and the deficit was the only topic to come up at all four debates, being the subject of 13 questions, almost twice as many as the next most popular question.[18] As Miliband left the stage, he stumbled. It was a trivial moment, but was made worse because he was so close to the camera. The trip was instantly and insistently rebroadcast on social networks. As usual, Miliband was ahead on Twitter approval ratings, although an ICM instant poll of a representative sample of voters in the real world had Cameron on 44% to the Labour leader's 38%. With hindsight, we can see that was more accurate than the regular campaign opinion polls on voting intention.

Table 11.2 TV debate questions

Topic	*26 March: Sky/Channel 4: Cameron and Miliband*	*2 April: ITV Leaders' Debate*	*16 April: BBC Challengers' Debate*	*30 April: BBC* Question Time *with Cameron, Miliband and Clegg*
Immigration		1	1	5
Police/crime	1			
Education				4
Public Spending/ deficit	5	1	1	6
Military			1	1
NHS	1	1		4
EU	2			4
Housing			1	
Welfare	2			5
Coalition making			1	6
Younger generation		1		
Political culture	2			3
Inequality	1			1
Poverty				2
Zero-hours contracts				2

Collectively, the TV debates should be seen as political theatre that tell stories and demonstrate character rather than as a gladiatorial combat where someone 'wins' and someone else 'loses'. Their significance in the campaign is the degree to which they challenge – or more likely confirm – public attitudes to the politician and the party they represent. They are what Daniel Dayan and Elihu Katz call 'Media Events' that have power to shape collective feelings.[19] The live reaction or instant 'post-match' analysis made possible by social media and continuous news coverage therefore may have a bias against understanding the real, long-term effects on eventual voting outcomes. As we will see below, there was plenty of other broadcast coverage of the election, but particularly in such a stage-managed campaign, these live set pieces still produced the most potent and useful political drama for those people who understood the political performance rather than the hype.

Other programmes

Apart from the news bulletins and the four main TV debates, there was a large amount of other special election programming, including a series of leader debate programmes in the different home nations. The variety of the output reflected a determination on the part of the broadcasters to find new ways to connect to a public that they feared was becoming increasingly tired of conventional politics and conventional political broadcasting. There was a particular attempt to target younger audiences and also a focus on the leaders' characters. Formats were more diverse and often more informal than before. Social media was a key element in this effort to engage viewers beyond the broadcast. TV and radio journalists were active on Twitter and Facebook, programme clips were uploaded onto platforms such as YouTube and special content was created such as ITV's one-minute film roundup *Daily Dose* designed for a short-attention-span online audience.

New or younger voters were a key target. Sky News created a special website and social media campaign 'Stand Up Be Counted' that encouraged young people to interact with election news and debate, but also to create their own content for the forum. BBC Three ran a special series of its live *Free Speech* debate programme that featured politicians from all parties answering unscripted questions from an 18–34-year-old audience. Radio 1's Newsbeat even created *BallotBots*, an online election game. Perhaps the boldest attempt to get young people to take an active interest in the campaign was ITV's collaboration with the 'party-neutral, youth democracy movement' charity Bite The Ballot. They worked together to create a social media-enhanced series of programmes where party leaders (except David Cameron) agreed to face an audience of young people as well as take online questions. Many of the questioners in the studio had strong followings on platforms such as YouTube and the conversation was actively fostered through social media such as Twitter. However, it seems that while these networked initiatives had some impact, it was largely on young people already interested in politics.

More mainstream was the focus on the individual party leaders, who were all interrogated at length. The BBC's Andrew Marr quizzed all of them in his usual intelligent and persistent way, but his pessimistic theory about the increasing artificiality of political interviews was largely borne out: 'In our trade we become too aggressive ... partly because of our fury at a lack of answers, so we get more aggressive. Politicians note this and find ways of blocking us, usually by obfuscating using dull language.'[20] The one moment that his own programme really came alive was when Boris Johnson accused Ed Miliband of 'back-stabbing' his brother, which resulted in a spirited and revealing exchange needing no mediation from Marr. The BBC's Evan Davis also interviewed the party leaders for a series of special programmes, with the edition featuring Nigel Farage pulling in the most viewers at 2.5 million, but the *Newsnight* presenter's cerebral style generated little heat and few headlines. Arguably the BBC's most incisive political interviewer, Andrew Neil, was not given interviews with the leaders, but as well as his regular *Daily Politics* programme, he conducted a series of one-hour policy debates with party spokesmen on welfare, home affairs, the economy, defence and foreign affairs.

ITV sought to present the leaders in less formal settings. All the leaders appeared live on Tom Bradby's *The Agenda*, where politicians were able to speak in a more relaxed chat-show format. Ed Miliband, for example, found himself with an actor, a comedian and a businesswoman. Bradby and Julie Etchingham also presented film portraits of the party leaders which drew upon their biographical hinterlands as well as exploring their visions for the country. Other programmes were also given time with the leaders, such as Jon Snow's ten-minute sit-downs for *Channel 4 News*. Phillip Schofield's ITV's *This Morning* viewer call-ins with the party leaders produced one moment of edgy humour when Cameron referred off-camera to Alex Salmond as a pickpocket.

At the local level, BBC Radio put on around 200 constituency level debates. In terms of volume and variety, broadcasters produced more election-related non-news material than ever before. Much of it was also available on-demand, online with supplementary data, comment and analysis. Very few news lines emerged from this huge amount of content, but no one could argue that the broadcasters had not tried to provide opportunities for the public to find out about the parties' policies and personalities.

BBC, ITV and Sky all produced excellent results programmes, although it was the BBC that topped the ratings and was the centre of attention on the evening of 7 May.[21] The conventional wisdom had been that we were in for a long night, picking through marginal contests with an expectation of surprises from the Greens or UKIP. In practice, Labour's

'I'll only agree to do this debate...'

Morten Morland, *The Times*, 12 January 2015 (© Morten Morland)

fox was shot by the 10 pm exit poll and, as the results began to come in, speculation about a 'false' exit poll soon evaporated (see Chapter 9). All channels handled this drama with coolness despite the evident shock to journalistic sensibilities. In his diary, Nick Robinson, the BBC's Political Editor, captured the reaction when he first saw the seat projection as he sat in the election night studio with a throat still recovering from the side-effects of cancer treatment: 'I want to shout, "Really? Labour go backwards and the Lib Dems collapse? Why the hell haven't the polls shown that happening?"'[22]

The campaign news coverage

Election broadcasting does not happen in isolation. During this campaign there were major stories such as the investigation into the Germanwings 'suicide' plane crash, a migrant boat disaster off Libya and an earthquake in Nepal that dominated the bulletins and people's news-related conversations for days. In total, in 45% of the broadcast bulletins analysed, the election was not the lead story (see Table 11.3). *Channel 4 News*, a programme with a mandate to cover a different agenda from other broadcasters, led on the election in 41% of its bulletins compared to *BBC News at 10*, which led with the campaign 66% of the time. The main news bulletins were not extended, although the BBC did lengthen its regional news programmes to give more space to the campaign, and programmes such as BBC Radio 4's *Today* had dedicated slots. As we have seen, there was also extensive special election programming outside the bulletins. It is therefore difficult to make any kind of case that the broadcasters did not pay attention to the campaign or provide a substantial amount of coverage. But how good was it, especially the regular news bulletins that still provide most people with their dominant impression of the campaign narrative?

Table 11.3 Election lead stories by outlet

Outlet	*% Election leads*
BBC News, 10 pm	66%
ITV News, 1.30 pm	61%
Sky News, 7 pm	46%
Channel 4 News, 7 pm	41%
BBC Radio 4, *Today* programme (8.00–8.30 am)	59%
BBC Radio 4, *PM* (4.00–4.30 pm)	61%
Average	56%

Horse race v. policy analysis

One of the consequences of the misleading opinion polling was a greater focus on the tactical political competition and the possibility of a minority Labour government, though given the close final result, this attention to tactics and potential outcomes would still have been the case had the polls been more accurate. Even in the digital era, TV bulletins have time limits, so this focus on process can be seen to have reduced space for debate and analysis of the issues. Broadcasters argue that with such a 'close' election, it was inevitable that attention focused on whether the campaign was going to move public opinion far enough to change the result. Likewise, it made discussion of minority or coalition permutations more relevant. Coverage of the so-called 'horse race' was also justified because the competition was so complex, with more parties and more constituencies in play. This was complicated further by Lord Ashcroft's marginal polling that drew journalists' attention to the minutiae of the many local horse races. The issues were reported, but often in relation to the fight to win. Broadcasters were much better than newspapers at not reporting individual polls in isolation, but like the on-screen poll graphic constantly blinking away on Sky News, the polls were an underlying assumption. Research shows that the BBC was less prone to horse race over policy, but as its Head of News, James Harding, later admitted, it had also become thoroughly 'infected' by the poll obsession and allowed 'coalitionology' too much airtime.[23]

As Table 11.4 shows, the horse race dominated at the beginning of the six-week campaign period (66% of programmes mentioned it) and then reduced for a while (down to 8% in week 4) before returning strongly at the end (71% in week 6). Polling was mentioned in 66% of bulletins in the first week, dropping to just 29% in week five, although even this means that even at its lowest, almost a third of bulletins were reporting polls. Then, in the final week, 72% of broadcasts talked about the close poll numbers. These findings show that the broadcasters were setting out what was at stake, then detouring to pay attention to the issues before returning to what was then thought to be the story: a tight election possibly resulting in a deal-making minority government.[24] It was arguably too often fruitless speculation. As one senior journalist said: 'Why keep bashing the politicians in the last week about what they would do after the election when they were quite rightly refusing to talk about that and insisted on addressing the issues?'

Table 11.4 Horse race coverage by campaign week

Campaign week	*Horse race coverage present in all broadcasts*
Week one	64%
Week two	31%
Week three	47%
Week four	32%
Week five	71%
Week six	86%

The broadcasters had taken seriously their public service obligation to attempt to provide the public with a wide range of information on policy. But they acknowledged that they had also accepted the false framing of the close race too easily. In that sense, the BBC's own guidance on reporting polls was not followed properly:

> We should always bear in mind that even properly conducted opinion polls by trusted companies can be wrong. When we report the result of a poll, no matter how convincing it may seem or what the attitude

> of the rest of the media, we should always ask how much of the rest of our story, and its prominence, is dependent on the poll's accuracy.[25]

Broadcasters insist that journalism during an election campaign is not just meant to provide information; it is also supposed to report on the contest for power and the political dynamics of that competition. With hindsight we can see that the horse race was somewhat misreported because of the misleading polls, but it was an understandable editorial focus.

Balance and framing

Not only were issues less discussed at times, but some issues were less discussed than others. The NHS and education were both topics that voters claimed were important to them, but neither featured strongly over the election as a whole. Health featured in 22% of bulletins in week 2, but barely at all at other periods. The economy was a bigger subject category, but it registered in only 18% of coverage averaged over the entire campaign. Coalition speculation was the lead issue in 18% of all of the broadcasts. This selectivity was a form of 'bias' that might favour one party over another. However, topic selection has a complex relationship to impartiality. It cannot be assumed that talking about the economy, for example, is necessarily pro-Conservative. The NHS is seen as a safe topic for Labour, but Tory promises on increased spending early on in the campaign helped neutralise the issue and push it down, though not off, the broadcast news agenda.

During an election where the press was more partisan than ever before and was largely in favour of the Conservatives (see Chapter 12), the broadcasters' obligation to strive for impartiality became even more important. There were moments when they did appear overly keen to follow up on newspaper stories. A *Daily Telegraph* front page featuring a letter from small business people that turned out very quickly to be a stunt cooked up by the Conservative Party was still reported on by the news programmes. As shown in Chapter 7, this became a major issue for the Labour Party. At times it seemed that the argument was still being made that if it is in the papers – even as a process row – then it must be a story. The single most contentious and important accusation of bias was aimed at the BBC by Labour's head of communications, Tom Baldwin:

> Our biggest dispute with the BBC was over the prominence it gave to the idea of a deal between Labour and the SNP that was never on the cards. After the first 237 incarnations on news bulletins, I

> struggled to see how this theme could be developed further, yet the BBC continued to lead with speculation about bizarre consequences of a Labour–SNP government for the economy, tax, and even road schemes. At no stage was there an examination of David Cameron, Nicola Sturgeon and Nick Clegg's motives in playing tag-team with almost identical messages on the same non-existent deal.[26]

The charge was that the BBC framed this issue in too similar a way to the (generally right-wing) press. Yet according to the (erroneous) polling, the result of a Labour minority government with a strong SNP presence in Parliament was an extremely likely post-election scenario. Indeed, Labour made the same assumption. The broadcasters argue that this was the key dynamic of the last phase of the campaign and they had to focus on it. The Tories adapted their campaign tactics more nimbly to expose a core weakness for Labour in the eyes of the public, and the reporting reflected that reality. Politically, the Conservatives were astute at shaping the narrative of a close campaign to attack Labour, who struggled to clarify their position on post-election deals. The question is whether broadcasters queried the Conservative framing strongly enough.

This election showed how difficult it is for broadcasting to guarantee 'fairness' in an electoral system designed to be disproportionate. The smaller parties had a higher profile than before, partly thanks to the election debates that gave them a national platform alongside the major figures. They also received relatively significant space on current affairs programming and general interviews on radio and TV. Yet, despite all the pre-election talk of the rise of the minor parties, the end result saw the two major parties secure two-thirds of the vote. So it was less surprising that Labour and the Conservatives were given the most coverage, as they were the parties most likely to form the next government. However, more coverage does not mean it is 'positive'. *Channel 4 News*, for example, gave significantly more airtime to the Conservatives and UKIP at times during the campaign, but much of that was framed critically.[27] Considering it was only standing in Scotland, the SNP received proportionately far more coverage, but that was because of its wider potential importance. The Lib Dems received far more airtime than their final seat tally merited, but they had been the third party and were in government. Broadcasters were less 'presidential' in their coverage than newspapers, quoting a wider range of party spokespeople, according to Loughborough University research.[28] Leaders like Nick Clegg got slightly more coverage than his party, while Cameron got slightly less.

Stage-management

The professionalisation of political communications in the UK abetted by Australian and American consultants continued its remorseless advance in 2015 to create ever more closely controlled messaging and tightly orchestrated appearances. This was partly in response to the speeding-up of the news cycle and the increase in its potential volatility thanks to continuous news and social media. All parties feared a repeat of the Gordon Brown 'bigoted woman' episode from 2010. This meant that the material generated by the parties for general broadcast coverage was highly constrained. The fixed-term Parliament arguably also contributed to this shift to the US-style permanent campaign.[29]

At some of the rallies, journalists were not even allowed to hold the microphone when asking questions to discourage follow-ups. The two main party leaders especially avoided any uncontrolled contact with public or journalists. Speeches were held in closed venues with journalists literally corralled. Party activists crowded around camera-friendly backdrops. Broadcast journalists shelled out to be on the battle buses and rarely showed wide shots of the fake stunts. Broadcasters argue that it would have been self-regarding, but there were few on-screen challenges to the stage-management.[30] From the main parties' point of view, this was successful and it was a largely gaffe-free election. Journalists were briefly excited by small slips such as when Cameron forgot which football team he supported (see p. 194), but this had no consequence beyond providing a moment of human error in a robotic campaign.

It is naïve to expect the parties to do anything that might harm their chances. In the 'jungle' of the hyper-fast 24/7 digital news cycle, they had everything to lose and little to gain from greater openness. Party leaders were interviewed endlessly, including at length. All of them took part in the 'debate' programmes. Questions were allowed at events and a range of media from local to national had access to the politicians every day. Before blaming the politicians, broadcasters, like journalists in general, need to ask themselves what they could have done better.

Human interest

Broadcasters struggled to find a way to animate the coverage. All channels featured vox-pop slots with voters talking about what mattered to them. *Newsnight* made the stylish 'This House Believes' series of films where 'ordinary' families chatted about politics over a meal. But the danger was that the voters themselves often went unchallenged and this 'abbreviated public comment' could feel like a way of showing 'involvement' when it was nothing of the sort.[31]

Journalists sought to bring out the 'personalities' of the leaders to help connect them to the public. Interviewing politicians in kitchens is nothing new, but in this election it delivered one of the very few scoops of the campaign and set off a bizarre hoopla about false social modesty. In a conversation during salad preparation in his Cotswold home kitchen with the BBC's James Landale, the Prime Minister revealed mid-chat that he would not be seeking a third term in office. In contrast, when the Milibands posed in their north London home, the revelation was not what they said, but the fact that they had invited the cameras into the more spartan of their two kitchens. This was reported as a cheeky attempt to downplay their 'poshness'. The 'visual syntax' of broadcast coverage is an integral part of political communications, but in this campaign the essential triviality of these two incidents perhaps shows how hard it was for the broadcasters to bring empathy, let alone enlightenment into the coverage.[32] Ultimately, it is up to the politicians, not the journalists, to be 'authentic', but whatever that magic quality is, the style of this campaign did little to promote it.[33]

Future policy

In the context of this full but flat coverage, the election debates provided much-needed variation. They attracted reasonable audiences with extensive further engagement via social media and newspaper reportage. They allowed the public to judge the leaders under pressure and evaluate their arguments in competition with others. They also served an important role in demonstrating that democracy is about putting yourself directly before the public and answering their questions.

All the broadcasters and political parties largely accept that after 2015, something similar now has a place in future campaigns. However, almost everyone rules out any kind of formal regulatory or legislative framework as unrealistic and undesirable. Now that we have had two elections with debates, it seems less likely (but by no means impossible) to imagine one without any set-piece encounters. The fact that broadcasters were flexible in 2015 makes it harder for parties to refuse to accept adjusted arrangements on any kind of absolute principle. The next test will be how the various stakeholders come up with an arrangement for the EU referendum and the European elections.

Regardless though of what happens for those polls, the next general election will be subject to negotiation. While a formal independent structure to organise debates sounds attractive, it raises questions about who would have the final say and how adaptable it would be if the political landscape continues to evolve.[34] A debate commission sounds like a practical step, but the parties will not agree to one unless it gives them more power. Broadcasters are better served by maintaining their independence. However, there are useful principles to abide by. Broadcasters should produce an offer and, as with every other kind of programme making, the subject has the right not to take part. Broadcasters need to maintain a united front and produce as simple a proposal as possible. They have to stress the public value of these debates, but that includes the potential for robust and direct exchanges with the speakers and the public. They should have proposals ready on time, but they should also then be open-minded about adjusting the model right up to a short period before transmission.

There are dangers in leaving it to political bartering. The parties may insist on tighter control over, for example, audience selection in an effort to make the events less risky. The spiral of media management may continue to circle inwards. So the debates become ever more important as a way to orchestrate some kind of space for real deliberation and convincing and engaging political theatre.

Conclusion

It would be simplistic to separate out the different news media because they are all networked into each other. Yet social media was clearly the worst offender in creating a self-referential bubble, especially on the left. In a mirror image, the right-wing newspapers that were panicked by an apparently close race redoubled their efforts to drive home the horrors of Ed, Nicola and Nigel. But TV and radio were key brokers in this campaign of mistaken premises. Broadcasting remains the medium with the most impact on voters: 38% said that they 'were influenced' by the TV debates and 23% said the same of news bulletins.[35] On the one hand, the broadcasters did try much harder than the newspapers and social networks to cover a broad range of topics and they did deliver an unprecedented slew of information and balanced analysis. However, on the other hand, they went along with the banal theatre of the tightest, most sterile, stage-managed campaign ever.

In the end, the process of election broadcast journalism and its relationship with the politicians will always be political, just like every other aspect of the campaign. The Conservatives' tactics were more successful in focusing attention on the SNP factor and in the same way they were the most successful in handling the TV debate negotiations – as well as managing the wider media frame – than Labour were.

The media, let alone one platform such as broadcasting, cannot make politics interesting by itself; that depends on the politicians and the public. One needs to avoid either nostalgia for some golden age of a vibrant public sphere or getting sucked into digital delusions of engagement. But consider an election without TV debates and it is clear that broadcasting has a key role in trying to counter apathy. For all their faults, the so-called TV debates are now a significant part of the UK election campaigns' claim to democratic authority. As the limits of newspaper and online coverage become clearer, broadcasting as a whole remains absolutely vital.

Notes

1. Thanks to research assistance from Brooks Decillia, Emily Revess, Isha Vermani, Matilde Giglio and Richard Kirsch.
2. 'The Ofcom Broadcasting Code' (March 2013–July 2015), Ofcom, March 2013.
3. 'Election Brings Record BBC Traffic, But News Chief "Quite Astonished" by "Ferocity and Frequency" of Party Complaints', *Press Gazette*, 2 June 2015.
4. Nick Robinson, *Election Notebook*. Bantam, 2015, p. 357.
5. Dennis Kavanagh and Philip Cowley, *The British General Election of 2015*. Palgrave Macmillan, 2010, p. 147.
6. *BBC Radio Manchester*, 16 April 2014.
7. 'BBC, ITV, Channel 4 and Sky Join Forces for Party Leader Debates Proposal', BBC Media Centre, 13 October 2014.
8. 'Review of Ofcom List of Major Political Parties for Elections Taking Place on 7 May 2015', Ofcom, 8 January 2015.
9. HC Deb 14 January 2015, col. 849.
10. 'Lord Grade Defends David Cameron from Bullying Broadcasters', *The Guardian*, 11 March 2015.
11. The 211 broadcasts draw on six news programmes over the course of the six weeks of the campaign: *BBC News* at 10 pm; *ITV News* at 1.30 pm; *Sky News* at 7 pm; *Channel 4 News* at 7 pm; BBC Radio Four's *Today* programme (between 8 and 8.30 pm) and *PM* (between 5 and 5.30 pm).
12. There were almost 500 complaints to Ofcom, more than all the other election debate programmes combined.
13. Sylvia Shaw, 'Winning and Losing the "Battle for Number 10"', UK Election Analysis 2015.
14. Colin J. Davis, Jeffrey S. Bowers and Amina Memon, 'Social Influence in Televised Election Debates: A Potential Distortion of Democracy', *PLoS ONE*, 6(3) (2011): e18154.

15. 'Why David Cameron's Victory in the Leaders' Interviews Matters', *The Guardian*, 27 March 2015.
16. 'So Who Won the ITV General Election Leaders' Debate?', *Daily Telegraph*, 3 April 2015.
17. 'Who Won BBC Leaders Debate According to the Data?', *Daily Mirror*, 16 April 2015.
18. Next came questions on immigration and post-election coalition formation, both of which were the subject of seven questions.
19. Daniel Dayan and Elihu Katz, *Media Events*. Harvard University Press, 1992.
20. Talk at LSE, 28 March 2015.
21. In addition, Channel 4 broadcast *Channel 4's Alternative Election Night.*
22. Robinson, *Election Notebook*, p. 363.
23. 'BBC Has Focused More on Policy in Election Coverage, Study Finds', *The Guardian*, 16 April 2015; BBC Election Coverage Became "Infected" by Speculation of Labour–SNP Coalition, Head of News Admits', *The Independent*, 2 June 2015.
24. 'TV News Focuses on Election Race at Expense of Policy Issues', *The Guardian*, 7 May 2015.
25. BBC Editorial Guidelines, *Section 10: Politics, Public Policy and Polls – Opinion Polls, Surveys and Votes.*
26. 'The BBC was Not in the Pocket of Labour This Election. Quite the Opposite', *The Guardian*, 13 May 2015.
27. 'Channels 4 and 5 Giving Tories More Airtime Than Other Broadcasters', *The Guardian*, 24 April 2015.
28. Loughborough University General Election 2015, *Media Coverage of the 2015 Campaign (Report 5)*, 11 May 2015.
29. I. Lamond (2015) 'Oh What A Circus: Reflecting on the 2015 General Election As An Event', in Dan Jackson and Einar Thorsen (eds) *UK Election Analysis 2015: Media, Voters and the Campaign*. Bournemouth University of the Study of Journalism, Culture and Community, 2015.
30. 'Why is the British Media So Supine in the Face of Control from the Big Parties?', www.capx.co, 22 April 2015.
31. Richard Scullion, 'Liars, Bullies, Confused and Infantilised, and That's Just the Electorate', in Jackson and Thorsen (eds), *UK Election Analysis 2015.*
32. Rutherford, 'Standing behind the Leaders', UK Election Analysis 2015.
33. Frances Smith, 'Ordinariness and Authenticity in the 2015 General Election Campaign', in Jackson and Thorsen (eds), *UK Election Analysis 2015.*
34. 'The Guardian View on Televised Election Debates: Shine the Light', *The Guardian*, 14 January 2015.
35. 'Election 2015: TV Debates "Most Influential" for Voters', BBC News website, 9 May 2015.

12
Still Life in the Old Attack Dogs: The Press

David Deacon and Dominic Wring

During the 2015 campaign, there was considerable negativity and partiality in much press reporting; it was not difficult to find examples of robust political partisanship descending into personal vilification. Some of this was the kind of journalism that had been repeatedly highlighted and criticised only a few years before, following the 2011 hacking scandal and during the ensuing year-long Leveson Inquiry. Some commentators believed that this election might witness digital platforms operating as a counterbalance, assuming a more significant, potentially influential role in framing public participation in, and perceptions of, the contest. At the close of the campaign, Alastair Campbell observed: 'Why has social media been so important? Politicians aren't trusted anymore, business isn't trusted like it was, the media is certainly not trusted like it was ... The genius of social media, and the genius of Facebook is the concept of the friend. We trust our friends.'[1]

Those who believed social media were potentially transformative during the election suggested that the new online forums would host rather than lead opinion, enabling citizens to take a more active role in the campaign – drawing up their own informational diet, mobilising the like-minded, sharing insights and evidence, challenging journalistic falsehoods, subverting party imagery through memes and so on. For their part, the main parties invested considerable efforts in trying to accommodate the 'wonderful world' of Web 2.0. The most celebrated example of this came in the last week of the campaign when Ed Miliband was interviewed by the celebrity and activist Russell Brand on his YouTube channel, 'The Trews' (see p. 200). Amongst many things, the unexpected outright victory of the Conservatives provided a reality check to some of the more outlandish claims made of the democratising potential of social media. Similarly, 'Milifandom' – a Twitter-led ebullition of ardour for the Labour leader led by teenage admirers – did not make it past the ballot box. Although there are dangers in writing off the significance of social media too readily (and in the process over-emphasising its distinctiveness from traditional news journalism), Steven Barnett believes that digital platforms generally provided more of an 'echo chamber' than a megaphone.[2] These forums appear to have been a means for communing with the like-minded rather than converting the unconvinced. By contrast, there is substantial circumstantial evidence that the influence of 'legacy' media lives on, not least in the national printed press, discussion of which forms the basis of this chapter.

Still a critical mass medium

There is no question that the UK press has experienced challenging market conditions in the five years since the last general election. Tables 12.1 and 12.2 compare circulation and readership figures for print copies of national daily and Sunday newspapers in 2010 and 2015. There was a 31% decline in daily circulation and a 36% drop in Sunday newspaper circulation in this period alone. Readership has also reduced substantially, down 34% for the dailies and 36% for the Sunday editions. The reduction in readership has been mitigated by the growth of online readership of several titles (see Table 12.1), but the continuing struggle to find a viable digital business model has meant that this has done little to alleviate the financial pressures facing the industry. News UK's introduction of paywalls for the digital content of both its dailies (*The Sun* and *The Times*) may have generated additional revenue, but, as the figures show, it has reduced their online presence.

Despite the challenge facing the traditional print media industry, the figures in Tables 12.1 and 12.2 also show that the UK national press still has considerable reach. Daily readership of hard-copy newspapers (excluding the *Financial Times*) averaged 16.7 million in April 2015, and this figure increases to 22.3 million when online readerships are included. National Readership Survey data show that press readership is strongly biased towards older people, with 80% of readers being over 35 years of age. This demographic group also constitutes the section of the electorate most likely to vote, underlining the enduring significance

Table 12.1 Daily newspapers' partisanship and circulation[3]

Title *Proprietor* *(Chair)* *Editor*	*Declaration* *(2010)*	*Circulation*[a] *(2010)* *(000s)*	*Print readership*[b] *(000s)*	*Print and online*[c] *(000s)*
Daily Mirror Trinity Mirror (David Grigson) Lloyd Embley	Very strong Labour (Strong Labour)	882 (1,240)	2,211 (3,425)	2,726
Daily Express Northern and Shell (Richard Desmond) Hugh Whittow	Very strong UKIP (Very strong Conservative)	438 (666)	993 (1,577)	1,145
Daily Star Northern and Shell (Richard Desmond) Dawn Neesom	No declaration (No declaration)	420 (823)	943 (1,965)	1,065
The Sun News UK (Rupert Murdoch) David Dinsmore	Very strong Conservative (Strong Conservative)	1,858 (2,956)	5,178 (7,761)	5,237
Daily Mail Associated Newspapers (Lord Rothermere) Paul Dacre	Very strong Conservative (Strong Conservative)	1,631 (2,096)	3,704 (4,934)	5,463
Daily Telegraph Telegraph Group (Barclay Brothers) Ian MacGregor	Very strong Conservative (Moderate Conservative)	486 (683)	1,119 (1,905)	2,138
The Guardian Scott Trust (Liz Forgan) Alan Rusbridger	Moderate Labour (Moderate Liberal Democrat)	176 (289)	761 (1,147)	2,130
The Times News UK (Rupert Murdoch) John Witherow	Moderate Conservative–Liberal Democrat Coalition (Weak Conservative)	394 (507)	788 (1,773)	1,367
The Independent/i Independent Print Limited (Evgeny Lebedev) Amol Rajan (The Independent)/ Oliver Duff (i)	Weak Liberal Democrat–Conservative Coalition (Moderate Liberal Democrat)	*The Independent* 59 (188) *i* 276	995 (671)	1,026
Financial Times Pearson plc (Glen Moreno)	Conservative–Liberal Democrat Coalition (Very weak Conservative)	212 (387)	Not available	Not available

[a] Audit Bureau of Circulation (April 2015)
[b] National Readership Survey (April 2014–March 2015)
[c] National Readership Survey and Comm Score (April 2014–March 2015)

Table 12.2 Sunday newspapers' partisanship and circulation

Title	*Declaration (2010)*	*Circulation (2010) (000s)*[a]	*Readership (2010) (000s)*[b]
Sunday Mirror	Very strong Labour (Strong Labour)	833 (1,124)	2,401 (3,826)
Sunday Express	Very strong UKIP (Very strong Conservative)	385 (574)	1,150 (1,622)
Sun on Sunday (News of the World)	Strong Conservative (Very strong Conservative)	1,474 (2,906)	4,207 (7,602)
The People	Moderate Labour (None)	324 (530)	674 (1,331)
Mail on Sunday	Strong Conservative (Strong Conservative)	1,447 (1,983)	4,007 (5,213)
Star on Sunday	No declaration (No declaration)	254 (348)	254 (348)
Sunday Telegraph	Strong Conservative (Strong Conservative)	371 (510)	1,150 (1,677)
Observer	Moderate Labour (Moderate Liberal Democrat)	196 (332)	723 (1,212)
Sunday Times	Moderate Conservative (Strong Conservative)	809 (1,135)	2,010 (3,219)
Independent on Sunday	No declaration (No declaration)	99 (168)	363 (600)

[a] Audit Bureau of Circulation (April 2015)
[b] National Readership Survey (April 2014–March 2015)

of printed newspapers. Given that many of these readers still largely engage with the medium in its hard-copy format, this non-interactive version is by design obviously less 'social' in construction. For David Thorburn, the way in which this news is consumed is important because these titles 'organize the world each day in a coherent way, and even to choose not to read a particular article is to make contact with and become aware of another angle or perspective on the world'.[4] It is this structured management of news and views that makes these newspapers' interventions potentially so compelling for the still significant numbers of loyal readers.

The perception that this would be a close-run election did little to encourage even-handedness in many quarters; indeed, it appears to have stimulated partiality within sections of the print media. This inevitably drew attention to *cui bono* questions: whose interests were being served by such propagandising and what were their motives? Concerns about the influence of newspaper proprietors surfaced during the campaign when *The Independent* published a story about News UK owner Rupert Murdoch two weeks before polling day.[5] This report suggested that Murdoch had visited London in February to personally instruct staff on his *The Sun* newspaper to get their 'act together' and help prevent Ed Miliband becoming Prime Minister. It was widely speculated that the veteran proprietor was seeking revenge on a Labour leader who had been vocal in his criticism of News International (as News UK was previously known) during the 2011 hacking scandal. The episode had also embarrassed David Cameron when it was revealed that his former spin doctor Andy Coulson was implicated because of his prior editorship of the *News of the World*, the paper at the centre of a highly publicised scandal involving allegations of illegal phone hacking (a scandal which ultimately led to the paper's closure). Cameron felt pressured to launch the Leveson Inquiry, but ultimately distanced himself from the subsequent Report's recommendations, despite having pledged to support them unless they were 'bonkers'.[6] A Miliband-led government's preparedness to revisit the issue presented an obvious threat to Murdoch's interests.

The Sun's official response to *The Independent*'s story about Murdoch's alleged interference was to state that its editorial line 'is informed by how the political parties approach the issues that matter most to our readers'.[7] But the credibility of this claim was strained further in the last days of the election when it emerged that a PR agency working for the newspaper had offered paid incentives for 'case studies' for coverage in the guise of '(ideally *Sun* readers) who are going to vote Conservative and have a good news story to tell'.[8] Close relations between newspapers and political parties of this kind are, of course, nothing new.[9] But there were several instances that exposed the scale of this cooperation, even connivance, in 2015. Richard Desmond, owner of the *Express* and *Star* newspapers, was more upfront in making his support for UKIP public when he donated £1 million to the party during the campaign. It therefore came as no surprise when the *Express* newspapers formally declared their backing for Nigel Farage. The *Mirror* newspapers too continued their longer-established association with Labour and, as will be shown, articulated key themes from the party's campaign in their coverage of the election. Perhaps reflecting this, David Cameron, guided by media advisors including Craig Oliver, rejected an invitation to be interviewed by the *Sunday People* and was duly 'empty chaired' by the title (5 April). The Labour press operation was accused of instituting a 'ban' on press critics attending the party's campaign launch (*The Sun*, 28 March).

Allegations of proprietorial influence were not restricted to the 'popular' press. The most notable came early on in the campaign when the *Daily Telegraph* influenced the news agenda through devoting its front page to an 'open letter' from 103 senior corporate executives hailing the successes of the Conservatives' economic policies and criticising opposition plans.[10] The story led most broadcast news bulletins that day. But questions subsequently emerged about its provenance and independence, with several signatories revealed to be Tory donors and others insisting that their name be removed as they had been misled as to the letter's tone and purpose. After initial denials, there was an admission from Conservative Campaign Headquarters (CCHQ) that its officials had offered a 'guiding hand' in organising the intervention.[11] This was only one incident. As this chapter will demonstrate, the Conservatives in particular were able to harness and use the bulk of the print media for their own campaigning purposes.

Polarised and polemical: 'popular' partisanship

During their 1970s and 1980s heyday, the term 'tabloid' became synonymous with a polemical, irreverent kind of journalism, and politics was particularly subjected to this treatment. More recently, the adoption of the tabloid format, though not the associated style, by former broadsheets such as the *The Times* and *The Independent* has meant that their more populist rivals have been redefined as the 'populars'. The latter remain deeply political animals and still appear keen to cultivate and persuade their audiences, particularly during elections. So, for example, when the best-selling *The Sun* formally announced its long anticipated endorsement of the Conservatives, it did so by making a jokey allusion to another major story, the then imminent birth of Princess Charlotte, by depicting Cameron as a newborn emblazoned with headline 'It's a Tory!' (30 April). The editorial praised the party's economic policy and decision to hold an EU referendum while warning of the threat posed by the 'saboteurs' of the Scottish National Party (SNP). In sharp contrast, the *Scottish Sun* endorsed Nicola Sturgeon on a front page that depicted her as *Star Wars* hero Princess Leia ('Stur Wars – A New Hope, May the 7th Be with You: Why it's Time to Vote SNP', 30 April). The English edition of the paper had earlier superimposed Sturgeon's face on a photo of singer Miley Cyrus atop a wrecking ball (a scene from the latter's music video) to warn that the SNP would demolish the British economy if it gained any leverage over a Labour-led coalition government ('Tartan Barmy', *The Sun*, 10 March).

The various ominous forces that *The Sun* suggested would dominate Prime Minister Miliband were a recurrent theme of its election coverage and were collectively illustrated as a mythical hydra monster: 'The Six Edded Beast' (29 April). Sturgeon's was one among the creature's half-dozen demonic heads along with Miliband himself, his deputy Harriet Harman, union leader Len McCluskey, celebrity activist Russell Brand and Sinn Fein President Gerry Adams. Adams' inclusion referenced a previous claim that normally absentionist Irish republican MPs might take up their Westminster seats for the first time after the election to help Labour form the government ('Desperate Labour Wooing Sinn Fein', *The Sun*, 28 January). Although the party vehemently denied the story, the Conservatives issued an advert emblazoned with the aforementioned headline that depicted Alex Salmond with his arm around Miliband alongside a smiling Adams.

The Sun recognised the threat to the Conservatives posed by UKIP's advance and was quick to highlight any perceived downturn in its polling fortunes ('UKIP's Slump', 7 April). Similarly, 'UKIP... U Lose' informed readers about 'the 26 marginals where voting for Farage's party would allow Labour to steal a win on Thursday' (*The Sun*, 5 May). The same feature also listed the 14 seats where it claimed supporting the Liberal Democrats could help 'get Cam in No 10'. The paper reinforced its warning about the consequences of supporting UKIP in a front-page story featuring 'White Van Dan'. The man in question, Dan Ware, was the owner of the house decorated with St George flags that MP Emily Thornberry had publicised on Twitter during the 2014 Rochester by-election. Thornberry was duly sacked from Labour's frontbench, having been accused of snobbery by *The Sun*, which subsequently interviewed Mr Ware. The paper returned to 'Dan' during the campaign as a representative of 'hard-working families' and subsequently confirmed that he would be voting Conservative, disliked the 'racist' UKIP and also supported staying in the European Union ('Van of the People', *The Sun*, 28 April). In sharp contrast, the paper portrayed Mike Holpin, 'Britain's Most Shameless Dad – 40 Kids by 20 Women', as the ultimate example of what the same day's editorial denounced as Labour's 'bloated benefits culture' (1 April).

The single most memorable intervention by *The Sun* during the campaign came in its eve of its poll edition. The front page was given over to the by then widely publicised and very unflattering photograph of Ed Miliband eating breakfast on an early morning visit to Covent

Garden during the 2014 European elections.[12] *The Sun* reproduced this image with the headline: 'Save Our Bacon: Don't Swallow His Porkies and Keep Him OUT'. The front-page editorial continued: 'This is the pig's ear Ed made of a helpless sarnie. In 48 hours he could be doing the same to Britain' (6 May). The attention-grabbing imagery provoked a reaction, but not all of it was favourable, with one contributor to *The Guardian* questioning whether the supposedly jokey piece contained a more sinister anti-Semitic message, given the Labour leader's Jewish heritage.[13]

The *Daily Mail* vied with *The Sun* to be the most polemical newspaper during the election. The paper's highly combative approach was demonstrated in a series of attacks on rival politicians, including the outgoing Deputy Prime Minister, who had clashed with Cameron in their face-to-face televised debate ('Treacherous Clegg Knifes Dave', 3 April). Following her perceived success in the same encounter, SNP leader Nicola Sturgeon was labelled the 'Most Dangerous Woman in Britain' (4 April). Similarly, even a seemingly innocuous photograph of a smiling First Minister was framed negatively: 'Sturgeon Gloats as SNP is Set to Win EVERY Seat in Scotland' (30 April). But this was mild, however, compared to *Daily Mail* columnist Dominic Lawson's attack on 'The Scottish Nasty Party' in which he denounced their 'intimidation and (an) intolerance of dissent (that) reeks of fascism' (20 April). The alleged threat posed by a powerful SNP was contrasted with the perceived weakness of Ed Miliband, who the *Daily Mail* feared would be dominated by the Nationalists in a coalition government ('Swaggering Salmond Boasts: I'll Be Writing Labour's Budget', 23 April). Miliband's vulnerability to pressure from Unite leader Len McCluskey also formed the basis of stories about his union's sponsorship of several parliamentary candidates ('Union's Sinister Hold over Miliband', 22 April; 'Red Len: I Own Labour', 24 April). This ridicule culminated with a front-page photograph of the prospective Prime Minister's meeting with activist Russell Brand accompanied by the headline: 'Do You Really Want this Clown Ruling Us? (And, No, We Don't Mean the One on the Left)' (29 April). Pointedly the editorial formally endorsing the Conservatives denounced Miliband as 'a class war zealot' and revived an earlier *Daily Mail* attack on him for being 'schooled by his Marxist father' ('For Sanity's Sake, Don't Let a Class War Zealot and the SNP Destroy Our Economy – and Our Very Nation', 6 May).[14]

The *Daily Mail* was more cautious in dealing with the threat to the Conservatives from Nigel Farage's party because, as the normally forthright columnist Stephen Glover observed: 'There's hardly a word

I disagree with in UKIP's manifesto. And I know the other parties are lying to me. But...' (16 April). The paper's 'mid-market' rival the *Daily Express* showed less reluctance in embracing the Eurosceptic party's cause. The title had long been prominent in its clear, unequivocal call for Britain to the leave the European Union. Links between the paper and UKIP had been forged over some time by former columnist turned MEP Patrick O'Flynn and proprietor Richard Desmond, who became a prominent donor. Consequently, during the campaign, the *Express* provided Farage and his colleagues with sympathetic coverage and this culminated with a formal endorsement on polling day itself: 'Vote UKIP and Help Britain to Break Free from the EU' (7 May). The *Sunday Express* took a similar line, arguing that the party 'is in touch with ordinary people' (3 May). But it should be noted that *Express* columnists also provided anti-Labour commentaries that were as potentially useful to the Tories as to UKIP.[15]

Richard Desmond's 'red-top' newspaper, the *Daily Star*, has not formally endorsed a party in the last two general elections.[16] This stance logically follows the title's decision not to publish dedicated editorial commentaries on any issue, political or otherwise. During the campaign, the *Daily Star* adopted a mocking tone, noting the number of 'ruddy days to go' each time it presented its limited electoral coverage. Nonetheless, the newspaper did highlight the link between Desmond and Nigel Farage in a report that featured a photograph of them announcing the proprietor's £1 million donation to UKIP. The businessman was quoted as liking the party's commitment to the 'common man' and hostility towards the 'elitists' running its electoral rivals (17 April). And although the *Star* did not emulate Desmond's other newspaper, the *Express*, and formally support UKIP, it did offer the party some sympathetic coverage. On St George's Day, for instance, the paper featured a smiling Farage posing with the national flag and beer in front of a pub to 'drink a toast to England's patron saint' ('Fly Flag for England', *Daily Star*, 23 April). The eve-of-poll edition also featured an advert of the UKIP leader with his now customary pint accompanied by the slogan 'Thirsty for Change?' and a signed letter urging readers to 'BELIEVE in BRITAIN' and vote for his party the following day (6 May).

Alone among the popular daily newspapers, the *Daily Mirror* and its various sister titles took a very different line on Europe as well as party politics more generally. Recycling phraseology that had originally accompanied the notorious anti-Labour *The Sun* election day 1992 front page, the paper warned that the Conservatives' planned EU referendum would trigger an exodus of businesses: 'If Cam Wins Will the Last Big Firm to Leave Britain Please Turn Out the Lights' (25 April). The newspaper routinely featured attacks on David Cameron and George Osborne that concluded with a front-page polling day exhortation to vote Labour in order to 'Send 'em Packing' courtesy of a 'Mirror Removals' van (7 May). Inside the editorial declared: 'Let's make today the dawn of a better day.' North of the border, the *Mirror*'s sibling, the *Daily Record*, counted down the number of days 'To Boot out the Tories'. The *Sunday People* also railed against the Conservatives. In an emotive endorsement of Labour, the paper's editorial cited that a primary motivation was to see an end to the 'hateful Bedroom Tax' that it claimed had caused suicides ('Vote in Memory of Them', 3 May). The *Mirror* papers also attacked other parties. Recognising their potential threat to Labour, veteran columnist Paul Routledge denounced UKIP as 'Nasty Nigel and the Little Englanders' (*Daily Mirror*, 29 April). The *Sunday Mirror* turned its attention to another rival in '50 shades of Green... Inside the Weird World of Party Leader Natalie Bennett' and accused her partner Jim Jepps of having controversial attitudes towards sex offenders (19 April). The *Mirror* also published more positive and supportive material, such as the front-page devoted to Ed Miliband in which he declared 'My Pledge' to help voters and their families because 'you can trust me' (13 April).

Qualified judgements

While the so-called 'popular' daily and Sunday newspapers were mostly keen to promote their partisan preferences during the campaign, what were once known as 'broadsheets' were, for the most part, more circumspect. And whereas the former allied themselves to a particular party, three of the five so-called 'qualities' endorsed the formation of another Conservative–Liberal Democrat coalition government. For its part, the *Financial Times* argued 'the compelling case for continuity' (1 May). The editorial credited several Conservative-led initiatives, but also made clear its support for continuing UK membership of the European Union, a stance most closely associated with the Liberal Democrats. Earlier on in the campaign, *The Independent* picked up on this issue through giving prominence to Nick Clegg's denunciation of the 'swivel-eyed' right-wing Conservative and UKIP MPs he feared would hold Cameron 'to ransom' over Britain's continuing role within the EU (10 April). The paper eventually declared for what it pointedly called a 'Lib–Con' government in an endorsement, 'in defence of liberal democracy', that applauded Clegg's party while calling for the Coalition's re-election, 'for all its faults' (*The Independent*, 5 May).

The Liberal Democrat leader was singled out in an editorial in *The Times*, 'Vote Clegg', which urged Conservative voters in his constituency to lend him their support on polling day (5 May). The newspaper's formal declaration, 'Britain's Vital Choice', the following day called for the re-election of the Coalition because it had taken 'tough decisions' on the economy (*The Times*, 6 May). It did, however, lament over how 'the Conservatives have strayed rashly from the fiscal probity that is supposed to be their hallmark'. Although decidedly Eurosceptic in tone, the editorial acknowledged polls indicating that Liberal Democrat support would be needed to ensure a continuation of what it believed had been a successful government. The statement warned against the 'tyranny' posed by the SNP, a prospective partner in an alternative centre-left coalition. The Nationalists also featured in the *Sunday Times*' endorsement, 'A Conservative Case for the Conservatives' (3 May). Reflecting on a 'dull campaign' in which 'politicians have droned us into bored submission', the editorial presented the case for a Cameron-led government. Although the statement acknowledged the merits of supporting Clegg and his 'closest Lib Dem' ministerial colleagues, it concentrated on comparing the Conservative economic plans with Labour's 'populist 'soak the rich' policies', which it contended would 'deter inward investment'.

The *Daily Telegraph* was the quality newspaper that provided by far the most strident endorsement of a party, even writing to subscribers imploring them to vote Conservative.[17] Its declaration of there being 'A clear choice for Britain' was followed by an attack on 'a Labour campaign strewn with gimmicks, half-truths and downright lies' (7 May). It conjured up a vision of future 'economic and social wreckage' with the party having 'lurched to the Left' under a leader who espoused 'an insidious anti-wealth, soak-the-rich ethos'. Although it acknowledged that the Tories had 'made mistakes' in office, the *Sunday Telegraph* also made clear its position, declaring 'Vote Conservative for the good of the country' (3 May). Predictably, the left-leaning *The Guardian* came to a very different conclusion. Having abandoned Labour for the Liberal Democrats in 2010, the paper reversed this decision, having acknowledged the 'visceral' antipathy of rival newspapers towards Ed Miliband. The paper believed that these 'personal' attacks were in part motivated by the politician's reformist media policy (1 April). During the closing stages of the campaign, a leader comment concluded that 'Britain confronts a profound choice. Labour offers the best chance of a new direction' and urged readers to think of those less fortunate than themselves when voting (2 May). *The Observer* agreed with its daily sister paper. Writing that the country was at a 'crossroads', it suggested that a new direction was necessary and that 'only Labour offers that vision' (3 May).

Front-page news

Table 12.3 details the front-page story of the ten main daily newspapers during the short campaign. (Where the paper has a distinct Scottish version, the table gives the front-page story of the version south of the border.) Overall, the election ran as a front-page story in almost exactly half of these papers' front pages during the campaign, although this masks large differences between the 'quality' and 'popular' papers. All of the latter ran front-page election stories in under half of the days of the campaign – the *Daily Star* doing so on just three occasions (two of those involving Russell Brand). At the other end of the scale, *The Times* ran an election story on its front page on all but four days, and all of the 'quality' papers apart from the *sui generis Financial Times* had the election as their front-page story for more than half of the days of the campaign. It is also noticeable how often these front-page stories are about the party (or the leader of the party) which is *not* being supported by that paper. *The Telegraph*, for example, had 11 front-page leads on Ed Miliband (all of which were negative), *The Sun* had five (ditto) and *The Times* 11 (all but one negative). *The Times* also led on three occasions with threat of SNP influence over Labour. Similarly, of *The Mirror*'s front-page election stories, more than half were about how terrible the Conservatives were.

The 'horse race' campaign

Process is a term describing much of the so-called 'horse race' style of reporting that features quite prominently in modern election campaigns. It made up the single largest component of papers' coverage of the election, accounting for 44.5% of all coverage (see Table 12.4). The largest single component of that was discussion of party strategies and tactics (which alone accounted for 16.7% of coverage), more than any substantive policy issue. Electoral process also refers to the coverage devoted to the likelihood of there being another hung parliament and coalition government. This widely anticipated outcome to the election encouraged a significant amount of news reporting to make routine and copious references to the various polling findings published throughout the campaign. Many of these surveys were commissioned by rival

Table 12.3 Front-page lead stories, 30 March–7 May

Date	*Daily Mirror*	*Daily Express*	*The Sun*	*Daily Mail*	*Daily Star*	*Daily Telegraph*	*The Guardian*	*The Times*	*The Independent*	*Financial Times*
30 March	(Killer pilot's girlfriend pregnant with his baby)	(Gales chaos to last a week)	(Swinger dies at 007 orgy)	(Your pension secrets sold to conmen for 5 pence)	(I am having killer pilot's baby)	Miliband top donor backs the Tories	EU referendum will play havoc with business, Miliband warns	Labour will raise tax bill by £3,000, says Cameron	Labour seeks legal advice to stop PM 'squatting' in No 10	Miliband woos business bosses with warning over EU exit risk
31 March	(E-cigs timebomb)	(Murdered in each other's arms)	(Load of hot heir)	(Now they are selling your health secrets)	('Pilot had a death wish years ago')	Miliband stung by business backlash	They're off: with row over tax and a personal attack	Miliband faces threat of mutiny over cuts	Secret ballot: Cameron and Miliband accused of hiding their cuts	(Global tie-ups hit $811bn in fastest start since 2007)
1 April	(40 kids... with 20 mums)	(Father of 16 costs you £2m)	(40 kids by 20 women)	(Your secrets for sale: now NHS in the dock)	(Zayn and Perrie flee on love)	100 business chiefs: Labour threatens Britain's recovery	Lib Dems seek US-style first amendment	(Schools fear Easter terror exodus)	Labour lays down the gauntlet on zero hours	Miliband puts clampdown on zero-hours at heart of policy
2 April	(We won £1m... twice)	(Why watching TV gives you diabetes)	(More chance of seeing Elvis in Tesco)	Red Ed's zero hours hypocrisy	(Couple win £1m lotto twice in 2 years and still live in a caravan)	Miliband rift with business deepens	Labour fights back on Tory business letter	Panic in the markets as poll jitters hit sterling	(Teachers face storm of bullying – by parent)	(Obama declares hacking threats from abroad a 'national emergency)

Date	*Daily Mirror*	*Daily Express*	*The Sun*	*Daily Mail*	*Daily Star*	*Daily Telegraph*	*The Guardian*	*The Times*	*The Independent*	*Financial Times*
3 April	(£53m lotto winner: I thought it was April fool)	(Drug reverses memory loss)	Oops! I just lost my election: Miliband blows his chance on TV	Runaway Jihadi's father is Labour activist	(Easter footies travel chaos)	Miliband flops as outsiders shine	Seven-way debate points again to coalition Britain	Enter the outsiders: Farage and Sturgeon top Times poll after seven-way debate	The technicolour vote	NOT PUBLISHED (GOOD FRIDAY)
4 April	('100-year-old' girl dies aged 17)	(Foreign aid bill to soar to £1bn)	Lost the plod [UKIP candidate cautioned for 'bribing' voters with sausage rolls]	Most dangerous woman in Britain	(EastEnders Alfie and Kat get own show)	Sturgeon's secret backing for Cameron	Warning: 'pay-NHS is coming'	Sturgeon triumph has Labour in turmoil	Huntsmen step up Tory support – and expect repeal of ban in return	(Nuclear deal first step to less hostile relationship with west, says Tehran)
6 April	(Skint families have to be DIY dentists)	(70f! Summer is on its way)	The reem ticket: a party political broadside on behalf of hard-working Brits	(Pensions shake-up shambles)	(Strewth! Britain's hotter than Oz)	(80,000 could die in superbug outbreak)	(Minister warns: don't blow your pension today)	Miliband 'is insane' to risk defeat in TV debate	Tories: we're for the bosses, you're for the workers	(Billionaire Fridman targets US and Europe in $16bn telecoms spree)
7 April	(Slaughter of the seals in Britain)	(How to live for longer)	(Killer lag on the lash)	(Snowden: the damning truth)	(Zayn's babes in a big bro house)	It's time to come home, PM tells UKIP voters	Cameron's EU vote threatens chaos – Blair	(Yorkshire teens slip net to Syria)	Tories search for a more positive message	Collapse in efficiency leaves NHS black hole deeper than admitted

Date	*Daily Mirror*	*Daily Express*	*The Sun*	*Daily Mail*	*Daily Star*	*Daily Telegraph*	*The Guardian*	*The Times*	*The Independent*	*Financial Times*
8 April	(NHS treating transgender kids aged 3)	Outrage at plot to block EU vote	(Blingo: raiders tunnel to steal £200m in gems and cash)	Blair's toxic embrace	(Ocean's gang in £100m gems heist)	(Children who fail Sats will face resits)	'We'll end non-dom tax status' – Miliband	Miliband raids rich in purge of non-doms	Labour to scrap 'non-dom' tax status	Miliband vow to ban rules that make UK 'a tax haven' for rich
9 April	(£53m winner goes back to work)	(Now Britain's on 77f health alert)	(Find the king of diamonds)	(£13m NHS bill for suncream)	(Flutter madness: £200m riding on Grand National meet)	Labour tax plan to spark exodus	Tories play the Trident card	'Backstabber' Miliband attacked over Trident	(Sex crime is 'genetically influenced' find biggest study yet)	(Shell's £47bn swoop on BG group fuels hopes for wave of energy deals)
10 April	(We've struck oil)	We'll give you what you deserve: Cameron: We've woken up to the challenge from UKIP	(£1m compo 'terrorist')	(Cataract ops: jump NHS queue by paying)	(Oil!)	Tories duck pledge to spend 2pc on defence	The day the polls turned	Tories freeze rail fares as Labour edges ahead	Clegg lashes out at 'swivel-eyed' Tories	Political uncertainty hits markets as sterling signals volatility ahead
11 April	(The diamond geezers)	(Free £2 bet)	Kids Web porn axe [Tories to protect under-18 Web users]	(Camilla shouldn't be queen say public)	(£260m bet frenzy)	(Death of the credit card perk)	Tories pledge extra £8bn a year for NHS	Midwife for every new mother, says Miliband	Tories switch to campaign pan B	(GE returns to its industrial roots)

Date	*Daily Mirror*	*Daily Express*	*The Sun*	*Daily Mail*	*Daily Star*	*Daily Telegraph*	*The Guardian*	*The Times*	*The Independent*	*Financial Times*
13 April	My pledge [by Ed Miliband]	(Simple way to beat back pain)	No Ed for business: Miliband slated in letter from 100 small traders	(Show passport to use the NHS)	(Brit bake off starts now)	Labour plea to voters: the economy is safe with us	Labour's big promise: no extra spending	Passionate Cameron outlines his Tory dream	'Economic credibility' at the heart of Labour's manifesto	(Shareholder payouts set to top $1tn as US group rein in capex)
14 April	Nurses don't have time to feed sick	Maggie's 'Right to buy' dream is back	(Balloony)	Right to buy: a new revolution	(Big Bro fix new series with secret cast)	We are the true party of working people	('End subsidy on fossil fuels now')	Right to buy for 1.3m families	Cameron banks on Thatcher's legacy	Cameron builds on Right to Buy in effort to regain edge from Miliband
15 April	(Take Top Gear job and we'll kill you)	(Drug to beat Alzheimer's)	Happy ever grafter: Cam boost for workers	Housing Fat Cats' hypocrisy	(Cowell: Rita's got the seX factor)	Return of the good life	Clegg: we will not sell out in coalition talks	Brussels vows to block Cameron on EU treaty	(Alzheimer's breakthrough gives new hope to millions)	(Brussels to charge Google with abusing its market dominance)
16 April	Cam's bribes will cost every family £1,439 a year	(Gardening key to longer life)	We DO have two kitchens... nanny uses the one downstairs [Miliband]	Labour's queen of hypocrisy [Emily Thornberry]	(Magaluf hols kids given free hippy crack)	(Scramble for houses as market shrinks)	('No accident': stadium fire that killed 56)	(Law chief drops child abuse case against peer)	(One thousand troops stricken by MoD's anti-malaria drug)	IMF dismisses prospect of Britain balancing the books this decade

Date	*Daily Mirror*	*Daily Express*	*The Sun*	*Daily Mail*	*Daily Star*	*Daily Telegraph*	*The Guardian*	*The Times*	*The Independent*	*Financial Times*
17 April	Tories too right wing to win	Why I'm giving £1.3m to UKIP	(The safe house bigamist)	Migrant on way to UK rapes and kills girl, 9	(Masterchef babes get their baps out to win)	Sturgeon offer to Miliband: I'll make you MP	Call for new Bradford fire inquiry	Join me or you'll pay, Sturgeon tells Labour	(Justice denied)	(Goldman and Citi signal end to long malaise on Wall Street)
18 April	(Daddy became mummy and now I love her even more)	(Judge backs Muslim veil)	(Crown Persecution Service)	(Best fixed rate mortgage ever)	(BGT in boyband 'fix')	Gove rules out UKIP deal	Tories are 'panic–stricken' says top Miliband adviser	Revealed: Miliband's plan for power in Downing Street	One million Britons using food banks	(HSBC hastens global retreat with pullback from emerging markets)
20 April	Your country needs you … to vote [for Labour]	(Elderly dumped in care factories)	(Mind benders)	(Greed of the NHS fat cats)	(Zayn dumps Perrie to rejoin 1D mates)	SNP's ransom note to Miliband	(Hundreds feared dead as migrant vessel capsizes)	We will hold UK defence to ransom, SNP warns	(The EU's darkest day)	(Deutsche Bank prepares spin-off for Postbank in strategic rethink)
21 April	(Too many vitamins can give you cancer)	(Vitamin pill health alert)	Slave Labour	(Cosy tax deals of the NHS fat cats)	(Cowell & 11m fans tricked by £10 magic kit)	A dose of political blackmail	PM's Sturgeon tactics put UK at risk, says Tory peer	Major warns of SNP coup	(A plea to Europe: stop this tide of death)	Fresh economy alert raises fears for long-term growth prospects
22 April	Thicky Wiki [Tory Co-Chairman accused of altering websites]	(Drug reverses Alzheimer's)	(Deadly diet pills a click away)	Union's sinister hold over Labour	(Shocking 2,000 Brits fighting for ISIS)	(Briton held over £500bn Wall Street 'Flash crash')	Shapps accused of secret slurs against top Tories	(Law chief faces new onslaught over Janner)	(Home Office told to bring back child it deported to Nigeria)	(British futures trader charged by US prosecutors over 'flash crash')

Date	*Daily Mirror*	*Daily Express*	*The Sun*	*Daily Mail*	*Daily Star*	*Daily Telegraph*	*The Guardian*	*The Times*	*The Independent*	*Financial Times*
23 April	(Teddy… youngest organ donor ever)	(EU will force up mortgages)	(Number 9… It's time for a line)	Voters tell Cameron to act on migration	(Missing Claudia: three men held)	Miliband SNP pact would cost families £350 each	(EU emergency summit will offer safe-haven to only 5,000 refugees)	Boris eyes the top prize	The Green betrayal	('Flash crash' charges spark alarm over weaknesses of US markets)
24 April	(Sign up for Teddy)	(Pension shock for millions)	(Skin up all night)	Miliband will bring back uncontrolled migration	(Top Gear is back)	Labour minister attacks Miliband	PM's gamble on English tax	Labour's £1,000 tax on families	(EU vows to capture and destroy trafficker boats)	Business jitters at Tory tactics as Cameron bets on the ground war
25 April	(To have and to old)	(Mushroom cure for arthritis)	(Crony prosecutor: DPP worked at same firm as paedo rap Lord she let off	(Janner: the stench grows)	(1D Louis is smoking hot!)	Farage: truth about my health	('Spoof trader' now linked to City elite)	Sturgeon: I will use influence on Labour	Miliband is winning the waverers, says Ashcroft	(Hong Kong's welcome adds force to HSBC threat to quit Britain)
27 April	Put your house on Ed	(Race to rescue quake Britons)	(Race to save 7 Everest Brits)	(Over 75? Sign here if you're ready for death)	(70 Brits dead in quake horror)	'Businesses like ours have helped create 1,000 jobs a day since 2010'	(Grief and fear amid the ruin)	Labour's sweetener to help buy first home: relief from stamp duty is worth up to £5,000	('Please pray for us')	Miliband to woo first-time buyers with pledge to scrap stamp duty
28 April	Tory MP: make people wait longer at A&E	(Diabetes: new breakthrough)	White Van Dan: Cam's my man	Miliband the landgrabber	(Amanda Holden sister trapped in quake hell)	(Switching to organic milk can harm an unborn baby)	Bank's Libor fine will be used for apprenticeships says PM	Cameron: ten days to save the Union	Fear of SNP alliance dents Labour support	(Varoufakis sidelined as Greece shakes up bailout talks team)

Date	Daily Mirror	Daily Express	The Sun	Daily Mail	Daily Star	Daily Telegraph	The Guardian	The Times	The Independent	Financial Times
29 April	(McCanns win £358k payout from cop)	Freeze on VAT and income tax	Monster raving Labour Party: 'Mockney' Miliband cosies up with Brand	(Ministers' shame on killer salt)	Red Ed & Brand talk total ballots	Cameron's pledge: no tax rises for five years	Miliband's tactical gamble	Labour chief given £1.5m shares from tax haven	(Nepal death toll hits 5,000 as survivor's freeze in Himalayas)	Cameron in election pledge to ban tax rises in life of next parliament
30 April	(Cocaine found in Kate's hospital toilet)	(Why we are all living longer)	It's a Tory!	40% of voters still can't decide	(Pop gear)	Miliband heads for wipeout in Scotland	Revealed: Tory plan to slash £8bn benefits	Lib Dems to revolt over fresh pact with Tories	(Revealed: London's secret exodus of the poor)	(Fed concedes US recovery has lost momentum)
1 May	Betrayal of our school kids	(Alzheimer's: drug can defeat it)	(I'm eating myself to death)	The night real voters finally had their say	Russell Brand: I want to be PM!	Miliband stumbles over his spending record	Miliband hardens his line: I will not deal with the SNP	Miliband savaged for 'lies' over spending	Miliband: I will not deal with SNP to become PM	(US tech faces wider probe as EU eyes tighter web regulation)
2 May	(24-stone primary school boy)	£1,000 pension boost for all	(Carla quits Corrie)	(For sale: your crash details)	(Amanda faces BGT axe in 'bully' row)	Revealed: what life would look like under the SNP	Values – not the SNP – are key, says Miliband	(Power to the people in energy revolution)	(Thousands of police investigated for brutality)	Sterling suffers sell-off as tight campaign climax strains nerves

Date	*Daily Mirror*	*Daily Express*	*The Sun*	*Daily Mail*	*Daily Star*	*Daily Telegraph*	*The Guardian*	*The Times*	*The Independent*	*Financial Times*
4 May	(Harry: my niece is a real beauty)	(Diabetes bill rockets to £10bn a year)	(Corrie Craig: I quit too)	(And now for my audience with the Queen!)	(Mum's the word for new princess)	The 100,000 voters who could win Tories power	Clarke: chaos of second vote will fix nothing	Win right to govern, Miliband is warned	Tory election chief's firm aimed to expand private healthcare	Cameron and Clegg prepared to move quickly to form coalition
5 May	Ed: nurses face axe at 66% of hospitals	(In honour of Charles, Diana and the Queen)	(Charlie and Di)	(For the mother he lost)	(Lottes of Love)	A vote for UKIP 'is a suicide note for Britain'	Miliband's warning – NHS faces financial bombshell	Miliband asks unions to save his No 10 bid	Sixty percent want voting reform	(China's migrant miracle grinds to halt as rural labour supply runs dry)
6 May	Major fail [former PM on the state of Britain]	Why you must vote for UKIP	Save our bacon: don't swallow his porkies and keep him OUT	(The doctor will see you in a month!)	(Brits live sex show on Magaluf booze cruise)	Nightmare on Downing Street	Revealed: hit list of welfare cuts facing next chancellor	Miliband trying to con way into No 10, says PM	Post-election 'shambles' looms as legitimacy crisis worsens	Party leaders scramble to line up durable coalition deals
7 May	Send 'em packing [Cameron and Osborne from Downing St]	Vote to keep Britain great	Well hung: make sure YOU vote today to stop Labour ballsing up Britain	(Gagging of mother forced to hand baby to gay dad)	Never mind the ballots... here's the party, party. Sex up the election and get Pist-oled	Don't do something you'll regret	It couldn't be closer	Queen to take control of election aftermath	Over to you	(Oil price jump quickens sell-off in international debt markets)

newspapers and cumulatively helped create a narrative that the race was too close to call. Dedicated analysis was provided by polling experts YouGov President Peter Kellner for *The Times*, Alberto Nardelli of *The Guardian* and Professor John Curtice writing in *The Independent*.

When citing polling in campaign reports, newspapers tended to give particular prominence to those surveys supporting their favoured election outcome. So, for example, the *Daily Mirror* keenly reported an apparent 'surge' of support of 4% for Labour during the campaign ('Ed's Up Again', 10 April). Conversely, a Tory-leaning newspaper appeared to revel in publishing a 'leaked' survey report on the Thanet South constituency indicating that the UKIP leader was unlikely to become its MP ('Farage Buries "Loser" Poll', *Mail on Sunday*, 5 April). Polling was noticeably integral to newspaper analysis of the televised debate between the seven leaders. Survey figures were selectively used to frame perceptions of the rival candidates' performances. In a report entitled 'Oops! I Just Lost My Election', *The Sun* suggested that Miliband had failed as the 'PM Comes Out Fighting' (3 April). The 'quality' press were not averse to making selective interpretations, albeit with greater subtlety. Whereas a front-page report in *The Guardian* suggested 'Labour Buoyed as Miliband Edges Cameron in Snap Poll', the same day's *Daily Telegraph* declared 'Miliband Flops as Outsiders Shine' (3 April).

Table 12.4 Top 10 campaign issues in the press

Rank	*Press*	%
1	Election process*	44.5
2	Economy	10.5
3	Taxation	6.5
4	Standards	3.8
5	Constitutional	3.7
6	NHS	3.7
7	Immigration/race	3.5
8	Europe	3.4
9	Employment	2.9
10	Business	2.6

Source: Loughborough Communication Research Centre[18]

*('Televised leadership events'=3.6%; 'Hung parliament – prospect and implications'=6.1%; 'Opinion polls'=4%'; 'Public engagement with the election'=3.7%; 'Party strategies and tactics'=16.7%; 'Other election process'=10.4%)

The perceived closeness of the election race as reported in successive newspaper polls created a widespread expectation of another hung parliament. Successive reports reinforced this view, with Peter Kellner confidently predicting that 'there will be a second election before the end of 2015' (*The Times*, 22 April). Similarly, fellow *The Times* contributor Sam Coates forecast that 'the next government will teeter on the edge every night. Political journalists will be taking camp beds to work' (16 April). Some questioned the prevailing consensus and the polling on which it was based. Reflecting on a 1992 Conservative victory that had not been anticipated by the preceding polls, John Rentoul suggested that 'Cameron's best hope is the return of the "shy Tories"' (*Independent on Sunday*, 12 April). Rachel Sylvester also cautioned that Likud's surprising triumph in the recent Israeli election was an example of how voter surveys do not necessarily accurately predict outcomes ('Labour and Tories Turn Up the Fear Factor', *The Times*, 28 April).

David Cameron was in his tenth year as party leader and fifth as Prime Minister, so was already reasonably well known to a voting public, who, by the time of the general election, were likely to have formed an opinion of him. For media detractors such as Kevin Maguire, 'cynical' Cameron was 'the posh boy who vowed to mend what he called a Broken Britain' (*Daily Mirror*, 30 March). The Prime Minister appeared keen to counter such criticisms through favourable press coverage. On one occasion, when he was supposedly having a 'day off' campaigning, he was photographed bottle-feeding a small farm animal and the image widely disseminated by various newspapers ('"Lamb Cam!" PM with Lamb', *Daily Mail*, 6 April). An informal-looking Cameron was also interviewed alongside colleague, friend and potential successor George Osborne ('The Blue Brothers', *The Sun*, 1 April). Following on from her high-profile role during the last campaign, Samantha Cameron made prominent appearances in newspapers most sympathetic to the Conservatives. *The Sun* published a two-page spread in which the Prime Minister's wife talked about their late son ('SAM CAM.I.AM', 6 April). The impact of caring for their disabled child informed the headlines of her interviews with both the *Daily Mail* and the *Daily Telegraph* in which family photographs of the couple's children were used to illustrate the features ('Dave and Sam: Our Crisis over Ivan', *Daily Mail*, 6 April; 'The Strain of Caring for Ivan Took Dave and Me to the Limit', *Daily Telegraph*, 6 April).

It was noteworthy how much less human interest coverage the Liberal Democrat leader and his family received compared with the 'Cleggmania' of the last election. *The Independent* featured one of the few interviews with the Deputy Prime Minister's wife, albeit an encounter that focused more on her work as a food writer than as a political spouse (22 April).

Understandably, there was greater scrutiny of the Labour leader and his family. In response to this, and possibly Mrs Cameron's intervention, Justine Miliband featured in her own sympathetic interview with the *Daily Mirror*, in which she talked about her family life and how she had got to know her husband: 'Ed Bandaged Me Up after I was Bitten by a Doberman and I Fell in Love' (9 April). The seeming conventionality of Ed Miliband was, however, challenged the following day. In 'Red Ed's Very Tangled Love Life', *Daily Mail* columnist Andrew Pierce suggested that Miliband had been romantically involved with four members of an 'incestuous, privileged clique' comprising well-connected women in journalism and politics (10 April). Rather than harming the Labour leader, the article in some ways flattered him. But even sympathetic print journalists acknowledged that Miliband had an image problem and still had some way to go before overcoming it. So when he replied 'hell, yes!' in response to Jeremy Paxman's question as to whether he was 'tough enough' to be Prime Minister (see p. 161), Kevin Maguire compared his reaction to that of comedic character and personification of naff Alan Partridge (*Daily Mirror*, 30 March). Later in the campaign, John Rentoul speculated as to whether Miliband might have peaked too soon, having managed to change the 'narrative' about him in his favour (*Independent on Sunday*, 26 April).

The Labour leader's vulnerability was symbolically highlighted when he stumbled on stage during the BBC *Question Time Leaders' Special*, the last major televised broadcast of the campaign. But it was his deployment of the so-called 'Ed Stone', a huge tablet carved with six key pledges, in the final week of the campaign that attracted most disdain (see pp. 194–5). Labour sympathising *The Times* columnist Philip Collins dismissed the photo opportunity as the 'most risible political stunt' (5 May). The *Daily Telegraph* likened the incident to the '"Kinnock" gaffe moment', a poignant reference to the rally shortly before his 1992 defeat in which Miliband's mentor had appeared to prematurely celebrate, and thereby undermine, his party's chances of victory (4 May). Other critics ridiculed the Labour leader for agreeing to be interviewed by celebrity activist Russell Brand for his online news service 'The Trews'. The *Daily Star*, like David Cameron, dismissed the encounter as a joke, while *The Times* suggested that 'Ed's Attempt at Brand Awareness Backfires' ('Red Ed & Brand Talk Total Ballots', *Daily Star*, 29 April; *The Times*, 29 April). Brand was also heavily criticised, with one former partner calling him 'a misogynist' (*Mail on Sunday*, 3 May). Predictably it was *The Guardian* which took the opposing view, suggesting Miliband's attempt to cultivate younger voters was a 'tactical gamble' that columnist Owen Jones believed might work (29 April).

If Russell Brand became a late convert to Ed Miliband's cause, other celebrities proved far more willing. High-profile endorsements by famous supporters have sometimes been dismissed as an irrelevance, but the *Daily Star*, the least political of newspapers, might not have reported on a Labour rally but for the presence of comedian Eddie Izzard, chef Delia Smith and a range of other familiar faces (5 May). Famous Conservatives like Andrew Lloyd-Webber also made electoral interventions, warning *Mail on Sunday* readers 'don't sleepwalk to disaster' in an article accompanied with a mock-up of Sturgeon and Miliband as characters from the composer's *Phantom of the Opera* musical (26 April). Reality television celebrity Amy Childs from ITV2 programme *The Only Way Is Essex* made a front-page denunciation of 'scroungers' before later reappearing in *The Sun* with a blue rosette to endorse Cameron (6 April). Actor Tom Conti, a self-confessed 'life-long Labour luvvie', confirmed he had switched allegiance to the Tories in an article for the *Daily Mail* (6 May). Performers also featured in Labour Party election broadcasts, the first of which was introduced by the actor Martin Freeman. Freeman was subsequently dismissed as 'Red Ed's celebrity phony' by the *Daily Mail* for having schooled his children privately and having not paid his partner's outstanding tax bill despite reportedly being a multi-millionaire (1 April).

Follow the money

The economy was the major substantive policy issue in terms of newspaper reporting of the election (Table 12.4). Much of this coverage was filtered through the prism of the title's editorial standpoint and here a reinvigorated 'Tory press' really came into its own.[19] The most prominent example of an agenda-setting story was the *Daily Telegraph*'s publication of the letter signed by corporate executives: '100 Business Chiefs: Labour Threatens Britain's Recovery' (1 April). A feature in the following day's *The Times* reinforced this message: 'Labour has alarmed businesses with its attitude to lower taxes and a flexible labour market. These are vital to a strong economy' (2 April). *The Sun* promoted similar concerns in a feature, '120 Execs Come Out Backing Tories', focusing on criticisms of Miliband's proposed ban on zero-hours contracts (2 April). Employment had previously featured in 'We're Just the Job', which pointedly applauded the 1.9 million 'jobs created in the last 5 years under (the) Tories' rather than the Coalition (*The Sun*, 31 March). *The*

Sun also published its own list of 100 small businesspeople supporting the Conservatives, including some former Labour voters who were quoted in the piece ('Shop Keepers of the World Unite', 13 April). Two weeks later, Baroness Karren Brady exceeded this effort by a considerable margin when she revealed the names of 5,000 self-employed workers who were going to vote Tory (*Daily Telegraph*, 27 April).

In a guest *Sunday Telegraph* column, David Cameron set out his key campaign theme: 'We've Saved the Economy from Ruin: Don't Let Miliband Spoil it' (26 April). Cameron's view was echoed by a range of sympathetic commentators, most notably in *The Times*, which ran an editorial, 'Clear Cut', claiming that the government's austerity was both successful and a necessity (1 April). The newspaper also made several pointed references to the Labour leader ('Miliband Would Send Britain £90Bn Further into the Red', 24 April; 'Miliband is Bad for Business, Warn FTSE Executives' and 'Miliband Savaged for "Lies" over Spending', both 1 May) and his allegedly flawed budgetary plans ('Labour Manifesto Leaves Voters Clueless on Cuts, Experts Claim', 14 April). Other print media commentators were more circumspect in their economic analysis. *The Observer* challenged the rival campaigners to be more candid and provide fuller details as to their budgetary plans ('Politicians, Be Honest about Britain's Finances', editorial, 26 April). Writing in the *Financial Times*, the influential journalist Martin Wolf questioned prevailing orthodoxy when he argued that 'economics is the loser in this political contest'. Wolf further suggested that neither of the main parties was 'competent' and that they both lacked a 'healthy scepticism' towards the financial services industry and over the state of the housing market, two factors he believed had helped to cause the 2008 crisis (6 May).

Closely linked to economics, taxation also featured prominently in newspaper reporting of the campaign. Following George Osborne's announcement that he was raising the inheritance threshold, the *Daily Express* welcomed the move against what it called the 'hated death tax' (13 April). The *Mail on Sunday* was similarly effusive, applauding the measure in an interview featuring the Chancellor ('Cheers! George, £1million Tax Gift', 12 April). Osborne, a possible successor to Cameron, featured prominently in 'St George's Pay', a story in *The Sun* with a mock-up of him as the nation's patron saint and the declaration that 'he vows lowers tax for English workers' (24 April). In sharp contrast, the paper had earlier warned of the '£3,028 Cost of Voting Ed' from additional taxes that would be levied on households in the event of a Miliband victory (28 March).

The *Daily Mirror* articulated the Labour case on tax and associated credits, claiming '4.3M families could lose out on £1,000-a-year child benefit' under proposals drawn up by the Conservatives (8 April). Similarly, its Sunday sister reported: 'Osborne Plans Top Rate Tax Cut as Rest of Us Struggle' (*Sunday Mirror*, 5 April). The *Mirror* titles also gave prominence to another supposed instance of Tory favouritism towards the rich when it criticised the party's failure to act over the status of so-called 'non-dom' citizens while simultaneously welcoming Labour's plans to 'home in on tax avoiders' ('Non-Doms Doomsday', *Daily Mirror*, 8 April). The paper further alleged that the Prime Minister's late father had been a high-profile beneficiary of allegedly dubious financial arrangements ('Cam's Dad Dodged Tax', 1 May). Although *The Times* dismissed Labour's 'non-dom' policy as counterproductive 'Tax Twaddle' (9 April), Jonathan Guthrie of the *Financial Times* pointedly disagreed, questioning whether it was credible to defend the status quo (8 April). But ultimately Miliband and his strategists must have felt impotent in trying to rebut the Conservatives' single-minded economic argument while simultaneously trying to articulate their own courtesy of a largely hostile print media.

The constitution and other issues

The Coalition's promotion of austerity measures guaranteed that the economy and taxation would feature prominently in the campaign. Similarly, the 2014 Scottish independence referendum transformed the electoral landscape, and not just north of the border, ensuring that the future of the Union would also be a major campaign issue (see Table 12.4). The SNP's subsequent rise in the polls led to widespread speculation that it would play a decisive role in a hung parliament. Following Nicola Sturgeon's confirmation that she would never support the Conservatives in such a scenario, several newspapers speculated on what the *Financial Times* called the 'wish list' the First Minister was likely to present Miliband as the price of power (21 April). An editorial in *The Times* presented 'The SNP Challenge' as a 'dangerous trap' for Labour (17 April) before returning to the subject in a front-page story days later ('We Will Hold UK Defence to Ransom, SNP Warns', 20 April). For Janet Daley, the prospect of a pact between the Nationalists and Labour 'would be an outrage to democracy' (*Sunday Telegraph*, 26 April). Daley's colleagues on the daily sister paper believed it would precipitate a 'Nightmare in Downing Street' (*Daily Telegraph*, 6 May). Underlying such a view was the contention, articulated by Robert Hardiman among others, that SNP politicians were 'bungling, neurotic far-Left dinosaurs who'll wreck their booming economy' (*Daily Mail*, 18 April).

The press rhetoric attacking the SNP became highly personalised and aimed on Nicola Sturgeon following her well-received performance in the seven-way leader debate. In a hyperbolic front-page *Daily Mail* story on the 'Queens of Scots', Sturgeon was, as has been previously noted, labelled the 'Most Dangerous Woman in Britain' (4 April). A similar *Sunday Express* story even suggested there was a 'cult' around the First Minister (5 April). In sharp contrast to her sympathetic portrayal in its Scottish edition, the English version of *The Sun* profiled Sturgeon as 'The Scotweiler', a reference to her supposed ruthlessness that extended back to childhood when the paper claimed she had cut the hair off her sister's doll. The same feature also likened the SNP leader to the diminutive 1980s comedy character Jimmy Krankie (*The Sun*, 25 April). More cerebral commentators like Jonathan Freedland questioned whether this kind of coverage might further alienate the Scots and hasten the end of the Union (*The Guardian*, 25 April). *The Guardian* followed this up with a piece by Democratic Unionist Party leader Nigel Dodds, who warned that political expediency, in the guise of the fierce rhetoric being directed at the SNP, threatened to undermine the integrity of the UK (*The Guardian*, 27 April).

Integrity of a different kind had been a major theme in coverage of the last general election following the MPs' expenses scandal. This time around, politicians' standard of conduct was an issue, but press reports on the subject included a more varied range of alleged misdemeanours. Certain UKIP activists were, for instance, identified as having been involved in far-right groups such as the English Defence League and the National Front ('Manifestoads', *Daily Mirror*, 16 April; *Mail on Sunday*, 3 May). But most of this kind of coverage focused on the perceived flaws of leading politicians. Prior to the campaign, *Daily Mail* columnist Sarah Vine had criticised the 'bland, functional, humourless, cold' character of a utility room she had wrongly believed – following a television profile – to be the Labour leader's family kitchen.[20] Although this assumption was soon corrected, *The Sun* revisited the controversy by accusing Miliband of being an elitist hypocrite. In a front-page piece, the paper depicted the politician as an aristocratic character from popular period drama *Downton Abbey*: 'We DO Have Two Kitchens... Nanny Uses the One Downstairs' (*The Sun*, 16 April). Toby Young, guest columnist on the paper's Sunday sister, had earlier suggested that 'Ed has two faces' in a wide-ranging critique that also attacked the 'hypocrisy' of the prospective Prime Minister and questioned his fitness to govern (*Sun on Sunday*, 12 April). Young also criticised Miliband for having, in his view, betrayed his brother David to win the party leadership. 'Bozfather' Boris Johnson reiterated this point in an interview with the paper: 'Ed stabbed his own brother in the back ... family don't do that' (*Sun on Sunday*, 26 April). The interview with Johnson was illustrated with a photograph from classic film *The Godfather* of the eponymous character and the errant brother he murdered.

The charge of hypocrisy was levelled at Labour politicians other than Miliband. Shadow Chancellor Ed Balls' alleged failure to pay a window installer was highlighted by the *Mail on Sunday* in an attempt to question his financial probity ('Exposed: Balls the Cheque Bouncer', 3 May). The payment of £4 an hour by another prospective minister, Toby Perkins, to campaign interns (a level well below the minimum wage) led to a front-page denunciation in *The Sun* of 'Slave Labour' (21 April). Conservative candidates also found themselves accused of impropriety, with Sir Paul Beresford challenged by the *Daily Mirror* over why he was reportedly 'filling his boots' through spending the campaign working at his dental practice rather than meeting constituents (2 May). More embarrassing were the same paper's front-page allegations of online misconduct levelled against Tory Co-Chairman Grant Shapps ('Thicky Wiki', 22 April). The charge that Shapps had doctored Wikipedia entries for senior party colleagues was challenged by a *Daily Telegraph* report that claimed his accuser was a politically motivated 'Lib Dem activist' (*Daily Telegraph*, 23 April). The Tory (press) ability to refute accusations of impropriety had been earlier demonstrated by the swift rebuttal, via *The Times*, of a potentially damaging claim by Danny Alexander (which had made the *Independent* front page) that a then Conservative colleague had told him 'we're for the bosses, you're for the workers' when both were members of the Cabinet (*The Independent*, 6 April; *The Times*, 7 April).

Labour focused on the NHS as a major theme of their campaign. Perhaps partly because of this, the issue did not rank higher up the print media agenda (Table 12.3). George Osborne chose *The Guardian* to write a report on his intention to provide an extra £8 billion in health funding a year (11 April). But more often it was Labour-inclined newspapers that tried to move the debate onto the future of the NHS. Emulating an approach deployed by rival titles, *The Guardian* published a letter to the paper from 100 eminent clinicians in an attempt to highlight concerns over the future of the health service ('Senior Doctors Assess the Government's Record on the NHS', 8 April). The *Daily Mirror* also ran a series of stories alleging the Conservatives had broken promises on GP recruitment ('Dr No', 7 April) and a warning from Labour-supporting celebrity chef Delia Smith that the health service could not go on being 'treated like a supermarket' (4 May). The last *Sunday Mirror* before polling day featured Ed Miliband warning of a 'Tory plague' and alerting readers to the 1,000 reasons not to trust the Conservatives on health. Miliband advised readers that there were '100 Hours to Save the NHS' by voting Labour (3 May).

If health was the key issue for Labour, immigration had long been a prominent theme for UKIP campaigners. And although it did not formally endorse Nigel Farage, the *Daily Star* ran several prominent stories on the topic, despite consciously devoting less attention to the election than any of its rivals. The paper approvingly reported comments by a Polish-born party candidate that 'immigration is great – but Britain is too overcrowded' ('UKIP Dead Right on Says Pole', 4 May). Farage was also quoted attacking Labour for 'betraying working-class voters' through siding with 'multinational corporations which benefit from mass immigration while damaging small firms and local communities' (20 April). The *Daily Star* itself took to criticising the Conservatives with a blunt message: 'Get Tougher on Migrants, Dave' (24 April). The same feature cited an Ipsos MORI poll to argue that 'voters want the Tories to be far tougher on mass immigration'. Perhaps anticipating this kind of critique, David Cameron offered a personal response in a rival newspaper the same day ('Why You Can Only Trust the Tories on Migration', *Daily Mail*, 24 April). But overall the issue did not register on the election agenda as it had done in previous campaigns. This was despite an ongoing crisis in the Mediterranean involving displaced people fleeing Libya and incendiary comments by *The Sun* columnist Katie Hopkins that likened them to 'cockroaches' ('Rescue Boats? I'd Use Gunships to Stop Migrants', *The Sun*, 17 April).

Voting by newspaper

People tend to buy newspapers that conform with and confirm their own views. The most obvious examples are the high proportions of Labour and Conservative voters reading the *Daily Mirror* and the *Daily Telegraph* respectively. Table 12.5 provides Ipsos MORI data on the voting patterns of these and other titles' readers in the 2015 general election along with the corresponding figures for 2010. It is noteworthy that, for the most part, levels of support for the major two parties are broadly consistent for each newspaper across the two elections. By contrast, there were dramatic falls in backing for the Liberal Democrats among readers of both the popular and quality titles, reflecting the decline in the party's fortunes since the 2010 election.[21] It is equally striking how support for UKIP has grown among newspapers readers. Those buying popular titles were noticeably more likely to vote for Farage's party than the public as a whole. This may reflect the ageing profile and other demographic factors associated with the audiences in question. It should obviously not be assumed that these former Liberal Democrat supporters have simply defected to UKIP; rather, there has been a considerable amount of churn whereby readers have abandoned the Liberal Democrats for other parties, which in turn have lost support to UKIP.

Table 12.5 Voting by newspaper readership (equivalent figures for 2010 in brackets)

	Party/Vote % (2010 figure in brackets)						
	Cons	*Labour*	*Lib Dem*	*UKIP*	*SNP*	*Green*	*Other*
Mirror	14 (16)	62 (59)	2 (17)	19 (–)	1 (–)	1 (–)	1 (8)
Express	44 (53)	16 (19)	4 (18)	33 (–)	1 (–)	1 (–)	1 (10)
Sun	39 (43)	27 (28)	3 (18)	23 (–)	6 (–)	1 (–)	2 (10)
Mail	57 (59)	16 (16)	6 (16)	18 (–)	2 (–)	1 (–)	1 (10)
Telegraph	72 (70)	8 (7)	5 (18)	11 (–)	1 (–)	1 (–)	1 (5)
Guardian	16 (9)	50 (46)	13 (37)	2 (–)	7 (–)	10 (–)	2 (8)
Times	60 (49)	17 (22)	11 (24)	6 (–)	3 (–)	2 (–)	3 (5)
Independent	17 (14)	47 (32)	16 (44)	4 (–)	3 (–)	11 (–)	1 (10)
Election	37 (36)	30 (29)	8 (23)	13 (3)	5 (2)	4 (1)	3 (6)

Source: Ipsos MORI[22]

The voting figures for readership confirm a longer-term trend, specifically that there have always been significant minorities who have not supported their newspaper's electoral choice. More than a quarter of *The Sun* readers voted Labour, roughly the same proportion as had in 2010. But 2015 has seen marked growth in support and publicity for other parties, and this fragmentation partly explains some of the striking disparities between the voters' partisan choices and the editorial stances of their favoured newspapers. For example, around one-fifth of *The Sun* and *Daily Mirror* readers voted for UKIP, thereby disregarding the very strong preference of their newspapers, which are well known for being, respectively, antagonistic and sympathetic towards the European Union. Similarly, UKIP's endorsement by the *Express* still resulted in the Conservatives securing a greater level of support among the paper's readers than Nigel Farage's party. Evidence of independent thinking on the part of readers is not surprising: people buy newspapers for many reasons and their decision as to how to vote is the product of a complex set of interacting factors. Some commentators believe that the print media were influential in 2015 because of the more stridently partisan coverage discussed earlier in the chapter.[23] But whether or not this was the case, the actions of both the politicians and editors suggest that they at least share a belief in the opinion-forming power of the traditional press.

Conclusion

The campaign witnessed the return to the kind of robust press partisanship not seen since 1992, when *The Sun* (in)famously published a highly negative front-page denunciation of the then Labour leader Neil Kinnock. The paper repeated this in 2015 with another eve-of-poll attempt to demolish the credibility of the opposition. And it was this and other similarly polemical editorialising that led former *Sunday Times*-turned-BBC broadcaster Andrew Neil to describe the 'British press at (its) partisan worst' and lament the end of 'all pretence of separation between news and opinion gone'.[24] This was evident in so-called 'quality' as well as 'popular' titles, with the *Daily Telegraph* and *The Guardian* joining the *The Sun* and the *Daily Mirror* in their attempts to frame events in ways that reinforced their favoured party's interpretations. Much newspaper reporting of the campaign was therefore coloured by editorial judgement: readers solely reliant on their newspaper for coverage would have received a highly partial, selective account of the election. And although press circulations were down by a third compared to 2010, the sales of printed copies ensured that this most traditional news medium still reached millions of voters. These readers will have included many who buy their paper for largely non-political reasons, but who will nonetheless have been exposed to stridently partisan news and views during the campaign.

It is noteworthy that UKIP, the party experiencing the most significant rise in its electoral support, did even better among newspaper readers than the public as a whole. This was despite the party only having the formal endorsement of the *Daily* and *Sunday Express*. These are two of the newspapers that traditionally appeal most to older readers, who in turn are more likely to vote (and also support UKIP) than younger people. More broadly, whether or not these and other titles have influenced their consumers' partisan preferences remains a contentious issue. It has been notoriously difficult to isolate the significance of media effects in previous campaigns when sales of printed newspapers were much higher than now. In the 2015 election, it would seem the most plausible interpretation of the influence of the anti-Labour coverage is that it might have marginally improved the Conservatives' position while more significantly boosting the UKIP campaign. This seems paradoxical given the imbalance in these parties' respective editorial endorsements. But the multitude of newspaper stories that were hostile to Labour and its SNP 'allies' might have been as potentially beneficial to the UKIP as the Conservative cause. *The Sun* and other members of the 'Tory press' may have formally campaigned for a Cameron victory in 2015, but they simultaneously promoted an ideological agenda on the economy, Europe and immigration that also favoured electoral rival Nigel Farage.

Notes

1. Alastair Campbell, 'Newspaper Election Coverage is Beyond Parody', www.theguardian.com/uk, 7 May 2015. Unless otherwise stated, all newspaper references in the chapter are to printed, hard-copy versions of the item.
2. Steven Barnett, 'Four Reasons Why a Partisan Press Helped Win it for the Tories', in Dan Jackson and Einar Thorsen (eds), *UK Election Analysis 2015: Media, Voters and the Campaign*. Bournemouth University Centre of the Study of Journalism, Culture and Community, 2015. See also Dominic Wring and Stephen Ward, 'Exit Velocity: The Media Campaign', in Andrew Geddes and Jonathan Tonge (eds), *Britain Votes 2015*. Oxford University Press, 2015.
3. The equivalent figures for 2010 in brackets are courtesy of Dominic Wring and David Deacon, 'Patterns of Press Partisanship in the 2010 General Election', *British Politics*, 5 (2010): 436–54. When considering press partisanship, it is important to account for the choice of party a given newspaper chooses to support, but also the strength of that endorsement. The key piece of information to determine this is the editorial declaration. Traditionally this used to be published on polling day itself, but now increasingly appears in the days and even the week before. Although the statement is, by definition, limited in terms of both time and space, it is nonetheless of significance. The editorial declaration conveys a viewpoint that normally reflects the newspaper's political outlook as expressed in the preceding campaign. It is also something that the key decision-making editors, proprietors and/or journalists traditionally take very seriously.

   Close analysis of editorials provides the most accessible way of comparing newspapers with the strength (or not) of both their rivals' as well as their own previous allegiances. Thus, when sections of the so-called 'Tory press' morphed into the Blair-supporting so-called 'Tony press' during the 1990s, it became important to understand that this shift of partisan allegiance did not necessarily mean a change in the more fundamental ideological outlook of a given title. Consequently, it was important to analyse and qualify this apparent shift in support from one party to another. *The Sun*'s endorsement of Tony Blair was, for instance, more a personal vote of confidence in him than his party and was characteristically 'weak' compared to the 'strong' support given to the Margaret Thatcher-led Conservatives.

Where a newspaper endorsement has been deemed 'very strong', it reflects the one-sided nature of the editorial, which can often be more negative about the opposition than positive about the preferred party. The description 'strong' applies to a statement that contains some qualification about the paper's chosen politicians. This, however, is still a clearer signal of intent compared to the 'moderate' endorsement, a stance that delivers an identifiable judgement, but with caveats. 'Weak' statements are characteristically tentative and highly qualified. 'Very weak' endorsements state a preference, but do so in the mildest of ways. Partisanship has in the past been attributed to newspapers without these evaluations and this only provides limited insight into the nature rather than the intensity of that media support for a particular party. For more on this, see David Deacon and Dominic Wring, 'Partisan Dealignment and the British Press', in John Bartle, Ivor Crewe and Brian Gosschalk (eds), *Political Communications: The British General Election of 2001*. Frank Cass, 2002, pp. 197–211.

4. Marie Thibault (ed.), 'Why Newspapers Matter', MIT Communications Forum, October 2006.
5. Adam Sherwin and Oliver Wright, 'Murdoch Berated "Sun" Journalists for Not Doing Enough to Attack Miliband', *The Independent*, 21 April 2015.
6. Nick Davies, *Hack Attack*. Faber & Faber, 2014.
7. Sherwin and Wright, 'Murdoch Berated "Sun" Journalists'.
8. Jessica Elgot, '*The Sun* Criticised over Offer to Pay £100 to Tory Voters for "Good News" Stories', www.theguardian.com/uk, 6 May 2015.
9. Colin Seymour-Ure, *The Political Impact of the Media*. Constable, 1974.
10. '100 Business chiefs: Labour Threatens Britain's Recovery', 1 April.
11. Rajeev Syal, 'Three Business Leaders Distance Themselves from Pro-Tory Letter', www.theguardian.com/uk, 2 April.
12. Joe Murphy, 'Ed Miliband Battles with a Bacon Sandwich as He Buys Flowers for His Wife at London Market', *Evening Standard*, 21 May 2014.
13. Keith Kahn-Harris, 'Is the Sun's "Save Our Bacon" Front Page Anti-Semitic?', www.theguardian.com/uk, 6 May, 2015.
14. The *Daily Mail* had previously courted controversy in the autumn of 2013 when it published an article by Geoffrey Levy claiming Ed Miliband's academic father was 'The Man Who Hated Britain' on account of his Marxist views. The newspaper found itself having to defend its stance: 'Daily Mail's Position on Miliband Unravelling – Labour', *BBC News*, 4 October 2013.
15. Leo McKinstry, 'A Miliband Victory Would Be a Total Disaster for the UK', *Daily Express*, 4 May 2015; Stephen Pollard, 'Miliband Would Take Britain Back to the 1970s', *Daily Express*, 22 April 2015.
16. Wring and Deacon, 'Patterns of Press Partisanship in the 2010 General Election'.
17. Jon Stone, 'The Daily Telegraph's Editor Just Emailed its Subscribers Telling Them to Vote Tory', www.independent.co.uk, 7 May 2015.
18. David Deacon, John Downey, James Stanyer and Dominic Wring, 'News Media Performance in the 2015 General Election Campaign', in Jackson and Thorsen (eds), *UK Election Analysis 2015*.

19. Ivor Gaber, 'The "Tory Press" Rides Again', in Jackson and Thorsen (eds), *UK Election Analysis 2015*.
20. Sarah Vine, 'Why Their Kitchen Tells You All You Need to Know about the Mirthless Milibands... and Why There's Nothing to Suggest that Ed and Justine are Not, in Fact, Aliens', www.dailymail.co.uk, 12 March 2015.
21. Margaret Scammell and Charlie Beckett, 'Labour No More: The Press', in Dennis Kavanagh and Philip Cowley, *The British General Election of 2010*. Palgrave Macmillan, 2010.
22. Thanks to Roger Mortimore of Ipsos MORI for the figures in Table 12.5. Note: the 2010 figures for the 'other' parties include support for UKIP, SNP and the Greens.
23. See Barnett, Four Reasons Why a Partisan Press Helped Win it for the Tories'; and also Roy Greenslade, 'Yes, Rightwing Newspaper Coverage Did Cause Ed Miliband's Downfall', www.theguardian.com/uk, 11 May 2015.
24. Jack Sommers, 'General Election Front Pages Show the British Press at its "Partisan Worst", BBC's Andrew Neil Says', www.huffingtonpost.co.uk, 6 May 2015.

13
Variable Diversity: MPs and Candidates

Byron Criddle

The composition of the House of Commons elected in May 2015 was the most diverse in 100 years. Its diversity was the product of two contrasting forces: one of continuity, the other of change. The continuity lay in the further diversification of its social composition as it more closely reflected the composition of the electorate, especially in terms of gender, ethnicity and sexuality. The increased numbers of women, of ethnic minority MPs and of gay, lesbian and bisexual MPs in 2015 built upon previously record numbers in 2010.

But increased diversity was also reflected in dramatic change in the Commons' political composition with the oddly symmetrical collapse of the Liberal Democrats from 57 to 8 MPs and the dramatic upsurge of the Scottish National Party (SNP) from 6 to 56, the latter's advance constituting the arrival at Westminster of a secessionist party on a scale unknown since the election of 73 Sinn Fein candidates in 1918.

A total of 3,971 candidates contested the election, an average of 6.1 per constituency, down on 6.3 in 2010. The Conservatives contested every mainland seat apart from the Speaker's seat of Buckingham and 16 of the Northern Ireland seats, a total of 647. Labour and the Liberal Democrats contested all 631 GB seats except the Speaker's, the SNP fought all 59 Scottish seats and Plaid Cymru all 40 in Wales. UKIP fielded candidates in 624 seats (up from 558 in 2010) and the Green Party 573 (up from 335). These previously fourth- and fifth-placed parties were now outdoing the Referendum Party's spread of 547 candidates in 1997.

The new intake of MPs totalled 182 and comprised 74 Conservatives, 53 Labour, 50 SNP, 1 Plaid Cymru, 2 Ulster Unionist Party (UUP), 1 Democratic Unionist Party (DUP) and 1 Sinn Fein. The 74 new Conservatives comprised 22% of their party's MPs, close to the 23% of the Parliamentary Labour Party (PLP) formed by the 53 new Labour MPs. Five of the new MPs were 'retreads', previous MPs, either in the case of Labour's three returning in the same seat they had lost in 2010 (Dawn Butler (Brent Central), Joan Ryan (Enfield North) and Rob Marris (Wolverhampton South West)), or the Conservative Boris Johnson returning for Uxbridge and South Ruislip, having represented Henley from 2001 to 2007, and Alex Salmond of the SNP, returning for Gordon having sat for Banff and Buchan from 1987 to 2010. A further 18 former MPs sought unsuccessfully to return to the Commons.[1]

The size of new intakes varies depending on the nature of the election. At the end of an electoral cycle, where one party's long incumbency is ending, as in 1997, when the new intake of 260 represented 40% of the Commons, or in 2010, when the 232 new MPs comprised 36% of all MPs, the numbers are high, both through high levels of retirement and of seats changing hands. At elections occurring in mid-cycle and maintaining the political status quo, as in 2001, when the 123-strong intake covered 19% of the House, or in 2005, when 99 new MPs comprised 15%, the numbers are lower. The new intake of 182 in 2015, accounting for 28% of the Commons, was at the higher end of the range, and yet it was not an election where there was expectation of a dramatic change of government. The two major parties were level in terms of poll ratings in the run-up to the election and the numbers of MPs retiring were spread evenly across the parties, with 38 Conservative and 39 Labour MPs leaving the Commons. What inflated the new intake in 2015 was the dramatic SNP surge in Scotland and the heavy collapse of the Lib Dems everywhere.

Most of the retirements were attributable to age, some to personal factors other than age and a few to political difficulties. The great majority were over 60 or would soon reach that age in a new parliament. The oldest leaving was the 84-year-old Sir Peter Tapsell, who had been Father of the House since 2010 and was retiring after 49 years as a Lincolnshire MP since 1966 and, before that, in Nottingham from 1959 to 1964. His retirement removed the last MP from the 1950s. Following him from the Conservatives was a clutch of former Cabinet ministers: Andrew Lansley (58), Stephen Dorrell (62) and Sir George Young (71), along with William Hague, the former Leader and one-time boy prodigy of his party, who was leaving at the early age of 53 to write books on history.

What attracted attention on the Conservative side were nine young retirements from the 2010 intake. The Eurosceptic Chris Kelly (36) was returning to his family business and Laura Sandys (50) cited 'family demands'. But Aidan Burley was going after attracting adverse publicity for attending a Nazi-themed stag party and describing the opening ceremony of the London Olympics as 'leftie multicultural crap'. Another, Mike Weatherley, was leaving through ill-health. The retirement of the former Deputy Chief Whip Sir John Randall, who won the then hyper-marginal seat of Uxbridge in a by-election just after Labour's huge landslide win in 1997 (and whose beard inclined him to be mistaken for a Labour MP), paved the way for Boris Johnson's return.

However, three Conservative retirements were unintended: those of Tim Yeo, Anne McIntosh and Sir Malcolm Rifkind. Yeo (68) and McIntosh (60) were deselected within days of each other early in 2014.

Yeo, the Chairman of the Energy and Climate Change Select Committee, lost a local ballot of 600 members in Suffolk South. He had been criticised for having extensive business interests in companies linked to the green energy industry while chairing the relevant committee, and had been caught up in a sting by *Sunday Times* reporters and allegations that he had offered to lobby ministers and coached an associate who was due to give evidence to the Committee. Strongly denying all claims, he was cleared by the Standards Committee.

McIntosh, Chairman of the DEFRA Select Committee, who had represented Thirsk and Malton (or its predecessor seat Vale of York) since 1997, was dropped by her constituency after falling out with local personalities who alleged her insufficient support for their business concerns. Resisting the result of one ballot with the support of Conservative Campaign Headquarters (CCHQ), she lost the second in February 2014 and was rumoured to be thinking of standing as an Independent, but went quietly.

The demise of Sir Malcolm Rifkind (68), MP for Kensington, who had been the last Foreign Secretary in John Major's government and was Chairman of Parliament's Intelligence and Security Committee, in February 2015 was inglorious. He was filmed in a 'cash-for-access' sting offering consultancy services to reporters from the *Daily Telegraph* and Channel 4 posing as representatives of a bogus Chinese company. He was recorded as claiming to be self-employed, that nobody paid him a salary, that he had to earn his income and stating what his usual fee would be for half-a-day's work. He announced he would give up his seat at the Dissolution.

Of Labour's 39 retiring MPs, 33 were over 60, including two over 80, Joe Benton (born 1933 and MP for Bootle since 1990) and Austin Mitchell (born 1934 and MP for Grimsby since 1977), the former a very quiet backbencher, the latter a politically incorrect off-message performer on such subjects as the inadequacy of the beneficiaries of all-women shortlists.

A large clear-out of Labour Cabinet ministers of the Blair/Brown era (Jack Straw, David Blunkett, Alistair Darling, Frank Dobson, Peter Hain, John Denham and Paul Murphy) accompanied these two, led by former Prime Minister Gordon Brown himself. His departure meant that there was, again, no ex-Prime Minister in the Commons. Jack Straw's long political career, which began as an aide to Barbara Castle and involved four Cabinet posts in 13 years, notably as a tough law-and-order Home Secretary and, more awkwardly, as Foreign Secretary at the time of the Iraq War, was marred, like Sir Malcolm Rifkind's, by a cash-for-access sting in which he too was filmed in February 2015 talking about his influential paid consultancy work, though his decision to retire had by then already been announced. David Blunkett's departure removed a man whose remarkable long career had been in spite of major disability, and that of Shaun Woodward, the one-time Oxfordshire Tory MP married to a Sainsbury heiress, whose floor-crossing to Labour in 1999, and insertion into a safe Labour seat in St Helens and, in time, the Cabinet, had symbolised the hegemony of the Blair years.

None of Labour's retirements was political, though one, that of Eric Joyce in Falkirk, was messy and led to a serious row over the selection of a replacement candidate. A sometime squaddie risen to major in the Education Corps before becoming a Labour MP in 2000, he had been the subject of damaging press coverage of alcohol-related incidents including a brawl in a Commons bar, and court appearances, leading to his resignation from the Labour Party in 2012. He sat as an Independent for the rest of the Parliament.

Ten Lib Dem MPs retired (probably thankful after the election that they had gone before being unceremoniously pushed), again mostly on grounds of age, including the former Leader, Sir Menzies Campbell (73) and Sir Alan Beith (71), his party's longest-serving Member, having won the Berwick-on-Tweed by-election in 1973. Two Lib Dem MPs were certainly young to be retiring. Jeremy Browne, the 44-year-old Member for Taunton, had served as a minister in two posts under the Coalition, but was dropped in 2013 and, being on the right of his party, was the subject of perennial press speculation about joining the Conservatives. More clearly political was the departure of Sarah Teather (44), who had won the formerly Labour seat of Brent South at a by-election during the Iraq War in 2003. She served as a Coalition minister, but had been dropped in 2012 for rebelliousness over welfare cuts, after which she criticised her party's record on social justice and integration, and announced her decision to leave.

In addition to all these retirements, three other MPs had left the House during the Parliament for breaches of procedures, involving false expenses claims in the cases of the Labour MPs Eric Illsley and Denis MacShane (both going to jail), and for paid advocacy in the case of the Conservative Patrick Mercer.

The stage was set for the candidate selection process after 2010 by the Report of the Speaker's Conference on Parliamentary Representation, which had been set up in 2008 and which reported in early 2010. Its aim was 'to consider and make recommendations for rectifying the disparity between the representation of women, ethnic minorities and disabled people in the House of Commons and their representation in the UK population at large'. Its membership reflected the Labour majority in the 2005 House of Commons and it addressed its themes in a manner congenial to the arrangements that the Labour Party had employed to deal with the under-representation of women and ethnic minorities. The Report stated that the way to restore the standing of Parliament in public life was to make sure that the House reflected more closely a diverse society, noting that 52% of the population were women, 13% black and minority ethnic (BAME), that 'experiences of disability' affected one in five people and that '6 to 9%' of the population was lesbian, gay, bisexual and transgender (LGBT). Against those figures, it noted that (in the 2005–10 Parliament) 80% of MPs were men, one in 43 was from a BAME community, only a handful identified as disabled and only two MPs were under 30, that there was only one out-lesbian and no Asian woman. It recommended too that political parties should be required to monitor and publish details of their candidate selections in order to ensure representation of the nation, an objective justified on grounds of justice, effectiveness and enhanced legitimacy, all themes taken from current academic discourse.

Accompanying the Speaker's Conference Report had been the Equality Act 2010, a final act of the Labour government which reaffirmed anti-discrimination law relating to personal characteristics while providing continued exemption to the practice of all-women shortlisting used by the Labour Party. The provisions of the Act served to mirror the concerns over diversity addressed in the Speaker's Conference.

The Labour Party entered the candidate selection round after the 2010 election fully attuned to the ethos of the Report and, before starting to select, made changes to its selection procedures, principal among which was the suspension of its National Parliamentary Panel of approved candidates, who had all been carefully screened by interview and written test, and who formed the pool of eligible people from which parliamentary candidates traditionally had to be selected. It did so for two reasons. The process of maintaining the list, of some 3,000 names, was expensive in terms of time and effort, and the claim that the list might exclude would-be candidates put off by having to meet its entry requirements. Instead of needing to be on the approved list, any party member could now apply for an advertised vacant candidacy by 'self-nomination'. The length of the candidate selection process was also reduced from 12–14 to 6–8 weeks so as to cut costs of time and expense which also might inhibit some candidates. Local party selection committees were also required to be gender-balanced and, in an albeit unexplained way, to reflect the demography of the constituency. The selection process, including longlisting and shortlisting, was to be overseen by a central party official tasked to 'ensure due consideration is given to applications from BAME candidates, people with disabilities and LGBT candidates'. These rule changes were accompanied by telling phrases in the procedural guidelines, notably that the aim was 'to select more candidates who reflect the full diversity of our society in terms of gender, race, sexual orientation and disability, and to increase working class representation'.[2] A 'Future Candidates Programme' was introduced to train and mentor candidates with the aim of meeting these objectives.

Labour candidate selections were thereafter accompanied by a monitoring system which recorded whether selection in all the seats was by open or all-women shortlist. In a sample of 164 constituencies, monitoring involved detailed identities of all applicants for selection under the headings 'male, female, Asian, black, mixed, white British, white other, disabled, LGBT', recording the numbers within each identity who remained in the process at all successive stages from application, through longlisting and shortlisting, to the final selection. All this information was used by officials to track the progress of the diversity agenda. This did not, however, include monitoring for 'working class representation', even though its desirability was being variously alluded to, primarily because of the definitional problems of doing so.[3]

Class had been put on the agenda by statements of the party leader, Ed Miliband, and as a coded response to the perception that authenticity had been drained from politics by the ubiquity of the career politician, variously comprising special advisers and/or party staffers engaged in political work since reading politics at university and on the lookout, in Labour's case, for a safe seat on a defunct coalfield 100 miles north of London with a good rail link – a description, as it happens, of Ed Miliband himself, who had in 2005 been elected MP for Doncaster North.

According to the MP Diane Abbott, 'the Labour Party has paid a price for parachuting one too many special advisers into industrial seats. There is a great deal of hand-wringing about UKIP and its inroads into previously rock solid Labour seats, but one cause of disaffection among core Labour voters is the sense that there is a remote Westminster class which doesn't relate to them'.[4] Reflecting this was the tendency in 2015 for candidates' CVs to be peppered with claims that they were not career politicians, that they were the first in their family to go to university or that they grew up on a council estate with a single-parent mother.

To an extent, the concern for 'working class' representation, which was being expressed by union leaders such as Unite's Len McCluskey, was a metaphor for more radical policies in a party that was now in opposition, after 13 years of the compromises and disappointments of government, and reflected in a revival of factional conflict long suppressed in the governing years. The role in this factional unrest provided by Unite was highlighted in the contentious selection process in 2013 to replace Eric Joyce in Falkirk, where allegations of mass recruitment of Unite members to the local party, with their fees being paid en bloc by the union in a constituency with a withered membership base, in order to select the Unite-backed union official Karie Murphy, led to threats of legal action, reference to the police, and the suspension and investigation of the constituency party by Labour's National Executive Committee (NEC), and eventually the selection of a candidate of which the Labour leadership approved. Karie Murphy insisted that she and the Falkirk Party Chairman, Steve Deans, a powerful local Unite official who had been suspended with her during this dispute, had done nothing wrong. She was later to reappear in the selection race at Halifax just before the election, where her omission from an NEC-drawn-up all-women shortlist was attacked by the retiring left-wing Halifax MP Linda Riordan.

The Falkirk selection dispute had repercussions for the unions' power within the party (see p. 83). It also in effect underlined the long-term decline of union influence from the glory days before the 1997 election when full-blown trade union financial sponsorship of Labour MPs and a delegate-based rather than a membership-based method of candidate selection had meant, in the 1992 Parliament, a 271-strong PLP containing 143 union-sponsored MPs. The interest of unions such as Unite in the selection round represented both the decline of union power as well as a revival of factionalism on the left of the party.

Aside from this re-emergence of Labour factional strife, the party proceeded with a selection strategy in which it had become well-versed, namely the application of selection by all-women shortlist (AWS) in 77 constituencies across the country, with distribution determined by the availability of the seats of retiring MPs and the marginality of target seats. In the case of seven of the 24 most marginal target seats, the application of AWS was avoided because of the presence of the seat's former male MPs wishing to attempt a comeback. Such exemptions aside, the principle of prioritising women's selection had become unassailable. From Labour's headquarters, the view was that the culture in the party was now accepting of AWS, with any reluctance confined to those who wished it to be employed in seats other than their own.

AWSs were applied in half the seats needing to be gained for a parliamentary majority, that is to say in 36 of the 68 seats required for a bare majority, and in 11 of the further 20 seats required for a seat total of 346. In the 40 seats where MPs were retiring, the application of AWS covered two-thirds of the seats, with the selection of 25 women being guaranteed, in place of only ten women among the 40 retiring. By these means, the party aimed at and achieved its target of a 40% female PLP.

The course to this objective was inevitably marred by some resistance here and there, and with allegations of attempts to parachute-in favoured Westminster insiders close to the election by way of NEC-determined shortlists, as in Coventry North West, where the elderly Geoffrey Robinson decided, in the event, not to retire. But none of these situations equalled the messiness of the confrontation with Unite at Falkirk.

Conservative Party selection procedures, having been innovative before 2010, were more traditional in the run-up to 2015. Before the 2010 election, the party had boosted female selections by imposing a gender-balanced 'A' list of favoured candidates and by introducing open primary selections in 116 constituencies to widen candidate selection to non-party members, and in two cases to organise selection by postal ballot of the entire electorate of the constituency. This latter innovation had produced the independent-minded Totnes MP, Dr Sarah Wollaston.

In November 2014, a full constituency ballot was held to select the candidate to challenge Mark Reckless, the deserter to UKIP, in the Rochester and Strood by-election. On a very low turnout of under 6,000, Kelly Tolhurst narrowly won selection. Although she lost the by-election, she went on to retrieve the seat at the general election, perhaps assisted by publicity obtained from all the balloting.

Primaries in general were seen by CCHQ as having the virtue of potentially recruiting membership. But ordinary open primaries involving selection at a public meeting, followed by the need for endorsement at a members-only meeting, were nevertheless held in only 31 constituencies, equally divided between Conservative-held and some (mostly Lib Dem-held) target seats.

Resistance to selection from the 'A' list in the 2005 Parliament had led to its partial withdrawal by making its use optional in advance of the 2010 election, and it was claimed that CCHQ had no intention after 2010 of exercising pressure from the centre to select women or ethnic minority candidates. There was, in any case, a view held in CCHQ that grassroots constituency officers were now more favourable to the selection of women, seeing them as better able to appeal to target voters with a greater capacity to empathise. It certainly appeared that CCHQ had made no special arrangement of the sort used by the Labour Party to monitor elaborately for diversity in the selection process. The approved list of candidates had been reconstituted after the 2010 election, reducing its size, and with full reappraisal of all those who wished to remain on it. CCHQ was satisfied that because of that renewal of the list, the party had a fully representative range of candidates. That the party selected women in 14 of the 38 seats where MPs were retiring and where there had been only four retiring women suggested either a change of culture in the grassroots or, notwithstanding denials of putting pressure on constituency officers, the traditional hidden hand of CCHQ, or indeed both.

The view of CCHQ was that culture in the grassroots 'is changing', but its assumed retreat into a more passive and quietly exhorting mode did not convince all commentators, one of whom observed that 'a glance at the names of those who have been selected to inherit the safest constituencies shows that something has been going on behind the scenes' and that 'there is an "A" list in everything but name ... dominated by women and ethnic minorities'.[5] By way of balanced or even all-women shortlists, a group of women and BAME candidates, including the future MPs Heidi Allen, Jo Churchill, Lucy Frazer, Helen Whately, Suella Fernandes and Nusrat Ghani, all appeared on the shortlists in a sequence of geographically distributed seats until they struck lucky. Of the seven safe constituencies that selected ethnic minority candidates (Braintree, Fareham, Hampshire North East, Havant, Richmond Yorkshire, South Ribble and Wealden), only two of the candidates selected, the banker Ranil Jayawardena in Hampshire North East and the lawyer Seema Kennedy in South Ribble, had a discernible connection with the area.

Occasionally the process by which these allegedly favoured suitors obtained their seats stumbled. The primary in Cambridgeshire South East selecting the barrister Lucy Frazer was found to have involved a miscounted ballot, but her defeated rival, the company director Heidi Allen, was soon compensated by winning selection in neighbouring Cambridgeshire South. More embarrassingly at Bexhill and Battle, where a white man, the City lawyer Huw Merriman, was selected, the chairman of the local association injudiciously remarked that a shortlisted Asian woman, the barrister Suella Fernandes, had not been selected because of 'the double whammy of being brown and a woman'. With four shortlistings behind her, she subsequently found her berth at Fareham. Even more peripatetic was the management consultant Helen Whately, whose passage to the nomination at Faversham was preceded by a trail of shortlists in five other safe seats spread across the Home Counties.

But if a favoured raft of aspirants were being accommodated in safe seats, the limited use of primaries included ten in targeted Lib Dem-occupied seats where some wider local engagement in selection was thought prudent. Instead of the apparent disregard for the local status of candidates in many safe seat selections, in the Lib Dem-targeted seats, especially in the south-west, more attention was paid to local credentials and it may well have been Cornwall they had in mind when a CCHQ source remarked that among more ordinary people featuring in the new intake, alongside the traditional lawyers and company directors, were 'a postman and a Methodist preacher'.

The Lib Dems, unlike the other two parties, had never been able to address the matter of diversity within their parliamentary ranks because of the small number of seats safe enough to permit experiments in the type of candidates presented. In addition, the seats they managed to hold continuously relied heavily on the personal appeal and reputation of incumbents. The party had never elected more than ten women MPs, when at its high water mark of 62 seats in 2005, and only one ethnic minority MP when Parmjit Singh Gill won the Leicester South by-election in 2004 and lost it a year later. Nor was the party prepared, with its belief in a liberal meritocracy, to use devices such as primaries or all-women shortlists, although it required gender balancing in its selection procedures.

Following the 2010 election, the party introduced a 'Leadership Programme', with some connotations of the Conservative Party's discarded 'A' list. It was designed to diversify the pool of candidates by creating a small group of 30 approved candidates supported by finance and training, made up of 50% women, 20% BAME, 20% LGBT and the rest for other minorities, including those with disabilities. The intention was to target such candidates at winnable seats where they would be prioritised in shortlisting.

But the collapse of the party's electoral support after entering coalition with the Conservatives made such efforts seem rather irrelevant. With very large seat losses in municipal and European elections in the course of the Parliament and the prospect of worse at the general election, morale sank and the pace at which parliamentary selections were made became so slow that by the start of 2015, only 206 candidates were in place, with 400 still to be chosen. This alarming situation was attributed internally to the effect of the fixed-term Parliament removing the need for urgency in candidate selection, but more telling was the fact that when all selections were completed by April 2015, of the candidates in the 584 non-Lib Dem-held seats, 254 were people who had stood in previous parliamentary contests; 35 had been in over four such contests, in one case in as many as seven stretching back to 1983, and in another in five contests beginning 40 years earlier in 1974. These recycled candidates accounted for as many as 44% of the total, a proportion far higher than the 18% of Conservative and 16% of Labour candidates who had fought earlier Westminster elections. The internal explanation for this apparent problem with the supply of candidates was that it was in the nature of a small party to rely on candidates with local roots and good name recognition.

With the lowering of expectations as the election neared and speculation turning to the matter of how many seats the party could simply expect to hold, the Lib Dems' publicity illustrated the impact of candidates produced from their 'Leadership Programme' by referring to the identities of the people replacing incumbents in the ten seats where their MPs were retiring. All the MPs were white and two were women, but of their replacements, six were woman, two ethnic minority and one LGBT. But of these, both BAME candidates withdrew before the election. In any case, the election saw the party reduced to the least diverse parliamentary representation in 30 years, as a rump of eight white men.

Table 13.1 Women candidates 2010–15

	Conservative	*Labour*	*Liberal Democrat*
2015	169 (26%)	214 (34%)	166 (26%)
2010	153 (24%)	191 (30%)	134 (20%)

Table 13.2 Women MPs 2010–15

	2010	*By-elections 2010–15*	*Retiring 2015*	*Defeated 2015*	*New MPs*	*Total*
Conservative	49	-1	–4	–3	27	68 (20%)
Labour	81	+6	–10	–12	34	99 (43%)
Liberal Democrat	7	–	–2	–5	–	0
SNP	1		–	–	19	20 (36%)
Plaid Cymru	0	–	–	–	1	1
SDLP	1	–	–	–	–	1
Alliance	1	–	–	–1	–	0
SinnFein	1	–	–	–1	–	0
Independent	1	–	–	–	–	1
Green	1	–	–	–	–	1
TOTAL	143	+5	–16	–22	+81	191

Between them, Labour, the Conservatives and the Lib Dems fielded 549 women candidates, in all cases representing a higher percentage than in 2010 (see Table 13.1). UKIP, by contrast, selected a lower proportion of women candidates, with 78, or 13%. For the major parties, total numbers were less important than the placing of candidates in winnable seats. The record number of 191 MPs had been secured, first, by the Labour Party using AWSs in most of its seats vacated by retiring MPs, second, by the Conservatives equally installing women candidates in 14 of their 38 safe retirement seats rather than targeted marginals, and, third, by the unexpected boost to numbers provided by the 19 women borne in on the SNP's tidal wave. That the Conservatives elected almost as many new women MPs as Labour without a mechanism precluding the selection of men attested to the changed culture in a party that historically had trailed Labour in electing women MPs. As noted, Conservative women had been conspicuous in the peripatetic trail of aspiring candidates making the shortlist in a sequence of safe seat selections. More new women MPs came from safe seats (14

Conservative, 16 Labour) than from the few marginal seats with women candidates exchanged between those parties (3 Conservative and 6 Labour), though 9 new Conservative women and 7 new Labour women came from the large Lib Dem losses.

Across the House, including the four women elected for smaller parties, women comprised 29% of the Commons, up from 22% in 2010. Labour had the highest proportion (43%) of women MPs, twice the Conservatives' (20%), and yet Conservative numbers were strong. Their total of new women MPs was close to Labour's, even if the gap between the parties' total numbers was similar to that of 2010.

Table 13.3 BAME MPs 2010–15

	2010	*By-elections 2010–15*	*Death 2010–15*	*Defeated 2015*	*New MPs 2015*	*Total 2015*
Conservative	11	–	–	–1	+7	17
Labour	16	+1	–1	–1	+8	23
LibDem	0	–	–	–	–	0
SNP	0	–	–	–	+1	1
Total	27	+1	–1	–2	+16	41

The number of BAME MPs rose from 27 to 41 in 2015, as shown in Table 13.3. The three parties fielded (allowing for difficulties of classification) numbers of candidates not very different from those in 2010: Conservatives 58 (43 in 2010), Labour 52 (46), Lib Dems 54 (46), totalling 164 (135). Of the other parties, UKIP fielded a similar number (42), though in the 120 seats where it came second, only four of its candidates were ethnic minority.

Labour's selection monitoring system confirmed that the great majority of BAME applicants for selection, and of those succeeding, were Asian rather than black. Of the 15 new Labour and Conservative MPs in 2015, 10 were Asian (7 of them women), 4 black (2 of them women) and 1 Chinese. The SNP ethnic minority MP was a half-Asian woman.

Numbers were low, but as with women, what mattered was the location of the candidacy. Traditionally, Labour had been most involved in furthering BAME representation, with most of its ethnic minority MPs located in safe Labour seats with large BAME populations. But in 2010 the Conservatives audaciously challenged the assumption that a BAME candidate had to be matched with a BAME electorate by placing ethnic minority candidates in six almost wholly white safe Conservative seats. They persisted with this strategy in 2015, with seven more ethnic minority candidates in a range of seats in none of which the white population comprised less than 92% of the total.

Labour, on the other hand, had selected only two BAME candidates in any of its 40 vacant seats, Tulip Siddiq (Hampstead and Kilburn) and Kate Osamor (Edmonton), and in only six of the top 60 marginals, although at Brent Central, Dawn Butler, a former MP returning in an area she had previously represented, was elected with a large majority. The selection at Edmonton had come on the eve of the election, attracting a very large number of applications and from an open-list selection produced an all-women all-BAME shortlist, thus meeting calls from MP David Lammy and BAME–Labour lobbyists for all-black shortlists, but beyond mandatory longlisting of BAME applications (which was in Labour's selection rule book), anything more would not be lawful.

The Conservative advance had been without positive discrimination, and by placing its ethnic minority candidates in safe seats, it made a more permanent contribution to parliamentary numbers than Labour's reliance in 2015 on gains in marginal seats. The Conservatives also provided, in Alan Mak (Havant), the first ethnic minority MP of Chinese origin.

As interesting as the rise in the total number of non-white MPs was the increase in that of ethnic minority women, where Labour led the Conservatives by 13 to 5, and specifically among Asian women, by 9 to 4. Of particular interest among the new Asian women MPs was Tulip Siddiq, a political adviser, and granddaughter of the founding President of Bangladesh, Sheikh Mujibur Rahman, and Naseem Shah (Bradford West), a former NHS manager and local woman with a personal history illustrative of Asian cultural conservatism, who was selected close to the election in March 2015 to replace another Asian but London-based woman who had withdrawn within days of being selected. In a toxic campaign, Shah regained for Labour a constituency lost at a 2012 by-election to the fluent but mercurial and divisive maverick George Galloway.

The election saw the return of 32 LGBT MPs out of 155 candidates, 42 of them Conservative, 36 Labour, 39 Lib Dems and 7 (all elected) SNP. The total of 32 MPs was an increase on the 26 LGBT MPs before the election, both totals being internationally unequalled.[6] All three main traditional parties had LGBT lobby groups which had published lists of their candidates and Parliament had seen the passage of the Equal Marriage Act by a Conservative-led government, and whilst the Conservative MP Crispin Blunt had faced and won in 2013 a deselection ballot in Reigate over his LGBT identity, the issue seemed to be relatively depoliticised and the proportion of the Commons represented by the 32 Members (4.9%) was broadly equivalent to the estimated size of the LGBT population.

Table 13.4 Age of candidates

	Conservative		*Labour*		*Liberal Democrat*		*SNP*
	Elected	*Unelected*	*Elected*	*Unelected*	*Elected*	*Unelected*	*Elected*
Age (as at 1 January 2015)							
Under 20	–	2	–	5	–	6	–
20–29	6	51	3	57	–	69	7
30–39	49	114	38	95	–	99	10
40–49	122	89	59	100	5	119	20
50–59	112	42	74	87	2	149	15
60–69	33	18	44	52	1	104	4
70–79	8	1	11	3	–	17	–
80–89	–	–	3	–	–	–	–
Unknown	–	–	–	–	–	60	–
Total	330	317	232	399	8	623	56
Median age							
2015	48	39	53	43	49	49	45
2010	47	39	52	45	50	47	48

The age profile of MPs (see Table 13.4) remained unchanged, notwithstanding much press coverage of the arrival of the youngest MP since 1832, Mhairi Black, a 20-year-old Glasgow University politics student (born 1994) who had to return to Glasgow to sit her final examinations once she had taken her seat as one of the 50 new MPs swept in on the Nationalist tsunami. The oldest MP was 84-year-old Sir Gerald Kaufman (born June 1930), who was older at the start of a parliament than any MP since David Logan, who had represented Liverpool Scotland for Labour from 1929 to 1964 (and who was 87 at the time of his last election in 1959, dying aged 92 in 1964). In Sir Gerald's wake came two fellow octogenarians, Dennis Skinner (born 1932) and David Winnick (born 1933). Behind them on the Labour benches were 11 MPs in their seventies.[7] The oldest Conservatives were the 77-year-old Sir Alan Haselhurst, Sir Bill Cash (born 1940), Kenneth Clarke (born 1940), Dame Angela Watkinson (born 1941), Sir Roger Gale (born 1943), Peter Lilley (born 1943), Glyn Davies (born 1944) and Sir Peter Bottomley (born 1944). These combined Labour and Conservative lists totalled 22

MPs over the age of 70, an increase on the start of the 2010 House, when the total was 15 (3 Conservative and 12 Labour).

Meanwhile, at the other end of the age range, numbers among the Conservative and Labour Parties were falling. Five Conservative MPs were in their twenties, with the youngest being Tom Pursglove (born November 1988), followed by William Wragg (born December 1987), Ranil Jayawardena (born September 1986), Ben Howlett (born August 1986) and Luke Hall (born July 1986). Labour had three MPs under 30, the youngest being Louise Haigh (born July 1987), followed by Holly Lynch (born October 1986) and Cat Smith (born June 1986). Comparing this total of eight Conservative and Labour MPs under 30 with the total of 15 in 2010 would indicate a decline in the number of young MPs in their twenties. But the SNP had six more, apart from Mhairi Black, who were under 30. They were Stuart Donaldson (born September 1991), Angela Crawley (born June 1987), Stewart McDonald (born August 1986), Kirsty Blackman (born March 1986), Neil Gray (born March 1986) and Callum McCaig (born January 1985). Thus, it was only through the impact of the SNP's youthful incursion that the number of MPs under 30, at 15, equalled the combined Conservative, Labour and Lib Dem total of 15 in 2010.

Table 13.5 Parliamentary experience of MPs

First elected	*Conservative*	*Labour*	*Liberal Democrat*	*SNP*
1966–79	3	8	–	–
1980–92	35	24	–	–
1993–97	20	40	1	–
1998–2005	64	46	7	5
2006–10	135	52	–	1
2011–15	73	62	–	50
Total	330	232	8	56

The parliamentary experience of MPs is set out in Table 13.5. With the retirement of Sir Peter Tapsell, the longest continuously serving MP became Labour's Sir Gerald Kaufman, MP originally for Manchester Ardwick, but latterly for Manchester Gorton. He was first elected in 1970, along with Kenneth Clarke (Conservative), Michael Meacher (Labour) and Dennis Skinner (Labour), but having taken the Oath before them had seniority. A journalist member of Harold Wilson's Downing Street staff in the 1960s, his career as a Labour parliamentary candidate had begun in the 1950s when he stood against Harold Macmillan in Bromley in 1955, and later contested the 1959 election in Gillingham.

The last surviving MP from the 1960s, before Sir Gerald's arrival, was David Winnick, who had won Croydon South in 1966, but was defeated in 1970. He later returned as MP for Walsall North in 1979. The other survivors of elections in the 1970s were Labour's Dame Margaret Beckett, first elected by defeating the ex-Labour MP Dick Taverne at Lincoln in October 1974, a seat she duly lost in 1979, but was then returned at Derby South from 1983; the Conservative Sir Peter Bottomley (elected in 1975), Geoffrey Robinson (Labour, 1976–), Sir Alan Haselhurst (Conservative, 1970–74 and 1977–), Frank Field (Labour, 1979–), and Barry Sheerman (Labour, 1979–), making a total of 11 MPs whose careers began in (or in one case before) the 1970s.

Fewer than 60 MPs remained from the ideologically polarised years of the Thatcher ascendancy, and only 37 Labour MPs remained from the landslide in 1997, when 183 new Labour MPs were swept in on Tony Blair's coat tails and experienced the easy supremacy of the first two Labour-dominated Parliaments (1997–2005). The Blairite cohort of that time had now virtually disappeared. After the 2015 election, the PLP was comprised of those elected in more fractious times. Almost half had known only the vagaries of opposition since 2010 and, if they were part of the new intake, were being launched in 2015 into a bitterly divisive leadership election. Two-thirds of Conservative MPs, meanwhile, knew only the period of government office after 2010, although the stress of coalition had stimulated a culture of dissent which could unsettle a government with a small majority.

The family connections of MPs have become a matter of some interest, it being assumed that family influence assisted political advancement. The numbers were not, however, entirely convincing. In 2015, 17 MPs were the children of former MPs, slightly fewer than the average figure of 18 across the four previous parliaments since 1997. Of the 17, 12 were Conservative, 4 Labour and 1 DUP.[8] At the election, the number of MPs whose fathers had been MPs declined with the retirement of the Conservatives James Arbuthnot, Francis Maude and Laura Sandys, and with the defeat of three Labour MPs, Anas Sarwar, Andrew Sawford and Alison Seabeck. These six were replaced by only three incoming MPs whose fathers had been MPs: the Conservatives Victoria Prentis and Victoria Atkins, and Labour's Stephen Kinnock.

Prior to the 2015 election there had been media speculation about the sons of leading Labour figures, dubbed 'Red Princes', being selected for safe seats, four being mentioned: the sons of Tony Blair, John Prescott,

Jack Straw and Neil Kinnock. In the event, of these four, Euan Blair appeared nowhere (despite speculation connecting him with Bootle and the Coventry seat of Geoffrey Robinson, who did not, in the event, retire); David Prescott was selected for the unwinnable Conservative seat of Gainsborough; and Will Straw was selected for marginal Rossendale and Darwen next door to the Blackburn seat vacated by his father, which he duly lost. Only Stephen Kinnock, by being selected for the safe seat of Aberavon, was launched on a parliamentary career. In so doing, he became the third Labour leader's son to follow his father into the Commons, his two predecessors having been Malcolm MacDonald (son of Ramsay MacDonald), who represented Bassetlaw from 1929 to 1935 and Ross and Cromarty from 1936 to 1945, and Arthur Henderson (son of Arthur Henderson), who represented Cardiff South (1923–4), Kingswinford (1935–50) and Rowley Regis and Tipton (1950–66). The incidence of successful parental patronage was not that obvious.

As the numbers of MPs children continued to flatline, so did that of MPs who comprised married couples or were siblings. In 2015, retirement or defeat reduced the number of married couples from four to two (Harriet Harman and Jack Dromey, and Jenny Chapman and Nick Smith), and the sibling count of three in 2010, though reduced to two – the sisters Angela and Maria Eagle, and the brother and sister Keith and Valerie Vaz – by the departure of David Miliband in 2011, was sustained by the arrival of Boris Johnson to join his brother Jo. The new House contained in the new intake a few more who had Westminster political relatives, such as Richard Burgon (nephew of former MP John Burgon); James Cartlidge (son-in-law of Sir Gerald Howarth MP), Christina Rees (ex-wife of former MP Ron Davies) and Peter Dowd, who was elected for Bootle, a seat held from 1955 to 1979 by his great-uncle Simon Mahon, whose brother Peter had been MP for Preston South (1964–70).

The House already had a group of eight political grandchildren, 5 Conservative and 3 Labour, and that number was augmented in 2015 by the arrival of the SNP MP Stuart Donaldson, grandson of Hamish Watt, SNP for Banffshire (1974–9), and the son of the SNP MSP and minister in the Scottish government Maureen Watt.[9]

However, historical dynastic connections had declined. The Hurd and Benn families had been present as MPs for four generations, but more impressive dynastic credentials, with each generation producing MPs for 200 or 300 years, were now confined, and through the female line, to only two MPs: Nicholas Soames, of the Spencer-Churchill (Marlborough) family, and Zac Goldsmith, of the Vane-Tempest-Stewart

(Londonderry) family. Although the last two were Old Etonians, that did not reflect the broader picture, as shown below.

Table 13.6 Education of candidates

	Conservative		*Labour*		*Liberal Democrat*		*SNP*	
	Elected	*Unelected*	*Elected*	*Unelected*	*Elected*	*Unelected*	*Elected*	*Unelected*
Secondary schl	21	25	17	25	–	40	6	2
Secondary schl +poly/coll	22	28	35	44	–	85	7	–
Secondary sch +univ	121	159	144	264	7	360	39	–
Private schl	5	–	–	–	–	7	1	–
Private schl +poly/coll	15	9	2	–	–	10	–	–
Private schl +univ	145	78	34	33	1	102	3	1
Unknown	–	18	–	33	–	19	–	–
TOTAL	330*	317	232	399	8	623	56	3
Oxford	65	21	30	22	1	37	–	–
Cambridge	35	18	19	13	–	38	–	–
Other univs	166	199	129	262	7	387	42	1
TOTAL univs	266 (81%)	238 (75%)	178 (77%)	297 (74%)	8 (100%)	462 (74%)	42 (75%)	1
Eton	19	5	–	–	–	4	–	1
Harrow	3	1	–	–	–	–	–	–
Winchester	5	–	–	–	–	2	–	–
Other private	138	81	36	33	1	113	4	–
TOTAL private Schls	165 (50%)	87 (27%)	36 (16%)	33 (9%)	1	119 (19%)	4 (7%)	1

*One MP who was 'home-schooled' is omitted from this total

The education table (Table 13.6) is mainly instructive for what it says about schooling, given that the effect of broadening higher education has been that virtually all MPs have become graduates, albeit at a wide range of institutions. Schooling is an important measure of social status and has most importance in its analysis of the Conservative Party, which has traditionally drawn the majority of its MPs from the privately educated.

The traditional pattern has, however, been in decline for 50 years. Taking all elections since the 1970s where the party won a similar total of seats to the 330 in 2015 (from 339 in 1979 to 306 in 2010), the proportion of privately educated Conservative MPs had moved from 72% (1979), 62% (1992) and 54% (2010) to parity with the state-educated in 2015. Clearly the elitist educational character of the party was undergoing long-term decline, albeit not quickly enough for those who sought to make it more representative of the wider society. Whilst by 2015 the parliamentary party comprised 165 privately schooled MPs and 164 state-schooled (with one other 'home-schooled'), the balance within the 74-strong new intake more clearly showed the trend, with 54% of new MPs being state-educated. Within that part of the new intake made up of the 38 MPs who had inherited mostly safe seats, as distinct from the new MPs who had gained their seats at the election, the private-state distinction still favoured the former (by 55% to 45%), but there was a clear rise in the percentage of state-educated MPs among those gaining rather than inheriting seats. Nor were many of the new MPs who had been privately educated from the grand boarding schools, but rather from former direct grant day grammar schools which had become independent, even if three of the new MPs had attended Winchester and one, Boris Johnson, Eton.

The preoccupation of commentators with the assumed role of Eton in contemporary politics owed everything to the presence of David Cameron as the first 'Eton and Oxford' Prime Minister since Sir Alec Douglas-Home in 1963. At the election, two out of 20 Etonians had retired, meaning that the return to the Commons of Boris Johnson did not sustain the previous total. Thus, in 2015, the number of MPs who had attended Eton fell to 19, which, if not its lowest total ever, represented the lowest proportion ever that Etonians comprised of all Conservative MPs: 5.8%. In 1959, Harold Macmillan could call upon the services of 73 fellow Etonians or one in four (23%) of all Conservative MPs.[10]

As shown in Table 13.6, in addition to the 19 Etonian Conservative MPs returned in 2015, a further ten Etonians unsuccessfully fought the election, five for the Conservatives and four for the Liberal Democrats, including John Thurso, who lost his Caithness, Sutherland and Easter Ross seat to the SNP. Another bizarrely enough, given his party's populist demeanour, was the SNP's Etonian Danus Skene in Orkney and Shetland, one of only three seats the party failed to win. The 29 Etonian candidates comprised 1.5% of the grand total of 1,968 candidates fielded in the election by the Conservatives, Labour, the Lib Dems and the SNP, suggesting that the school's motto, 'Floreat Etona', did not apply at the ballot box.

The other traditional measure of elitism is an education at Oxford or Cambridge. Of 330 Conservative MPs, 30% were Oxbridge graduates.

This, as in private schooling, represented a further downward trend across the years, from 50% in 1979, 45% in 1992 to 34% in 2010. Moreover, Oxford and Cambridge supplied only 24% of the new intake of 74 Conservative MPs.

The Labour Party's proportion of private school-educated MPs had never been high, averaging 17% across 60 years. In 2015, it was, at 16%, up slightly on 14% in 2010. Its Oxbridge component was in 2015, at 21%, up on 2010 (18%), which had itself been up on 2005 (16%). But that figure had also fluctuated trendlessly across the decades. The percentage of Oxbridge graduates in the new Labour intake, at 19%, was similar to that in 2010 (20%).

The Lib Dems' educational profile had, when returning 40 or 50 MPs, comprised about 40% private school-educated and 30% from Oxbridge. In 2015, of its eight MPs, only one, Nick Clegg, had a private school or Oxbridge education. When the party last returned as small a number as in 2015, with nine Liberal MPs in 1964, four had been privately educated: two at Eton (Jo Grimond and Jeremy Thorpe) and one at Harrow (Eric Lubbock).

Meanwhile, the SNP's MPs were conspicuous for their state education. Only four had attended private schools and 42 of the 56 were graduates, all but one from Scottish universities.

Categorisation of MPs' previous occupations is notoriously difficult. Many MPs and candidates no longer follow a single career path. The exercise has an element of broad brush and can be seen as much of a work of art as of science. One of the salient questions in 2015 was to determine the number of professional politicians, given the attention paid in the media to the matter. Table 13.7 shows high numbers of Labour MPs in this category, having served predominantly as party staffers, MPs' aides, ministers' special advisers, political think tank employees or full-time councillors. Such political work was often interwoven with activity in the voluntary sector, which had largely replaced activities once dealt with by the now retreating public sector. In all, 59 (or 26%) of the PLP were in political or quasi-political occupations.[11] This percentage was mirrored by at least 14 career politicians out of the 53 MPs comprising the new intake, and if the number of trade union officials was added, Labour's so-defined professional politicians comprised over one in three (36%) of the PLP. And of course others will have had some experience of political work.

This pattern was a contrast to the Conservative Party, where the 40 MPs with strictly political careers comprised only 12%, and with few (7, or 10%) in the new intake, albeit including the Downing Street

Table 13.7 Occupation of candidates

	Conservative		*Labour*		*Liberal Democrat*		*SNP*
	Elected	*Unelected*	*Elected*	*Unelected*	*Elected*	*Unelected*	*Elected*
Professions:							
Barrister	28	10	9	11	–	11	1
Solicitor	28	24	17	22	2	19	4
Doctor/Dentist	8	8	–	9	–	6	2
Architect/Surveyor	4	–	2	2	–	7	1
Civil/Chrtrd Engineer	2	9	2	4	–	35	1
Accountant	14	10	1	5	–	19	1
Civ. Serv/Loc. Govt	2	7	10	19	2	24	2
Armed services	12	6	1	3	–	2	–
Teachers: Univ.	–	4	8	14	–	26	1
Poly/college	1	1	4	10	–	6	2
School	5	8	7	30	2	53	2
Other consultants	3	4	2	4	–	15	–
Science/research	–	–	1	5	–	7	–
Total	107	91	64	138	6	230	17
	(32%)	(29%)	(28%)	(35%)		(37%)	(30%)
Business:							
Company director	61	35	3	10	–	29	2
Company executive	50	38	11	22	2	64	6
Commerce/insurance	10	13	3	12	–	21	5
Managerial/clerical	3	9	3	10	–	14	–
General business	12	24	5	20	–	33	6
Management cnsltnt	9	6	1	3	–	9	–
Total	145	125	26	77	2	170	19
	(44%)	(40%)	(11%)	(19%)		(27%)	(34%)
Miscellaneous:							
Misc. white collar	4	18	11	17	–	43	1
Politician	40	33	59	57	–	57	8
Union official	–	–	23	20	–	–	–
Journalist/publisher	16	13	14	17	–	18	4
Public relations	6	14	3	9	–	19	1
Charity/voluntary sector	2	8	16	31	–	37	4
Farmer	7	7	–	–	–	6	–
Student	–	5	–	5	–	17	2
Total	75	98	126	156	0	197	20
	(23%)	(30%)	(54%)	(40%)		(32%)	(36%)
Manual	3	3	16	24	0	16	0
	(1%)	(1%)	(7%)	(6%)		(3%)	
Unknown	–	–	–	5	–	10	
GRAND TOTAL	330	317	232	399	8	623	56

aide, Oliver Dowden. The Conservative commentator Paul Goodman suggested that Conservative political advisers lacked the same political career ambitions as Labour's, with few therefore being on CCHQ's candidates list, unlike the more numerous lawyers and businesspeople who comprised as much of the new intake (60%) as they did of all Conservative MPs.[12] Whilst Labour's party and union staffers swelled its ranks, the Conservatives had reinforced their strength in the business sector, where Labour remained noticeably weak.

The SNP's occupational profile, as befitted a populist catch-all party, was evenly spread across the three main sections of the occupation table, with traditional professionals such as lawyers, medics and teachers balanced by people in the business sector, as well as those from journalism and political occupations. The latter had been stimulated by the creation of the Scottish Parliament and more particularly the SNP's occupancy of power in Edinburgh since 2007 which had created many political jobs at Holyrood. Although the SNP made much of their candidates who had been brought into politics as a result of the independence referendum, at least one in six of the SNP group had been aides to MSPs.

If there was no reversal in the rise of the professional politician, there was equally no reversal of the decline of the working class MP, which owed much to the long-term restructuring of employment and to deindustrialisation. When the mining industry was strong, the National Union of Mineworkers was able, by way of Labour's system of delegate-based selection and union sponsorship, to advance otherwise poorly resourced miners straight into the House of Commons. But where once virtually all MPs representing seats on the Yorkshire coalfield were miners, by the late 1990s with the collapse of the mining industry and candidate selection changes weakening union influence, they were more likely to be London-based political advisers. Elsewhere, moreover, many manual workers had not entered Parliament straight from a manual job, as in the case of the sometime postman Alan Johnson, who reached the Commons in 1997 as the leader of a trade union. Whilst there were some women in Labour's new intake in 2015 from clearly impoverished backgrounds, they had experienced social mobility to become union officials, social workers or health service managers before selection and election in 2015. By that point, their occupational class classification had materially changed.

If concerns over the diversity of the House of Commons in relation to gender and race had been attended to, clearly other more complex questions beyond the remit of the Speaker's Conference, such as political professionalism and class, remained to be addressed. Arguably of greater salience as the new Parliament advanced would be not its social, but its political diversity; the presence of a large secessionist party whose claim for attention had the potential for creating more intractable difficulties.

Notes

1. Of these, 14 were Labour (11 in the same seat they had lost, 1 in a different seat and 2 who were contesting the election for other parties) and 4 Liberal Democrats (2 in the same seat they had lost). One further outgoing MP, the former Liberal Democrat Mike Hancock, was contesting his Portsmouth South seat as an Independent. Former Labour MPs seeking re-election in the same seat were: Bob Blizzard (Waveney), Paul Clark (Gillingham and Rainham), Andrew Dismore (Hendon), David Drew (Stroud), Patrick Hall (Bedford), Sally Keeble (Northampton North), Mike O'Brien (Warwickshire North), Nick Palmer (Broxtowe), Kerry Pollard (St Albans), Anne Snellgrove (Swindon South) and Gareth Thomas (Clwyd West). John Grogan, defeated at Selby in 2010, fought Keighley. The two ex-Labour MPs seeking a return under different colours were Tony Clarke, who had lost Northampton South in 2005 and was trying a comeback in Northampton North for the Green Party, and Dave Nellist, who had represented Coventry South from 1983 to 1992, when he lost it as Independent Labour (having been expelled from the party) and was fighting another Coventry seat (this time Coventry North West) as he had done perennially ever since, now for the Trade Union and Socialist Coalition. The Liberal Democrat would-be returning MPs were Julia Goldsworthy (Camborne and Redruth), Richard Younger-Ross (Newton Abbott), David Rendel, who had represented Newbury (1993–2005) and was now seeking to defend the Liberal Democrat-held seat of Somerton and Frome, and Parmjit Singh Gill (Leicester South), who had briefly represented the seat from 2004 to 2005.
2. Labour Party, 'Selection Procedure: Parliamentary Candidates', May 2013.
3. Labour did, however, experiment with reviewing all candidate selections once made against Mosaic data. The conclusions reached from such monitoring were not publicly disclosed, but established a benchmark for future comparison.
4. Diane Abbott, 'Why Ed Miliband Needs to Widen Labour's MP Selection Pool', *The Guardian*, 18 November 2014.
5. Harry Cole, 'David Cameron's Secret "A" List', *Spectator Life*, May 2015.
6. Andrew Reynolds, 'The UK Broke its Own record for LGBT Representation', *New Statesman*, 13 May 2015.
7. Paul Flynn (born 1935), Ann Clwyd (born 1937 and the oldest woman MP), Geoffrey Robinson (born 1938), Michael Meacher (born 1939), Barry Sheerman (born 1940), Jim Cunningham (born 1941), Kelvin Hopkins (born 1941), Frank Field (born 1942), Dame Margaret Beckett (born 1943), Ronnie Campbell (born 1943) and Margaret Hodge (born 1944).
8. They were: Victoria Atkins, Richard Benyon, Dominic Grieve, Ben Gummer, Nick Hurd, Bernard Jenkin, Andrew Mitchell, Mark Pawsey, Victoria Prentis, Nicholas Soames, Robin Walker and Bill Wiggin (all Conservative); Hilary

Benn, John Cryer, Lindsay Hoyle and Stephen Kinnock (Labour); Ian Paisley (DUP).

9. Other grandchildren in 2015: Geoffrey Clifton-Brown, Philip Dunne; Zac Goldsmith, Nick Hurd and Nicholas Soames (all Conservative); Hilary Benn, Fiona MacTaggart and Lisa Nandy (Labour).
10. In the 2010 book in this series, the total of Etonian Conservative MPs was incorrectly shown as 19, but another MP came to light early in the new Parliament, taking the total to 20, or 6.5% of all Conservative MPs. The total of Etonian Conservatives had been lower than the 19 elected in 2015, when in 1997 the number fell to 15, but it then comprised as much as 9% of the 165 Conservative MPs returned at that election, the smallest number since 1945.
11. The CV of Jo Cox (Batley and Spen), one of the new Labour intake, amply describes the political adviser's career path: born 1974; Heckmondwike Grammar School; Pembroke College, Cambridge; LSE; political adviser to Joan Walley MP (2 years); Head of Campaign, Britain in Europe (2 years); political adviser to Glenys Kinnock MEP (2 years); Oxfam, including Head of its EU Office (7 years); chair, Maternal Mortality Campaign (involving PM Gordon Brown's wife) (2 years); 'strategy consultant' with Save the Children and the anti-slavery Freedom Fund; director, Labour Women's Network... and then selection for Batley and Spen.
12. Paul Goodman, 'Cameron's Children: The Next Generation of Conservative MPs', www.conservativehome.com, 3 February 2015.

14
Out of the Blue: The Campaign in Retrospect

The Conservative election victory of 2015 overturned many expectations. It had been widely expected that the fragmentation of the party system would produce yet another hung parliament, out of which would emerge another coalition or post-election deal. The era of one-party majority government seemed to be over. David Cameron's victory also belied predictions – made, for example, by Mervyn King, the Governor of the Bank of England – that the measures needed to deal with the economy would be so unpopular that they would keep the winner of the 2010 election out of office for a generation.[1]

For much of the short campaign, commentators wondered, given the Conservatives' advantages on many key issues and their overwhelming press support, why the polls did not show the party doing better. None of the party's policy offers, on the Budget, inheritance tax or right-to-buy, seemed to be game-changers. Even Conservative commentators were unimpressed with the campaign and complained that George Osborne's much-touted long-term economic plan lacked vision.[2] For the Conservatives, it seemed that the economic recovery had been voteless, reminiscent of the fate of John Major's government in 1997. On 7 April 2015, Ed Conway in *The Times* claimed that the election appeared to be overturning the rule that the economy decided elections: 'It is obviously not the economy at all, stupid.' On 7 May, *The Guardian* headline had read 'It Couldn't Be Closer', with the paper's polls showing the two parties neck and neck, and with the sub-head: 'Parties Prepare for Coalition Talks.'

Instead, the Conservatives achieved a stunning victory. Cameron formed the first majority Conservative government for 23 years and was the first Tory Prime Minister to increase his party's vote share in 60 years. He was backed by record numbers of female (68), ethnic minority (17) and state-educated Conservative MPs (164). Twenty-four hours after the polls closed, the British electoral landscape had been transformed. Scotland had become virtually a one-party state in which the Scottish National Party (SNP) held 56 of the 59 seats. The Liberal Democrats had been massacred, reduced to just eight seats overall. For much of the Parliament, UKIP had been seen as the insurgent party which would damage the Conservatives, and some right-wing Conservatives warned that unless the party came to an arrangement with UKIP, it would lose the election badly. In the event, whilst UKIP garnered an impressive number of votes, it was another self-declared insurgent party (albeit one that had been in government for eight years), the SNP, who had the greater impact and damaged Labour.

Commentators struggled to find a new script in the early hours of 8 May for the unexpected outcome. The new narrative concentrated on why Labour had lost and what was so effective about the Conservative campaign. The extended analyses of why the opinion polls had been so badly mistaken were rarely accompanied by much self-criticism by the commentators – including many academics – who had followed the polls blindly. Indeed, the polls' catastrophic failure in 2015 makes a systematic examination of the election outcome harder than it would normally be. Given that the polls were so wrong in their pre-election estimates, how can we trust anything else they tell us about the voters? As we argued in Chapter 9, we need to be particularly careful about questions involving the headline intention to vote figures, since these were so wrong, although we can have somewhat more confidence in findings drawn from some of the underlying questions about secondary characteristics, if only because these were never as narrowly balanced as the headline figures. There is little reason to doubt a poll showing the Conservatives ahead on, say, economic competence in a poll that in any case under-estimates Conservative support. Moreover, most post-election surveys can at least weight their results to match the actual outcome of the election. This diminishes polling error, although it does not necessarily eliminate it.[3]

Those who followed the polling on these fundamentals were less likely to get the election outcome wrong. As one of the Labour team put it: 'Throughout the entire campaign, I was thinking: I must know nothing about politics. Why on earth are we still in with a chance? They had a very clear and powerful message. We had this weird guy. And we're going to have to do deals with the SNP. It just didn't make any sense. How is this possible? And then you got the exit poll, and you think, actually that makes perfect sense.'

The election campaign was criticised for being negative, as is usual. Labour and the Conservatives raised the stakes by warning of the disasters that would follow if the other was in government. A Labour government 'propped up' or 'held to ransom' by the SNP would be a risk to the economic recovery and the maintenance of the UK. In turn, Labour warned that the Conservative programme of steep spending cuts would return Britain to the 1930s and would destroy the NHS. The Liberal Democrats attacked both parties and offered themselves as a head for Labour and heart for the Conservatives. On-message politicians campaigned on 'the long-term economic plan', 'competence versus chaos', 'a millionaires' tax cut' and a '100 hours to save the NHS'. Those who expected a Socratic dialogue about Great Matters of State would have been disappointed, but then they would be disappointed by every election. Voters thought the major parties all pretty equally negative, but were slightly more positive about the behaviour of the other parties.[4]

Among the heated rhetoric, some key issues were neglected, including foreign policy, Europe, the reform of public services and, despite the increased presence of the Greens, climate change.[5] No party made clear where the inevitable cuts in spending programmes would be made. And it was difficult for the Conservatives to argue for the importance of spending cuts – which they claimed made necessary their continuance in government – given their offerings on childcare, the NHS, tax cuts and a generally brighter tomorrow. On 5 May, Janan Ganesh in the *Financial Times* wished 'good riddance to a carnival of nonsense and futility [which] has embarrassed the country with its studious avoidance of little things such as fiscal reality and the state of the world'. But again, this was hardly a new complaint.

For all the talk of the election being exciting and close, the turnout increased by a mere 1% to 66%. In Scotland, because of the high turnout in the referendum, turnout increased by 7% to 71%. Of the ten seats with the highest turnout, five were in Scotland. But the Scottish circumstances – a highly polarising referendum on an existential issue – may well have galvanised a level of political commitment in the short term which spilled over into the subsequent general election, but they are *sui generis* and it is not clear how long such an effect will last. In general, and despite the slight rise, turnouts that would have seemed shockingly low a generation ago now seem to be the norm in British elections.

Even once the election was formally under way, it was not always the top news story noticed by the public. Of the stories that the public noticed most (see Table 14.1) in the first week of the election campaign, the plane crash in the Alps dominated, the election coming second, and of the six weeks of the campaign, election news was only the most-noticed story in three. It was always the first– or second-most noticed story, but sometimes was mentioned by as few as 14% of people, and often not by many more people than had noticed no news story at all. Only in the very last week of the campaign did the percentage citing the election rise above 30% – and even then, fewer than half of respondents mentioned the election as their most-noticed story of the week.[6]

Table 14.1 Stories the public noticed

Week ending	*Most noticed story*	*General election (if not first)*	*% saying none*
2 April	Alps plane crash (60%)	Second place (14%)	13
10 April	General election (24%)		27
17 April	General election (29%)		28
24 April	Mediterranean migrants (38%)	Second place (17%)	22
1 May	Earthquake in Nepal (57%)	Second place (18%)	13
8 May	General election (40%)		14

Source: Populus. Populus polled around 2,000 people aged 18+ each week; the question was open-ended and respondents could name any news story.

The overseas influence on British elections was again evident in terms of personnel as well as techniques. The Conservatives had imported Jim Messina for ground war strategy and Bill Knapp for debate preparations, as well as Lynton Crosby and Mark Textor from Australia. Labour also called on veterans of the Obama election, including the pollster Stan Greenberg, David Axelrod on messaging and the British Matthew McGregor, based in New York, for digital work. The Lib Dems turned to Ryan Coetzee, a South African.

In 2015, the leaders' campaigns were heavily stage-managed, often appearing before pre-selected and politically supportive or otherwise safe audiences for televised events. The size and enthusiasm of the audiences shown on clips on TV programmes were somewhat misleading. Lip service is sometimes paid to the importance of the

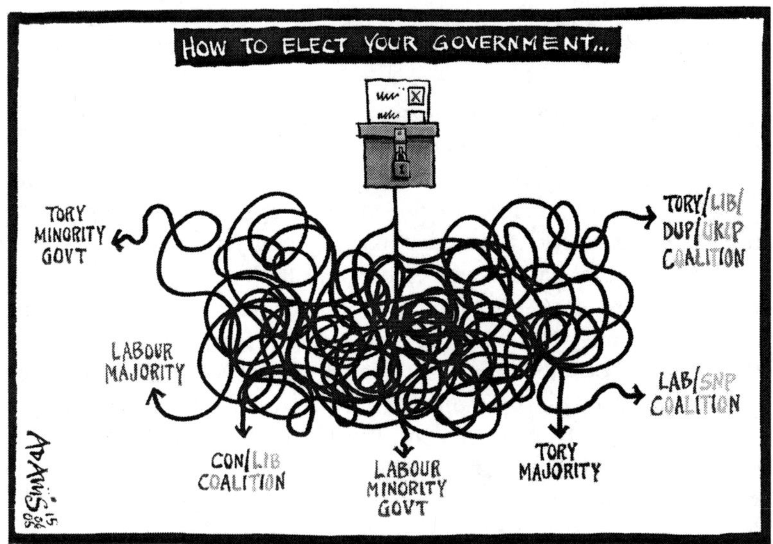

'How to elect your government...'

Christian Adams, *Daily Telegraph*, 6 May 2015 (© Adams/*The Telegraph*)

'team', but party leaders continued to be the most prominent voices for their parties' messages – a trend not helped by the disappearance of the party's morning press conferences, which had necessitated at least some sharing of the limelight previously. The top five politicians to feature in the media were the leaders of the Conservatives, Labour, the Lib Dems, the SNP and UKIP in that order.[7] David Cameron was featured in the media almost four times as often as the second most-featured Conservative politician, George Osborne, whilst Ed Miliband featured almost six times as often as the second most-prominent Labour politician, Ed Balls. The disparity was even starker for the smaller parties. There was only one other Lib Dem apart from Nick Clegg in the top 20 politicians seen on the media and only one other SNP politician apart from Nicola Sturgeon.[8] For UKIP, Plaid Cymru and the Greens, their leader was the only politician to feature in the top 20, for which the bar was to appear in just 0.5% or more of stories.

It is interesting to note what was expected but did not happen. The introduction of leaders' debates in 2010 was thought to have set a precedent. But although some debates did take place in 2015, head-to-head debates between the main party leaders did not, largely because of Cameron's refusal to participate. The painful nature of the negotiations and the shape of the eventual debates – involving representatives of up to seven parties – were themselves testimony to how British politics was mutating beyond the three 'main' parties. The results in 2015 in turn make the possibility of a return to the three-way debates of 2010 even less likely.

The combined circulation of the newspapers was the lowest it has been in any election since 1945. But newspapers still mattered, both directly and in terms of the way they helped determine the broadcast agenda. As one of Labour's press team put it: 'The Tories had, it's not too strong a word, cheerleaders in multiple papers. All we had was the *Mirror.*' And once a story was running on multiple papers' front pages, 'then the BBC decide it's an important story, and we get a double lock and get it high up on their running order as well'.[9] Whilst social media emerged as a partial counterpoint, it was still only a very partial one. After the election, many Labour politicians worried that all it had done was to create an echo chamber, in which those on the left convinced themselves they were virtuous and that no sane person would vote for the Conservatives. 2015 was certainly the first election in which digital campaigning really mattered, but it was more a conduit to broadcast partisan material to voters as anything which fundamentally changed the terms of trade.

The verdict of commentators on the 1987 and 1992 general elections had been that Labour had fought the best campaign, but still lost both decisively. Many within the Labour campaign felt that the 2015 campaign was considerably better run than most recent campaigns – and much better than the dysfunctional 2010 campaign. As one said: 'Of the three I've been closely involved with this was the most collegiate, the most fun, and the most professional.' Yet, once again, the result was nothing short of a disaster.

The relatively small Conservative majority – of just 12 seats – may make the election look close, but Labour was more than six percentage points behind, trailing by just shy of 100 seats. The party lost 40 (of 41) seats in Scotland and made net gains of only 14 in England and Wales, and a net gain of just two from the Conservatives. The party piled up votes in Greater Manchester, Merseyside and inner London, where most of its seats were safe, but fell short where it needed to win. Having thought they were so close to office when the polls closed on 7 May, on the morning of 8 May, Labour woke up facing an electoral mountain. Of the 180 seats in the south outside of London, Labour holds just 12. Within 3,000 votes of victory in only 24 seats, it will need a result of

1997 proportions, gaining over 90 seats (mainly Conservative) and a swing of over 9% to secure a majority in 2020. A minority Labour government, dependent on other parties, may be more achievable, but even here the hurdles are formidable, even before a boundary review that will probably gift the Conservatives another 20 or so seats.

Labour's position is redolent of that identified in the report *Southern Discomfort* which followed the 1992 election defeat.[10] This report had warned that the party needed to regain ground in the south-east and it would not do so by being seen as the party mainly for the poor and under-privileged. Yet in many ways Labour's position is now worse than it was in 1992. The need to recover ground from the SNP in Scotland and ward off UKIP in England and Wales have been added to the perennial challenge of making gains in the south-east and among the middle class. There was no shortage of post-2015 equivalents to *Southern Discomfort*. In the days following 7 May, there were multiple reports into what had gone wrong for Labour, from the Fabian Society's *The Mountain to Climb* to the Smith Institute's *Red Alert*, from Lord Ashcroft's *Project Red Dawn* to Policy Network's *Can Labour Win?* The last of these was co-authored by Giles Radice, who had written the original *Southern Discomfort*. The Trades Union Congress (TUC) and Jon Cruddas, the latter on behalf of groups supporting the Labour Party, also ran research projects into Labour's failure, as did Labour internally. The interim Labour leader Harriet Harman quickly commissioned an inquiry led by Margaret Beckett called 'Learning the Lessons', and largely written by Alan Buckle from KPMG. It was not published. Nor was the other, more empirical, internal report entitled '2015: What Happened?' The Conservatives conducted a happier exercise but their report, 'How the Conservatives Won. Myths and Realities' also remained off limits for all but a handful of insiders. Transparency did not extend outside of party headquarters. Although the reports differed on details, they largely came to the same broad conclusion: Labour lost not because of things it did in the six weeks of the election campaign or because of events in the year or so before, but because it failed on fundamentals about the economy, spending and immigration.

Like Gordon Brown in 2010, Ed Miliband was a dampener on his party's vote. Reactions to Miliband in focus groups – as well as to Labour canvassers and candidates – were often disheartening. When public (and private) polls showed the Conservatives and Labour level-pegging in terms of voting intention, forced questions asking voters to choose between a Conservative government led by Cameron and a Labour one led by Miliband showed the former moving into a narrow but clear lead. On leadership, Cameron led Miliband throughout the Parliament apart from a brief period in spring 2012. On strength, competence, being good in a crisis and willingness to take unpopular decisions, he handsomely outscored Miliband even if he trailed on the question of understanding the concerns of ordinary people and being on their side. A substantial minority of Labour voters preferred Cameron as a leader and UKIP and Lib Dem supporters also preferred him.

Yet many of the internal criticisms made of Miliband were less to do with how he appeared to voters than with his policy choices. It was his campaign and he made the key decisions, despite the reservations of some of his close associates. One of them reflected: 'Ed said what he wanted, did not trim his sails and told me he had "left it all out in the field".' That mood informed his decision to resign once it was clear that Labour had lost. Another criticism levelled was a slightly sterile debate about whether Labour's manifesto was too 'left-wing'. Insofar as voters think in terms of left and right (which they largely do not), the purely technical answer seemed to be 'no'.[11] But the real critique was much more nuanced than this; it was that Labour's appeal seemed to be aimed at only part of the electorate with its promised action on zero-hours contracts, the minimum wage, and freezing some rents and energy prices. There was no vision of the future encompassing economic growth, a more balanced economy or generally feeling good about the country, a contrast to the party campaigns in 1964 or 1997. One of Labour's team was fond of citing a phrase of Tony Judt's, 'The social democracy of fear', as summarising Labour's message: 'The Tories will take away your tax credits, the Tories will take away your pension, the Tories will take away your child benefit, you name it, the Tories will take it away.' But he added: 'Scaring people shitless worked in 2010. But it doesn't work in the same way when you're trying to fight an offensive campaign.' In an offensive campaign, you 'needed some hope'.

Crucially, however, the party never overcame the perceptions of the last Labour government's economic record and the effectiveness of a highly negative Conservative narrative about it. A YouGov post-election poll found by 38% to 32% that voters were still blaming Labour 'for the current spending cuts'. The party had lost the reputation for economic prudence it established during the first two terms of Tony Blair's government. The long 2010–15 campaign was therefore an abject failure in that Labour singularly failed to change the public's perception on its big weaknesses from 2010. A Miliband strategist stated: 'It was not our stance but the record of the last government that was the problem and we never got away from it.' Another key figure described it as a clear case of 'brand failure'. It may be that Miliband would not have been able to reverse the negative perceptions of the party, but it is a fundamental criticism of his leadership that he never really appeared to realise how important it was to do so.

Key Lib Dem contributions to the Coalition – the pupil premium and personal tax allowance – hardly figured in the election campaign, and in government they had failed to win the referendum on the Alternative Vote or deliver House of Lords reform. Surveys at the end of the Parliament showed that the party was seen as largely irrelevant.[12] An Ashcroft focus group in January 2015 had asked people what animal they thought the party leaders would be: one response for Nick Clegg was: 'A Chihuahua in David Cameron's handbag.' Yet despite their poor standing in the polls, the Lib Dems' campaign team had banked on the local reputations of their MPs to enable them to defy electoral gravity. Privately, the party had been still hopeful of holding at least 20 seats, with an upper target of 30 – a figure that should have been enough to keep it involved in post-election negotiations. As shown on p. 402, there was still an incumbency advantage accruing to Lib Dem MPs, but it was not sufficient to withstand the tidal wave that hit them. Ryan Coetzee reflected: 'The result trumped much Lib Dem folklore as the national tide swamped incumbency and local factors.'

In terms of both vote share and seats won, 2015 was the worst result for the Lib Dems, or their predecessors, since 1970. On that measure alone, the 2015 election represented the reversal of a generation's work growing the party. But the true picture was much worse than that. There have been only two occasions since 1832 when a major political party has suffered over one electoral cycle the scale of vote loss experienced

by the Lib Dems between 2010 and 2015.[13] As a proportion of the vote gained or lost, it was even worse. In 2015, the Lib Dems polled just over a third of their 2010 vote; there is only one precedent since 1832 for a major party suffering that sort of a drop.[14] The party held just 14% of the seats it had won in 2010. That is a worse record than in every contest of any major party since 1832; it is even worse than Labour's electoral disaster of 1931. Ever since the formation and rise of the Labour Party, and even when it was in the electoral doldrums, the Liberals were at least the third party in British politics. Whether measured in terms of seats or votes, that is no longer true. And in large parts of the country, the picture is even worse than this implies. Just over half of Lib Dem candidates came fourth, but over a quarter came fifth, and there were more sixth places than first places. The party is only in second place in 63 seats, and the majority of those are seats it held until May 2015.[15]

The scale of the defeat in 2015 was such that the discussion of alternate strategies post-2010 – the various what-ifs discussed on p. 100 – suddenly became otiose. However damaging those alternate strategies might have been, they almost certainly would not have been worse than what actually transpired. Whatever the Lib Dems would have done in 2010 or in the years after – to have allied with an unstable rainbow coalition with Labour, to have refused to join office at all, to have exited the Coalition early – there seems almost no way in which the outcome could have been worse than being reduced to the same number of MPs as the Democratic Unionist Party (DUP).[16]

On top of that, there was the damage that five years of Coalition had inflicted on the party's local government base, or in the Scottish Parliament or in the European Parliament. Shortly after the 2015 election, the Liberal Democrat History Group held a seminar at the House of Commons to discuss the results. The seminar's title: 'Catastrophe.' It was difficult to disagree. The question – which only the Lib Dems can really answer – is whether it was worth it.

For all the talk of the party system fragmenting, the share of the vote gained by the two main parties was broadly similar to most recent elections at just over two-thirds, and the two main parties continued to campaign as though the contest was a binary choice of government between themselves. Indeed, both major parties saw their vote shares increase. Rather than fragmenting further, the British party system both changed and diverged.

The total number of MPs not sitting for either Labour or the Conservatives was, at 87, just two up on 2010. But their make-up was very different. The majority of 'other' MPs in 2010 were Lib Dems. In 2015, by contrast, they sat for the SNP, who had replaced the Lib Dems as the third-placed party in terms of seats in the Commons. The rise in the number of SNP MPs between 2010 and 2015 was greater than that achieved by any party since Sinn Fein in 1918. The precedent cannot be of comfort to unionists given that the partition of Ireland and the creation of the Irish Free State followed within four years. The SNP was all-conquering: the Lib Dems recorded their weakest performance in Scotland since 1970; Labour's share of the vote in Scotland was its lowest since 1918; the Conservatives were at their lowest ever. And despite their impressive performances in England and Wales, UKIP and the Greens were swept aside by the SNP in Scotland; between them, the two parties gained less than 3% of the Scottish vote. The SNP increased their vote most in Labour's safe seats and in which many previously Labour supporters had voted yes in the referendum.

The SNP were helped by a surge in members and a powerful ground operation – and by a very competent and impressive leader. Scottish reaction to the SNP was like nothing else seen in the UK. When asked which party fought the most positive campaign or which was the most likeable, the SNP was by a large margin regarded as the most positive. The British Election Study (BES) asked a question about the emotions associated with each party. Some 42% of (Scottish) respondents said they were proud of the SNP, way above the next highest – the 15% of (Britain-wide) respondents who said they were proud of the Conservatives. The SNP also topped the ratings for 'hopeful', with 34%.[17] In Scotland, when the popularity of the party leaders was tested, Nicola Sturgeon won by the proverbial country mile. Yet it is taking nothing away from the success of the SNP to ask how much any of this was the result of things they were doing during the campaign or even in its build-up. Indeed, those around Sturgeon were very aware of how there were bigger forces at play. 'The campaign ran itself', said one of the SNP team. 'It was going so well ... what do you do?' Or as another key member of the Sturgeon team put it simply: 'The thing about this campaign, it didn't have to be complicated ... It was a campaign whose time had come ... Something had moved.'

In terms of votes, the UK's third party was now UKIP, which simultaneously achieved both a wonderful and a terrible result in 2015. The party gained 3.8 million votes, 13% of the total, compared to 3% in 2010. Despite a slight squeeze in its vote as the election approached, those who had predicted that UKIP's bubble would burst were proved wrong. As the analysis in Appendix 1 shows, the rise in UKIP support was particularly strong in seats which had suffered an above-average rise in unemployment and which had a predominantly white working-class electorate. These, though, are the areas where UKIP's vote increased *most*. It increased, to some extent, almost everywhere – except in Scotland. And although there were certain types of voters who were particularly likely to vote UKIP (see Table 14.2) – older, working class, less educated – the party still polled well amongst other demographic groups. Amongst ABs, for example, it polled at 10% and amongst those aged 18–29 at 9%. Even these would have seemed remarkable figures for a supposedly fringe party at the beginning of the Parliament.

UKIP achieved an impressive 120 second places, often with little more than token candidates. But they failed to convert this support into seats, and even ended the election campaign with fewer MPs than they began it with. The party bested many people's estimates in terms of its vote share, but under-achieved many estimates in terms of seats. Any serious electoral force would want the relationship the other way round. The pre-election debate about where UKIP got its votes from, and which party it would hurt most, ended in a score-draw. In terms of 2010 votes, UKIP took about 2.5 votes off the Conservatives for every vote they took from Labour.[18] But in terms of seats, Labour's internal post-election report concluded that UKIP 'ultimately hurt the electoral prospects of the Labour Party significantly more than those of the Conservatives', both by stopping Labour taking key marginals and by hurting them in those marginal seats that they were attempting to hold from the Conservatives. In other words, UKIP took their votes disproportionately from the Conservatives, but because of the geographical distribution of those votes, they disproportionately hurt Labour in terms of seats.

All leaders dominated their parties' campaigns in 2015, but of none was this truer than of Nigel Farage and UKIP. Farage was UKIP and UKIP

'Labour isn't working'. Bob, *Daily Telegraph*, 9 May 2015 (© Bob/*The Telegraph*)

was Farage. Yet Farage was a divisive figure in the country at large – by far the most disliked party leader in many surveys – and, according to post-election revelations, he was not universally liked within the party either. And despite immense efforts on behalf of the party, he failed to reach Westminster again.

Seen as a base, the result in 2015 was an impressive achievement, albeit less so as a destination. But in order for it to be a base for UKIP's 2020 strategy, UKIP need to be able to build on it. The party's immediate post-election in-fighting did not bode well for its future success, and only in two of the seats in which it is in second place seats does it need a swing of less than 5% to move into first place. Certainly, UKIP can look forward to the EU referendum when Europe and immigration are bound to be more prominent, but the hurdles against the party's progress remain immense. Moreover, whilst it is possible to focus on internal reasons for UKIP's failure (did they target the wrong seats, should they have gone for a less divisive strategy?), part of the reason UKIP fell short was that the other parties – and especially the Conservatives – began to work out how to fight back against them. Having just seen what had happened to their colleagues in Scotland, Labour MPs who now find UKIP in second place are not complacent about the situation in which they find themselves. As one Midlands Labour MP put it after the election: 'This is an existential crisis for the Labour Party. UKIP could SNP us in England, if they just hold their nerve. If we don't get this right, there won't be a Labour Party in 2020.' The possibility of a UKIP surge rivalling the SNP may be slight, but it will not be treated lightly.[19]

Long before the votes were counted, the Green Party knew that they had failed to achieve gains in any of their target seats, although they knew they would comfortably hold on to Brighton Pavilion. And, as with UKIP, in terms of votes, their support was both a record for the party and a potential base for forthcoming elections in London, Wales and Liverpool. But the Greens continued to draw support from a very specific and limited part of the electorate (see p. 408), beyond which they struggled to expand.[20]

The polls consistently indicated that voters preferred a single-party government to a coalition, despite apparently collectively denying a majority to any one party. It is yet another indicator of the failure of the Lib Dems' strategy that after spending five years trying to demonstrate the benefits of coalition, the dangers of a hung parliament became such a major issue in the 2015 campaign. Stephan Shakespeare on 3 May wrote that he found voters split 50:50 between supporting a Cameron-led minority government and a Miliband-led one. But when it came to a choice of coalitions, voters preferred the Conservatives, supported by the Lib Dems, over Labour relying on the goodwill of the SNP, by 58% to 42%. Paradoxically, of course, the warnings about the SNP only worked if the polls were correct in forecasting a close-run race between Labour and the Conservatives. Yet, after 7 May, Lynton Crosby and Jim Messina claimed the Conservatives had long held a clear lead. They should perhaps have been grateful that the public polls were so wrong.

All elections are followed by 'if onlys'. Some members of Miliband's team, including Miliband himself, reflected after 7 May that if the polls had reported a clear Conservative lead over previous months, the media coverage would have been very different. The broadcasters and the press would not have been relentlessly discussing the consequences of a Labour–SNP accommodation, but would have provided greater scrutiny of the policies a majority Conservative government would implement. Rather than extensive media coverage of the SNP holding Miliband to 'ransom', a scenario which depended entirely on the parties being neck and neck in the polls, there might have been more discussion of the impact of Conservative welfare cuts. The Miliband adviser Tom Baldwin said: 'I remain convinced that the media focus on us in the last half of the campaign may have delivered a Tory majority rather than a hung Parliament.'[21] Nick Clegg reached a similar conclusion:

> Basically what happened was the massive amount of broadcast coverage devoted to the possible hypothetical outcome of a Labour/SNP government was like giving the richest party in British politics, the Conservatives, hundreds of millions of pounds of additional attack advertising funding ... It had a determining effect on the outcome and meant the government that was elected wasn't rigorously scrutinised.[22]

The claim that if the media had believed a majority Conservative government had been possible, they would have reported the election in a different way, and one which would have focused more on the Conservatives and less on the possibility of a Labour–SNP accommodation, seems unarguable – and after the election many journalists accepted this. But it was not just pollsters and the media who thought that the election would not result in a majority government. The parties thought the same: it is difficult for the Lib Dems to complain that the media reported the near-certainty of a hung parliament, given that the Lib Dems were consistently making the same claim as a key part of their appeal to voters in a campaign in which they publicly set out red lines for post-election negotiations. Moreover, even if the polls had been completely accurate, they would only have been reporting a

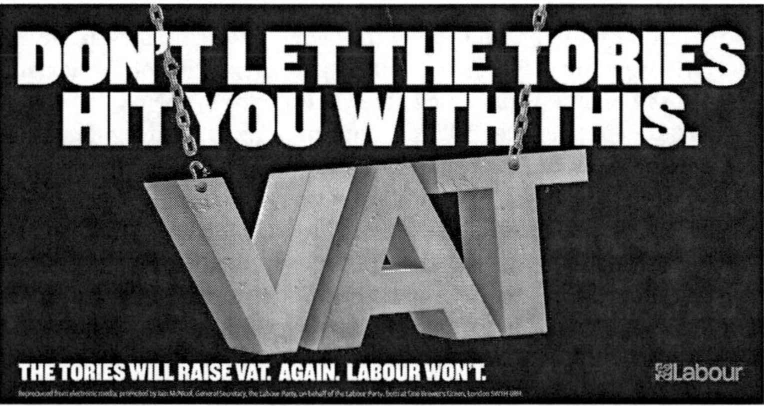

projected Conservative majority of 12, a slim enough majority that the margin of error alone could have reduced the government to minority status (and, at the upper end of the margin of error, never raised its majority above comfortable). There would presumably still have been considerable speculation about the possibility of a hung parliament and the role that the SNP might play in it. In any case, as we argue in Chapter 9, if the polls had been accurately reporting the public's views *throughout* the Parliament, they may have put the Conservatives ahead in the polls by as early as 2013, which may then have led to a very different second half of the Parliament in lots of ways. What the Miliband/Baldwin analysis overlooks is that the polls probably protected Ed Miliband. Had they shown a 6% lead for the Conservatives earlier in the Parliament, his position could have become untenable much earlier than 8 May. That is a much larger counterfactual than the effect that the polls and the media had on the short campaign.

After the election, the BES claimed to have found no evidence that the rise of the SNP played a role in influencing the outcome of the election in England and Wales.[23] This is a conclusion that needs to be treated with some caution, and not just for the reason that the BES – like all polls – got the election result wrong, under-reporting Conservative support whilst over-reporting Labour. For one thing, noting that there is no evidence for something is not quite the same as that thing not existing. And whilst the BES contained multiple questions about Scottish politics, they were asked almost exclusively in Scotland. Only late in the day, for example, did it begin to ask questions about either the SNP or its leadership to voters in England and Wales. Moreover, many of the questions it did ask were not ideal.[24] There is a danger of putting too much emphasis on polling data that we know is problematic and that asked poorly constructed questions of the wrong people. Moreover, even within the various polling data, there are plenty of signs of people in England and Wales becoming concerned about the rise of the SNP in Scotland. Nicola Sturgeon and the SNP may have been popular in Scotland, but the phenomenon did not travel well. In the TUC/Greenberg Quinlan Rosner Research (GQRR) post-election survey, for example, the fear that a Labour government would be 'bossed around by Nicola Sturgeon and the Scottish nationalists' was the third-biggest doubt voters had about voting Labour; it was the second-biggest doubt for those aged over 55, or men, or those who had only considered voting Labour. Even the BES noticed that UKIP supporters – who took a dim view of the SNP – went back to the Conservatives in greater numbers than they would have predicted. Why might UKIP voters – many of whom identify strongly as English and resent foreign political forces telling them what to do – respond to an anti-SNP campaign? It does not seem counter-intuitive.

On the other hand, the key party strategists for Labour, the Conservatives and the Lib Dems have absolutely no doubt that the rise of the SNP had a major influence on the result of the election south of the border. Multiple local candidates – of all parties –talk about the issue coming up repeatedly. To take just a handful of examples:

> The whole debate about Sturgeon, propping up a weak Labour government, I had that repeated back to me, unprompted, on the doorstep. (Conservative backbench MP)

> There was a belief that Scotland got more of the cake anyway; didn't want them getting even more. (Conservative Cabinet minister)

> It was just the idea that Scotland might be getting a better deal out of the government than they would in Bolton. (Labour Shadow Cabinet member)

> We fully understood the problem, but we didn't realise the scale of it. But what could we have done if we had? The terror of the SNP, propping up an unpopular Labour government, just swamped us. (Lib Dem strategist)

Here too, however, we need to be careful. As these quotes show, if there was an SNP effect, it operated in multiple ways. At its most indirect, as noted in Chapter 7, it dominated the media agenda and prevented Labour from getting its message across. Second, whilst for some people in England and Wales the fear of the SNP playing a role in government may have been sufficiently strong on its own, for others it will have reinforced existing doubts about Labour and Ed Miliband. A key member of the Conservative campaign team was explicit about this during the last few days of the campaign. When we put it to him that it seemed a distraction from the core Conservative messages about leadership and the economy to be talking so much about the SNP, he replied that, on the contrary, it helped to reinforce the key Conservative messages. Labour's own internal report into the election noted that 'SNP threat messaging had a strong impact with middle-class families in England', but it went on: 'This line of messaging also played into concerns around Labour's leadership.' Or, as another of Labour's team put it: 'Had we done real repair work on the brand, we would have been less vulnerable

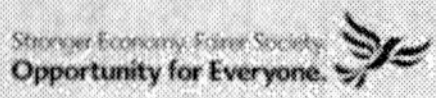

to the attacks; we couldn't survive it because we were so weak.' For some within Labour and the Lib Dems, the attraction of focusing on the rise of the SNP is obvious: it provides an easy excuse, enabling them to dodge the more fundamental failings with their campaigns and with the way in which their party or leadership was perceived. This political get-out-of-jail-free card is too convenient, and not just because the rise of the SNP in Scotland was hardly exogenous to the behaviour of the other political parties in the first place.

The various fundamental problems with the opinion polls mean that we may never get a definitive answer to the question of how significant the rise of the SNP was to voters in England and Wales, and to what extent it drove voters back to the Conservative fold – or kept them from straying in the first place. But to us it seems unlikely that it did not have an effect from which the Conservatives benefited, even if a necessary condition for that effect to exist was Labour's own weaknesses – and it at least seems plausible that without that effect, there would have been no Conservative majority government in 2015.

For all that politicians talk of concerns about voter engagement and turnout, campaigners are now more interested in who votes and where than in national levels of turnout. They invest heavily in micro-targeting of undecided voters in marginal seats, using opinions polls and social media. An effect of such targeting is that personal experience of the campaign can bypass many voters.

The major parties devoted more resources than ever to their field campaigns in 2015. But the election result raised questions about what constitutes effective campaigning. Labour made more contacts with voters than other parties, had more workers in the field and were widely thought to be winning the ground war. Once the results were known, some campaign organisers and candidates questioned the relevance of the party's message and the quality of the conversations that activists had with target voters. Many voters told Labour canvassers and pollsters they would vote for the party, but, according to Ipsos MORI and the BES, did not do so on polling day. So much for the impact of Labour's get-out-the-vote operation. The party's total vote increased by more than 700,000 compared to 2010, but it fell short of what it expected. Ipsos MORI blamed 'lazy' Labour supporters for not turning out on 7 May. Labour's vote share in their key seats increased by just over 1%, which was pretty similar to the national picture.

The Conservative ground war was clearly effective in achieving a more efficient distribution of votes than in recent elections. The party's vote share fell by 2% in its safe seats, but increased by the same level in marginal seats. That efficiency saw it take twice as many seats from the Lib Dems as Labour did, and eight from Labour. The Conservatives also did well among demographic groups (the middle class and the over-55s) which turned out strongly on polling day. And the incumbency 'bonus' for MPs who had first been elected in 2010 of 4.5% exceeded expectations.

Yet for all the praise which the Conservative ground team acquired, it is not obvious that they were doing very much differently from Labour. As one of those in charge of Labour's ground operation – admittedly *parti pris* – put it: 'Everyone is praising them to the skies, because they won. We were doing all of that, and we lost.' Beyond the hype, it is difficult to identify many structural differences between the Labour and Conservative ground operations. They all micro-targeted in a sophisticated way, combining polling data, canvass returns and commercially available data; they all used segmented direct mail and paid adverts on social media. The difference is that the Conservatives invested more resources into this than Labour were able to do, and for longer. That element often gets left out of slightly self-serving accounts given by the Conservatives of how brilliant their ground operation was. In addition, no matter how good a ground operation is, it cannot remedy larger problems. As another member of Labour's ground team put it: 'I'm pretty sure we were targeting the right people but they just didn't like the product.'

Table 14.2 shows how the electorate voted on 7 May based on a survey weighted to the election outcome. The Conservatives led Labour among the 60+ age group by 45% to 25%, among private sector workers by 43% to 26%, and among C2s (skilled manual workers) by 36% to 31%. Labour led among trade unionists 39% to 30%, and by 43% to 27% among those unionists in the public sector. The Lib Dems suffered big falls among all types of voters, but especially among students (down by 26 percentage points) and the young (down 24 percentage points amongst those aged 18–29). The biggest party difference was among press readership, with the *Daily Mirror* and *The Guardian* attracting an overwhelmingly Labour readership, and the *Daily Telegraph* a Conservative one.

The analysis in Appendix 1 confirms that the Conservatives did better in seats with above-average household incomes, lower levels of unemployment and a smaller proportion of those in public sector employment. In seats with the opposite features and more ethnically diverse electorates, Labour did better.

An Ashcroft survey of 12,000 people conducted on polling day conveys some idea of why the electorate voted as it did.[25] Even allowing for its under-reporting of the Conservative vote, the results are striking. The two most popular reasons Conservatives gave for their vote were that Cameron would make the best Prime Minister and that they trusted Conservative motives and values (both mentioned by 71%). Some 49% preferred the Conservatives' promises and 46% thought they would make a more competent government. Only 39% of Labour voters mentioned the Labour leader as making the best Prime Minister, while 75% preferred the party's motives and values, and 66% their promises. On motives and values, Labour were just ahead, but the party's vote was not based primarily on its leadership or competence, while Conservatives were three times more likely to mention these two reasons.

Ashcroft also found that a key difference between Labour and Conservative supporters was the greater optimism and life satisfaction among the latter. By a margin of 2:1, Conservatives thought that life for most children would be better than it was for their parents. Labour voters, on the other hand, were more likely to believe that life was better 30 years ago and were less likely to agree that people could succeed if they worked hard regardless of their social background. The differences were reflected in the campaigns of the two parties, with Cameron promising better times ahead and Miliband emphasising the unfairness of life in modern Britain. In this respect, Labour voters had more in common with UKIP's voters, who were often mourning a better yesterday.

When asked about 'the most important issue for me and my family', the top three issues mentioned by Conservatives were the economy/ jobs, improving the NHS and the cost of living. The second and third

Table 14.2 How the nation voted (GB)

	Con	Lab	UKIP	Lib Dem	Green	Con lead	Change since 2010		
	%	%	%	%	%		Con	Lab	LD
All	38	31	13	8	4	*7*	+1	+1	−16
Men	37	29	15	8	4	*8*	−1	−1	−15
Women	38	33	12	8	4	*5*	+2	+1	−17
Age 18–29	32	36	9	9	7	*−4*	+2	+3	−24
Age 30–39	36	34	10	8	5	*2*	+4	+3	−20
Age 40–49	33	33	14	7	4	*0*	+1	+1	−17
Age 50–59	36	32	16	7	3	*4*	+1	−1	−15
Age 60+	45	25	16	7	2	*20*	+1	−2	−12
AB social grade (professional/managerial)	44	28	9	10	4	*16*	+4	0	−16
C1 (white collar)	38	30	11	9	5	*8*	+2	+2	−18
C2 (skilled manual)	36	31	17	6	3	*5*	−1	−2	−16
DE (semi–/unskilled)	29	37	18	6	3	*−8*	−4	0	−14
Highest education: GCSE or lower	38	30	20	5	2	*8*	−2	−1	−13
Highest education: A-level	37	31	11	8	5	*6*	0	+2	−17
University graduates	35	34	6	11	6	*1*	+3	+5	−21
Own home outright	47	23	15	8	3	*24*	+2	−1	−14
Mortgage-payers	42	29	12	8	3	*13*	+2	0	−18
Social housing	20	45	18	5	3	*−25*	−4	+3	−15
Privately renting	34	32	12	9	7	*2*	+1	+5	−24
Work in private sector	43	26	14	7	4	*17*	+1	0	−17
Work in public sector	33	36	11	9	4	*−3*	+1	+4	−18
Unemployed	21	43	16	6	6	*−22*	−5	+5	−20
Full-time students	29	37	6	11	9	*−8*	+4	0	−26
Trade union members	30	39	12	8	4	*−9*	+2	+5	−21
Indian subcontinent roots	33	54	3	5	3	*−21*	+5	+4	−15
Asian roots (not Indian subcontinent)	47	34	4	9	4	*13*	+6	−6	−10
Caribbean/African roots	21	67	2	4	3	*−46*	−1	+1	−11
Household income less than £20k per year	29	36	17	7	4	*−7*	−2	+2	−17
Household income £20–39k p.a	37	32	14	8	4	*5*	0	+1	−7
Household income £40–69k p.a	42	29	10	9	4	*13*	+4	−1	−17
Household income more than £70k per year	51	23	7	10	3	*28*	+5	0	−15
Telegraph readers	69	8	12	8	1	*61*	0	−3	−8
Daily Mail readers	59	14	19	5	1	*45*	−1	−3	−11
Times readers	55	20	6	13	3	*35*	+7	0	−13
Express readers	51	13	27	5	1	*38*	−7	−4	−11
Sun readers	47	24	19	4	1	*23*	−2	−5	−10
Star readers	25	41	26	3	1	*−16*	−3	−4	−19
Independent readers	17	47	4	16	11	*−30*	0	+11	−30
Mirror readers	11	67	9	5	2	*−56*	+2	+1	−12
Guardian readers	6	62	1	11	14	*−56*	+1	+11	−32

Source: '2015 Analysis of Vote. How People Voted', YouGov, 30 May 2015. The sample is 100,000, conducted between 6–18 May 2015, weighted to reflect the overall result in England, Wales and Scotland.

of these were thought to be Labour issues. The NHS was Labour's strongest card and the issue steadily rose in salience towards the end of the Parliament – Labour always had a decisive lead as the party most trusted to deal with it. But issue preferences are only part of the picture; what also matters are perceptions of the party's competence and ability to deliver on acceptable terms. It was telling that the Ashcroft poll conducted on 7 May found that the over-65s, the age group that included the heaviest users of the service and those most likely to vote, trusted the Conservatives more than Labour on the NHS (42% to 26%).

Peter Kellner analysed the 10% of voters who told YouGov they had thought of voting Labour, but in the end did not. He found that most of them preferred income tax cuts over giving higher benefits to poorer families. For Labour loyalists, on the other hand, those preferences were reversed. Polling for Jon Cruddas' Independent Review into the party's defeat showed that many Labour voters, who were often socially liberal and progressive, were losing touch with the views, often socially conservative, of the voters the party had lost and needed to recapture. Although voters thought that the way the economy worked was often unfair and needed radical reform, they also agreed with the proposition that 'the country needs to live within its means'.[26]

Not for the first time, the effects of the British first-past-the-post electoral system came under critical scrutiny. Critics wondered if it was no longer fit for purpose in the era of multi-party politics, being neither representative nor likely to produce a stable majority government. In 2015 a majority for one party emerged, but there were some gross imbalances between share of votes and share of seats. In Scotland the electoral system had benefited Labour in the past, but in 2015 the SNP's 50% share of the vote provided the party with more than 90% of Scottish seats. On average, an SNP MP needed just 25,000 votes to be elected, compared to the one Green MP, whose party gained 1.1 million, and the UKIP MP, who needed 3.8 million. While the SNP benefited from concentrating their vote, gaining 56 seats for 4.7% of the vote, UKIP gained one seat for nearly 13%. The Conservatives needed 34,000 votes per MP, while Labour needed 40,000 votes.

UKIP lost out because their support was evenly spread across England. There was nothing new about this. The Lib Dems, and their predecessors, had suffered massively for spreading their vote too evenly under the first-past-the-post system, particularly in 1983 and 1987. Nor was there anything new in a government gaining a majority of seats with less than 38% of the vote. Labour had a comfortable majority in

2005 on 35%. Electoral reform for Westminster had been comprehensively defeated in the referendum in 2011 and, however much those on the wrong side of the system complained after the election about its 'unfairness', reforming the electoral system was unlikely to be a priority for Cameron in the remaining years of his premiership. Yet, as the analysis in Appendix 1 shows, there is nothing inevitable about the electoral system producing majority outcomes in the future, and consequently it is still easy enough to imagine circumstances in which electoral reform could become one of the planks in a post-election negotiation in the future.

The election confirmed more strongly than ever that party vote shares do not go up or down by the same amount in all constituencies, but, as shown in Appendix 1, the outcome in seats would have been similar to the actual result if the changes in party support had been uniform across constituencies within each nation. There was no longer a UK party system, but different patterns of party competition across the nations. In England the lead party was the Conservatives, in Wales Labour, in Scotland the SNP and in Northern Ireland the DUP. And within England, the regional differences are stark. Labour, dominant in the north of England, is as weak as ever in the south-east (outside of London) and the south-west.

Less noticed, but of huge significance in explaining the outcome of the election, was the reversal of the pro-Labour bias in the electoral system – something on which many Labour supporters had been depending to drag them over the finishing line. Because of the collapse of the Lib Dem vote and the rise of the SNP, British electoral geography, having hampered the Conservatives for decades, now helped them. The analysis in Appendix 1 shows how the Conservatives have suddenly become the beneficiary of the electoral system; with similar shares of the vote, they would be 46 seats ahead of Labour.

For all the sound and fury, many elections do not matter as much as their protagonists claim at the time. Policy choices are driven by much more than any single election, however exciting, and events can scupper even the largest electoral mandate. But the potential significance of the 2015 election was clear almost as soon as the ballot boxes were opened. The Conservative victory ushered in the promised referendum on EU membership, to take place by 2017, with Britain's exit from the EU a realistic prospect, if far from a racing certainty. That alone would be one of the most significant constitutional developments for a generation or more. But were it to happen, it would then make a second Scottish independence referendum almost inevitable, in which the chances of a vote for independence would likely be higher than before. And even without an out vote occurring in the EU referendum, the chances of a second Scottish referendum are high, and despite the SNP's claims to not want a Conservative government, it was not just the most cynical who could see the benefits to the SNP of a Conservative administration at Westminster, against which they could fulminate. A majority Conservative government at Westminster, supported by a record low proportion of the Scottish electorate, is a political gift to Nicola Sturgeon, however much she claims it is not a welcome one.

With Ed Miliband's immediate resignation as Labour leader, the Labour Party fell into another leadership contest. Despite the various post-election diagnoses of Labour's failure, all stressing the need to attract Tory voters and deal with the doubts that centrist voters had about the party, the left claimed that a radical platform would enthuse the young and non-voters, and would bring back voters from the SNP and UKIP. The candidate espousing the latter view, Jeremy Corbyn, won the leadership comfortably, aided by a mass influx of new party members and supporters. Almost all psephological analysis of Labour's support between 2010 and 2015, as well as what we know about non-voters, the UKIP vote or indeed the nature of support for the SNP, would indicate that the Corbyn strategy is a route to an electoral brick wall.

Yet psephological analysis had not predicted a Conservative victory in 2015. Indeed, the last volume in this series argued that the Conservatives would need to have a double-digit lead over Labour to secure a majority, only for David Cameron to secure his 2015 majority despite the Conservatives' lead over Labour narrowing.[27] Similarly, at the beginning of the 2010 Parliament, few people – however eminent – predicted that the SNP would win a majority in the Scottish Parliament and secure a referendum that they would come (relatively) close to winning. Even by early 2014, almost no one predicted that the SNP would do well in the following year's general election, let alone achieve a near-clean sweep. And almost no one – least of all the man himself – predicted that Jeremy Corbyn would become leader of Her Majesty's Opposition. It is therefore perhaps better to approach the road to 2020 with a more open mind.

Notes

1. 'Mervyn King Warned That Election Victor Will Be Out of Power for a Generation, Claims Economist', *The Guardian*, 29 April 2010.

2. See, for example, James Kirkup, 'Whatever Happened to the Conservatives' Boring, Disciplined Campaign?', *Daily Telegraph*, 10 April 2015; Rachel Sylvester, 'Conservatives are Swerving All Over the Place', *The Times*, 21 April 2015; Tim Montgomerie, 'Nine Ideas to Rejig the Conservative Election Campaign', *The Times*, 13 April 2015. Or, from before the short campaign, see Peter Kellner, 'Why aren't the Tories Doing Better?', *Sunday Times*, 22 February 2015; Lord (Michael) Ashcroft, 'Why aren't the Tories Running Away with the Election?', lordashcroftpolls.com, 18 March 2015; 'Why aren't the Tories Winning?', *The Spectator*, 4 April 2015.
3. Much depends on why the polls were originally wrong, as discussed in Chapter 9.
4. The British Election Study included a question asking about the tone of the campaigns. Respondents were asked to place the parties on a 1–5 scale, where 1 meant a party had focused mainly on criticising other parties (negative) or 5 (where it had focused mainly on putting forward its own policies and personalities). In order of increasing positivity, the scores were: Labour, 2.7; the Conservatives and the Lib Dems, both 2.8; UKIP, 3.0; Plaid Cymru, 3.2; the Greens, 3.3; the SNP, 3.5. The figures for Plaid and the SNP are for Wales and Scotland only respectively. The stand-out figure is the SNP. Just 11% of people gave the Conservatives the most positive score, just 8% gave it to Labour and just 7% gave it to the Lib Dems – but in Scotland, a full 38% gave the SNP a score of 5.
5. Andrew Gamble, 'The Economy' in Andrew Geddes and Jon Tonge (eds), *Britain Votes 2015*. Oxford University Press, 2015.
6. As well as the general category of 'general election', respondents would occasionally give more specific responses, but these were always very small numbers, always fewer than 10%, such as the 'EdStone' (1%), Ed Miliband and Russell Brand (1%), David Cameron ruling out a third term (1%), the party manifestos (never more than 8%) or the leaders' debates (never more than 6%).
7. Data drawn from the Loughborough University Communication Research Centre research: blog.lboro.ac.uk/general-election. The figures refer to media appearances in a range of press and broadcast media between 30 March and 7 May 2015.
8. These were Danny Alexander and Alex Salmond, both with less than 1% of appearances.
9. He added: 'Even the *Guardian* were much more studious and independent ... Various people in the office were just as annoyed with the *Guardian* as with the *Telegraph*.'
10. Giles Radice, *Southern Discomfort*. Fabian Society, 1992.
11. Jane Green and Chris Prosser, 'Learning the Right Lessons from Labour's 2015 Defeat'. *Juncture*, 2015, 22.2.
12. See D. Cutts and A. Russell, 'From Coalition to Catastrophe: The Electoral Meltdown of the Liberal Democrats' in Geddes and Tonge (eds), *Britain Votes 2015*.
13. Both were the Liberals, between 1910 and 1918, and 1929 and 1931. Neither were good omens.
14. Again, the Liberals between 1929 and 1931.

15. The majority of their other second place seats are those they held recently until 2010 or 2005.
16. As this book goes to press, even one of these is still being contested in the courts.
17. The SNP were also the party with the lowest figure for 'none'; people had reactions to the SNP. Source: Wave 6, British Election Study, core weighting.
18. Although, as mentioned above (see p. 114), trace people's voting back further than 2010 and the relationship becomes messier.
19. As one member of Labour's National Executive Committee (NEC) put it, there were real problems with the possibility of Labour being seen as the party of the establishment in any EU referendum: 'You cannot go around saying to people, "you could lose all of this", if they haven't got anything to begin with.'
20. In terms of the Mosaic categories, Green support is strongest amongst four groups, especially the so-called 'Liberal Opinions'. This last group is the type of voter amongst whom UKIP did worst.
21. T. Baldwin, 'The BBC was Not in the Pocket of Labour This Election. Quite the Opposite', *The Guardian*, 13 May 2015.
22. Speech to the Royal Television Society conference, Cambridge, 18 September 2015.
23. Green and Prosser, 'Learning the Right Lessons from Labour's 2015 Defeat'.
24. As an example, the BES contained a question about whether a party had a 'real chance' of being in government or not, 'either forming a government by itself or as part of a coalition'. But this excludes other ways in which parties might be involved in government, such as confidence and supply agreements. This question was asked after the SNP, for example, had ruled out a coalition with Labour (and vice versa), after which the 'correct' response to this question about the SNP was 'no'. But would a 'no' response indicate that the respondent is very clued-up about politics, understands that the SNP would not be in coalition but might still have an influence, or does it just indicate they did not think the SNP would have any influence? Who knows?
25. Lord Ashcroft, 'Why Did People Vote as They Did? My Post-vote Poll', lordashcroftpolls.com, 8 May 2015.
26. 'Labour Stands on the Brink of Becoming Irrelevant to the Majority of Working People', labourlist.org, 13 August 2015.
27. See John Curtice, Stephen Fisher and Robert Ford, 'Appendix 2: An Analysis of the Results' in Dennis Kavanagh and Philip Cowley, *The British General Election of 2010*. Palgrave Macmillan, 2010, p. 416.

Appendix 1: The Results Analysed

John Curtice, Stephen D. Fisher and Robert Ford

Introduction

At first glance, the outcome of the 2015 election looks like a return to normality. In 2010, no one party managed to secure an overall majority, only the second time that this had happened since 1945, and the country found itself undergoing the uncommon experience of being governed by a peacetime coalition. This time around, however, one party did manage to secure a majority and Britain returned to single-party majority government. True, at just 12 seats, the Conservatives' majority still looks rather small by the standards of many a previous post-war British election, and indeed it may not be enough to ensure that the party has a majority throughout its five-year term.[1] But given that at 6.6 points (in Great Britain), the Conservatives' lead in votes was rather smaller than it had been in 2010 (7.3 points), the first-past-the-post electoral system had at least proven rather more effective at delivering a clear majoritarian outcome than had been the case in 2010.

Yet if we look more closely, the outcome of the 2015 election also looks nothing like 'normal'. In many respects it represented a radical break with the past. The Liberal Democrats won fewer votes and seats than at any time since 1970 and the party lost its position as the third party in British politics, which it had occupied ever since 1922. Third place in terms of votes was now held instead by the United Kingdom Independence Party (UKIP), a party that was only founded in 1993 and which had previously never managed to win more than 3% of the vote in a general election. However, when it came to seats, it was the Scottish National Party (SNP), which had hitherto never had more than 11 MPs, that now claimed the honour by winning no less than 56 of Scotland's 59 seats. In achieving that feat, the nationalists shattered Labour's previous dominance of Scottish politics, leaving the party with its worst Scottish result since 1918. Meanwhile, the Greens, who had been fighting elections for 40 years without a great deal to show for it, also secured a higher share of the vote than ever before.

One consequence of these developments is that rather than comprising one Britain-wide election, the 2015 election looks like two separate contests – one in England and Wales, and the other in Scotland.[2] For, as an examination of Table A2.4 in Appendix 2 shows, the outcomes in these two parts of Britain were very different from each other. Both the Conservatives and Labour enjoyed a modest increase in support in England and Wales (the first time that this has happened since 1951), with Labour advancing the more. In Scotland both parties fell back, Labour especially so. UKIP registered a double-digit increase in its share of the vote in England and in Wales, but in Scotland barely advanced at all. Equally, the increase in support for the Greens was much weaker north of the border. Above all, not only did the SNP win almost every seat in Scotland, it also secured half the vote, whereas the party's counterpart in Wales, Plaid Cymru, barely did any better than in 2010.

We therefore have a relatively familiar question to address: how and why did the Conservatives manage to win the principal battle for power with Labour? That contest has preoccupied the analysis of many a previous British election.[3] But we also have three more unusual questions to consider. First, how did the Liberal Democrats manage to fall so far? Second, what lies behind the unprecedented success of UKIP on the one hand and the Greens on the other? And, third, what did happen in the apparently wholly *sui generis* contest in Scotland?

Our evidence consists of the election results themselves. In particular, we focus on how the level of support for the parties changed between 2010 and 2015, how this change varied from one kind of constituency to another, and how the parties' performances were reflected and refracted by the electoral system. This is far from being the only way of addressing our questions. Much analysis and commentary about voting behaviour is based on the evidence of sample surveys, and such surveys are invaluable to any attempt to ascertain why, in general, voters behaved as they did. However, voters do not vote in isolation, but do so in particular constituencies that differ in terms of their social character and political complexion. By examining where parties did particularly well and particularly badly, we can secure vital clues as to how voters might have been influenced by these considerations. Meanwhile, it is only by examining the election results themselves that we can understand how the electoral system converted votes into seats.

Measuring change

Usually, measuring the extent to which a party's vote has risen or fallen since the last election is relatively straightforward. We simply ascertain the difference between the percentage of the vote a party won this time and the share it won at the previous election. Moreover, we do so irrespective of the share of the vote that a party won last time around. We do not anticipate that the change in a party's share of the vote will or should be proportional to (or in any other way related to) the share of the vote it won last time around.[4]

Table A1.1 summarises the level and distribution (across all constituencies in Great Britain) of this measure of change in the share of the vote for those parties that fought all or most of the seats in 2015. It shows the change in each party's overall share of the vote across Britain as a whole, the average (mean) change in that share across all of the seats that the party contested this time and last time, and the median of the change across all those constituencies, that is, the value which divides those changes into two equally sized groups. The table also shows the standard deviation, a measure of the extent to which the change in vote share varied from one constituency to another.

What immediately stands out is the scale of the losses suffered by the Liberal Democrats. On average, their vote fell by around 15 percentage points. However, we can also see that, as measured by the standard deviation, the scale of the party's losses varied considerably from constituency to constituency. At 5.0, this figure is higher than at any previous election since the then Liberal Party started fighting elections on a Britain-wide basis in 1974. Moreover, at 14.6, the median drop in the party's share of the vote is rather less than the mean drop; this indicates that there were some constituencies where the Liberal Democrat vote fell especially heavily, falls not counterbalanced by a similar number of particularly small drops.

There is a simple reason why this is the case. Given that the party only won 24% of the vote in 2010, there were many constituencies – no less than 152 – where the party did not win as much as 15.5% of the vote in 2010. In these places it was arithmetically impossible for the Liberal Democrat vote to fall by as much as it did nationally. Consequently, the Liberal Democrat vote must to some degree have fallen more heavily in those places where the party had previously been stronger – and perhaps on occasion very heavily indeed.

The extent to which this happened is illustrated in Table A1.2, which shows the average drop in the Liberal Democrat share of the vote broken down by how well the party performed in 2010. In seats where the Liberal Democrats won less than 16% of the vote in 2010, the party's vote fell on average by just over ten points. In those where it won more than 28% five years previously, its vote fell by almost twice as much, that is, by nearly 20 points. This does not mean that the scale

Table A1.1 Measures of change since 2010

	Overall	*Mean*	*Median*	*Standard deviation*
Change in Con vote	+0.8	+1.0	+1.2	3.9
Change in Lab vote	+1.5	+1.4	+2.6	8.0
Change in Lib Dem vote	–15.5	–15.4	–14.6	5.1
Change in UKIP vote	+9.7	+10.3	+10.1	4.8
Total vote swing	–0.7	–0.2	–0.3	4.3
Two-party swing	–0.7	–1.0	–1.4	5.5
Change in turnout	+1.1	+1.1	+0.6	3.1

Note: Buckingham (no Labour or Liberal Democrat candidates in 2010 and 2015) is excluded from the calculation of the mean, median and standard deviation of all statistics apart from turnout. The seat is also excluded from all analysis of party performance in this appendix. Note that UKIP did not fight 19 seats (all of them in Scotland) and, of the remaining 614, only fought 552 seats in 2010 as well. Total vote swing is the average of the change in the Conservative share of the vote and the Labour share of the vote. Two-party swing is the change in the Conservative share of the votes cast for Conservative and Labour only (that is, the two-party vote). In both cases a plus sign indicates a swing to the Conservatives and a minus sign a swing to Labour.

of the Liberal Democrat losses was simply proportional to their share of the vote – the losses in the seats where the party was weakest represent 80% of the vote the party won in these seats in 2010, whereas the losses in those where it was strongest constitute only just over half of its previous vote. But the pattern does mean that in assessing how well a party performed in a constituency, we often need to take into account how strong the Liberal Democrats were in that seat beforehand. In some cases the change in a party's share of the vote may be relatively low or high simply because there were relatively few or relatively many Liberal Democrat votes to be lost.

Table A1.2 Change in Liberal Democrat share of the vote since 2010 by Liberal Democrat share of the vote in 2010

Liberal Democrat % share of the vote 2010	*Mean change in Liberal Democrat % share of the vote 2010–15*	*Seats*
Less than 16%	–10.4	170
16–22%	–14.4	179
22–28%	–17.8	121
More than 28%	–19.8	161
All seats	–15.4	631

This is potentially less of a problem if we deploy one of the traditional tools of British psephology to assess the performance of the Conservatives and Labour: swing. Swing is a measure of the relative performance of the two main parties. So long as both parties suffer or profit equally from a relatively large or small drop in the Liberal Democrat vote, the swing should be unaffected.[5] There is more than one way of measuring swing, but at this election, the two measures give very similar results. We have thus opted to use the more familiar measure, total vote swing, which is simply the change in the Conservative percentage share of all votes cast less the equivalent Labour change, with the resulting sum divided by two.

We begin by examining the performances of the parties in England and Wales, starting with the Conservatives and Labour before turning to the performance of the smaller parties. Our analysis of what happened south of the border then concludes with an assessment of the degree to which some voters might have voted tactically in their constituency. We then turn to the results in Scotland. Finally, after looking at the pattern of turnout across Britain as a whole, we assess how the electoral system rewarded – or otherwise – the performances that the parties did achieve.

England and Wales

The Conservatives and Labour

Governments are often thought to be rewarded for economic good times and punished for bad times.[6] The economy, together with the state of the country's public finances, was a central concern and point of political contention during the Coalition's term of office (see pp. 6–9), and there is thus every reason to anticipate that the reaction of voters and communities to the Conservatives' record in office would depend on both the state of the economy locally and the degree to which the area was reliant on a reduced number of public sector workers. The Conservatives might be expected to perform better (and perhaps consequently Labour worse) in places where the economy was more robust, as measured, for example, by the level of unemployment. Equally, voters in areas with relatively large numbers of public sector workers might have reacted less favourably to the Conservatives' record in office than those where private sector employment predominated.

However, before we embark on whether these expectations are fulfilled, we need to assess the extent to which the performance of both the Conservatives and Labour depended on the prior strength of the Liberal Democrats. Table A1.3 shows quite clearly that both the Conservatives and Labour performed better the bigger the Liberal Democrat share of the vote last time. For example, support for the

Conservatives actually fell back slightly on average in those seats where the Liberal Democrats won less than 16% of the vote in 2010, whereas it increased by two and a half points in constituencies where the Liberal Democrats won more than 28%. Yet there is little evidence that either the Conservatives or Labour consistently secured a relative advantage where the Liberal Democrats were at risk of losing an especially large share of the vote. The average total vote swing (which anticipates that any gains from the Liberal Democrats will be shared equally between the Conservatives and Labour) is much the same in those places where the Liberal Democrats were previously strongest as it is in those places where the Liberal Democrats had been hitherto weakest.

Table A1.3 Conservative and Labour performance in England and Wales by Liberal Democrat share of the vote in 2010

Liberal Democrat share of the vote, 2010	*Mean change in percentage share of the vote 2010–15*			
	Conservative	*Labour*	*Total vote swing*	*Seats*
Less than 16%	–0.6	+1.4	–1.0	134
16–22%	+1.3	+2.2	–0.5	172
22–28%	+1.8	+4.4	–1.3	121
More than 28%	+2.5	+5.7	–1.6	145
All Seats	+1.2	+3.3	–1.1	572

This is not to say that this is necessarily true of every constituency. In Table A1.4 we look in particular at the fortunes of the Conservatives and Labour in those seats that the Liberal Democrats were trying to defend, distinguishing between those where the Conservatives had been second in 2010 and those where Labour had been. It shows that Labour's vote advanced very strongly indeed – on average by more than 12 points – in those seats in which the party had started off second to the Liberal Democrats, while the Conservatives, if anything, performed less well in these circumstances (an observation to which we will return in our discussion below about tactical voting). In contrast, the total vote swing in seats where the Conservatives had previously been second is little different from that across England and Wales as a whole. A not dissimilar, though much less marked, difference is also apparent between those seats in which the Liberal Democrats started off second to the Conservatives (and won at least 28% of the vote in 2010) and those where they were behind Labour. In the former, there was on average a –0.3 total vote swing to Labour, whereas in the latter there was a –3.4 swing. In short, it looks as though former Liberal Democrat voters were more likely to switch to Labour in areas of relative Labour strength, perhaps because in such seats these voters were more likely to be ex-Labour supporters in the first place.[7]

Table A1.4 Conservative and Labour performance in England and Wales in seats being defended by the Liberal Democrats

	Mean change in percentage share of the vote 2010–15			
Second party 2010	*Conservative*	*Labour*	*Total vote swing*	*Seats*
Conservative	+2.0	+4.3	–1.2	34
Labour	–3.3	+12.3	–7.8	11

Note: one seat, Ceredigion, where Plaid Cymru was the second party in 2010, is excluded.

So we need to bear in mind the link between past Liberal Democrat strength and the change in Conservative and Labour support when looking at whether the Conservatives performed better (and Labour worse) in seats where the economy was relatively buoyant and where public sector workers are relatively few and far between. It could be the case, for example, that the Liberal Democrats were previously relatively weak in seats where the local economy was relatively buoyant; in that event, any link between Conservative performance and the local state of the economy could be an artefact of the pattern of the collapse in Liberal Democrat support. But first of all in Table A1.5, we examine whether there is any apparent link between party performance and the state of the local economy at all. The latter is measured with reference to the level of unemployment as a proportion of the electorate as measured shortly before the election.[8]

Table A1.5 Conservative and Labour performance in England and Wales by local level of unemployment

	Mean change in percentage share of the vote 2010–15			
Unemployment level	*Conservative*	*Labour*	*Total vote swing*	*Seats*
Less than 1%	+3.0	+2.7	+0.1	155
1–1.7%	+2.2	+2.1	+0.1	146
1.7–2.5%	+0.8	+2.5	–0.8	121
More than 2.5%	–1.1	+6.0	–3.6	150

Note: Unemployment level: Jobseeker's Allowance claimants as a proportion of the registered electorate in March 2015.

The table shows that the higher the level of unemployment, the less well the Conservatives performed. Indeed, the party's vote actually fell on average in those seats with the highest level of unemployment. In the case of Labour, the picture is not quite so clear – while the party performed especially well in those seats with the highest level of unemployment, its performance did not vary consistently with the local level of unemployment. It appears that while voters were less willing to back the Conservatives in places where the local economy was relatively weak, Labour was not always the beneficiary of this apparent disenchantment.[9]

But does this pattern still stand once we take into account the previous level of the Liberal Democrat vote locally? It does. Indeed, if anything it becomes clearer, and especially as far as Labour is concerned. In Table A1.6 we illustrate this point by looking at the link between the local level of unemployment and party performance in just those seats where the Liberal Democrats won between 16% and 22% in 2010. It remains the case that the Conservatives performed less well where unemployment was higher, while the opposite is now consistently true of Labour. The equivalent analyses for seats with other levels of Liberal Democrat support in 2010 show much the same pattern.[10]

Table A1.6 Conservative and Labour performance by local level of unemployment in seats in England and Wales where the Liberal Democrats won between 16% and 22% of the vote in 2010

	Mean change in percentage share of the vote 2010–15			
Unemployment level	*Conservative*	*Labour*	*Total vote swing*	*Seats*
Less than 1%	+2.4	+0.4	+1.0	30
1–1.7%	+2.5	+1.6	+0.4	56
1.7–2.5%	+1.2	+2.1	−0.5	45
More than 2.5%	−1.1	+4.4	−2.8	41

Note: Unemployment level: Jobseeker's Allowance claimants as a proportion of the registered electorate in March 2015.

Other evidence also points to a link between local economic prosperity and party performance. For example, the Conservative share of the vote fell on average by one point in seats where the average household income was less than £23,000 a year, but rose by 2.4 points in those constituencies where the average income was more than £30,000 a year.[11] It looks as though voters were more likely to back the Conservatives if the area in which they were living was relatively prosperous and thus perhaps was more likely to feel that it was enjoying some of the fruits of economic recovery.

But what of the suggestion that voters were less willing to support the Conservatives in places that were relatively dependent on public sector employment?[12] Table A1.7 suggests that there is at least some truth in this. Support for the Conservatives increased by just over one point less in seats with a relatively high proportion of public sector workers than it did in those with relatively few such workers. The opposite is true of Labour. This remains the case when we take into account the level of support for the Liberal Democrats in a constituency in 2010 (and indeed the state of the local economy). Given that a similar pattern was also evident in 2010,[13] it seems that the electoral division between those working in the public and the private sector has recently become a more prominent feature of British electoral politics.[14]

Table A1.7 Conservative and Labour performance in England and Wales by local level of public sector employment

% of workforce employed in public sector	*Mean change in percentage share of the vote 2010–15*			
	Conservative	*Labour*	*Total vote swing*	*Seats*
Less than 26%	+2.0	+2.9	–0.5	130
26–29%	+1.2	+3.2	–1.0	189
29–32%	+1.0	+3.5	–1.2	143
More than 32%	+0.8	+4.1	–1.7	110

Note: % of workforce in public sector: % of those aged 16–74 and in employment who are engaged in public administration and defence, health or education according to the 2011 Census.

Another pattern that was in evidence in 2010 and again in 2015 was a tendency for Labour to perform rather better in seats with relatively large numbers of voters from an ethnic minority background.[15] In seats where, according to the 2011 Census, more than 15% come from such a background, Labour's share of the vote increased by 6.8 points, or more than twice the increase the party enjoyed on average across England and Wales as a whole. Nearly all of these seats are ones in which there is a relatively large Muslim population and it is in these that Labour's advance was strongest; in seats where over 4% told the 2011 Census that they were Muslim, Labour's vote increased on average by 7.1 points. Following the UK's involvement in the Iraq War, Labour lost ground heavily in 2005 in constituencies with relatively large Muslim communities. That erosion of Labour support, already seemingly partially reversed in 2010,[16] was apparently repaired yet further at this election.

However, Labour's performance in more ethnically diverse constituencies also depended on the ethnic background of the party's candidate. In line with previous research showing that ethnic minority voters are more likely than white British voters to vote for such candidates,[17] those Labour candidates in these constituencies who were from a minority background themselves saw their vote increase on average by 2.1 points more than did those from a white background. In contrast, in seats with fewer than 15% from an ethnic minority background, ethnic minority Labour candidates on average saw their vote increase by 1.7 points less than their white counterparts. A similar pattern is apparent wherever an ethnic minority (Labour or Conservative) candidate replaced a white one or vice versa. But whereas Labour increased their number of ethnic minority MPs from 16 to 23 mainly by fielding more such candidates in ethnically diverse constituencies (including five seats they had not previously won), the number of Conservative ethnic minority MPs rose from 11 to 17 as a result of more ethnic minority candidates fighting safe Conservative seats in which ethnic minority voters are relatively rare. Only one ethnic minority Conservative MP represents a constituency in which more than 15% of the population belong to an ethnic minority, whereas all but two Labour ethnic minority MPs do.

Many of the seats with relatively large ethnic minority populations (some 45% of them) are in London. This largely accounts for the relatively large increase in Labour support in the capital (see Table A2.4), making it an increasingly fruitful battleground for the party. At 7.2 points, the average increase in the Labour vote in seats in London with a relatively large ethnic minority population is little different from that in similarly diverse seats elsewhere (6.5 points). Meanwhile, in the half-dozen seats in the capital that do not have a substantial ethnic minority population, Labour's vote only increased on average by 2.6 points, slightly less than the average increase in the party's support across England and Wales as a whole.

But not all of the regional variation evident in Table A2.4 can be accounted for by the patterns we have examined so far. Although unemployment in Wales was slightly above that across Britain as a whole, Labour's vote increased least there, and as a result there was actually a small net swing to the Conservatives. Meanwhile, in a partial echo of the long-term tendency for the North of England to become relatively fertile territory for Labour while the Conservatives have become relatively strong in the South and the Midlands, on average the Conservative performance was weaker and the Labour one stronger in both the North West and in Yorkshire & the Humber.[18] Indeed, these were the only two regions where support for the Conservatives actually fell, albeit only slightly. This finding cannot be accounted for by any of the patterns that we have identified so far. For example, in the 49 seats across the two regions in which the unemployed represented more than 2.5% of the electorate, the Conservative vote fell on average by 2.2 points, twice the 1.1 point drop found in all seats in England and Wales with similar levels of unemployment (see Table A1.5). Equally, at 6.7 points, the increase in the Labour vote is rather higher too.

However, the relatively strong Labour performance is not universal across these two regions. While it is apparent in the more urban environments of, for example, Merseyside, Greater Manchester and South Yorkshire, it is not for the most part to be found in more rural counties such as Cheshire, Cumbria or North Yorkshire. Although the average swing in the North East region as a whole was little different from that in England and Wales as a whole, Labour did relatively well in Tyne & Wear, but not in Northumberland or Durham. In short, despite the Conservatives' proposal to offer more devolution for provincial England's metropolitan centres, the party appears to have had particular difficulty in winning over voters in and around many of the North of England's large cities.[19]

If the Conservatives' promises of more devolution brought them little apparent benefit, they do seem to have profited from another phenomenon that has become a regular feature of recent British elections. It involves MPs who are defending for the first time a seat that they gained at the last election from their principal opponents. MPs who have won a seat in this way have a strong incentive to be active locally in the hope that having a high profile in their constituency might enable them to win a 'personal' vote. Recent elections have suggested that such activity does indeed make a difference.[20]

Because the Conservatives made as many as 87 gains from Labour in 2010, there were plenty of Conservative-held seats being defended by first-term incumbent Conservative MPs who five years previously had captured their seats from Labour. Table A1.8 shows that, on average, these MPs clearly outperformed their party. The pattern was strongest in those seats – shown in the first row of the table – where an incumbent Conservative MP was defending for the first time a seat he or she had wrested in 2010 from an incumbent Labour MP who was not standing again. In these seats, not only had the new Tory MP had a chance to develop a personal vote during the previous five years, but any personal vote that may have been developed by the former Labour MP would most likely have been lost. And in these seats the Conservative vote rose on average by no less than 4.5 points, while Labour support actually fell back a little.

Of course, if the former Labour MP did stand again, then he or she might succeed in retaining some of his or her personal vote. Certainly the second row of Table A1.8 suggests that in these circumstances, the Conservatives' relative advantage, though still noticeable, was rather less. Meanwhile, if in fact the former Labour MP never defended his or her seat in 2010 in the first place, then his or her personal vote may well have already been lost five years ago, and certainly the third row suggests that in this circumstance, the Conservative advantage was again rather less.

Table A1.8 The incumbency effect in Conservative/Labour contests in England and Wales

	Mean change in percentage share of the vote 2010–15			
Incumbency status	*Conservative*	*Labour*	*Total vote swing*	*Seats*
Con incumbent won against Lab incumbent 2010	+4.5	–0.9	+2.7	38
Con incumbent won against Lab incumbent 2010; ex-Lab MP stood again	+3.8	+1.3	+1.2	10
Con incumbent won seat from Lab 2010 when Lab incumbent did not stand	+3.7	+1.9	+0.9	32
Con won seat from Lab 2010; Con incumbent did not stand again; ex-Lab MP did not stand	+1.0	+0.7	+0.2	7
Con held seat before 2010; Con incumbent stood again; 2010 majority less than 20%	+1.1	+1.9	–0.4	11

Given that most of the constituencies where any of these three sets of circumstances pertained were marginal seats, we might equally suggest that an above-average Conservative performance in these seats was occasioned by a successful concentration of the party's campaigning efforts in such constituencies. But if that were the case, we would expect the Conservatives to have performed well in such seats irrespective of who was defending the seat for the party. However, the last two rows of Table A1.8 show that is not the case. The fourth row indicates that the Conservative advance was much weaker in those seats that the party had captured from Labour in 2010, but where the incumbent Conservative MP did not stand again. Meanwhile, although they might not be regarded as the most marginal of seats, in the just under a dozen constituencies where the 2010 Conservative majority was no more than 20 points and which were being defended by a Conservative MP who had held the seat since before 2010, again the increase in the Conservative vote was not particularly high. In these seats there was actually a small swing to Labour.[21]

So how voters in England and Wales responded to both the Conservatives and Labour was shaped by the experience of the previous five years. Voters were more inclined to back the Conservatives in places where the economy was relatively buoyant and which were less dependent on public sector employment. At the same time, voters were seemingly more resistant to the Conservatives in ethnically more diverse Britain and in many of the more urban areas in the North of England. In combination, these patterns helped ensure that England and Wales became yet politically more divided. While there was a clear total vote swing to Labour of 2.4 points on average in those seats that the party already held, there was actually a small swing (of 0.3 points) to the Conservatives in places that they were defending. Yet it was in marginal seats that were being defended by first-term Conservative MPs that the Conservatives performed especially well, thanks not so much to what voters thought of the party's record in government as what they thought of their local MP. Far from simply reflecting a uniform nationwide judgement, this was an election in which locality mattered.

The Liberal Democrats

As already noted, the Liberal Democrat vote fell more heavily the better the party had performed in 2010, an almost inevitable consequence of the fact that the party lost as much as two-thirds of the vote it won in 2010. A party that had long profited from its ability to garner the support of voters who were wanting to register a protest against the performance of the party in government (or indeed politics in general),[22] it now found itself losing ground heavily as a result of voters' disillusion with its own performance in office.

No decision had caused the Liberal Democrats more difficulty than the increase in university tuition fees, in direct contradiction of the party's manifesto pledge to abolish them entirely (see pp. 103–6). This policy had seemingly enabled the party to perform particularly well at recent elections in seats containing large numbers of university students.[23] We might anticipate that the party would have suffered especially badly in these circumstances. Of this there is some sign, at least in those seats where the party had previously been relatively strong and where it may well have been particularly successful in winning support from students. Amongst those seats where the party won over 28% of the vote in 2010 and which were not being defended by an incumbent Liberal Democrat MP (on which see further below), the party's vote fell on average by 23.9 points where students are relatively numerous compared with 21.0 points where they are relatively few.[24] A similar, though smaller, gap (a drop of 17.7 points versus one of 19.3 points) is also evident in those seats where the party won between 22% and 28% of the vote last time.

Yet if the party to some extent lost ground in student communities, this was not true of those constituencies where university graduates are relatively numerous. Relatively liberal as they tend to be in their social and political attitudes, those in receipt of a university education have long been disproportionately likely to support the Liberal Democrats and their predecessors.[25] Thus, more likely perhaps to be attracted to the party by its core beliefs rather than as a vehicle of protest, they might be expected to have proved relatively loyal at a time when the party was haemorrhaging support. Certainly, as Table A1.9 shows, once we take into account how well the party performed locally in 2010, the drop in Liberal Democrat support tended to be a little less marked – albeit no more than that – in seats that contained a relatively large proportion of graduates.

Table A1.9 Average change in Liberal Democrat share of the vote in England and Wales by prior strength and proportion of graduates

	% of adults with a degree		
	Less than 20%	*Between 20 and 35%*	*More than 35%*
Lib Dem 2010 share of vote			
Less than 16%	–11.3 (58)	–10.7 (68)	–10.2 (8)
16–22%	–14.7 (45)	–14.4 (111)	–13.5 (16)
22–28%	–18.6 (11)	–17.8 (83)	–17.4 (27)
More than 28%	–20.7 (7)	–20.5 (109)	–19.5 (28)

Note: figures in brackets show the number of seats on which the mean change is calculated. Note that in this table, the result in Bradford East, where the result for all the main parties was unusual, is excluded.

In contrast, the party certainly did not profit from a locally buoyant economy. In fact, support for the Liberal Democrats actually fell away rather more in places with relatively low unemployment (–17.6) than it did in those with relatively high levels of joblessness (–15.5). True, this gap disappears once we take into account the strength of the Liberal Democrats locally – unemployment was typically low in places where the Liberal Democrats had previously been strong and this explains why its support fell so heavily on average in such seats – but the party's hopes that it might receive some of the credit where the Coalition's economic policies appeared to be paying dividends were apparently dashed. That credit was evidently all too easily garnered by their Conservative coalition partners.

But perhaps the biggest hope that the party carried into the election was that voters would be willing to vote for their local Liberal Democrat MP irrespective of what they thought of the record of the Coalition. It has long been the case that the ability of Liberal Democrat MPs to win and retain their seats has rested not so much on the national standing of the party as on their own ability to develop a personal profile for getting things done in their constituency, combined with intense local campaigning by their constituency party.[26] If this continued to be the case, then perhaps many of the party's MPs would be able to save their seats even if the party was losing ground heavily across the country as a whole.

In the event, those Liberal Democrat MPs who were attempting to defend their seats often did perform relatively well. On average, their support fell by 14.9 points, well below the 24.6 point drop suffered by the party where the Liberal Democrat MP was not attempting to defend his or her seat (and thus where that MP's personal vote was at risk of being lost), or indeed the 21.8 point drop that occurred on average in those seats that the party did not win in 2010, but where it won more than 28% of the vote. The 14.9 point drop also proves on average to be 10.8 points less than the 25.7 point drop that would have been expected if the relationship between the level of Liberal Democrat support in 2010 and the fall in Liberal Democrat support had been in line with the relationship between those two phenomena in those seats that the party did not win in 2010.[27]

But relatively good though the performance of Liberal Democrat MPs might have been, given how many votes they had to defend, this still meant that on average their support fell by almost as much as the party's vote did across England and Wales as a whole (–15.8 points). The party's expectation that the personal popularity of Liberal Democrat

MPs would mean that their vote would drop by much less than the party's vote was falling across the whole country was not fulfilled – with the inevitable consequence that the party was left with just a handful of seats. Nevertheless, if incumbent Liberal Democrat MPs had not typically performed relatively well, the party would have won even fewer seats, with perhaps Tim Farron in Westmorland and Lonsdale left as the only Liberal Democrat MP anywhere in England and Wales.

As we might expect, one group of incumbents that did particularly well are those (seven in all) who were defending their seat for the first time, and thus who had had the opportunity during the previous five years to develop a personal vote for the first time. Their vote fell on average by just 9.9 points, though this still proved insufficient to save any of what were typically relatively marginal seats. Much of the relatively strong performance of this group is accounted for by the outcome in three seats (Burnley, Bradford East and Cambridge) where the MP was a relatively regular rebel in parliamentary divisions. In these three cases, Liberal Democrat support fell on average by just 4.9 points, whereas in the case of the other new MPs, it dropped by as much as 13.7 points. More generally, the dozen more experienced MPs who were ministers in the Coalition at the time of the election saw their vote fall on average by 17.0 points, whereas the dozen MPs who had never had been ministers in the Coalition – and who had been free to speak out against it – saw their vote fall by 14.9 points. The Coalition was, it seems, nothing but toxic for the party.

UKIP

UKIP stood in all 573 seats in England and Wales, the first time it had done so. Of these, 529 were seats in which the party also stood in 2010, and our analysis here focuses on the change in the party's share of the vote in these seats, which averaged 10.7 points. As we might anticipate given that it was advancing from a relatively low base, the kinds of places where the party's vote increased most since 2010 are also the kinds of places where its share of the vote was highest, albeit that the only seat the party won, Clacton, was amongst the minority of seats that the party did not contest in 2010.

Analysis of UKIP's growth before the election suggested that the party's support would come primarily from economically struggling 'left behind' white working-class voters with few educational qualifications and for whom immigration was a particular concern.[28] Table A1.10 reveals that those expectations were largely fulfilled. It shows how the increase in UKIP's share of the vote between 2010 and 2015 varied according to a constituency's demographic characteristics. To simplify matters, we simply show how the party performed in those constituencies where the characteristic in question is relatively common and those where it is relatively rare.

Table A1.10 Change in UKIP support 2010–15 in England and Wales by demographic character of constituency

Mean change in UKIP % share of the vote 2010–15 in constituencies where incidence of characteristic is:	*Low*	*High*
% with a degree	+14.9 (142)	+6.4 (132)
% unemployed 2015	+9.3 (150)	+11.8 (129)
Change in % unemployed 2001–11	+8.5 (126)	+13.1 (130)
% born in the UK	+7.9 (148)	+11.7 (149)
% white British	+8.2 (125)	+11.5 (125)

Note: % with a degree: Low = less than 21% of adults with a degree; High = more than 31%. % unemployed 2015: Low = Jobseeker's Allowance claimants represented less than 1% of the registered electorate in March 2015; High = represented more than 2.5%. Change in % unemployed 2001–11: Low = % of 16–74 year olds who said they were unemployed fell by two percentage points between 2001 and 2011; High = Proportion increased by more than 1.4 points. % born in the UK: Low = less than 86% of the resident population born in the UK; High = more than 95%. White British: Low = less than 79% describe themselves as 'white British'; High = more than 95%. The data come from the 2011 Census, except the % unemployed 2015, which is based on Jobseeker's Allowance statistics reported by the Department for Work and Pensions (March 2015 release).
Numbers in brackets show the number of seats on which the average is based.

The educational background of those living in a constituency was especially important in distinguishing between those places where UKIP did particularly well and those where its advance was less marked. As the table shows, the increase in UKIP's support was as much as 8.5 points higher in seats containing relatively few graduates than it was in those where graduates are relatively plentiful. This pattern helps explain why Douglas Carswell was able to retain the Clacton seat that he had won in a parliamentary by-election the previous year. Only 13.4% of adults in his constituency have a degree, one of the lowest proportions of any constituency in the country. Meanwhile, UKIP performed even better if a constituency not only had relatively few graduates but also relatively few public sector workers.[29]

UKIP also performed relatively well in less economically prosperous constituencies. As Table A1.10 shows, UKIP support increased on average by 2.5 points more in seats where unemployment was currently relatively high than it did in those where it was relatively low. However, the contrast is even more marked if we compare constituencies in which unemployment fell most between the 2001 and 2011 Censuses

– not least perhaps because they were particularly affected by the 2008 economic crisis – and those where unemployment rose most.[30] Here the equivalent gap is almost five points.

However, while economic conditions played a role in UKIP's growth, it has been issues of identity and immigration that have been emphasised most by the party. That though does not mean that the party performed especially well in places which have experienced relatively high levels of immigration. Rather, as Table A1.10 shows, UKIP typically did less well in those places where a relatively large proportion of the population was born outside the UK. This is because the largest migrant inflows during the past decade have tended to be in seats in London and other large cities that have ethnically diverse populations, large numbers of graduates and buoyant economies, all circumstances that are the very opposite of where UKIP typically does well.

In order to understand how immigration influenced UKIP's performance, we have also to take into account the existing ethnic composition and sense of identity of those living in a constituency. UKIP advanced by over three points more in seats in which a relatively large proportion of the population described themselves on the 2011 Census as 'white British' than it did in constituencies where relatively few people did so (see Table A1.10). And it was in these, the less ethnically diverse parts of England and Wales, where UKIP's anti-immigration message, and especially its attacks on migration from those Eastern European countries that joined the EU in 2004, mattered. As Table A1.11 shows, in seats in which over 85% considered themselves to be 'white British', UKIP's vote increased by nearly three points more where a relatively large proportion of the population was born in one of the EU accession states than it did in those constituencies where relatively few were born in that part of the EU. In contrast, UKIP performed relatively badly in seats that contain a relatively large proportion of people born in Eastern Europe but where the population is also diverse in other ways.

Table A1.11 Change in UKIP share of the vote 2010–15 in England and Wales by proportion with a white British identity and the proportion born in one of the EU accession states

% population born in a EU accession state	*% describing themselves as 'White British'*	
	Less than 85%	*More than 85%*
Below 1%	+12.3 (10)	+11.2 (189)
Above 2.5%	+8.1 (95)	+14.0 (24)

Note: figures in brackets show the number of seats on which that statistic is based.

The strongest UKIP performances thus came in seats that are not ethnically diverse, have populations with relatively low levels of educational attainment, rising unemployment and a high level of concern about immigration. This pattern is very similar to that for support for the British National Party (BNP), a more extreme radical-right party that also focused on immigration, which won on average 3.8% of the vote in the 338 seats it fought in 2010, only to collapse financially and organisationally shortly thereafter. UKIP's vote increased by no less than 17.0 points between 2010 and 2015 in those seats where the BNP won over 5% of the vote in 2010, by only 9.6 points in those constituencies where the BNP won less than 3%, and just 8.3 points where the BNP did not stand at all. This may in part be the result of former BNP voters switching directly to UKIP (the former BNP party leader, Nick Griffin, endorsed UKIP in 2015), but it is also most likely the result of the success of both parties in mobilising a similar set of concerns – political disaffection, economic exclusion, ethnic identity politics and anxiety about immigration.

But what impact did UKIP's performance have on that of the Conservatives, Labour and the Liberal Democrats? The common expectation in the run-up to the 2015 election was that UKIP would primarily damage the Conservative Party by 'splitting the right'. Support for UKIP's core messages of Euroscepticism, opposition to immigration and English nationalism was higher among Conservative voters than amongst supporters of other parties, and survey evidence consistently suggested that UKIP was winning over more support from 2010 Conservative voters than Labour or Liberal Democrat backers.[31] However, even if that is the position amongst voters across the country a whole, it does not necessarily follow that the Conservatives will have suffered particularly badly where UKIP advanced most. UKIP may have appealed to a somewhat different combination of voters where it did particularly well. Moreover, perhaps when UKIP did do particularly well, the party was picking up voters who, if they had not voted UKIP, would have voted Labour or Liberal Democrats even though they might not have voted for those parties in 2010.

The Conservatives certainly lost more support where UKIP did best. But then the same also happened to Labour (though once we take into account how well the Liberal Democrats performed in a constituency in 2010, it seems that how well or badly UKIP did had no impact at all on the Liberal Democrats' fortunes). As a result, it seems that an above-average UKIP performance had at most only a marginally greater impact on the Conservatives than Labour. This can be seen by comparing the third row with the second row of Table A1.12. In seats where UKIP's vote increased by more than 13.5 points, the Conservative vote fell on average by 0.7 points, whereas in seats where UKIP's vote rose between 7.5 and 13.5 points, it rose on average by 2.2 points, a difference of 2.9 points. In contrast, the equivalent figures in Labour's case are increases of 1.6 and 2.6 points respectively, a difference of just one point. This contrast in the performance of the two largest parties is reflected in the slightly higher total vote swing to Labour in seats where UKIP performed well.

However, even this difference needs to be interpreted with care. As we have already noted, many of the seats in which UKIP advanced most were seats in which the BNP performed relatively well. And where the BNP performed well in 2010, they did so primarily at Labour's expense.[32] Thus, one possible reason why the Conservatives appear to have suffered slightly more where UKIP advanced most is that some former Labour voters had already switched in 2010 to a party with a strong anti-immigration message. Certainly, if we leave aside those seats where the BNP won over 4% of the vote in 2010, the total vote swing in seats where UKIP advanced by more than 13.5 points (–0.1) was on average almost exactly the same as it was in seats where it advanced between 7.5 and 13.5 points (–0.0), suggesting that in these seats at least, an especially strong UKIP performance hurt the Conservatives and Labour to much the same extent.

Table A1.12 Change in Conservative and Labour share of the vote 2010–15 by change in UKIP share of the vote 2010–15 in England and Wales

Change in UKIP % share 2010–15	*Mean change in percentage share of the vote 2010–15*			
	Conservative	*Labour*	*Total vote swing*	*Seats*
Up less than 7.5	+1.4	+6.9	–2.7	133
Up between 7.5 and 13.5	+2.2	+2.6	–0.2	284
Up by more than 13.5	–0.7	+1.6	–1.2	155

Note: in this table, seats not contested by UKIP in 2010 are classified according to the share of the vote won by UKIP in 2015.

Moreover, the astute reader will also have noticed something else – that, according to the first row of Table A1.12, it was Labour that did especially well where UKIP's advance was relatively weak. This is certainly not consistent with a story that suggests that UKIP's success in the 2015 election simply hurt the Conservatives; rather, it suggests that it is Labour that might have benefited the more if UKIP had not enjoyed the record-breaking advance it achieved in 2015, profiting more perhaps from the political and economic disillusion that in practice helped feed UKIP support.

We might wonder whether there are other features of those seats where UKIP advanced less that helps explain why Labour did so well in them. They tend, as we have seen, to be seats that are more ethnically diverse and Labour generally did relatively well in such seats. But they also tend to be seats where unemployment was relatively low, and those were not the kind of seats where Labour tends to do relatively well. In practice, the pattern is still in evidence even if we take into account the ethnic composition or the economic circumstances of a constituency,[33] although it is less strong in seats that were won by Labour in 2010 than in those won by the Conservatives.

The suggestion that UKIP might have been winning some votes that might otherwise be going to Labour secures further support if, as in Table A1.13, we look at the relationship between the performances of the parties over two election cycles rather than just one, that is, since 2005. Here we find that Labour have actually increased their vote on average in seats where UKIP's long-term advance has been weakest, whereas the party's support has fallen heavily elsewhere. In contrast, the Conservatives' advance has been only been very slightly higher in seats where UKIP have made little progress than it has in places where UKIP have advanced strongly.

Table A1.13 Change in Conservative and Labour share of the vote 2005–15 by change in UKIP share of the vote 2005–15 in England and Wales

Change in UKIP % share 2005–15	*Mean change in percentage share of the vote 2005–15*			
	Conservative	*Labour*	*Total vote swing*	*Seats*
Up less than 7.5	+5.4	+3.2	+1.1	117
Up between 7.5 and 13.5	+6.3	–4.6	+5.5	261
Up by more than 13.5	+4.0	–7.8	+5.9	194

Note: in this table, seats not contested by UKIP in 2005 are classified according to the share of the vote won by UKIP in 2015. The 2005 result in each constituency is an estimate of what the outcome in that seat would have been if that election had been fought on the same boundaries as those that were in force at the 2010 and 2015 general elections.[34]

In part, this divergent pattern reflects the fact that the kind of constituencies in which UKIP have prospered most are the kinds of places that rejected Labour most heavily in 2010. In 2010 Labour did worst in relatively working-class seats that had experienced a sharp increase in unemployment between 2005 and 2010, had low proportions of public sector workers and were not ethnically diverse.[35] The overlap between the places where Labour did badly in 2010 and UKIP performed well in 2015 does not necessarily mean there has been a direct switch of support from Labour to UKIP in these constituencies, but it does suggest that UKIP have prospered most in areas where disenchantment with the previous Labour government was most widespread.

The Greens

Although UKIP's advance was the more dramatic, the Greens also enjoyed their best general election result ever. The party stood in 542 constituencies in England and Wales. On average, the party won 4.3% of the vote in the seats that it fought, compared with just 1.7% in 2010. But with its vote still relatively evenly spread, the party did no more than retain the Brighton Pavilion seat that Caroline Lucas first won in 2010. Moreover, it only managed to secure second place in four seats, in only one of which, Bristol West (Labour majority, 8.8%), did it come anything like close to winning.

As at previous elections, support for the party was strongest in areas with large concentrations of university graduates and students, reflecting the appeal of the party's socially liberal and environmental politics for such voters. On average, the party won 5.6% of the vote in seats where more than 31% of adults are graduates, compared with 2.9% in those where less than 21% fall into that category. Equally, in those seats that the party also fought in 2010, its share of the vote increased on average by 3.8 points in places where graduates were relatively plentiful and by only 1.8 points where they were scarce. The Greens also performed better in constituencies where unemployment fell markedly between 2001 and 2011 than they did in seats where unemployment had increased most during that period, suggesting that, despite their opposition to the Coalition's financial austerity policy, their appeal was stronger in places that had been insulated from the worst effects of the financial crisis.[36]

At previous elections, a relatively strong Green performance has often seemed to come at the particular expense of the Liberal Democrats, reflecting an overlap in the ideological values and social bases of the two parties.[37] It thus comes as little surprise that the party performed particularly well where the Liberal Democrat vote fell most. The party's share of the vote rose by as much as 4.7 points on average in seats where the Liberal Democrat vote fell by more than 20 points, but by only 1.8 points in constituencies where Liberal Democrat support fell by less than ten points. Equally, Liberal Democrat support fell most heavily where the Greens performed best. In contrast, and despite much speculation that the advance of the Greens posed a risk to Labour, Labour often performed relatively well in the same seats as the Greens. For example, Labour's vote increased by 5.5 points in those seats where Green support in 2015 was four points or more higher than in 2010, much larger than the 2.7 point increase in the Labour vote registered elsewhere.[38]

Plaid Cymru

The surge in nationalist support in Scotland was not in evidence in Wales, even though Plaid Cymru, the country's nationalist party, received considerable UK-wide media attention thanks to the appearance of Leanne Wood in two of the three televised leaders' debates. The party won 12.1% of the vote in Wales, up 0.8 of a point on 2010, but still below the record 14.3% the party won in 2001. It retained the three seats it already held, but added no others to its tally, though once again it ran Labour close in Ynys Môn.

Unlike her predecessors as Plaid Cymru leader, Wood lives in South Wales rather than in heavily Welsh-speaking North and West Wales, and indeed is not a native Welsh speaker. She is also on the left of the party, and shared much the same anti-austerity position adopted by the SNP and the Greens. These characteristics appear to have had some impact on the party's progress. Although its support was still heavily concentrated in those seats where Welsh is widely spoken, its support fell on average by 1.1 points in the 12 seats where more than one-fifth of the population speak at least some Welsh, whereas elsewhere it increased by 1.8 points. Support for the party increased on average by 2.5 points in the 20 Welsh seats with the highest levels of unemployment at the time of the election, whereas it fell by 0.7 of a point in the 20 seats with the lowest levels of joblessness. But it is still some way from being the party of all of Wales as opposed to the country's Welsh-speaking heartlands.

Tactical voting

One of the notable features of how voters behaved at the three elections that Labour won between 1997 and 2005 was a marked willingness amongst both Labour and Liberal Democrat voters to vote tactically in order to try and secure the defeat of the local Conservative candidate.[39] Where the Liberal Democrats were placed third, some of the party's supporters switched to backing Labour. Conversely, where Labour started off in third place, some of the party's supporters switched to the Liberal Democrats. Moreover, there was no consistent evidence that this pattern reversed itself in 2010, even though by this stage the Conservatives were not so unpopular.[40]

The formation of the Coalition between the Conservatives and the Liberal Democrats might be expected to have caused some of these tactical voters to reassess their options. Third-placed Labour supporters might feel there was little point voting tactically for a Liberal Democrat party that had gone on to share power with the Conservatives. Meanwhile, third-placed Liberal Democrat voters might feel less impetus to help Labour defeat the candidate who was representing their Conservative coalition partners locally. On the other hand, we might find that third-placed Conservative supporters were now willing to lend their support to their local Liberal Democrat candidate in the hope that this might help defeat Labour locally.

If the previous pattern of tactical switching between Labour and the Liberal Democrats did unravel, we should find that Labour performed relatively well in places where the party started off third, while the Liberal Democrat vote should have fallen back especially heavily in seats where the Liberal Democrats were previously third. However, as we have already seen in Table A1.3 above, there is little sign that Labour did especially well in those seats that the Liberal Democrats were trying to defend against a Conservative challenger. Labour's vote increased in these seats by just one point more than it did across England and Wales as a whole, while the Conservative vote increased by 0.8 of a point more too. In short, both parties seemingly profited from the Liberal Democrats' difficulties. The picture is little different in those Conservative-held seats where the Liberal Democrats were in second place with more than 28% of the vote in 2010. Despite the typically very heavy drop in Liberal Democrat support in these circumstances (on average it fell by 21.2 points), Labour's vote again only increased by 4.3 points, just a point above the England and Wales average. It appears that those who at recent elections had opted to vote tactically for the Liberal Democrats were no more likely than those who had voted sincerely for the party to have switched back to Labour.

Meanwhile, there is little sign that the Liberal Democrat vote fell away particularly heavily in seats that were marginal between the Conservatives and Labour. Amongst those seats where the Liberal Democrats won less than 16% of the vote in 2010 and which the Conservatives held with less than a five point lead over Labour, the Liberal Democrat vote fell on average by 11.4 points. The drop amongst seats with a similar level of Liberal Democrat support in 2010 but where the Conservatives enjoyed more than a 20 point lead over Labour was, at 11.3 points, almost exactly the same. Similar analyses of those seats where the Liberal Democrats won between 16% and 22% of the vote and of those seats that Labour were defending also fails to show any substantial or systematic difference between marginal and safe seats so far as the scale of the Liberal Democrat decline is concerned.

However, as we had noted earlier, the Conservatives did perform relatively poorly in seats that the Liberal Democrats were trying to defend against a Labour challenge. Table A1.3 showed that the Conservative vote fell on average by over three points in these circumstances. Indeed, where the incumbent Liberal Democrat MP was standing again, the average drop in Conservative support was no less than 5.3 points. This suggests that in these seats, some third-placed Conservative supporters made a tactical switch in favour of the Liberal Democrats. Conservative support also fell away heavily (on average by 9.3 points) in three Liberal Democrat seats in which, although the Conservatives started off in second place, they were less than ten points ahead of Labour in 2010 and where, as a result, Labour might also have been thought capable of mounting (and indeed in practice did mount) a challenge locally.[41] As it happens, the tactical support of third-placed Conservative voters proved insufficient to enable the Liberal Democrats to stave off defeat against any of their second-placed Labour challengers, but it appears to have been instrumental in enabling the Liberal Democrats to retain two of the three seats where previously second-placed Conservative supporters switched to the Liberal Democrats.[42]

So much for how the local tactical situation influenced support for the three parties that have traditionally dominated elections in England and Wales. However, the rise of UKIP and the Greens raises another possibility we should consider. This is that, aware of the fact that their preferred party was unlikely to win, some UKIP and Green supporters may have been especially likely to have been discouraged from voting UKIP or Green in those seats which were marginal between two or more other parties, instead opting to vote for whichever of those two parties they preferred to win.

Table A1.14 suggests that this pressure did have some impact on both UIKIP and Green support. UKIP support increased on average by one and a half points less in those seats where the two leading contenders were less than 5% apart locally in 2010 than it did in those seats where the winner locally enjoyed more than a 20 point lead. In the case of the Greens, there is a similar difference of just over half of a point. These differences cannot easily be accounted for by the social character of marginal seats; on average, they are little different from the country as a whole when it comes to those demographic or economic characteristics that we showed earlier generally made a difference to the level of UKIP and Green support.

Table A1.14 Mean change in UKIP and Green support in England and Wales by marginality of seat

Lead of the largest party over the second party 2010	*Mean change in UKIP % share of vote 2010–15*	*Seats*	*Mean change in Green % share of the vote 2010–15*	*Seats*
0–5%	+9.5	78	+2.6	45
5–10%	+10.0	97	+2.9	49
10–20%	+11.4	138	+3.3	84
More than 20%	+11.0	216	+3.2	127

Note: based on all seats fought by the party in question in both 2010 and 2015, except that in the case of the Greens, Brighton Pavilion, which was won by the party in 2010, is excluded.

The rise in UKIP support was especially low in marginal seats that the Conservatives were defending. In seats where the Conservatives started off just five points ahead of Labour, UKIP support increased on average by 8.8 points, while in those where the Conservatives had previously only been narrowly ahead of the Liberal Democrats, the UKIP rise was no more than 7.2 points. This might be thought to indicate a wish on the part of some UKIP supporters not to see the Conservatives defeated locally. However, it is far from clear whether the apparent squeeze on UKIP support in marginal seats was of particular benefit to the Conservatives. Across all seats in which the lead of the winning party in 2010 was less than ten points and UKIP's vote increased by less than 7.5 points, there was on average a total vote swing to Labour of 1.5 points. The swing was almost exactly the same (1.4 points) in seats where UKIP's vote increased by 13.5 points or more. Meanwhile, as in our earlier analysis of UKIP performance, if we confine our attention to just those seats that were previously marginal between Conservative and Labour, it was Labour rather than the Conservatives that performed relatively well where the UKIP advance was weakest.[43]

Scotland

One feature dominates the election outcome in Scotland: a 30 point increase in SNP support that left the party with just under half (49.97%) of the vote. This result far outshone the nationalists' previous best performance in a UK general election (30.4% in October 1974) and even the 45% that the party won in the 2011 Scottish Parliament election. It was the biggest advance between two UK elections registered by any party since that achieved by Sinn Fein in Ireland in 1918. However, the SNP did just fail to emulate the Conservatives' record achievement, 50.1% of the Scottish vote, in 1955.

Labour's share of the Scottish vote, meanwhile, fell to its lowest level since 1918. Much like the Liberal Democrats across Britain as a whole (and in part for the same arithmetical reason), in general the stronger Labour had been in a seat in 2010, the more the party's vote fell (subject only to the extent to which the Liberal Democrat vote was declining locally), while equally it was in areas where Labour had previously been strongest – and where often the Yes vote had been relatively high in the independence referendum held the previous September – that the SNP advanced most. On average, in seats where Labour won over 40% of the vote in 2010, its vote fell by 22.5 points compared with just 9.9 points elsewhere, while the SNP vote increased by 33.6 points, well above the 23.8 point increase in other constituencies. Conversely, the nationalist advance was typically weakest in those seats where not only had Labour previously not been especially strong, but where the SNP itself had been. In seven seats where the SNP won over 25% of the vote in 2010 (six of which they had won) and Labour less than 40%, the SNP vote increased on average by a relatively modest 14.8 points. Whereas hitherto SNP-held constituencies had been relatively isolated beacons of nationalist strength, now those beacons look much like the rest of the country.[44]

The prospect that the SNP might perform exceptionally well had persuaded some of those who want Scotland to remain in the Union to urge voters to vote tactically for whichever candidate appeared best placed locally to defeat the SNP. Some Conservative voters certainly appear to have responded to this call (and in so doing helped push the Conservative vote to its lowest level ever). The phenomenon was most apparent in seats that the party's coalition partners, the Liberal Democrats, were trying to defend. On average, support for the Conservatives fell by 5.4 points in such seats; indeed, Conservative support even fell, with one exception,[45] in those Liberal Democrat-held seats where the Conservatives had been second in 2010 – in stark contrast with what happened in equivalent seats in England and Wales (see pp. 392–3).

However, Conservative support also often – though not always – fell in seats that Labour was trying to defend, and especially so in more middle-class parts of Scotland where the Conservatives themselves were still relatively strong.[46] In nine Labour-held seats where the

Conservatives won over 20% of the vote in 2010, the party's vote fell on average by 2.9 points. A particularly striking example was the 8.4 point drop in Conservative support in the East Renfrewshire seat of the Scottish Labour leader, Jim Murphy. But perhaps the most important instance was Edinburgh South, where the Conservative vote fell by 4.1 points. This seemingly tactically induced drop in the Conservative vote, in combination with a very sharp fall in the Liberal Democrat vote (see further below), may well have helped Labour to retain what proved to be its one and only Scottish seat. Otherwise the campaign to promote tactical voting had very little to show for its efforts so far as seats saved is concerned.[47]

Thanks to the apparent willingness of some Conservative supporters to vote tactically for the Liberal Democrats,[48] many Scottish Liberal Democrat MPs were relatively successful at stemming the outgoing tide for their party. The party's vote fell on average by 11.7 points in the nine seats where an incumbent Liberal Democrat was trying to defend, not only far less than the 28.6 point drop that the party suffered in other seats in Scotland where it had won at least 28% of the vote last time (a group that included Edinburgh South, where the party suffered a 30.3 point drop) but also noticeably better than the 14.9 point drop that Liberal Democrat MPs suffered on average in England and Wales. However, similar to the position south of the border, this pattern of relative success in seats that the party was trying to defend (which, however, unlike in England and Wales, also extended to the two seats where the incumbent Liberal Democrat MP stood down)[49] simply meant that on average the party's vote fell in these seats in line with the drop in the party's share of the vote across Scotland as a whole. Otherwise, as in England and Wales, the more popular the party had been in 2010, the more heavily its support fell. However, because it was not very popular in much of Scotland in the first place, overall the party's vote simply had less far to fall.

UKIP has never enjoyed the same degree of popularity in Scotland as it has done in England and Wales. The party's relative weakness was reflected in the fact that it fought just 41 of Scotland's 59 seats, of which it had contested just 22 in 2010. The party managed on average to win just 2.3% of the vote where it stood, and increased its share by just 0.9 of a point where it had fielded a candidate in 2010. In stark contrast to the position in England and Wales, UKIP remained a bit player north of the border. The Greens too fared less well than elsewhere. The party won on average just 2.6% of the vote in the 31 seats that it fought. That represented an average increase in support of only 1.2 points in the 16 seats that the party also contested in 2010, little more than a third of the increase that the party secured on average in England and Wales. In short, Scotland emerged from the election looking in almost every respect like a very different country politically from the rest of Great Britain.

Turnout across Great Britain

The officially recorded level of turnout depends in the first instance on how many voters are recorded as registered to vote. That figure was influenced at this election by the initial steps that had been taken to switch from a process of household to individual registration. The change particularly affected university students living in a hall of residence as well as anyone who had recently moved (a group that consists disproportionately of younger people). Although the switch also involved the introduction of a new online system of registration, which was quite heavily used (see pp. 22–3), the growth in the electorate in seats where younger people and students were more numerous was still relatively low. In seats in England and Wales with the most students, for example, just over 250 more names appeared on the register than had done five years ago, well down on the average of just under 800 across England and Wales as a whole.[50]

Amongst those affected by the change of procedure but who were determined to vote, there is little reason to believe that the changes to the system of registration acted as a barrier to registering. On the other hand, amongst those with less interest in the election, there might have been a risk that they did not make it on to the register. If so, then we should find that the official level of turnout increased most in constituencies where the registered number of voters had grown least since 2010.

This is indeed what we find. Across England and Wales as a whole, turnout increased on average by just half a point. But in those 183 seats in which there were fewer registered voters than in 2010, turnout increased on average by 1.6 points. Conversely, it actually fell slightly – by 0.4 of a point – in those 175 seats where the electorate had increased by more than 1,600 voters. Equally, turnout increased rather more in constituencies with more young people and more students.[51] True, some of this difference might be attributed to differential changes in the accuracy of the register, that is, that in seats where the electorate had fallen, greater efforts had been made to exclude from the register those who should not have been there in the first place. However, the pattern is certainly consistent with the proposition that, thanks to the change of procedure, those who were inclined to abstain in the election were less likely to appear on the electoral register than had been the case five years previously.[52]

There were certainly plenty of voters in England and Wales who did abstain. At 66.0%, the overall level of turnout in this part of the UK was still well below the turnout recorded at any election between 1922 and 1997, when turnout never fell below 70%. This is despite the fact that the opinion polls had suggested that the outcome would be close and that more parties than ever before appeared to have a realistic prospect of winning a significant share of the vote. This election appeared to confirm, if confirmation were needed, that there has been a long-term decline in the willingness of voters to make it to the polling station.

There was, however, one marked exception to this picture of low and largely stable turnout – Scotland. The referendum on Scottish independence held the previous September had secured a turnout of 84.6%, higher than at any previous nationwide vote in Scotland since the advent of the mass franchise. The importance of the choice and the intensity of the referendum debate had seemingly made an impression on voters, and this continued through to the general election. At 71.0%, turnout north of the border was 7.2 points higher than in 2010. The increase was on average rather higher in less affluent constituencies, in many of which the vote in favour of independence had been relatively high the previous year.[53] Nevertheless, the level of turnout was still lower than that recorded north of the border at any election between 1950 and 1997. Even the intense political debate during and since the referendum did not ensure that turnout returned to a level that would once have been regarded as the norm.

The electoral system

After the 2010 election, we wrote that the electoral system continued to be strongly biased towards Labour and that, given the high level of support for and seats won by third parties, it would be difficult for the Conservatives to secure an overall majority in future unless they secured a double-digit lead over Labour.[54] Yet they proceeded to win a majority, even though their lead over Labour was actually 0.6 points lower than in 2010. How did they manage it? And does this mean the electoral system is now likely to produce single-party majorities in future?

Extrapolations of how many seats a party might win for any given share of the vote are commonly made on the basis of the assumption that the changes in party support will be 'uniform' across Britain as a whole. If a party's support is up overall by say, two points, we assume that its support will increase by two points in each and every constituency. Of course, we do not anticipate that this is exactly what will happen, but we do assume that any seats that a party gains because it does better locally than it is doing nationally will be counterbalanced by a similar number of seats that it fails to win because it underperforms locally. In effect, we are assuming that the overall geographical distribution of each party's support across constituencies stays the same.

However, if we extrapolate the Britain-wide changes in party support to seats in Scotland and Wales, we in effect have to assume that there is little or no change in the level of support for, and thus seats won by, the nationalist parties that only contest elections in those two parts of the UK. Because those parties fight relatively few seats, the Britain-wide change in their support will always be relatively small – even the surge in SNP support between 2010 and 2015 represented an increase of only 3.2 points in the party's share of the Britain-wide vote. While the assumption of little or no change in nationalist support is one that can again be applied in Wales, it is manifestly not one that can be used on this occasion in Scotland. Consequently, any attempt to estimate how the electoral system would have treated the parties if the ups and downs in party support had been 'uniform' has to be made on the basis of two separate calculations. In other words, we assume that the overall changes in party support across England and Wales would have applied in each and every constituency there, while in Scotland we assume that the outcome in every seat would have reflected the (very different) overall changes in party support that were in evidence in that part of the UK.

If that had indeed been what had happened at this election, the Conservatives would not have won an overall majority – but they would not have been far short of one. The party would have won 320 seats, six short of an overall majority, while Labour would have 243, the SNP 55, the Liberal Democrats 10, Plaid Cymru three and the Greens one. UKIP, meanwhile, would not have won any representation at all. While the Conservatives would have lost a dozen seats to Labour, they would have won no less than 26 from the Liberal Democrats. From this it is clear that the collapse in support for their junior coalition partners was a crucial foundation of the Conservatives' success.[55] On the other hand, all that would have happened to the Conservatives in Scotland under our extrapolation is that the party would have lost their one and only seat – so the divergent outcome north of the border is not in any way responsible for the Conservatives' success.

But how did the Conservatives manage to win an overall majority rather than just falling short? Here what is crucial is the party's success at avoiding losses to Labour. If the outcome had been in line everywhere with our model of uniform change, the party would have lost a dozen seats to Labour. In the event, it suffered a net loss of just two. There were in fact exactly ten seats that the Conservatives successfully held that would have been lost if the outcome had been in line with our uniform change projection.[56] Eight of these were constituencies where the seat was being defended by a Conservative MP who gained the seat in 2010 from Labour, circumstances in which we have seen there was typically a swing to the Conservatives. It was above all – perhaps somewhat paradoxically – the personal votes won by first-time incumbent Conservative MPs as a result of their local constituency activity that gave the party the crucial additional stepping stone it needed to win a nationwide majority.[57]

These were not the only seats being contested between the Conservatives and Labour that failed to conform to the pattern of uniform change. In fact, the Conservatives gained as many as eight seats from Labour against the tide, only for these gains to be matched by eight gains that Labour made from the Conservatives where the swing required for victory was greater than our model of uniform change would anticipate. In truth, given that it was an election in which in England and Wales at least there was only a relatively small swing between the two parties (exactly 1% to Labour), some gains and losses in both directions were likely to occur simply as a result of random variation from one constituency to another. There was, however, some pattern to these gains and losses.

No less than five of the eight 'unexpected' gains made by Labour were seats with relatively large ethnic minority populations, and indeed all five of these seats are amongst the top 10% of constituencies in respect of the proportion of Muslims that they contain. We showed earlier that Labour generally performed well in such seats. Of the remaining three seats, two were in the North West, where Labour performed relatively well, while one was a seat in which the incumbent Conservative MP stood down. However, we should also note that all but one of them were seats where UKIP's advance was relatively weak, circumstances in which, as we have shown, Labour consistently did better, underlining our earlier conclusion that UKIP's advance was not self-evidently simply a problem for the Conservatives.

In contrast, the eight seats the Conservatives gained from Labour are more variegated in character.[58] Two were constituencies in which the incumbent Labour MP retired, while two (including one of the seats where the MP retired) were in Wales where there was a small net swing to the Conservatives (see Table A2.4). At the same time, in none of the seats was unemployment particularly high, while three had relatively low proportions of people working in the public sector. But beyond this, there is little about these constituencies that would lead one to anticipate a swing from Labour to the Conservatives. It looks as though in many cases, specifically local circumstances played a role in bringing about a Conservative victory, the most notable of which was the capture of the Morley and Outwood seat of the Labour Shadow Chancellor, Ed Balls.

Apart from these three sets of seats involving the Conservatives and Labour, there are relatively few discrepancies between the expectations generated by our model of uniform change and the actual outcome. UKIP held one of its two by-election gains (Clacton) from the Conservatives, thereby ensuring that the party was not entirely denied representation. The SNP made three gains where the swing required locally was greater than that occurring across Scotland as a whole,[59] but in each case this simply reflected the fact that Labour's vote was falling more heavily, and the SNP's vote increasing most, in seats where Labour had previously been strongest. As we noted earlier, Labour saved one Scottish seat (Edinburgh South) from the SNP thanks to anti-nationalist tactical voting, while the Conservatives hung on to their one and only Scottish seat (Dumfriesshire, Clydesdale and Tweeddale) by increasing their vote in line with the party's performance south of the border and also perhaps as a result of some tactical voting. Although the Liberal Democrats retained two seats that they might have been expected to have lost to the Conservatives, they lost three others they might have hoped to retain (including one where the incumbent MP stood down).[60] The party also lost one 'extra' seat, Bristol West, to Labour, almost undoubtedly as a result of the 23.1 point increase in the Green vote in the constituency, the highest in the country. But none of the departures from the expectations of a model of uniform change involving one of the smaller parties had a major impact on the overall outcome.

This leaves us with a paradox about the way in which the electoral system operated at this election. For all of the parties, the amount by which their vote increased or fell varied from one constituency to another to a greater extent than at any other recent election (see the standard deviation figures in Table A1.1), while some were experiencing falls in support that made it impossible for their performance to be uniform across the country. This suggests that the outcome should have been very different from what we would expect if the pattern of movement were largely uniform. Yet we have to take just two sources of geographical variation into consideration to be able almost wholly to account for the outcome in seats – these are the very different outcomes for nearly all of the parties in Scotland and the relative success of the Conservatives in fending off a Labour challenge in marginal seats being defended by a first-time incumbent. There was nothing inevitable about this – there was, for example, no necessary reason why the Liberal Democrats' performance in seats being defended by an incumbent Liberal Democrat MP should have more or less matched the drop in the party's support across the country as a whole. It just so happened that for the most part, the various sources of variation largely cancelled themselves out so far as each party's tally of seats was concerned.

But that does not mean that the way in which the electoral system operated largely remained unchanged. The Conservatives' success in defending a number of marginal seats against the tide, the collapse in Liberal Democrat support and the rise of the SNP in Scotland between them had profound implications for the way in which the system now translated votes into seats. Moreover, despite the Conservatives' success in winning an overall majority even though they enjoyed a lower lead over Labour in terms of votes, the ability of the system to ensure that whichever party comes first in votes secures a majority in the Commons – one of the system's key attributes according to its advocates – remains in question.

The ability of the single-member plurality system to provide whichever of the Conservatives or Labour secures most votes with a majority in the House of Commons – even though that party may have much less than 50% of the vote – depends on three phenomena.[61] First, there needs to be a reasonably large number of seats that are marginal between those two parties and which thus can be expected to change hands in response to what might be no more than a switch from a small lead nationally for one party to a small lead for the other. Second, the system needs to be even-handed in its treatment of the Conservatives and Labour; if the two parties secure the same share of the vote, they should win the same number of seats, such that, for example, a two point lead nationally for, say, the Conservatives should result in the same-sized majority as a two point lead for Labour. Third, the system should give third parties little or no representation, for the more third party MPs there are in the House of Commons, the greater the probability that no one party will win an overall majority.

In some ways the system did what it was meant to do so far as the treatment of third parties is concerned. The UKIP upsurge was rewarded with just one seat. The collapse in Liberal Democrat support saw the party's representation plummet. As a result, less than 2% of the seats in England and Wales were won by third parties, fewer than at any time since 1979. Nevertheless, the overall tally of third party MPs was still as high as 87, two more than were elected in 2010 and second only to the 92 that entered the Commons in 2005. The explanation, of course, lies in the success of the SNP. Far from discriminating against this party, the 4.7% of the UK-wide vote that it won was rewarded with no less than 8.6% of the seats in the House of Commons. Here at least was one third party that profited from the first-past-the-post system.

The contrast between the way in which the system treated the SNP and the way in which it gave the Liberal Democrats and (especially) UKIP just a few spoils is, of course, a reflection of the very different way in which those parties' votes are distributed geographically. The SNP's vote is confined to Scotland and was big enough there to sweep almost everything before it. In contrast, support for the Liberal Democrats and (especially) that for UKIP, is scattered relatively evenly across the country.[62] At the same time, all 18 seats in Northern Ireland are entirely the preserve of parties (and an independent) that do not contest elections in Britain, while Plaid Cymru can gain representation thanks to a concentration of its support in those parts of Wales where Welsh is widely spoken. The ability of the first-past-the-post system to discriminate against third parties has always been contingent on the geography of their support;[63] what this election did was to provide a vivid illustration of that truth. It does, however, mean, that the system ensures that third parties that represent particular territorial interests and identities may find it easier to secure leverage in the House of Commons than those that represent much larger bodies of voters scattered across the UK as a whole.

But if the electoral system proved relatively ineffective at keeping third parties out of the House of Commons, has there been any increase in the number of seats that are marginal between Conservative and Labour, thereby making it more likely that the largest party will secure an overall majority? Previous research has uncovered a long-term decline in the number of such seats.[64] And the number of such seats fell even further at this election. We can define as a marginal seat a seat in which the Conservative share of the votes cast for Conservative and Labour (the two-party vote) would lie between 45% and 55% should both parties secure the same share of the vote across Britain as a whole.

The number of seats falling within this category fell from 85 in 2010 to 74 now, fewer than ever before.

The reason for this is simple. As we have shown, within England and Wales, Conservative support generally increased most in relatively affluent constituencies, those with few public sector workers and those with predominantly white populations, all characteristics that tend to be associated with relatively high Conservative support in the first place. The fact that the party performed relatively well in such seats meant that England and Wales polarised yet further politically, with the Conservatives' share of the two-party vote falling less on average in seats that the party already held (by 0.9 of a point) than in those that were already in Labour's hands (2.4). As a result, there were yet fewer constituencies in which the two parties are likely to be close combatants in an election that is closely fought across the country as a whole.

So if the number of marginal seats fell, how then did we still end up with a Conservative majority? The answer lies in how some of the patterns of geographical variation we have identified, together with the collapse in Liberal Democrat support, turned a system that hitherto appeared to be biased in Labour's favour into one that now treats the Conservatives more kindly than it does their principal opponents.

The first crucial reason why this happened was the success of Conservative incumbents who were defending a marginal seat for the first time. Under the first-past-the-post system, a party will always be more richly rewarded if it wins plenty of seats by relatively small margins rather than piling up large majorities in safe seats or losing narrowly in marginal ones. At recent elections, it has been Labour's vote that has been the more efficiently distributed in this way.[65] However, the relative success of the Conservatives in the most marginal seats that they were defending meant that this advantage was reversed. Of the 74 seats that we defined earlier as marginal, 45 would be won by the Conservatives if the two parties were equal nationally, while only 29 would be won by Labour.[66]

The second reason lies in the profound change that occurred in the character of third party representation. Because the Liberal Democrats have tended to perform better in seats where the Conservatives are relatively strong, and because hitherto the principal third party has been the Liberal Democrats, until now the Conservatives have 'wasted' more votes than Labour in seats that were won by a third party. For example, while Labour on average won 16.6% of the vote in seats won by third parties in 2010, the Conservatives won 28.4% of the vote in such circumstances. But the collapse of the Liberal Democrats in 2015 meant that the Conservatives now wasted far fewer votes in seats captured by that party, while 40 of the 50 seats gained by the SNP were constituencies that had previously been held by Labour. It was Labour (average vote in third party seats 23.3%) that was now piling up more votes in third party seats, not the Conservatives (15.6%).

So, rather than representing a restoration of the electoral system's ability to deliver an overall majority to the largest party in a reliable and consistent manner, the Conservative success in winning an overall majority was the product of a reversal of the unequal way in which it treated the two largest parties.[67] Even then, thanks to the fact that there are fewer marginal seats nowadays, the Conservative overall majority of 12 is less than that enjoyed by the party in 1955, 1959 or 1970, or indeed the majority that Labour won in 2005, even though at each of those elections the lead of the largest party in votes was smaller than the 6.5 point lead the Conservatives enjoyed on this occasion. The result is that if the level and character of third party support remains as it is at present, the system still does not look like one that can be relied upon to produce overall majorities.

This feature – together with the way in which the system now treats the Conservatives more favourably – is illustrated in Table A1.15, which shows what the outcome would be as the result of various possible swings from Conservative to Labour, assuming: (i) that these occurred uniformly in each and every constituency; (ii) that the current parliamentary boundaries remain in place; and (iii) that the level and distribution of support for third parties is unchanged. First of all, we should note the wide range of results, that is, anything in between a Conservative lead of 5.8 points to a Labour lead of 12.5 points, which would, if our assumptions held, result in a hung parliament. Never before has this range been as wide as it has proven to be after the 2015 election.

Table A1.15 The relationship between votes and seats following the 2015 general election

Swing to Con from 2015 result	*Con lead over Lab (% GB Vote)*	*Seats (UK)*		
		Con	*Lab*	*Others*
–0.4	5.8	327	236	87
–3.3	0.0	302	256	92
–6.9	–3.7	279	278	93
–9.6	–12.5	229	326	95

Meanwhile, we can observe that the range is asymmetric. In order to be able to win an overall majority, Labour need more than twice as large a lead as the Conservatives. That in itself is an indication of the way in which the system now treats the Conservatives more favourably. But, in addition, we can note that the Conservatives would win 46 more seats than Labour if the two parties were to win the same share of the vote and that Labour would need to be 3.7 points ahead of the Conservatives before they achieved parity in terms of seats. In 2010, in contrast, the equivalent calculations put Labour 51 seats ahead in the event of a tie in votes, while the Conservatives needed to be 4.1 points ahead in order to win as many seats as Labour.

Not the least of the reasons why Labour would require such a large lead to win an overall majority is that even a 9.6% swing from the Conservatives to Labour would result in the party gaining just one seat from the SNP, so far ahead are the SNP in most of the seats that they won. The electoral system is, in truth, likely to continue to operate to Labour's relative disadvantage for so long as the SNP are anything like as successful in Scotland as they were in 2015. On the other hand, if SNP support were to decline as well as Labour's to rise, then Labour would begin to win back seats. For example, if SNP support fell by 9.6 points everywhere at the same time as Labour's increased by that amount, Labour would capture a dozen seats from their nationalist opponents.

However, the next election is not only due to be fought under new, more equal electoral boundaries, but also following a reduction in the number of constituencies from 650 to 600 (see p. 22). Making the sizes of constituencies more equal is likely to make the system even less favourable to Labour because the average Labour held seat contains some 3,800 fewer registered voters than the average Conservative constituency. However, reducing the number of constituencies could make the system somewhat better able to produce overall majorities as increasing the sizes of constituencies increases the likelihood that they are socially and thus politically more heterogeneous.

Although the single-member plurality system has been the only system used to elect MPs since 1950, there was nothing inevitable about its continued use at this election. It only continued to be used because in 2011 voters rejected in a referendum a proposal to use the Alternative Vote system instead (see p. 20). Yet, ironically, according to calculations made by the Electoral Reform Society, it would have made very little difference if voters had backed the Alternative Vote system, under which voters are invited to place candidates in rank order and the votes of less successful candidates are redistributed in accordance with voters' second and lower preferences until one candidate secures a majority of all votes cast.[68] It is estimated that the Conservatives would have won 337 seats (six more than they actually won), Labour 227 (–5), SNP 54 (–2) and the Liberal Democrats 9 (+1), while UKIP and the Greens would still have had just one seat each. It is perhaps ironic that the Conservatives might have been the principal beneficiary of a system whose possible introduction they strongly opposed, while the Liberal Democrats, who insisted that the referendum be held as their price for participating in the Coalition, would apparently have profited little. In any event, the likely similarity of the result in 2015 suggests that the Alternative Vote system is unlikely to be regarded as a worthwhile alternative by critics of the current system in future.

Rather, these critics are likely to point to the extent of the mismatch between votes won and seats secured across all the parties that contested the 2015 election. According to one index of disproportionality at least, only on one previous occasion (1983) was the outcome as disproportionate as that in 2015.[69] Far from signalling a return to service as normal, the way in which the electoral system operated in 2015 seems set to ensure that the debate about its merits will continue.

Notes

1. As indeed proved to be the fate of the last majority Conservative government to be elected, that is, the one elected in 1992 with an initial majority of 21.
2. This appendix does not attempt to analyse the result in Northern Ireland, where elections are dominated by parties that do not field candidates in Great Britain. Although the Conservatives, the Greens and UKIP stood in some constituencies in Northern Ireland, they each won less than 3% of the vote. The results in the 18 constituencies in Northern Ireland are shown in Table A2.5, while Table A2.3 provides a summary for the region as a whole.
3. For example, see, J. Curtice, S. Fisher and M. Steed, 'Appendix 2: The Results Analysed' in D. Kavanagh and D. Butler, *The British General Election of 2005*. Palgrave Macmillan, 2005; J. Curtice, S. Fisher and R. Ford, 'Appendix 2: The Results Analysed' in D. Kavanagh and P. Cowley, *The British General Election of 2010*. Palgrave Macmillan, 2010.
4. I. McLean, 'The Problem of Proportionate Swing', *Political Studies*, 21(1) (1973): 57–63.
5. Though the two measures of swing define 'suffer or profit equally' differently. See M. Steed, 'Appendix II: An Analysis of the Results' in D. Butler and A. King, *The British General Election of 1964*. Macmillan, 1965, pp. 337–8.
6. See, e.g., R. Duch and R. Stevenson, *The Economic Vote*. Cambridge University Press, 2008 and citations therein.
7. Even so, the two-party swing (which anticipates that former Liberal Democrat voters would switch to the Conservatives and Labour in proportion to their prior strength) was higher (–10.7) in Liberal Democrat seats where Labour

started off second than it was in those where the Conservatives had been second (–6.7).

8. The measure of unemployment is the share of the registered electorate who were claiming Jobseeker's Allowance in March 2015, the latest month for which data were available prior to the election (ONS regional labour market statistic JSA02 – Claimant Count for Parliamentary Constituencies). This 'claimant count' measure produces a lower estimate of unemployment than others, such as the Labour Force Survey, which counts people who are looking for work but are not claiming unemployment benefits. However, it is more regularly updated and the two series track each other closely (Office for National Statistics, 'UK Labour Market March 2015', www.ons.gov.uk). Unemployment statistics are commonly reported as a share of the active labour force, but we report them as a share of the electorate as this is the more relevant measure for our purposes: the political impact of economic changes will be more muted in areas where many voters are out of the labour force through, for example, retirement or full-time study.
9. J. Curtice, 'A Defeat to Reckon with: On Scotland, Economic Competence, and the Complexities of Labour's Losses', *Juncture*, 22(1) (2015): 42–7.
10. Regression analysis confirms that the relationship between the local level of unemployment and both Conservative and Labour performance is statistically significant after controlling for the prior Liberal Democrat share of the vote.
11. Data on incomes by parliamentary constituency are for the tax year 2012/13 and come from the Survey of Personal Incomes. See www.gov.uk/government/statistics/income-and-tax-by-parliamentary-constituency-2010-to-2011.
12. Exact data on the proportion of people in each constituency who are employed in the public sector are not available. But those who work in the industrial sectors, 'public administration and defence', 'education' and 'health and social care' for which data are available from the 2011 Census are mostly employed in the public sector and these groups constitute the majority of public sector workers.
13. Curtice, Fisher and Ford, 'Appendix 2', pp. 390–1.
14. P. Dunleavy, 'The Political Implications of Sectoral Cleavages and the Growth of State Employment: Part 2, Cleavage Structures and Political Alignment', *Political Studies*, 28(4) (1980): 527–49.
15. Curtice, Fisher and Ford, 'Appendix 2', pp. 391–2.
16. *Ibid.*
17. S. Fisher, A. Heath, D. Sanders and M. Sobolewska, 'Candidate Ethnicity and Vote Choice in Britain', *British Journal of Political Science*, 45(4) (2015): 883–905.
18. References to regions of England here and later in this appendix are to the UK government region of that name.
19. Thus, in the 40 seats in the North of England with a population density of more than 25 persons per hectare (as measured by the 2001 Census), the Conservative vote fell on average by 2.1 points, while Labour's increased by 6.9 points. In contrast, in the 24 seats with a population density of less than three persons per hectare, the Conservative vote actually increased slightly more (by 2.3 points) than did the Labour vote (1.7 points).

20. See, for example, T. Smith, 'Are You Sitting Comfortably? Estimating Incumbency Advantage in the UK: 1983–2010 – A Research Note', *Electoral Studies*, 32(1) (2013): 167–73 and citations therein.
21. Further evidence in support of the argument that incumbency mattered comes from the fact that although there were no instances of a Labour MP defending a seat gained from the Conservatives in 2010, whether or not a seat was being defended by the incumbent MP also made a difference to Labour's performance in the seats that it was defending. The party's vote increased on average by 3.4 points in seats in which the incumbent retired, but by 5.1 points where the local MP was standing again.
22. A. Russell, E. Fieldhouse and I. MacAllister, *Neither Left nor Right: The Liberal Democrats and the Electorate*. Manchester University Press, 2004.
23. See S. Fisher and N. Hillman, 'Do Students Swing Elections? Registration, Turnout and Voting Behaviour among Full-Time Students', www.hepi.ac.uk (2014) and citations therein.
24. Seats with relatively large numbers of students are defined as those in which more than 9% of those aged 16–74 were classified as students in the 2011 Census. Those with relatively few students are those in which less than 6% were classified as students.
25. A. Heath, R, Jowell and J. Curtice, *How Britain Votes*. Pergamon Press, 1985.
26. Smith, 'Are You Sitting Comfortably?' and citations therein.
27. This observation is based on a regression model of the relationship between prior Liberal Democrat strength and the fall in Liberal Democrat support that is confined to those seats the party did not win in 2010. It includes both linear and log-linear terms that between them summarise the pattern whereby Liberal Democrat support fell more heavily the better the party did in 2010, but that in places where the party was stronger, the drop represented a smaller proportion of the party's prior support. This, of course, presumes that we can extrapolate accurately from this model what would have happened in seats in which the party won very high shares of the vote in 2010, in all of which, inevitably, the party came first.
28. R. Ford and M. Goodwin, *Revolt on the Right*. Routledge, 2014.
29. As defined in Table A1.7 above. UKIP's vote increased on average by 15.5 points in seats with less than 29% employed in the public sector.
30. As a percentage of those aged 16–74 who were economically active.
31. See, e.g., G. Evans and J. Mellon, 'Working Class Votes and Conservative Losses: Solving the UKIP Puzzle', *Parliamentary Affairs* (2015); R. Ford and M. Goodwin, 'Different Class? UKIP's Social Base and Political Impact: A Reply to Evans and Mellon', *Parliamentary Affairs* (2015).
32. Curtice, Fisher and Ford, 'Appendix 2', pp. 407–8.
33. In any event, it might be the case that one of the reasons why Labour performed relatively well and UKIP relatively badly in many ethnically diverse constituencies is that Labour voters in such seats were less willing to switch to UKIP.
34. C. Rallings and M. Thrasher, *Media Guide to the New Parliamentary Constituencies*. Local Government Chronicle Elections Centre, 2007.
35. Curtice, Fisher and Ford, 'Appendix 2', pp. 389–93.
36. In seats where the proportion of those aged 16–74 classified by the Census as unemployed fell by two points or more, the Greens won on average 5.7%

of the vote and saw their vote increase by 4.2 points in those seats they also fought in 2010. In contrast, where the proportion unemployed had increased by 1.4 points, the Greens won just 3.2% of the vote on average and saw their vote increase by 2.1 points. However, there is little discernible relationship between Green performance and the level of unemployment in 2015.

37. See, for example, Curtice, Fisher and Ford, 'Appendix 2'.
38. This calculation is based on all seats that the party fought in 2015. Where the party did not fight the constituency in 2010 the increase in its share of the vote since 2010 is simply the share of the vote it won in 2015.
39. S. Fisher and J. Curtice, 'Tactical Unwind? Changes in Party Preference Structure and Tactical Voting from 2001 to 2005', *Journal of Elections, Public Opinion and Parties*, 16(1) (2006): 55–76 and citations therein.
40. Curtice, Fisher and Ford, 'Appendix 2', pp. 400–1.
41. Labour support increased on average by 13.5 points in these seats, a performance that emulated that achieved by the party on average in those seats where it started off second to the Liberal Democrats.
42. The two seats that were retained were Leeds North West and Sheffield Hallam. Cambridge, in contrast, was narrowly lost by the Liberal Democrats.
43. In Conservative/Labour marginals where UKIP's vote increased by less than 7.5 points, there was a swing to Labour of 0.6 points. In contrast, in seats where the increase was more than 13.5 points, there was a swing of 2.1 points to the Conservatives, while in seats where the increase was between 7.5 points and 13.5 points, there was a 2.5 point swing in the Conservatives' favour.
44. Not that the support for the party was the same everywhere. It was typically highest in less affluent constituencies as well as those where more people were born in Scotland or acknowledged a Scottish identity. For example, on average the party won 54.0% in seats where the current unemployment level represented more than 2% of the electorate, compared with 46.2% elsewhere. At the same time, the party won 53.3% in seats where, according to the 2011 Census, more than 83% of people were born in Scotland, compared with 46.0% elsewhere. Indeed, in both cases, the difference in the level of SNP support between the two types of seat was rather greater than it was in 2010.
45. This was Berwickshire, Roxburgh and Selkirk, where the Conservative vote increased by 2.2 points, where the party's credibility may have been unusually strong locally because polling undertaken by Lord Ashcroft had suggested the Conservatives might be able to win the seat, and because the Conservatives currently held the nearest equivalent Scottish Parliament constituency.
46. Indeed, we should note that in contrast to the pattern we have seen in England and Wales, there is no evidence that Conservative support fell less in places with relatively low levels of unemployment, while in fact Labour's vote fell most (and the SNP's rose most) in places with relatively high levels of unemployment.
47. Apart from Edinburgh South, it is possible that the Tories' success in narrowly retaining Dumfriesshire, Clydesdale and Tweeddale was assisted by a small amount of tactical switching by both Liberal Democrat and Labour voters.

Both of those parties suffered a slightly bigger drop in support (of around two points) in the constituency than might have otherwise have been expected, given their respective prior levels of strength in the constituency in 2010.

48. And in a few instances probably Labour voters too. This certainly seems to be what happened in East Dunbartonshire, where Labour's vote fell by 21.8 points, well above the drop elsewhere in seats with a similarly sized Labour vote in 2010 and enough to ensure that the fall in the Liberal Democrat vote there (–2.8 points) was the lowest anywhere in Britain. But Labour's vote also fell by slightly more than we would otherwise expect (that is, given its previous strength locally) in the handful of other seats in which the party started off second to the Liberal Democrats.
49. The Liberal Democrat vote fell by just 3.3 points in Gordon, where Malcolm Bruce stood down and the seat was being contested for the SNP by the former Scottish First Minister, Alex Salmond, while in Fife North East (where Sir Menzies Campbell retired), the party's vote fell by 13.0 points.
50. Defined as constituencies in which more than 12% of those aged 16–74 were classified by the 2011 Census as students.
51. For example, turnout increased on average by 1.8 points in those seats where over 12% of those aged 16–74 were classified in the 2011 Census as students, well above the average of 0.5 of a point across all seats in England and Wales. As seats with relatively large numbers of students were disproportionately constituencies where Labour and the Liberal Democrats shared second place, this means that turnout also rose most in such contests, contests in which on average Labour tended to perform relatively well. However, given the apparent impact of the change of procedure on the level of registration in such seats, we clearly cannot presume that the relatively strong Labour performance in such seats was occasioned by the increase in turnout.
52. But note that although the level of turnout continued to be lower in places with relatively high levels of social deprivation, there is no evidence that the gap widened. Turnout increased on average by around half a point irrespective of the proportion of the population that in the 2011 Census said that they were in good health.
53. For example, on average turnout increased by 8.8 points in those seats where less than 79% said in the 2011 Census that they were in good health, compared with 6.6 points in those where more than 82% said they were in good health.
54. Curtice, Fisher and Ford, 'Appendix 2', pp. 410–17. See also M. Thrasher, G. Borisyuk, C. Rallings and R. Johnston, 'Electoral Bias at the 2010 General Election: Evaluating its Extent in a Three-Party System', *Electoral Studies*, 21(2) (2011): 279–94.
55. This calculation is itself not unproblematic. As we noted earlier, in around one in four seats the fall in the Liberal Democrat share of the vote was greater than the party's share of the vote locally last time, and thus it was arithmetically impossible for the Liberal Democrat vote to have fallen by the same amount everywhere. Equally, the Scotland-wide fall in Labour support was greater than its share of the vote locally in nine seats north of the border. However, examination of the cases where the uniform change assumption produces an estimated negative share for a party gives no reason

to believe that in any instance the outcome could have been different, not least because in most cases the projected negative share for the Liberal Democrats/Labour is less than the projected majority for the winning party.

56. These constituencies were Amber Valley, Broxtowe, Cardiff North, Hendon, Morecambe and Lunesdale, Sherwood, Stockton South, Thurrock, Warwickshire North, and Waveney.
57. If we add to our model of uniform change an estimate, derived from regression analysis of the party's performance, of the bonus that first-time Conservative incumbents secured on average (3.7 points), we secure the Conservatives' exact tally of 331 seats. The two other seats that the party held against the uniform trend were Cardiff North and Warwickshire North, in both of which the (first-time) Conservative incumbent actually stood down. There was, however, as we note below, a slight net swing to the Conservatives in Wales, which helps account for the result in Cardiff North, while Warwickshire North enjoyed relatively low unemployment and is home to relatively few public sector workers, both factors associated with an above-average Conservative performance in England and Wales.
58. These constituencies were Bolton West, Derby North, Gower, Morley and Outwood, Plymouth Moor View, Southampton Itchen, Telford, and Vale of Clwyd.
59. These seats are Coatbridge, Chryston and Bellshill, Glasgow North East, and Kirkcaldy and Cowdenbeath.
60. The party held Carshalton and Wallington against the tide, together with Southport, but lost out in Bath, Twickenham, and Yeovil.
61. G. Gudgin and P. Taylor, *Seats, Votes and the Spatial Organization of Elections*. Pion, 1979.
62. The standard deviation of the Liberal Democrat vote across all constituencies is now 8.4, down from 10.4 in 2010. Meanwhile, the equivalent figure for UKIP (here also taking into account the ten seats it contested in Northern Ireland) is just 6.2. Support for both parties is markedly more evenly spread than that for both the Conservatives (standard deviation 16.9, after including 16 seats fought in Northern Ireland) and Labour (16.5).
63. Gudgin and Taylor, *Seats, Votes and the Spatial Organisation of Elections*.
64. J. Curtice, 'So What Went Wrong with the Electoral System? The 2010 Election Result and the Debate about Electoral Reform', *Parliamentary Affairs*, 68(suppl 1) (2010), 623–38.
65. *Ibid.*
66. More generally, the relative efficiency of the Conservative vote is indicated by the fact that the median Conservative share of the two-party vote across all constituencies is 2.1 points higher than the mean share. Because the median is less sensitive than the mean to especially high or low values, this difference suggests that, as compared with Labour, the Conservatives waste fewer votes through winning seats by relatively large majorities. See C. Soper and J. Rydon, 'Under-Representation and Electoral Prediction', *Australian Journal of Politics and History*, 4(1) (1958): 94–106.
67. There is, however, one way in which the system continued to be biased in Labour's favour. This is a long-standing tendency for fewer votes to be cast in seats won by Labour than in those won by the Conservatives. This time, nearly 7,400 fewer votes were cast in the seats Labour won. This is both

because there were some 3,800 fewer registered voters in Labour seats (see also further below), while, at 61.9%, turnout in Labour-held constituencies was nearly seven points less than that in Conservative-held seats (68.7%). The Conservatives had hoped to reduce this source of bias against them by securing a redrawing of the parliamentary boundaries, but their plans were scuppered by their Liberal Democrat coalition partners (see p. 22). In the event, the size of this particular source of bias remained much the same as in 2010.

68. J. Garland and C. Terry, *The 2015 General Election: A Voting System in Crisis*. Electoral Reform Society, 2015.
69. This is the so-called Loosemore–Hanby index (see J. Loosemore and V. Hanby, 'The Theoretical Limits of Maximum Distortion: Some Analytic Expressions for Electoral Systems', *British Journal of Political Science*, 1(4) (1971): 467–77), which is the sum of the differences between the parties' shares of the vote and their shares of the vote divided by two. This index (calculated for the result across the whole of the UK) is 23.9, the same as in 1983. However, according to an alternative index which places greater weight on large discrepancies between votes and seats, the result in 2015 was slightly less disproportionate than in 2010, and the least disproportionate since and including 1997 (see M. Gallagher, 'Proportionality, Disproportionality and Electoral Systems', *Electoral Studies*, 10(1) (1991): 33–51).

Appendix 2 :The Voting Statistics

Table A2.1 Votes and seats, 1945–2015

	Electorate/ turnout	*Votes/ seats*	*Conservative*[a]	*Labour*	*Liberal (Democrats)*[b]	*Scottish and Welsh Nationalists*	*Other*
1945[c]	73.3%	100%–640	39.8%–213	48.3%–393	9.1%–12	0.20%	2.5%–22
	32,836,419	24,082,612	9,577,667	11,632,191	2,197,191	46,612	628,251
1950	84.0%	100%–625	43.5%–299	46.1%–315	9.1%–9	0.10%	1.2%–2
	34,269,770	28,772,671	12,502,567	13,266,592	2,621,548	27,288	354,676
1951	82.5%	100%–625	48.%–321	48.8%–295	2.5%–6	0.10%	0.6%–3
	34,645,573	28,595,668	13,717,538	13,948,605	730,556	18,219	180,750
1955	76.8%	100%–630	49.7%–345	46.4%–277	2.7%–6	0.20%	0.9%–2
	34,858,263	26,760,493	13,311,936	12,404,970	722,405	57,231	263,951
1959	78.7%	100%–630	49.4%–365	43.8%–258	5.9%–6	0.40%	0.6%–1
	35,397,080	27,859,241	13,749,830	12,215,538	1,638,571	99,309	175,987
1964	77.1%	100%–630	43.4%–304	44.1%–317	11.2%–9	0.50%	0.8%–0
	35,892,572	27,655,374	12,001,396	12,205,814	3,092,878	133,551	215,363
1966	75.8%	100%–630	41.9%–253	47.9%–363	8.5%–12	0.70%	0.9%–2
	35,964,684	27,263,606	11,418,433	13,064,951	2,327,533	189,545	263,144
1970	72.0%	100%–630	46.4%–330	43.%–288	7.5%–6	1.3%–1	1.8%–5
	39,342,013	28,344,798	13,145,123	12,178,295	2,117,033	381,819	524,527
Feb 1974	78.1%	100%–635	37.8%–297	37.1%–301	19.3%–14	2.6%–9	3.2%–14
	39,770,724	31,340,162	11,872,180	11,646,391	6,058,744	804,554	991,036

Oct 1974	72.8%	100%–635	35.8%–277	39.2%–319	18.3%–13	3.5%–14	3.2%–12
	40,072,971	29,189,178	10,464,817	11,457,079	5,346,754	1,005,938	914,590
1979	76.0%	100%–635	43.9%–339	37.%–269	13.8%–11	2.%–4	3.3%–12
	41,093,264	31,221,361	13,697,923	11,532,218	4,313,804	636,890	1,039,563
1983	72.7%	100%–650	42.4%–397	27.6%–209	25.4%–23	1.5%–4	3.1%–17
	42,197,344	30,671,136	13,012,315	8,456,934	7,780,949	457,676	144,723
1987	75.3%	100%–650	42.3%–376	30.8%–229	22.6%–22	1.7%–6	2.6%–17
	43,181,321	32,536,137	13,763,066	10,029,778	7,341,290	543,559	852,368
1992	77.7%	100%–651	41.9%–336	34.4%–271	17.8%–20	2.3%–7	3.5%–17
	43,249,721	33,612,693	14,092,891	11,559,735	5,999,384	783,991	1,176,692
1997	71.5%	100%–659	30.7%–165	43.2%–418	16.8%–46	2.5%–10	6.8%–20
	43,757,478	31,286,597	9,602,857	13,516,632	5,242,894	782,570	2,141,644
2001	59.4%	100%–659	31.7%–166	40.7%–412	18.3%–52	2.5%–9	6.8%–20
	44,403,238	26,368,798	8,357,622	10,724,895	4,812,833	660,197	1,813,251
2005	61.2%	100%–646	32.4%–198	35.2%–356	22.0%–62	2.2%–9	8.2%–22
	44,261,545	27,123,652	8,772,473	9,547,944	5,981,874	567,105	2,234,267
2010	65.1%	100%–650	36.1%–307	29.0%–258	23.0%–57	2.2%–9	9.6%–19
	45,610,369	29,687,409	10,726,555	8,606,518	6,836,188	656,780	2,861,368
2015	66.2%	100%–650	36.9%–331	30.4%–232	7.9%–8	5.3%–59	19.4%–20
	46,354,197	30,697,525	11,334,226	9,347,273	2,415,916	1,636,140	5,963,964

Notes:

[a] Includes Ulster Unionists 1945–70.

[b] Liberals 1945–79; Liberal–SDP Alliance 1983–7; Liberal Democrats 1992–.

[c] The 1945 figures exclude university seats and are adjusted for double counting in the 15 two-member seats.

Table A2.2 Party performance (UK)

Party	*Votes*	*% share (change)*	*Average % share*	*Seats (change)*	*Candidates*	*Lost deposits*
Conservative	11,334,226	36.9 (+0.8)	35.8	331 (+24)	648	18
Labour	9,347,273	30.4 (+1.5)	32.3	232 (–26)	631	3
United Kingdom Independence Party (UKIP)	3,881,099	12.6 (+9.5)	13.4	1 (+1)	624	79
Liberal Democrats	2,415,916	7.9 (–15.2)	7.8	8 (–49)	631	341
Scottish National Party (SNP)	1,454,436	4.7 (+3.1)	50.2	56 (+50)	59	0
Green	1,157,630	3.8 (+2.8)	4.2	1 (0)	573	442
Democratic Unionist Party (DUP)	184,260	0.6 (0)	29.9	8 (0)	16	0
Plaid Cymru	181,704	0.6 (0)	12.8	3 (0)	40	8
Sinn Fein	176,232	0.6 (0)	23.6	4 (–1)	18	4
Ulster Unionist Party (UUP)	114,935	0.4 (0)	18.1	2 (+2)	15	2
Social Democratic and Labour Party (SDLP)	99,809	0.3 (0)	13.7	3 (0)	18	3
Alliance Party of Northern Ireland (APNI)	61,556	0.2 (+0.1)	8.9	0 (–1)	18	8
Trade Unionist and Socialist Coalition	36,368	0.1 (+0.1)	0.6	–	134	134
National Health Action (NHA)	20,210	0.1 (0)	3.3	–	12	10
Traditional Unionist Voice (TUV)	16,538	0.1 (0)	6.1	–	7	3
Respect	9,989	0 (–0.1)	6.1	–	4	3
Cannabis is Safer Than Alcohol (CISTA)	8,419	0 (0)	0.6	–	32	32
Yorkshire First	6,811	0 (0)	1.1	–	14	14
English Democrats	6,531	0 (–0.2)	0.5	–	32	32

Note: the cut-off for inclusion was 5,000 votes. Below that line are a variety of other parties, including the Monster Raving Loony Party, the Socialist Labour Party, the Christian Peoples Alliance, the Christian Party, the Workers' Party and the British National Party. The last polled just 1,667 votes in 2015, down from 564,321 in 2010. Not included is Lady Sylvia Hermon, who won North Down as an independent.

Table A2.3 Party performance (Northern Ireland)

Party	*Votes*	*% share (change)*	*Average % share*	*Seats (change)*	*Candidates*	*Lost deposits*
Democratic Unionist Party (DUP)	184,260	25.7 (+0.7)	29.9	8 (0)	16	0
Sinn Fein	176,232	24.5 (–1.0)	23.6	4 (–1)	18	4
Ulster Unionist Party (UUP)	114,935	16 (+0.8)	18.1	2 (+2)	15	2
Social Democratic and Labour Party (SDLP)	99,809	13.9 (–2.6)	13.7	3 (0)	18	3
Alliance Party of Northern Ireland (APNI)	61,556	8.6 (+2.2)	8.9	0 (–1)	18	8
United Kingdom Independence Party (UKIP)	18,324	2.6 (+2.6)	4.9	–	10	6
Traditional Unionist Voice (TUV)	16,538	2.3 (–1.6)	6.1	–	7	3
Conservative	9,055	1.3 (+1.3)	1.5	–	16	15
Green	6,822	1 (+0.4)	3.5	–	5	3
Cannabis is Safer Than Alcohol (CISTA)	1,853	0.3 (+0.3)	1.2	–	4	4

Note: the calculations for the UUP are based on comparisons with the UCU in 2010. As in Table A2.2, not included is Lady Sylvia Hermon, who won North Down as an independent.

Table A2.4 National and regional results

UK

Seats won in 2015 (change since 2010)						Share of votes cast in 2015 (change since 2010)						
Con	*Lab*	*LD*	*Nat and other*		*Turnout*	*Con*	*Lab*	*Lib Dem*	*Nat*	*UKIP*	*Green*	*Other*
319 (+21)	206 (+15)	6 (–37)	2 (+1)	**England**	66.0 (+0.5)	41.0 (+1.4)	31.6 (+3.6)	8.2 (–16.0)	0 (0)	14.1 (+10.7)	4.2 (+3.2)	0.8 (–2.8)
44 (+1)	110 (+6)	4 (–7)	0 (0)	North	63.5 (+1.2)	30.7 (0)	43.1 (+4.7)	6.7 (–15.7)	0 (0)	15.0 (+12.0)	3.4 (+2.8)	1.1 (–3.8)
66 (+2)	39 (0)	0 (–2)	0 (0)	Midlands	65.2 (–0.4)	42.5 (+2.3)	32.3 (+2.1)	5.5 (–15.1)	0 (0)	15.7 (+12.1)	3.1 (+2.6)	0.7 (–3.9)
209 (+18)	57 (+9)	2 (–28)	2 (+1)	South	67.7 (+0.5)	45.7 (+1.8)	25.5 (+3.5)	9.9 (–16.6)	0 (0)	13.1 (+9.5)	5.0 (+3.6)	0.8 (–1.8)
11 (+3)	25 (–1)	1 (–2)	3 (0)	**Wales**	65.7 (+0.9)	27.2 (+1.1)	36.9 (+0.6)	6.5 (–13.6)	12.1 (+0.9)	13.6 (+11.2)	2.6 (+2.1)	1.0 (–2.4)
1 (0)	1 (–40)	1 (–10)	56 (+50)	**Scotland**	71.0 (+7.2)	14.9 (–1.8)	24.3 (–17.7)	7.5 (–11.3)	50.0 (+30.0)	1.6 (+0.9)	1.3 (+0.7)	0.3 (–0.8)
331 (+24)	232 (–26)	8 (–49)	61 (+51)	**Great Britain**	66.4 (+1.1)	37.8 (+0.8)	31.2 (+1.5)	8.1 (–15.5)	5.5 (+3.2)	12.9 (+9.7)	3.8 (+2.9)	0.8 (–2.6)
0 (0)	0 (0)	0 (0)	18 (0)	**Northern Ireland**	58.1 (+0.4)	1.3 (+1.3)	0 (0)	0 (0)	0 (0)	2.6 (+2.6)	1.0 (+0.4)	95.2 (–4.2)
331 (+24)	232 (–26)	8 (–49)	79 (+51)	**UK**	66.2 (+1.1)	36.9 (+0.8)	30.4 (+1.5)	7.9 (–15.2)	5.3 (+3.1)	12.6 (+9.5)	3.8 (+2.8)	3.0 (–2.6)

Regions

Seats won in 2015 (change since 2010)						Share of votes cast in 2015 (change since 2010)						
Con	*Lab*	*LD*	*Nat and other*		*Turnout*	*Con*	*Lab*	*Lib Dem*	*Nat*	*UKIP*	*Green*	*Other*
138 (+3)	51 (+7)	1 (–11)	2 (+1)	**South East**	67.2 (+0.5)	45.3 (+1.2)	28.2 (+3.9)	8.4 (–15.6)	0 (0)	12.7 (+9.4)	4.7 (+3.3)	0.7 (–2.2)
27 (–1)	45 (+7)	1 (–6)	0 (0)	Greater London*	65.4 (+0.9)	34.9 (+0.4)	43.7 (+7.1)	7.7 (–14.4)	0 (0)	8.1 (+6.4)	4.9 (+3.3)	0.8 (–2.7)
5 (0)	23 (+2)	0 (–2)	0 (0)	Inner London	63.3 (+1.5)	26.8 (+0.7)	52.4 (+8.4)	7.9 (–15.8)	0 (0)	4.6 (+3.7)	7.1 (+5.0)	1.2 (–2.1)
22 (–1)	22 (+5)	1 (–4)	0 (0)	Outer London	66.8 (+0.6)	39.9 (+0.3)	38.3 (+6.1)	7.6 (–13.6)	0 (0)	10.3 (+8.0)	3.4 (+2.2)	0.5 (–3.0)
111 (+4)	6 (0)	0 (–5)	2 (+1)	Rest of South East	68.3 (+0.3)	51.3 (+1.8)	19.3 (+1.9)	8.8 (–16.2)	0 (0)	15.3 (+11.2)	4.6 (+3.4)	0.7 (–2.0)
59 (0)	3 (0)	0 (0)	0 (0)	Outer Met. Area	68.3 (0)	53.1 (+2.1)	19.7 (+2.3)	7.8 (–15.9)	0 (0)	14.9 (+11.1)	3.7 (+2.9)	0.8 (–2.4)
52 (+4)	3 (0)	0 (–5)	2 (+1)	Other South East	68.2 (+0.7)	49.4 (+1.4)	18.8 (+1.5)	9.8 (–16.6)	0 (0)	15.6 (+11.4)	5.6 (+3.9)	0.7 (–1.6)
51 (+15)	4 (0)	0 (–15)	0 (0)	**South West***	69.5 (+0.5)	46.5 (+3.7)	17.7 (+2.3)	15.1 (–19.6)	0 (0)	13.6 (+9.1)	5.9 (+4.8)	1.2 (–0.3)
17 (+6)	1 (–1)	0 (–5)	0 (0)	Devon and Cornwall	69.4 (+1.1)	45.2 (+2.6)	16.2 (+3.7)	16.2 (–19.8)	0 (0)	14.4 (+8.6)	5.7 (+4.2)	2.4 (+0.7)
34 (+9)	3 (+1)	0 (–10)	0 (0)	Rest of South West	69.6 (+0.3)	47.2 (+4.2)	18.4 (+1.6)	14.6 (–19.5)	0 (0)	13.2 (+9.3)	6.0 (+5.1)	0.6 (–0.8)
20 (0)	2 (+2)	1 (–2)	0 (0)	**East Anglia***	67.5 (–0.4)	46.9 (+2.2)	22.6 (+3.8)	9.8 (–17.2)	0 (0)	15.7 (+10.7)	4.9 (+2.5)	0.2 (–2.0)
32 (+1)	14 (–1)	0 (0)	0 (0)	**East Midlands***	66.5 (–0.3)	43.5 (+2.3)	31.6 (+1.9)	5.6 (–15.3)	0 (0)	15.8 (+12.5)	3.0 (+2.4)	0.6 (–3.9)

34 (+1)	25 (+1)	0 (−2)	0 (0)	**West Midlands***	64.1 (−0.6)	41.8 (+2.2)	32.9 (+2.3)	5.5 (−14.9)	0 (0)	15.7 (+11.7)	3.3 (+2.7)	0.8 (−4.0)
7 (0)	21 (+2)	0 (−2)	0 (0)	W. Mids. Met. Co.	60.5 (−0.9)	33.1 (−0.4)	42.5 (+4.8)	5.5 (−13.8)	0 (0)	15.5 (+11.6)	2.9 (+2.4)	0.6 (−4.6)
27 (+1)	4 (−1)	0 (0)	0 (0)	Rest of W. Mids.	67.2 (−0.3)	48.7 (+4.3)	25.3 (+0.3)	5.5 (−15.8)	0 (0)	15.9 (+11.8)	3.6 (+2.9)	1.0 (−3.5)
19 (0)	33 (+1)	2 (−1)	0 (0)	**Yorks and Humber***	63.3 (+0.4)	32.6 (−0.2)	39.1 (+4.8)	7.1 (−15.8)	0 (0)	16.0 (+13.2)	3.5 (+2.7)	1.6 (−4.6)
0 (0)	13 (0)	1 (0)	0 (0)	S. Yorks Met. Co.	60.5 (−0.4)	17.4 (−3.2)	49.5 (+7.5)	8.2 (−15.6)	0 (0)	20.8 (+16.4)	2.7 (+2.1)	1.6 (−7.2)
7 (0)	14 (+1)	1 (−1)	0 (0)	W. Yorks Met. Co.	64.5 (+0.5)	32.7 (−0.2)	42.2 (+4.8)	6.4 (−14.3)	0 (0)	13.6 (+12.3)	3.6 (+2.6)	1.6 (−5.1)
12 (0)	6 (0)	0 (0)	0 (0)	Rest of Yorks and Humb	63.9 (+1.0)	43.5 (+1.8)	28.0 (+3.0)	7.3 (−17.8)	0 (0)	15.6 (+12.0)	4.1 (+3.2)	1.6 (−2.1)
20 (0)	48 (+4)	1 (−4)	0 (0)	**North West**	64.1 (+2.3)	30.4 (−0.6)	45.9 (+5.7)	6.0 (−15.4)	0 (0)	13.7 (+10.5)	3.2 (+2.7)	0.8 (−2.8)
5 (+3)	22 (0)	0 (−3)	0 (0)	Gtr. Mancs. Met. Co.	61.3 (+1.9)	26.4 (−0.9)	46.1 (+5.8)	7.1 (−16.7)	0 (0)	16.1 (+12.9)	3.5 (+3.0)	0.8 (−4.0)
0 (−1)	14 (+1)	1 (0)	0 (0)	Merseyside Met. Co.	65.7 (+5.0)	18.1 (−3.0)	61.7 (+9.4)	5.5 (−15.3)	0 (0)	10.3 (+7.1)	3.6 (+3.3)	0.8 (−1.5)
15 (−2)	12 (+3)	0 (−1)	0 (0)	Rest of North West	66.3 (+1.3)	40.9 (+1.3)	37.3 (+3.3)	5.1 (−14.3)	0 (0)	13.3 (+9.9)	2.6 (+2.1)	0.8 (−2.3)
5 (+1)	29 (+1)	1 (−2)	0 (0)	**North**	62.6 (+0.3)	28.1 (+1.5)	43.8 (+2.6)	7.7 (−16.0)	0 (0)	16.0 (+13.4)	3.6 (+3.2)	0.8 (−4.7)
0 (0)	12 (0)	0 (0)	0 (0)	Tyne and Wear Met. Co.	60.6 (+0.8)	20.3 (−1.1)	52.1 (+3.4)	5.5 (−16.1)	0 (0)	17.3 (+15.5)	4.1 (+3.4)	0.7 (−5.1)
5 (+1)	17 (+1)	1 (−2)	0 (0)	Rest of North	63.6 (+0.1)	32.1 (+2.9)	39.6 (+2.1)	8.8 (−15.9)	0 (0)	15.3 (+12.3)	3.3 (+3.1)	0.9 (−4.5)
11 (+3)	25 (−1)	1 (−2)	3 (0)	**Wales***	65.7 (+0.9)	27.2 (+1.1)	36.9 (+0.6)	6.5 (−13.6)	12.1 (+0.9)	13.6 (+11.2)	2.6 (+2.1)	1.0 (−2.4)
4 (+1)	20 (0)	0 (−1)	0 (0)	Industrial South Wales	64.5 (+1.1)	24.1 (+1.2)	42.9 (+1.1)	5.2 (−14.4)	9.9 (+1.4)	14.3 (+11.9)	2.7 (+2.1)	1.0 (−3.3)
7 (+2)	5 (−1)	1 (−1)	3 (0)	Rural Wales	67.7 (+0.6)	32.3 (+1.1)	27.2 (−0.3)	8.7 (−12.2)	15.8 (+0.1)	12.5 (+10.0)	2.3 (+2.2)	1.2 (−0.8)
1 (0)	1 (−40)	1 (−10)	56 (+50)	**Scotland***	71.0 (+7.2)	14.9 (−1.8)	24.3 (−17.7)	7.5 (−11.3)	50.0 (+30.0)	1.6 (+0.9)	1.3 (+0.7)	0.3 (−0.8)
1 (0)	0 (−5)	0 (−1)	6 (+6)	Ayrshire and Borders	73.1 (+7.9)	24.4 (−1.4)	22.3 (−17.5)	4.3 (−11.9)	46.6 (+29.5)	1.8 (+1.2)	0.6 (+0.4)	0 (−0.3)
0 (0)	0 (−19)	0 (−1)	20 (+20)	Clydeside	68.9 (+7.3)	9.3 (−2.1)	31.0 (−24.3)	3.8 (−9.0)	53.1 (+35.3)	1.3 (+0.9)	1.0 (+0.4)	0.5 (−1.2)
0 (0)	1 (−9)	0 (−1)	10 (+10)	Rest of Central Belt	72.7 (+5.9)	15.0 (−1.8)	28.1 (−14.2)	5.6 (−14.6)	46.7 (+28.5)	2.0 (+1.4)	2.5 (+1.1)	0.1 (−0.5)
0 (0)	0 (−7)	0 (−3)	15 (+10)	North East and Fife	70.7 (+7.2)	19.2 (−0.2)	18.1 (−14.5)	8.6 (−11.8)	51.2 (+25.7)	1.3 (+0.4)	1.3 (+1.0)	0.3 (−0.6)
0 (0)	0 (0)	1 (−4)	5 (+4)	Highlands and Islands	73.6 (+8.9)	8.6 (−6.0)	9.4 (−11.7)	30.9 (−9.5)	46.8 (+27.4)	2.4 (+1.1)	1.1 (−0.2)	0.7 (−1.2)
0 (0)	0 (0)	0 (0)	18 (0)	**N Ireland**	58.1 (+0.4)	1.3 (+1.3)	0 (0)	0 (0)	0 (0)	2.6 (+2.6)	1.0 (+0.4)	95.2 (−4.2)

Notes:
The English Regions are the eight *Standard Regions*, now obsolete but used by the OPCS until the 1990s.

The *Outer Metropolitan Area* compromises those seats wholly or mostly in the Outer Metropolitan Area as defined by the OPCS. It includes: the whole of Surrey and Hertfordshire; the whole of Berkshire except Newbury; and the constituencies of Bedfordshire South West; Luton North; Luton South (Bedfordshire); Beaconsfield; Chesham and Amersham; Wycombe (Buckinghamshire); Basildon and Billericay; Basildon South and East Thurrock; Brentwood and Ongar; Castle Point; Chelmsford; Epping Forest; Harlow; Rayleigh and Wickford; Rochford and Southend East; Southend West; Thurrock

(Essex); Aldershot; Hampshire North East (Hampshire); Chatham and Aylesford; Dartford; Faversham and Kent Mid; Gillingham and Rainham; Gravesham; Maidstone and The Weald; Rochester and Strood; Sevenoaks; Tonbridge and Malling; Tunbridge Wells (Kent); Arundel and South Downs; Crawley; Horsham; Sussex Mid (West Sussex).

Industrial Wales (a description that is no longer entirely accurate, but which has been used for continuity with previous volumes) includes Gwent, the whole of Glamorgan, and the Llanelli constituency in Dyfed.

Ayrshire and Borders comprises: Ayr, Carrick and Cumnock; Ayrshire Central; Ayrshire North and Arran; Berwickshire, Roxburgh and Selkirk; Dumfries and Galloway; Dumfriesshire, Clydesdale and Tweeddale; and Kilmarnock and Loudoun.

Clydeside includes all Glasgow seats, both Dunbartonshire seats, both Paisley and Renfrewshire seats, plus Airdrie and Shotts; Coatbridge, Chryston and Bellshill; Cumbernauld, Kilsyth and Kirkintilloch East; East Kilbride, Strathaven and Lesmahagow; Inverclyde; Lanark and Hamilton East; Motherwell and Wishaw; Renfrewshire East; and Rutherglen and Hamilton West.

Rest of Central Belt includes all Edinburgh seats, plus East Lothian; Falkirk; Linlithgow and East Falkirk; Livingston; Midlothian; and Stirling.

NE and Fife includes both Aberdeen seats, both Dundee seats, plus Aberdeenshire West and Kincardine; Angus; Banff and Buchan; Dunfermline and West Fife; Fife North East; Glenrothes; Gordon; Kirkcaldy and Cowdenbeath; Moray; Ochil and South Perthshire; and Perth and North Perthshire.

Highlands and Islands includes Argyll and Bute; Caithness, Sutherland and Easter Ross; Inverness, Nairn, Badenoch and Strathspey; Na h-Eileanan an Iar; Orkney and Shetland; Ross, Skye and Lochaber.

In all but four cases, the European constituencies are covered in the table above. These constituencies are indicated with an asterisk (*). The results for the four other European constituencies are:

Seats won in 2015 (change since 2010)						*Share of votes cast in 2015 (change since 2010)*						
Con	*Lab*	*LD*	*Nat and other*		*Turnout*	*Con*	*Lab*	*Lib Dem*	*Nat*	*UKIP*	*Green*	*Other*
3 (+1)	26 (+1)	0 (–2)	0 (0)	**North East**	61.8 (+0.7)	25.3 (+1.6)	46.9 (+3.3)	6.5 (–17.1)	0 (0)	16.7 (+14.0)	3.6 (+3.3)	0.9 (–5.2)
22 (0)	51 (+4)	2 (–4)	0 (0)	**North West**	64.3 (+2.0)	31.2 (–0.5)	44.6 (+5.2)	6.5 (–15.1)	0 (0)	13.6 (+10.5)	3.2 (+2.7)	0.7 (–2.8)
52 (0)	4 (+2)	1 (–3)	1 (+1)	**Eastern**	67.5 (–0.1)	49.0 (+1.9)	22.0 (+2.4)	8.2 (–15.8)	0 (0)	16.2 (+12.0)	3.9 (+2.5)	0.5 (–2.9)
79 (+4)	4 (0)	0 (–4)	1 (0)	**South East**	68.6 (+0.4)	51.6 (+1.8)	18.3 (+2.1)	9.4 (–16.8)	0 (0)	14.7 (+10.6)	5.2 (+3.7)	0.7 (–1.4)

Table A2.5 Constituency results

These tables list the votes in each constituency in percentage terms.

With the exception of Scotland, the constituencies are listed alphabetically within counties, as defined in 1974. In Greater London the constituencies are listed alphabetically within each borough (and allocated to a single borough in cases where they cross borough boundaries). The Scottish results are not arranged within counties as too many of the constituencies cross boundaries.

The figure in the 'Other' column is the total percentage received by all other candidates than the parties listed in the table.

* denotes a seat won by different parties in 2010 and 2015.
† denotes a seat that changed hands in a by-election between 2010 and 2015.
‡ denotes a seat held by the Speaker in 2010 or 2015.

The table provides a figure for the change in the share of the vote only where candidates from a party stood in both 2010 and 2015. There were six seats in which UKIP stood in 2010, but not in 2015. These were: Dunbartonshire West (2010 share: 1.6%); Dundee East (1.1%); Dunfermline and West Fife (1.3%); Fife North East (2.6%); Glenrothes (1.0%); and Stirling (0.8%). Similarly, there were nine seats in which the Greens stood in 2010, but not in 2015: Argyll and Bute (2010 share: 1.7%); Bolton West (1.1%); Chester, City of (1.1%); Devon East (1.5%); East Kilbride, Strathaven and Lesmahagow (2.0%); Gordon (1.5%); Hertsmere (1.3%); Ochil and South Perthshire (1.2%); and Swansea East (1.0%).

Swing is given in the conventional (total vote or 'Butler') form – the average of the Conservative % gain (or loss) and the Labour % loss (or gain) (measured as % of the total poll). It is only reported for seats where those parties occupied the top two places in 2005 and 2010. This is the practice followed by previous books in this series since 1955.

ENGLAND	*Turnout %*	*Turnout +/–*	*Con %*	*Con +/–*	*Lab %*	*Lab +/–*	*LD %*	*LD +/–*	*UKIP %*	*UKIP +/–*	*Grn %*	*Grn +/–*	*Other No and %*	*Swing*
Avon, Bath*	74.8	+4.2	37.8	+6.4	13.2	+6.3	29.7	–26.9	6.2	+4.3	11.9	+9.6	2 (1.2)	–
Bristol East	64.9	+0.1	30.7	+2.3	39.3	+2.7	5.8	–18.6	15.5	+12.1	8.3	+6.5	1 (0.5)	–0.2
North West	69.3	+0.8	43.9	+6.0	34.4	+8.5	6.2	–25.3	9.4	+7.1	5.7	+4.7	1 (0.3)	–
South	62.4	+0.8	24.3	+1.4	38.4	–0.1	8.7	–20.0	16.5	+13.9	11.5	+9.0	1 (0.6)	–
West*	70.4	+3.5	15.2	–3.2	35.7	+8.1	18.8	–29.2	3.0	+1.8	26.8	+23.0	2 (0.5)	–
Filton and Bradley Stoke	68.9	–1.1	46.7	+5.9	26.6	+0.2	7.3	–18.0	14.8	+11.7	4.6	+3.7	–	+2.9
Kingswood	70.6	–1.6	48.3	+7.9	29.6	–5.7	3.8	–13.1	14.8	+11.6	2.8	+2.0	3 (0.6)	+6.8
Somerset North	73.5	–1.4	53.5	+4.2	14.3	+3.2	12.7	–23.0	13.0	+9.1	6.5	–	–	–
Somerset North East	73.7	–1.8	49.8	+8.5	24.8	–6.8	7.9	–14.4	12.0	+8.6	5.5	+4.2	–	+7.7
Thornbury and Yate*	73.5	–1.7	41.0	+3.9	7.8	+0.8	37.9	–14.0	10.6	+7.0	2.7	–	–	–
Weston-Super-Mare	65.4	–1.7	48.0	+3.7	18.3	+7.3	10.4	–28.8	17.8	+15.2	4.9	–	1 (0.6)	–
Bedfordshire, Bedford	66.5	+0.7	42.6	+3.7	40.2	+4.3	4.2	–15.6	9.6	+7.1	3.1	+2.2	1 (0.3)	–0.3
Bedfordshire Mid	74.0	+2.0	56.1	+3.6	15.9	+1.1	7.2	–17.7	15.4	+10.3	4.2	+2.8	2 (1.2)	–
North East	70.2	–0.9	59.5	+3.7	15.8	–0.4	5.8	–15.9	14.6	+10.5	4.3	–	–	–
South West	64.7	–1.6	55.0	+2.2	20.3	+0.7	5.2	–14.9	15.5	+11.3	4.1	–	–	–
Luton North	63.2	–2.3	29.9	–1.9	52.2	+3.0	3.1	–8.1	12.5	+8.9	2.3	+1.1	–	–2.4
South	62.3	–2.4	30.7	+1.3	44.2	+9.3	7.5	–15.1	12.1	+9.8	2.9	+2.1	2 (2.5)	–4.0
Berkshire, Bracknell	65.3	–2.5	55.8	+3.4	16.9	+0.1	7.5	–14.8	15.7	+11.3	4.1	+2.6	–	–
Maidenhead	72.6	–1.2	65.8	+6.4	11.9	+4.8	9.9	–18.3	8.4	+6.1	3.6	+2.7	2 (0.4)	–
Newbury	72.1	–2.0	61.0	+4.6	8.4	+4.2	15.0	–20.5	10.8	+8.3	4.1	+3.2	3 (0.6)	–
Reading East	69.0	+2.2	46.0	+3.4	33.1	+7.6	7.4	–20.0	7.2	+5.0	6.4	+4.2	–	–
West	66.7	+0.8	47.7	+4.5	33.9	+3.4	4.9	–15.2	10.0	+6.8	2.9	+1.7	3 (0.6)	+0.6
Slough	55.9	–5.7	33.3	–1.0	48.5	+2.7	2.6	–11.9	13.0	+9.8	2.5	+1.4	–	–1.8
Windsor	70.1	–1.2	63.4	+2.5	13.4	+3.5	8.6	–13.8	10.0	+6.7	3.7	+2.4	1 (1)	–
Wokingham	71.9	+0.5	57.7	+5.0	14.5	+4.4	13.5	–14.5	9.9	+6.8	3.7	+2.7	1 (0.6)	–
Buckinghamshire, Aylesbury	69.0	+0.7	50.7	–1.5	15.1	+2.5	10.6	–17.8	19.7	+12.9	3.9	–	–	–
Beaconsfield	71.1	+1.1	63.2	+2.2	11.4	–0.3	7.4	–12.2	13.8	+8.8	4.2	+2.7	–	–
Buckingham‡	69.3	+4.9	64.5	+17.2	–	–	–	–	21.7	+4.4	13.8	–	–	–
Chesham and Amersham	72.7	–1.9	59.1	–1.3	12.7	+7.1	9.0	–19.5	13.7	+9.6	5.5	+4.0	–	–
Milton Keynes North	66.4	+1.1	47.2	+3.8	30.3	+3.5	6.2	–15.9	11.9	+8.6	3.9	+2.5	2 (0.5)	+0.1
South	65.8	+1.8	46.8	+5.2	32.1	–0.1	3.9	–13.8	13.2	+9.5	3.3	+1.9	2 (0.6)	+2.7

Wycombe	67.4	+2.4	51.4	+2.8	22.5	+5.2	8.8	–20.0	10.1	+5.7	6.0	–	1 (1.1)	–
Cambridgeshire, Cambridge*	62.1	–5.0	15.7	–9.9	36.0	+11.7	34.9	–4.3	5.2	+2.8	7.9	+0.3	1 (0.4)	–
Cambridgeshire North East	62.4	–8.7	55.1	+3.5	14.4	–3.4	4.5	–15.6	22.5	+17.1	3.5	–	–	–
North West	67.6	+2.1	52.5	+2.0	17.9	+0.9	5.7	–16.2	20.1	+11.8	3.5	–	1 (0.3)	–
South	73.1	–1.6	51.1	+3.7	17.6	+7.4	15.2	–18.9	9.8	+6.6	6.3	+4.5	–	–
South East	70.4	+1.0	48.5	+0.5	15.1	+7.5	20.2	–17.5	11.1	+7.4	5.1	+3.8	–	–
Huntingdon	67.7	+2.8	53.0	+4.2	18.3	+7.3	7.8	–21.1	16.9	+10.9	3.9	+2.7	–	–
Peterborough	64.9	+1.0	39.7	–0.7	35.6	+6.1	3.8	–15.9	15.9	+9.2	2.6	+1.4	2 (2.5)	–3.4
Cheshire, Chester, City of*	68.7	+2.0	43.1	+2.5	43.2	+8.2	5.6	–13.5	8.1	+5.5	–	–	–	–2.9
Congleton	70.3	+0.1	53.3	+7.5	20.4	+3.2	9.1	–22.8	13.6	+9.4	3.7	–	–	–
Crewe and Nantwich	67.3	+3.2	45.0	–0.9	37.7	+3.7	2.8	–12.2	14.5	+11.8	–	–	–	–2.3
Eddisbury	69.1	+6.1	51.0	–0.6	23.6	+2.1	9.1	–13.4	12.2	+8.0	3.4	–	1 (0.6)	–
Ellesmere Port and Neston	67.5	+1.0	34.3	–0.5	47.8	+3.1	3.3	–11.7	12.0	+8.3	2.1	–	2 (0.5)	–1.8
Halton	61.8	+1.8	17.8	–2.4	62.8	+5.2	2.4	–11.4	14.1	+11.1	2.3	+0.7	1 (0.6)	–3.8
Macclesfield	69.2	+2.7	52.5	+5.6	22.7	+2.4	7.7	–15.3	12.2	+9.3	4.8	+3.2	–	–
Tatton	69.7	+1.9	58.6	+4.0	18.3	+1.1	8.5	–14.1	10.8	–	3.8	–	–	–
Warrington North	63.0	+0.3	28.2	–2.1	47.8	+2.3	4.1	–16.7	17.1	–	2.8	–	–	–2.2
South	70.0	+0.7	43.7	+7.9	39.1	+6.1	5.6	–21.9	8.3	+5.3	3.0	+2.2	1 (0.4)	+0.9
Weaver Vale	68.5	+3.1	43.2	+4.6	41.4	+5.2	3.0	–15.7	9.7	+7.4	2.5	+1.8	1 (0.2)	–0.3
Cleveland, Hartlepool	56.5	+1.0	20.9	–7.2	35.6	–6.9	1.9	–15.2	28.0	+21.0	3.4	–	3 (10.1)	–0.2
Middlesbrough	52.9	+1.5	16.5	–2.3	56.8	+10.9	3.7	–16.2	18.7	+15.0	4.3	–	–	–
South and Cleveland East	64.2	+0.6	37.1	+1.4	42.0	+2.8	3.4	–12.5	15.2	+11.1	2.3	–	–	–0.7
Redcar*	63.1	+0.6	16.2	+2.4	43.9	+11.1	18.5	–26.7	18.4	+13.9	2.2	–	1 (1)	–
Stockton North	59.8	+0.7	28.0	+2.0	49.1	+6.3	2.2	–13.8	19.2	+15.2	–	–	1 (1.5)	–2.1
South	69.0	+0.9	46.8	+7.8	37.0	–1.3	2.6	–12.5	10.6	+7.7	1.8	–	1 (1.2)	+4.5
Cornwall, Camborne and Redruth	68.5	+2.1	40.2	+2.6	25.0	+8.6	12.4	–25.0	14.8	+9.7	5.7	+4.3	1 (2)	–
Cornwall North*	71.8	+2.9	45.0	+3.3	5.4	+1.2	31.2	–16.8	12.7	+7.8	4.3	–	2 (1.4)	–
South East	71.1	+1.5	50.5	+5.4	9.3	+2.2	16.9	–21.8	15.2	+9.0	5.4	+3.7	2 (2.7)	–
St Austell and Newquay*	65.7	+3.0	40.2	+0.2	10.2	+3.1	24.0	–18.8	16.9	+13.2	4.6	–	1 (4.1)	–
St Ives*	73.7	+5.1	38.3	–0.7	9.3	+1.2	33.2	–9.6	11.8	+6.3	6.3	+3.5	1 (1.1)	–
Truro and Falmouth	70.0	+1.0	44.0	+2.3	15.2	+5.5	16.8	–24.0	11.6	+7.7	8.7	+6.9	4 (3.7)	–
Cumbria, Barrow and Furness	63.3	–0.7	40.5	+4.2	42.3	–5.8	2.7	–7.3	11.7	+9.8	2.5	+1.3	1 (0.3)	+5.0
Carlisle	64.7	0.0	44.3	+5.0	37.8	+0.5	2.6	–13.0	12.4	+10.1	2.6	+1.2	1 (0.3)	+2.2
Copeland	63.8	–3.9	35.8	–1.3	42.3	–3.8	3.5	–6.7	15.5	+13.2	3.0	+2.1	–	+1.2
Penrith and The Border	67.4	–2.6	59.7	+6.3	14.4	+1.4	8.5	–19.9	12.2	+9.4	5.3	–	–	–

ENGLAND	*Turnout* %	*Turnout* +/–	*Con* %	*Con* +/–	*Lab* %	*Lab* +/–	*LD* %	*LD* +/–	*UKIP* %	*UKIP* +/–	*Grn* %	*Grn* +/–	*Other* No and %	*Swing*
Westmorland and Lonsdale	74.3	–2.6	33.2	–3.0	5.4	+3.2	51.5	–8.5	6.2	+4.6	3.7	–	–	–
Workington	65.6	–0.2	30.1	–3.7	42.3	–3.2	4.4	–9.1	19.6	+17.4	3.0	–	1 (0.5)	–0.3
Derbyshire, Amber Valley	65.8	+0.3	44.0	+5.4	34.8	–2.7	3.0	–11.5	15.9	+13.9	2.4	–	–	+4.0
Bolsover	61.1	+0.7	24.5	–0.1	51.2	+1.2	3.3	–12.2	21.0	+17.1	–	–	–	–0.7
Chesterfield	63.6	–0.2	18.1	+2.3	47.9	+8.9	13.8	–24.0	16.5	+13.4	3.0	+1.7	2 (0.7)	–
Derby North*	64.1	+1.0	36.7	+5.0	36.6	+3.5	8.6	–19.5	14.6	+12.8	3.6	–	–	+0.7
South	58.1	+0.1	27.4	–1.1	49.0	+5.7	4.2	–16.3	15.5	+11.1	3.0	–	2 (0.9)	–3.4
Derbyshire Dales	74.6	+0.8	52.4	+0.3	22.7	+3.4	8.4	–14.1	11.6	+7.8	4.6	+2.9	1 (0.3)	–
Mid	70.7	–0.9	52.2	+3.9	25.4	+1.0	4.8	–15.7	13.6	+11.0	4.0	–	–	+1.5
North East	67.1	+1.2	36.7	+3.8	40.6	+2.5	4.2	–19.1	15.9	+10.3	2.2	–	1 (0.3)	+0.6
South	68.7	–2.7	49.4	+3.9	26.8	–4.6	3.7	–12.2	17.7	+15.3	2.4	–	–	+4.2
Erewash	67.2	–1.2	42.7	+3.2	35.3	+1.1	3.4	–14.1	16.1	+14.3	2.5	+1.3	–	+1.1
High Peak	69.3	–1.2	45.0	+4.1	35.3	+3.7	4.7	–17.1	11.4	+8.1	3.6	+1.7	–	+0.2
Devon, Devon Central	74.9	–0.8	52.2	+0.7	12.8	+5.9	12.2	–22.2	13.2	+7.8	8.9	+7.0	1 (0.6)	–
East	71.5	–1.1	46.4	–1.9	10.2	–0.6	6.8	–24.4	12.6	+4.4	–	–	1 (24)	–
North*	70.0	+1.1	42.7	+6.7	7.1	+1.9	29.4	–17.9	14.8	+7.5	5.8	+4.4	1 (0.3)	–
South West	70.9	+0.5	56.6	+0.6	16.7	+4.2	7.5	–16.7	14.5	+8.3	4.8	+3.5	–	–
West and Torridge	72.0	+0.5	50.9	+5.2	10.6	+5.4	13.2	–27.1	18.3	+12.9	7.0	+5.1	–	–
Exeter	70.2	+2.5	33.1	+0.1	46.4	+8.2	4.3	–16.0	9.4	+5.7	6.5	+4.9	1 (0.4)	–4.0
Newton Abbot	69.0	–0.6	47.2	+4.2	9.8	+2.8	24.0	–18.0	13.9	+7.5	4.6	+3.1	1 (0.5)	–
Plymouth Moor View*	62.4	+1.4	37.6	+4.3	35.2	–2.0	3.0	–13.9	21.5	+13.8	2.4	+1.4	1 (0.4)	+3.1
Sutton and Devonport	65.5	+5.3	37.8	+3.5	36.7	+5.0	4.2	–20.5	14.0	+7.5	7.1	+5.0	1 (0.2)	–0.8
Tiverton and Honiton	70.5	–1.0	54.0	+3.7	12.7	+3.8	10.5	–22.9	16.5	+10.5	6.4	+4.9	–	–
Torbay*	63.0	–1.6	40.7	+2.0	8.7	+2.1	33.8	–13.2	13.6	+8.3	3.2	+2.3	–	–
Totnes	68.6	–1.8	53.0	+7.1	12.7	+5.3	9.9	–25.7	14.1	+8.1	10.3	+7.8	–	–
Dorset, Bournemouth East	62.0	+0.1	49.2	+0.8	16.6	+3.4	8.4	–22.5	16.5	+9.6	7.3	–	1 (2)	–
West	58.0	–0.1	48.2	+3.1	17.7	+2.9	7.9	–23.9	18.5	+11.3	7.4	–	1 (0.2)	–
Christchurch	71.7	0.0	58.1	+1.7	9.5	–0.3	6.6	–18.7	21.5	+13.0	4.3	–	–	–
Dorset Mid and Poole North*	72.3	0.0	50.8	+6.3	6.0	+0.1	28.2	–16.9	12.2	+7.7	2.8	–	–	–
North	72.4	–1.0	56.6	+5.6	9.0	+3.6	11.7	–25.3	17.1	+11.9	5.7	+4.7	–	–
South	67.9	–0.6	48.9	+3.8	24.2	–6.1	6.0	–13.0	15.0	+11.0	4.7	+3.5	2 (1.2)	+4.9

West	72.4	−2.2	50.2	+2.6	10.0	+3.3	21.6	−19.1	12.5	+8.7	5.7	+4.6	–	–
Poole	65.3	0.0	50.1	+2.6	12.9	+0.1	11.8	−19.8	16.8	+11.5	4.6	–	2 (3.8)	–
Durham, Bishop Auckland	59.6	−0.6	32.5	+6.2	41.4	+2.4	4.4	−18.0	17.8	+15.1	3.9	–	–	+1.9
Darlington	62.5	−0.5	35.2	+3.7	42.9	+3.5	4.8	−18.6	13.1	+10.3	3.5	–	1 (0.5)	+0.1
Durham, City Of	66.5	−0.7	22.2	+9.0	47.3	+3.0	11.3	−26.4	11.5	+9.6	5.9	–	2 (1.8)	–
North	61.4	+0.8	20.9	−0.1	54.9	+4.4	5.1	−15.9	16.0	+12.7	3.1	–	–	−2.3
North West	61.3	−1.0	23.4	+3.4	46.9	+4.6	9.1	−15.8	17.0	+14.1	3.7	–	–	–
Easington	56.2	+1.5	12.9	−0.8	61.0	+2.1	2.4	−13.6	18.7	+14.1	2.1	–	2 (2.8)	–
Sedgefield	61.6	−0.5	29.5	+6.0	47.2	+2.1	3.5	−16.4	16.6	+12.9	3.1	–	–	+2.0
East Sussex, Bexhill and Battle	70.1	+2.7	54.8	+3.2	14.1	+2.2	7.6	−20.4	18.4	–	5.1	–	–	–
Brighton Kemptown	66.8	+2.1	40.7	+2.7	39.2	+4.3	3.0	−15.0	9.8	+6.6	7.0	+1.6	2 (0.3)	−0.8
Pavilion	71.4	+1.4	22.8	−0.9	27.3	−1.7	2.8	−11.0	5.0	+3.2	41.8	+10.5	2 (0.4)	–
Eastbourne*	67.6	+0.6	39.6	−1.1	7.8	+3.0	38.2	−9.1	11.6	+9.1	2.6	–	1 (0.3)	–
Hastings and Rye	67.8	+3.1	44.5	+3.5	35.1	−2.0	3.2	−12.5	13.3	+10.5	3.8	–	–	+2.7
Hove*	71.0	+1.6	39.9	+3.2	42.3	+9.3	3.6	−19.0	6.3	+3.8	6.8	+1.7	3 (1.1)	−3.1
Lewes*	72.7	−0.2	38.0	+1.3	9.9	+4.9	35.9	−16.1	10.7	+7.3	5.5	+4.1	–	–
Wealden	71.1	−0.8	57.0	+0.5	10.8	+1.2	9.1	−16.2	16.7	+10.7	6.4	+3.8	–	–
Essex, Basildon and Billericay	64.9	+1.4	52.7	−0.1	23.7	+0.6	3.8	−11.9	19.8	+16.0	–	–	–	−0.3
Basildon South and East Thurrock	64.1	+1.8	43.4	−0.5	25.2	−5.8	3.0	−10.4	26.5	+20.6	–	–	3 (1.9)	+2.6
Braintree	68.4	−0.8	53.8	+1.2	18.5	−1.4	4.9	−13.8	18.8	+13.8	3.1	+1.7	2 (0.8)	+1.3
Brentwood and Ongar	72.2	−0.8	58.8	+1.9	12.5	+2.6	8.8	−14.6	16.8	+12.8	2.7	+1.5	1 (0.3)	–
Castle Point	66.7	−0.2	50.9	+6.9	13.8	−0.9	1.8	−7.6	31.2	–	2.4	–	–	–
Chelmsford	68.5	−1.9	51.5	+5.4	17.6	+6.7	11.9	−24.9	14.2	+11.4	3.5	+2.6	1 (1.2)	–
Clacton†*	64.1	0.0	36.7	−16.4	14.4	−10.6	1.8	−11.1	44.4	–	2.7	+1.4	–	−2.9
Colchester*	65.5	+3.2	38.9	+6.1	16.2	+3.8	27.5	−20.5	12.1	+9.2	5.1	+3.6	1 (0.2)	–
Epping Forest	67.2	+2.7	54.8	+0.8	16.1	+1.9	7.0	−14.5	18.3	+14.4	3.6	+2.2	1 (0.2)	–
Harlow	65.1	+0.2	48.9	+4.0	30.0	−3.7	2.0	−11.6	16.3	+12.7	2.2	–	2 (0.7)	+3.8
Harwich and North Essex	69.9	+0.6	51.0	+4.1	19.7	−0.2	7.4	−16.2	17.5	+12.3	4.4	+2.5	–	–
Maldon	69.6	−0.1	60.6	+0.8	11.8	−0.8	4.5	−14.8	14.7	+9.6	3.1	–	2 (5.3)	–
Rayleigh and Wickford	69.0	−0.2	54.7	−3.1	12.6	−1.9	3.0	−12.1	22.3	+18.1	2.9	–	1 (4.5)	–
Rochford and Southend East	60.6	+2.4	46.4	−0.4	24.7	+4.4	3.3	−16.1	20.5	+14.7	5.0	+3.3	–	−2.4
Saffron Walden	71.4	−0.1	57.2	+1.7	11.8	+2.1	10.6	−16.9	13.8	+9.7	3.8	+2.4	1 (2.9)	–
Southend West	66.6	+1.4	49.8	+3.8	18.3	+4.9	9.3	−20.1	17.5	+13.6	4.7	+3.2	1 (0.4)	–
Thurrock	63.9	+5.0	33.7	−3.1	32.6	−4.0	1.3	−9.4	31.7	+24.3	–	–	3 (0.7)	+0.4
Witham	70.3	+0.4	57.5	+5.3	15.8	−2.7	6.1	−13.6	16.0	+9.5	4.3	+1.3	1 (0.2)	–

ENGLAND	Turnout %	Turnout +/–	Con %	Con +/–	Lab %	Lab +/–	LD %	LD +/–	UKIP %	UKIP +/–	Grn %	Grn +/–	Other No and %	Swing
Gloucestershire, Cheltenham*	69.5	+2.7	46.1	+5.0	7.3	+2.1	34.0	–16.5	7.1	+4.8	5.0	–	1 (0.5)	–
Cotswolds, The	72.4	+0.9	56.5	+3.5	9.2	–1.5	18.6	–10.9	10.9	+6.7	4.6	+2.9	–	–
Forest of Dean	70.9	–0.4	46.8	0.0	24.6	+0.5	5.3	–16.6	17.8	+12.6	5.5	+3.6	–	–0.3
Gloucester	63.4	–0.6	45.3	+5.4	31.5	–3.6	5.4	–13.9	14.3	+10.7	2.8	+1.8	2 (0.7)	+4.5
Stroud	75.5	+1.5	45.7	+4.9	37.7	–0.9	3.4	–12.0	8.0	+5.7	4.6	+1.9	2 (0.6)	+2.9
Tewkesbury	70.1	–0.3	54.5	+7.3	14.8	+3.2	13.8	–21.7	12.9	+8.7	4.0	+3.0	–	–
Greater London														
Barking and Dagenham, Barking	58.2	–3.2	16.3	–1.5	57.7	+3.4	1.3	–6.9	22.2	+19.3	2.1	+1.4	1 (0.4)	–2.4
Dagenham and Rainham	62.3	–1.1	24.4	–10.0	41.4	+1.1	1.7	–6.9	29.8	+26.3	1.9	+1.2	3 (0.8)	–5.5
Barnet, Chipping Barnet	68.1	+0.8	48.6	–0.2	34.1	+8.9	4.5	–15.7	7.8	+5.0	4.7	+2.7	1 (0.2)	–4.6
Finchley and Golders Green	70.0	+3.3	50.9	+4.9	39.7	+6.1	3.3	–13.8	3.4	+1.7	2.7	+1.1	–	–0.6
Hendon	65.9	+2.3	49.0	+6.7	41.5	–0.6	2.2	–10.2	5.2	+3.2	2.0	+0.9	–	+3.6
Bexley, Bexleyheath and Crayford	67.4	+1.0	47.3	–3.2	26.2	–0.3	3.0	–9.7	21.0	+17.4	2.2	+1.3	1 (0.3)	–1.5
Erith and Thamesmead	60.5	–0.2	27.4	–4.0	49.8	+4.9	2.3	–9.8	17.3	+14.6	2.2	+1.4	2 (1)	–4.5
Old Bexley and Sidcup	70.8	+1.5	52.8	–1.3	19.0	–0.3	3.5	–11.9	18.2	+14.9	2.9	+2.0	3 (3.6)	–0.5
Brent, Brent Central*	61.1	–0.2	20.3	+9.2	62.1	+20.9	8.4	–35.8	3.9	–	4.1	+2.6	3 (1.2)	–
North	63.5	+1.2	33.5	+2.0	54.3	+7.4	5.0	–12.0	3.9	+3.1	2.9	+1.6	1 (0.4)	–2.7
Bromley, Beckenham	72.4	+0.4	57.3	–0.6	19.4	+5.0	6.9	–13.7	12.5	+9.3	3.8	+2.6	–	–
Bromley and Chislehurst	67.3	0.0	53.0	–0.5	22.2	+5.6	6.4	–15.5	14.3	+11.0	4.1	+2.8	–	–
Orpington	72.0	–0.2	57.4	–2.3	15.6	+6.6	6.8	–17.7	16.7	+13.9	3.5	+2.5	–	–
Camden, Hampstead and Kilburn	67.3	+1.6	42.3	+9.6	44.4	+11.6	5.6	–25.6	2.8	+2.1	4.4	+3.0	2 (0.4)	–1.0
Holborn and St Pancras	63.3	+0.2	21.9	+1.5	52.9	+6.8	6.5	–21.4	5.0	+3.9	12.8	+10.1	3 (1)	–
Croydon, Croydon Central	67.7	+2.7	43.0	+3.6	42.7	+9.1	2.2	–11.0	9.1	+7.1	2.7	+1.6	2 (0.3)	–2.7
North	62.3	+1.6	22.7	–1.4	62.6	+6.6	3.6	–10.4	5.4	+3.7	4.7	+2.7	3 (1)	–4.0
South	70.0	+0.8	54.5	+3.6	24.8	+4.8	6.0	–16.9	10.5	+6.1	3.7	+2.0	2 (0.5)	–
Ealing, Ealing Central and Acton*	71.3	+4.1	42.7	+4.7	43.2	+13.1	6.1	–21.5	3.8	+2.2	3.6	+2.1	4 (0.6)	–4.2
North	65.7	+0.4	29.7	–1.2	55.1	+4.7	3.2	–9.9	8.1	+6.6	3.4	+2.3	1 (0.4)	–3.0
Southall	66.0	+2.2	21.7	–8.1	65.0	+13.5	3.6	–11.4	4.1	–	4.6	+3.0	1 (1.1)	–10.8
Enfield, Edmonton	62.6	–0.6	24.1	–5.7	61.4	+7.8	2.2	–8.4	8.1	+5.6	3.3	+2.0	1 (0.9)	–6.7
Enfield North*	67.7	+0.6	41.4	–0.9	43.7	+5.2	2.3	–9.9	9.0	+6.8	2.8	+1.7	2 (0.8)	–3.1
Southgate	70.5	+1.4	49.4	–0.1	39.0	+6.8	3.3	–10.5	4.6	+3.5	3.7	+2.3	–	–3.4

Greenwich, Eltham	67.4	+0.4	36.4	–1.2	42.6	+1.1	3.0	–9.6	15.0	+12.6	3.0	+2.0	–	–1.1
Greenwich and Woolwich	63.7	+0.8	26.6	+2.1	52.2	+3.0	5.7	–12.5	8.3	–	6.4	+3.8	1 (0.8)	–0.5
Hackney, Hackney North and														
Stoke Newington	56.6	–6.3	14.7	+0.2	62.9	+7.9	5.0	–18.9	2.2	–	14.6	+10.0	2 (0.6)	–
South and Shoreditch	56.0	–2.8	13.5	0.0	64.4	+8.6	4.6	–17.8	3.8	+2.3	11.6	+8.1	6 (2.1)	–
Hammersmith	66.4	+0.8	36.4	0.0	50.0	+6.1	4.6	–11.3	4.4	+3.2	4.4	+2.9	1 (0.2)	–3.1
Haringey, Hornsey and Wood Green*	72.9	+3.0	9.3	–7.4	50.9	+16.9	31.8	–14.7	2.2	–	5.4	+3.2	3 (0.4)	–
Tottenham	60.1	+1.0	12.0	–2.9	67.3	+8.0	4.1	–13.6	3.6	+2.4	9.2	+6.8	2 (3.8)	–
Harrow, Harrow East	69.0	+0.9	50.3	+5.7	40.6	+3.1	2.1	–12.2	4.8	+2.9	1.7	+0.1	1 (0.4)	+1.3
West	66.9	–0.4	42.2	+5.4	47.0	+3.4	3.4	–12.8	4.4	+2.3	2.8	+1.5	1 (0.3)	+1.0
Havering, Hornchurch and Upminster	69.6	+1.7	49.0	–2.5	20.1	–0.7	2.7	–11.2	25.3	+20.0	2.6	+1.5	1 (0.3)	–0.9
Romford	67.7	+2.6	51.0	–5.0	20.9	+1.4	2.9	–9.1	22.8	+18.4	2.5	+1.5	–	–3.2
Hillingdon, Hayes and Harlington	60.2	–0.5	24.7	–4.7	59.6	+4.7	2.0	–6.8	12.0	–	1.8	+0.9	–	–4.7
Ruislip, Northwood and Pinner	70.0	–0.9	59.6	+2.1	20.1	+0.6	5.0	–11.7	10.9	+8.2	3.5	+2.0	2 (0.9)	+0.8
Uxbridge and South Ruislip	63.4	+0.1	50.2	+2.0	26.4	+3.0	4.9	–15.0	14.2	+11.4	3.2	+2.1	8 (1.1)	–0.5
Hounslow, Brentford and Isleworth*	67.8	+3.4	42.9	+5.7	43.8	+10.2	4.0	–19.6	5.6	+4.0	3.7	+2.2	–	–2.2
Feltham and Heston	60.0	+0.1	29.1	–4.9	52.3	+8.7	3.2	–10.6	12.6	+10.5	2.8	+1.7	–	–6.8
Islington, Islington North	67.1	+1.7	17.2	+3.0	60.2	+5.8	8.1	–18.6	4.0	+2.4	10.2	+7.2	1 (0.2)	–
South and Finsbury	65.0	+0.6	22.2	+2.8	50.9	+8.7	10.9	–23.2	7.6	+6.0	7.6	+6.0	1 (0.7)	–
Kensington and Chelsea, Kensington	57.0	+3.7	52.3	+2.2	31.1	+5.6	5.6	–13.9	4.5	+2.3	5.1	+2.9	4 (1.5)	–1.7
Chelsea and Fulham	63.4	+3.2	62.9	+2.5	23.1	+4.6	5.2	–11.0	5.1	+3.9	3.7	+2.0	–	–1.1
Kingston and Surbiton*	72.9	+2.5	39.2	+2.7	14.5	+5.1	34.5	–15.3	7.3	+4.8	3.9	+2.9	2 (0.6)	–
Lambeth, Streatham	63.1	+0.3	25.1	+6.8	53.0	+10.2	9.0	–26.8	3.2	–	8.9	+7.0	3 (0.8)	–
Vauxhall	58.3	+0.6	27.3	+5.7	53.8	+4.0	6.9	–18.2	2.9	–	7.6	+6.0	5 (1.5)	–
Lewisham, Lewisham Deptford	64.6	+3.1	14.9	+1.4	60.2	+6.6	5.3	–18.1	4.2	–	12.5	+5.8	5 (2.9)	–
East	64.1	+0.9	22.3	–1.3	55.7	+12.6	5.7	–22.4	9.1	+7.2	5.7	+4.2	2 (1.6)	–
West and Penge	66.6	+1.3	24.2	–1.3	50.6	+9.5	7.7	–20.4	7.8	+5.3	8.5	+6.4	3 (1.2)	–
Merton, Mitcham and Morden	65.9	–0.5	23.2	–2.1	60.7	+4.2	3.1	–8.8	9.5	+7.5	3.2	+2.3	1 (0.5)	–3.1
Wimbledon	73.5	+1.4	52.1	+3.0	26.0	+3.8	12.7	–12.3	5.1	+3.2	4.1	+2.9	–	–
Newham, East Ham	59.8	+4.3	12.1	–3.1	77.6	+7.2	1.6	–10.0	5.0	–	2.5	+1.3	2 (1.2)	–5.1
West Ham	58.2	+3.2	15.4	+0.8	68.4	+5.8	2.7	–8.8	7.5	+5.9	5.0	+3.6	2 (0.9)	–2.5
Redbridge, Ilford North*	65.0	0.0	42.7	–3.1	43.9	+9.6	2.3	–10.4	8.9	+7.0	2.1	+0.9	1 (0.2)	–6.3
South	56.4	–2.9	25.9	–1.5	64.0	+14.6	2.0	–15.0	5.2	+3.0	2.9	+0.3	–	–8.0
Richmond, Richmond Park	76.5	+0.2	58.2	+8.5	12.3	+7.3	19.3	–23.5	4.2	+3.0	6.0	+5.0	–	–
Twickenham*	77.3	+3.1	41.3	+7.2	11.5	+3.8	38.0	–16.4	4.9	+3.5	4.0	+2.8	2 (0.3)	–

ENGLAND	Turnout %	Turnout +/–	Con %	Con +/–	Lab %	Lab +/–	LD %	LD +/–	UKIP %	UKIP +/–	Grn %	Grn +/–	Other No and %	Swing
Southwark, Camberwell and Peckham	62.3	+3.0	13.2	+0.1	63.3	+4.1	5.0	–17.4	4.7	–	10.1	+7.1	6 (3.8)	–
Bermondsey and Old Southwark*	61.7	+4.2	11.8	–5.3	43.1	+13.8	34.3	–14.0	6.3	–	3.9	+2.3	4 (0.6)	–
Dulwich and West Norwood	67.1	+0.9	22.7	+0.5	54.1	+7.5	9.8	–17.3	3.1	+1.7	9.4	+6.8	3 (0.8)	–
Sutton, Carshalton and Wallington	68.0	–1.0	31.7	–5.1	15.0	+6.3	34.9	–13.4	14.8	+11.9	3.1	+2.4	2 (0.5)	–
Sutton and Cheam*	72.1	–0.7	41.5	–0.8	11.1	+4.2	33.7	–12.0	10.7	+8.7	2.1	+1.6	2 (0.8)	–
Tower Hamlets, Bethnal Green and Bow	64.0	+1.5	15.2	+1.3	61.2	+18.3	4.5	–15.6	6.1	–	9.3	+7.6	6 (3.7)	–
Poplar and Limehouse	62.2	–0.1	25.4	–1.7	58.5	+18.6	4.2	–6.9	6.1	+4.9	4.8	+3.9	2 (0.9)	–10.1
Waltham Forest, Chingford and Woodford Green	65.7	–0.8	47.9	–4.8	28.8	+6.1	5.5	–11.3	12.9	+10.3	4.2	+2.7	2 (0.7)	–5.5
Leyton and Wanstead	63.0	–0.2	22.0	–0.3	58.6	+15.0	5.7	–22.0	5.8	+3.1	7.3	+5.9	1 (0.7)	–
Walthamstow	62.4	–1.1	13.4	–0.6	68.9	+17.0	4.0	–24.7	6.0	+4.0	6.4	+4.5	3 (1.4)	–
Wandsworth, Battersea	67.0	+1.4	52.4	+5.0	36.8	+1.7	4.4	–10.3	3.1	+2.1	3.3	+2.2	–	+1.7
Putney	67.0	+2.6	53.8	+1.7	30.0	+2.6	6.3	–10.6	4.6	+3.6	4.8	+3.4	1 (0.4)	–0.4
Tooting	69.7	+1.1	41.9	+3.4	47.2	+3.7	3.9	–10.9	2.9	+1.6	4.1	+2.9	–	–0.2
Westminster, Cities of London and W.	59.3	+4.1	54.1	+1.9	27.4	+5.2	7.0	–13.5	5.2	+3.4	5.4	+3.3	3 (1)	–1.6
Westminster North	63.4	+4.0	41.8	+3.3	46.8	+2.9	3.7	–10.2	3.8	+3.0	3.3	+2.1	2 (0.5)	+0.2
Greater Manchester, Altrincham and Sale W.	70.6	+2.2	53.0	+4.0	26.7	+4.3	8.4	–17.1	8.0	+4.8	3.9	–	–	–
Ashton-under-Lyne	56.9	+0.2	22.1	–2.6	49.8	+1.4	2.4	–12.4	21.8	+17.4	3.9	–	–	–2.0
Blackley and Broughton	51.6	+2.4	15.0	–3.3	61.9	+7.7	2.4	–11.9	16.5	+13.8	4.2	–	–	–5.5
Bolton North East	63.6	–1.2	32.8	–3.7	43.0	–3.0	2.9	–10.1	18.8	+14.6	2.6	–	–	–0.4
South East	58.5	+1.5	20.3	–5.3	50.5	+3.0	2.6	–13.2	23.6	+19.7	2.9	+1.4	–	–4.2
West*	66.8	+0.1	40.6	+2.3	39.0	+0.5	4.0	–13.2	15.3	+11.3	–	–	2 (1.1)	+0.9
Bury North	66.9	–0.4	41.9	+1.8	41.1	+5.9	2.1	–14.9	12.4	+9.5	2.5	–	–	–2.1
South	63.9	–1.7	34.6	+1.0	45.1	+4.6	3.6	–14.6	13.3	+11.2	3.0	+2.0	1 (0.4)	–1.8
Cheadle*	72.5	–0.8	43.1	+2.3	16.3	+7.0	31.0	–16.1	8.3	+5.6	–	–	3 (1.3)	–
Denton and Reddish	58.5	+1.7	23.7	–1.2	50.8	–0.2	2.5	–15.4	18.7	+13.2	3.8	–	1 (0.6)	–0.5
Hazel Grove*	68.5	+1.1	41.4	+7.8	17.5	+5.1	26.2	–22.6	12.2	+7.1	2.6	–	–	–
Heywood and Middleton	60.7	+3.1	19.1	–8.1	43.1	+3.0	3.3	–19.4	32.2	+29.6	2.3	–	–	–5.5
Leigh	59.4	+1.0	22.6	+1.7	53.9	+5.8	2.5	–15.6	19.7	+16.3	–	–	1 (1.2)	–2.1
Makerfield	60.3	+1.0	19.5	+0.8	51.8	+4.5	3.7	–12.5	22.4	–	2.5	–	–	–1.9

Manchester Central	52.7	+8.4	13.5	+1.7	61.3	+8.5	4.1	−22.5	11.1	+9.6	8.5	+6.2	3 (1.5)	–
Gorton	57.6	+7.1	9.7	−1.4	67.1	+17.0	4.2	−28.4	8.2	–	9.8	+7.0	2 (1.1)	–
Withington*	67.4	+6.9	9.8	−1.4	53.7	+13.3	24.0	−20.7	4.3	+2.8	8.1	+6.3	1 (0.1)	–
Oldham East and Saddleworth	62.2	+0.9	25.9	−0.5	39.4	+7.5	12.9	−18.8	19.2	+15.4	2.6	–	–	–
West and Royton	60.2	+0.9	19.0	−4.7	54.8	+9.3	3.7	−15.4	20.6	+17.4	1.9	–	–	−7.0
Rochdale	58.8	+0.7	17.0	−1.0	46.1	+9.8	10.3	−24.2	18.8	+14.4	3.0	–	3 (4.8)	–
Salford and Eccles	58.2	+3.2	20.4	−0.1	49.4	+9.3	3.7	−22.6	18.0	+15.4	5.2	–	3 (3.2)	–
Stalybridge and Hyde	57.5	−1.7	28.7	−4.2	45.0	+5.4	3.1	−14.0	18.8	+15.5	4.5	+2.8	–	−4.8
Stockport	62.0	−0.2	24.5	−0.8	49.9	+7.2	7.7	−17.3	13.1	+10.9	4.4	+2.7	1 (0.4)	−4.0
Stretford and Urmston	67.2	+3.9	27.8	−0.8	53.0	+4.4	2.9	−14.0	10.9	+7.6	4.7	+2.7	2 (0.5)	−2.6
Wigan	59.6	+1.1	20.7	−4.0	52.2	+3.7	2.8	−12.6	19.5	+13.8	2.8	–	2 (2.1)	−3.8
Worsley and Eccles South	58.3	+0.7	30.1	−2.4	44.2	+1.3	2.6	−13.9	18.3	+13.4	3.0	–	3 (1.8)	−1.9
Wythenshawe and Sale East	56.9	+5.9	25.7	+0.2	50.1	+6.0	4.5	−17.9	14.7	+11.2	3.8	–	2 (1.2)	−2.9
Hampshire, Aldershot	63.8	+0.3	50.6	+3.9	18.3	+6.2	8.8	−25.6	17.9	+13.4	4.4	–	–	–
Basingstoke	66.6	−0.5	48.6	−2.0	27.7	+7.3	7.4	−17.1	15.6	+11.5	–	–	1 (0.7)	–
Eastleigh*	69.7	+0.4	42.3	+2.9	12.9	+3.3	25.8	−20.7	15.8	+12.2	2.7	–	2 (0.4)	–
Fareham	70.9	−0.7	56.1	+0.8	14.3	+0.1	8.8	−15.0	15.4	+11.3	3.9	+2.4	2 (1.5)	–
Gosport	65.1	+0.6	55.3	+3.5	14.5	−2.4	6.9	−14.1	19.4	+16.3	3.6	+2.4	1 (0.2)	–
Hampshire East	72.7	+1.7	60.7	+3.9	10.1	+2.2	11.1	−19.4	12.0	+9.1	6.1	–	–	–
North East	70.2	−3.1	65.9	+5.3	9.8	0.0	10.5	−15.0	8.8	+4.6	4.4	–	1 (0.7)	–
North West	69.7	+0.2	58.1	−0.2	13.3	+0.2	9.3	−14.1	14.7	+9.5	4.6	–	–	–
Havant	63.5	+0.5	51.7	+0.6	15.9	−1.8	6.5	−16.9	20.6	+14.7	5.2	–	–	–
Meon Valley	71.1	−1.6	61.1	+4.8	10.9	+4.6	9.6	−22.9	14.8	+11.9	3.5	–	–	–
New Forest East	68.0	−0.7	56.3	+3.4	12.2	+2.3	9.4	−20.9	17.5	+12.5	4.7	+2.7	–	–
West	69.3	−0.4	59.9	+1.1	10.8	+1.0	6.9	−16.4	16.5	+10.6	5.8	+3.6	–	–
Portsmouth North	62.1	−0.6	47.0	+2.7	23.8	−3.9	6.2	−13.9	19.1	+15.0	3.2	+2.1	2 (0.7)	+3.3
South*	58.5	−0.3	34.8	+1.6	19.5	+5.9	22.3	−23.6	13.4	+11.2	7.5	+5.8	3 (2.5)	–
Romsey and Southampton North	72.8	+1.0	54.3	+4.6	11.9	+5.5	17.7	−23.5	11.4	+8.8	4.7	–	–	–
Southampton Itchen*	61.9	+2.3	41.7	+5.4	36.5	−0.2	3.6	−17.3	13.4	+9.1	4.2	+2.8	1 (0.5)	+2.8
Test	62.1	+0.7	32.5	−0.5	41.3	+2.8	4.9	−17.5	12.8	+8.8	5.9	+3.9	2 (2.7)	−1.6
Winchester	74.6	−1.2	55.0	+6.5	8.3	+2.9	24.4	−18.7	7.5	+5.4	4.8	–	–	–
Hereford and Worcester, Bromsgrove	71.2	+0.5	53.8	+10.2	22.2	+0.4	5.0	−14.6	15.6	+9.9	3.3	–	–	+4.9
Hereford and South Herefordshire	66.1	−1.1	52.6	+6.3	12.8	+5.5	10.6	−30.5	16.8	+13.4	7.2	–	–	–
Herefordshire North	70.7	−0.4	55.6	+3.9	11.4	+4.3	12.0	−19.0	14.0	+8.3	7.0	+3.7	–	–
Redditch	67.3	+1.2	47.1	+3.6	31.1	+0.9	3.1	−14.5	16.2	+12.8	2.2	+1.3	1 (0.4)	+1.4

ENGLAND	Turnout %	Turnout +/–	Con %	Con +/–	Lab %	Lab +/–	LD %	LD +/–	UKIP %	UKIP +/–	Grn %	Grn +/–	Other No and %	Swing
Worcester	68.6	+1.4	45.3	+5.8	34.0	+0.5	3.4	–16.1	12.8	+10.1	4.1	+2.6	2 (0.4)	+2.6
Worcestershire Mid	71.5	+0.9	57.0	+2.5	14.5	–0.5	7.2	–16.2	17.7	+11.7	3.7	+2.5	–	–
West	73.7	–0.6	56.1	+5.8	13.4	+6.6	9.7	–28.1	14.4	+10.4	6.5	+5.3	–	–
Wyre Forest	63.9	–2.5	45.3	+8.4	19.3	+4.9	2.5	–9.4	16.1	+13.2	2.3	–	1 (14.6)	–
Hertfordshire, Broxbourne	63.1	–0.9	56.1	–2.7	18.4	+0.8	3.2	–10.2	19.7	+15.6	2.6	–	–	–1.8
Hemel Hempstead	66.5	–1.5	52.9	+2.9	23.8	+3.0	4.8	–18.0	14.6	+12.1	3.3	–	1 (0.5)	–
Hertford and Stortford	69.8	–0.8	56.1	+2.3	17.9	+4.2	7.8	–18.2	13.4	+10.3	4.8	–	–	–
Hertfordshire North East	70.7	+0.8	55.4	+1.8	18.9	+2.4	7.6	–15.8	12.9	+8.8	5.3	+3.6	–	–
South West	71.9	–0.6	56.9	+2.7	16.3	+4.8	10.3	–17.7	11.5	+9.0	4.5	–	1 (0.4)	–
Hertsmere	67.9	+3.2	59.3	+3.3	22.4	+3.7	5.5	–11.8	12.7	+9.1	–	–	–	–0.2
Hitchin and Harpenden	68.9	–5.1	56.9	+2.3	20.6	+7.1	8.1	–18.6	8.9	+5.8	5.5	+4.0	–	–
St Albans	71.8	–3.6	46.6	+5.9	23.3	+5.7	18.5	–17.9	7.8	+4.0	3.7	+2.3	–	–
Stevenage	67.7	+2.9	44.5	+3.1	34.2	+0.8	3.3	–13.3	14.4	+9.9	2.9	–	3 (0.7)	+1.2
Watford	67.2	–1.1	43.5	+8.5	26.0	–0.7	18.1	–14.3	9.8	+7.6	2.4	+0.8	1 (0.3)	–
Welwyn Hatfield	68.5	+0.6	50.4	–6.6	26.1	+4.8	6.3	–10.1	13.1	+9.7	3.5	+1.8	2 (0.7)	–5.7
Humberside, Beverley and Holderness	65.2	–1.9	48.1	+1.0	25.0	+3.9	5.5	–17.2	16.7	+13.2	3.4	+2.1	1 (1.2)	–
Brigg and Goole	63.2	–2.0	53.0	+8.2	27.2	–5.9	1.8	–12.9	15.5	+11.5	2.1	–	2 (0.4)	+7.0
Cleethorpes	63.5	–0.5	46.6	+4.5	29.1	–3.4	3.0	–15.2	18.5	+11.4	2.2	–	1 (0.5)	+4.0
Great Grimsby	57.0	+3.2	26.3	–4.2	39.8	+7.1	5.0	–17.4	25.0	+18.8	2.3	–	2 (1.7)	–5.6
Haltemprice and Howden	68.5	–0.9	54.2	+3.9	21.0	+5.3	6.3	–20.2	13.9	–	3.7	+2.3	1 (1)	–
Hull East	53.5	+2.9	15.9	–0.7	51.7	+3.8	6.5	–16.3	22.4	+14.3	2.3	–	3 (1.2)	–
North	55.1	+3.1	15.0	+1.9	52.8	+13.6	9.0	–28.3	16.3	+12.2	5.8	+4.4	1 (1)	–
West and Hessle	53.8	–1.2	17.5	–2.7	49.2	+6.7	10.0	–14.3	19.9	+14.5	3.0	–	1 (0.5)	–
Scunthorpe	57.7	–1.0	33.2	+0.5	41.7	+2.1	2.1	–16.2	17.1	+12.6	2.4	+1.3	2 (3.5)	–0.8
Yorkshire East	61.7	–2.3	50.6	+3.1	20.7	+0.4	5.9	–15.2	17.9	+13.7	3.5	+2.0	1 (1.4)	–
Isle of Wight, Isle of Wight	64.6	+0.7	40.7	–6.0	12.8	+1.2	7.4	–24.3	21.2	+17.7	13.4	+12.1	1 (4.5)	–
Kent, Ashford	67.4	–0.5	52.5	–1.7	18.4	+1.8	6.0	–16.8	18.8	+14.3	4.3	+2.5	–	–
Canterbury	65.7	–0.7	42.9	–1.9	24.5	+8.4	11.6	–20.9	13.6	+9.8	7.0	+4.7	1 (0.3)	–
Chatham and Aylesford	64.9	+0.5	50.2	+4.0	23.6	–8.7	3.2	–10.2	19.9	+16.9	2.6	+1.7	2 (0.6)	+6.4
Dartford	69.7	+4.0	49.0	+0.2	25.4	–2.1	2.8	–11.9	19.9	+16.2	2.5	–	1 (0.4)	+1.2
Dover	68.9	–1.3	43.3	–0.7	30.7	–2.8	3.1	–12.7	20.3	+16.8	2.6	–	–	+1.0

Faversham and Kent Mid	65.9	–2.0	54.4	–1.8	16.2	–0.4	6.6	–13.0	18.0	+14.3	3.9	+2.0	2 (1)	–
Folkestone and Hythe	65.8	–1.9	47.9	–1.6	14.4	+3.6	8.9	–21.4	22.8	+18.2	5.4	+4.2	3 (0.7)	–
Gillingham and Rainham	66.3	+0.3	48.0	+1.8	25.6	–2.0	3.6	–14.5	19.5	+16.3	2.4	+1.6	3 (0.8)	+1.9
Gravesham	69.6	+2.2	46.8	–1.7	30.1	+1.3	2.2	–11.1	18.6	+13.8	2.2	+0.8	–	–1.5
Maidstone and The Weald	68.3	–0.5	45.5	–2.5	10.5	+0.8	24.1	–11.9	15.9	+12.5	2.8	+1.5	2 (1.3)	–
Rochester and Strood†	68.1	+3.1	44.1	–5.1	19.8	–8.7	2.4	–13.9	30.5	–	2.9	+1.4	1 (0.4)	+1.8
Sevenoaks	69.7	–1.3	56.9	+0.1	12.9	–0.4	7.9	–13.5	17.9	+14.3	4.5	–	–	–
Sittingbourne and Sheppey	65.0	+0.9	49.5	–0.6	19.6	–5.0	3.2	–13.2	24.8	+19.4	2.4	–	1 (0.6)	+2.2
Thanet North	65.8	+2.6	49.0	–3.7	17.9	–3.6	3.5	–15.9	25.7	+19.2	3.7	–	1 (0.3)	–0.1
South	69.6	+4.0	38.1	–9.9	23.8	–7.6	1.9	–13.2	32.4	+26.9	2.2	–	6 (1.6)	–1.1
Tonbridge and Malling	71.7	+0.2	59.4	+1.5	14.2	+1.5	6.8	–15.7	15.2	+11.5	4.4	+2.9	–	–
Tunbridge Wells	70.0	+1.9	58.7	+2.4	14.2	+3.4	8.4	–16.8	12.6	+8.5	5.2	+3.4	1 (0.9)	–
Lancashire, Blackburn	60.1	–2.8	27.3	+1.1	56.3	+8.5	2.2	–13.0	14.3	+12.2	–	–	–	–3.7
Blackpool North and Cleveleys	63.1	+1.6	44.4	+2.7	36.0	–0.5	2.4	–10.9	14.8	+10.7	2.3	–	1 (0.1)	+1.6
South	56.5	+0.7	33.8	–2.0	41.8	+0.7	2.3	–12.2	17.3	+13.5	2.6	–	2 (2.2)	–1.4
Burnley*	61.6	–1.2	13.5	–3.1	37.6	+6.3	29.5	–6.2	17.3	+15.0	2.1	–	–	–
Chorley	69.2	–0.9	36.3	–1.7	45.1	+1.9	2.6	–11.4	13.5	+9.5	2.1	–	1 (0.3)	–1.8
Fylde	66.3	0.0	49.1	–3.1	18.8	–1.0	3.7	–18.3	12.8	+8.3	3.2	+1.7	2 (12.4)	–
Hyndburn	62.8	–0.7	31.9	–2.0	42.1	+1.1	2.0	–9.8	21.3	+17.9	2.6	+1.5	–	–1.5
Lancashire West	70.1	+4.4	32.4	–3.7	49.3	+4.1	2.6	–10.9	12.2	+8.5	3.2	+2.2	1 (0.3)	–3.9
Lancaster and Fleetwood*	67.4	+4.0	39.2	+3.2	42.3	+7.0	3.3	–15.8	9.7	+7.3	5.0	+0.6	1 (0.4)	–1.9
Morecambe and Lunesdale	64.6	+2.1	45.5	+4.0	34.9	–4.6	3.7	–9.6	12.4	+8.1	3.2	+1.8	1 (0.2)	+4.3
Pendle	68.8	+1.0	47.2	+8.3	34.9	+4.0	3.3	–16.8	12.2	+8.9	2.3	–	–	+2.2
Preston	55.8	+2.7	20.0	–1.7	56.0	+7.8	3.7	–20.7	15.4	+10.9	4.9	–	–	–
Ribble Valley	67.5	+0.3	48.6	–1.7	22.6	+0.5	5.3	–15.2	15.8	+9.1	4.2	–	3 (3.5)	–1.1
Rossendale and Darwen	66.4	+2.1	46.6	+4.8	35.1	+2.8	1.6	–16.5	14.0	+10.6	2.1	–	3 (0.6)	+1.0
South Ribble	68.5	+0.6	46.4	+1.0	35.1	+0.4	4.4	–9.7	14.1	+10.4	–	–	–	+0.3
Wyre and Preston North	70.6	–2.5	53.2	+0.8	24.8	+3.5	5.4	–16.1	13.2	+8.4	3.4	–	–	–
Leicestershire, Bosworth	67.2	–3.0	42.8	+0.2	17.5	+1.5	22.3	–11.0	17.4	+15.4	–	–	–	–
Charnwood	67.6	–4.3	54.3	+4.7	21.9	+2.2	6.9	–14.6	15.9	+12.6	–	–	1 (0.9)	–
Harborough	67.5	–3.0	52.7	+3.8	15.3	+2.6	13.4	–17.7	14.4	+11.7	4.1	–	–	–
Leicester East	63.7	–2.0	23.0	–1.5	61.1	+7.4	2.6	–11.6	8.9	+7.4	3.1	+1.5	2 (1.4)	–4.4
South	62.5	+1.4	21.0	–0.4	59.8	+14.2	4.6	–22.3	8.3	+6.8	5.5	+3.9	1 (0.8)	–
West	54.6	–0.6	25.6	–1.5	46.5	+8.1	4.4	–18.3	17.2	+14.8	5.4	+3.7	1 (0.8)	–4.8
North West	71.4	–1.5	49.5	+4.9	27.4	–2.7	3.9	–12.7	16.9	+14.7	2.3	–	–	+3.8

ENGLAND	*Turnout* %	*Turnout* +/–	*Con* %	*Con* +/–	*Lab* %	*Lab* +/–	*LD* %	*LD* +/–	*UKIP* %	*UKIP* +/–	*Grn* %	*Grn* +/–	*Other* No and %	*Swing*
South	70.2	–1.0	53.2	+3.7	22.0	+1.1	7.4	–13.6	17.4	+13.7	–	–	–	–
Loughborough	69.2	+1.0	49.5	+7.9	31.9	–2.6	4.1	–14.2	11.0	+9.2	3.5	–	–	+5.3
Rutland and Melton	68.5	–3.0	55.6	+4.5	15.4	+1.1	8.1	–17.7	15.9	+11.3	4.3	–	1 (0.8)	–
Lincolnshire, Boston and Skegness	64.6	+0.4	43.8	–5.7	16.5	–4.2	2.3	–12.4	33.8	+24.3	1.8	–	4 (1.7)	–0.7
Gainsborough	66.0	–1.6	52.7	+3.4	21.3	+5.7	6.7	–21.2	15.7	+11.5	2.6	–	1 (1)	–
Grantham and Stamford	66.2	–1.4	52.8	+2.5	16.9	–1.1	6.1	–16.1	17.5	+14.5	3.5	–	2 (3.2)	–
Lincoln	63.2	+1.0	42.6	+5.1	39.6	+4.3	4.3	–16.0	12.2	+10.0	–	–	2 (1.3)	+0.4
Louth and Horncastle	67.2	+2.2	51.2	+1.5	18.0	+0.7	4.5	–17.7	21.4	+17.1	3.1	–	2 (1.8)	–
Sleaford and North Hykeham	70.4	+0.2	56.2	+4.6	17.3	+0.4	5.7	–12.5	15.7	+12.1	–	–	1 (5.2)	–
South Holland and The Deepings	64.4	–1.5	59.6	+0.5	12.4	–1.6	3.0	–12.5	21.8	+15.4	3.2	+1.8	–	–
Merseyside, Birkenhead	62.7	+6.4	14.9	–4.1	67.6	+5.1	3.6	–15.0	9.8	–	4.2	–	–	–4.6
Bootle	64.4	+6.6	8.1	–0.9	74.5	+8.0	2.2	–13.0	10.9	+4.8	3.3	–	1 (1.1)	–
Garston and Halewood	66.4	+6.4	13.7	–2.5	69.1	+9.6	4.7	–15.5	9.2	+5.6	3.5	–	–	–
Knowsley	64.1	+8.0	6.6	–2.3	78.1	+7.2	2.9	–10.4	9.8	+7.2	2.5	–	–	–
Liverpool Riverside	62.5	+10.4	9.6	–1.3	67.4	+8.1	3.9	–18.9	5.7	+3.9	12.1	+8.6	1 (1.3)	–
Walton	62.0	+7.2	4.7	–1.8	81.3	+9.3	2.3	–11.9	9.0	+6.4	2.5	–	2 (0.2)	–
Wavertree	66.6	+5.9	10.0	+2.5	69.3	+16.2	6.0	–28.2	8.2	+5.9	5.2	+3.6	2 (1.2)	–
West Derby	64.5	+7.7	6.6	–2.6	75.2	+11.0	2.3	–10.2	8.5	+5.4	2.4	–	1 (5)	–
St Helens North	61.5	+2.0	19.6	–2.7	57.0	+5.3	4.4	–15.8	15.1	+10.4	3.8	–	–	–4.0
South	62.3	+3.2	15.9	–1.9	59.8	+6.9	5.7	–16.6	14.0	+11.3	4.6	–	–	–
Sefton Central	72.4	+0.6	29.6	–4.3	53.8	+11.9	4.3	–15.7	10.0	+5.7	2.4	–	–	–8.1
Southport	65.5	+0.4	28.0	–7.9	19.2	+9.8	31.0	–18.7	16.8	+11.7	2.8	–	1 (2.2)	–
Wallasey	66.2	+3.0	22.7	–8.7	60.4	+8.6	2.3	–11.3	11.7	+8.8	3.0	–	–	–8.6
Wirral South	73.5	+2.3	37.2	–2.2	48.2	+7.4	3.5	–13.0	8.9	+5.7	2.1	–	–	–4.8
West*	75.6	+4.1	44.2	+1.7	45.1	+8.9	3.4	–13.4	6.6	+4.3	–	–	1 (0.7)	–3.6
Norfolk, Broadland	72.2	–0.5	50.5	+4.3	18.8	+4.9	9.8	–22.6	16.7	+12.2	4.2	+2.8	–	–
Great Yarmouth	63.7	+2.5	42.9	–0.2	29.1	–4.1	2.3	–12.1	23.1	+18.3	2.2	+1.2	1 (0.4)	+2.0
Norfolk Mid	67.7	–0.7	52.1	+2.6	18.4	+0.9	6.3	–15.9	19.0	+13.5	4.2	+1.3	–	–
North	71.8	–1.4	30.9	–1.2	10.2	+4.4	39.1	–16.4	16.9	+11.5	3.0	+2.0	–	–
North West	63.7	–1.7	52.2	–2.0	22.8	+9.5	3.5	–19.7	17.8	+13.9	3.8	+2.2	–	–
South	70.8	–1.4	54.3	+4.9	18.4	+5.2	8.2	–21.2	13.7	+9.5	5.4	+3.6	–	–

South West	65.1	–1.5	50.9	+2.6	17.3	–1.3	4.4	–17.2	23.3	+17.0	4.1	+2.5	–	–
Norwich North	67.6	+1.9	43.7	+3.1	33.5	+2.0	4.3	–13.9	13.7	+9.3	4.4	+1.5	1 (0.3)	+0.5
South*	64.7	+0.2	23.5	+0.6	39.3	+10.6	13.6	–15.7	9.4	+7.0	13.9	–1.0	2 (0.3)	–
North Yorkshire, Harrogate and Knaresborough.	69.9	–1.2	52.7	+7.0	10.1	+3.7	22.1	–21.7	10.6	+8.7	4.4	–	–	–
Richmond (Yorks)	68.3	+2.0	51.4	–11.4	13.2	–2.1	6.4	–12.7	15.2	–	4.3	+1.4	2 (9.6)	–
Scarborough and Whitby	64.9	–0.4	43.2	+0.3	30.2	+3.9	4.5	–18.0	17.1	+14.1	4.6	+3.1	1 (0.4)	–1.8
Selby and Ainsty	69.4	–1.6	52.5	+3.1	26.8	+1.1	3.6	–14.1	14.0	+10.8	2.8	–	1 (0.3)	+1.0
Skipton and Ripon	71.2	+0.5	55.4	+4.9	17.4	+7.3	7.4	–25.0	14.0	+10.5	5.7	–	–	–
Thirsk and Malton	67.6	+17.7	52.6	–0.3	15.4	+1.9	9.0	–14.3	14.9	+8.3	4.6	–	2 (3.5)	–
York Central	63.3	+2.5	28.3	+2.2	42.4	+2.4	8.0	–17.2	10.1	+7.7	10.0	+6.5	2 (1.2)	–0.1
Outer	68.6	–1.6	49.1	+6.1	24.8	+7.7	11.6	–24.4	9.7	+7.7	4.7	–	–	–
Northamptonshire, Corby†	70.4	+0.9	42.8	+0.6	38.5	–0.2	2.6	–11.8	13.7	–	2.4	–	–	+0.4
Daventry	72.1	–0.4	58.2	+1.7	18.1	+2.3	4.5	–15.0	15.8	+11.3	3.5	+2.0	–	–
Kettering	67.3	–1.5	51.8	+2.7	25.2	–4.8	3.2	–12.7	16.1	–	3.5	–	1 (0.3)	+3.7
Northampton North	66.6	+1.5	42.4	+8.3	34.1	+4.8	3.6	–24.4	16.1	+13.0	3.8	+2.7	–	+1.7
South	63.4	+1.7	41.6	+0.7	31.8	+6.4	4.3	–15.1	18.3	+13.4	3.6	+2.7	1 (0.4)	–2.8
Northamptonshire South	71.0	–2.1	60.1	+4.9	16.7	–0.6	5.9	–15.1	13.5	+9.5	3.7	+2.5	–	–
Wellingborough	67.9	+0.6	52.1	+3.8	19.5	–5.9	4.4	–12.7	19.6	+16.4	4.4	+3.5	–	+4.9
Northumberland, Berwick-upon-Tweed*	71.0	+3.0	41.1	+4.4	14.9	+1.8	28.9	–14.8	11.2	+7.9	3.7	–	1 (0.2)	–
Blyth Valley	62.8	+1.5	21.7	+5.1	46.3	+1.8	5.9	–21.3	22.3	+18.0	3.8	–	–	–
Hexham	72.6	+0.6	52.7	+9.5	24.9	+5.9	6.8	–23.1	9.9	–	5.6	–	–	–
Wansbeck	63.5	+1.5	21.8	+4.2	50.0	+4.2	6.2	–21.2	18.2	+15.7	3.8	+2.2	–	–
Nottinghamshire, Ashfield	61.5	–0.8	22.4	+0.2	41.0	+7.3	14.8	–18.5	21.4	+19.5	–	–	1 (0.3)	–
Bassetlaw	64.2	–0.6	30.7	–3.2	48.6	–1.8	2.7	–8.5	16.0	+12.4	2.0	–	–	–0.7
Broxtowe	74.5	+1.3	45.2	+6.2	37.2	–1.1	4.0	–12.9	10.6	+8.4	2.9	+2.1	1 (0.1)	+3.6
Gedling	68.6	+0.6	36.1	–1.2	42.3	+1.2	4.0	–11.3	14.4	+11.4	3.2	–	–	–1.2
Mansfield	60.9	+0.4	28.2	+1.8	39.4	+0.7	3.5	–12.0	25.1	+18.9	3.1	–	1 (0.7)	+0.6
Newark	70.9	–0.5	57.0	+3.2	21.7	–0.6	4.6	–15.4	12.0	+8.2	3.4	–	1 (1.2)	+1.9
Nottingham East	58.2	+1.8	20.8	–2.9	54.6	+9.2	4.2	–20.1	9.9	+6.5	9.9	+7.1	2 (0.7)	–
North	53.6	–0.6	21.0	–3.8	54.6	+6.0	2.4	–14.7	18.5	+14.6	3.1	–	1 (0.5)	–4.9
South	63.0	+2.5	31.7	–1.3	47.6	+10.3	3.5	–19.5	11.3	+8.9	5.4	+3.9	1 (0.5)	–5.8
Rushcliffe	75.3	+1.7	51.4	+0.2	26.3	+5.6	5.0	–16.7	10.8	+6.7	6.5	+4.1	–	–
Sherwood	69.1	+0.6	45.0	+5.8	35.9	–2.9	2.2	–12.7	14.6	+11.6	2.2	–	1 (0.2)	+4.4
Oxfordshire, Banbury	67.1	+0.5	53.0	+0.2	21.3	+2.1	5.9	–14.5	13.9	+8.9	4.6	+2.9	1 (1.3)	–

ENGLAND	Turnout %	Turnout +/–	Con %	Con +/–	Lab %	Lab +/–	LD %	LD +/–	UKIP %	UKIP +/–	Grn %	Grn +/–	Other No and %	Swing
Henley	70.9	–2.3	58.5	+2.3	12.5	+1.6	11.2	–13.9	10.9	+7.5	6.9	+4.4	–	–
Oxford East	64.2	+1.1	19.9	+1.0	50.0	+7.5	10.8	–22.8	6.8	+4.5	11.6	+9.2	4 (0.9)	–
West and Abingdon	75.2	+9.8	45.7	+3.4	12.7	+2.1	28.9	–13.1	6.9	+4.2	4.4	+2.3	2 (1.4)	–
Wantage	70.3	+0.3	53.3	+1.3	16.0	+2.1	13.1	–14.9	12.5	+8.2	5.1	+3.3	–	–
Witney	73.3	0.0	60.2	+1.4	17.2	+4.2	6.8	–12.7	9.2	+5.7	5.1	+0.9	7 (1.6)	–
Shropshire, Ludlow	72.4	–0.7	54.3	+1.5	12.3	+5.6	13.5	–19.3	14.9	+10.5	5.1	+4.1	–	–
Shrewsbury and Atcham	70.8	+0.5	45.5	+1.6	27.8	+7.3	7.9	–21.1	14.4	+11.4	4.2	+3.1	1 (0.2)	–
Shropshire North	66.7	+1.0	51.4	0.0	20.1	+1.9	6.0	–15.0	17.6	+12.9	4.9	+3.3	–	–
Telford*	61.4	–2.1	39.6	+3.3	37.8	–0.9	2.3	–13.2	18.0	+12.2	2.3	–	–	+2.1
Wrekin, The	68.9	–1.2	49.7	+2.0	26.0	–1.1	4.3	–13.1	16.8	+12.3	3.2	–	–	+1.5
Somerset, Bridgwater and West Somerset	67.6	+1.3	46.0	+0.7	17.6	+0.5	12.4	–15.9	19.2	+14.4	4.8	+3.3	–	–
Somerton and Frome*	72.4	–1.9	53.0	+8.5	7.3	+2.9	19.4	–28.1	10.7	+7.5	9.0	–	1 (0.6)	–
Taunton Deane*	69.6	–0.9	48.1	+5.9	9.2	+4.1	21.3	–27.7	12.0	+8.3	4.5	–	3 (4.8)	–
Wells*	71.7	+1.3	46.1	+3.6	6.6	–0.9	32.8	–11.2	9.9	+6.9	4.1	+3.0	3 (0.4)	–
Yeovil*	69.1	–0.4	42.5	+9.6	7.1	+1.9	33.1	–22.6	13.4	+9.3	3.8	–	–	–
South Yorkshire, Barnsley Central	56.7	+0.2	15.0	–2.3	55.7	+8.5	2.1	–15.2	21.7	+17.1	2.6	–	2 (2.9)	–
East	55.7	–0.4	14.6	–1.9	54.7	+7.7	3.2	–15.0	23.5	+19.0	–	–	4 (4)	–
Don Valley	59.6	–0.2	25.3	–4.4	46.2	+8.2	3.5	–13.6	23.5	+19.1	–	–	2 (1.6)	–6.3
Doncaster Central	56.8	–0.4	20.7	–4.0	49.1	+9.4	4.2	–16.8	24.1	+20.7	–	–	2 (1.8)	–6.7
North	55.6	–2.2	18.3	–2.7	52.4	+5.1	2.5	–12.3	22.6	+18.3	1.9	–	3 (2.2)	–3.9
Penistone and Stocksbridge	66.2	–1.8	27.7	–3.5	42.0	+4.3	6.3	–14.8	22.9	+18.8	–	–	1 (1.1)	–3.9
Rother Valley	63.3	–0.9	23.3	–5.1	43.6	+2.7	4.2	–13.1	28.1	+22.5	–	–	1 (0.8)	–3.9
Rotherham	59.4	+0.4	12.3	–4.4	52.5	+7.9	2.9	–13.1	30.2	+24.3	–	–	3 (2.1)	–6.2
Sheffield Brightside and Hillsborough	56.5	–0.9	11.0	–0.5	56.6	+1.6	4.5	–15.5	22.1	+18.0	4.3	–	2 (1.5)	–
Central	61.1	–0.3	11.1	+1.0	55.0	+13.7	9.7	–31.2	7.5	+5.9	15.8	+12.1	5 (0.8)	–
Hallam	76.7	+2.4	13.6	–9.9	35.8	+19.7	40.0	–13.4	6.4	+4.1	3.2	+1.4	3 (0.9)	–
Heeley	61.9	–0.5	16.2	–1.2	48.2	+5.6	11.3	–17.1	17.4	+13.7	6.1	+3.7	2 (0.9)	–
South East	59.2	–2.5	17.4	0.0	51.4	+2.7	5.3	–18.0	21.9	+17.3	2.7	–	3 (1.3)	–
Wentworth and Dearne	58.1	+0.1	14.9	–2.7	56.9	+6.3	2.6	–13.5	24.9	+16.7	–	–	1 (0.7)	–4.5
Staffordshire, Burton	65.1	–1.5	49.8	+5.2	27.5	–4.3	2.5	–13.3	17.7	+14.8	2.5	–	–	+4.8
Cannock Chase	63.2	+2.0	44.2	+4.1	33.7	+0.6	2.7	–14.3	17.5	+14.0	1.9	–	–	+1.7

Lichfield	69.3	–1.7	55.2	+0.8	19.8	0.0	5.2	–14.9	15.7	+10.0	3.8	–	1 (0.2)	–
Newcastle-under-Lyme	63.6	+1.4	36.9	+2.5	38.4	+0.5	4.2	–15.4	16.9	+8.8	2.9	–	1 (0.7)	+1.0
Stafford	71.0	–0.1	48.4	+4.5	29.6	–3.4	2.8	–13.6	12.9	+9.5	2.9	+1.7	1 (3.5)	+4.0
Staffordshire Moorlands	67.5	–3.0	51.1	+5.9	27.2	–2.7	4.1	–12.6	14.6	+6.5	2.9	–	–	+4.3
South	68.2	–0.1	59.4	+6.2	18.4	–1.9	2.9	–13.8	16.7	+11.2	2.6	–	–	+4.1
Stoke-on-Trent Central	51.3	–2.0	22.5	+1.5	39.3	+0.5	4.2	–17.5	22.7	+18.3	3.6	–	3 (7.7)	–
North	54.1	–1.7	27.4	+3.6	39.9	–4.4	2.9	–14.8	24.7	+18.5	2.8	–	2 (2.2)	+4.0
South	57.4	–1.1	32.7	+4.3	39.2	+0.4	3.3	–12.5	21.2	+17.8	2.6	–	1 (1)	+1.9
Stone	69.8	–0.6	54.7	+4.1	20.2	–0.5	5.3	–17.2	16.2	+10.9	2.5	+1.5	1 (1.1)	–
Tamworth	65.6	+1.1	50.0	+4.3	26.1	–6.6	3.0	–13.2	18.5	+13.6	2.4	–	–	+5.4
Suffolk, Bury St Edmunds	69.0	–0.3	53.6	+6.1	17.7	+1.1	6.0	–20.4	14.7	+9.6	7.9	+3.6	–	–
Ipswich	65.4	+3.4	44.8	+5.6	37.1	+2.4	2.9	–15.4	11.7	+8.8	3.6	+1.9	–	+1.6
Suffolk Central and Ipswich North	70.6	+0.1	56.1	+5.3	18.8	+2.6	6.1	–18.8	13.8	+9.4	4.9	+2.2	1 (0.3)	–
Coastal	71.4	–0.2	51.9	+5.5	18.0	+2.0	8.6	–21.2	15.6	+9.8	5.9	+3.9	–	–
South	70.3	–0.6	53.1	+5.3	19.3	+4.9	7.8	–23.1	15.2	+8.1	4.3	–	1 (0.3)	–
West	64.6	0.0	52.2	+1.6	17.5	+2.7	5.0	–18.4	21.7	+15.3	3.6	–	–	–
Waveney	65.1	0.0	42.3	+2.1	37.7	–1.0	2.0	–11.3	14.5	+9.3	3.4	+1.1	–	+1.6
Surrey, Epsom and Ewell	72.7	+3.9	58.3	+2.1	15.5	+3.6	8.8	–18.1	12.5	+7.8	3.7	–	2 (1.3)	–
Esher and Walton	71.3	–1.1	62.9	+4.0	12.7	+2.0	9.4	–15.4	9.7	+6.5	4.1	–	2 (1.1)	–
Guildford	71.3	–0.8	57.1	+3.8	12.1	+7.0	15.5	–23.8	8.8	+7.0	4.7	–	3 (1.8)	–
Mole Valley	74.5	–0.7	60.6	+3.1	8.3	+1.3	14.5	–14.3	11.2	+6.1	5.4	+3.8	–	–
Reigate	69.9	+0.1	56.8	+3.4	12.8	+1.5	10.5	–15.7	13.3	+9.1	6.7	+4.5	–	–
Runnymede and Weybridge	67.8	+1.5	59.7	+3.8	15.5	+2.1	6.7	–14.9	13.9	+7.4	4.1	+2.7	–	–
Spelthorne	68.6	+1.4	49.7	+2.6	18.6	+2.1	6.4	–19.4	20.9	+12.4	3.5	–	2 (0.9)	–
Surrey East	70.4	–0.7	57.4	+0.7	11.8	+2.8	9.2	–16.6	17.0	+10.1	3.8	–	1 (0.6)	–
Heath	68.5	–1.1	59.9	+2.2	11.2	+1.0	9.1	–16.8	14.3	+8.0	4.4	–	2 (1.2)	–
South West	73.7	–1.2	59.9	+1.2	9.5	+3.5	6.3	–23.9	9.9	+7.3	5.4	+4.2	2 (9.1)	–
Woking	70.0	–1.5	56.2	+5.9	16.1	+8.1	11.6	–25.8	11.3	+7.5	4.1	–	3 (0.7)	–
Tyne and Wear, Blaydon	66.2	–0.1	17.4	+1.5	49.2	–0.5	12.2	–17.1	17.5	–	3.7	–	–	–
Gateshead	58.8	+1.3	14.5	–0.4	56.8	+2.6	6.8	–14.5	17.8	+14.9	4.1	+3.1	–	–
Houghton and Sunderland South	56.3	+1.0	18.5	–3.0	55.1	+4.8	2.1	–11.9	21.5	+18.8	2.8	–	–	–3.9
Jarrow	60.3	0.0	17.1	–3.6	55.7	+1.7	3.2	–15.3	19.7	–	3.4	–	1 (1)	–2.7
Newcastle upon Tyne Central	60.3	+3.9	18.9	–0.5	55.0	+9.1	6.3	–17.8	14.9	+12.7	4.9	+3.3	–	–
East	61.1	+2.4	17.6	+1.5	49.4	+4.4	11.0	–22.2	12.5	–	8.7	+7.1	2 (0.7)	–
North	66.1	+0.6	23.5	+5.3	46.1	+5.2	9.7	–23.4	16.6	+13.7	3.4	+2.6	1 (0.8)	–

ENGLAND	Turnout %	Turnout +/–	Con %	Con +/–	Lab %	Lab +/–	LD %	LD +/–	UKIP %	UKIP +/–	Grn %	Grn +/–	Other No and %	Swing
South Shields	57.8	+0.8	16.6	–5.0	51.3	–0.8	1.8	–12.4	22.0	–	4.5	+2.4	1 (3.9)	–2.1
Sunderland Central	57.2	+0.2	23.4	–6.7	50.2	+4.3	2.6	–14.3	19.1	+16.6	4.1	–	1 (0.5)	–5.5
Tynemouth	69.0	–0.6	32.8	–1.6	48.2	+2.9	3.0	–11.9	12.2	+10.5	3.8	+2.7	–	–2.3
Tyneside North	59.0	–0.7	19.2	+0.9	55.9	+5.3	4.4	–18.5	16.3	+13.5	3.1	–	2 (1.1)	–
Washington and Sunderland West	54.6	+0.5	18.9	–3.0	55.0	+2.4	2.7	–14.4	19.6	+16.3	2.9	–	1 (0.9)	–2.7
Warwickshire, Kenilworth and Southam	76.3	+1.0	58.4	+4.8	15.3	+1.0	10.1	–17.6	11.2	+8.7	4.0	+2.8	2 (1)	–
Nuneaton	67.2	+1.4	45.5	+4.0	34.9	–2.0	1.8	–13.6	14.4	–	2.8	–	2 (0.7)	+3.0
Rugby	68.4	–0.5	49.1	+5.0	27.9	–3.4	5.7	–14.2	14.0	+13.1	2.9	+1.9	1 (0.5)	+4.2
Stratford-on-Avon	72.2	–0.5	57.7	+6.1	13.0	+3.5	12.0	–17.1	13.2	+9.6	4.1	+3.1	–	–
Warwick and Leamington	70.7	–1.7	47.9	+5.4	34.9	–0.5	5.0	–13.3	8.3	+6.4	3.9	+2.5	–	+2.9
Warwickshire North	67.5	+0.1	42.3	+2.1	36.0	–4.0	2.1	–9.5	17.4	+14.6	1.9	–	1 (0.3)	+3.1
West Midlands, Aldridge-Brownhills	65.6	0.0	52.0	–7.3	22.4	+2.6	3.4	–14.3	19.6	–	2.1	–0.1	1 (0.5)	–4.9
Birmingham Edgbaston	63.0	+2.3	38.3	+0.7	44.8	+4.2	2.9	–12.5	10.1	+8.3	3.3	+2.2	2 (0.6)	–1.7
Erdington	53.3	–0.3	30.8	–1.8	45.6	+3.8	2.8	–13.4	17.4	+15.0	2.7	–	1 (0.6)	–2.8
Hall Green	61.6	–2.0	17.7	+2.7	59.8	+26.9	11.6	–13.0	4.5	+2.6	4.7	–	1 (1.7)	–
Hodge Hill	54.5	–2.1	11.5	–0.2	68.4	+16.4	6.4	–21.3	11.3	+9.7	2.0	–	1 (0.4)	–
Ladywood	52.7	+4.1	12.7	+0.8	73.6	+18.0	3.8	–23.6	5.0	+2.5	4.2	+1.8	1 (0.6)	–
Northfield	59.4	+0.8	35.7	+2.1	41.6	+1.3	3.2	–12.5	16.7	+13.5	2.8	+1.8	–	+0.4
Perry Barr	59.0	0.0	21.5	+0.2	57.4	+7.1	4.8	–17.1	12.2	+8.2	3.2	–	1 (0.8)	–
Selly Oak	60.3	–1.9	29.0	–2.1	47.7	+9.1	5.6	–16.7	12.7	+10.3	5.1	+3.7	–	–5.6
Yardley*	57.0	+0.6	14.0	–5.2	41.6	+9.4	25.6	–14.0	16.1	+13.2	1.7	–	3 (1)	–
Coventry North East	56.0	–3.4	23.1	+0.9	52.2	+2.9	4.8	–11.9	14.9	+11.9	2.9	–	2 (2.2)	–1.0
North West	61.5	–2.4	31.0	+1.7	41.0	–1.8	4.0	–13.9	15.7	+12.9	4.3	+3.3	1 (3.9)	+1.8
South	62.1	–0.3	35.0	+1.5	42.3	+0.5	4.1	–14.0	13.1	+9.2	3.9	+2.5	2 (1.7)	+0.5
Dudley North	62.6	–0.9	30.8	–6.2	41.8	+3.2	1.3	–9.3	24.0	+15.5	1.4	–	2 (0.8)	–4.7
South	63.3	+0.3	43.8	+0.7	32.6	–0.4	2.2	–13.5	18.9	+10.7	2.5	–	–	+0.5
Halesowen and Rowley Regis	66.3	–2.7	43.2	+2.0	36.2	–0.4	2.1	–12.7	16.6	+10.2	1.9	–	–	+1.2
Meriden	64.2	+0.8	54.7	+3.1	19.0	–1.5	5.0	–12.8	16.9	+14.3	4.1	+2.8	1 (0.2)	+2.3
Solihull*	70.3	–2.0	49.2	+6.7	10.4	+1.5	25.7	–17.2	11.6	+9.4	3.0	–	2 (0.2)	–
Stourbridge	66.6	–1.2	46.0	+3.4	31.5	–0.2	3.3	–13.0	16.9	+12.4	2.2	+1.4	–	+1.8
Sutton Coldfield	67.8	–0.1	54.6	+0.7	22.3	+2.0	5.2	–12.9	14.7	+11.6	2.8	+1.7	1 (0.3)	–0.7

Walsall North	55.0	–1.5	33.8	–0.5	39.0	+2.0	2.3	–10.9	22.0	+17.2	1.4	–	1 (1.5)	–1.3
South	61.8	–1.7	32.8	–2.5	47.2	+7.5	1.6	–12.8	15.6	+7.2	2.7	–	–	–5.0
Warley	59.4	–1.6	19.3	–5.5	58.2	+5.3	2.1	–13.4	16.5	+9.6	3.9	–	–	–5.4
West Bromwich East	58.9	–1.6	24.9	–4.0	50.2	+3.7	2.0	–11.2	21.2	+18.6	1.7	–	–	–3.8
West	53.5	–2.3	23.9	–5.5	47.3	+2.4	1.6	–10.4	25.2	+20.9	2.0	–	–	–3.9
Wolverhampton North East	55.7	–3.5	29.9	–4.4	46.1	+4.7	2.7	–10.8	19.2	+15.9	2.1	–	–	–4.5
South East	55.6	–2.4	22.3	–6.2	53.3	+5.8	2.3	–12.9	20.3	+12.6	1.7	–	–	–6.0
South West*	66.6	–1.6	41.2	+0.5	43.2	+4.2	2.1	–13.9	10.7	+7.0	2.6	–	1 (0.1)	–1.9
West Sussex, Arundel and South Downs	73.1	+0.3	60.8	+3.0	11.2	+2.6	7.2	–20.7	14.4	+8.8	6.4	–	–	–
Bognor Regis and Littlehampton	64.5	–1.6	51.3	–0.1	13.8	–0.2	9.0	–14.5	21.7	+15.3	4.1	–	–	–
Chichester	68.5	–1.1	57.7	+2.3	12.1	+1.7	8.5	–18.9	14.9	+8.1	6.5	–	1 (0.2)	–
Crawley	65.7	+0.4	47.0	+2.3	33.6	+1.3	2.8	–11.6	14.4	+11.5	2.3	+1.0	–	+0.5
Horsham	72.0	0.0	57.3	+4.6	11.4	+3.9	11.7	–20.5	14.0	+8.9	3.9	+2.8	3 (1.7)	–
Sussex Mid	70.9	–1.4	56.1	+5.4	13.9	+7.3	11.5	–26.0	12.0	+9.5	4.3	+3.1	2 (2.2)	–
Worthing East and Shoreham	66.7	+1.3	49.5	+1.0	19.5	+2.8	6.7	–18.8	16.6	+10.4	5.2	+2.9	1 (2.5)	–
West	67.1	+2.4	51.5	–0.3	15.7	+3.9	8.8	–19.0	18.3	+12.3	5.8	+3.8	–	–
West Yorkshire, Batley and Spen	64.4	–2.2	31.2	–2.3	43.2	+1.0	4.7	–11.1	18.0	–	2.4	+1.3	2 (0.3)	–1.7
Bradford East*	62.6	+0.5	11.3	–15.5	46.6	+13.8	29.5	–4.2	9.9	–	2.1	–	1 (0.5)	–
South	59.1	–0.7	26.3	–2.8	43.4	+2.2	2.9	–15.4	24.1	+20.6	3.3	–	–	–2.5
West†	63.6	–1.3	15.3	–15.9	49.6	+4.2	2.9	–8.8	7.8	+5.8	2.7	+0.4	3 (21.7)	–10.0
Calder Valley	68.9	+1.5	43.6	+4.2	35.4	+8.4	5.0	–20.2	11.1	+8.8	3.9	+2.2	2 (1)	–2.1
Colne Valley	68.8	–0.2	44.4	+7.5	35.0	+8.6	6.0	–22.2	10.1	+8.0	3.4	+1.8	2 (1.1)	–
Dewsbury*	67.2	–1.2	39.1	+4.1	41.8	+9.6	3.6	–13.4	12.4	–	2.5	+1.0	2 (0.6)	–2.8
Elmet and Rothwell	73.0	+1.3	48.4	+5.8	33.7	–0.8	4.6	–11.8	11.1	+8.3	2.2	–	–	+3.3
Halifax	62.1	+0.2	39.0	+5.0	40.0	+2.6	3.7	–15.4	12.8	+11.3	2.6	–	2 (1.8)	+1.2
Hemsworth	58.3	+0.3	22.9	–1.5	51.3	+4.6	3.2	–9.7	20.2	–	–	–	1 (2.4)	–3.0
Huddersfield	62.0	+0.9	26.8	–1.0	44.9	+6.1	5.8	–18.9	14.7	–	6.9	+2.9	1 (0.8)	–3.6
Keighley	71.3	–1.0	44.3	+2.4	38.1	+2.3	2.7	–12.1	11.5	+8.4	3.4	–	–	0.0
Leeds Central	55.1	+9.1	17.3	–2.9	55.0	+5.7	3.4	–17.4	15.7	–	7.9	–	1 (0.7)	–
East	59.0	+0.5	20.9	–2.2	53.7	+3.4	3.4	–14.1	19.0	–	2.9	–	–	–2.8
North East	69.9	–0.1	32.9	–0.2	47.9	+5.2	5.3	–14.3	7.7	+5.9	5.3	–	1 (0.9)	–2.7
North West	70.0	+3.5	18.6	–7.9	30.1	+9.1	36.8	–10.7	6.9	+5.5	7.0	+5.8	3 (0.6)	–
West	59.2	+1.7	20.1	+0.4	48.0	+5.7	3.9	–20.3	18.5	+15.5	8.4	+3.6	2 (1.1)	–
Morley and Outwood*	63.6	–1.6	38.9	+3.6	38.0	+0.4	3.0	–13.8	16.5	+13.4	2.6	–	1 (1)	+1.6
Normanton, Pontefract and Castleford	55.6	–0.6	20.8	–3.6	54.9	+6.7	2.9	–13.5	21.3	–	–	–	–	–5.2

ENGLAND	Turnout %	Turnout +/–	Con %	Con +/–	Lab %	Lab +/–	LD %	LD +/–	UKIP %	UKIP +/–	Grn %	Grn +/–	Other No and %	Swing
Pudsey	72.2	+1.3	46.4	+8.0	37.6	+2.5	3.8	–17.0	9.2	+6.7	3.0	–	–	+2.7
Shipley	71.7	–1.3	50.0	+1.4	31.0	+2.5	3.9	–16.2	8.9	–	5.3	+2.3	1 (1.1)	–0.5
Wakefield	60.9	–1.8	34.2	–1.5	40.3	+1.0	3.5	–12.9	18.3	–	2.5	+0.5	2 (1.3)	–1.2
Wiltshire, Chippenham*	74.7	+2.0	47.6	+6.5	8.2	+1.3	29.4	–16.4	10.6	+7.2	4.2	+3.4	–	–
Devizes	70.8	+2.0	57.7	+2.7	13.0	+2.8	8.1	–18.9	15.4	+10.9	5.8	+4.1	–	–
Salisbury	72.9	+1.0	55.6	+6.4	15.3	+7.7	10.1	–26.9	12.1	+9.3	5.4	+4.4	1 (1.4)	–
Swindon North	64.5	+0.3	50.3	+5.8	27.8	–2.7	3.3	–14.0	15.3	+11.7	3.3	+2.3	–	+4.3
South	66.6	+1.8	46.2	+4.5	34.5	+0.2	3.7	–13.9	12.0	+7.7	3.6	+2.3	–	+2.1
Wiltshire North	74.5	+1.1	57.2	+5.7	9.8	+3.1	15.6	–20.6	11.5	+7.6	4.6	+3.4	2 (1.3)	–
South West	70.7	+2.3	52.7	+1.0	13.5	+2.0	10.6	–19.9	17.5	+12.0	5.8	–	–	–

WALES	Turnout %	Turnout +/–	Con %	Con +/–	Lab %	Lab +/–	LD %	LD +/–	Plaid %	Plaid +/–	UKIP %	UKIP +/–	Grn %	Grn +/–	Others No and %	Swing
Clwyd, Aberconwy	66.2	–1.0	41.5	+5.7	28.2	+3.8	4.6	–14.7	11.7	–6.1	11.5	+9.4	2.4	–	–	+1.0
Alyn and Deeside	66.6	+1.1	31.9	–0.3	40.0	+0.4	4.2	–14.1	3.9	0.0	17.6	+15.0	2.4	–	–	–0.4
Clwyd South	63.8	–0.8	30.4	+0.2	37.2	–1.2	3.8	–13.4	10.3	+1.6	15.6	+13.3	2.6	–	–	+0.7
West	64.8	–1.0	43.3	+1.7	25.6	+0.9	3.6	–11.6	12.2	–3.2	13.1	+10.8	–	–	2 (2.1)	+0.4
Delyn	69.8	+0.7	32.7	–1.9	40.5	–0.2	3.7	–11.9	4.8	–0.2	16.4	+14.6	1.8	–	–	–0.8
Vale of Clwyd*	62.4	–1.3	39.0	+3.8	38.4	–3.9	2.6	–10.0	7.1	+1.2	13.0	+11.5	–	–	–	+3.9
Wrexham	64.2	–0.7	31.6	+6.2	37.2	+0.4	5.3	–20.5	7.6	+1.5	15.5	+13.2	2.0	–	1 (0.6)	–
Dyfed, Carmarthen East and Dinefwr	70.7	–1.9	21.2	–1.2	24.2	–2.3	2.4	–9.8	38.4	+2.8	11.1	+7.7	2.8	–	–	–
West and Pembrokeshire South	69.9	+0.2	43.7	+2.6	28.7	–4.0	2.4	–9.7	10.4	0.0	11.6	+8.8	3.2	–	–	+3.3
Ceredigion	69.0	+5.1	11.0	–0.5	9.7	+3.9	35.9	–14.2	27.7	–0.6	10.2	+7.7	5.6	+3.8	–	–
Llanelli	65.0	–2.3	14.3	0.0	41.3	–1.1	1.9	–8.5	23.0	–7.0	16.3	+13.5	1.8	–	2 (1.4)	–
Preseli Pembrokeshire	70.8	+1.8	40.4	–2.4	28.1	–3.0	1.9	–12.6	6.2	–3.0	10.5	+8.2	3.6	–	2 (9.3)	+0.3
Gwent, Blaenau Gwent	61.7	–0.1	10.8	+3.8	58.0	+5.6	2.0	–8.2	9.0	+4.9	17.9	+16.4	2.3	–	–	–
Islwyn	63.6	+0.3	15.2	+1.2	49.0	–0.2	2.7	–7.7	10.7	–2.3	19.6	+16.9	1.9	–	2 (1)	+0.7
Monmouth	76.2	+4.2	49.9	+1.6	26.8	+0.9	5.3	–14.1	4.0	+1.2	10.4	+8.0	3.4	+2.2	1 (0.2)	+0.4

Newport East	62.7	–0.6	27.3	+4.3	40.7	+3.7	6.4	–25.8	3.5	+1.4	18.4	+16.5	2.5	–	1 (1.1)	–
West	64.9	+1.0	32.5	+0.2	41.2	0.0	3.9	–12.7	4.0	+1.2	15.2	+12.3	3.2	+2.0	–	+0.1
Torfaen	61.3	–0.2	23.1	+3.1	44.6	–0.1	3.4	–13.3	5.7	+0.4	19.0	+16.7	2.0	+0.8	2 (2.2)	+1.6
Gwynedd, Arfon	66.3	+3.0	13.1	–3.8	30.3	–0.1	2.7	–11.4	43.9	+8.0	8.5	+5.9	–	–	1 (1.5)	–
Dwyfor Meirionnydd	65.1	+1.4	22.7	+0.4	13.5	–0.4	4.0	–8.3	40.9	–3.5	10.8	+8.1	3.4	–	1 (4.8)	–
Ynys Mon	69.9	+1.2	21.2	–1.3	31.1	–2.2	2.2	–5.4	30.5	+4.3	14.7	+11.2	–	–	1 (0.4)	–
Mid-Glamorgan, Bridgend	65.8	+0.4	32.2	+1.8	37.1	+0.7	4.2	–18.4	7.1	+1.1	15.0	+12.9	1.9	–	4 (2.7)	+0.5
Caerphilly	63.3	+1.1	16.6	–0.5	44.3	–0.6	2.3	–12.4	14.6	–2.1	19.3	+17.0	2.3	–	1 (0.4)	0.0
Cynon Valley	59.3	+0.3	12.1	+2.0	47.7	–4.8	2.7	–11.1	16.8	–3.5	16.3	+13.0	2.6	–	1 (1.7)	–
Merthyr Tydfil	53.0	–5.6	10.1	+2.5	53.9	+10.2	4.1	–26.9	9.5	+4.4	18.7	+15.9	1.8	–	2 (2)	–
Ogmore	63.4	+1.0	15.9	+0.4	52.9	–0.9	3.0	–12.1	10.1	+0.5	15.4	+13.1	2.1	–	1 (0.5)	+0.6
Pontypridd	64.3	+1.3	17.3	+1.2	41.1	+2.3	12.9	–18.2	11.5	+4.2	13.4	+10.1	2.6	+1.6	2 (1.1)	–
Rhondda	60.9	+0.6	6.7	+0.3	50.7	–4.6	1.5	–9.1	27.0	+8.9	12.7	+11.5	1.4	–	–	–
Powys, Brecon and Radnorshire*	73.6	+1.1	41.1	+4.5	14.7	+4.2	28.3	–17.8	4.4	+1.9	8.3	+6.1	3.1	+2.3	–	–
Montgomeryshire	69.3	–0.1	45.0	+3.7	5.6	–1.5	29.3	–8.6	5.2	–3.1	11.2	+7.8	3.7	–	–	–
South Glamorgan, Cardiff Central*	67.3	+8.2	14.7	–6.9	40.0	+11.2	27.1	–14.3	5.0	+1.5	6.5	+4.4	6.4	+4.8	2 (0.4)	–
North	76.1	+3.5	42.4	+4.9	38.3	+1.2	3.8	–14.5	4.5	+1.2	7.7	+5.4	2.5	+1.7	2 (0.8)	+1.9
South and Penarth	61.4	+1.2	26.8	–1.5	42.8	+3.9	5.0	–17.3	7.4	+3.2	13.8	+11.2	3.7	+2.5	1 (0.6)	–2.7
West	65.6	+0.4	25.2	–4.5	40.7	–0.6	4.7	–12.8	13.9	+6.9	11.2	+8.5	3.9	+2.1	1 (0.4)	–2.0
Vale of Glamorgan	70.5	+1.1	46.0	+4.2	32.6	–0.3	2.6	–12.7	5.6	+0.1	10.7	+7.6	2.1	+1.1	1 (0.5)	+2.3
West Glamorgan, Aberavon	63.3	+2.4	11.9	–2.4	48.9	–3.0	4.4	–11.8	11.6	+4.5	15.8	+14.2	2.3	–	3 (5.1)	–
Gower*	69.2	+1.6	37.1	+5.1	37.0	–1.4	3.6	–15.4	7.1	+0.5	11.2	+9.6	2.7	–	3 (1.2)	+3.3
Neath	66.2	+1.4	15.3	+2.3	43.8	–2.4	3.2	–11.8	18.1	–1.8	16.4	+14.2	3.2	–	–	–
Swansea East	58.0	+3.3	15.3	+0.5	53.0	+1.5	4.1	–14.2	10.4	+3.7	17.2	+14.6	–	–	–	–
West	59.8	+1.8	22.6	+1.7	42.6	+7.9	9.0	–24.2	6.4	+2.4	13.5	+11.5	5.1	+3.9	3 (0.8)	–

SCOTLAND	*Turnout* %	*Turnout* +/–	*Con* %	*Con* +/–	*Lab* %	*Lab* +/–	*LD* %	*LD* +/–	*SNP* %	*SNP* +/–	UKIP %	*UKIP* +/–	*Grn*	*Grn*	*Others* No and %	*Swing*
Aberdeen North*	64.9	+6.7	12.1	–0.3	25.9	–18.5	4.7	–13.9	56.4	+34.2	2.5	–	–	–	–	–
South*	71.3	+4.1	22.8	+2.1	26.8	–9.8	4.6	–23.7	41.6	+29.8	–	–	1.3	–	–	–
Aberdeenshire West and Kincardine*	75.2	+6.8	28.8	–1.4	4.5	–9.1	21.4	–17.0	41.6	+25.9	2.4	–	–	–	–	–
Airdrie and Shotts*	66.3	+8.8	7.7	–1.1	34.1	–24.0	1.5	–6.6	53.9	+30.4	2.4	+1.2	1.1	–	1 (0.2)	–

SCOTLAND	Turnout %	Turnout +/–	Con %	Con +/–	Lab %	Lab +/–	LD %	LD +/–	SNP %	SNP +/–	UKIP %	UKIP +/–	Grn	Grn	Others No and %	Swing
Angus	67.6	+7.2	29.0	–1.9	8.8	–8.4	2.7	–8.0	54.2	+14.7	2.3	+1.0	–	–	–	–
Argyll and Bute*	75.3	+8.0	14.9	–9.1	10.4	–12.3	27.9	–3.7	44.3	+25.3	2.8	+1.4	1.6	+0.5	–	–
Ayr, Carrick and Cumnock*	71.5	+8.9	19.8	–5.7	27.3	–19.9	1.6	–7.7	48.8	+30.8	–	–	–	–	–	+7.1
Ayrshire Central*	72.5	+8.3	17.3	–3.0	26.4	–21.3	1.8	–10.1	53.2	+34.1	2.5	–	–	–	1 (0.3)	+9.1
North and Arran*	71.1	+8.9	14.8	–0.8	28.0	–19.4	1.7	–8.4	53.2	+27.2	2.1	–	–	–	–	–
Banff and Buchan	66.5	+6.7	28.8	–2.0	5.8	–8.2	5.1	–6.2	60.2	+19.0	–	–	–	–	–	–
Berwickshire, Roxburgh and Selkirk*	74.2	+7.8	36.0	+2.2	4.9	–5.3	18.7	–26.7	36.6	+27.4	1.0	–0.1	1.5	–	–	–
Caithness, Sutherland and Easter Ross*	71.9	+11.0	6.8	–6.2	9.0	–15.7	35.1	–6.3	46.3	+27.1	–	–	–	–	1 (1)	–
Coatbridge, Chryston and Bellshill*	68.6	+9.2	6.3	–1.8	33.9	–32.7	1.1	–7.4	56.6	+39.8	2.0	–	–	–	1 (0.5)	–
Cumbernauld, Kilsyth and Kirkintilloch East*	73.6	+9.3	7.9	–0.4	30.0	–27.2	2.2	–7.3	59.9	+36.1	2.0	+1.2	4.0	+1.3	3 (0.9)	–
Dumfries and Galloway*	75.2	+5.3	29.9	–1.7	24.7	–21.2	1.7	–7.1	41.4	+29.1	2.6	+2.0	0.9	–	1 (0.5)	+9.7
Dumfriesshire, Clydesdale and Tweeddale	76.1	+7.2	39.8	+1.8	14.8	–14.1	2.7	–17.1	38.3	+27.5	1.3	–	6.2	+3.0	2 (0.9)	+7.9
Dunbartonshire East*	81.9	+6.8	8.6	–6.9	12.3	–21.8	36.3	–2.4	40.3	+29.7	–	–	1.6	–	2 (1.2)	–
West*	73.9	+9.9	7.0	–0.6	31.3	–30.0	1.6	–6.5	59.0	+38.9	–	–	2.7	+0.2	2 (0.8)	–
Dundee East	71.0	+9.1	15.0	–0.3	19.9	–13.4	2.9	–7.7	59.7	+21.9	–	–	2.9	+0.5	1 (0.6)	–
West*	67.8	+8.9	8.6	–0.7	23.7	–24.8	2.4	–9.0	61.9	+33.0	2.4	–	1.2	–	1 (0.4)	–
Dunfermline and West Fife*	71.6	+5.1	11.9	+5.1	31.7	–14.5	4.0	–31.1	50.3	+39.6	1.6	+0.4	–	–	1 (0.5)	–
East Kilbride, Strathaven and Lesmahagow*	72.8	+6.2	11.8	–1.2	28.3	–23.2	1.7	–8.2	55.6	+32.6	2.6	+1.3	–	–	–	–
East Lothian*	74.2	+7.2	19.5	–0.1	31.0	–13.6	2.6	–14.3	42.5	+26.5	2.7	–	–	–	–	+6.7
Edinburgh East*	70.1	+4.7	9.9	–1.0	29.9	–13.5	2.8	–16.6	49.2	+28.8	–	–	1.4	–	2 (0.8)	–
North and Leith*	71.7	+3.3	16.2	+1.2	31.3	–6.2	4.5	–29.3	40.9	+31.3	–	–	–	–	1 (0.6)	–
South	74.9	+1.1	17.5	–4.1	39.1	+4.4	3.7	–30.3	33.8	+26.1	1.6	+0.8	–	–	–	–
South West*	71.5	+3.0	20.2	–4.0	27.2	–15.6	3.7	–14.3	43.0	+30.8	2.3	+0.8	–	–	1 (0.6)	+5.8
West*	76.5	+5.2	12.3	–10.9	11.7	–16.0	33.1	–2.8	39.0	+25.8	2.0	+0.9	2.1	+0.4	1 (0.3)	–
Falkirk*	72.4	+10.3	12.1	+0.9	25.1	–20.6	2.0	–8.3	57.7	+27.5	1.9	–	6.0	+0.9	1 (0.2)	–
Fife North East*	73.0	+9.2	16.3	–5.5	7.7	–9.5	31.3	–13.0	40.9	+26.7	1.5	–	5.4	+3.2	1 (0.2)	–
Glasgow Central*	55.4	+4.5	6.0	–1.1	33.1	–19.0	1.6	–14.8	52.5	+35.0	1.2	–	4.2	+2.2	1 (0.4)	–

East*	60.3	+8.3	6.0	+1.5	32.4	−29.2	0.7	−4.3	56.9	+32.1	2.1	–	3.8	+1.9	–	–
North*	61.4	+3.9	7.9	+0.8	27.9	−16.6	2.7	−28.6	53.1	+41.2	1.9	–	2.1	–	–	–
North East*	56.8	+7.6	4.7	−0.7	33.7	−34.7	0.8	−6.9	58.1	+43.9	3.0	+0.5	–	–	–	–
North West*	64.1	+5.8	8.4	−1.5	30.9	−23.2	2.7	−13.1	54.5	+39.3	2.7	–	–	–	1 (0.2)	–
South*	65.9	+4.3	9.7	−1.7	29.7	−22.0	2.1	−9.7	54.9	+34.7	3.1	+2.1	–	–	–	–
South West*	61.8	+7.2	5.0	−1.6	32.8	−29.7	1.0	−8.0	57.2	+40.8	2.4	+1.5	2.5	+1.0	–	–
Glenrothes*	68.2	+8.4	7.7	+0.5	30.6	−31.7	1.9	−5.8	59.8	+38.1	–	–	3.1	+1.5	–	–
Gordon*	73.3	+6.8	11.7	−7.0	5.9	−14.2	32.7	−3.3	47.7	+25.5	–	–	–	–	2 (0.9)	–
Inverclyde*	75.2	+11.8	10.0	−2.0	30.3	−25.6	2.5	−10.9	55.1	+37.6	1.8	–	2.0	+1.0	1 (0.3)	–
Inverness, Nairn, Badenoch and Strathspey*	74.2	+9.3	5.9	−7.4	7.5	−14.6	31.3	−9.4	50.1	+31.4	1.8	+0.9	1.6	–	1 (0.3)	–
Kilmarnock and Loudoun*	71.6	+8.8	12.5	−1.6	30.4	−22.2	1.5	−5.9	55.7	+29.7	3.0	+1.5	2.2	–	–	–
Kirkcaldy and Cowdenbeath*	69.6	+7.4	9.9	+0.6	33.4	−31.2	2.2	−7.1	52.2	+37.9	–	–	–	–	–	–
Lanark and Hamilton East*	69.1	+6.8	15.9	+0.9	30.5	−19.4	2.2	−9.1	48.8	+27.8	–	–	1.9	+0.5	2 (0.7)	–
Linlithgow and East Falkirk*	70.8	+7.2	12.0	0.0	31.0	−18.8	2.0	−10.8	52.0	+26.6	–	–	2.7	–	1 (0.7)	–
Livingston*	69.9	+6.8	10.3	−0.5	27.6	−20.8	2.1	−9.0	56.9	+31.0	–	–	2.1	–	–	–
Midlothian*	71.2	+7.3	11.9	0.0	30.2	−16.8	2.3	−14.8	50.6	+30.0	–	–	3.1	–	1 (0.7)	–
Moray	68.7	+6.5	31.1	+5.0	9.9	−7.1	2.8	−11.7	49.5	+9.8	–	–	–	–	–	–
Motherwell and Wishaw*	68.6	+10.2	7.7	−1.7	31.9	−29.2	1.2	−8.6	56.5	+38.4	2.0	–	–	–	–	–
Na h-Eileanan an Iar	73.2	+5.6	7.6	+3.2	28.6	−4.3	2.9	−4.6	54.3	+8.7	2.3	+0.7	–	–	–	–
Ochil and South Perthshire*	74.8	+7.6	20.7	+0.2	28.4	−9.5	2.6	−8.8	46.0	+18.4	3.9	+1.3	2.7	–	–	–
Orkney and Shetland	65.8	+7.3	8.9	−1.6	7.1	−3.5	41.4	−20.6	37.8	+27.2	2.3	+0.9	–	–	–	–
Paisley and Renfrewshire North*	76.2	+7.6	12.3	−2.3	32.7	−21.3	2.1	−8.4	50.7	+31.7	2.0	–	2.1	–	1 (0.7)	–
South*	75.4	+10.1	7.6	−2.3	38.6	−21.0	2.2	−7.3	50.9	+32.9	2.5	–	–	–	–	–
Perth and North Perthshire	74.8	+7.9	32.7	+2.2	8.1	−8.3	3.8	−8.5	50.5	+10.9	2.9	–	–	–	–	–
Renfrewshire East*	81.1	+3.8	22.0	−8.4	34.0	−16.8	1.9	−7.3	40.6	+31.7	2.1	+0.9	2.4	+0.7	1 (0.7)	+4.2
Ross, Skye and Lochaber*	77.2	+10.0	6.2	−6.0	4.9	−10.2	35.9	−16.8	48.1	+33.0	–	–	–	–	1 (6.6)	–
Rutherglen and Hamilton West*	69.6	+8.1	7.6	−2.1	35.2	−25.6	1.8	−10.2	52.6	+36.5	4.8	−1.6	–	–	–	–
Stirling*	77.5	+6.7	23.1	−0.9	25.5	−16.2	2.7	−11.8	45.6	+28.3	1.9	+0.1	2.5	+0.3	1 (0.5)	+7.7

NORTHERN IRELAND	*Turnout* %	*Turnout* +/–	*UUP* %	*UUP* +/–	*DUP* %	*DUP* +/–	*APNI* %	*APNI* +/–	*SF* %	*SF* +/–	*SDLP* %	*SDLP* +/–	*Other* %
Antrim East	53.3	+2.7	18.8	–4.8	36.1	–9.7	15.0	+3.9	6.9	+0.1	4.9	–1.7	18.2
North	55.2	–2.6	12.1	+1.1	43.2	–3.2	5.6	+2.4	12.3	–0.1	7.0	–1.8	19.9
South*	54.2	+0.2	32.7	+2.3	30.1	–3.8	9.8	+2.1	12.9	–1.0	8.2	–0.5	6.4
Belfast East*	62.8	+4.4	–	–	49.3	+16.5	42.8	+5.6	2.1	–0.3	0.3	–0.7	5.5
North	59.2	+2.7	–	–	47.0	+7.0	7.2	+2.4	33.9	–0.1	8.2	–4.1	3.6
South	60.0	+2.6	9.1	–8.2	22.2	–1.5	17.2	+2.3	13.9		24.5	–16.5	13.0
West	56.3	+2.4	3.1	0.0	7.8	+0.3	1.8	–0.1	54.2	–16.8	9.8	–6.5	23.2
Down North	56.0	+0.8	–	–	23.6		8.6	+3.0	0.8	0.0	1.0	–1.0	66.1
South	56.8	–3.4	9.3	+2.0	8.2	–0.4	3.8	+2.5	28.5	–0.2	42.3	–6.1	7.9
Fermanagh and South Tyrone*	72.6	+3.6	46.4	–	–	–	1.3	+0.4	45.4	–0.1	5.4	–2.3	1.5
Foyle	52.8	–4.7	3.3	+0.1	12.4	+0.5	2.3	+1.7	31.6	–0.4	47.9	+3.2	2.6
Lagan Valley	55.9	–0.1	15.2	–5.9	47.9	–1.9	13.9	+2.5	2.9	–1.1	6.3	+1.3	13.8
Londonderry East	51.9	–3.4	15.4	–2.4	42.2	+7.6	7.6	+2.1	19.8	+0.5	12.3	–3.2	2.7
Newry and Armagh	64.2	+3.8	32.7	+13.6	–	–	1.7	+0.5	41.1	–0.9	24.1	+0.7	0.4
Strangford	52.8	–0.9	14.3	–13.5	44.4	–1.5	13.8	+5.1	2.6	–1.0	6.9	+0.2	18.0
Tyrone West	60.5	–0.4	15.9	+1.7	17.5	–2.3	2.2	–0.1	43.5	–4.9	16.7	+2.7	4.3
Ulster Mid	60.3	–2.9	15.4	+4.4	13.4	–1.0	1.9	+0.9	48.7	–3.3	12.4	–1.9	8.2
Upper Bann	59.0	+3.6	27.9	+2.2	32.7	–1.2	3.8	+0.8	24.6	–0.2	9.0	–3.8	2.1

Notes:
UUP: Ulster Unionist Party. Comparison with 2010 is with the Ulster Conservatives and Unionists – New Force
DUP: Democratic Unionist Party
APNI: Alliance Party of Northern Ireland
SF: Sinn Fein
SDLP: Social Democratic and Labour Party

Table A2.6 Seats changing hands

Con gains from Labour
Bolton West
Derby North
Gower
Morley and Outwood
Plymouth Moor View
Southampton Itchen
Telford
Vale of Clwyd

Con gains from Lib Dems
Bath
Berwick-upon-Tweed
Brecon and Radnorshire
Cheadle
Cheltenham
Chippenham
Colchester
Cornwall North
Devon North
Dorset Mid and Poole North
Eastbourne
Eastleigh
Hazel Grove
Kingston and Surbiton
Lewes
Portsmouth South
Solihull
Somerton and Frome
St Austell and Newquay
St Ives
Sutton and Cheam
Taunton Deane
Thornbury and Yate
Torbay
Twickenham
Wells
Yeovil

Labour gains from Con
Brentford and Isleworth
Chester, City of
Dewsbury
Ealing Central and Acton
Enfield North
Hove
Ilford North
Lancaster and Fleetwood
Wirral West
Wolverhampton South West

Labour gains from Lib Dems
Bermondsey and Old Southwark
Birmingham Yardley
Bradford East
Brent Central
Bristol West
Burnley
Cambridge
Cardiff Central
Hornsey and Wood Green
Manchester Withington
Norwich South
Redcar

SNP gains from Labour
Aberdeen North
Aberdeen South
Airdrie and Shotts
Ayr, Carrick and Cumnock
Ayrshire Central
Ayrshire North and Arran
Coatbridge, Chryston and Bellshill
Cumbernauld, Kilsyth and Kirkintilloch East
Dumfries and Galloway
Dunbartonshire West
Dundee West
Dunfermline and West Fife
East Kilbride, Strathaven and Lesmahagow
East Lothian
Edinburgh East
Edinburgh North and Leith
Edinburgh South West
Falkirk
Glasgow Central
Glasgow East
Glasgow North
Glasgow North East
Glasgow North West
Glasgow South
Glasgow South West
Glenrothes

Inverclyde
Kilmarnock and Loudoun
Kirkcaldy and Cowdenbeath
Lanark and Hamilton East
Linlithgow and Falkirk East
Livingston
Midlothian
Motherwell and Wishaw
Ochil and South Perthshire
Paisley and Renfrewshire North
Paisley and Renfrewshire South
Renfrewshire East
Rutherglen and Hamilton West
Stirling

SNP gains from Lib Dems
Aberdeenshire West and Kincardine
Argyll and Bute
Berwickshire, Roxburgh and Selkirk
Caithness, Sutherland and Easter Ross
Dunbartonshire East
Edinburgh West
Fife North East
Gordon
Inverness, Nairn, Badenoch and Strathspey
Ross, Skye and Lochaber

Other gains
Clacton UKIP from Con
Belfast East DUP from Alliance
South Antrim UUP from DUP
Fermanagh and South Tyrone UUP from SF

Table A2.7 Exceptional results

TURNOUT

10 largest and smallest % turnout	
Dunbartonshire East	81.9
Renfrewshire East	81.1
Stirling	77.5
Twickenham	77.3
Ross, Skye and Lochaber	77.2
Sheffield Hallam	76.7
Edinburgh West	76.5
Richmond Park	76.5
Kenilworth and Southam	76.3
Monmouth	76.3
[...]	
Birmingham Erdington	53.3
Merthyr Tydfil and Rhymney	53.0
Middlesbrough	52.9
Foyle	52.8
Strangford	52.8
Birmingham Ladywood	52.7
Manchester Central	52.7
East Londonderry	51.9
Blackley and Broughton	51.6
Stoke-on-Trent Central	51.3

10 largest increases and decreases in % turnout	
Thirsk and Malton*	+17.7
Inverclyde	+11.8
Caithness, Sutherland and Easter Ross	+11.0
Liverpool Riverside	+10.4
Falkirk	+10.4
Motherwell and Wishaw	+10.2
Paisley and Renfrewshire South	+10.1
Ross, Skye and Lochaber	+10.0
Dunbartonshire West	+9.9
Oxford West and Abingdon	+9.8
[...]	
St Albans	–3.6
Copeland	–3.9
Charnwood	–4.3
Foyle	–4.7
Cambridge	–5.0
Hitchin and Harpenden	–5.2
Merthyr Tydfil and Rhymney	–5.6
Slough	–5.7
Hackney North and Stoke Newington	–6.3
Cambridgeshire North East	–8.7

Note: the election in Thirsk and Malton was delayed in 2010 due to the death of one candidate and was therefore held after the general election.

MARGINALITY

10 largest and smallest % majorities

		N	
Liverpool Walton	Lab		72.3
Knowsley	Lab		68.3
Liverpool West Derby	Lab		66.7
East Ham	Lab		65.5
Bootle	Lab		63.6
Birmingham Ladywood	Lab		60.9
Liverpool Wavertree	Lab		59.3
Manchester Gorton	Lab		57.3
Birmingham Hodge Hill	Lab		56.9
Walthamstow	Lab		55.5
[...]			
Bury North	Con	378	0.8
Brentford and Isleworth	Lab	465	0.8
Vale of Clwyd	Con	237	0.7
Ynys Mon	Lab	229	0.7
Berwickshire, Roxburgh and Selkirk	SNP	328	0.6
Ealing Central and Acton	Lab	274	0.5
Croydon Central	Con	165	0.3
Chester, City of	Lab	93	0.2
Derby North	Con	41	0.1
Gower	Con	27	0.1

CONSERVATIVE

10 largest rises and falls in % vote share

Bromsgrove	+10.2
Hampstead and Kilburn	+9.6
Yeovil	+9.6
Hexham	+9.5
Brent Central	+9.2
Durham, City of	+9.0
Watford	+8.5
Somerset North East	+8.5
Richmond Park	+8.5
Somerton and Frome	+8.5
[...]	
Argyll and Bute	–9.1
Thanet South	–9.9
Cambridge	–9.9
Sheffield Hallam	–10.0
Dagenham and Rainham	–10.0
Edinburgh West	–10.9
Richmond (Yorks)	–11.4
Bradford East	–15.5
Bradford West	–15.9
Clacton	–16.4

Note: this excludes Buckingham, where the Speaker (a former Conservative) was seeking re-election.

10 highest and lowest % vote share (GB)

Hampshire North East	65.9
Maidenhead	65.8
Buckingham	64.5
Windsor	63.4
Beaconsfield	63.2
Chelsea and Fulham	63.0
Esher and Walton	62.9
Meon Valley	61.1
Newbury	61.0
Arundel and South Downs	60.8
[...]	
Knowsley	6.6
Liverpool West Derby	6.6
Coatbridge, Chryston and Bellshill	6.3
Ross, Skye and Lochaber	6.2
Glasgow Central	6.0
Glasgow East	6.0
Inverness, Nairn, Badenoch and Strathspey	5.9
Glasgow South West	5.0
Liverpool Walton	4.7
Glasgow North East	4.7

Note: this list excludes Buckingham, where the Speaker (a former Conservative) was seeking re-election. It also excludes Northern Ireland. The worst Conservative performances all came in Northern Ireland. They polled lower than in any seat in Great Britain in all but one of the 16 constituencies in which they stood, and below 1% in eight. They saved a deposit in just one (Strangford, where they polled 6.39%).

LABOUR

10 largest rises and falls in % vote share

Birmingham Hall Green	+26.9
Brent Central	+20.9
Sheffield Hallam	+19.7
Poplar and Limehouse	+18.6

Bethnal Green and Bow	+18.3
Birmingham Ladywood	+18.0
Walthamstow	+17.0
Manchester Gorton	+17.0
Hornsey and Wood Green	+16.9
Birmingham Hodge Hill	+16.4
[...]	
Inverclyde	–25.7
Cumbernauld, Kilsyth and Kirkintilloch East	–27.2
Glasgow East	–29.2
Motherwell and Wishaw	–29.2
Glasgow South West	–29.7
Dunbartonshire West	–30.0
Kirkcaldy and Cowdenbeath	–31.2
Glenrothes	–31.7
Coatbridge, Chryston and Bellshill	–32.7
Glasgow North East	–34.7

10 largest falls in % vote share (England and Wales)

Wellingborough	–5.9
Brigg and Goole	–5.9
Dorset South	–6.1
Tamworth	–6.6
Somerset North East	–6.8
Hartlepool	–6.9
Thanet South	–7.6
Rochester and Strood	–8.7
Chatham and Aylesford	–8.7
Clacton	–10.7

10 highest and lowest % vote share

Liverpool Walton	81.3
Knowsley	78.1
East Ham	77.6
Liverpool West Derby	75.2
Bootle	74.5
Birmingham Ladywood	73.6
Liverpool Wavertree	69.3
Garston and Halewood	69.1
Walthamstow	68.9
West Ham	68.4
[...]	
Wells	6.6
Dorset Mid and Poole North	6.0
Gordon	5.9
Banff and Buchan	5.8
Montgomeryshire	5.6
Westmorland and Lonsdale	5.4
Cornwall North	5.4
Berwickshire, Roxburgh and Selkirk	4.9
Ross, Skye and Lochaber	4.9
Aberdeenshire West and Kincardine	4.5

LIBERAL DEMOCRATS

10 least and greatest falls in % vote share

Dunbartonshire East	–2.4
Edinburgh West	–2.8
Gordon	–3.3
Argyll and Bute	–3.7
Bradford East	–4.2
Glasgow East	–4.3
Cambridge	–4.3
Na h-Eileanan an Iar	–4.6
Ynys Mon	–5.4
Glenrothes	–5.8
[...]	
Manchester Gorton	–28.4
Glasgow North	–28.6
Weston-Super-Mare	–28.8
Bristol West	–29.2
Edinburgh North and Leith	–29.3
Edinburgh South	–30.3
Hereford and Herefordshire South	–30.5
Dunfermline and West Fife	–31.1
Sheffield Central	–31.3
Brent Central	–35.8

Note: the Liberal Democrats lost vote share in every seat, thus making a table listing rises and falls impossible.

10 highest and lowest % vote share

Westmorland and Lonsdale	51.5
Orkney and Shetland	41.4
Sheffield Hallam	40.0
Norfolk North	39.1
Eastbourne	38.2
Twickenham	38.0
Thornbury and Yate	37.9
Leeds North West	36.8
Dunbartonshire East	36.3

Ross, Skye and Lochaber	35.9
[...]	
Rhondda	1.5
Kilmarnock and Loudoun	1.5
Barking	1.3
Thurrock	1.3
Dudley North	1.3
Motherwell and Wishaw	1.3
Coatbridge, Chryston and Bellshill	1.1
Glasgow South West	1.0
Glasgow North East	0.8
Glasgow East	0.8

UKIP

10 largest rises and falls in % vote share

Heywood and Middleton	+29.6
Thanet South	+26.9
Dagenham and Rainham	+26.3
Boston and Skegness	+24.3
Thurrock	+24.3
Rotherham	+24.3
Rother Valley	+22.5
Hartlepool	+21.0
West Bromwich West	+20.9
Doncaster Central	+20.7
[...]	
Inverness, Nairn, Badenoch and Strathspey	+0.9
East Lothian	+0.9
Renfrewshire East	+0.8
Rutherglen and Hamilton West	+0.8
Kirkcaldy and Cowdenbeath	+0.7
Falkirk	+0.5
Inverclyde	+0.5
Ross, Skye and Lochaber	+0.1
Dunbartonshire East	–0.1
Orkney and Shetland	–1.6

Note: the table lists constituencies in which UKIP candidates stood in both 2010 and 2015. The following three constituencies saw even larger increases in vote share, but where no UKIP candidate stood in 2010: Clacton (+44.4); Castle Point (+31.2); Rochester and Strood (+30.5).

10 highest and lowest % vote share

Clacton	44.4
Boston and Skegness	33.8
Thanet South	32.4
Heywood and Middleton	32.2
Thurrock	31.7
Castle Point	31.2
Rochester and Strood	30.5
Rotherham	30.2
Dagenham and Rainham	29.9
Rother Valley	28.1
[...]	
Edinburgh East	1.9
Edinburgh West	1.9
Aberdeen South	1.9
Aberdeenshire West and Kincardine	1.8
Inverclyde	1.6
Renfrewshire East	1.6
Edinburgh North and Leith	1.5
Glasgow North	1.3
Edinburgh South	1.2
Dunbartonshire East	1.0

10 lowest % vote share (England and Wales)

Finchley and Golders Green	3.4
Streatham	3.2
Dulwich and West Norwood	3.1
Battersea	3.1
Bristol West	3.0
Vauxhall	2.9
Tooting	2.9
Hampstead and Kilburn	2.8
Hornsey and Wood Green	2.2
Hackney North and Stoke Newington	2.2

GREENS

10 largest rises and falls in % vote share

Bristol West	+23.1
Sheffield Central	+12.1
Isle of Wight	+12.1
Brighton Pavilion	+10.5
Holborn and St Pancras	+10.1
Hackney North and Stoke Newington	+10.0
Bath	+9.6

Oxford East	+9.2
Bristol South	+9.0
Liverpool Riverside	+8.6
[...]	
Dumfriesshire, Clydesdale and Tweeddale	+0.5
Bradford West	+0.4
East Lothian	+0.4
Cambridge	+0.4
Ilford South	+0.3
Ross, Skye and Lochaber	+0.3
Glasgow North West	+0.2
Harrow East	+0.1
Aldridge-Brownhills	–0.1
Norwich South	–0.1

Note: the table lists constituencies in which Green candidates stood in both 2010 and 2015. The following two constituencies saw larger or similar increases in vote share, but where no Green candidate stood in 2010: Buckingham (+13.8); Somerton and Frome (+9.0). The Greens increased their vote share in all but two seats where they stood in both of the last two elections.

10 highest and lowest % vote share

Brighton Pavilion	41.8
Bristol West	26.8
Sheffield Central	15.8
Hackney North and Stoke Newington	14.6
Norwich South	13.9
Buckingham	13.8
Isle of Wight	13.4
Holborn and St Pancras	12.8
Lewisham Deptford	12.5
Liverpool Riverside	12.1
[...]	
Fermanagh and South Tyrone	1.6
Dunbartonshire East	1.5
Rhondda	1.4
Walsall North	1.4
Paisley and Renfrewshire North	1.4
Dudley North	1.4
Ayrshire Central	1.3
Glasgow South West	1.2
Berwickshire, Roxburgh and Selkirk	1.2
Glasgow East	0.9

SNP

10 largest and smallest rises in % vote share

Glasgow North East	+43.9
Glasgow North	+41.2
Glasgow South West	+40.8
Coatbridge, Chryston and Bellshill	+39.8
Dunfermline and West Fife	+39.6
Glasgow North West	+39.3
Dunbartonshire West	+38.9
Motherwell and Wishaw	+38.4
Glenrothes	+38.1
Kirkcaldy and Cowdenbeath	+37.9
[...]	
Edinburgh West	+25.8
Gordon	+25.5
Argyll and Bute	+25.3
Dundee East	+21.9
Banff and Buchan	+19.0
Ochil and South Perthshire	+18.4
Angus	+14.7
Perth and Perthshire North	+10.9
Moray	+9.8
Na h-Eileanan an Iar	+8.7

Note: the SNP gained vote share in every seat in Scotland, thus making a table listing rises and falls impossible.

10 highest and lowest % vote share

Dundee West	61.9
Banff and Buchan	60.2
Cumbernauld, Kilsyth and Kirkintilloch East	59.9
Glenrothes	59.8
Dundee East	59.7
Dunbartonshire West	59.1
Glasgow North East	58.1
Falkirk	57.7
Glasgow South West	57.2
Livingston	56.9
[...]	
Dumfries and Galloway	41.4
Edinburgh North and Leith	40.9
Fife North East	40.9
Renfrewshire East	40.6
Dunbartonshire East	40.3

Edinburgh West	39.0
Dumfriesshire, Clydesdale and Tweeddale	38.3
Orkney and Shetland	37.8
Berwickshire, Roxburgh and Selkirk	36.6
Edinburgh South	33.8

PLAID CYMRU

10 largest rises and falls in % vote share

Rhondda	+8.9
Arfon	+8.0
Cardiff West	+6.9
Blaenau Gwent	+4.9
Aberavon	+4.5
Merthyr Tydfil and Rhymney	+4.4
Ynys Mon	+4.3
Pontypridd	+4.2
Swansea East	+3.7
Cardiff South and Penarth	+3.2
[...]	
Neath	–1.8
Caerphilly	–2.1
Islwyn	–2.3
Preseli Pembrokeshire	–3.0
Montgomeryshire	–3.1
Clwyd West	–3.2
Cynon Valley	–3.5
Dwyfor Meirionnydd	–3.5
Aberconwy	–6.1
Llanelli	–7.0

10 highest and lowest % vote share

Arfon	43.9
Dwyfor Meirionnydd	40.9
Carmarthen East and Dinefwr	38.4
Ynys Mon	30.5
Ceredigion	27.7
Rhondda	27.0
Llanelli	23.0
Neath	18.1
Cynon Valley	16.8
Caerphilly	14.6
[...]	
Vale of Glamorgan	5.6
Montgomeryshire	5.2
Cardiff Central	5.0
Delyn	4.8
Cardiff North	4.5
Brecon and Radnorshire	4.4
Newport West	4.0
Monmouth	4.0
Alyn and Deeside	3.9
Newport East	3.5

INDEPENDENT

10 best Independent results

North Down	49.2
Devon East	24.0
Fylde	11.9
Preseli Pembrokeshire	9.2
Hartlepool	7.5
Stoke-on-Trent Central	6.8
Richmond (Yorks)	6.2
Maldon	5.1
Dwyfor Meirionnydd	4.8
Isle of Wight	4.6

Table A2.8 By-election results, 2010–15

	Date	*Con*	*Lab*	*Lib Dem*	*UKIP*	*Best other*	*Other candidates (N)*	*Turnout*
Oldham East and Saddleworth	13.1.11	12.8	**42.1**	31.9	5.8	BNP (4.5)	5	48.0
Barnsley Central	3.3.11	8.3	**60.8**	4.2	12.2	BNP (6.0)	4	37.0
Leicester South	5.5.11	15.1	**57.8**	22.5	2.9	MRL (1.6)	0	43.9
		(SF)	(SDLP)	(PBP)	(DUP)	N/A	0	37.4
Belfast West	9.6.11	**70.6**	13.5	7.6	6.1			
Inverclyde	30.6.11	9.9	**53.8**	2.2	4.9	SNP (33.0)	0	45.4
Feltham and Heston	15.12.11	27.7	**54.4**	5.9	5.5	BNP (2.3)	4	28.7
Bradford West	29.3.12	8.4	25.0	4.6	3.3	**Respect (55.9)**	3	50.8
Respect gain at by-election								
Labour regain at 2015 general election								
Cardiff South and Penarth	15.11.12	19.9	**47.3**	10.8	6.1	Plaid Cymru (9.5)	3	25.7
Corby	15.11.12	26.5	**48.3**	4.9	14.3	BNP (1.7)	9	44.8
Labour gain at by-election								
Conservatives regain at 2015 general election								
Manchester Central	15.11.12	4.5	**69.1**	9.4	4.5	Green (3.9)	7	18.2
Croydon North	29.11.12	16.8	**64.7**	3.5	5.7	Green (3.5)	7	26.4
Middlesbrough	29.11.12	6.3	**60.5**	9.9	11.8	Peace (6.3)	3	25.9
Rotherham	29.11.12	5.4	**46.5**	2.1	21.7	BNP (8.4)	6	33.8
Eastleigh	28.2.13	25.4	9.8	**32.1**	27.8	Independent (1.8)	9	52.7
Conservatives gain at 2015 general election								

		(SF)	(Ind)	(SDLP)				
Mid Ulster	7.3.13	**46.9**	34.4	17.4	–	Alliance (1.3)	0	55.4
South Shields	2.5.13	11.5	**50.5**	1.4	24.2	Independent (5.4)	4	39.3
Wythenshawe and Sale East	13.2.14	14.5	**55.3**	4.9	18.0	Green (3.1)	2	28.2
Newark	5.6.14	**45.0**	17.7	2.6	25.9	Independent (4.9)	6	52.7
Clacton	1.10.14	24.6	11.2	1.4	**59.7**	Green (1.9)	3	51.5
UKIP gain at by-election								
UKIP hold at 2015 general election								
Heywood and Middleton	9.10.14	12.3	**40.9**	5.1	38.7	Green (3.1)	0	36.0
Rochester and Strood	20.11.14	34.8	16.8	0.9	**42.1**	Green (4.2)	8	50.6
UKIP gain at by-election								
Conservatives regain at 2015 general election								

Note: winning party at the by-election in bold. All held by the incumbent party, in both by-election and then 2015 general election, unless indicated otherwise.

Index

Page numbers in italics refer to illustrations or charts. An 'n' after the page number indicates a note (with the note number following) and 'tab' refers to tables.